T0202768

Lecture Notes in Computer Science 14526

Founding Editors

Gerhard Goos
Juris Hartmanis

Editorial Board Members

The series Lecture Notes in Computer Science (LNCS), including its subseries Lecture Notes in Artificial Intelligence (LNAI) and Lecture Notes in Bioinformatics (LNBI), has established itself as a medium for the publication of new developments in computer science and information technology research, teaching, and education.

LNCS enjoys close cooperation with the computer science R & D community, the series counts many renowned academics among its volume editors and paper authors, and collaborates with prestigious societies. Its mission is to serve this international community by providing an invaluable service, mainly focused on the publication of conference and workshop proceedings and postproceedings. LNCS commenced publication in 1973.

Chunpeng Ge · Moti Yung
Editors

Information Security and Cryptology

19th International Conference, Inscrypt 2023
Hangzhou, China, December 9–10, 2023
Revised Selected Papers, Part I

 Springer

Editors
Chunpeng Ge
Shandong University
Jinan, China

Moti Yung 🆔
Columbia University
New York, NY, USA

ISSN 0302-9743   ISSN 1611-3349 (electronic)
Lecture Notes in Computer Science
ISBN 978-981-97-0941-0   ISBN 978-981-97-0942-7 (eBook)
https://doi.org/10.1007/978-981-97-0942-7

This Springer imprint is published by the registered company Springer Nature Singapore Pte Ltd.
The registered company address is: 152 Beach Road, #21-01/04 Gateway East, Singapore 189721, Singapore

Paper in this product is recyclable.

Preface

The 19th International Conference on Information Security and Cryptology (Inscrypt 2022) was held December 9–10, 2023. The conference was hosted by Hangzhou Dianzi University and co-organized by Zhejiang Lab. Inscrypt is an international conference on information security, cryptology, and their applications. Inscrypt is designed to be a forum for theoreticians, scheme and application designers, protocol developers and practitioners to discuss and express their views on the current trends, challenges, and state-of-the-art solutions related to various issues in information security and cryptography. Topics of interests include, but are not limited to, information security and cryptography for asymmetric cryptography, symmetric cryptography, cryptography foundations, privacy and anonymity technologies, secure cryptographic protocols and applications, security notions, approaches, and paradigms, leakage-resilient cryptography, lattice-based cryptography and post-quantum cryptography, blockchain and cryptocurrency, IoT security, cloud security, and access control.

The conference received 152 submissions. Each submission was reviewed by at least three program committee members or external reviewers. The program committee members accepted 38 full papers, 7 short papers and 6 posters to be included in the conference program. The program committee members selected one best paper "Compact Ring Signatures with Post-Quantum Security in Standard Model" by Tuong Ngoc Nguyen, Willy Susilo, Dung Hoang Duong, Fuchun Guo, Kazuhide Fukushima and Shinsaku Kiyomoto, and one best student paper "Text Laundering: Mitigating Malicious Features through Knowledge Distillation from Language Foundation Models" by Yi Jiang, Chenghui Shi, Oubo Ma, Youliang Tian and Shouling Ji.

We thank the Program Committee members and the external reviewers for their hard work in reviewing the submissions. We thank the Organizing Committee and all volunteers for their time and effort dedicated to arranging the conference.

December 2023

Chunpeng Ge
Moti Yung

Organization

Honorary Co-chairs

Dongdai Lin   University of Chinese Academy of Sciences, China

Guojin Ma   Hangzhou Dianzi University, China

General Co-chairs

Zhidong Zhao   Hangzhou Dianzi University, China

Zhe Liu   Zhejiang Lab, China

Program Co-chairs

Chunpeng Ge   Shandong University, China

Moti Yung   Columbia University, USA

Program Committee

Junqing Gong   East China Normal University, China

Long Yuan   Nanjing University of Science and Technology, China

Jianchang Lai   Southeast University, China

Shi Bai   Florida Atlantic University, USA

Savio Sciancalepore   Eindhoven University of Technology (TU/e), Netherlands

Shihui Fu   TU Delft, Netherlands

Aydin Abadi   University College London, UK

Thang Hoang   Virginia Tech, USA

Kirill Morozov   University of North Texas, USA

Hongbo Liu   University of Electronic Science and Technology of China, China

Haoyu Ma   Zhejiang Lab, China

Tao Xiang   Chongqing University, China

Peng He   Hubei University, China

Publicity Chairs

Weizhi Meng   Technical University of Denmark, Denmark
Chuan Ma   Zhejiang Lab, China

Organizing Committee Co-chairs

Yizhi Ren   Hangzhou Dianzi University, China
Liming Fang   Nanjing University of Aeronautics and
                               Astronautics, China

Contents – Part I

Contents – Part II

Cryptanalysis

Short Papers

Poster

Signature

TVES: Threshold Verifiably Encrypted Signature and Its Applications

Chen Li[1,2], Haibo Tian[1,2], and Fangguo Zhang[1,2(✉)]

[1] School of Computer Science and Engineering, Sun Yat-sen University,
Guangzhou 510006, China
lich368@mail2.sysu.edu.cn, {tianhb,isszhfg}@mail.sysu.edu.cn
[2] Guangdong Province Key Laboratory of Information Security Technology,
Guangzhou 510006, China

Abstract. Verifiably Encrypted Signature (VES) is useful to enable fair exchange in online contract signing. This cryptographic primitive introduces the adjudicator, a trusted third party, to keep the signature a secret but verifiable. The ordinary signature can be revealed at a later stage. In this paper, we propose Threshold Verifiably Encrypted Signature (TVES), which applies threshold cryptography to both signer and adjudicator parties to decentralize the adjudicator's power and achieve better fairness in multiparty contract signing where participants do not trust each other. We give TVES's definition and security notions, then present a concrete construction from bilinear pairings based on BLS short signature scheme and analyze its security and performance. We also show a practical application of TVES in the multiparty contract signing and exchange scenario.

Keywords: Fair exchange · Verifiably encrypted signature (VES) · Threshold cryptography · Bilinear pairings

1 Introduction

1.1 Background

Fair exchange is the problem of designing a protocol that exchanges digital assets between untrusted parties and guarantees all the honest parties obtain the assets they expect or no useful information about the assets is leaked if the protocol is terminated [28]. Fair exchange is mainly used in certified mail [39], electronic commerce [27], contract signing [3], etc.

In contract signing, suppose that Alice has signed the contract and sent her signature to Bob. Bob might refuse to send his signature to Alice or claim that he has not received Alice's signature. This is unfair to Alice because her signature is leaked. In this case, Alice wants to show Bob that she has signed the contract, but does not want Bob to possess the signature immediately.

Verifiably encrypted signature (VES) is purposed to enable fair exchange in contract signing [1]. It introduces a trusted third party called *Adjudicator* to the

C. Ge and M. Yung (Eds.): Inscrypt 2023, LNCS 14526, pp. 3–22, 2024.
https://doi.org/10.1007/978-981-97-0942-7_1

original digital signature scheme. Back to the example above, now Alice encrypts her ordinary signature with the adjudicator's public key before sending it to Bob. It is easy for Bob to verify that the encrypted signature is true of Alice and valid on the given contract (message) with Alice and the adjudicator's public key. But Bob is unable to decrypt Alice's encrypted signature by himself. In other words, no information about Alice's ordinary signature is leaked. Bob can obtain the ordinary signature from Alice if the contract is successfully executed, or ask the adjudicator to decrypt Alice's encrypted signature with his secret key in case of disputes (if Alice is unwilling to cooperate with Bob or reveal her ordinary signature, for example).

Threshold signature is another variant of the digital signature scheme that works with Multi-Party Computation. A (t, n)-threshold signature scheme involves n signers and requires at least t honest signers to create a valid signature of the given message. Conversely, it is infeasible for an adversary who corrupts at most $t - 1$ signers to create a valid signature. Therefore we often refer to t as the *threshold* of the scheme. Threshold signature is used heavily in blockchain systems and cryptocurrencies to sign and verify transactions due to the scheme's fault-tolerant nature that we can tolerate a subset of signers (or nodes) to be offline or corrupted [32].

Threshold signature eliminates single points of failure in basic digital signature schemes. If we put the focus back on VES schemes, we may notice that VES also suffers from single points of failure. When it comes to disputes between signers, adjudication is required to resolve the dispute and we notice that most existing VES schemes ideally assume that the adjudication service is always available. However, the adjudicator may go offline for various reasons in real-world applications such as blockchain systems, making the signature scheme not work properly. Moreover, even if the adjudicator appears as a "trusted" third party, the possibility of collusion between the adjudicator and other participants in the scheme still exists (refusing to reveal the ordinary signature under a participant's bribe, for example), which impairs the fairness of the scheme. Participants should not trust each other in multiparty contract signing scenarios. Therefore, it is also important to avoid the appearance of a single adjudicator as a trusted third party to achieve better fairness. Threshold cryptography is the way to decentralize the single adjudicator's power among multiple mutually untrusted adjudicators.

1.2   Related Works

Verifiably Encrypted Signature. After the concept of VES was purposed, several researchers were trying to design VES schemes based on existing signature schemes including RSA, ECDSA, BLS, ZSS and Fiat-Shamir style lattice-based schemes etc. [6,22,30,35–37].

Threshold Signature. The prototype of threshold signature was purposed by Desmedt *et al.* [8]. Their further research purposed a threshold signature scheme based on RSA and Shamir's secret sharing [10,29]. Harn [14] and Gennaro *et al.* [19] presented their threshold signature scheme based on ElGamal and DSA respectively, the signature share size is smaller than the RSA version. However, these threshold signature schemes require interaction, which means that there is an additional communication overhead between signers. Shoup's [31] threshold RSA signature is the first non-interactive threshold signature scheme, although it still suffers from the disadvantage of RSA signature's huge key size. After this, a lot of research on building non-interactive threshold signature schemes using ElGamal, Schnorr, DSA, ECDSA, BLS etc. appeared [2,4,9,13,14,16,21,33].

Applying Threshold Cryptography on Verifiably Encrypted Signature Schemes. It was noted in Boneh *et al.* 's paper that the adjudicator's secret key can be shared using a (t, n)-threshold cryptography as an extension of their VES scheme based on BLS [6]. Subsequently, Gorantla *et al.* [17] gave a more formal definition and security analysis of this extension based on a slightly modified version of BLS named H-BLS [34]. This is the first work to introduce threshold adjudication into the VES scheme. However, no VES scheme that applies threshold cryptography on both signer and adjudicator parties has been proposed.

1.3 Our Contributions

The contributions we have made in this paper can be summarized as follows:

- We propose a new cryptographic primitive called *Threshold Verifiably Encrypted Signature (TVES)* and give a definition of its model and security notions.
- We also give a concrete construction of the TVES scheme from bilinear pairings based on Boneh *et al.* 's [7] BLS short signature scheme and prove that the construction is valid and secure in the random oracle model.
- We use a practical application to show how TVES works in multiparty contract signing and it is more difficult for a malicious participant to break the protocol than in original VES schemes.

TVES applies threshold cryptography to both signer and adjudicator parties simultaneously (the threshold can be represented as (t_s, n_s, t_a, n_a)), which achieves better fairness in multiparty contract signing. This primitive describes a more general scenario compared to the previously mentioned studies since the original VES schemes and the VES schemes with a (t, n)-threshold applied on the adjudicator or signer party can be considered as special cases of $(1, 1, 1, 1)$, $(1, 1, t, n)$ and $(t, n, 1, 1)$-TVES. To the best of our knowledge, there is no similar primitive or scheme has been proposed in previous studies.

1.4 Organization

The rest of the paper is organized as follows. Section 2 gives some preliminaries on secret sharing, bilinear pairings and BLS short signature scheme. In Sect. 3, we present the definitions and security notions of TVES schemes. Our construction of the scheme from bilinear pairings is presented in Sect. 4. The construction's security proofs and the analysis of computation consumption are presented in Sect. 5. We also present an application of TVES for multiparty contract signing and exchange in Sect. 6. Section 7 concludes our work.

2   Preliminaries

2.1   Secret Sharing and Distributed Key Generation (DKG)

Secret sharing provides a secure way to distribute secret information among a distributed group. In a (t, n)-secret sharing scheme, the secret is divided into n shares and can be reconstructed only if at least t shares are gathered together. This requirement plays the role of a threshold. Shamir proposed the first secret sharing scheme relies on Lagrange interpolation theorem on polynomials [29]. There is a dealer who chooses a polynomial $f(x)$ of degree $t - 1$ related to the secret (equals to $f(0)$) and sends point $(i, f(i))$ to each participant i. The participant i can reconstruct the secret by interpolation $(f(0) = \sum_i f(i) \prod_{j \neq i} \frac{j}{j-i})$.

The shares received by the participants might be tampered. Verifiable Secret Sharing (VSS) was purposed to solve this problem by revealing additional commitments of corresponding shares to make these shares verifiable. Feldman's [12] VSS scheme is one of the most commonly used VSS schemes based on Shamir's secret sharing. Pedersen's [26] VSS scheme provides perfect secrecy of the secret [15] at the cost of higher computational complexity.

Distributed Key Generation (DKG) is purposed to get rid of the trusted third-party dealer by running a VSS instance on each participant. DKG also prevents any participant from getting access to the secret. We mainly concentrate on discrete logarithm-based DKG protocols in this paper. The security of these protocols comes from the hardness of computing discrete logarithms in cyclic groups $G = \langle g \rangle$ of large prime order p.

Definition 1 (DKG Protocol). *A (t, n)-DKG protocol is a protocol executed among n participants $P_1, \cdots, P_n$ which outputs secret key share sk_i for each participant P_i, public key shares $(pk_1, \cdots, pk_i)$ and the public key pk.*

The protocol consists of two phases:

1. *Sharing phase: Each participant P_i creates a secret z_i then plays the role of VSS's dealer, sends shares s_{ij} of z_i to other participants and reveals commitments s'_{ij}. As a result, there are n VSS schemes running in parallel.*
2. *Reconstruction phase: After disqualifying malicious participants, each participant P_i reconstruct his secret key share sk_i from s_{ij} and the public key pk from s'_{ij}. In theory, the secret key sk can be reconstructed from z_i. However, since z_i must be kept as a secret by P_i, the reconstruction is impossible.*

The protocol must satisfy the following properties [2, 15]:

- *Consistency: All subsets of t honest participants output the same uniformly-distributed secret key $sk \in \mathbb{Z}_p$ and the corresponding public key $pk = g^{sk}$ mod p.*
- *Correctness: There exists a polynomial $f(x) \in \mathbb{Z}_p[X]$ of degree $t-1$ satisfying the following properties whenever at most t participants are corrupted: $\forall i \in \{1, \cdots, n\} : sk_i = f(i), pk_i = g^{f(i)}$. Moreover, $pk = g^{f(0)}$.*
- *Unpredictability: An adversary who knows the public key pk and all participants' public key share pk_i can't learn any information of the secret key sk whenever at most $t-1$ participants are corrupted. The probability of recovering sk by the adversary is negligible.*

Pedersen's [25] JF-DKG and Gennaro's [15] New-DKG are two very classical discrete logarithm-based DKG protocols.

2.2   Bilinear Pairings

Let $G_1 = \langle g_1 \rangle$, $G_2 = \langle g_2 \rangle$ and G_T be three cyclic groups of prime order p (using the multiplicative form, generally constructed using elliptic curves). A *bilinear pairing* (or *bilinear map*) is a map $e : G_1 \times G_2 \to G_T$, which satisfies the following properties:

- Bilinearity: $\forall u \in G_1, v \in G_2, p, q \in \mathbb{Z}_p : e(u^a, v^b) = e(u^{ab}, v) = e(u, v^{ab}) = e(u, v)^{ab}$
- Non-degeneracy: $\exists u \in G_1, v \in G_2 : e(u, v) \neq 1_{G_T}$
- Computability: $\forall u \in G_1, v \in G_2$, there exists an efficient algorithm to compute $e(u, v)$ in polynomial time.

It can be further deduced that:

- $\forall u \in G_1, v, w \in G_2 : e(u, vw) = e(u, v)e(u, w)$
- $\forall u, v \in G_1 : e(u, \psi(v)) = e(v, \psi(u))$, ψ is a map from G_1 to G_2.

We call that e is a *symmetric bilinear pairing* if $G_1 = G_2 = G$ (the generator is $g_1 = g_2 = g$).

The first application of bilinear pairings in cryptography is the Tripartite Diffie-Hellman protocol purposed by Joux [20]. After then, bilinear pairings are used widely in cryptography researches such as Boneh *et al.* 's [5] Identity-Based encryption scheme, Boneh *et al.* 's [7] and Zhang *et al.* 's [38] short signature schemes, Groth's [18] group signature scheme and so forth.

2.3   BLS Short Signature Scheme

BLS short signature scheme was purposed by Boneh *et al.* [7] in 2001. The security of the scheme is based on the properties of co-Diffie-Hellman group pairs (co-GDH).

Definition 2 (Co-Gap Diffie-Hellman (co-GDH) Group Pair). *Consider the following two problems on group pair (G_1, G_2):*

- *Computational co-Diffie-Hellman (co-CDH) problem: Given $g_2, g_2^a \in G_2$ and $g_1^b \in G_1$ as input, compute $g_1^{ab} \in G_1$.*
- *Decision co-Diffie-Hellman (co-DDH) problem: Given $g_2, g_2^a \in G_2$ and $g_1^b, g_1^{bc} \in G_1$ as input, return 1 if and only if $a = c$ holds, otherwise return 0.*

If the co-CDH problem is hard and the co-DDH problem is easy on (G_1, G_2), then (G_1, G_2) is a co-Gap Diffie-Hellman (co-GDH) group pair.

We briefly describe the signature scheme here. Let (G_1, G_2) be a co-Gap Diffie-Hellman (co-GDH) group pair, $\{0,1\}^*$ be the message space and $H : \{0,1\}^* \rightarrow G_1$ be a cryptographic full-domain hash function. The message is $m \in \{0,1\}^*$. $e : G_1 \times G_2 \rightarrow G_T$ is a bilinear pairing. The algorithms of BLS short signature scheme (KeyGen, Sign, Verify) are defined as follows:

- KeyGen: Choose secret key $sk \in \mathbb{Z}_p$ randomly, then compute the public key $pk = g_2^{sk} \in G_2$.
- Sign: Use the secret key to compute the message's signature $\sigma = H(m)^{sk} \in G_1$.
- Verify: Accept the signature and return 1 if and only if $e(\sigma, g_2) = e(H(m), pk)$ holds, otherwise return 0.

3   Threshold Verifiably Encrypted Signature (TVES) Scheme

In this section, we introduce the definitions and security notions of a TVES scheme.

3.1   Definition

In simple terms, a TVES scheme involves three kinds of roles:

- *Signers* produce ordinary signature shares of the given message secretly, then encrypt the shares with adjudicators' public keys and make them public. A representative of the signers then verifies these encrypted shares and aggregates them into a verifiably encrypted signature.
- *Adjudicators* provide their public key for the signers to encrypt the ordinary signature shares. In case of disputes, they use their secret key shares to decrypt the aggregated verifiably encrypted signature and get signature shares. Notice that these decrypted shares are also public and different from signers' ordinary signature shares. Similarly, a representative of the adjudicators then verifies these decrypted shares and aggregates them into the ordinary signature.
- *Verifiers* verify that the signers-encrypted and adjudicators-decrypted shares are valid under their public key.

The TVES scheme is a (t_s, n_s, t_a, n_a)-threshold scheme, that is to say, there are n_s signers and n_a adjudicators, and the scheme holds whenever at most $t_s - 1$ signers and $t_a - 1$ adjudicators are corrupted. The ordinary signature can be aggregated from t_s signers' ordinary shares or t_a adjudicator-decrypted shares in case of disputes. Figure 1 shows the flow of executing the TVES scheme between n_s signers (represented by s_i) and n_a adjudicators (represented by a_i).

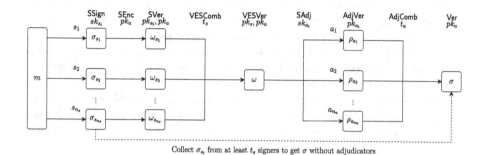

Collect σ_{s_i} from at least t_s signers to get σ without adjudicators

Fig. 1. Flow chart of the TVES scheme. s_i represent signers and a_i represent adjudicators. The algorithms, keys and threshold used in each phase are labeled above.

The scheme's algorithms are described below.

Definition 3 (TVES Scheme). *A* (t_s, n_s, t_a, n_a)-Threshold Verifiably Encrypted Signature (TVES) scheme *is a tuple of algorithms* $\sum = ($SDKG, AdjDKG, SSign, SEnc, SVer, VESComb, VESVer, SAdj, AdjVer, AdjComb, Ver$)$ *with the following properties:*

- $((sk_{s_1}, pk_{s_1}), (sk_{s_2}, pk_{s_2}), \cdots, (sk_{s_{n_s}}, pk_{s_{n_s}}), pk_s) \leftarrow$ SDKG(1^λ): *Signers use a DKG protocol to generate their secret key shares* $(sk_{s_1}, sk_{s_2}, \cdots, sk_{s_{n_s}})$, *public key shares* $(pk_{s_1}, pk_{s_2}, \cdots, pk_{s_{n_s}})$ *and a public key* pk_s.
- $((sk_{a_1}, pk_{a_1}), (sk_{a_2}, pk_{a_2}), \cdots, (sk_{a_{n_a}}, pk_{a_{n_a}}), pk_a) \leftarrow$ AdjDKG(1^λ): *Similar to* SDKG. *Adjudicators use a DKG protocol to generate secret key shares* $(sk_{a_1}, sk_{a_2}, \cdots, sk_{a_{n_a}})$, *public key shares* $(pk_{a_1}, pk_{a_2}, \cdots, pk_{a_{n_a}})$ *and a public key* pk_a.
- $\sigma_{s_i} \leftarrow$ SSign(sk_{s_i}, m): *Given a signer's secret key* sk_{s_i} *and a message* m, *the algorithm outputs an ordinary signature share* σ_{s_i} *of the message. The signer should keep* σ_{s_i} *as a secret. This algorithm is actually the signing algorithm of some basic signature schemes without verifiably encrypting or thresholding.*
- $\omega_{s_i} \leftarrow$ SEnc(σ_{s_i}, pk_a): *Given an ordinary signature share* σ_{s_i} *and adjudicators' public key* pk_a, *the algorithm outputs a verifiably encrypted signature share* ω_{s_i}, *which is revealed to the public.*
- 0 *or* 1 $\leftarrow$ SVer$(\omega_{s_i}, m, pk_{s_i}, pk_a)$: *Given a verifiably encrypted signature share* ω_{s_i}, *the message* m, *the signer's public key* pk_{s_i} *and adjudicators' public key* pk_a, *the algorithm verifies that* ω_{s_i} *is a valid verifiably encrypted signature share of the message under* pk_{s_i} *and* pk_a.

- $\omega \leftarrow$ VESComb($\{(s_i, \omega_{s_i}), \cdots \}$): *Given a set of t_s pairs of SVer-verified verifiably encrypted signature share and corresponding signer (s_i, ω_{s_i}), the algorithm outputs an aggregated verifiably encrypted signature ω of the message or $\perp$ if the set is not exist. If there are more than t_s valid pairs, choosing any of t_s pairs as input to the algorithm may give different results, but they should all be valid.*
- 0 or $1 \leftarrow$ VESVer(ω, m, pk_s, pk_a): *Given the aggregated verifiably encrypted signature ω, the message m, the signers' public key pk_s and adjudicators' public key pk_a, the algorithm verifies that ω is a valid aggregated verifiably encrypted signature of the message under pk_s and pk_a.*
- $\rho_{a_i} \leftarrow$ SAdj(sk_{a_i}, ω): *Given a adjudicator's secret key sk_{a_i} and the aggregated verifiably encrypted signature ω, the algorithm outputs a decrypted signature share ρ_{a_i}, which is revealed to the public.*
- 0 or $1 \leftarrow$ AdjVer($\omega, \rho_{a_i}, pk_{a_i}$): *Given the aggregated verifiably encrypted signature ω, a decrypted signature share ρ_{a_i} and the adjudicator's public key pk_{a_i}, the algorithm verifies that ρ_{a_i} is a valid decrypted signature share under pk_{a_i}.*
- $\sigma \leftarrow$ AdjComb($\{(a_i, \rho_{a_i}), \cdots \}$): *Given a set of t_a pairs of AdjVer-verified decrypted signature shares and corresponding adjudicators (a_i, ρ_{a_i}), the algorithm outputs the ordinary signature σ of the message or $\perp$ if the set is not exist. If there are more than t_s valid pairs, then choosing any of the t_s pairs as input to the algorithm should give the same result.*
- 0 or $1 \leftarrow$ Ver(σ, m, pk_s): *Given the ordinary signature σ, the message m and the signers' public key pk_s, the algorithm verifies that σ is a valid ordinary signature of the message under pk_s. Similar to SSign, this algorithm is also the same as the verifying algorithm of some basic signature schemes.*

3.2   Security Notions

The security of TVES is defined by validity, unforgeability and opacity. These security notions are similar to VES but with additional requirements related to thresholds. The following are formal definitions of these properties.

Definition 4 (Secure TVES Scheme). *A (t_s, n_s, t_a, n_a)-TVES scheme is secure if the following hold:*

- *Validity: Let m denotes the message to be signed, $\mathcal{P}$ and $\mathcal{Q}$ denotes a subset of honest signers and adjudicators, s_i and a_i denotes a particular honest signer and adjudicator. The following equations must hold for all messages and all properly generated keypairs if $|\mathcal{P}| = t_s$ and $|\mathcal{Q}| = t_a$ (the set's sizes meet the threshold requirement):*
  - *For verifiably encrypted signature shares ω_{s_i}:*

$$\Pr \left[\begin{matrix} \omega_{s_i} = \text{SEnc}(\sigma_{s_i}, pk_a) \\ \text{SVer}(\omega_{s_i}, m, pk_{s_i}, pk_a) = 1 \end{matrix} \right] = 1 \tag{1}$$

- *For aggregated verifiably encrypted signature ω:*

$$\Pr \left[\begin{array}{c} \omega = \mathsf{VESComb}(\{(s_i, \omega_{s_i}) \mid s_i \in \mathcal{P}\}) \\ \mathsf{VESVer}(\omega, m, pk_s, pk_a) = 1 \end{array} \right] = 1 \qquad (2)$$

- *For decrypted signature shares ρ_{a_i}:*

$$\Pr \left[\begin{array}{c} \rho_{a_i} = \mathsf{SAdj}(\omega, sk_{a_i}) \\ \mathsf{AdjVer}(\rho_{a_i}, \omega, pk_{a_i}) = 1 \end{array} \right] = 1 \qquad (3)$$

- *For ordinary signature σ:*

$$\Pr \left[\begin{array}{c} \sigma = \mathsf{AdjComb}(\{(a_i, \rho_{a_i}) \mid a_i \in \mathcal{Q}\}) \\ \mathsf{Ver}(\sigma, m, pk_s) = 1 \end{array} \right] = 1 \qquad (4)$$

– *Unforgeability: No polynomial-time adversary, who is allowed to corrupt up to $t_s - 1$ signers and any number of adjudicators (even if n_a), can output an existential forgery of the verifiably encrypted signature pair (m, ω) which satisfies $\mathsf{VESVer}(\omega, m, pk_s, pk_a) = 1$. Otherwise, the adversary can subsequently obtain a valid (m, σ) from at least t_a corrupted adjudicators.*

– *Opacity: No polynomial-time adversary, who is allowed to corrupt up to $t_s - 1$ signers or t_a adjudicators and given a verifiably encrypted signature pair (m, ω), can extract the ordinary signature pair (m, σ) which satisfies $\mathsf{Ver}(\sigma, m, pk_s) = 1$. The extraction may be accomplished in two ways:*

- *Corrupt up to $t_s - 1$ signers, then output a forgery (m, σ) of the basic threshold signature scheme.*
- *Corrupt up to $t_a - 1$ adjudicators, then extracts σ from ω.*

4   A Concrete Construction of TVES: TVES$_{\mathsf{BP}}$ from Bilinear Pairings

We present our concrete construction of the TVES scheme TVES$_{\mathsf{BP}}$ from bilinear pairings, which is built on Boldyreva's [2] BLS-based threshold signature scheme and Gorantla *et al.* 's [17] BLS-based verifiably encrypted signature scheme with threshold applied on the adjudicator party as the starting point. By using the correctness of DKG protocols and the multiplicative homorphic property of ElGamal encryption [11], we are able to apply threshold on both the signer and adjudicator parties.

Scheme 1 (TVES Scheme from Bilinear Pairings). *Let $G = \langle g \rangle$ be a cyclic group of prime order p. The bilinear pairing is given by $e : G \times G \to G_T$. Define a cryptographic full-domain hash function $H : \{0,1\}^* \to G$ and a DKG protocol* DKG. *The message is $m \in \{0,1\}^*$. The algorithms of the (t_s, n_s, t_a, n_a)-TVES scheme* TVES$_{\mathsf{BP}}$ = (SDKG, AdjDKG, SSign, SEnc, SVer, VESComb, VESVer, SAdj, AdjVer, AdjComb) *from bilinear pairings are defined as follows:*

- SDKG: *Input a security parameter* 1^λ *and use* DKG *to generate keypair* $(sk_{s_i}, pk_{s_i}) = (S(s_i), g^{S(s_i)})$ *for each signer* s_i. $S(x) \in \mathbb{Z}_p[X]$ *is a polynomial of degree* $t_s - 1$ *and cannot be reconstructed by at most* $t_s - 1$ *signers. Moreover,* $pk_s = g^{S(0)}$.
- AdjDKG: *Similar to* SDKG. *Use* DKG *to generate keypair* $(sk_{a_i}, pk_{a_i}) = (A(a_i), g^{A(a_i)})$ *for each adjudicator* a_i. $A(x) \in \mathbb{Z}_p[X]$ *is a polynomial of degree* $t_a - 1$ *and cannot be reconstructed by at most* $t_a - 1$ *adjudicators. Moreover,* $pk_a = g^{A(0)}$.
- SSign: *For a particular signer* s_i, *input* $sk_{s_i} \in G$ *and* m, *output an ordinary signature share* $\sigma_{s_i} = H(m)^{sk_{s_i}}$.
- SEnc: *For a particular signer* s_i, *choose* $r_{s_i} \in \mathbb{Z}_p$ *randomly, input* σ_{s_i} *and* pk_a, *output a verifiably encrypted signature share*

$$(\mu_{s_i}, \omega_{s_i}) = (g^{r_{s_i}}, \sigma_{s_i} pk_a^{r_{s_i}}). \tag{5}$$

This is equivalent to using ElGamal encryption on σ_{s_i}.
- SVer: *Input* $(\mu_{s_i}, \omega_{s_i})$, m, pk_{s_i} *and* pk_a, *accept the verifiably encrypted signature share and return* 1 *if and only if*

$$e(g, \omega_{s_i}) = e(pk_{s_i}, H(m))e(pk_a, \mu_{s_i}) \tag{6}$$

holds, otherwise return 0.
- VESComb: *Input a set* $\mathcal{P}$ *of signers* $(|\mathcal{P}| = t_s)$, *run* SVer *for all* $s_i \in \mathcal{P}$ *with their verifiably encrypted signature share* $(\mu_{s_i}, \omega_{s_i})$ *and public key* pk_{s_i}. *Return* $\perp$ *if any of these calls return* 0. *Otherwise return the aggregated verifiably encrypted signature*

$$(\mu, \omega) = (\prod_{s_i \in \mathcal{P}} \mu_{s_i}^{L_{s_i}}, \prod_{s_i \in \mathcal{P}} \omega_{s_i}^{L_{s_i}}), \tag{7}$$

where $L_{s_i} = \prod_{s_j \in \mathcal{P} \backslash \{s_i\}} \frac{s_j}{s_j - s_i}$ *is the* s_i*th Lagrange coefficient of the polynomial* S.
- VESVer: *Input* (μ, ω), m, pk_s *and* pk_a, *accept the aggregated verifiably encrypted signature and return* 1 *if and only if*

$$e(g, \omega) = e(pk_s, H(m))e(pk_a, \mu) \tag{8}$$

holds, otherwise return 0.
- SAdj: *For a particular adjudicator* a_i, *input* (μ, ω) *and* sk_{a_i}, *output a decrypted signature share* $\rho_{a_i} = \omega \cdot (\mu^{sk_{a_i}})^{-1}$.
- AdjVer: *Input* ρ_{a_i}, (μ, ω) *and* pk_{a_i}, *accept the decrypted signature share and return* 1 *if and only if*

$$e(g, \rho_{a_i}) = e(g, \omega)e(pk_{a_i}, \mu^{-1}) \tag{9}$$

holds, otherwise return 0.

– AdjComb: *Input a set $\mathcal{Q}$ of adjudicators ($|\mathcal{Q}| = t_a$), run AdjVer for all $a_i \in \mathcal{Q}$ with their decrypted signature share ρ_{a_i} and public key pk_{a_i}. Return $\perp$ if any of these calls return 0. Otherwise return the ordinary signature*

$$\sigma = \omega \prod_{a_i \in \mathcal{Q}} (\rho_{a_i} \cdot \omega^{-1})^{M_{a_i}}, \tag{10}$$

where $M_{a_i} = \prod_{a_j \in \mathcal{Q}\backslash\{a_i\}} \frac{a_j}{a_j - a_i}$ is the a_ith Lagrange coefficient of the polynomial A.

– Ver: *Input σ, m and pk_s, accept the ordinary signature and return 1 if and only if $e(g, \sigma) = e(pk_s, H(m))$ holds, otherwise return 0.*

5 Security and Performance Analysis

5.1 Validity

Theorem 1. *The validity of $\mathsf{TVES_{BP}}$ holds if the DKG protocol used and ElGamal encryption are correct.*

Proof. For SVer : $e(g, \omega_{s_i}) \overset{?}{=} e(pk_{s_i}, H(m))e(pk_a, \mu_{s_i})$ and SEnc : $(\mu_{s_i}, \omega_{s_i}) = (g^{r_{s_i}}, \sigma_{s_i} pk_a^{r_{s_i}})$, we have

$$\begin{aligned}
e(g, \omega_{s_i}) &= e(g, \sigma_{s_i} pk_a^{r_{s_i}}) \\
&= e(g, H(m)^{sk_{s_i}} g^{sk_a r_{s_i}}) \\
&= e(g, H(m)^{sk_{s_i}})e(g, g^{sk_a r_{s_i}}) \\
&= e(g^{sk_{s_i}}, H(m))e(g^{sk_a}, g^{r_{s_i}}) \quad = e(pk_{s_i}, H(m))e(pk_a, \mu_{s_i})
\end{aligned} \tag{11}$$

which shows that $\Pr\left[\begin{array}{l} \omega_{s_i} = \mathsf{SEnc}(\sigma_{s_i}, pk_a) \\ \mathsf{SVer}(\omega_{s_i}, m, pk_{s_i}, pk_a) = 1 \end{array}\right] = 1$ holds.

For VESVer : $e(g, \omega) \overset{?}{=} e(pk_s, H(m))e(pk_a, \mu)$ and VESComb : $(\mu, \omega) = (\prod_{s_i \in \mathcal{P}} \mu_{s_i}^{L_{s_i}}, \prod_{s_i \in \mathcal{P}} \omega_{s_i}^{L_{s_i}})$, we have

$$\begin{aligned}
\mu &= \prod_{s_i \in \mathcal{P}} \mu_{s_i}^{L_{s_i}} = \prod_{s_i \in \mathcal{P}} g^{r_{s_i} L_{s_i}} = g^{\sum_{s_i \in \mathcal{P}} r_{s_i} L_{s_i}} \\
\omega &= \prod_{s_i \in \mathcal{P}} \omega_{s_i}^{L_{s_i}} = \prod_{s_i \in \mathcal{P}} \sigma_{s_i}^{L_{s_i}} pk_a^{r_{s_i} L_{s_i}} = H(m)^{\sum_{s_i \in \mathcal{P}} sk_{s_i} L_{s_i}} pk_a^{\sum_{s_i \in \mathcal{P}} r_{s_i} L_{s_i}}
\end{aligned} \tag{12}$$

$$\begin{aligned}
e(g, \omega) &= e(g, H(m)^{\sum_{s_i \in \mathcal{P}} sk_{s_i} L_{s_i}} pk_a^{\sum_{s_i \in \mathcal{P}} r_{s_i} L_{s_i}}) \\
&= e(g, H(m)^{\sum_{s_i \in \mathcal{P}} sk_{s_i} L_{s_i}})e(g, g^{sk_a \sum_{s_i \in \mathcal{P}} r_{s_i} L_{s_i}}) \\
&= e(g^{\sum_{s_i \in \mathcal{P}} sk_{s_i} L_{s_i}}, H(m))e(g^{sk_a}, g^{\sum_{s_i \in \mathcal{P}} r_{s_i} L_{s_i}}) \quad = e(pk_s, H(m))e(pk_a, \mu)
\end{aligned} \tag{13}$$

which shows that $\Pr\left[\begin{array}{l} \omega = \mathsf{VESComb}(\{(s_i, \omega_{s_i}) \mid s_i \in \mathcal{P}\}) \\ \mathsf{VESVer}(\omega, m, pk_s, pk_a) = 1 \end{array}\right] = 1$ holds.

For AdjVer : $e(g, \rho_{a_i}) \overset{?}{=} e(g, \omega)e(pk_{a_i}, \mu^{-1})$ and SAdj : $\rho_{a_i} = \omega \cdot (\mu^{sk_{a_i}})^{-1}$, we have

$$
\begin{aligned}
e(g, \rho_{a_i}) &= e(g, \omega \cdot (\mu^{sk_{a_i}})^{-1}) \\
&= e(g, \omega)e(g, (\mu^{sk_{a_i}})^{-1}) \\
&= e(g, \omega)e(g^{sk_{a_i}}, \mu^{-1}) \qquad = e(g, \omega)e(pk_{a_i}, \mu^{-1})
\end{aligned}
\tag{14}
$$

which shows that $\Pr\left[\begin{array}{c} \rho_{a_i} = \mathsf{SAdj}(\omega, sk_{a_i}) \\ \mathsf{AdjVer}(\rho_{a_i}, \omega, pk_{a_i}) = 1 \end{array} \right] = 1$ holds.

For Ver : $e(g, \sigma) \overset{?}{=} e(pk_s, H(m))$, we first need to show that the ordinary signature σ aggregated from t_a adjudicator-decrypted shares using AdjComb : $\sigma = \omega \prod_{a_i \in \mathcal{Q}} (\rho_{a_i} \cdot \omega^{-1})^{M_{a_i}}$ $(M_{a_i} = \prod_{a_j \in \mathcal{Q} \setminus \{a_i\}} \frac{a_j}{a_j - a_i})$ can also be aggregated from t_s signers' ordinary shares produced by SSign : $\sigma_{s_i} = H(m)^{sk_{s_i}}$.

$$
\begin{aligned}
\sigma &= \omega \prod_{a_i \in \mathcal{Q}} (\rho_{a_i} \cdot \omega^{-1})^{M_{a_i}} \\
&= \omega \prod_{a_i \in \mathcal{Q}} (\mu^{sk_{a_i} M_{a_i}})^{-1} \\
&= \omega \cdot (\mu^{\sum_{a_i \in \mathcal{Q}} sk_{a_i} M_{a_i}})^{-1} \\
&= \omega \cdot (\mu^{sk_a})^{-1} \\
&= H(m)^{\sum_{s_i \in \mathcal{P}} sk_{s_i} L_{s_i}} pk_a^{\sum_{s_i \in \mathcal{P}} r_{s_i} L_{s_i}} \cdot (g^{sk_a \sum_{s_i \in \mathcal{P}} r_{s_i} L_{s_i}})^{-1} \\
&= H(m)^{\sum_{s_i \in \mathcal{P}} sk_{s_i} L_{s_i}} g^{sk_a \sum_{s_i \in \mathcal{P}} r_{s_i} L_{s_i}} \cdot (g^{sk_a \sum_{s_i \in \mathcal{P}} r_{s_i} L_{s_i}})^{-1} \\
&= H(m)^{\sum_{s_i \in \mathcal{P}} sk_{s_i} L_{s_i}} \\
&= \prod_{s_i \in \mathcal{P}} H(m)^{sk_{s_i} L_{s_i}} \\
&= \prod_{s_i \in \mathcal{P}} \sigma_{s_i}^{L_{s_i}}
\end{aligned}
\tag{15}
$$

According to DKG's correctness

$$
pk_s = g^{S(0)} = g^{\sum_{s_i} sk_{s_i} L_{s_i}} \quad (L_{s_i} = \prod_{s_j \in \mathcal{P} \setminus \{s_i\}} \frac{s_j}{s_j - s_i}),
\tag{16}
$$

we have

$$
\begin{aligned}
e(g, \sigma) &= e(g, \prod_{s_i \in \mathcal{P}} \sigma_{s_i}^{L_{s_i}}) \\
&= e(g, \prod_{s_i \in \mathcal{P}} H(m)^{sk_{s_i} L_{s_i}}) \\
&= e(g, H(m)^{\sum_{s_i \in \mathcal{P}} sk_{s_i} L_{s_i}}) \\
&= e(g^{\sum_{s_i \in \mathcal{P}} sk_{s_i} L_{s_i}}, H(m)) \qquad = e(pk_s, H(m))
\end{aligned}
\tag{17}
$$

which shows that $\Pr\left[\begin{array}{c} \sigma = \mathsf{AdjComb}(\{(a_i, \rho_{a_i}) \mid a_i \in \mathcal{Q}\}) \\ \mathsf{Ver}(\sigma, m, pk_s) = 1 \end{array} \right] = 1$ holds. $\square$

5.2   Unforgeability

Theorem 2. *If Boldyreva's [4] BLS-based threshold signature scheme* TBLS *is existentially unforgeable under chosen message attack, then* TVES$_{BP}$ *is also existentially unforgeable under chosen message attack.*

Proof. We will use a simulation-based proof to reduce TVES$_{BP}$'s unforgeability to TBLS's unforgeability. Given a polynomial-time adversary $\mathcal{A}$ who can forge (t_s, n_s, t_a, n_a) − TVES$_{BP}$, then we can construct another polynomial-time forger $\mathcal{F}$ for (t_s, n_s) − TBLS who uses $\mathcal{A}$ as a subroutine. $\mathcal{F}$ needs to simulate $\mathcal{A}$'s input and oracle queries, making them indistinguishable from the real execution of TVES$_{BP}$ for the view of $\mathcal{A}$.

Formally, $\mathcal{A}$ conducts the following experiment $\mathsf{Forge}_{\mathcal{A}, \mathsf{TVES}_{BP}}^{EF-CMA}(t_s, n_s, t_a, n_a)$:

1. Setup: SDKG(1^λ) and AdjDKG(1^λ) are run to obtain n_s signers' keypairs $\left((sk_{s_1}, pk_{s_1}), \cdots, (sk_{s_{n_s}}, pk_{s_{n_s}})\right)$, n_a adjudicators' keypairs $\left((sk_{a_1}, pk_{a_1}), \cdots, (sk_{a_{n_a}}, pk_{a_{n_a}})\right)$, signers' public key pk_s and adjudicators' public key pk_a respectively.
2. Query: $\mathcal{A}$ is given $(pk_{s_1}, \cdots, pk_{s_{n_s}})$, $(pk_{a_1}, \cdots, pk_{a_{n_a}})$, pk_s and pk_a. $\mathcal{A}$ is also given access to two oracles $\mathsf{Corrupt}_{sk_{s_i}}(\cdot)$ and $\mathsf{VES}_{sk_s}(\cdot)$, and can make the following two kinds of queries:
   – Corruption Queries: Query $\mathsf{Corrupt}_{sk_{s_i}}(\cdot)$ with a corrupted signer s_i to get its secret key sk_{s_i}. After $\mathsf{Corrupt}_{sk_{s_i}}(\cdot)$ gives $t_s - 1$ different answers, $\perp$ is returned for all subsequent queries.
   – VES Queries: Query $\mathsf{VES}_{sk_s}(\cdot)$ with a chosen message m to get its valid verifiably encrypted signature (μ, ω).
3. Output: $\mathcal{A}$ outputs another verifiably encrypted signature pair $(m, (\mu, \omega))$. The output of the experiment is defined to be 1 if and only if:
   – $\mathcal{A}$ have not made any query to $\mathsf{VES}_{sk_s}(\cdot)$ with m.
   – VESVer : $e(g, \omega) = e(pk_s, H(m))e(pk_a, \mu)$ holds.

We use $\Pr[\mathsf{Forge}_{\mathcal{A}, \mathsf{TVES}_{BP}}^{EF-CMA}(t_s, n_s, t_a, n_a) = 1]$ to denote the probability that $\mathcal{A}$ successfully outputs an existential forgery of TVES$_{BP}$. Similarly, $\Pr[\mathsf{Forge}_{\mathcal{F}, \mathsf{TBLS}}^{EF-CMA}(t_s, n_s) = 1]$ denotes the probability that $\mathcal{F}$ successfully outputs an existential forgery of TBLS.

We now describe the algorithms of $\mathcal{F}$ to forge TBLS. In the setup phase, $\mathcal{F}$ takes the public keys $(pk_{s_1}, \cdots, pk_{s_{n_s}})$ and pk_s generated in TBLS's key generation algorithm as input to $\mathcal{A}$. Since these public keys and the public keys generated using TVES$_{BLS}$'s SDKG are generated using the same DKG protocol and have the same properties, they are indistinguishable for the view of $\mathcal{A}$. Similarly, when $\mathcal{A}$ queries $\mathsf{Corrupt}_{sk_{s_i}}(\cdot)$ with s_i, $\mathcal{F}$ queries its corruption oracle to obtain the corrupted signer's secret key sk_{s_i} as the return of $\mathcal{A}$'s query, the return value is also indistinguishable.

For adjudicator-related keys, $\mathcal{F}$ randomly chooses a polynomial $f(x) \in \mathbb{Z}_p[X]$ of degree $t - 1$, then use $(f(1), \cdots, f(n_a))$, $(g^{f(1)}, \cdots, g^{f(n_a)})$, $f(0)$, $g^{f(0)}$ to simulate $(sk_{a_1}, \cdots, sk_{a_{n_a}})$, $(pk_{a_1}, \cdots, pk_{a_{n_a}})$, sk_a and pk_a. This is consistent with the correctness of DKG, so it is also indistinguishable for $\mathcal{A}$.

When $\mathcal{A}$ requests a verifiably encrypted signature on a message m, $\mathcal{F}$ randomly chooses $r \in \mathbb{Z}_p$ and queries its own signing oracle with m to obtain an ordinary signature σ, then returns $\mathcal{A}$ with $(\mu, \omega) = (g^r, \sigma pk_a^r)$. Since (m, σ) is a valid ordinary signature pair in TBLS, that is to say $e(\sigma, g) = e(H(m), pk_s)$ holds, $(m, (\mu, \omega))$ is also a valid verifiably encrypted signature pair in TVES$_{\text{BLS}}$. Therefore, the simulation of VES$_{sk_s}(\cdot)$ is indistinguishable for $\mathcal{A}$.

$$
\begin{aligned}
e(g, \omega) &= e(g, \sigma pk_a^r) \\
&= e(g, \sigma)e(g, pk_a^r) \\
&= e(g, H(m)^{sk_s})e(g, g^{sk_a r}) \\
&= e(pk_s, H(m))e(g^{sk_a}, g^r) \quad = e(pk_s, H(m))e(pk_a, \mu)
\end{aligned}
\tag{18}
$$

Finally, if $\mathcal{A}$ outputs the forged verifiably encrypted signature pair $(m, (\mu, \omega))$, then $\mathcal{F}$ can also output a forgery $(m, \sigma) = (m, \omega \cdot (\mu^{sk_a})^{-1})$ of TBLS. From the above analysis, it is clear that $\Pr[\text{Forge}_{\mathcal{A}, \text{TVES}_{\text{BP}}}^{\text{EF-CMA}}(t_s, n_s, t_a, n_a) = 1] \leq \Pr[\text{Forge}_{\mathcal{F}, \text{TBLS}}^{\text{EF-CMA}}(t_s, n_s) = 1]$. Hence, if TBLS is existentially unforgeable (this has been proved in [4]) so it satisfies $\Pr[\text{Forge}_{\mathcal{F}, \text{TBLS}}^{\text{EF-CMA}}(t_s, n_s) = 1] \leq \text{negl}(\lambda)$, then $\Pr[\text{Forge}_{\mathcal{A}, \text{TVES}_{\text{BP}}}^{\text{EF-CMA}}(t_s, n_s, t_a, n_a) = 1] \leq \text{negl}(\lambda)$ which completes the proof.

5.3   Opacity

Theorem 3. *If Boldyreva's [4] BLS-based threshold signature scheme* TBLS *is existentially unforgeable, discrete logarithm problem is hard in G, threshold ElGamal encryption [9] is secure and the DKG protocol used is unpredictable, then* TVES$_{\text{BP}}$ *is secure against extraction.*

Proof. The two possible ways of extracting the ordinary signature pair (m, σ) from a verifiably encrypted signature pair $(m, (\mu, \omega))$ have been given in the previous security notions of TVES. From [4] we know that TBLS is existentially unforgeable. Hence, a polynomial-time adversary cannot perform the forgery (m, σ) of the ordinary signature.

In addition, since we have AdjComb : $\sigma = \omega \prod_{a_i \in \mathcal{Q}} (\rho_{a_i} \cdot \omega^{-1})^{M_{a_i}}$, the adversary can extract the original signature σ if the adjudicators' secret key sk_a can be recovered:

$$
\begin{aligned}
\sigma &= \omega \prod_{a_i \in \mathcal{Q}} (\rho_{a_i} \cdot \omega^{-1})^{M_{a_i}} \\
&= \omega \prod_{a_i \in \mathcal{Q}} (\mu^{sk_{a_i} M_{a_i}})^{-1} \\
&= \omega \cdot (\mu^{\sum_{a_i \in \mathcal{Q}} sk_{a_i} M_{a_i}})^{-1} \\
&= \omega \cdot (\mu^{sk_a})^{-1}
\end{aligned}
\tag{19}
$$

However, since the adversary can only corrupt up to $t_a - 1$ adjudicators, it is impossible to recover sk_a according to the unpredictability property of DKG protocols. Computing the discrete logarithm $sk_a = \log_g pk_a$ is also impossible because of the hardness of discrete logarithm problem. In fact, since SEnc is equivalent to using ElGamal encryption on σ_{s_i}, VESComb combines these verifiably encrypted signature shares using multiplication and ElGamal encryption is multiplicative homomorphic, extracting σ from (μ, ω) is equivalent to breaking threshold ElGamal encryption.   □

5.4   Efficiency

Computation Consumptions. The computation consumptions of each algorithm for $\mathsf{TVES_{BP}}$ are shown in Table 1. We denote Ad the point addition and doubling on G (expressed as multiplication in the multiplicative group), Pm the point scalar multiplication on G (expressed as exponentiation in the multiplicative group), Pa the pairing operation, Mul the multiplication on $\mathbb{Z}_p$ and Inv the inversion in $\mathbb{Z}_p$. Addition on $\mathbb{Z}_p$ and Inversion in G are omitted since these operations are trivial and the time is negligible. The computation consumption is also related to the size of the threshold (t_s, n_s, t_a, n_a).

Table 1. Computation consumptions of algorithms for $\mathsf{TVES_{BP}}$

Algorithm	Computation
SSign	Pm
SEnc	$\mathrm{Ad} + 2\mathrm{Pm}$
SVer	$\mathrm{Ad} + 3\mathrm{Pa}$
VESComb	$(2t_s - 2)\mathrm{Ad} + 2t_s\mathrm{Pm} + (2t_s^2 - 3t_s)\mathrm{Mul} + (t_s^2 - t_s)\mathrm{Inv}$
VESVer	$\mathrm{Ad} + 3\mathrm{Pa}$
SAdj	$\mathrm{Ad} + \mathrm{Pm}$
AdjVer	$\mathrm{Ad} + 3\mathrm{Pa}$
AdjComb	$2t_a\mathrm{Ad} + t_a\mathrm{Pm} + (2t_a^2 - 3t_a)\mathrm{Mul} + (t_a^2 - t_a)\mathrm{Inv}$
Ver	$2\mathrm{Pa}$

During the execution of $\mathsf{TVES_{BP}}$, one signer can be selected as the representative of signers to run VESComb only once to create the aggregated verifiably encrypted signature and send it to other signers. It is similar for AdjComb.

If it is desired to reduce the number of communication rounds, it is also feasible to have each signer run VESComb individually by selecting $(s_i, (\mu_{s_i}, \omega_{s_i}))$ according to some pre-defined rules (e.g., selecting the first t_s valid pairs submitted) to ensure getting the same result.

Running Time. We have implemented TVES$_{BP}$ using the PBC library [24] and measured the running time of each algorithm under several different thresholds. The implementation is written in C programming language, compiled with GCC 12.3.0 with `-Ofast -march=native` extra flags enabled and executed on the Inter Core i7-7820X CPU and Ubuntu 22.04 on Windows Subsystem for Linux for Windows 11. The elliptic curve used in this implementation is $y^2 = x^3 + x$ over the field F_q for some 512-bit prime $q = 3 \mod 4$ with embedding degree 2 [23], which is denoted as Type A curves in PBC library's documentation. The curve's parameters are chosen from the `param/a.param` file that comes with the PBC library. The results are shown in Table 2.

Table 2. Running time of algorithms for TVES$_{BP}$ in milliseconds

Algorithm	Running time
SSign	0.863
SEnc	1.736
SVer	1.854
VESVer	1.838
SAdj	0.867
AdjVer	1.840
Ver	1.219

Algorithm	Running time in different t_s or t_a *			
	$t = 3$	$t = 5$	$t = 10$	$t = 20$
VESComb	1.837	3.534	8.564	18.285
AdjComb	0.878	1.774	4.542	9.421

* The running time of VESComb is only related to t_s, and the running time of AdjComb is only related to t_a. For simplicity, they are both denoted as t in the table header.

Signature Size. For the signature size, the ordinary signature (share) $\sigma_{(s_i)}$ and the decrypted signature ρ_{a_i} are one element of G, and the verifiably encrypted signature (share) $(\mu_{(s_i)}, \omega_{(s_i)})$ is two elements. With the chosen elliptic curve parameters, their sizes are 65 and 130 bytes using the compressed form.

6   Application

Here we present a practical application of TVES for multiparty contract signing and exchange.

Suppose there are two companies denoted as S and T that need to sign a contract together. S and T need to exchange their signatures σ_s and σ_t with each other on the contract, which is the previously mentioned message m. In the case of using TVES, each company can elect multiple representatives $(s_1, \cdots, s_{n_s})$ and $(t_1, \cdots, t_{n_t})$ (e.g. from board members) to participate in the signature process. They also choose multiple individual adjudicators $(a_1, \cdots, a_{n_a})$. This constitutes two separate executions of TVES using (t_s, n_s, t_a, n_a) and (t_t, n_t, t_a, n_a) thresholds as shown in Fig. 2.

The contract can only be successfully signed and exchanged if not less than t_s and t_t representatives of S and T agree. If S does not receive T's ordinary signature σ_t, S can resort to at least t_a honest adjudicators to reveal the signature as shown in Fig. 3. If T wants to break the protocol and get σ_s without giving the ordinary signature σ_t, it needs to corrupt at least t_s representatives of T and t_a adjudicators to obtain their decrypted or ordinary signature shares and prevent the adjudicators from revealing ω_t. Since the number of participants that need to be corrupted has become larger, this is much more difficult (and secure) than the original Verifiably Encrypted Signature scheme.

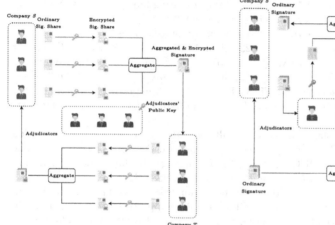

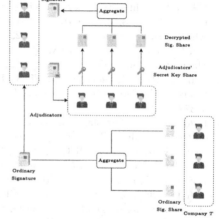

Fig. 2. Company S and T exchange verifiably encrypted signature ω_s and ω_t with adjudicators' public key in a TVES scheme.

Fig. 3. Company S gets the other company T's ordinary signature σ_t from T's representatives. S can also resort to adjudicators to reveal σ_t from previously obtained ω_t if it does not receive σ_t from T.

7   Conclusion

Verifiably Encrypted Signature is useful to enable fair exchange in online contract signing. Threshold cryptography is also usually used as a building block to construct more complex protocols due to its fault tolerance and decentralized power properties. In this paper, we combined these two important cryptographic primitives and proposed a new cryptographic primitive called Threshold Verifiably Encrypted Signature (TVES). We gave its definition, security notions and then a concrete construction TVES$_{BP}$ from bilinear pairings based on BLS short signature scheme. We proved that TVES$_{BP}$ is valid and secure against existential forgery and extraction. We also analyzed TVES$_{BP}$'s computation consumption. We showed that the purpose of TVES is to achieve better security and fairness in contract signing through a practical application example. Future work includes integrating TVES into other efficient signature schemes.

Acknowledgement. This work is supported by the National R&D Key Program of China under Grant 2022YFB2701500 and the National Natural Science Foundation of China (No. 62272491).

References

1. Asokan, N., Schunter, M., Waidner, M.: Optimistic protocols for fair exchange. In: Proceedings of the 4th ACM Conference on Computer and Communications Security. pp. 7–17. CCS '97, Association for Computing Machinery, New York, NY, USA (1997). https://doi.org/10.1145/266420.266426
2. Bacho, R., Loss, J.: On the adaptive security of the threshold BLS signature scheme. In: Proceedings of the 2022 ACM SIGSAC Conference on Computer and Communications Security. pp. 193–207. CCS '22, Association for Computing Machinery, New York, NY, USA (2022). https://doi.org/10.1145/3548606.3560656
3. Ben-Or, M., Goldreich, O., Micali, S., Rivest, R.: A fair protocol for signing contracts. IEEE Trans. Inf. Theory **36**(1), 40–46 (1990). https://doi.org/10.1109/18.50372
4. Boldyreva, A.: Threshold signatures, multisignatures and blind signatures based on the gap-diffie-hellman-group signature scheme. In: Desmedt, Y.G. (ed.) Public Key Cryptography — PKC 2003, pp. 31–46. Springer Berlin Heidelberg, Berlin, Heidelberg (2002). https://doi.org/10.1007/3-540-36288-6_3
5. Boneh, D., Franklin, M.: Identity-based encryption from the weil pairing. In: Kilian, J. (ed.) Advances in Cryptology — CRYPTO 2001, pp. 213–229. Springer Berlin Heidelberg, Berlin, Heidelberg (2001). https://doi.org/10.1007/3-540-44647-8_13
6. Boneh, D., Gentry, C., Lynn, B., Shacham, H.: Aggregate and verifiably encrypted signatures from bilinear maps. In: Biham, E. (ed.) Advances in Cryptology — EUROCRYPT 2003, pp. 416–432. Springer Berlin Heidelberg, Berlin, Heidelberg (2003). https://doi.org/10.1007/3-540-39200-9_26
7. Boneh, D., Lynn, B., Shacham, H.: Short Signatures from the Weil Pairing. In: Boyd, C. (ed.) ASIACRYPT 2001. LNCS, vol. 2248, pp. 514–532. Springer, Heidelberg (2001). https://doi.org/10.1007/3-540-45682-1_30
8. Desmedt, Y.: Society and Group Oriented Cryptography: a New Concept. In: Pomerance, C. (ed.) CRYPTO 1987. LNCS, vol. 293, pp. 120–127. Springer, Heidelberg (1988). https://doi.org/10.1007/3-540-48184-2_8
9. Desmedt, Y., Frankel, Y.: Threshold cryptosystems. In: Brassard, G. (ed.) CRYPTO 1989. LNCS, vol. 435, pp. 307–315. Springer, New York (1990). https://doi.org/10.1007/0-387-34805-0_28
10. Desmedt, Y., Frankel, Y.: Shared generation of authenticators and signatures. In: Feigenbaum, J. (ed.) CRYPTO 1991. LNCS, vol. 576, pp. 457–469. Springer, Heidelberg (1992). https://doi.org/10.1007/3-540-46766-1_37

11. ElGamal, T.: A public key cryptosystem and a signature scheme based on discrete logarithms. IEEE Trans. Inf. Theory **31**(4), 469–472 (1985). https://doi.org/10.1109/TIT.1985.1057074

12. Feldman, P.: A practical scheme for non-interactive verifiable secret sharing. In: 28th Annual Symposium on Foundations of Computer Science (sfcs 1987), pp. 427–438 (1987). https://doi.org/10.1109/SFCS.1987.4

13. Gennaro, R., Goldfeder, S., Narayanan, A.: Threshold-Optimal DSA/ECDSA Signatures and an Application to Bitcoin Wallet Security. In: Manulis, M., Sadeghi, A.R., Schneider, S. (eds.) ACNS 2016. LNCS, vol. 9696, pp. 156–174. Springer, Cham (2016). https://doi.org/10.1007/978-3-319-39555-5_9

14. Gennaro, R., Jarecki, S., Krawczyk, H., Rabin, T.: Robust Threshold DSS Signatures. In: Maurer, U. (ed.) EUROCRYPT 1996. LNCS, vol. 1070, pp. 354–371. Springer, Heidelberg (1996). https://doi.org/10.1007/3-540-68339-9_31

15. Gennaro, R., Jarecki, S., Krawczyk, H., Rabin, T.: Secure distributed key generation for discrete-log based cryptosystems. J. Cryptology **20**(1), 51–83 (2007). https://doi.org/10.1007/s00145-006-0347-3

16. Goldfeder, S., Gennaro, R., Kalodner, H., Bonneau, J., Kroll, J.A., Felten, E.W., Narayanan, A.: Securing bitcoin wallets via a new DSA/ECDSA threshold signature scheme (2015). http://stevengoldfeder.com/papers/threshold_sigs.pdf

17. Gorantla, M.C., Saxena, A.: Verifiably encrypted signature scheme with threshold adjudication. Cryptology ePrint Archive, Paper 2006/343 (2006), https://eprint.iacr.org/2006/343

18. Groth, J.: Fully anonymous group signatures without random oracles. In: Kurosawa, K. (ed.) ASIACRYPT 2007. LNCS, vol. 4833, pp. 164–180. Springer, Heidelberg (2007). https://doi.org/10.1007/978-3-540-76900-2_10

19. Harn, L.: Group-oriented (t, n) threshold digital signature scheme and digital multisignature. IEE Proceedings - Comput. Digital Tech. **141**, 307–313 (1994)

20. Joux, A.: A one round protocol for tripartite Diffie–Hellman. In: Bosma, W. (ed.) ANTS 2000. LNCS, vol. 1838, pp. 385–393. Springer, Heidelberg (2000). https://doi.org/10.1007/10722028_23

21. Komlo, C., Goldberg, I.: FROST: Flexible Round-Optimized Schnorr Threshold Signatures. In: Dunkelman, O., Jacobson, Jr., M.J., O'Flynn, C. (eds.) SAC 2020. LNCS, vol. 12804, pp. 34–65. Springer, Cham (2021). https://doi.org/10.1007/978-3-030-81652-0_2

22. Lu, X., Yin, W., Zhang, P.: Lattice-based verifiably encrypted signature scheme without gaussian sampling for privacy protection in blockchain. Sustainability **14**(21) (2022). https://doi.org/10.3390/su142114225

23. Lynn, B.: On the implementation of pairing-based cryptosystems (2007). http://crypto.stanford.edu/pbc/thesis.pdf

24. Lynn, B.: PBC library - the pairing-based cryptography library (2013). https://crypto.stanford.edu/pbc/

25. Pedersen, T.P.: A threshold cryptosystem without a trusted party. In: Davies, D.W. (ed.) EUROCRYPT 1991. LNCS, vol. 547, pp. 522–526. Springer, Heidelberg (1991). https://doi.org/10.1007/3-540-46416-6_47

26. Pedersen, T.P.: Non-Interactive and information-theoretic secure verifiable secret sharing. In: Feigenbaum, J. (ed.) CRYPTO 1991. LNCS, vol. 576, pp. 129–140. Springer, Heidelberg (1992). https://doi.org/10.1007/3-540-46766-1_9

27. Ray, I., Ray, I., Natarajan, N.: An anonymous and failure resilient fair-exchange e-commerce protocol. Decis. Support Syst. **39**(3), 267–292 (2005). https://doi.org/10.1016/j.dss.2003.10.011

28. van Tilborg, H.C.A., Jajodia, S. (eds.): Encyclopedia of Cryptography and Security. Springer, Boston, MA (2011). https://doi.org/10.1007/978-1-4419-5906-5

29. Shamir, A.: How to share a secret. Commun. ACM **22**(11), 612–613 (Nov 1979). https://doi.org/10.1145/359168.359176

30. Shao, Z., Gao, Y.: Certificate-based verifiably encrypted RSA signatures. Trans. Emerg. Telecommun. Technol. **26**(2), 276–289 (2015). https://doi.org/10.1002/ett.2607

31. Shoup, V.: Practical threshold signatures. In: Preneel, B. (ed.) EUROCRYPT 2000. LNCS, vol. 1807, pp. 207–220. Springer, Heidelberg (2000). https://doi.org/10.1007/3-540-45539-6_15

32. Stathakopoulou, C., Cachin, C.: Threshold signatures for blockchain systems. Tech. rep., Swiss Federal Institute of Technology (2017). https://dominoweb.draco.res.ibm.com/reports/rz3910.pdf

33. Takaragi, K., Miyazaki, K., Takahashi, M., et al.: A threshold digital signature issuing scheme without secret communication. IEEE P1363 Study **154** (2000)

34. Tan, C.H.: Key substitution attacks on provably secure short signature schemes. IEICE Trans. Fundam. Electron. Commun. Comput. Sci. **88**(2), 611–612 (2005). https://doi.org/10.1093/ietfec/e88-a.2.611

35. Yang, X., Lau, W.F., Ye, Q., Au, M.H., Liu, J.K., Cheng, J.: Practical escrow protocol for bitcoin. IEEE Trans. Inf. Forensics Secur. **15**, 3023–3034 (2020). https://doi.org/10.1109/TIFS.2020.2976607

36. Yang, X., Liu, M., Au, M.H., Luo, X., Ye, Q.: Efficient verifiably encrypted ECDSA-like signatures and their applications. IEEE Trans. Inf. Forensics Secur. **17**, 1573–1582 (2022). https://doi.org/10.1109/TIFS.2022.3165978

37. Zhang, F., Safavi-Naini, R., Susilo, W.: Efficient verifiably encrypted signature and partially blind signature from bilinear pairings. In: Johansson, T., Maitra, S. (eds.) INDOCRYPT 2003. LNCS, vol. 2904, pp. 191–204. Springer, Heidelberg (2003). https://doi.org/10.1007/978-3-540-24582-7_14

38. Zhang, F., Safavi-Naini, R., Susilo, W.: An Efficient Signature Scheme from Bilinear Pairings and Its Applications. In: Bao, F., Deng, R., Zhou, J. (eds.) PKC 2004. LNCS, vol. 2947, pp. 277–290. Springer, Heidelberg (2004). https://doi.org/10.1007/978-3-540-24632-9_20

39. Zhou, J., Deng, R., Bao, F.: Some remarks on a fair exchange protocol. In: Imai, H., Zheng, Y. (eds.) PKC 2000. LNCS, vol. 1751, pp. 46–57. Springer, Heidelberg (2000). https://doi.org/10.1007/978-3-540-46588-1_4

Compact Accountable Ring Signatures in the Plain Model

Thanh Xuan Khuc[1]([✉])[iD], Willy Susilo[1][iD], Dung Hoang Duong[1][iD],
Fuchun Guo[1][iD], Kazuhide Fukushima[2][iD], and Shinsaku Kiyomoto[2][iD]

[1] Institute of Cybersecurity and Cryptology, School of Computing and Information
Technology, University of Wollongong, Wollongong, Australia
xtk929@uowmail.edu.au, {wsusilo,hduong,fuchun}@uow.edu.au
[2] Information Security Laboratory, KDDI Research, Inc., Fujimino, Japan
{ka-fukushima,kiyomoto}@kddi-research.jp

Abstract. Accountable ring signatures close the gap between ring signatures and group signatures. They support a designated opener who can identify signers when necessary while allowing for the most excellent possible flexibility in selecting the ring. Accountable ring signatures were first informally defined by Xu and Yung at CARDIS 2004. They present a compiler that transforms a traditional ring signature scheme into an accountable one by using a trusted model on the smart cards. At ESORICS 2015, Bootle et al. introduced a formal security model for accountable ring signatures. In addition, they also present a generic construction for accountable ring signatures in the random oracle model. In terms of the security proof model, the plain model is preferable since it requires neither any assumptions that sometimes do not exist in practice nor any trusted setup assumptions. Until now, there has been no construction of accountable ring signatures in the plain model, even with a linear signature size. In this paper, we present the first generic construction of accountable ring signature schemes that have the logarithmic signature size and are secure in the plain model using standard assumptions.

Keywords: NIWI · ring signatures · accountable ring signatures · plain model · standard model

1 Introduction

Group signatures [9] and ring signatures [13] allow signers to remain anonymous inside a group of users. While anonymity is desirable, in certain circumstances, we also want to be assured of signature traceability which implies that anonymity can be revealed. The group signature scheme relies on a trust manager to achieve both anonymity and traceability of the signature. The manager identifies the group members and assigns each member a key pair. The signer is anonymous to other team members, but the manager can know the signer's identity and revoke the anonymity if desired. On the other hand, in a ring signature, we

C. Ge and M. Yung (Eds.): Inscrypt 2023, LNCS 14526, pp. 23–43, 2024.
https://doi.org/10.1007/978-981-97-0942-7_2

have no group manager, no particular setup for secret sharing among group members, and the dynamics of group choice. Ring signature allows a person to sign a message on behalf of a group of users, but no one (including users of that ring) can know who signed that message.

The gap between ring signatures and group signatures is closed by accountable ring signatures [14]. They give you the freedom to choose the ring of users when making a signature, and they also make sure people are responsible by having an opener who can open a signature and show who signed it. The mix of flexibility and accountability makes it useful in situations where ring or group signatures are not as good. For example, an online forum that wishes to provide anonymity to its users while also being able to identify those who transgress the code of conduct. A forum can accomplish this by permitting user posts with accountable ring signatures whose proprietor is the designated opener. This system is decentralised and adaptable because various forums can have their opener keys, and users are not required to register with each platform individually.

Informally, accountable ring signatures require several security requirements as follows: (i) *traceability* (a designated opener can trace anyone who makes signatures) (ii) *unforgeability* (even with a control over an opener, the adversary cannot come up with a valid forged signature without knowing the user's secret key in the ring) (iii) *anonymity* (as long as an opener does not reveal the identity of the signer, the signer's identity is indistinguishable from any of the possible ring members), (iv) *tracing soundness* (the adversary cannot accuse a user of having created a signature when this user did not generate it).

We can categorise the security proof models in cryptography into two catalogues: random oracle model (ROM) and standard model[1]. In ROM, we need to use the assumption of truly uniformly random output as a random oracle. However, this assumption may not exist in practice. Theoretical results show that several protocols are secure in the random oracle model but trivially insecure whenever the RO is instantiated with any hash function [7]. In the standard model, the adversary is limited in computing power and time. The standard model is also divided into two main types of models: (i) the common reference string model in which the parties are allowed access to a pre-set common information)and (ii) the plain model in which there is no need to pre-set anything other than public system parameters. Therefore, the plain model is the most desirable one to achieve, but also the most difficult to construct cryptographic schemes.

1.1 Related Work

Xu and Yung defined accountable ring signatures informally in [14]. They present a compiler that converts a traditional ring signature scheme into one that is accountable by employing a trusted model that can only be used on smart cards,

---

[1] The quantum random oracle model (QROM) was developed recently. This model also necessitates the existence of a quantum oracle that all parties involved in a scheme consult. Both the output and input of the QROM are represented by qubit.

such as requiring that the Certificate Authority (CA) is trusted in issuing public key certificates and that the smart cards are tamper-resistant and trusted not to leak its secrets. Bootle et al. revisit accountable ring signatures and provide a formal security model for the primitive in [4]. Their model offers robust security definitions that include protection against maliciously selected keys and, at the same time, flexibility in the selection of the ring and the opener. In the random model, they also provide a generic construction using standard tools instead of using the tools on smart cards as [14]. Fraser et al. present a novel type of ring signature called a report and trace ring signature in [6]. A designated opener can revoke a signer's anonymity if and only if a user reports malicious behaviour. In fact, report and trace ring signatures can be viewed as an extension of accountable ring signatures, where the opener's role is distributed, and the reporter is modelled as an anonymous system user. They also provide a generic construction of report and trace ring signature that is secure in the random oracle.

1.2   Our Contribution

The notable contributions and innovations of our work can be summarized as follows:

- We introduce the first generic construction of an accountable ring signature in the plain model. Our scheme can be built from falsifiable standard assumptions without the random oracle heuristic or trusted setup assumptions.
- Our proposed scheme has a compact signature size. Namely, it is logarithmic with the number of users in the ring.
- Our proposed scheme achieves anonymity against full key exposure. It ensures that even if the adversary can corrupt and control users, a signature does not disclose the signer's identity unless an opener reveals it. Our scheme also achieves unforgeability. Even if the adversary is able to determine the identity of honest signers via the opening functionality, the adversary cannot generate a valid signature on behalf of an honest user. Moreover, our scheme is tracing soundness. It ensures that an adversary cannot use opening functionality to blame for a non-signer even if the adversary can control the opener and corrupt a user.

1.3   Overview of Our Techniques

Our construction is inspired by [1,4]. We first present an overview of the approach in [1,4]. Then, we outline our approach to construct accountable ring signatures in the plain model with logarithmic size.

Outline of Approach in [1] to Build Ring Signatures in the Plain Mode. In their construction, each user has a public key $VK = (epk, spk)$ and a secret key $SK = (esk, ssk)$, where (epk, esk) and (spk, ssk) respectively are a pair of encryption and signature scheme keys. Consider a ring of l users $R = (VK_0, \ldots, VK_{l-1})$

and a message $m \in \{0,1\}^*$, and assume the signer has a signing secret key SK_i and the corresponding public key $VK_i \in R$. To generate a signature for the message m, the signer uses the secret key ssk_i to obtain the signature σ and then encrypts σ using the key epk_i to obtain a ciphertext ct_i. For any $j \neq i$, since the signer does not know the other user's secret keys, he computes the ciphertext ct_j using epk_j to encrypt a string 0. Finally, the signer uses a non-interactive witness-indistinguishable (NIWI) proof π for a language $\mathcal{L}$ with the statement $(m, ct_0, \ldots, ct_{l-1}, VK_0, \ldots, VK_{l-1})$ to prove that there is an index i such that ct_i encrypts a signature σ and σ is a valid signature of message m under the verification key spk_i. The ring signature Σ includes the ciphertexts and the NIWI protocol transcript, i.e., $\Sigma = (ct_0, \ldots, ct_{l-1}, \pi)$. To verify signature Σ, the verifier uses the verification process of the NIWI protocol to prove that the statement $(m, ct_0, \ldots, ct_{l-1}, VK_0, \ldots, VK_{l-1})$ has π as a proof. However, the signature size is linear in l since it includes l ciphertexts and the proof π which also is linear in l. To reduce signature to logarithmic size, instead of computing $ct_0, \ldots, ct_{l-1}$, the signer now computes only two ciphertext ct_0, ct_1, where $ct_0 = ct_i$ and ct_1 is chosen uniformly at random from ciphertext space of PKE scheme. The signer uses a somewhere perfectly binding (SPB) hashing scheme that allows collapsing a ring R of l verification keys into a ring of just two keys. The signer generates two hashing keys hk_0, hk_1 and computes the hash of the ring R under both hk_0 and hk_1, obtaining hash values h_0 and h_1. Finally, the signer i computes a NIWI scheme π using an OR-statement which proves that either (hk_0, h_1) binds to a key VK_i and that ct_0 encrypts a signature of m for spk_i or (hk_1, h_1) binds to a key VK_i and that ct_1 encrypts a signature of m for spk_i. A signature has the form $\Sigma = (ct_0, ct_1, hk_0, hk_1, \pi)$ and verification is straightforward.

Outline of Approach in [4] *to Build Accountable Ring Signatures in the ROM.* Each user has a pair of encryption and decryption keys (epk_i, esk_i). The opener also has an encryption scheme key (osk, opk). In the signing algorithm, the signer computes a ciphertext oct that encrypts epk_i under the opener's key opk. The signer then uses a NIZK scheme, denoted π, to prove that the signer has a decryption key esk_i and a random value r satisfying the relation that the encryption key epk_i is computed corresponding to the decryption key esk_i of the signer and that $epk \in R$ and that the ciphertext oct is correctly computed using opener's key opk, signer's key epk_i and random value r. The ciphertext ct becomes part of the ring signature Σ. Namely, $\Sigma = (ct, \pi)$. To verify a signature, the verifier uses the verifying algorithm of the NIZK scheme π to check the validity of the ring signature. Upon receiving the ring signature Σ, the opener can obtain the encryption key epk_i of the signer by decrypting oct using the opener's decryption key osk. To ensure the tracing soundness, the opener uses a NIZK scheme π', proving that the opener has the encryption key opk computed from the decryption key osk and that the decryption is correct. The opener returns (VK_i, π'). To check opening, the verifier uses the verifying algorithm of NIZK scheme π'. An open question is raised:

"Is it possible to construct compact accountable ring signatures in the plain model from falsifiable standard assumptions? "

Outline of our Approach: There are two major challenges in constructing accountable ring signatures in the plain model:

- *Challenge 1:* In the signing algorithm, the signer uses a NIZK scheme that requires a pre-setup with a common reference string to prove anonymity and unforgeability. *Can we switch to using the NIWI scheme that does not require any pre-setup and still ensures the above security properties?*
- *Challenge 2:* In the opening algorithm, the opener also uses a NIZK scheme to ensure tracing soundness. In fact, the tracing soundness is based on verifiable decryption. However, there does not exist an effective NIWI scheme for proving verifiable decryption. *Is it possible to achieve tracing soundness without using the NIZK or NIWI scheme?*

Challenge 1. Fortunately, we can combine the techniques in [1,4] together. The signer computes the ciphertext that encrypts the signer's key under the opener public key. Namely, the signer computes two ciphertexts $oct_{0,0}, oct_{0,1}$, where $oct_{0,0} = \mathsf{PKE}(opk, VK_i, or_{0,0})$ and $oct_{1,0}$ chosen at random in the ciphertext space of encryption scheme. The signer computes a NIWI scheme π for OR relation with statement $(m, oct_{0,0}, oct_{1,0}, ct_0, ct_1, h_0, h_1, hk_0, hk_1)$. There exists an index i such that

- (hk_0, h_0) bind to a key VK_i, and that $oct_{0,0}$ is an encryption of a key VK_i under the opener's key opk, and that ct_0 is an encryption of a signature on message $(oct_{0,0}||m)$ with respect to spk_i under the public key epk_i,
- or (hk_1, h_1) bind to a key VK_i, and that $oct_{1,0}$ is an encryption of a key VK_i under the opener's key opk, and that ct_1 is an encryption of a signature on message $(oct_{1,0}||m)$ with respect to spk_i under the public key epk_i.

The signer outputs a signature $\Sigma = (oct_{0,0}, oct_{1,0}, ct_0, ct_1, hk_0, hk_1, \pi)$. To verify a signature Σ for a ring $R = (VK_0, \ldots, VK_{l-1})$, a message m and an opener key opk, the verifier first computes the hashes h_0 and h_1 of R using hk_0 and hk_1 respectively. Now it checks if the NIWI scheme π verifies for $(m, oct_{0,0}, oct_{1,0}, ct_0, ct_1, h_0, h_1, hk_0, hk_1)$, and if so it outputs 1.

To prove unforgeability, the security of the scheme is reduced to the security of the underlying signature scheme Sig. To do this, the reduction receives a verification key spk_{i*} from the challenger, creates the remaining verification keys spk_i for $i \neq i^*$, also the public keys epk_i for all $i \in [l]$. Upon receiving an accountable ring signature forge from the adversary, the reduction decrypts both ct_0 and ct_1, to obtain σ_0 and σ_1, respectively. Then, check if any of σ_0, σ_1 is a valid signature under spk_{i*} on message m. If one of them is valid, the reduction outputs it as the valid forge for Sig scheme. By the perfect correctness of the SPB hashing and perfect soundness of the NIWI, the reduction outputs a valid forge with non-negligible probability.

Establishing anonymity relies on the witness indistinguishability of the NIWI scheme. We transform a signature computed with SK_0 into a signature under SK_1 via a sequence of hybrids. The sequence of hybrids starts by replacing $oct_{1,0}$ with encryption of VK_1 under opener key opk. Then, we return ct_1 with encryption of a valid signature under spk_1. This change goes unnoticed since the PKE has pseudorandom ciphertexts. Next, we switch the index i the witness used to create the proof π from SK_0 to SK_1 using the witness-indistinguishability of the NIWI scheme.

However, this construction method fails to ensure tracing soundness. Indeed, upon receiving Σ, the opener computes $VK_i = \mathsf{PKE.Dec}(osk, ct_{0,0})$ and returns VK_i. In this case, the verifier can only check if VK_i is in R. Hence, the adversary who controls the opener can issue any public key.

Challenge 2. This is the biggest obstacle since we can no longer use the known techniques such as in [4,6]. To find a novelty technique, we look closer at the tracing soundness. In this property, the adversary $\mathcal{A}$ gains control over both the opener and a user in the ring. The adversary wants to slander (to his advantage or disadvantage) a user that this user-generated a signature, but actually, this user did not make that signature. We see that there are only two ways an adversary can do this.

Scenario 1: The Adversary Uses a Signature That is Generated by an Honest User VK_{i^*} and Proves That this Signature Comes from a Dishonest User VK_j. To avoid this scenario, we require the opener to provide a commitment and unveil information that was previously computed by the honest user VK_{i^*}. Using a perfectly binding commitment scheme, we can be assured that $\mathcal{A}$ cannot issue a public key VK_j and an unveil that equals a commitment value computed by honest user VK_{i^*}. Namely, the signer computes $(com_0, \gamma_0) \leftarrow \mathsf{CS.Com}(1^\lambda, VK_{i^*})$, and $(com_1, \gamma_1) \leftarrow \mathsf{CS.Com}(1^\lambda, 0)$. Besides computing $oct_{0,0}$ and $oct_{1,0}$ as Challenge 1, the signer also computes $oct_{0,1}$ is an encryption of a unveil γ_0 under the opener public key opk and $oct_{1,1}$ is chosen uniformly at random from ciphertext space of PKE scheme.

Now, the signer computes a new NIWI scheme π by adding one more new relation in OR relation. In addition to satisfying relations as Challenge 1, a new relation also holds that ($\mathsf{CS.Verify}(com_0, VK_{i^*}, \gamma_0) = 1$ and $\mathsf{PKE.Enc}(opk, \gamma_0, or_{0,1}) = oct_{0,1}$) OR ($\mathsf{CS.Verify}(com_1, VK_{i^*}, \gamma_1) = 1$ and $\mathsf{PKE.Enc}(opk, \gamma_1, or_{1,1}) = oct_{1,1}$). The signer outputs a signature $\Sigma = (com_0, com_1, oct_{0,0}, oct_{0,1}, oct_{1,0}, oct_{1,1}, ct_0, ct_1, hk_0, hk_1, \pi)$.

Upon receiving Σ, the opener computes $VK_{i^*} = \mathsf{PKE.Dec}(osk, ct_{0,0})$, and $\gamma_0 = \mathsf{PKE.Dec}(osk, ct_{0,1})$, then returns (VK_{i^*}, γ_0) as an output of opening algorithm. The verifier not only checks if VK_{i^*} is in R but also verify $\mathsf{CS.Verify}(com_0, VK_{i^*}, \gamma_0) = 1$. By perfect binding of commitment scheme, it holds that $\mathcal{A}$ cannot find a tuple $(com_0, VK_{i^*}, \gamma_0, VK_j, \gamma_j)$ such that ($\mathsf{CS.Verify}(com_0, VK_{i^*}, \gamma_0) = 1$ and $\mathsf{CS.Verify}(com_0, VK_j, \gamma_j) = 1$) OR a tuple $(com_1, 0, \gamma_1, VK_j, \gamma_j)$ such that ($\mathsf{CS.Verify}(com_1, 0, \gamma_1) = 1$ and $\mathsf{CS.Verify}(com_1, VK_j, \gamma_j) = 1$).

Scenario 2: From a signature of the dishonest user VK_j, the adversary proves that this signature was generated by an honest user VK_{i^*}. To avoid this scenario, the opener is required to output a signature on a message that is signed under the signing key ssk_{i^*} of the honest user VK_{i^*}. To avoid the trivial case where an adversary uses a signature on a previously signed message, we require that the signature given by the opener be the signature on a previously unsigned message by honest user VK_{i^*}. A secure signature scheme holds that only an honest user can issue such a signature. Namely, the signer computes $oct_{0,2} = \mathsf{PKE.Enc}(opk, \sigma, or_{0,2})$, where $\sigma = \mathsf{Sig.Sign}(ssk_{i^*}, com_0 \| oct_{0,0} \| oct_{0,1} \| m)$. Moreover, the signer chooses $oct_{1,2}$ uniformly at random from the ciphertext space of PKE scheme.

The signer adds one more new relation in the OR relation. Namely, the OR relation now holds for all old relations as Scenario 1 and that $oct_{0,2}$ is an encryption of a signature under opener's key opk, OR $oct_{1,2}$ is an encryption of a signature under opener's key opk. The signer outputs a signature $\Sigma = (com_0, com_1, oct_{0,0}, oct_{0,1}, oct_{0,2}, oct_{1,0}, oct_{1,1}, oct_{1,2}, ct_0, ct_1, hk_0, hk_1, \pi)$.

In opening algorithm, the opener decrypts $\sigma = \mathsf{PKE.Dec}(osk, oct_{0,2})$, then returns $(VK_{i^*}, \gamma_0, \sigma)$. The verifier checks $VK_{i^*} \in R$, $\mathsf{CS.Com}(com_0, VK_{i^*}, \gamma_0) = 1$ and $\mathsf{Sig.Verify}(spk_{i^*}, com_0 \| oct_{0,0} \| oct_{0,1} \| m, \sigma) = 1$. By EU-CMA of the signature scheme, it holds that $\mathcal{A}$ cannot find such a signature.

We note that an accountable ring signature must satisfy both scenarios. If one of the two is satisfied, it is not secure for the other case.

Efficiency of Our Construction: Our signature includes two commitment values and eight ciphertexts. These elements are logarithmic in size and independent of the number of users in the ring. Using an efficiency SPB hashing scheme, the hashing key hk_0, hk_1 and the proof π are logarithmic size. Hence, the signature is logarithmic size. In addition, since there is no need to use non-interactive protocols such as NIZK in the opening and verify opening algorithms, our accountable ring signature scheme is more efficient than the previous scheme [4].

2   Preliminaries

This section will recall some cryptographic primitives that are building blocks for our construction. We will use λ as a main security parameter. We denote by $[l]$ the set $\{0, 1, \ldots, l-1\}$. Let $r \leftarrow_{\$} S$ denote r be chosen uniformly random from the set S.

Definition 1 (Public Key Encryption, [1]). *A public key encryption scheme* PKE *consists of the algorithms* $(\mathsf{PKE.KeyGen}, \mathsf{PKE.Enc}, \mathsf{PKE.Dec})$ *with the following syntax:*

- $(epk, esk) \leftarrow \mathsf{PKE.KeyGen}(1^\lambda)$. *On input a security parameter* 1^λ, *this PPT algorithm outputs a pair of public and secret keys* (epk, esk).
- $ct \leftarrow \mathsf{PKE.Enc}(epk, m, r)$. *On input a public key epk, a message m and a randomness r, this PPT algorithm outputs a ciphertext ct.*
- $m \leftarrow \mathsf{PKE.Dec}(esk, ct)$. *On input a secret key esk and a ciphertext ct, this deterministic algorithm outputs a message m.*

We require the following properties of a PKE scheme. Firstly, the property of *perfect correctness* guarantees that the original plaintext can be obtained through decryption if the keys and ciphertexts were generated honestly. Secondly, *pseudorandom ciphertexts* guarantees that ciphertexts are computationally indistinguishable from uniform. Thirdly, *perfect binding* ensures that every unbounded adversary cannot output two pairs of distinct messages and randomness such that it computes the same ciphertext. PKE schemes that satisfy pseudorandom ciphertexts and perfect binding can be instantiated based on DDH [10].

Definition 2 (Signature Schemes, [1]). *A signature scheme* Sig *is 3-tuple* (Sig.KeyGen, Sig.Sign, Sig.Verfify) *with the following syntax:*

- $(spk, ssk) \leftarrow$ Sig.KeyGen(1^λ) : *On input a security parameter* 1^λ, *this PPT algorithm outputs a public verification key spk and corresponding secret key ssk.*
- $\sigma \leftarrow$ Sig.Sign(ssk, m) : *On input the secret key ssk and a message m, this PPT algorithm outputs a signature* σ.
- $b \leftarrow$ Sig.Verify(spk, m, σ). *On input a verification key spk, a message m, and a signature* σ, *this deterministic algorithm outputs a single bit b.*

We require the signature scheme Sig to be *correctness* and *EU-CMA* secure. A signature scheme is EU-CMA if any polynomial-time adversary, after seeing signatures of messages of its choice, should not be able to output a valid signature for a new message.

Definition 3 (Commitment Schemes, [1]). *A commitment scheme* CS *consists of two algorithms* (CS.Com, CS.Verify) *defined as the following:*

- $(com, \gamma) \leftarrow$ CS.Com($1^\lambda, m$): *On input a security parameter* 1^λ, *a message m, this PPT algorithm outputs a commitment value com and unveil information* γ.
- $b \leftarrow$ CS.Verify(com, m, γ): *On input a commitment value com, a message m, and unveil information* γ, *this deterministic algorithm outputs a single bit* $b \in \{0, 1\}$.

We require the commitment scheme CS to be *correctness*, *perfect binding* and *computational hiding*. A commitment scheme is perfectly binding if every unbounded adversary cannot change the committed message after the commitment phase. It is hiding if any computational adversary cannot distinguish the commitments of two different messages.

Definition 4 (Somewhere Perfectly Binding Hashing, [1]). *A somewhere perfectly binding hash family with private local opening* SPB *consists of four algorithms* (SPB.KeyGen, SPB.Hash, SPB.Open, SPB.Verify) *defined as the following:*

- $(hk, shk) \leftarrow$ SPB.KeyGen($1^\lambda, n, ind$). *On input a security parameter* 1^λ, *a database size n and an index ind, this PPT algorithm outputs public hashing key hk and corresponding secret hashing key shk.*
- $h \leftarrow$ SPB.Hash(hk, db). *On input a hashing key hk, a database db of size n, this deterministic algorithm outputs a hash value h.*

- $\tau \leftarrow$ SPB.Open(hk, shk, db, ind). *On input a hashing key hk, private hashing key shk, a database db of size n, and index ind, this algorithm outputs a witness τ.*
- $b \leftarrow$ SPB.Verify(hk, h, ind, x, τ). *On input a hashing key hk, a hash value h, and an index ind, this algorithm outputs a single bit $b \in \{0, 1\}$.*

The somewhere perfect binding satisfies the following properties. Firstly, *correctness* ensures that if the keys, hashes, and openings are generated truthfully, the verification process will be successful. Secondly, *efficiency* provides that the size of public hashing hk and witnesses τ is logarithmic with the number of ring users. Moreover, the Verify algorithm can be computed by a circuit of size $\log(n) \cdot \mathsf{poly}(\lambda)$. Thirdly, *somewhere perfectly binding* ensures that if a particular index i and value x pass verification, all valid openings for that index must result in x. Lastly, *index hiding* means that an efficient adversary cannot determine the index i from the public hashing key. SPB scheme can be constructed from somewhere statistically binding hashing (SSB). In [Appendix A.2, [1]], they present how to transform SSB into an SPB scheme. Moreover, SBB schemes can be constructed from the hardness of assumptions such as DDH, QR, LWE [12].

Let $\mathcal{R}$ be an efficiently computable binary relation, where for $(x, w) \in \mathcal{R}$ (x is a statement and w is the witness). The language $\mathcal{L}$ is defined as all statements that have a valid witness in $\mathcal{R}$, i.e. $\mathcal{L} := \{x | \exists w : (x, w) \in \mathcal{R}\}$.

Definition 5 (Non-Interactive Proof System, [1]). *Let $\mathcal{R}$ be an efficiently computable witness relation, and $\mathcal{L}$ be the language accepted by $\mathcal{R}$. A non-interactive witness-indistinguishable proof system NIWI for $\mathcal{L}$ includes* (NIWI.Prove, NIWI.Verify) *with the following syntax:*

- $\pi \leftarrow$ NIWI.Prove$(1^\lambda, x, w)$. *On input a security parameter 1^λ, a statement x and a witness w, it outputs a proof π.*
- $b \leftarrow$ NIWI.Verify(x, π). *Given a statement x and a proof π, it outputs a bit b.*

We require the following four properties for a Non-Interactive Witness Indistinguishable (NIWI) proof system. Firstly, *perfect completeness* ensures that correct statements can always be proven. Secondly, *perfect soundness* prevents the generation of valid proofs for false statements. Thirdly, *witness indistinguishability* states that given two valid witnesses for a statement, no efficient adversary can determine which witness was used to compute the proof. Last one, the *proof-size* requires that π is polynomial size with security parameter λ.

NIWI scheme can be constructed from pairing assumptions [11] as pointed out in [1,5] for classical instantiation. For post-quantum instantiation, we can replace our NIWI by using ZAP (two-message public coin argument system) based on LWE [2], which can be found in [8].

3   Compact Accountable Ring Signatures

In this section, we first recall the definition and security model for accountable ring signatures in Sect. 3.1. Our construction of the compact accountable ring signature in the plain model is presented in Sect. 3.2.

3.1 Definition and Security Model

Definition 6 (Accountable Ring Signatures). *An accountable ring signature* ARS *scheme is given by 6-tuple algorithm* (ARS.OKeyGen, ARS.UKeyGen, ARS.Sign, ARS.Verify, ARS.Open, ARS.VerifyOpen) *defined as follows:*

- $(opk, osk) \leftarrow$ ARS.OKeyGen(1^{λ}). *On input a security parameter* 1^{λ}, *this PPT algorithm generates a public encryption key* opk *and a corresponding secret key* osk *for an opener.*
- $(VK, SK) \leftarrow$ ARS.UKeyGen(1^{λ}). *On input a security parameter* 1^{λ}, *this PPT algorithm generates a public verification key* VK *and a corresponding secret key* SK *for a user.*
- $\Sigma \leftarrow$ ARS.Sign(R, opk, m, SK). *On input a signing key* SK, *an opener public key* opk, *a ring* $R = (VK_0, VK_1, \ldots, VK_{l-1})$ *and a message* $m \in \{0,1\}^*$, *this PPT algorithm outputs a signature* Σ *on* m.
- $b \leftarrow$ ARS.Verify(R, opk, Σ, m). *On input a ring* R, *an opener public key* opk, *a signature* Σ *and a message* $m \in \{0,1\}^*$, *this deterministic algorithm outputs a bit* b.
- $(VK, \text{aux}) \leftarrow$ ARS.Open(R, osk, Σ, m). *On input a secret opener key* osk, *a ring* R, *a signature* Σ *and a message* $m \in \{0,1\}^*$, *this deterministic algorithm outputs a verification key of signer* VK, *and an auxiliary information* aux.
- $b \leftarrow$ ARS.VerifyOpen$(R, opk, \Sigma, m, VK, \text{aux})$. *On input a ring* R, *an opener public key* opk, *a signature* Σ, *a message* $m \in \{0,1\}^*$, *a verification key of signer* VK *and an auxiliary information* aux, *this deterministic algorithm outputs a bit* b.

We require five properties of a ARS scheme as the following. First, the *correctness* guarantees that a signature generated by honest users will always pass the verification algorithm.

Definition 7 (Correctness). *We say that an accountable ring signature* ARS *is correct, if for all* $\lambda \in \mathbb{N}$, *all* $l = \text{poly}(\lambda)$, *all* $i \in [l]$ *and all message* $m \in \{0,1\}^*$ *that if* $(opk, osk) \leftarrow$ ARS.OKeyGen, *for* $i \in [l]$, $(VK_i, SK_i) \leftarrow$ ARS.UKeyGen(1^{λ}), $R = (VK_i)_{[l]}$, $\Sigma \leftarrow$ ARS.Sign(R, opk, m, SK), *then it holds that*

$$\Pr[\text{ARS.Verify}(R, opk, \Sigma, m) = 1] = 1 - \text{negl}(\lambda).$$

Second, the *traceability* guarantees that an honestly generated signature must be traceable to the correct signer.

Definition 8 (Traceability). *We say that an accountable ring signature* ARS *is traceable, if for all* $\lambda \in \mathbb{N}$, *all* $l = \text{poly}(\lambda)$, *all* $i \in [l]$ *and all message* $m \in \{0,1\}^*$ *that if* $(opk, osk) \leftarrow$ ARS.OKeyGen, *for* $i \in [l]$, $(VK_i, SK_i) \leftarrow$ ARS.UKeyGen(1^{λ}), $R = (VK_i)_{[l]}$, $\Sigma \leftarrow$ ARS.Sign(R, opk, m, SK) *and* $(VK, \text{aux}) \leftarrow$ ARS.Open(R, osk, Σ, m) *then it holds that*

$$\Pr[\text{ARS.VerifyOpen}(R, opk, \Sigma, m, VK, \text{aux}) = 1] = 1 - \text{negl}(\lambda).$$

Third, the *anonymity* ensures that a signature does not disclose the signer's identity unless an opener reveals it. Our formal definition of anonymity captures anonymity against full key exposure as defined in [3]. Hence, assume that the adversary can corrupt and control users, but that the opener is honest. We require that, when presented with a challenging signature, the adversary cannot determine which of two potential honest signers generated the signature, provided the adversary does not obtain an opening for the challenging signature.

Definition 9 (Anonymity). *We say that an accountable ring signature* ARS *is anonymous if every PPT adversary* $\mathcal{A}$, *it holds that* $\mathcal{A}$ *has a negligible advantage in the following experiment.*
$\mathsf{Exp}_{\mathsf{ARS\text{-}Anon}}(\mathcal{A})$:

1. *For* $i = 0, 1$, *the experiment generates* $(VK_i, SK_i) \leftarrow \mathsf{ARS.UKeyGen}(1^\lambda, r_i)$. *Besides, the experiment generates* $(opk, osk) \leftarrow \mathsf{ARS.OKeyGen}(1^\lambda)$.
2. *Sample* $b \leftarrow_s \{0, 1\}$.
3. *The experiment provides* VK_0, VK_1, r_0, r_1 *and* opk *to* $\mathcal{A}$. *The adversary* $\mathcal{A}$ *can append new public keys to the global public key lists* R. *The experiment requires* VK_0, *and* VK_1 *must be included in* R. *Moreover,* $\mathcal{A}$ *can access signing oracles* $\mathsf{ARS.Sign}_{VK_b}, \mathsf{ARS.Sign}_{VK_0}, \mathsf{ARS.Sign}_{VK_1}$ *and opening oracles* $\mathsf{ARS.Open}$, *where*

    i. $\mathsf{ARS.Sign}_{VK_b}$ *is challenge signing oracle with respect to* VK_b *for signing* (R, opk, m). *The experiment computes* $\Sigma \leftarrow \mathsf{ARS.Sign}(R, opk, m, SK_b)$ *and returns* Σ.
    ii. $\mathsf{ARS.Sign}_{VK_0}$ *(resp.* $\mathsf{ARS.Sign}_{VK_1}$*) is the signing oracle with respect to* VK_0 *(resp.* VK_1*) for signing* (R, opk, m). *It computes* $\Sigma \leftarrow \mathsf{ARS.Sign}(R, opk, m, SK_0)$ *(resp.* $\Sigma \leftarrow \mathsf{ARS.Sign}(R, opk, m, SK_1)$ *and returns* Σ.
    iii. $\mathsf{ARS.Open}$ *is an opening oracle with respect to* (R, Σ, m). *If* Σ *is obtained by calling challenge signing oracle* $\mathsf{ARS.Sign}_{SK_b}$, *then return* $\bot$. *Otherwise, the experiment returns* $\mathsf{ARS.Open}(R, osk, \Sigma, m)$.
4. $\mathcal{A}$ *outputs a guess* $b' \in \{0, 1\}$. *The experiment outputs 1 if* $b' = b$. *Otherwise, outputs 0.*

Fourth, the *unforgeability* ensures that an adversary cannot generate a valid signature on behalf of an honest user, even if the adversary is able to determine the identity of honest signers via the opening functionality. Formally, we consider a definition of unforgeability analogous to the one presented in [3]. Therefore, in our experiment on unforgeability, we presume that the adversary controls the opener and can corrupt users. We require that an adversary cannot generate a valid signature for a ring of honest users if the signature is not the output of the signing oracle.

Definition 10 (Unforgeability). *We say that an accountable ring signature* ARS *is unforgeability if, for every PPT adversary* $\mathcal{A}$, *it holds that* $\mathcal{A}$ *has a negligible advantage in the following experiment.*
$\mathsf{Exp}_{\mathsf{ARS\text{-}Unf}}$:

1. *For all $i = 0, \ldots, q-1$, it generates $(VK_i, SK_i) \leftarrow$ ARS.UKeyGen$(1^\lambda, r_i)$ by using random coins r_i. The experiment sets $\mathcal{VK} = (VK_0, \ldots, VK_{q-1})$, $\mathcal{C}, \mathcal{Q} = \emptyset$ and provides $\mathcal{VK}$ to $\mathcal{A}$.*
2. *The adversary generates $(opk^*, osk^*) \leftarrow$ ARS.OKeyGen(1^λ) and provides opk^* to the experiment.*
3. *The adversary $\mathcal{A}$ now can make the queries as the following*
    ii. *Corrupt$_{VK_i}$ is a corruption oracle with respect to VK_i. The experiment returns r_i and adds $\mathcal{C} = \mathcal{C} \cup VK_i$.*
4. *In the end, the adversary $\mathcal{A}$ outputs a tuple $(R^*, opk^*, \Sigma^*, m^*)$.*
5. *The experiment outputs 1 if the following conditions hold:*
    i. $R^* \subset \mathcal{VK} \setminus \mathcal{C}$,
    ii. $(R^*, opk^*, \Sigma^*, m^*) \notin \mathcal{Q}$,
    iii. ARS.Verify$(R^*, opk^*, \Sigma^*, m^*) = 1$.

Fifth, the *tracing soundness* ensures that an adversary cannot output a valid opening such that the trace identifies a non-signer even if the adversary can control the opener and corrupt the user. Our formal definition of tracing soundness requires that at least one in two users in the valid opening is an honest user. Since we use a NIWI framework, we cannot achieve strong tracing soundness where two users can be corrupted user as defined in [4].

Definition 11 (Tracing Soundness). *We say that an accountable ring signature ARS is tracing soundness if, for every PPT adversary $\mathcal{A}$, it holds that $\mathcal{A}$ has a negligible advantage in the following experiment.*
Exp$_{\text{ARS-TrS}}$:

1. *For all $i = 0, \ldots, q-1$, it generates $(VK_i, SK_i) \leftarrow$ ARS.UKeyGen$(1^\lambda, r_i)$ by using random coins r_i. The experiment sets $\mathcal{VK} = (VK_0, \ldots, VK_{q-1})$, $\mathcal{C}, \mathcal{Q} = \emptyset$, and provides $\mathcal{VK}$ to $\mathcal{A}$.*
2. *The adversary generates $(opk^*, osk^*) \leftarrow$ ARS.OKeyGen(1^λ) and provides opk^* to the experiment.*
3. *The adversary $\mathcal{A}$ is now allowed to make the following queries.*
    i. *ARS.Sign$_{VK_i}$ is a signing oracle with respect to VK_i for (R, opk^*, m). It checks if $VK_i \in R$ and, if so, computes $\Sigma \leftarrow$ ARS.Sign(R, opk^*, m, SK_i) and returns Σ to $\mathcal{A}$. Besides, the experiment sets $\mathcal{Q} = \mathcal{Q} \cup (R, opk^*, \Sigma, m)$.*
    ii. *Corrupt$_{VK_i}$ is a corruption oracle with respect to VK_i. The experiment returns r_i and adds $\mathcal{C} = \mathcal{C} \cup VK_i$.*
4. *In the end, $\mathcal{A}$ outputs a tuple $(R^*, opk^*, m^*, \Sigma^*, VK_i, \text{aux}_i, VK_j, \text{aux}_j)$.*
5. *The experiment outputs 1 if the following conditions hold:*
    i. $VK_i, VK_j \in R^*$, $VK_i \neq VK_j$, *and at least one public key in $\{VK_i, VK_j\}$ does not belong to $\mathcal{C}$.*
    ii. ARS.Verify$(R^*, opk^*, \Sigma^*, m^*) = 1$, *and $(R^*, opk^*, \Sigma^*, m^*) \in \mathcal{Q}$ or the tuple (R^*, opk^*, m^*) is never asked to signing oracle.*
    iii. ARS.VerifyOpen$(R^*, opk^*, \Sigma^*, m^*, VK_i, \text{aux}_i) = 1$.
    iv. ARS.VerifyOpen$(R^*, opk^*, \Sigma^*, m^*, VK_j, \text{aux}_j) = 1$.

3.2 Our Compact Accountable Ring Signatures Construction

Our construction employs the following technical building blocks.

- Sig = (Sig.KeyGen, Sig.Sign, Sig.Verfify) be a signature scheme.
- PKE = (PKE.KeyGen, PKE.Enc, PKE.Dec) be a public encryption scheme.
- CS = (CS.Com, CS.Verfify) be a commitment scheme.
- SPB = (SPB.KeyGen, SPB.Hash, SPB.Open, SPB.Verify) be a somewhere perfectly binding hash function.
- NIWI = (NIWI.Prove, NIWI.Verify) be a NIWI proof system for the language $\mathcal{L}$ defined as in (1).

Firstly, we define a relation $\mathcal{R}_0$ consisting of (x_0, w_0), where

$$x_0 = (m, opk, com_0, oct_{0,0}, oct_{0,1}, oct_{0,2}, ct_0, h_0, hk_0)$$
$$w_0 = (i, VK_i, \sigma, \tau, \gamma, r_{ct}, or_0, or_1, or_2), \text{ where } VK_i = (spk_i, epk_i)$$

satisfying the following:

SPB.Verfify$(hk_0, h_0, i, VK_i, \tau) = 1$
and PKE.Enc$(epk_i, \sigma, r_{ct}) = ct_0$ and CS.Verify$(com_0, VK_i, \gamma) = 1$
and PKE.Enc$(opk, VK_i, or_0) = oct_{0,0}$ and PKE.Enc$(opk, \gamma, or_1) = oct_{0,1}$
and PKE.Enc$(opk, \sigma, or_2) = oct_{0,2}$
and Sig.Verify$(spk_i, com_0||oct_{0,0}||oct_{0,1}||m, \sigma) = 1$.

The relation $\mathcal{R}_1$ is exactly like $\mathcal{R}_0$ except that it is true for (x_1, w_1), where

$$x_1 = (m, opk, com_1, oct_{1,0}, oct_{1,1}, oct_{1,2}, ct_1, h_1, hk_1)$$
$$w_1 = (i, VK_i, \sigma, \tau, \gamma, r_{ct}, or_0, or_1, or_2), \text{ where } VK_i = (spk_i, epk_i)$$

Let $\mathcal{L}_0, \mathcal{L}_1$ be languages accepted by $\mathcal{R}_0$ and $\mathcal{R}_1$, respectively. We define the language $\mathcal{L}$ as the following:
$$\mathcal{L} := \mathcal{L}_0 \vee \mathcal{L}_1 \tag{1}$$
The statement and witness for $\mathcal{L}$ are defined as the following:

$$x = (m, opk, com_0, com_1, \{oct_{0,i}\}_{i \in [2]}, \{oct_{1,i}\}_{i \in [2]}, ct_0, ct_1, h_0, h_1, hk_0, hk_1)$$
$$w = (i, VK_i, \sigma, \tau, \gamma, r_{ct}, or_0, or_1, or_2), \text{ where } VK_i = (spk_i, epk_i)$$

Our accountable ring signatures ARS = (ARS.OKeyGen, ARS.UKeyGen, ARS.Sign, ARS.Verify, ARS.Open, ARS.VerifyOpen) consists of the algorithms defined as the following:

ARS.OKeyGen(1^λ) : On input a security parameter 1^λ, it works as follows.

- Compute $(opk, osk) \leftarrow$ PKE.KeyGen(1^λ).
- Return (opk, osk).

ARS.UKeyGen(1^λ) : On input a security parameter 1^λ, it does as follows.

- Compute $(spk, ssk) \leftarrow$ PKE.KeyGen(1^λ).
- Compute $(epk, esk) \leftarrow$ Sig.KeyGen(1^λ).
- Set $VK := (spk, epk)$ and $SK := (ssk, esk)$.
- Return (VK, SK).

ARS.Sign(R, opk, m, SK_i) : On input a ring R, opener public key opk, a message m and a secret key SK_i of the user i, this algorithm processes as the following.

- Parse $VK_i = (spk_i, epk_i)$ and $SK_i = (ssk_i, esk_i)$.
- Compute $(com_0, \gamma_0) \leftarrow$ CS.Com($1^\lambda, VK_i$).
- Compute
  $oct_{0,0} \leftarrow$ PKE.Enc($opk, VK_i, or_{0,0}$), $oct_{0,1} \leftarrow$ PKE.Enc($opk, \gamma_0, or_{0,1}$), where $or_{0,0}, or_{0,1}$ is the encryption randomness.
- Compute $\sigma \leftarrow$ Sig.Sign($ssk_i, com_0 || oct_{0,0} || oct_{0,1} || m$)
- Compute $oct_{0,2} \leftarrow$ PKE.Enc($opk, \sigma, or_{0,2}$), and $ct_0 \leftarrow$ PKE.Enc(epk_i, σ, r_{ct}) where $or_{0,2}, r_{ct}$ is the encryption randomness.
- Compute $(hk_j, skh_j) \leftarrow$ SPB.KeyGen($1^\lambda, |R|, i$) for all $j \in \{0, 1\}$.
- Compute $h_j \leftarrow$ SPB.Hash(hk_j, R) for all $j \in \{0, 1\}$.
- Compute $\tau \leftarrow$ SPB.Open(hk_0, shk_0, R, i).
- Compute $(com_1, \gamma_1) \leftarrow$ CS.Com($1^\lambda, 0$).
- Choose $oct_{1,0}, oct_{1,1}, oct_{1,2} \leftarrow_\$ \{0,1\}^{|ctl|}$ and $ct_1 \leftarrow_\$ \{0,1\}^{|ctl|}$.
- Statement $x = (m, opk, com_0, com_1, \{oct_{0,i}, oct_{1,i}\}_{i \in [2]}, \{ct_i, h_i, hk_i\}_{i \in [1]})$.
- Witness $w = (i, VK_i, \sigma, \tau, \gamma, r_{ct}, or_0, or_1, or_2)$, where $VK_i = (spk_i, epk_i)$, $or_0 = or_{0,0}$, $or_1 = or_{0,1}$, and $or_2 = or_{0,2}$.
- Compute $\pi \leftarrow$ NIWI.Prove(x, w).
- Return $\Sigma = (com_0, com_1, \{oct_{0,i}, oct_{1,i}\}_{i \in [2]}, ct_0, ct_1, hk_0, hk_1, \pi)$.

ARS.Verify(R, opk, Σ, m) : On input a ring R, an opener public key opk, a signature Σ, and a message m, do the following.

- Parse $\Sigma = (com_0, com_1, \{oct_{0,i}, oct_{1,i}\}_{i \in [2]}, ct_0, ct_1, hk_0, hk_1, \pi)$.
- Compute $h'_j =$ SPB.Hash(hk_j, R) for all $j \in \{0, 1\}$.
- Set $x = (m, opk, com_0, com_1, \{oct_{0,i}, oct_{1,i}\}_{i \in [2]}, ct_0, ct_1, h'_0, h'_1, hk_0, hk_1)$.
- Return NIWI.Verify(x, π).

ARS.Open(R, osk, Σ, m) : On input ring R, an opener secret key osk, a signature Σ, and a message m, do the following.

- If ARS.Verify(R, opk, Σ, m) = 0 , then return $\bot$.
- Parse $\Sigma = (com_0, com_1, \{oct_{0,i}, oct_{1,i}\}_{i \in [2]}, ct_0, ct_1, hk_0, hk_1, \pi)$.
- Compute $VK' =$ PKE.Dec($osk, oct_{0,0}$), $\gamma' =$ PKE.Dec($osk, oct_{0,1}$), and $\sigma' =$ PKE.Dec($osk, oct_{0,2}$).
- Compute $VK'' =$ PKE.Dec($osk, oct_{1,0}$) , $\gamma'' =$ PKE.Dec($osk, oct_{1,1}$), and $\sigma'' =$ PKE.Dec($osk, oct_{1,2}$).

- If $((VK' \in R) \wedge (\mathsf{CS.Verify}(com_0, VK', \gamma') = 1) \wedge (\mathsf{Sig.Verify}(spk', com_0||$
  $oct_{0,0}||oct_{0,1}||m, \sigma') = 1))$ and $((VK'' = \perp) \vee (VK'' \notin R))$ then return
  $(VK', \mathsf{aux} = (\gamma', \sigma'))$.
- If $((VK'' \in R) \wedge (\mathsf{CS.Verify}(com_1, VK'', \gamma'') = 1) \wedge (\mathsf{Sig.Verify}(spk'', com_1$
  $||oct_{1,0}||oct_{1,1}||m, \sigma'') = 1))$ and $((VK' = \perp) \vee (VK' \notin R))$ then return
  $(VK'', \mathsf{aux} = (\gamma'', \sigma''))$.
- Otherwise, return $\perp$.

$\mathsf{ARS.VerifyOpen}(R, opk, \Sigma, m, VK, \mathsf{aux})$: On input ring R, an opener public key
osk, a signature Σ, a message m, a signer public key VK, and an auxiliary
information aux, this algorithm works as the following.

- If $\mathsf{ARS.Verify}(R, opk, \Sigma, m) = 0$, then return 0.
- Parse $\Sigma = (com_0, com_1, \{oct_{0,i}, oct_{1,i}\}_{i \in [2]}, ct_0, ct_1, hk_0, hk_1, \pi)$.
- Parse $VK = (spk, epk)$ and $\mathsf{aux} = (\gamma, \sigma)$.
- If $\mathsf{CS.Verify}(com_0, VK, \gamma) = 1$ and $\mathsf{Sig.Verify}(spk, com_0||oct_{0,0}||oct_{0,1}||m, \sigma) = 1$, then return 1.
- If $\mathsf{CS.Verify}(com_1, VK, \gamma) = 1$ and $\mathsf{Sig.Verify}(spk, com_1||oct_{1,0}||oct_{1,1}||m, \sigma) = 1$, then return 1.
- Otherwise, return 0.

Theorem 1 (Correctness and Traceability). *If the* NIWI, Sig, PKE, CS *and*
SPB *schemes are correct then* ARS *is correct and traceable. Moreover, our ARS
scheme has a logarithmic signature size.*

Proof. We assume that $VK = (spk, epk), SK = (ssk, esk)$ were generated by
$\mathsf{ARS.UKeyGen}(1^\lambda)$ algorithm and $(opk, osk) \leftarrow \mathsf{ARS.OKeyGen}(1^\lambda)$. We suppose
that the signature $\Sigma = (com_0, com_1, \{oct_{0,i}\}_{i \in [2]}, \{oct_{1,i}\}_{i \in [2]}, ct_0, ct_1, hk_0,$
$hk_1, \pi)$ is an output of $\mathsf{ARS.Sign}(R, opk, m, SK)$ algorithm, where $R = \{VK_i\}_{[l]}$. Since SPB.Hash is a deterministic algorithm, we have $h'_0 = h_0$
and $h'_1 = h_1$. It also holds that $VK = VK_i \in R$. By the cor-
rectness of the SPB function, we have $\mathsf{SPB.Verify}(hk_0, h'_0, i, VK_i, \tau) = 1$.
Since PKE, Sig and CS are correctness, we have $\mathsf{PKE.Enc}(epk_i, \sigma, r_{ct}) = ct_0$, $\mathsf{PKE.Enc}(opk, VK_i, or_{0,0}) = oct_{0,0}$, $\mathsf{PKE.Enc}(opk, \gamma_0, or_{0,1}) = oct_{0,1}$,
$\mathsf{PKE.Enc}(opk, \sigma, or_{0,2}) = ct_{0,2}$, $\mathsf{CS.Verify}(com_0, VK_i, \gamma_0) = 1$, and $\mathsf{Sig.Verify}$
$(spk_i, com_0|| oct_{0,0}||oct_{0,1}||m, \sigma) = 1$ Therefore, we have $(x, w) \in L$, where
$x = (m, opk, com_0, com_1, \{oct_{0,i}\}_{i \in [2]}, \{oct_{1,i}\}_{i \in [2]}, ct_0, ct_1, h_0, h_1, hk_0, hk_1)$, and
$w = (i, VK_i = (spk_i, epk_i), \sigma, \tau, \gamma, r_{ct}, or_0 = or_{0,0}, or_1 = or_{0,1}, or_2 = or_{0,2})$. By
the correctness of the NIWI scheme, $\mathsf{NIWI.Verify}(x, \pi) = 1$. Therefore, our ARS
scheme is correct.

By the correctness of PKE, it implies $VK_i = \mathsf{PKE.Dec}(osk, oct_{0,0})$, $\gamma_i = \mathsf{PKE.Dec}(osk, oct_{0,1})$, and $\sigma = \mathsf{PKE.Dec}(osk, oct_{0,2})$. Hence $\mathsf{CS.Verify}(com_0,$
$VK_i, \gamma_i) = 1$ and $\mathsf{Sig.Verify}(spk_i, com_0 ||oct_{0,0}||oct_{0,1}||m, \sigma) = 1$ since CS and
Sig scheme are correctness,. Hence, our ARS scheme is traceable.

Let consider a signature $\Sigma = (com_0, com_1, \{oct_{0,i}\}_{i \in [2]}, \{oct_{1,i}\}_{i \in [2]}, ct_0, ct_1,$
$hk_0, hk_1, \pi)$. The size of elelemts $(com_0, com_1, \{oct_{0,i}\}_{i \in [2]}, \{oct_{1,i}\}_{i \in [2]}, ct_0, ct_1)$
are $\mathcal{O}(\mathsf{poly}(\lambda))$ and independent of the number of users l. By the efficiency

property of SPB, the sizes of the hashing keys hk_0, hk_1 are bounded by $\mathcal{O}(\log(l) \cdot \mathsf{poly}(\lambda))$. By the proof-size property of NIWI proof, it holds that the size of proof π is $\mathcal{O}(\log(l) \cdot \mathsf{poly}(\lambda))$. Therefore, the size of signatures Σ is $\mathcal{O}(\log(l) \cdot \mathsf{poly}(\lambda))$. The output of opener includes $(VK_i, \mathsf{aux} = (\sigma, \gamma))$ which also is logarithmic size.

4   Security Proofs

4.1   Anonymity

Theorem 2. *If NIWI is computationally witness-indistinguishable, PKE has pseudorandom ciphertexts, CS is computational hiding, SPB is index hiding, then ARS is anonymous.*

To prove anonymity, given two honestly generated verification keys VK_0 and VK_1, we will build a sequence of hybrids to prove that a signature created under VK_0 is computationally indistinguishable from a signature created under VK_1.

Proof. Let $\mathcal{A}$ be a PPT adversary against the anonymity experiment of ARS. Let $R = (VK_0, VK_1, VK_2, \dots, VK_{l-1})$, where (VK_0, VK_1) is challenge public key and $(VK_2, \dots, VK_{l-1})$ is new public keys that are appended by the adversary $\mathcal{A}$. We consider the following hybrids:

Hybrid $\mathcal{H}_0$: This is the real experiment $\mathsf{Exp}_{\mathsf{ARS\text{-}Anon}}$ with challenge bits $b = 0$. In this experiment, we use $(x_0, w_0) \in \mathcal{R}_0$ to compute $\tau \leftarrow$ NIWI.Prove(x, w), where $x = (m, opk, com_0, com_1, \{oct_{0,i}\}_{i \in [2]}, \{oct_{1,i}\}_{i \in [2]}, ct_0, ct_1, h_0, h_1, hk_0, hk_1)$ $x_0 = (m, opk, com_0, oct_{0,0}, oct_{0,1}, oct_{0,2}, ct_0, h_0, hk_0)$ and $w = w_0 = (i = 0, VK_0, \sigma, \tau, \gamma_0, r_{ct}, or_{0,0}, or_{0,1}, or_{0,2})$

Hybrid $\mathcal{H}_1$: This hybrid is similar to $\mathcal{H}_0$, except that we compute $hk_1 \leftarrow$ SPB.Key $(1^\lambda, |R|, i = 1)$ instead of $hk_1 \leftarrow$ SPB.Key$(1^\lambda, |R|, i = 0)$. Since SPB has index hiding, the hybrid $\mathcal{H}_0$ and $\mathcal{H}_1$ are computationally indistinguishable

Hybrid $\mathcal{H}_2$: It is similar to $\mathcal{H}_1$, except that $(com_1, \gamma_1) \leftarrow$ CS.Com$(1^\lambda, VK_1)$ instead of $(com_1, \gamma_1) \leftarrow$ CS.Com$(1^\lambda, 0)$. Since CS is computational hiding, the hybrid $\mathcal{H}_1$ and $\mathcal{H}_2$ are computationally indistinguishable.

Hybrid $\mathcal{H}_3$: This hybrid works exactly like the previous one, except that we compute $oct_{1,0} \leftarrow$ PKE.Enc$(opk, VK_1, or_{1,0})$ instead of $oct_{1,0} \leftarrow_\$ \{0,1\}^{|ct|}$ (i.e. chossing $oct_{1,0}$ uniformly random from the ciphertext space of PKE). The hybrid $\mathcal{H}_2$ and $\mathcal{H}_3$ are computationally indistinguishable since PKE has pesudorandom ciphertexts.

Hybrid $\mathcal{H}_4$: It is the same as $\mathcal{H}_3$, except that instead of sampling $oct_{1,1} \leftarrow \{0,1\}^{|ct|}$, we compute $oct_{1,1} \leftarrow$ PKE.Enc$(opk, \gamma_1, or_{1,1})$. By the pseudorandom ciphertext of PKE, the indistinguishability between hybrid $\mathcal{H}_3$ and $\mathcal{H}_4$ are negligible.

Hybrid $\mathcal{H}_5$: The same as $\mathcal{H}_4$, except that $oct_{1,2} \leftarrow$ PKE.Enc$(opk, \sigma', or_{1,2})$, where $\sigma' = $ Sig.Sign$(ssk_1, com_1 \| oct_{1,0} \| oct_{1,1} \| m)$ instead of $oct_{1,2} \leftarrow_\$ \{0,1\}^{|ct|}$. Since PKE has pesudorandom ciphertexts, the hybrid $\mathcal{H}_4$ and $\mathcal{H}_5$ are computationally indistinguishable.

Hybrid $\mathcal{H}_6$: This hybrid works the same as $\mathcal{H}_5$, except that instead of chossing $ct_1 \leftarrow_\$ \{0,1\}^{|ct|}$, we compute $ct_1 \leftarrow \mathsf{PKE.Enc}(epk_1, \sigma', r'_{ct})$. By pesudorandom ciphertexts of PKE, the hybrid $\mathcal{H}_5$ and $\mathcal{H}_6$ are computationally indistinguishable.

Hybrid $\mathcal{H}_7$: It is identical to $\mathcal{H}_6$, expect that we use a witness w_1 corresponding to statement x_1, and $(x_1, w_1) \in \mathcal{R}_1$ instead of using $(x_0, w_0) \in \mathcal{R}_0$ for compute $\pi = \mathsf{NIWI.Prove}(x, w)$, where $x = (m, opk, com_0, com_1, \{oct_{0,i}\}_{i \in [2]}, \{oct_{1,i}\}_{i \in [2]}, ct_0, ct_1, h_0, h_1, hk_0, hk_1)$, $x_1 = (m, opk, com_1, oct_{1,0}, oct_{1,1}, oct_{1,2}, ct_1, h_1, hk_1)$, $w = w_1 = (i = 1, VK_1, \sigma', \tau', \gamma_1, r'_{ct}, or_{1,0}, or_{1,1}, or_{1,2})$, and $\tau' = \mathsf{SPB.Open}(hk_1, shk_1, R, i = 1)$. The hybrid $\mathcal{H}_6$ and $\mathcal{H}_7$ are computationally indistinguishable since NIWI is computationally witness-indistinguishable. In this hybrid, the statement x is true with both witnesses w_0 and w_1. Hence, to avoid confusion when an adversary asks to open identify's signer of a signature, we have a small modification in the opening algorithm, called $\mathsf{ARS.Open}^*(R, osk, \Sigma, m)$. Let $\mathcal{O}$ be an opening query set. When an adversary queries $\mathsf{ARS.Sign}_{VK_0}$ (resp. $\mathsf{ARS.Sign}_{VK_1}$) for signing on (R, opk, m), we computes $\Sigma \leftarrow \mathsf{ARS.Sign}(R, opk, R, m, SK_0)$, and $\mathcal{O} = \mathcal{O} \cup (\Sigma, \mathsf{index} = 0)$ (resp. $\Sigma \leftarrow \mathsf{ARS.Sign}(R, osk, m, SK_1)$, $\mathcal{O} = \mathcal{O} \cup (\Sigma, \mathsf{index} = 1)$. If $\mathcal{A}$ queries to opening oracle on (R, Σ, m) then $\mathsf{ARS.Open}^*(R, osk, \Sigma, m)$ works as the following: If Σ was obtained by calling the challenge signing oracle $\mathsf{ARS.Sign}_{SK_b}$, then return $\bot$. If $\Sigma \in \mathcal{O}$ and Σ were not obtained by calling $\mathsf{ARS.Sign}_{SK_b}$, then the experiment returns $(VK_{\mathsf{index}}, \mathsf{aux}_{\mathsf{index}})$, where $\mathsf{aux}_{\mathsf{index}}$ is an output of $\mathsf{ARS.Open}(osk, R, \Sigma, m)$. If $\Sigma \notin \mathcal{O}$, the experiment returns $\mathsf{ARS.Open}(osk, R, \Sigma, m)$. Since we control the opener, the adversary cannot know these changes.

Hybrid $\mathcal{H}_8$: This hybrid is identical to $\mathcal{H}_7$, except that instead of computing $(com_0, \gamma_0) \leftarrow \mathsf{CS.Com}(1^\lambda, VK_0)$, we compute $(com_0, \gamma_0) \leftarrow \mathsf{CS.Com}(1^\lambda, 0)$. Since CS is computationally hiding, the hybrid $\mathcal{H}_7$ and $\mathcal{H}_8$ are computationally indistinguishable. In this hybrid, instead of using $\mathsf{ARS.Open}^*(osk, R, \Sigma, m)$, we use $\mathsf{ARS.Open}(osk, R, \Sigma, m)$.

Hybrid $\mathcal{H}_9, \mathcal{H}_{10}, \mathcal{H}_{11}$: These hybrids are the same as the previous one, except that $\{oct_{0,i}\}_{i \in [2]} \leftarrow_\$ \{0,1\}^{|ct|}$ instead of $oct_{0,0} \leftarrow \mathsf{PKE.Enc}(opk, VK_0, or_{0,0})$, $oct_{0,1} \leftarrow \mathsf{PKE.Enc}(opk, \gamma_0, or_{0,1})$, $oct_{0,2} \leftarrow \mathsf{PKE.Enc}(opk, \sigma, or_{0,2})$, where the signature $\sigma = \mathsf{Sig.Sign}(ssk_0, com_0 \| oct_{0,0} \| oct_{0,1} \| m)$. Since PKE has pesudorandom ciphertexts, the hybrid $\mathcal{H}_8$ to $\mathcal{H}_{11}$ are computationally indistinguishable.

Hybrid $\mathcal{H}_{12}$: This hybrid is identical to $\mathcal{H}_{11}$, except that $ct_0 \leftarrow_\$ \{0,1\}^{|ct|}$ instead of computing $ct_0 = \mathsf{PKE.Enc}(epk_0, \sigma, r_{ct})$. Since PKE has pesudorandom ciphertexts, the hybrid $\mathcal{H}_{11}$ and $\mathcal{H}_{12}$ are computationally indistinguishable.

Hybrid $\mathcal{H}_{13}$: The only change in this hybrid is that, with the only difference being that we generate $hk_0 \leftarrow \mathsf{SPB.Key}(1^\lambda, |R|, i = 1)$ instead of $hk_0 \leftarrow \mathsf{SPB.Key}(1^\lambda, |R|, i = 0)$. By index hiding of SPB, the hybrid $\mathcal{H}_{12}$ and $\mathcal{H}_{13}$ are computationally indistinguishable.

Hybrid $\mathcal{H}_{14}$: It works the same as the previous hybrid, except that we compute $(com_0, \gamma_0) \leftarrow \mathsf{CS.Com}(1^\lambda, VK_1)$ and instead of $(com_0, \gamma_0) \leftarrow \mathsf{CS.Com}(1^\lambda, 0)$. By the computational hiding of CS, the difference between hybrid $\mathcal{H}_{13}$ and $\mathcal{H}_{14}$ are computational indistinguishable.

Hybrid $\mathcal{H}_{15}, \mathcal{H}_{16}, \mathcal{H}_{17}$: These hybrids are the same as the previous one, except that we compute $oct_{0,0} \leftarrow$ PKE.Enc$(opk, VK_1, or_{0,0})$, $oct_{0,1} \leftarrow$ PKE.Enc$(opk, VK_1, or_{0,1})$ and $oct_{0,2} \leftarrow$ PKE.Enc$(opk, \sigma'', or_{1,2})$, where $\sigma'' =$ Sig.Sign$(ssk_1, com_0 \|oct_{0,0}\|oct_{0,1}\|m)$ instead of choosing $\{oct_{0,i}\}_{i \in [2]} \leftarrow_\$ \{0,1\}^{|ct|}$. By the pesudorandom ciphertexts of PKE, the difference between hybrid $\mathcal{H}_{14}$ to $\mathcal{H}_{17}$ are computational indistinguishable.

Hybrid $\mathcal{H}_{18}$: The same as $\mathcal{H}_{17}$, except that $ct_0 \leftarrow$ PKE.Enc$(epk_1, \sigma'', r_{ct})$, where $\sigma'' =$ Sig.Sign$(ssk_1, com_0 \|oct_{0,0}\|oct_{0,1}\|m)$ instead of $ct_0 \leftarrow_\$ \{0,1\}^{|ct|}$. Since PKE has pesudorandom ciphertexts, the hybrid $\mathcal{H}_{17}$ and $\mathcal{H}_{18}$ are computationally indistinguishable.

Hybrid $\mathcal{H}_{19}$: It is identical to $\mathcal{H}_{18}$, expect that we use a witness w_0 corresponding to statement x_0, $(x_0, w_0) \in \mathcal{R}_0$ instead of using $(x_1, w_1) \in \mathcal{R}_1$, to compute $\pi =$ NIWI.Prove(x, w), where $x = (m, opk, com_0, com_1, \{oct_{0,i}\}_{i \in [2]}, \{oct_{1,i}\}_{i \in [2]}, ct_0, ct_1, h_0, h_1, hk_0, hk_1)$, $x_0 = (m, opk, com_0, oct_{0,0}, oct_{0,1}, oct_{0,2}, ct_0, h_0, hk_0)$, $w = w_0 = (i = 1, VK_1 = (spk_1, epk_1), \sigma'', \tau'', \gamma_0, r_{ct}, or_{0,0}, or_{0,1}, or_{0,2}$ and $\tau'' =$ SPB.Open$(hk_0, shk_0, R, i = 1)$. The hybrid $\mathcal{H}_{18}$ and $\mathcal{H}_{19}$ are computationally indistinguishable since NIWI is computationally witness-indistinguishable. In this hybrid, we use ARS.Open$^*(osk, R, \Sigma, m)$ instead of ARS.Open(osk, R, Σ, m).

Hybrid $\mathcal{H}_{20}$: It works the same as the previous hybrid, except that we compute $(com_1, \gamma_1) \leftarrow$ CS.Com$(1^\lambda, 0)$ and instead of $(com_1, \gamma_1) \leftarrow$ CS.Com$(1^\lambda, VK_1)$. By the computational hiding of CS, the difference between hybrid $\mathcal{H}_{19}$ and $\mathcal{H}_{20}$ are computational indistinguishable. In this hybrid, instead of using ARS.Open$^*(osk, R, \Sigma, m)$, we use ARS.Open(osk, R, Σ, m).

Hybrid $\mathcal{H}_{21}, \mathcal{H}_{22}, \mathcal{H}_{23}$: These hybrids are the same as the previous one, except that instead of computing $oct_{1,0} \leftarrow$ PKE.Enc$(opk, VK_1, or_{1,0})$, $oct_{1,1} \leftarrow$ PKE.Enc$(opk, VK_1, or_{1,1})$, and $oct_{1,2} \leftarrow$ PKE.Enc$(opk, \sigma', or_{1,2})$, where $\sigma' =$ Sig.Sign$(ssk_1, com_1 \|oct_{1,0}\|oct_{1,1}\|m)$, we choose $\{oct_{1,i}\}_{i \in [2]} \leftarrow_\$ \{0,1\}^{|ct|}$. By the pesudorandom ciphertexts of PKE, the difference between hybrid $\mathcal{H}_{20}$ to $\mathcal{H}_{23}$ are computational indistinguishable.

Hybrid $\mathcal{H}_{24}$: This hybrid is the same as $\mathcal{H}_{23}$, except that $ct_1 \leftarrow_\$ \{0,1\}^{|ct|}$ instead of $ct_1 =$ PKE.Enc$(epk_1, \sigma', r'_{ct})$. The hybrid $\mathcal{H}_{23}$ and $\mathcal{H}_{24}$ are computationally indistinguishable, since PKE has pesudorandom ciphertexts. This hybrid is identical to the real experiment Exp$_{\text{ARS-Anon}}(\mathcal{A})$ with $b = 1$.

4.2 Unforgeability

At a high level, we can see that an adversary has only two methods to give a valid forgery signature, even if the adversary controls an opener. First, the adversary can give a valid forgery signature by using useful information in the opening algorithm and aiming to output a valid forgery signature. Second, the adversary can give a valid signature for any message without using information from the opening algorithm. In the first method, since PKE has perfect correctness and perfect binding, we will prove that the probability that the adversary wins is negligible. In the latter case, by the EU-CMA secure of the signature Sig, the adversary also has negligible success. In other words, we have reduced the security of the signature scheme Sig. This reduction receives a verification key spk_{i^*} from the challenger and generates spk_i for all $i \neq i^*$ and epk_i for all $i \in [l]$. The reduction decrypts both ct_0^* and ct_1^*, yielding σ_0^* and σ_1^*, respectively, upon receiving an accountable ring signature forgery from the adversary. Then, determine whether any of σ_0^*, σ_1^* is a valid signature for spk_{i^*}. If one of them is valid, the reduction will output that value as the valid forging for the Sig scheme. Due to the somewhere perfect binding of SPB hashing and the perfect soundness of the NIWI scheme, the reduction produces a valid forge with a probability non-negligible.

Theorem 3. *If* NIWI *has perfect soundness,* SPB *is somewhere perfectly binding,* Sig *has EU-CMA,* CS *is perfect correctness,* PKE *has perfect correctness and perfect binding, then* ARS *is unforgeable.*

Proof. The proof is presented in a full version of the paper.   □

4.3   Tracing Soundness

To prove tracing soundness, we show that an adversary has only two ways to win in the tracking soundness experiment. The first way, $\mathcal{A}$ uses a signature generated by an honest user VK_{i^*}, proving that this signature is from a dishonest user VK_j. In this case, we obtain a reduction to break the perfect binding of the CS scheme. The second way, from a dishonest user VK_j signature, the adversary proves that this signature was generated by an honest user VK_{i^*}. This implies a reduction that can break the EU-CMA security of Sig scheme.

Theorem 4. *If* NIWI *has perfect soundness,* Sig *has EU-CMA,* SPB *is somewhere perfectly binding,* PKE *is perfect correctness, and* CS *is perfect binding, then* ARS *is tracing soundness.*

Proof. The proof is presented in a full version of the paper.   □

5   Conclusion

A ring signature is a well-studied cryptographic primitive with many applications. An accountable ring signature is a stronger cryptographic primitive than a ring signature while retaining the ring signature's flexibility. This paper introduces the first construction of the accountable ring signature in the plain model. Our signature size is logarithmic in the number of ring members, using only standard assumptions and not requiring a trusted setup.

Acknowledgement. We are grateful to the Inscrypt 2023 anonymous reviewers for their helpful comments. This work is partially supported by the Australian Research Council Linkage Project LP190100984.

References

1. Backes, M., Döttling, N., Hanzlik, L., Kluczniak, K., Schneider, J.: Ring signatures: logarithmic-size, no setup—from standard assumptions. In: Ishai, Y., Rijmen, V. (eds.) EUROCRYPT 2019. LNCS, vol. 11478, pp. 281–311. Springer, Cham (2019). https://doi.org/10.1007/978-3-030-17659-4_10

2. Badrinarayanan, S., Fernando, R., Jain, A., Khurana, D., Sahai, A.: Statistical ZAP arguments. In: Canteaut, A., Ishai, Y. (eds.) EUROCRYPT 2020. LNCS, vol. 12107, pp. 642–667. Springer, Cham (2020). https://doi.org/10.1007/978-3-030-45727-3_22

3. Bender, A., Katz, J., Morselli, R.: Ring signatures: stronger definitions, and constructions without random oracles. In: Halevi, S., Rabin, T. (eds.) TCC 2006. LNCS, vol. 3876, pp. 60–79. Springer, Heidelberg (2006). https://doi.org/10.1007/11681878_4

4. Bootle, J., Cerulli, A., Chaidos, P., Ghadafi, E., Groth, J., Petit, C.: Short accountable ring signatures based on DDH. In: Pernul, G., Ryan, P.Y.A., Weippl, E. (eds.) ESORICS 2015. LNCS, vol. 9326, pp. 243–265. Springer, Cham (2015). https://doi.org/10.1007/978-3-319-24174-6_13

5. Branco, P., Döttling, N., Wohnig, S.: Universal ring signatures in the standard model. In: Advances in Cryptology-ASIACRYPT 2022: 28th International Conference on the Theory and Application of Cryptology and Information Security, Taipei, Taiwan, 5–9 December 2022, Proceedings, Part IV, pp. 249–278. Springer (2023). https://doi.org/10.1007/978-3-031-22972-5_9

6. Bultel, X., Fraser, A., Quaglia, E.A.: Improving the efficiency of report and trace ring signatures. In: International Symposium on Stabilizing, Safety, and Security of Distributed Systems, pp. 130–145. Springer (2022). https://doi.org/10.1007/978-3-031-21017-4_9

7. Canetti, R., Goldreich, O., Halevi, S.: The random oracle methodology, revisited. J. ACM (JACM) 51(4), 557–594 (2004)

8. Chatterjee, R., et al.: Compact ring signatures from learning with errors. In: Malkin, T., Peikert, C. (eds.) CRYPTO 2021. LNCS, vol. 12825, pp. 282–312. Springer, Cham (2021). https://doi.org/10.1007/978-3-030-84242-0_11

9. Chaum, D., Van Heyst, E.: Group signatures. In: Advances in Cryptology-EUROCRYPT 1991: Workshop on the Theory and Application of Cryptographic Techniques Brighton, UK, 8–11 April 1991 Proceedings 10, pp. 257–265. Springer (1991). https://doi.org/10.1007/978-1-4419-5906-5_20

10. ElGamal, T.: A public key cryptosystem and a signature scheme based on discrete logarithms. IEEE Trans. Inf. Theory 31(4), 469–472 (1985)

11. Groth, J., Ostrovsky, R., Sahai, A.: Non-interactive zaps and new techniques for NIZK. In: Dwork, C. (ed.) CRYPTO 2006. LNCS, vol. 4117, pp. 97–111. Springer, Heidelberg (2006). https://doi.org/10.1007/11818175_6

12. Okamoto, T., Pietrzak, K., Waters, B., Wichs, D.: New realizations of somewhere statistically binding hashing and positional accumulators. In: Iwata, T., Cheon, J.H. (eds.) ASIACRYPT 2015. LNCS, vol. 9452, pp. 121–145. Springer, Heidelberg (2015). https://doi.org/10.1007/978-3-662-48797-6_6

13. Rivest, R.L., Shamir, A., Tauman, Y.: How to leak a secret. In: Boyd, C. (ed.) ASIACRYPT 2001. LNCS, vol. 2248, pp. 552–565. Springer, Heidelberg (2001). https://doi.org/10.1007/3-540-45682-1_32
14. Xu, S., Yung, M.: Accountable ring signatures: a smart card approach. In: Quisquater, J.-J., Paradinas, P., Deswarte, Y., El Kalam, A.A. (eds.) CARDIS 2004. IIFIP, vol. 153, pp. 271–286. Springer, Boston, MA (2004). https://doi.org/10.1007/1-4020-8147-2_18

Universally Composable Key-Insulated and Privacy-Preserving Signature Scheme with Publicly Derived Public Key

Chunping Zhu[1] , Xingkai Wang[1] , and Zhen Liu[1,2](✉)

[1] Shanghai Jiao Tong University, Shanghai, China
{chengfengpolang,starshine87,liuzhen}@sjtu.edu.cn
[2] Shanghai Qizhi Institute, Shanghai, China

Abstract. In recent years, the rapid development of blockchain-based applications, such as cryptocurrencies, has raised concerns about privacy preservation within the blockchain community. One widely adopted technique for privacy preservation is the use of Stealth Address, which serves as a crucial component of Monero's Ring Confidential Transaction (RingCT) protocol. Liu et al. (EuroS&P'19) introduced and formalized a new signature variant called the Key-Insulated and Privacy-Preserving Signature Scheme with Publicly Derived Public Key (PDPKS), and gave a systematically definition on the Stealth Address in both syntax and security definition. This signature variant goes beyond defining the necessary functionality but also capturing safety and privacy requirements, by introducing two game-based security definitions respectively.

Rather than in a standalone mode, PDPKS protocol is typically executed alongside other secure components within a complex blockchain system to achieve various security objectives. However, achieving security of a comprehensive system requires additional analysis on the entire system, considering mutual impacts among protocols. Hence, it is crucial to introduce a unified and systematic definition that can describe the security in a universally composable (UC) manner.

This paper focuses on formalizing the security of PDPKS in the UC framework, which provides a stronger security definition and ensures that the protocol can be designed and analyzed modularly, so that any specific constructions that satisfy the security requirements defined in the proposed UC model can be securely used as building blocks in complex blockchain systems, without any security concerns. To have a concrete construction that satisfies the UC-security proposed in this paper, we conducted an analysis of the conventional game-based security definitions put forth by Liu et al., and proved that the equivalence between the UC-security of PDPKS and the simultaneous satisfaction of the two game-based security definitions. As a result, this implies that the construction proposed by Liu et al. is a UC-secure PDPKS construction. Besides, the proved equivalence also contributes to a general framework wherein any PDPKS construction that satisfies Liu et al.'s security definition will also satisfies UC-security. This framework enables the use of these PDPKS constructions as secure building blocks in the design and implementation of UC-secure blockchain systems.

C. Ge and M. Yung (Eds.): Inscrypt 2023, LNCS 14526, pp. 44–64, 2024.
https://doi.org/10.1007/978-981-97-0942-7_3

Keywords: Universal Composability · Privacy Preservation · Signature Scheme · Stealth Address · Deterministic Wallet

1   Introduction

Since the introduction of Bitcoin [12] by Nakamoto in 2008, the past decade has witnessed a remarkable advancement in the blockchain-based technology and cryptocurrencies. Privacy protection has emerged as one of the most desirable features in this domain. In Bitcoin-like cryptocurrency systems, digital signature [16] schemes play a crucial role in authorizing and authenticating transactions. Specifically, in these cryptocurrency systems, each coin is represented by a pair (pk, v), where the public key pk indicates the owner of the coin, and the value v denotes the denomination of the coin. Roughly speaking, each coin c is represented by a $(pk, value)$ pair, where pk specifies the owner of the coin and $value$ denotes the denomination. When the coin owner (i.e. the payer of the transaction) wants to spend the coin c on the public key pk and transfer it to a receiver (i.e. the payee of the transaction), he must initiate a new transaction tx, which consumes c and generates a new coin c' assigned to the receiver's public key pk', and utilize the digital signature scheme to sign the transaction using his secret signing key sk' corresponding to the public key pk'. Indeed, the transaction tx is authorized and authenticated due to the properties of digital signatures. In essence, the transaction procedure indicates that: the public key servers as the designated coin-receiving address, while the secret signing key functions as the coin-spending key.

For users of such cryptocurrencies, privacy is undoubtedly on of the most coveted features. In Bitcoin, transactions and coins are solely associated with public keys, and there are no direct connections between public keys and user identities. The privacy-preserving mechanism in Bitcoin, known as *pseudonymity*, has limitations as it does not provide *untraceability* or *unlinkability* [14,20]. For example, if a participant uses a single public key to receive multiple coins from various transactions, it becomes possible for the public to link these transactions to a shared owner [10,17]. Researchers have conducted extensive studies and research [5,11,18] to enhance privacy protection for users in the realm of blockchain technology. *Stealth Address* (SA) [19,20] is recognized as one of the privacy-preserving techniques that offers a straightforward yet effective approach to enhancing privacy in blockchain transaction by concealing the recipient of transactions [13]. Particularly, Monero adopts the one-time derived public key mechanism, which is originally proposed in CryptoNote [20]. This mechanism ensures that each coin's receiving address is a fresh public key, which is derived from the payee's long-term public key and the payer's random data. The primary advantage of utilizing such a solution is that each coin-receiving address is inherently unique. This feature eliminates the ability of observers to discern whether transactions were sent to a specific long-term public key or to link multiple coin-receiving addresses together with their corresponding coins and transactions. However, Liu et al. [8] identified a critical vulnerability in the key derivation algorithm employed by the aforementioned technique, that the leakage of a single derived secret key could result in the complete compromise of all secret keys derived from the same long-term key. This vulnerability poses a severe threat to the security of cryptocurrencies which adopt SA algorithm, including Monero, since it is highly challenging to maintain the security of all derived secret keys simultaneously.

In addition to the above privacy concerns, the management of multiple coins in cryptocurrency system involves the use of wallets to handle corresponding public-secret key pairs. These wallets facilitate various operations, such as key generation, storage, usage, and deletion, among others. In this context, an advanced wallet technique named *Deterministic Wallet* [9] has been proposed. This technique is considered an effective solution for Bitcoin, particularly in managing cold storage address conveniently while maintaining the privacy of receiving each coin at a fresh cold address. Deterministic Wallet offers several additional features that enhance the user experience, including low-maintenance while providing easy backup and recovery, the ability to conduct trustless audit, and the capability for treasurers to allocate funds to specific departments or entities. However, similar to the key derivation algorithm of Monero, the key derivation algorithm used in Bitcoin's Deterministic Wallet also shares a security vulnerability. Specifically, if an attacker manages to obtain the master public key, and compromise any secret key, he can compute the master secret key to obtain all the secret keys, and further compromise the whole wallet.

To mitigate the aforementioned critical vulnerabilities, Liu et al. [8] proposed and formalized the concept of Key-Insulated and Privacy-Preserving Signature Scheme with Publicly Derived Public Key (PDPKS). This scheme was specifically designed to address the security concerns associated with Stealth Addresses and Deterministic Wallets, whose security definitions capture the functionality, safety, and privacy requirements for practical implementations in cryptocurrencies. Furthermore, they present two different constructions that successfully satisfy the proposed security definition.

On the other side, cryptocurrency systems are generally complicated, consisting of a variety of cryptographic structures. However, it is important to recognize that a protocol which is secure in standalone manner is not necessarily remaining secure when executed alongside other protocols within a system. To address this concern, Canetti [3] introduced the Universal Composability (UC) framework as a means to analyze the security of cryptographic protocols, offering a stronger security requirement. A primitive that satisfies UC-security remains secure even when concurrently executed with other UC-secure primitives under the same adversarial manner. This property allows a UC-secure PDPKS protocol to be arbitrarily combined with other UC-secure components, such as sender private protocols and transaction amount preserving protocols. Therefore, defining the security of PDPKS within the UC model is an interesting and significant topic for investigation. Additionally, it is worthwhile to assess the strength of the newly defined security and to explore the existence of an efficient UC-secure PDPKS construction. The lack of research in UC-security of PDPKS significantly reduces its scalability and modularity as a vital component of cryptocurrency systems.

1.1 Our Results

In this paper, we revisit the security definition of PDPKS and explore its modularity and adaptability to other cryptographic primitives whin a comprehensive crytocurrency system. Our contributions can be summarized as follows:

- We provide a novel security definition of Signature Scheme with Publicly Derived Public Key (PDPKS) in the Universal Composability (UC) model. We define the ideal functionality, which simultaneously captures correctness, soundness (existantial unforgeability) and privacy (unlinkability) requirements.
- We further investigate the security level of the proposed security definition. Through rigorous analysis, we demonstrate that the proposed UC-security of PDPKS is equivalent to the concurrent satisfaction of master public key unlinkablility (MPK-UNL) and existentially unforgeability under chosen message attack (EUF-CMA) security.
- We establish that the ideal functionality can be securely realized by the previously proposed construction that achieves the former two security definitions. This finding indicates that, including the PDPKS constructions proposed in [8] and [7], all secure PDPKS constructions that satisfy the security definition of [8] are UC-secure, and can arbitrarily compose with other UC secure components in a complicated blockchain system.

1.2 Related Work

After Liu et al. [8] put forward a provably secure paring-based construction, Liu et al. [7] further proposed a lattice-based PDPKS protocol, based on the hardness of Learning With Errors (LWE) problem [15], which makes PDPKS achieving quantum resistance.

While our work is the first to specifically address the UC-security of PDPKS, it is worth noting that there have been various studies focusing on UC-secure signature schemes. Canetti [3] initially proposed a functionality for signature schems; however, there was a flaw in the definition that rendered it impossible to be securely realized. Later, Backes et al. [2] and Canetti [4] addressed the flaw, and demonstrated that the newly defined UC-security is equivalent to the game-based definition of EUF-CMA. In this paper, we employ a similar proven technique that circumvents the flaw identified in [3]. Besides typical signature schemes, Abe et al. [1] introduced the UC secure non-committing blind signature. More recently, Hong et al. [6] formally defined the UC security of proxy re-signature. We would like to emphasize that PDPKS is distinct from these signature-related primitives, as it possesses unique functionality and security features.

2 Preliminaries

In this section, we begin by introducing the notations that will be used throughout this paper. Next, we revisit the definition of PDPKS as proposed by Liu et al. [8]. Subsequently, we review the background of the universal composability (UC) framework, as well as the definition of UC security.

2.1 Notations

A probabilistic algorithm $A(x_1, ..., x_n; r)$ represents the random variable of the output produced by A when given inputs $x_1, ..., x_n$ and a random coin r. The notation $y \xleftarrow{R} A(x_1, ..., x_n; r)$ signifies that y is randomly selected from the distribution of $A(x_1, ..., x_n; r)$. When S is a finite set, $x \xleftarrow{U} S$ denotes that x is uniformly selected from S. If α is neither an algorithm nor a set, $x \leftarrow \alpha$ indicates that x is assigned the value of α.

We say that a function $f : \mathbb{N} \to \mathbb{R}$ is negligible in the security parameter k if, for every constant $c \in \mathbb{N}$, there exists a threshold $k_c \in \mathbb{N}$ such that $f(k) < k^{-c}$ for any $k > k_c$. Hereafter, we often employ $f < \nu(k)$ to signify that the function f is negligible in k. Conversely, we use $f > \nu(k)$ to indicate that the function f is non-negligible in k. A distribution ensemble $X = \{X(k, z)\}_{k \in \mathbb{N}, z \in \{0,1\}^*}$ is an infinite collection of probability distributions, where a distribution $X(k, z)$ is associated with each $k \in \mathbb{N}$ and $z \in \{0, 1\}^*$. In this paper, the ensembles under consideration represent the outputs of computations, where the parameter z represents the input to the computation, and k is taken to be the security parameter. We use $X \approx Y$ to denote that two binary distribution ensembles X and Y are statistically indistinguishable, if for any $c, d \in \mathbb{N}$ there exists a threshold $k_c \in \mathbb{N}$ such that for any $k > k_c$ and any $z \in \cup_{\kappa \leq k^d} \{0,1\}^\kappa$, $|Pr[X(k, z) = 1] - Pr[Y(k, z) = 1]| < k^{-c}$ holds.

2.2 PDPKS: Signature Scheme with Publicly Derived Public Key

Syntax. A PDPKS scheme consists of the following algorithms:

- Setup(k) $\to$ PP. Given input the security parameter k, the algorithm outputs a public parameter denoted as PP.
- MasterKeyGen(PP) $\to$ (mpk, msk). Given input the public parameter PP, the algorithm outputs a master public-secret key pair denotesd as (mpk, msk).
- DpkDerive(PP, mpk) $\to$ dpk. Given inputs the public parameter PP and a master public key mpk, the algorithm outputs a derived public key dpk, which is linked to mpk.
- DpkCheck(PP, mpk, msk, dpk) $\to$ $\{0, 1\}$. Given inputs the public parameter PP, a master key pair (mpk, msk), and a derived public key dpk, the algorithm outputs a bit $b \in \{0, 1\}$, with $b = 1$ indicating that dpk is a valid derived public key linked to mpk and $b = 0$ indicating the irrelevance conversely.

- DskDerive(PP, mpk, msk, dpk) → dsk. Given inputs the public parameter PP, a master key pair (mpk, msk), and a derived public key dpk that is linked to mpk, the algorithm outputs a derived secret key dsk corresponding to dpk.
- Sign(PP, dpk, m, dsk) → σ. Given inputs the public parameter PP, a derived public key dpk, a message m in message space $\mathcal{M}$, and a derived secret key dsk corresponding to dpk, the algorithm outputs a signature σ.
- Verify(PP, dpk, m, σ) → {0, 1}. Given inputs the public parameter PP, a derived public key dpk, a message m, and a signature σ, the algorithm outputs a bit $b \in \{0, 1\}$, with $b = 1$ indicating a valid signature and $b = 0$ signifying an invalid signature.

System Model. In our PDPKS scheme, apart from the system itself, there are a minimum of two participants, where one acts as the payee, say Alice, and the other acts as the payer, Bob. Alice intends to receive funds from Bob. (1) For a cryptocurrency system with PDPKS scheme, the system initialization begins by executing Setup() algorithm and publishes to all users the system public parameter PP, which consists of parameters common parameters including the underlying groups, hash functions, and other relevant system-specific parameters. (2) Each participant can run MasterKeyGen() algorithm to obtain his long-term master key pair (mpk, msk) and publish mpk. (3) The payer Bob runs DpkDerive() algorithm on Alice's master public key mpk_A, and assigns dpk_A to the output coin, without any interaction with Alice. (4) The payee Alice runs DpkCheck() algorithm to check whether she is the intended receiver of this coin, and Alice accepts such a coin into only if the running result is 1. (5) To spend such a coin, Alice runs DskDerive() algorithm to obtain the derived secret key dsk_A corresponding to dpk_A. (6) Then, she runs Sign() algorithm to sign the transaction for spending the coin. (7) For a transaction that consumes a coin with derived public key dpk_A, anyone can run the Verify() algorithm to check whether the associated signature is valid, only using the dpk_A, without the corresponding master public key.

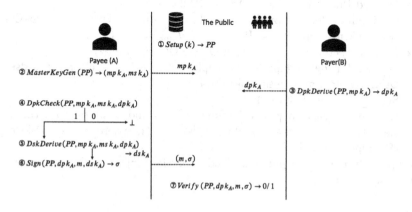

Fig. 1. System model.

Correctness. The scheme must satisfy the following correctness properties:

For any $PP \leftarrow Setup(1^\lambda)$, $(mpk, msk) \leftarrow MasterKeyGen(PP)$, $dpk \leftarrow DpkDerive(PP, mpk)$, $dsk \leftarrow DskDerive(PP, mpk, msk, dpk)$, and any message m, it holds that

$$Pr[DpkCheck(PP, mpk, msk, dpk) = 1] = 1 - negl(n),$$

and

$$Pr[Verify(PP, dpk, m, Sign(PP, dpk, m, dsk)) = 1] = 1 - negl(n).$$

Security Models. Note that PDPKS is actually a signature variant that considers key derivation and privacy-preserving, the security of PDPKS consists of unforgeability and unlinkability, which capture safety and privacy requirements respectively. Roughly speaking, unforgeability captures that, for a given derived verification key, without the corresponding derived signing key, no adversary can forge a valid signature. Unforgeability holds even if the derived verification key was generated by the adversary from a chosen master public key, and the adversary may also compromise the master secret key and an arbitrary number of derived signing keys for other verification keys, as long as the corresponding signing key and the master secret key of the derived verificatio key is remaining private. We follow the definition of existentially unforgeable security under an adaptive chosen-message attack (EUF-CMA) of PDPKS scheme in [8]. The definition is shown as follows.

Definition 1 (EUF-CMA security of PDPKS [8]). A PDPKS scheme is existentially unforgeably secure under an adaptive chosen-message attack (EUF-CMA) if for all probabilistic polynomial time (PPT) adversaries $\mathcal{A}$, the success probability of $\mathcal{A}$ in the following game $Game^{euf}$ is negligible.

- **Setup Phase.** $PP \leftarrow Setup(1^\lambda)$ and $(mpk, msk) \leftarrow MaterKeyGen(PP)$ are run. PP and mpk are given to $\mathcal{A}$. An empty set $L_{dpk} = \emptyset$.
- **Probing Phase.** $\mathcal{A}$ can adaptively query the following oracles:
  - Derived Public key Check Oracle $ODpkCheck(\cdot)$:
    On input a derived public key dpk, this oracle returns $c \leftarrow DpkCheck(PP, mpk, msk, dpk)$ to $\mathcal{A}$. If $c = 1$, set $L_{dpk} = L_{dpk} \cup \{dpk\}$.
  - Derived Secret Key Corruption Oracle $ODskCorrupt(\cdot)$:
    On input a derived public key $dpk \in L_{dpk}$, this oracle returns $dsk \leftarrow DskDerive(PP, mpk, msk, dpk)$ to $\mathcal{A}$.
  - Signing Oracle $OSign(\cdot, \cdot)$:
    On input a derived public key $dpk \in L_{dpk}$ and a message m, this oracle returns $\sigma \leftarrow Sign(PP, dpk, m, dsk)$ to $\mathcal{A}$, where $dsk \leftarrow DskDerive(PP, mpk, msk, dpk)$.
- **Output Phase.** $\mathcal{A}$ outputs a derived public key $dpk^* \in L_{dpk}$, a message m^*, and a signature σ^*.

$\mathcal{A}$ succeeds if $\mathsf{Verify}(\mathsf{PP}, \mathsf{dpk}^*, m^*, \sigma^*) = 1$ under the restrictions that (1) $\mathsf{ODskCorrupt}(\mathsf{dpk}^*)$ is never queried, and (2) $\mathsf{OSign}(\mathsf{dpk}^*, m^*)$ is never queried.

Unlinkability of PDPKS captures that neither the derived public keys or the corresponding signatures leak any information that can be linked to the origin master public key. Specifically, given a derived public key and corresponding signatures, an adversary cannot tell which master public key is that from which the verification key was derived, out of a set of given known master public keys. We follow the definition of master public-key unlinkable security (MPK-UNL) of PDPKS scheme in [8]. The definition is shown as follows.

Definition 2 (MPK-UNL security of PDPKS [8]). A PDPKS scheme is master public key unlinkable (MPK-UNL), if for all PPT adversaries $\mathcal{A}$, the advantage of $\mathcal{A}$ in the following game Game_{mpkunl}, denoted by $\mathbf{Adv}_{\mathcal{A}}^{mpkunl}$, is negligible.

- **Setup Phase.** $\mathsf{PP} \leftarrow \mathsf{Setup}(1^\lambda)$ is run and PP is given to $\mathcal{A}$. $(\mathsf{mpk}_0, \mathsf{msk}_0) \leftarrow \mathsf{MasterKeyGen}(\mathsf{PP})$ and $(\mathsf{mpk}_1, \mathsf{msk}_1) \leftarrow \mathsf{MasterKeyGen}(\mathsf{PP})$ are run, and $\mathsf{mpk}_0, \mathsf{mpk}_1$ are given to $\mathcal{A}$. Two empty sets $L_{\mathsf{dpk},0} = L_{\mathsf{dpk},1} = \emptyset$ are initialized.
- **Challenge Phase.** A random bit $b \leftarrow \{0, 1\}$ is chosen. $\mathsf{dpk}^* \leftarrow \mathsf{DpkDerive}(\mathsf{PP}, \mathsf{mpk}_b)$ is given to $\mathcal{A}$.
- **Probing Phase.** $\mathcal{A}$ can adaptively query the following oracles:
  - Derived Public Key Check Oracle $\mathsf{ODpkCheck}(\cdot, \cdot)$:
    On input a derived public key $\mathsf{dpk} \neq \mathsf{dpk}^*$ and an index $i \in \{0, 1\}$, the oracle returns $c \leftarrow \mathsf{DpkCheck}(\mathsf{PP}, \mathsf{mpk}_i, \mathsf{msk}_i, \mathsf{dpk})$ to $\mathcal{A}$. If $c = 1$, set $L_{\mathsf{dpk},i} = L_{\mathsf{dpk},i} \cup \{\mathsf{dpk}\}$.
  - Derived Secret Key Corruption Oracle $\mathsf{ODskCorrupt}(\cdot)$:
    On input a derived public key $\mathsf{dpk} \in L_{\mathsf{dpk},0} \cup L_{\mathsf{dpk},1}$, this oracle returns $\mathsf{dsk} \leftarrow \mathsf{DskDerive}(\mathsf{PP}, \mathsf{mpk}_i, \mathsf{msk}_i, \mathsf{dpk})$ to $\mathcal{A}$, with $i = 0$ if $\mathsf{dpk} \in L_{\mathsf{dpk},0}$, and $i = 1$ if $\mathsf{dpk} \in L_{\mathsf{dpk},1}$.
  - Signing Oracle $\mathsf{OSign}(\cdot, \cdot)$:
    On input a derived public key $\mathsf{dpk} \in L_{\mathsf{dpk},0} \cup L_{\mathsf{dpk},1} \cup \{\mathsf{dpk}^*\}$ and a message m, this oracle returns $\sigma \leftarrow \mathsf{Sign}(\mathsf{PP}, \mathsf{dpk}, m, \mathsf{dsk})$ to $\mathcal{A}$, where $\mathsf{dsk} \leftarrow \mathsf{DskDerive}(\mathsf{PP}, \mathsf{mpk}_i, \mathsf{msk}_i, \mathsf{dpk})$, with $i = 0$ if $\mathsf{dpk} \in L_{\mathsf{dpk},0}$, $i = 1$ if $\mathsf{dpk} \in L_{\mathsf{dpk},1}$, and $i = b$ if $\mathsf{dpk} = \mathsf{dpk}^*$.
- **Guessing Phase.** $\mathcal{A}$ outputs a bit $b' \in \{0, 1\}$ as its guess to b.

2.3 Universal Composability

We follow the notion of universally composable security as defined by Canetti [3]. The work provides a framework for defining the security properties of cryptographic primitives such that security is maintained under a general composition with an unbounded number of instances of arbitrary protocols running concurrently. In this framework, all protocols run in a given computational environment and the presence of an adversary. The computational environment models the arbitrary other protocols concurrently executing outside the protocol at hand. Considering that the communication is public without guarantee of messages delivery and asynchronous without guarantee of messages delivered in order in the real network, we assume the communication between parties is authenticated to ensure that messages sent by honest parties will not be modified. Next, we overview the model for protocol execution, called the real world model of computation, and then the ideal world model of computation and the general definition of security realizing an ideal functionality.

In the real world, there is an adversary $\mathcal{A}$ and a protocol π which realizes a functionality among some parties. Let $\mathsf{REAL}_{\pi,\mathcal{A},\mathcal{Z}}(k,z,r)$ denote the output of environment $\mathcal{Z}$ when interacting with adversary $\mathcal{A}$ and parties $P_1, ..., P_n$ running protocol π on security parameter k, auxiliary input z, and random input $r = (r_{\mathcal{Z}}, r_{\mathcal{A}}, r_1, ..., r_n)$, where each element represents the random tape the corresponding participant uses. Let $\mathsf{REAL}_{\pi,\mathcal{A},\mathcal{Z}}(k,z)$ denote the random variable describing $\mathsf{REAL}_{\pi,\mathcal{A},\mathcal{Z}}(k,z,r)$ when r is uniformly chosen.

In the ideal world, there is a simulator $\mathcal{S}$ that simulates the real life world, an ideal functionality $\mathcal{F}$, and n dummy parties for integrity of the simulation. Let $\mathsf{IDEAL}_{\mathcal{F},\mathcal{S},\mathcal{Z}}(k,z,r)$ denote the output of environment $\mathcal{Z}$ when interacting with adversary $\mathcal{S}$ and ideal functionality $\mathcal{F}$ on security parameter k, auxiliary input z, and a random input $r = (r_{\mathcal{Z}}, r_{\mathcal{S}}, r_{\mathcal{F}})$, where each element represents the random tape the corresponding participants uses. Let $\mathsf{IDEAL}_{\mathcal{F},\mathcal{S},\mathcal{Z}}(k,z)$ denote the random variable describing $\mathsf{IDEAL}_{\mathcal{F},\mathcal{S},\mathcal{Z}}(k,z,r)$ when r is uniformly chosen.

The definition of UC security of a protocol is defined as follows.

Definition 3 (UC security). *Let π be a protocol and $\mathcal{F}$ be its corresponding well-designed ideal functionality, we say that π is UC secure when π UC-realizes $\mathcal{F}$, if for all PPT adversary $\mathcal{A}$, there exists a simulator $\mathcal{S}$, such that for any environment $\mathcal{Z}$ the following holds:*

$$\mathsf{IDEAL}_{\mathcal{F},\mathcal{S},\mathcal{Z}} \approx \mathsf{REAL}_{\pi,\mathcal{A},\mathcal{Z}},$$

where $\mathcal{A}$, $\mathcal{S}$ and $\mathcal{Z}$ are probabilistic polynomial-time interactive Turing Machines.

3   Security Model of PDPKS in UC Framework

In this section, we will define the security model of PDPKS in the universal composability model, by presenting the newly designed ideal functionality $\mathcal{F}_{\mathsf{PDPKS}}$. We define the ideal functionality $\mathcal{F}_{\mathsf{PDPKS}}$ in Fig. 2. Our definition of $\mathcal{F}_{\mathsf{PDPKS}}$ follows for $\mathcal{F}_{\mathsf{PKE}}$ of regular public-key encryption schemes given by Canetti [3] and $\mathcal{F}_{\mathsf{SIG}}$ of digital signature scheme given by Backes et al. [2]. The idea of $\mathcal{F}_{\mathsf{PDPKS}}$ is to allow parties to obtain the master secret keys and derived secret keys by running the corresponding key generation algorithms, such that master secret keys and derived secret keys do not appear in the interface. The functionality is parameterized with a fixed system parameters PP, so as to omit the Setup interface and the judgment of whether PP is reasonable at the following interfaces.

Remark. Our definition in UC model captures the correctness, security and privacy of PDPKS simultaneously. Formal proof will be shown in Sect. 4.

4   A UC-Secure PDPKS Construction

In this section, we prove that the UC-Security of PDPKS defined above in Sect. 3 is equivalent to satisfying MPK-UNL and EUF-CMA simultaneously.

Let $\Sigma =$ (Setup, MasterKeyGen, DpkDerive, DpkCheck, DskDerive, Sign, Verify) be a PDPKS scheme. We define protocol π_Σ that is constructed from Σ and has the same interface with the environment as $\mathcal{F}_{\mathsf{PDPKS}}$. We define protocol π_Σ as in Fig. 3, which is constructed according to the above scheme Σ.

Below we prove that a UC secure PDPKS scheme implies a PDPKS scheme with existing unforgeability and master-public-key unlinkability, and vice versa.

Lemma 1. *Let Σ be a PDPKS scheme. If the corresponding protocol π_Σ securely realizes the ideal functionality $\mathcal{F}_{\mathsf{PDPKS}}$, then the PDPKS scheme Σ is both master public key unlinkable (MPK-UNL) and existentially unforgeable under an adaptive chosen-message attack (EUF-CMA).*

Proof. We prove the lemma by contradiction. In other words, if Σ is not MPK-UNL or not EUF-CMA, then π_Σ does not securely realize $\mathcal{F}_{\mathsf{PDPKS}}$.

First, if Σ is not MPK-UNL, there exists an adversary $\mathcal{G}$ that can break Σ in the sense of MPK-UNL with non-negligible probability, i.e. $\mathbf{Adv}_{\Sigma,\mathcal{G}}^{MPK-UNL} > \nu(k)$. There exists a PPT adversary $\mathcal{A}$ such that for all simulator $\mathcal{S}$, there exists an environment $\mathcal{Z}$ which could tell whether it is communicating with $(\mathcal{S}, \mathcal{F}_{\mathsf{PDPKS}})$ or $(\mathcal{A}, \pi_\Sigma)$ with non-negligible probability, under the help of $\mathcal{G}$. We prove the conclusion by construction. The environment $\mathcal{Z}$ proceeds as follows.

Functionality $\mathcal{F}_{\mathsf{PDPKS}}$

The functionality $\mathcal{F}_{\mathsf{PDPKS}}$ is parameterized with a fixed system parameters PP. The functionality $\mathcal{F}_{\mathsf{PDPKS}}$ interacts with n participants $P_1, ..., P_n$ and a simulator S. Empty sets $L_{\mathsf{dpk},i} = \emptyset$ are initialized where $i \in \{1, ..., n\}$.

•**MasterKeyGen:** Upon receiving value (**Keygen**, sid) from party P_i:
1. Hand (**Keygen**, sid, P_i) to S. Upon receiving value (**Keygened**, sid, P_i, mpk_i) from S, then send (**Keygened**, sid, mpk_i) to P_i.
2. Record (P_i, mpk_i).

•**DpkDerive:** Upon receiving value (**Dpkderive**, sid, mpk'_i, P_i) from any party P_j:
1. If $\mathsf{mpk}'_i \neq \mathsf{mpk}_i$ with (P_i, mpk_i), then ignore this request.
2. Otherwise, hand value (**Dpkderive**, sid, mpk'_i, P_i) to S. Upon receiving value (**Dpkderived**, sid, dpk_i, P_i) from S, send (**Dpkderived**, sid, dpk_i, P_i) to P_j, set $L_{\mathsf{dpk},i} = L_{\mathsf{dpk},i} \cup \{\mathsf{dpk}_i\}$.

•**DpkCheck:** Upon receiving value (**Dpkcheck**, sid, dpk_i) from party P_i:
1. Hand value (**Dpkcheck**, sid, dpk_i, P_i) to S. Upon receiving value (**Dpkchecked**, sid, dpk_i, P_i, g) from S where $g \in \{0, 1\}$, continue to the next step.
2. If P_i is uncorrupted and $\mathsf{dpk}_i \in L_{\mathsf{dpk},i}$, then set $f = 1$.
3. Else, set $f = g$. If $g = 1$, set $L_{\mathsf{dpk},i} = L_{\mathsf{dpk},i} \cup \{dpk_i\}$, otherwise record value $(\mathsf{dpk}_i, P_i, 0)$.
4. Send (**Dpkchecked**, sid, dpk_i, P_i, f) to P_i.

•**DskDerive:** Upon receiving value (**Dskderive**, sid, dpk_i) from party P_i:
1. Hand value (**Dskderive**, sid, dpk_i, P_i) to S, and receive value (**Dskderived**, sid, dpk_i, P_i, g) from S where $g \in \{0, 1\}$.
2. If P_i is uncorrupted, and $\mathsf{dpk}_i \notin L_{\mathsf{dpk},i}$ or there is an entry $(\mathsf{dpk}_i, P_i, 0)$ saved in memory, hand $\perp$ to P_i.
3. Otherwise, if $g = 1$, hand (**Dskderived**, sid, dpk_i) to P_i, else hand $\perp$ to P_i.

•**Sign:** Upon receiving value (**Sign**, sid, m, dpk_i) from party P_i:
1. Hand value (**Sign**, sid, m, dpk_i, P_i) to S, and receive value (**Signature**, sid, m, σ, dpk_i) from S.
2. If P_i is uncorrupted and $\mathsf{dpk}_i \notin L_{\mathsf{dpk},i}$, return an error message to P_i.
3. Otherwise, record value $(m, \sigma, \mathsf{dpk}_i, 1)$ and hand value (**Signature**, sid, m, σ, dpk_i) to P_i.

•**Verify:** Upon receiving value (**Verify**, sid, m, σ, dpk_i) from some party P_j:
1. If $\mathsf{dpk}_i \notin \{L_{\mathsf{dpk},i}\}_{i=1}^n$, send this value to S; upon receiving an answer (**Verified**, sid, m, σ, dpk_i, f) from S, forward the result to P_j.
2. If $\mathsf{dpk}_i \in \{L_{\mathsf{dpk},i}\}_{i=1}^n$, send this value to S, and receive an answer (**Verified**, sid, m, dpk_i, f') from S, answer with (**Verified**, sid, m, σ, dpk_i, f), where f is determined as follows:

 – If there is an entry $(m, \sigma, \mathsf{dpk}_i, g)$ saved in memory, then let $f = g$.
 – If the owner party P_i of dpk_i is uncorrupted and there is no entry $(m, \sigma, \mathsf{dpk}_i, g)$ for any g stored, let $f = 0$.
 – Else, let $f = f'$ and store the value $(m, \sigma, \mathsf{dpk}_i, f')$.

Fig. 2. Ideal Functionality of $\mathcal{F}_{\mathsf{PDPKS}}$

Protocol π_Σ

Setup: Upon input (**Setup**, sid, T) within some setup party T, T obtains the system parameters PP by running algorithm Setup($\cdot$) with a security parameter λ, then outputs PP.

MasterKeyGen: Upon input (**Masterkeygen**, sid, PP) within some party P_i, P_i obtains a master public-secret key pair (mpk_i, msk_i) by running the algorithm MasterKeyGen(PP), then outputs mpk_i.

DpkDerive: Upon input (**Dpkderive**, sid, mpk_i) within some party P_j, P_j obtains a derived public key dpk_i by running the algorithm DpkDerive(mpk_i, PP).

DpkCheck: Upon input (**Dpkcheck**, sid, dpk_i) within party P_i, P_i runs the DpkCheck algorithm and obtains a bit $b \in \{0, 1\}$ about the result whether dpk_i is generated from the mpk_i of party P_i or not.

DskDerive: Upon input (**Dskderive**, sid, dpk_i) within party P_i, P_i runs the DskDerive algorithm and obtains a dsk_i corresponding to the dpk_i or $\bot$.

Sign: Upon input (**Sign**, sid, m, dpk_i) within party P_i, P_i obtains a signature σ by running the Sign algorithm.

Verify: Upon input (**Verify**, sid, m, σ, dpk_i) within party some P_j, P_j obtains a bit $b \in \{0, 1\}$ by running the Verify algorithm, with $b = 1$ meaning valid and $b = 0$ invalid.

Fig. 3. A PDPKS Protocol π_Σ

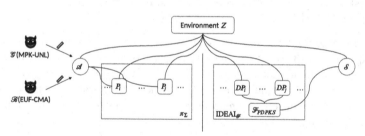

Fig. 4. Prove diagram of Lemma 1.

1. Activate party P_0 and P_1 with (**Keygen**, sid, PP), and obtain master public keys mpk_0 and mpk_1.
2. Hand mpk_0 and mpk_1 to $\mathcal{G}$, and play the roles of Derived Public Key Check Oracle ODpkCheck($\cdot$, $\cdot$), Derived Secret Key Corruption Oracle ODskCorrupt($\cdot$) and Signing Oracle OSign($\cdot$, $\cdot$) for adversary $\mathcal{G}$ in the MPK-UNL game. Two empty sets $L_{\text{dpk},0} = L_{\text{dpk},1} = \emptyset$ are initialized.
3. Choose a random bit $b \leftarrow \{0, 1\}$, and select an arbitrary party P_e, activate P_e with (**Dpkderive**, sid, mpk_b) and obtains dpk^*.
4. Hand dpk^* to $\mathcal{G}$ as the target derived public key.
5. Play the roles of ODpkCheck($\cdot$, $\cdot$), OSign($\cdot$, $\cdot$) and OSign($\cdot$, $\cdot$) for adversary $\mathcal{G}$ in the MPK-UNL game again, and obtain the guess result $b' \in \{0, 1\}$.

6. Output 1 if $b = b'$. Otherwise, output 0 and halt.

In Step 2, the adversary $\mathcal{G}$ issues queries $q_1, ..., q_m$. Moreover, these queries may be asked adaptively, which means that each query q_l may depend on the previous replies to $q_1, ..., q_{l-1}$. A single query q_l is one of the following:

1. Derived Public Key Check Oracle ODpkCheck$(\cdot, \cdot)$: When $\mathcal{Z}$ receives a derived public key check request about a dpk and an mpk$_i$ from $\mathcal{G}$ where $i \in \{0, 1\}$, $\mathcal{Z}$ hands it to the P_i corresponding to the owner of mpk$_i$. When $\mathcal{Z}$ receives the result $c \leftarrow$ DpkCheck(PP, mpk$_i$, msk$_i$, dpk) from party P_i, if $c = 1$, set $L_{\mathsf{dpk},i} = L_{\mathsf{dpk},i} \cup \{\mathsf{dpk}\}$, it hands the result c to $\mathcal{G}$.
2. Derived Secret Key Corruption Oracle ODskCorrupt$(\cdot)$: After receiving a derived public key corruption request about a dpk $\in L_{\mathsf{dpk},0} \cup L_{\mathsf{dpk},1}$, $\mathcal{Z}$ hands it to party P_i, with $i = 0$ if dpk $\in L_{\mathsf{dpk},0}$, and $i = 1$ if dpk $\in L_{\mathsf{dpk},1}$. When $\mathcal{Z}$ receives the result dsk $\leftarrow$ DskDerive(PP, mpk$_i$, msk$_i$, dpk) from party P_i, it hands the result dsk to $\mathcal{G}$.
3. Signing Oracle OSign$(\cdot, \cdot)$: After receiving a sign request about a dpk $\in L_{\mathsf{dpk},0} \cup L_{\mathsf{dpk},1}$ and a message m, $\mathcal{Z}$ hands it to party P_i, with $i = 0$ if dpk $\in L_{\mathsf{dpk},0}$, and $i = 1$ if dpk $\in L_{\mathsf{dpk},1}$.

When $\mathcal{Z}$ receives the result $\sigma \leftarrow$ Sign(PP, dpk, m, dsk) where dsk $\leftarrow$ DskDerive(PP, mpk$_i$, msk$_i$, dpk) from party P_i, it hands the result σ to $\mathcal{G}$.

In Step 5, the adversary $\mathcal{G}$ issues more queries $q_{m+1}, ..., q_n$ where query q_l may be asked adaptively as in Step 2, without ODpkCheck(dpk*, mpk$_i$), where $i \in \{0, 1\}$, and ODskCorrupt(dpk*) being queried.

Analysis: After $\mathcal{Z}$ interacts with $\mathcal{A}$ and π_Σ, $\mathcal{Z}$ obtains dpk* = DpkDerive (PP, mpk$_b$) in Step 3. $\mathcal{G}$ can break MPK-UNL security by interacting with $\mathcal{Z}$ with non-negligible advantage $\mathbf{Adv}_{\Sigma,\mathcal{G}}^{MPK-UNL}$. We let $\Pr[\mathcal{Z} \rightarrow 1 \mid \mathcal{Z} \leftrightarrow \text{REAL}]$ denote the probability that $\mathcal{Z}$ outputs 1 when $\mathcal{Z}$ interacts with $\mathcal{A}$ and π_Σ. Let $Evnt_i$ occur when dpk* is generated from the master public key mpk$_i$, and let $Game_i$ represent the event that $\mathsf{Game}_{\Sigma,\mathcal{G}}^{mpk-unl-i}(k) = 1$, where $i \in \{0, 1\}$ respectively. Then we have

$$\Pr[\mathcal{Z} \rightarrow 1 \mid \mathcal{Z} \leftrightarrow \text{REAL}]$$
$$= \Pr[\mathsf{mpk}_b = \mathsf{mpk}_0] \Pr[b' = 0 \mid Evnt_0] + \Pr[\mathsf{mpk}_b = \mathsf{mpk}_1] \Pr[b' = 1 \mid Evnt_1]$$
$$= \frac{1}{2}(1 - \Pr[b' = 1 \mid Evnt_0]) + \frac{1}{2}\Pr[b' = 1 \mid Evnt_1]$$
$$= \frac{1}{2} + \frac{1}{2}(\Pr[Game_1] - \Pr[Game_0]) > \frac{1}{2} + \frac{1}{2}\nu(k).$$

We notice that, when $\mathcal{Z}$ interacts with the ideal functionality $\mathcal{F}_{\mathsf{PDPKS}}$ and an arbitrary adversary, the view of $\mathcal{G}$ within $\mathcal{Z}$ is statistically independent of b. The reason is that the target derived public key dpk* received from $\mathcal{Z}$ is randomly generated by $\mathcal{S}$. Furthermore, all queries applied by $\mathcal{G}$ are independent of b. Thus, $b = b'$ with probability exactly one half.

We denote $\Pr[\mathcal{Z} \to 1 \mid \mathcal{Z} \leftrightarrow \mathsf{IDEAL}]$ as the probability that $\mathcal{Z}$ outputs 1 when $\mathcal{Z}$ interacts with $\mathcal{S}$ in the ideal process for functionality $\mathcal{F}_{\mathsf{PDPKS}}$. Further we have

$$
\begin{aligned}
&\Pr[\mathcal{Z} \to 1 \mid \mathcal{Z} \leftrightarrow \mathsf{IDEAL}] \\
&= \Pr[\mathsf{mpk}_b = \mathsf{mpk}_0] \Pr[b' = 0 \mid \mathsf{dpk}^* \leftarrow \mathcal{S}] + \\
&\quad \Pr[\mathsf{mpk}_b = \mathsf{mpk}_1] \Pr[b' = 1 \mid \mathsf{dpk}^* \leftarrow \mathcal{S}] \\
&= \frac{1}{2}(1 - \Pr[b' = 1 \mid \mathsf{dpk}^* \leftarrow \mathcal{S}] + \Pr[b' = 1 \mid \mathsf{dpk}^* \leftarrow \mathcal{S}]) = \frac{1}{2}.
\end{aligned}
$$

Thus, $\Pr[\mathcal{Z} \to 1 \mid \mathcal{Z} \leftrightarrow \mathsf{REAL}] - \Pr[\mathcal{Z} \to 1 \mid \mathcal{Z} \leftrightarrow \mathsf{IDEAL}] > \frac{1}{2}\nu(k)$. Therefore, $\mathcal{Z}$ can distinguish between executions with $(\pi_\Sigma, \mathcal{A})$ and $(\mathcal{F}_{\mathsf{PDPKS}}, \mathcal{S})$ with non-negligible probability. Hence we prove that UC security of PDPKS implies MPK-UNL of PDPKS.

Second, if Σ is not EUF-CMA, there exists a PPT adversary $\mathcal{B}$ that can forge the signature successfully and break Σ in the sense of EUF-CMA with non-negligible probability, i.e. $\mathbf{Adv}_{\Sigma,\mathcal{B}}^{EUF-CMA} > \nu(k)$. We will prove that there exists a PPT adversary $\mathcal{A}$ that for all simulator $\mathcal{S}$, such that there exists an environment $\mathcal{Z}$ which could tell whether it is communicated with $(\mathcal{S}, \mathcal{F}_{\mathsf{PDPKS}})$ or $(\mathcal{A}, \pi_\Sigma)$ under the help of $\mathcal{B}$. The interaction process between environment $\mathcal{Z}$ and $\mathcal{B}$ is as follows.

1. The environment $\mathcal{Z}$ first activates party P_i with input (**Keygen**, sid) to obtain an output (**Keygened**, sid, P_i, mpk_i). Then $\mathcal{Z}$ sends mpk_i to $\mathcal{B}$;
2. After $\mathcal{B}$ asks for a derived public key dpk_i, $\mathcal{Z}$ activates party P_i with input (**Dpkderive**, sid, mpk_i) and returns the obtained result to $\mathcal{B}$;
3. After $\mathcal{B}$ checks the validity of a derived public key dpk_i, $\mathcal{Z}$ activates party P_i with input (**Dpkcheck**, sid, dpk_i) and returns the obtained result to $\mathcal{B}$;
4. After $\mathcal{B}$ asks for the derived private key corresponding to a derived public key dpk_i, $\mathcal{Z}$ activates party P_i with input (**Dskderive**, sid, dpk_i) and returns the obtained result to $\mathcal{B}$;
5. After $\mathcal{B}$ asks the signature for a message m and a derived public key dpk_i of its choice, $\mathcal{Z}$ activates party P_i with input (**Sign**, sid, m, dpk_i) and returns the obtained result to $\mathcal{B}$.
6. After $\mathcal{B}$ outputs a signature σ for a message m and a valid derived public key dpk_i: if $\mathcal{B}$ has inquired about the derived private key corresponding to dpk_i or the signature of m and dpk_i, the environment $\mathcal{Z}$ outputs 0 and halts; otherwise, $\mathcal{Z}$ activates party P_j with the input (**Verify**, sid, m, σ, dpk_i) and outputs the verification value $f \in \{0, 1\}$.

Here, if $\mathcal{Z}$ is interacting with π_Σ and $\mathcal{A}$ in the real world, $\mathcal{Z}$ will output 1 when the signature σ is valid; if $\mathcal{Z}$ is interacting with the ideal functionality and $\mathcal{S}$ in the ideal world, $\mathcal{Z}$ will outputs 0, because dpk_i belongs to the set $L_{\mathsf{dpk},i}$, but $(m, \sigma, \mathsf{dpk}_i, 1)$ is not recorded in the ideal functionality $\mathcal{F}_{\mathsf{PDPKS}}$.

Since the probability of that $\mathcal{B}$ wins the game $\mathbf{Game}_{\mathsf{PDPKS}}^{euf-cma}$ cannot be ignored, the probability of that $\mathcal{Z}$ outputs 1 when interacting in the real world cannot be ignored. This means that $\mathcal{Z}$ is able to distinguish whether it is executed in real or ideal world with a non-negligible probability. And this contradicts the UC security of $\mathcal{Z}$, that $\mathcal{Z}$ can not distinguish the two models. That is, if π_Σ can UC-realize the ideal functionality $\mathcal{F}_{\mathsf{PDPKS}}$, then Σ satisfies the existentially unforgeable under an adaptive chosen-message attack. Hence we prove that UC security of PDPKS implies EUF-CMA of PDPKS. $\qquad\square$

Lemma 2. *If a PDPKS scheme Σ is master public key unlinkable (MPK-UNL) and existentially unforgeable under an adaptive chosen-message attack (EUF-CMA), the corresponding protocol π_Σ securely realizes the ideal functionality $\mathcal{F}_{\mathsf{PDPKS}}$.*

Proof. The proof can be divided into three parts, each corresponding to a different scenario based on the corruption of either P_i or P_j.

Case 1: P_i (the payee) is corrupted and P_j (the payer) is uncorrupted. We could construct a simulator $\mathcal{S}$ such that no $\mathcal{Z}$ can distinguish whether $\mathcal{Z}$ is executed with $(\mathcal{S}, \mathcal{F}_{\mathsf{PDPKS}})$ or $(\mathcal{A}, \pi_\Sigma)$, and the construction is as follows.

1. When $\mathcal{Z}$ sends (**Keygen**, sid) to the corrupted party P_i (i.e.,$\mathcal{S}$), $\mathcal{S}$ receives the message and sends it to $\mathcal{F}_{\mathsf{PDPKS}}$ on behalf of P_i and the simulated copy of $\mathcal{A}$, which returns a reply message to $\mathcal{S}$. When $\mathcal{S}$ receives (**Keygen**, sid, P_i) from $\mathcal{F}_{\mathsf{PDPKS}}$, $\mathcal{S}$ sends the reply of $\mathcal{A}$ to $\mathcal{F}_{\mathsf{PDPKS}}$.
2. When $\mathcal{Z}$ sends (**Dpkderive**, sid, mpk'_i, P_i) to party P_j, P_j forwards it to $\mathcal{F}_{\mathsf{PDPKS}}$. $\mathcal{F}_{\mathsf{PDPKS}}$ further sends it to $\mathcal{S}$, and then $\mathcal{S}$ randomly selects a derived public key dpk_i and returns (**Dpkderived**, sid, dpk_i, P_i) to $\mathcal{F}_{\mathsf{PDPKS}}$. Then, $\mathcal{F}_{\mathsf{PDPKS}}$ returns it to party P_j.
3. When $\mathcal{Z}$ sends (**Dpkcheck**, sid, dpk_i) to the corrupted party P_i (i.e.,$\mathcal{S}$), $\mathcal{S}$ receives the message and sends it to $\mathcal{F}_{\mathsf{PDPKS}}$ on behalf of P_i and the simulated copy of $\mathcal{A}$, which returns a reply message to $\mathcal{S}$. When $\mathcal{S}$ receives (**Dpkcheck**, sid, dpk_i, P_i) from $\mathcal{F}_{\mathsf{PDPKS}}$, $\mathcal{S}$ sends the reply of $\mathcal{A}$ to $\mathcal{F}_{\mathsf{PDPKS}}$.
4. When $\mathcal{Z}$ sends (**Dskderive**, sid, dpk_i) to the corrupted party P_i (i.e.,$\mathcal{S}$), $\mathcal{S}$ receives the message and sends it to $\mathcal{F}_{\mathsf{PDPKS}}$ on behalf of P_i and the simulated copy of $\mathcal{A}$, which returns a reply message to $\mathcal{S}$. When $\mathcal{S}$ receives (**Dskderive**, sid, dpk_i, P_i) from $\mathcal{F}_{\mathsf{PDPKS}}$, $\mathcal{S}$ sends the reply of $\mathcal{A}$ to $\mathcal{F}_{\mathsf{PDPKS}}$.
5. When $\mathcal{Z}$ sends (**Sign**, sid, m, dpk_i) to the corrupted party P_i (i.e.,$\mathcal{S}$), $\mathcal{S}$ receives the message and sends it to $\mathcal{F}_{\mathsf{PDPKS}}$ on behalf of P_i and the simulated copy of $\mathcal{A}$, which returns a reply message to $\mathcal{S}$. When $\mathcal{S}$ receives (**Sign**, sid, m, dpk_i, P_i) from $\mathcal{F}_{\mathsf{PDPKS}}$, $\mathcal{S}$ sends the reply of $\mathcal{A}$ to $\mathcal{F}_{\mathsf{PDPKS}}$.
6. When $\mathcal{Z}$ sends (**Verify**, sid, $m, \sigma, \mathsf{dpk}_i$) to party P_j, P_j forwards it to $\mathcal{F}_{\mathsf{PDPKS}}$.

$\mathcal{F}_{\mathsf{PDPKS}}$ then sends it to $\mathcal{S}$, and $\mathcal{S}$ returns (**Verified**, sid, m, dpk_i, f) to $\mathcal{F}_{\mathsf{PDPKS}}$. Then $\mathcal{F}_{\mathsf{PDPKS}}$ determines the value of f according to its own judgment and returns (**Verified**, sid, m, dpk_i, f) to P_j.

We claim that $\mathcal{Z}$ cannot distinguish whether $\mathcal{Z}$ is executed with $(\mathcal{S}, \mathcal{F}_{\mathsf{PDPKS}})$ or $(\mathcal{A}, \pi_\Sigma)$, because the message returned by $\mathcal{S}$ (using $\mathcal{A}$) as P_i in the ideal world is the same as that returned by $\mathcal{A}$ as P_i in the real world, hence (**Dpkderived**, sid, dpk_i, P_i) and (**Verified**, sid, m, dpk_i, f) returned by $\mathcal{F}_{\mathsf{PDPKS}}$ is exactly the same as that returned by P_j in the real world.

Case 2: P_j (the payer) is corrupted and P_i (the payee) is uncorrupted. We could construct a simulator $\mathcal{S}$ such that no $\mathcal{Z}$ can distinguish whether $\mathcal{Z}$ is executed with $(\mathcal{S}, \mathcal{F}_{\mathsf{PDPKS}})$ or $(\mathcal{A}, \pi_\Sigma)$, and the construction is as follows.

1. When $\mathcal{Z}$ sends (**Keygen**, sid) to party P_i, P_i forwards (**Keygen**, sid, P_i) to $\mathcal{F}_{\mathsf{PDPKS}}$. $\mathcal{F}_{\mathsf{PDPKS}}$ then sends it to $\mathcal{S}$, and $\mathcal{S}$ computes ($\mathsf{mpk}_i, \mathsf{msk}_i$) by running algorithm $\mathsf{KeyGen}(\cdot)$ and returns (**Keygened**, sid, P_i, mpk_i) to $\mathcal{F}_{\mathsf{PDPKS}}$.

2. When $\mathcal{Z}$ sends (**Dpkderive**, sid, mpk'_i, P_i) to the corrupted party P_j (i.e., $\mathcal{S}$), $\mathcal{S}$ receives the message and sends it to $\mathcal{F}_{\mathsf{PDPKS}}$ on behalf of P_j and the simulated copy of $\mathcal{A}$, which returns a reply message to $\mathcal{S}$. When $\mathcal{S}$ receives (**Dpkderive**, sid, mpk'_i, P_i) from $\mathcal{F}_{\mathsf{PDPKS}}$, $\mathcal{S}$ sends the reply of $\mathcal{A}$ to $\mathcal{F}_{\mathsf{PDPKS}}$.

3. When $\mathcal{Z}$ sends (**Dpkcheck**, sid, dpk_i) to party P_i, P_i forwards (**Dpkcheck**, sid, dpk_i) to $\mathcal{F}_{\mathsf{PDPKS}}$. $\mathcal{F}_{\mathsf{PDPKS}}$ then sends (**Dpkcheck**, sid, dpk_i, P_i) to $\mathcal{S}$, and $\mathcal{S}$ returns (**Dpkchecked**, sid, dpk_i, P_i, f) to $\mathcal{F}_{\mathsf{PDPKS}}$.

4. When $\mathcal{Z}$ sends (**Dskderive**, sid, dpk_i) to party P_i, P_i forwards (**Dskderive**, sid, dpk_i) to $\mathcal{F}_{\mathsf{PDPKS}}$. $\mathcal{F}_{\mathsf{PDPKS}}$ then sends (**Dskderive**, sid, dpk_i, P_i) to $\mathcal{S}$, and $\mathcal{S}$ returns (**Dskderived**, sid, dpk_i, P_i, f) to $\mathcal{F}_{\mathsf{PDPKS}}$.

5. When $\mathcal{Z}$ sends (**Sign**, sid, m, dpk_i) to party P_i, P_i forwards (**Sign**, sid, m, dpk_i) to $\mathcal{F}_{\mathsf{PDPKS}}$. $\mathcal{F}_{\mathsf{PDPKS}}$ then sends (**Sign**, sid, m, dpk_i) to $\mathcal{S}$, $\mathcal{S}$ returns (**Signature**, sid, m, σ, dpk_i) to $\mathcal{F}_{\mathsf{PDPKS}}$.

6. When $\mathcal{Z}$ sends (**Verify**, sid, m, σ, dpk_i) to corrupted party P_j (i.e., $\mathcal{S}$), $\mathcal{S}$ receives the message and sends it to $\mathcal{F}_{\mathsf{PDPKS}}$ on behalf of P_j and the simulated copy of $\mathcal{A}$, which returns a reply message to $\mathcal{S}$. When $\mathcal{S}$ receives (**Verify**, sid, m, σ, dpk_i) from $\mathcal{F}_{\mathsf{PDPKS}}$, $\mathcal{S}$ sends the reply of $\mathcal{A}$ to $\mathcal{F}_{\mathsf{PDPKS}}$.

We claim that $\mathcal{Z}$ cannot distinguish whether $\mathcal{Z}$ is executed with $(\mathcal{S}, \mathcal{F}_{\mathsf{PDPKS}})$ or $(\mathcal{A}, \pi_\Sigma)$, because the message returned by $\mathcal{S}$ (using $\mathcal{A}$) as P_j in the ideal world is the same as that returned by $\mathcal{A}$ as P_j in the real world, hence (**Keygened**, sid, mpk_i), (**Dpkchecked**, sid, dpk_i, P_i, f), (**Dskderived**, sid, dpk_i) (or $\bot$) and (**Signature**, sid, m, σ, dpk_i) returned by $\mathcal{F}_{\mathsf{PDPKS}}$ is exactly the same as that returned by P_i in the real world.

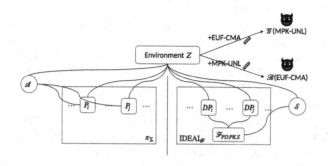

Fig. 5. Prove diagram of Lemma 2 Case 3.

Case 3: Both P_i (the payee) and P_j (the payer) are uncorrupted. We will prove the third case by contradiction. In other words, if π_Σ does not UC-realize $\mathcal{F}_{\mathsf{PDPKS}}$, then Σ is either not MPK-UNL or not EUF-CMA.

First, let us discuss the case that Σ is not MPK-UNL if π_Σ is EUF-CMA but does not UC-realize $\mathcal{F}_{\mathsf{PDPKS}}$. In more detail, we assume that there is real world adversary $\mathcal{A}$ such that for an arbitrary simulator $\mathcal{S}$, there exists an environment $\mathcal{Z}$ that can distinguish whether $\mathcal{Z}$ is executed with $(\mathcal{S}, \mathcal{F}_{\mathsf{PDPKS}})$ or $(\mathcal{A}, \pi_\Sigma)$. We then show that there exists a MPK-UNL attacker $\mathcal{G}$ against Σ by using $\mathcal{Z}$.

We could construct an adversary $\mathcal{G}$ that breaks MPK-UNL by using environment $\mathcal{Z}$. More precisely, we assume that there is a real-world adversary $\mathcal{A}$ such that for any ideal-world adversary $\mathcal{S}$, there exists an environment $\mathcal{Z}$ such that for a fixed security parameter k and a fixed input z for $\mathcal{Z}$, $|\ \mathsf{IDEAL}_{\mathcal{F}_{\mathsf{PDPKS}},\mathcal{S},\mathcal{Z}}(k, z) - \mathsf{REAL}_{\pi_\Sigma,\mathcal{A},\mathcal{Z}}(k, z)\ | > \nu(k)$.

We then show that there exists $\mathcal{G}_h$ whose advantage $\mathbf{Adv}_{\Sigma,\mathcal{G}_h}^{MPK-UNL}(k) > \nu(k)/l$ in the MPK-UNL game, where l is the total number of message that were used by uncorrupted party P_i. $\mathcal{G}_h$ is given the master public keys $\{\mathsf{mpk}_i\}_{i=1}^n$ of all parties, and is allowed to query three oracles as in above and also the derived public key derive oracle $\mathsf{ODpkderive}(\cdot, \cdot)$. $\mathcal{G}_h$ runs $\mathcal{Z}$ on the following simulated interaction with a system running π_Σ or $\mathcal{F}_{\mathsf{PDPKS}}$.

1. For the first $h - 1$ times that $\mathcal{Z}$ asks P_j to obtain a derived public key dpk_n about a mpk_i where $n \in \{1, ..., h - 1\}$, $\mathcal{G}_h$ lets P_j return $\mathsf{dpk}_n \leftarrow \mathsf{Dpkderive}(\mathsf{PP}, \mathsf{mpk}_i)$ to $\mathcal{Z}$.

2. For the h-th time that $\mathcal{Z}$ asks P_j to obtain a derived public key dpk_h about a mpk_i, $\mathcal{G}_h$ queries oracle $\mathsf{ODpkderive}(\cdot, \cdot)$ with the message pair $(\mathsf{mpk}_i, \mathsf{mpk}_r)$, where mpk_r is a fixed value generated from $\mathcal{G}_h$ running the master key generation algorithm randomly, and obtains target derived public key dpk_h. It then hands dpk_h to $\mathcal{Z}$ as the derived public key of mpk_i. In other words, $\mathsf{dpk}_h \leftarrow \mathsf{Dpkderive}(\mathsf{PP}, \mathsf{mpk}_i)$ if $b = 0$, and $\mathsf{dpk}_h \leftarrow \mathsf{Dpkderive}(\mathsf{PP}, \mathsf{mpk}_r)$ if $b = 1$.

3. For the remaining $l - h$ times that $\mathcal{Z}$ asks P_j to obtain a derive public key dpk_n about a mpk_i where $n \in \{h + 1, ..., l\}$, $\mathcal{G}_h$ lets P_j return $\mathsf{dpk}_n \leftarrow \mathsf{Dpkderive}(\mathsf{PP}, \mathsf{mpk}_r)$ to $\mathcal{Z}$.

4. Whenever party P_i is activated with input $(\mathbf{Dpkcheck}, \mathsf{sid}, \mathsf{dpk})$ where $\mathsf{dpk} \in L_{\mathsf{dpk},i}$, $\mathcal{G}_h$ lets P_i return the corresponding result f, with $f = 1$ meaning that dpk is linked to the master public key of P_i. Otherwise, $\mathcal{G}_h$ queries the oracle $\mathsf{ODpkCheck}(\cdot)$ on dpk, obtains value f, and lets P_i return it to $\mathcal{Z}$. This is a perfect simulation, so $\mathcal{Z}$ cannot distinguish between $(\mathcal{S}, \mathcal{F}_{\mathsf{pdpks}})$ and $(\mathcal{A}, \pi_\Sigma)$ in this step.

5. Whenever party P_i is activated with input $(\mathbf{Dskderive}, \mathsf{sid}, \mathsf{dpk})$ where $\mathsf{dpk} \in L_{\mathsf{dpk},i}$, $\mathcal{G}_h$ lets P_i output the execution result message $(\mathbf{Dskderived}, \mathsf{sid}, \mathsf{dpk})$ to $\mathcal{Z}$ from input of $\mathcal{G}_h$. Otherwise, $\mathcal{G}_h$ queries the oracle $\mathsf{ODskCorrupt}(\cdot)$ on dpk, obtains the corresponding dsk or $\bot$, and lets P_i return the message $(\mathbf{Dskderived}, \mathsf{sid}, \mathsf{dpk})$ or $\bot$ to $\mathcal{Z}$. This is a perfect simulation, so $\mathcal{Z}$ cannot distinguish between $(\mathcal{S}, \mathcal{F}_{\mathsf{pdpks}})$ and $(\mathcal{A}, \pi_\Sigma)$ in this step.

6. Whenever party P_i is activated with input (**Sign**, sid, m, dpk) where dpk $\in$ $L_{\mathsf{dpk},i}$, $\mathcal{G}_h$ lets P_i output the execution result (**Signature**, sid, m, σ, dpk) to $\mathcal{Z}$. Otherwise, $\mathcal{G}_h$ queries the oracle $\mathsf{OSign}(\cdot, \cdot)$ on dpk and m, obtains the corresponding signature σ, and lets P_i return the message (**Signature**, sid, m, σ, dpk) to $\mathcal{Z}$. This is a perfect simulation, so $\mathcal{Z}$ cannot distinguish between $(\mathcal{S}, \mathcal{F}_{\mathsf{pdpks}})$ or $(\mathcal{A}, \pi_\Sigma)$ in this step.

7. Whenever party P_j is activated with input (**Verify**, sid, m, σ, dpk_i), $\mathcal{G}_h$ lets P_j output the execution result (**Verified**, sid, m, dpk_i, f) to $\mathcal{Z}$. This is a perfect simulation, so $\mathcal{Z}$ cannot distinguish between $(\mathcal{S}, \mathcal{F}_{\mathsf{pdpks}})$ or $(\mathcal{A}, \pi_\Sigma)$ in this step.

8. When $\mathcal{Z}$ halts, $\mathcal{G}_h$ outputs whatever $\mathcal{Z}$ outputs and halts.

We apply a standard hybrid argument for analyzing the success probability of $\mathcal{G}_h$. For $j \in \{0, ..., l\}$, let **Env**$_j$ be an event that $\mathcal{Z}$ interacts with $\mathcal{S}$ in the ideal process, with the exception that the first j derived public keys are computed as a derived public key of the real master public key mpk_i, rather than mpk_r. The replies to $\mathcal{Z}$ from party P_i are the same as those shown in Step 4, 5, 6, and 7 above. Let H_j be $\Pr[\mathcal{Z} \rightarrow 1 \mid \mathbf{Env}_j]$. Notice that in Steps 4, 5, 6, and 7, $\mathcal{Z}$ cannot distinguish whether it is interacting with $\mathcal{A}$ and π_Σ or with $\mathcal{S}$ in the ideal world for $\mathcal{F}_{\mathsf{PDPKS}}$, because $\mathcal{G}_h$ offers a perfect simulation.

It is easy to see that H_0 is identical to the probability that $\mathcal{Z}$ outputs 1 in the ideal process, and that H_l is identical to the probability that $\mathcal{Z}$ outputs 1 in the real life model. Furthermore, in a run of $\mathcal{G}_h$, if dpk_h that $\mathcal{G}_h$ obtains from its derived public key oracle generates from the real master public key mpk_i, the probability that $\mathcal{Z}$ outputs 1 is identical to H_h. If dpk_h is a derived public key that generated by the randomly selected master public key mpk_r, the probability that $\mathcal{Z}$ outputs 1 is identical to H_{h-1}. We have $\sum_{i=1}^{l} |H_{i-1} - H_i| \geq \left| \sum_{i=1}^{l} (H_{i-1} - H_i) \right| = |H_0 - H_l| = |\mathbf{IDEAL}_{\mathcal{F}_{\mathsf{PDPKS}}, \mathcal{S}, \mathcal{Z}}(k, z) - \mathbf{REAL}_{\pi_\Sigma, \mathcal{A}, \mathcal{Z}}(k, z)| > \nu(k)$.

Therefore, there exists some $h \in \{0, ..., l\}$ such that $| H_{h-1} - H_h | > \nu(k)/l$. Here, w.l.o.g, let $|H_{h-1} - H_h| > \nu(k)/l$. We have the advantage of adversary $\mathcal{G}_h$ as follows:

$$\mathbf{Adv}_{\Sigma, \mathcal{G}_h}^{mpk-unl}(k) = \Pr[\mathbf{Exp}_{\Sigma, \mathcal{A}}^{mpk-unl-1}(k) = 1] - \Pr[\mathbf{Exp}_{\Sigma, \mathcal{A}}^{mpk-unl-0}(k) = 1]$$
$$= \Pr[\mathcal{G}_h \rightarrow 1 \mid \mathsf{dpk}_h \leftarrow \mathsf{DpkDerive}(\mathsf{PP}, \mathsf{mpk}_i)]$$
$$- \Pr[\mathcal{G}_h \rightarrow 1 \mid \mathsf{dpk}_h \leftarrow \mathsf{DpkDerive}(\mathsf{PP}, \mathsf{mpk}_r)]$$
$$= H_h - H_{h-1} > \nu(k)/l$$

In other words, $\mathcal{G}$ has non-negligible advantage in k since l is polynomially bounded in k.

Second, we will show that if π_Σ is MPK-UNL but does not UC-realize $\mathcal{F}_{\mathsf{PDPKS}}$, Σ is not EUF-CMA-secure. In more detail, we assume that there is real world adversary $\mathcal{A}$ such that for any ideal world adversary $\mathcal{S}$ there exists an environment $\mathcal{Z}$ that can distinguish whether it is executed with $(\mathcal{S}, \mathcal{F}_{\mathsf{PDPKS}})$

or $(\mathcal{A}, \pi_\Sigma)$. We then show that there exists an EUF-CMA attacker against Σ by using $\mathcal{Z}$.

We can use the real attacker $\mathcal{A}$ and the environment $\mathcal{Z}$ to construct a PPT attacker $\mathcal{B}$ who can forge a signature. The attack approach of $\mathcal{B}$ is to simulate the ideal attacker $\mathcal{S}$ and the ideal functionality $\mathcal{F}_{\mathsf{PDPKS}}$, and forge the signature by distinguishing between *ideal* and *real* through the environment $\mathcal{Z}$.

$\mathcal{B}$ simulates the ideal attacker $\mathcal{S}$ and the ideal functionality $\mathcal{F}_{\mathsf{PDPKS}}$ in the following way: $\mathcal{B}$ obtains the party P_i's master public key mpk_i from $\mathcal{Z}$.

1. Upon receiving the input of environment $\mathcal{Z}$, $\mathcal{B}$ takes the input to $\mathcal{A}$ and copies the output of $\mathcal{A}$ as its own output.
2. For the message $(\mathbf{Dpkderive}, \mathsf{sid}, \mathsf{mpk}_i')$ received by $\mathcal{F}_{\mathsf{PDPKS}}$, $\mathcal{B}$ first judges whether mpk_i' is equal to mpk_i. If negative, ignore this message; otherwise runs the algorithm $\mathsf{DpkDerive}(\mathsf{mpk}_i)$ to return one of the derived public keys dpk_i corresponding to the mpk_i.
3. For the message $(\mathbf{Dpkcheck}, \mathsf{sid}, \mathsf{dpk}_i)$ received by $\mathcal{F}_{\mathsf{PDPKS}}$, $\mathcal{B}$ asks the Derived Public Key Check Oracle $\mathsf{ODpkCheck}(\cdot)$ to test whether dpk_i is generated by mpk_i and returns the result $(\mathbf{Dpkchecked}, \mathsf{sid}, \mathsf{dpk}_i, f)$ to $\mathcal{Z}$.
4. For the message $(\mathbf{Dskderive}, \mathsf{sid}, \mathsf{dpk}_i)$ received by $\mathcal{F}_{\mathsf{PDPKS}}$, $\mathcal{B}$ asks the Derived Secret Key Corruption Oracle $\mathsf{ODskCorrupt}(\cdot)$ to obtain the derived private key for the existing valid derived public key dpk_i, and returns the boolean value of whether to obtain the derived private key.
5. For the message $(\mathbf{Sign}, \mathsf{sid}, m, \mathsf{dpk}_i)$ received by $\mathcal{F}_{\mathsf{PDPKS}}$, $\mathcal{B}$ asks the Signing Oracle $\mathsf{OSign}(\cdot, \cdot)$ to obtain the signature σ of message m and derived public key dpk_i, and returns $(\mathbf{Signature}, \mathsf{sid}, m, \sigma, \mathsf{dpk}_i)$ to $\mathcal{Z}$.
6. For the message $(\mathbf{Verify}, \mathsf{sid}, m, \sigma, \mathsf{dpk}_i)$ received by $\mathcal{F}_{\mathsf{PDPKS}}$, $\mathcal{B}$ runs the verify algorithm to obtain the verification value f and returns $(\mathbf{Verified}, \mathsf{sid}, m, \mathsf{dpk}_i, f)$ to $\mathcal{Z}$.

Obviously, during the above interactions, through there exists query oracles and the call of algorithms, the $\mathcal{S}$ and $\mathcal{F}_{\mathsf{PDPKS}}$ simulated by $\mathcal{B}$ are indistinguishable from the real $\mathcal{S}$ and $\mathcal{F}_{\mathsf{PDPKS}}$.

When the environment $\mathcal{Z}$ uses the input $(\mathbf{Verify}, \mathsf{sid}, m^*, \sigma^*, \mathsf{dpk}_i^*)$ to activates a party P_j, $\mathcal{B}$ verifies whether the signature is valid. If the signature is valid and satisfies the requirement that $\mathcal{B}$ does not ask the orcale $\mathsf{ODskCorrupt}(\mathsf{dpk}^*)$ and the orcale $\mathsf{OSign}(m^*, \mathsf{dpk}^*)$, $\mathcal{B}$ outputs the pair $(m^*, \sigma^*, \mathsf{dpk}_i^*)$ and halts. In other words, $\mathcal{B}$ obtains a forged signature. Otherwise, $\mathcal{B}$ continues the simulation.

If $\mathcal{B}$ can get a forged signature, for the input $(\mathbf{Verify}, \mathsf{sid}, m^*, \sigma^*, \mathsf{dpk}_i^*)$, if $\mathcal{Z}$ interacts with the real protocol π_Σ, the output observed by $\mathcal{Z}$ is 1 because of the signature is valid. Otherwise, if $\mathcal{Z}$ interacts with the ideal protocol, the output observed by $\mathcal{Z}$ is 0, because there is no record $(m^*, \sigma^*, \mathsf{dpk}_i^*, 1)$ stored. In other words, $\mathcal{Z}$ can distinguish its interaction with real protocols π_Σ and ideal functionality $\mathcal{F}_{\mathsf{PDPKS}}$. Therefore, if the probability of successful forgery of $\mathcal{B}$ is negligible, the probability that environment $\mathcal{Z}$ can distinguish its interaction with real and ideal protocol is also negligible, which is contradict to the assumption. Therefore, $\mathcal{B}$ can forge successfully if Σ does not satisfy the existentially unforgeable under an adaptive chosen-message attack.

In summary, if Σ satisfies the master public key unlinkable (MPK-UNL) and existentially unforgeable under an adaptive chosen-message attack (EUF-CMA) at the same time, π_Σ can UC-realize the ideal functionality $\mathcal{F}_{\mathsf{PDPKS}}$.   □

Finally, we have the following theorem.

Theorem 1. *Let Σ be a PDPKS scheme. The corresponding protocol π_Σ securely realizes the ideal functionality $\mathcal{F}_{\mathsf{PDPKS}}$ if and only if the scheme Σ is both master public key unlinkable (MPK-UNL) and existentially unforgeable under an adaptive chosen-message attack (EUF-CMA).*

Proof. The proof can be derived from the former two lemmas.   □

5   Conclusion

The Key-Insulated and Privacy-Preserving Signature Scheme with Publicly Derived Public Key (PDPKS) is a recently proposed signature scheme which captures the correctness, security and privacy requirements of applications like Stealth Address and Deterministic Wallet in blockchain systems. However, the scalability of PDPKS has received limited discussion. This concern becomes particularly significant in the context of complex blockchain systems where numerous cryptographic primitives are executed simultaneously. In this paper, we aim to address this gap by revisiting the definition and formalizing the ideal functionality of PDPKS in the Universal Composability (UC) model, capturing all of the correctness, security and privacy requirements. Furthermore, we prove that the newly proposed UC security of PDPKS is equivalent to the concurrent satisfaction of MPK-UNL and EUF-CMA, which are the two game-based security properties of PDPKS. This conclusion implies the previously presented secure PDPKS constructions are remaining secure in the UC framework, and may arbitrarily combined with other UC secure primitives in a blockchain system.

Acknowledgement. This work was supported by the National Natural Science Foundation of China (No. 62072305, 62132013).

References

1. Abe, M., Ohkubo, M.: A framework for universally composable non-committing blind signatures. In: International Conference on the Theory and Application of Cryptology and Information Security, pp. 435–450. Springer (2009)
2. Backes, M., Hofheinz, D.: How to break and repair a universally composable signature functionality. In: Zhang, K., Zheng, Y. (eds.) ISC 2004. LNCS, vol. 3225, pp. 61–72. Springer, Heidelberg (2004). https://doi.org/10.1007/978-3-540-30144-8_6
3. Canetti, R.: Universally composable security: a new paradigm for cryptographic protocols. In: Proceedings 42nd IEEE Symposium on Foundations of Computer Science, pp. 136–145. IEEE (2001)

4. Canetti, R.: Universally composable signature, certification, and authentication. In: Proceedings 17th IEEE Computer Security Foundations Workshop, 2004, pp. 219–233. IEEE (2004)
5. Heilman, E., Alshenibr, L., Baldimtsi, F., Scafuro, A., Goldberg, S.: Tumblebit: An untrusted bitcoin-compatible anonymous payment hub. In: Network and Distributed System Security Symposium (2017)
6. Hong, X., Gao, J., Pan, J., Zhang, B.: Universally composable secure proxy re-signature scheme with effective calculation. Clust. Comput. **22**(4), 10075–10084 (2019)
7. Liu, W., Liu, Z., Nguyen, K., Yang, G., Yu, Yu.: A lattice-based key-insulated and privacy-preserving signature scheme with publicly derived public key. In: Chen, L., Li, N., Liang, K., Schneider, S. (eds.) ESORICS 2020. LNCS, vol. 12309, pp. 357–377. Springer, Cham (2020). https://doi.org/10.1007/978-3-030-59013-0_18
8. Liu, Z., Yang, G., Wong, D.S., Nguyen, K., Wang, H.: Key-insulated and privacy-preserving signature scheme with publicly derived public key. In: 2019 IEEE European Symposium on Security and Privacy (EuroS&P), pp. 215–230. IEEE (2019)
9. Maxwell, G., Bentov, I.: Deterministic wallets (2011)
10. Meiklejohn, S., et al.: A fistful of bitcoins: characterizing payments among men with no names. In: Proceedings of the 2013 Conference on Internet Measurement Conference, pp. 127–140 (2013)
11. Miers, I., Garman, C., Green, M., Rubin, A.D.: Zerocoin: anonymous distributed e-cash from bitcoin. In: 2013 IEEE Symposium on Security and Privacy, pp. 397–411. IEEE (2013)
12. Nakamoto, S.: Bitcoin: A peer-to-peer electronic cash system, p. 21260 (2008)
13. Noether, S., Mackenzie, A., et al.: Ring confidential transactions. Ledger **1**, 1–18 (2016)
14. Okamoto, T., Ohta, K.: Universal electronic cash. In: Annual International Cryptology Conference, pp. 324–337. Springer (1991)
15. Regev, O.: On lattices, learning with errors, random linear codes, and cryptography. J. ACM (JACM) **56**(6), 1–40 (2009)
16. Rivest, R.L., Shamir, A., Adleman, L.: A method for obtaining digital signatures and public-key cryptosystems. Commun. ACM **21**(2), 120–126 (1978)
17. Ron, D., Shamir, A.: Quantitative analysis of the full bitcoin transaction graph. In: International Conference on Financial Cryptography and Data Security, pp. 6–24. Springer (2013)
18. Sasson, E.B., et al.: Zerocash: Decentralized anonymous payments from bitcoin. In: 2014 IEEE Symposium on Security and Privacy, pp. 459–474. IEEE (2014)
19. Todd, P.: Stealth addresses (2014)
20. Van Saberhagen, N.: Cryptonote v 2.0 (2013)

Compact Ring Signatures with Post-Quantum Security in Standard Model

Tuong Ngoc Nguyen[1]($\boxtimes$)(iD), Willy Susilo[1](iD), Dung Hoang Duong[1](iD),
Fuchun Guo[1](iD), Kazuhide Fukushima[2](iD), and Shinsaku Kiyomoto[2](iD)

[1] Institute of Cybersecurity and Cryptology, School of Computing and Information
Technology, University of Wollongong, Wollongong, Australia
ntn807@uowmail.edu.au, {wsusilo,hduong,fuchun}@uow.edu.au
[2] Information Security Laboratory, KDDI Research, Inc., Fujimino, Japan
{ka-fukushima,kiyomoto}@kddi-research.jp

Abstract. Ring signatures allow a ring member to produce signatures on behalf of all ring users but remain anonymous. At PKC 2022, Chatterjee *et al.* defined post-quantum ring signatures with post-quantum anonymity and post-quantum blind-unforgeability. Assuming the hardness of the learning with errors problem, they proposed a generic construction that transforms any blind-unforgeable (BU) secure signature into a post-quantum ring signature in the standard model. However, the signature size grows linearly to the number of ring members.

In this paper, we revisit the construction of Chatterjee et al. and present a compiler converting any BU secure signature into a compact (i.e., the signature size is logarithmically (or lower) dependent on the ring size) post-quantum ring signature in the standard model. Additionally, inspired by the work of Boneh et al. at CRYPTO 2013, we show how to transform any existentially unforgeable under a chosen message attack (EUF-CMA) secure signature into a BU secure signature. Hence, through our work, one can easily build a compact post-quantum ring signature in the standard model directly from any EUF-CMA secure signature.

Keywords: ring signatures · blind-unforgeability · post-quantum cryptography

1 Introduction

1.1 Literature Review and Motivation

Rivest *et al.* [17] firstly presented the primitive "ring signature" (RS) in which any member can sign messages on behalf of the ring without being revealed. There have been many works related to ring signatures were based on either classical hardness assumptions (Discrete Logarithm Problem, Integer Factorization Problem) [8,12,18], or quantum secure hardness assumptions (lattices, coding,

C. Ge and M. Yung (Eds.): Inscrypt 2023, LNCS 14526, pp. 65–84, 2024.
https://doi.org/10.1007/978-981-97-0942-7_4

etc.) [16,19]. However, these constructions are provably secure against adversaries who can only make classical queries to the random oracle (RO) and/or the signing oracle. In [3], Boneh *et al.* proposes a new primitive "quantum random oracle" (QRO) in which an adversary can make queries in superposition to the random oracle. This interesting topic immediately grabs cryptography researchers' attention. As a result, many works have investigated QROM security proposed in recent years [9,15]. However, Zhandry [20] showed that it is not sufficiently secure against quantum adversaries if we only consider classical signing queries. Boneh *et al.* [4] presented an example showing that adversaries with quantum-chosen message queries have more power than classical chosen message queries, which results in several existing signature schemes that are currently secure under classical chosen message attack might no longer be secure in the quantum setting where adversaries have enough hardware power to make quantum signing queries. Therefore, it is essential to have (ring) signatures that are secure against such attackers. In a classical existential unforgeability under chosen message attack (EUF-CMA) experiment, an adversary can arbitrarily choose messages and ask a challenger to provide valid signatures. For each query, the challenger updates a list of signed messages. Finally, the adversary needs to produce a valid message/signature pair such that the message has never been queried before, i.e., not in the list. Unfortunately, it is unclear how the challenger can record the list without disturbing its states in quantum settings.

To address the issue, Boneh *et al.* [4] proposed the security notion "quantum chosen message attack" or "one-more unforgeability" for signatures. In this experiment, the challenger does not need to record any signed messages; the adversary is allowed to make at most q quantum queries to the signing oracle, but in the end, instead of producing one forgery, it is required to produce $(q+1)$ distinct valid message/signature pairs. Therefore, even if the adversary uses at most q asked valid message/signature pairs, it has to generate at least one valid pair itself. Nevertheless, this definition does not sufficiently consider all cases with quantum unforgeability [1,10]. To overcome the disadvantage, Alagic *et al.* [1] introduced blind-unforgeability (BU). In the experiment, the challenger first defines a blindset, the subset of the message space. Next, in the query phase, an adversary is only allowed to ask signing queries on messages that are not in the blindset. Then, upon receiving the forgery from the adversary, the challenger checks if the message is on the blindset; if so, the forgery is accepted. Thereby, the challenger can ensure the adversary has never received a valid signature for the message without recording any signed messages. Chatterjee *et al.* [6] extended BU definition to obtain Post-Quantum Blind-Unforgeability (PQBU) and Post-Quantum Anonymity for ring signatures. They call such ring signatures by the term "Post-Quantum Ring Signatures" (PQRS). In terms of constructions, they propose a framework converting any BU secure signature into a PQRS assuming the hardness of the quantum Learning with Errors (QLWE) in the standard model. However, the ring signature scheme does not satisfy *compactness*, i.e., the signature size is not logarithmically (or lower) dependent on the number of ring members. Naturally, a question, which is also an open problem in [6], arises:

*Can we build a generic construction that transforms any BU secure signature
into a **compact** PQRS in the standard model?*

Chatterjee *et al.* [6] showed that the GPV signature [11] is BU secure in the
QROM by applying quantum pseudorandom functions [20]. They also design a
short (i.e., the signature size is independent of message size) BU secure signature
in the standard model based on the QLWE hardness assumption. To the best
of our knowledge, only these schemes are BU secure, and most of the current
signature schemes have been provably EUF-CMA secure. However, according
to the definition, EUF-CMA signatures do not have the appropriate properties
for post-quantum security. Thus, it is not easy to construct a PQRS from most
of the signature schemes since we must start from a BU signature to obtain a
PQRS. Therefore, there exists one more question:

*Can we have a compiler that converts any EUF-CMA secure signatures into a
BU secure signature?*

Interestingly, if we can solve these two questions, one can now obtain a compact
PQRS directly from any EUF-CMA secure signatures.

1.2   Our Contributions

We focus on proposing feasible solutions for the aforementioned questions. We
present the result for the second issue first and then discuss the resolution for the
first one later. Hence, the organization is (1) from EUF-CMA secure signatures
to BU secure signatures and (2) from BU secure signatures to PQRS. We believe
this order would be easier for readers to follow. Our main contributions are:

1. We solve the second question by proving that the generic construction from
   [4] can convert any EUF-CMA secure signature into a BU secure signature.
2. For the first question, we propose a compiler generically turning any BU
   secure signature into a compact PQRS. We prove our scheme enjoins Post-
   Quantum Anonymity and Post-Quantum Blind-Unforgeability.

1.3   Technical Overview

BU Signatures. We begin with the generic construction for quantum-secure
signatures in [4]. To sign a message, we first use the chameleon hash function
[14] to hash the message and then sign the hash using an EUF-CMA secure signature. To prove one can obtain a BU secure signature from a EUF-CMA secure
one, we attempt to go through two security reductions: (1) from BU to EUF-
RMA and (2) from EUF-RMA to EUF-CMA. Since the latter can be quickly
followed [13], the challenge is how we argue that any EUF-RMA secure signature
can be transformed into a BU secure signature. Our way out of this conundrum
is to take advantage of the properties of chameleon hash functions and quantum oracle indistinguishability of families of pairwise independent functions [21].
Then, assuming the underlying signature is EUF-RMA secure, we assert that the
generic construction is BU secure.

Compact Post-Quantum Ring Signatures. Our starting point is the generic construction in [6] based on LWE assumption. The construction takes a BU secure signature Sig, pair-wise independent hash functions, a lossy public key encryption LE and a ZAP for special super-complement languages as building blocks. Each ring member owns a verification key containing the verification key vk of Sig, the public key pk of LE, and the first message ρ for ZAP. To produce a ring signature Σ on a message m, a signer first computes a signature σ on $R||m$ using Sig; then, it encrypts σ and a random string with pseudo-randomness r_{c_1}, r_{c_2} using LE, respectively, to obtain two ciphertexts c_1, c_2, where r_{c_1}, r_{c_2} are computed from two pairwise-independent functions. Finally, it produces a proof π using ZAP.P on a statement $x = (R, m, c_1, c_2)$ and a witness $w = (vk, pk, \sigma, r_{c_1})$ proving that one of the ciphertexts is computed using a public key in R. The ring signature Σ contains c_1, c_2 and π. To prove the PQBU, they need to reduce from the PQBU to the BU of the underlying signature; therefore, signing directly on $R||m$ facilitating them to have a "smooth" reduction: the blindset B_ε^{RS} (in the PQBU experiment) and the blindset B_ε^S (in the BU experiment of the signature) are identical, i.e., both of them are generated by choosing a pair (R, m) with same probability ε. However, by doing this, their scheme does not achieve compactness since the ring signature Σ consists of a proof π generated by ZAP.P whose size is linearly dependent on the ring size. The reason is the size of the proof π depends on the size of x_1 in the statement $x = (x_1 = (R, m, c_1, c_2), x_2 = \emptyset)$. To solve this, instead of signing $R||m$, we sign on $H(R)||m$ where H is a collision-resistant hash function. By doing that, we update our statement x_1 not to contain R but $H(R)$ (and other components which we will discuss in Sect. 4.3); as a result, its size no longer depends on R. However, since we remove R in x_1, we cannot use (vk, pk) in witness w to prove the membership of the signer's verification key in the ring R. We notice that the size of proof π is also dependent on the size of the witness w and its verification circuit's length; therefore, a logarithmic-size witness w is required to obtain a compact π. To overcome the issue, we use somewhere perfect binding hash functions with private local opening [2], which produces a logarithmic-size witness τ for checking the membership in L; we then add τ to the witness w. Finally, we define a ZAP super-complement language $\tilde{L}$ and apply the ZAP construction from [7] for the updated statement and witness to obtain a compact proof π. The next challenge is proving the PQBU of our construction as with our modification, the blindsets in the PQBU experiment and the BU experiment are no longer identical. We argue that the two blindsets only need to satisfy some specific conditions. Our proof takes advantage of a collision-resistant hash function H to create an intermediate blindset B^{HRS} which helps us argue these conditions and correctly reduce the PQBU of the ring signature to the BU of the signature, more details is in Section 4.5.

2   Preliminaries

Notation. Let $[N]$ denote the set of $\{1, 2, 3, \cdots, N\}$. Note that all of the security notions presented in the paper are required to hold against (at least) Quantum Polynomial Time (QPT) adversaries.

2.1 Quantum Oracle Indistinguishability

Lemma 1 ([20]). *There is a universal constant C_0 such that, for any sets $\mathcal{X}$ and $\mathcal{Y}$, distribution D on $\mathcal{Y}$, any integer ℓ, and any quantum algorithm A making q queries to an oracle $H : \mathcal{X} \to \mathcal{Y}$, the following two cases are indistinguishable, except with probability less than $C_0 q^3 / \ell$:*

- *$H(x) = y_x$ where y_x is a list of samples of D of size $|\mathcal{X}|$.*
- *H is drawn from the small-range distribution with ℓ samples of D.*

Lemma 2 ([21]). *Let H be an oracle drawn from a $2q$-wise independent distribution. Then, the advantage of any quantum algorithm making at most q queries to H in distinguishing H from a truly random function is 0.*

Lemma 3 ([4]). *Let $\mathcal{X}$ and $\mathcal{Y}$ be sets, and for each $x \in \mathcal{X}$, let D_x and D_x' be distributions on $\mathcal{Y}$ such that $|(D_x - D_x')| \leq \varepsilon$ for some value ε that is independent of x. Let $O : \mathcal{X} \to \mathcal{Y}$ be a function where, for each x, $O(x)$ is drawn from D_x and let $O'(x)$ be a function where, for each x, $O'(x)$ is drawn from $D'(x)$. Then any quantum algorithm making at most q queries to either O or O' cannot distinguish the two, except with probability at most $\sqrt{8 C_0 q^3 \varepsilon}$.*

2.2 Chameleon Hash Functions

Definition 1 (Chameleon Hash Functions). *A chameleon hash function H consists of the following algorithms:*
$(sk, pk) \leftarrow \mathsf{H.Gen}(1^\lambda)$: *Given a security parameter λ, it returns a key pair of secret key sk and public key pk.*
$h \leftarrow \mathsf{H.Eval}(pk, m, r)$: *Given a public key pk, a value m, and a randomness r, it returns a digest h.*
$r \leftarrow \mathsf{H.Sample}(1^\lambda)$: *Given a security parameter λ, it returns a randomness r such that $h \leftarrow \mathsf{H.Eval}(pk, m, r)$ is uniformly distributed for any pk and m.*
$r \leftarrow \mathsf{H.Inv}(sk, h, m)$: *Given a secret key sk, a digest h and a value m, it returns a randomness r such that $\mathsf{H.Eval}(pk, m, r) = h$ and the statistical distance between r and $\mathsf{H.Sample}(1^\lambda)$ conditioned on $\mathsf{H.Sample}(1^\lambda)$ is negligible.*

An SIS instantiation of the hash function was proposed in [5].

2.3 Somewhere Perfectly Binding Hash Functions

Definition 2 (SPB Hash). *A somewhere perfectly binding hash function SPB with private local openings consists of the following algorithms:*
$(hk, shk) \leftarrow \mathsf{SPB.Gen}(1^\lambda, n, \mathsf{ind})$: *Given security parameter λ, a database size n, an index ind, it returns a public hashing key hk and a private opening key shk.*
$h \leftarrow \mathsf{SPB.Hash}(hk, \mathsf{db})$: *Given a public hashing key hk, a database db, it returns a digest value h.*
$\tau \leftarrow \mathsf{SPB.Open}(hk, shk, \mathsf{db}, \mathsf{ind})$: *Given a public hashing key hk, a private opening key shk, a database db, and an index ind, it returns a witness τ.*
$0/1 \leftarrow \mathsf{SPB.Verify}(hk, h, \mathsf{ind}, x, \tau)$: *Given a public hashing key hk, a digest value h, an index ind, a value x, and a witness τ, it returns $0/1$ if rejected/accepted.*

Correctness. Given $\forall \lambda \in \mathbb{N}, n = \text{poly}(\lambda)$, $\forall \text{ind} \in [n]$, and all size n databases db, with $(hk, shk) \leftarrow \text{SPB.Gen}(1^\lambda, n, \text{ind})$, $h \leftarrow \text{SPB.Hash}(hk, \text{db})$, $\tau \leftarrow \text{SPB.Open}(hk, shk, \text{db}, \text{ind})$, we have $\Pr[\text{SPB.Verify}(hk, h, \text{ind}, x, \tau) = 1] = 1$.

Efficiency. Sizes of all hashing key hk and witnesses τ are logarithmic to the size of the database, i.e., $\log(n) \cdot \text{poly}(\lambda)$. Also, one can compute the verification algorithm $\text{SPB.Verify}(hk, h, \text{ind}, x, \tau)$ by a circuit of size $\log(n) \cdot \text{poly}(\lambda)$.

Somewhere Perfectly Binding. Given $\forall \lambda \in \mathbb{N}, n = \text{poly}(\lambda)$, $\forall \text{ind} \in [n]$, all size n databases db, all database values x, and all witnesses τ, there exists only one $x = \text{db}_{\text{ind}}$ such that $\text{SPB.Verify}(hk, h, \text{ind}, x, \tau) = 1$, where $h \leftarrow \text{SPB.Hash}(hk, \text{db})$.

Index Hiding. Given $\forall n \in \mathbb{N}$, and any two indices ind_0, ind_1, we have

$$\{hk : (hk, shk) \leftarrow \text{SPB.Gen}(1^\lambda, n, \text{ind}_0)\} \approx_c \{hk : (hk, shk) \leftarrow \text{SPB.Gen}(1^\lambda, n, \text{ind}_1)\}.$$

Lemma 4 ([2]). *There exists such an SPB hash based on the LWE assumption.*

2.4 Lossy PKEs

Definition 3 (Special Lossy PKE). *A special lossy public key encryption scheme* LE *consists of the following algorithms:*

$(\{pk_i\}_{i=1}^N, msk) \leftarrow \text{LE.MSKGen}(1^\lambda, N)$: *Given a security parameter* λ *and a number* $N \in \mathbb{N}$, *it returns a list of injective public keys* $\{pk_i\}_{i=1}^N$ *and a master secret key* msk.

$sk \leftarrow \text{LE.MSKExt}(msk, pk)$: *Given a master secret key* msk *and a public key* pk, *it returns a corresponding secret key* sk.

$pk_{\text{ls}} \leftarrow \text{LE.KSam}(1^\lambda)$: *Give a security parameter* λ, *it returns a lossy public key* pk_{ls}.

$0/1 \leftarrow \text{LE.Valid}(pk, sk)$: *Given a public key* pk *and a secret key* sk, *it returns 1 if* sk *is associated with* pk, *otherwise, it returns 0.*

$r \leftarrow \text{LE.RndExt}(pk)$: *Given a public key* pk, *it returns a randomness* r.

$ct \leftarrow \text{LE.Enc}(pk, m)$: *Given a public key* pk *and a message* $m \in \mathcal{M}_\lambda$, *it returns a ciphertext* ct.

$m \leftarrow \text{LE.Dec}(sk, ct)$: *Given a secret key* sk *and a ciphertext* ct, *it returns a valid plaintext* $m \in \mathcal{M}_\lambda$.

Completeness. Given $\forall \lambda \in \mathbb{N}, \forall (pk, sk)$ s.t. $\text{LE.Valid}(pk, sk) = 1, \forall m \in \mathcal{M}_\lambda$:

$$\Pr[\text{LE.Dec}(sk, \text{LE.Enc}(pk, m)) = m] = 1.$$

Lossiness of Lossy Public Keys. Given $\forall \lambda \in \mathbb{N}$, for any $pk_{\mathsf{ls}} \leftarrow \mathsf{LE.KSam}(1^\lambda)$, $pk'_{\mathsf{ls}} \leftarrow \mathsf{LE.KSam}(1^\lambda)$, and two messages $m_0, m_1 \in \mathcal{M}_\lambda$, we have

$$\{ct_0 \leftarrow \mathsf{LE.Enc}(pk_{\mathsf{ls}}, m_0)\} \approx_s \{ct_1 \leftarrow \mathsf{LE.Enc}(pk'_{\mathsf{ls}}, m_1)\} \approx_s u,$$

where u is uniformly random.

Completeness of Master Secret Keys. Given $\forall N = \mathsf{poly}(\lambda)$, for all $i \in [n]$, we have

$$\Pr[\mathsf{LE.Valid}(pk_i, sk_i) = 1] = 1 - \mathsf{negl}(\lambda),$$

where $(\{pk_i\}_{i=1}^N, msk) \leftarrow \mathsf{LE.MSKGen}(1^\lambda, N)$, and $sk_i \leftarrow \mathsf{LE.MSKExt}(msk, pk_i)$.

Indistinguishability. Given $\forall N = \mathsf{poly}(\lambda)$, for all $i \in [N]$, we have

$$\{(pk_i, r_i) | pk_i \leftarrow \mathsf{LE.KSam}(1^\lambda, r_i)\}$$
$$\approx_c \{(pk_i, \mathsf{LE.RndExt}(pk_i)) | (\{pk_i\}_{i=1}^N, msk) \leftarrow \mathsf{LE.MSKGen}(1^\lambda, N)\}.$$

Almost-Unique Secret Key. Given $\forall N = \mathsf{poly}(\lambda)$, for all $i \in [N]$ and $j \neq i$:

$$\Pr[\mathsf{LE.Valid}(pk_i, sk_j) = 1] = \mathsf{negl}(\lambda),$$

where $(\{pk_i\}_{i=1}^N, msk) \leftarrow \mathsf{LE.MSKGen}(1^\lambda, N)$, and $sk_j \neq \mathsf{LE.MSKExt}(msk, pk_i)$.

We apply an instantiation of LE scheme based on dual mode LWE commitments [6]. Since it is based on the lossy (statistically hiding) mode, any ciphertext is statistically indistinguishable from a random matrix, which implies two different ciphertexts encrypted using two different lossy public keys are statistically indistinguishable. Based on that, we extend the Lossiness property from [6] to one in Definition 3 to support our security proof.

2.5 ZAPs

Definition 4 (Super-Complement [7]). *Let $L, \tilde{L}$ be two languages where the elements of $\tilde{L}$ are represented as pairs of bit strings. We say $\tilde{L}$ is a super-complement of L, if $\tilde{L} \subseteq (\{0,1\}^* \setminus L) \times \{0,1\}^*)$, i.e, $\tilde{L}$ is a super complement of L if for any $x = (x_1, x_2)$, $x \in \tilde{L} \Rightarrow x_1 \notin L$.*

In the paper, we apply the *compact relaxed ZAPs for* NP $\cap$ coNP from [7].

Definition 5 (Compact relaxed ZAPs [7]). *Let $L, \tilde{L} \in$ NP be two languages such that $\tilde{L}$ is a super complement of L. By R and $\tilde{R}$ denote the NP relations corresponding to L an $\tilde{L}$ respectively. Let $\{C_{n,\ell}\}_{n,\ell \in N}$ and $\{\tilde{C}_{n,\ell}\}_{n,\ell \in N}$ be the NP verification circuits for L and $\tilde{L}$ respectively. Let $\tilde{d} = \tilde{d}(n, \ell)$ be the depth of $\tilde{C}_{n,\ell}$. A compact relaxed ZAP for $L, \tilde{L}$ is a tuple of PPT algorithms $(\mathsf{V}, \mathsf{P}, \mathsf{Verify})$ defined as follows (where $1^n, 1^\lambda$ are implicit inputs to $\mathsf{P}, \mathsf{Verify}$):*

$\rho \leftarrow \mathsf{ZAP.V}(1^\lambda, 1^n, 1^{\tilde{\ell}}, 1^{\tilde{D}})$: *Given a security parameter λ, statement length n for L, witness length $\tilde{\ell}$ for $\tilde{L}$, and NP verifier circuit depth upper-bound $\tilde{D}$ for $\tilde{L}$, it returns a first message ρ.*

$\pi \leftarrow \mathsf{ZAP.P}(\rho, x = (x_1, x_2), w)$: *Given a string ρ, a statement $(x_1 \in \{0,1\}^n, x_2)$, and a witness w such that $(x_1, w) \in R$, it returns a proof π.*

$0/1 \leftarrow \mathsf{ZAP.Verify}(\rho, x = (x_1, x_2), \pi)$: *Given a string ρ, a statement x, and a proof π, it returns 1 if accepts, or 0 otherwise.*

Completeness. Given $\forall x \in L, \forall \tilde{\ell} \in \mathbb{N}, \forall \tilde{D} \geq \tilde{d}(|x|, \tilde{\ell})$, and $\forall \lambda \in \mathbb{N}$, we have

$$\Pr\left[\text{ZAP.Verify}(\rho, x, \pi) = 1 | \rho \leftarrow \text{ZAP.V}(1^\lambda, 1^{|x|}, 1^{\tilde{\ell}}, 1^{\tilde{D}}) \wedge \pi \leftarrow \text{ZAP.P}(\rho, x, w)\right] = 1.$$

Public coin. The output of $\text{ZAP.V}(1^\lambda, 1^n, 1^{\tilde{\ell}}, 1^{\tilde{D}})$ is a uniformly random string.

Selective Non-Witness Adaptive-Statement Soundness. Given $\forall n, \forall \tilde{D} \in \mathbb{N}$, every non-witnesses $\tilde{w} \in \{0,1\}^*$, for any non-uniform QPT prover P_λ^*, we have

$$\Pr\left[\text{ZAP.Verify}(\rho, x, \pi^*) = 1 \wedge (x, \tilde{w}) \in \tilde{R}\right] = \mathsf{negl}(\lambda),$$

where $\rho \leftarrow \text{ZAP.V}(1^\lambda, 1^n, 1^{\tilde{\ell}}, 1^{\tilde{D}})$, $(x, \pi^*) \leftarrow P_\lambda^*(\rho)$, and $\tilde{D} \geq \tilde{d}(|x|, |\tilde{w}|)$.

Statistical Witness Indistinguishability. Given $\forall n, \forall \tilde{\ell}, \forall \tilde{D} \in \mathbb{N}$, for any (possibly unbounded) cheating verifier $\tilde{V} = (V^*, \text{Verify}^*)$, we have

$$\Pr[\text{Verify}^*(\rho, x, \pi) = 1] - \Pr[\text{Verify}^*(\rho, x, \pi') = 1] = \mathsf{negl}(\lambda),$$

where

$$\begin{cases} (\rho, x, w, w') \leftarrow V^*(1^\lambda, 1^n, 1^{\tilde{\ell}}, 1^{\tilde{D}}) \wedge \pi \leftarrow P(\rho, x, w), \\ (\rho, x, w, w') \leftarrow V^*(1^\lambda, 1^n, 1^{\tilde{\ell}}, 1^{\tilde{D}}) \wedge \pi' \leftarrow P(\rho, x, w'). \end{cases}$$

Compactness. The size of the proof π is independent of the size of $\tilde{C}$ and x_2, and it is polynomially dependent on $n, \tilde{\ell}, \tilde{D}, \lambda$ and the size of C. In other words, the bit-size of π for $x = (x_1, x_2)$ is dependent on the size of x_1, but not x_2.

Lemma 5 ([7]). *There exists such a ZAP based on the LWE assumption.*

3 Blind-Unforgeable Signatures

3.1 Security Model

We show the Blind-Unforgeability experiment [6] for signatures in Fig. 1.

Completeness. Given security parameter $\lambda, \forall m \in \mathcal{M}_\lambda$, a signature S is complete if: $\Pr[\text{S.Verify}(pk, m, \text{S.Sign}(sk, m)) = 1 | (pk, sk) \leftarrow \text{S.Gen}(\lambda)] = 1 - \mathsf{negl}(\lambda)$.

Definition 6 (Blind-Unforgeable Signatures). *Given security parameter λ, and $Q = \text{poly}(\lambda)$, a signature S is post-quantum blind-unforgeable if for any QPT adversary $\mathcal{A}$ in Experiment 1, we have*

$$\Pr\left[\text{Adv}_{\text{BU}}^{\lambda, Q}(\mathcal{A}) = 1\right] \leq \mathsf{negl}(\lambda).$$

We also provide the definition of EUF-RMA secure signatures.

Definition 7 (EUF-RMA [4]). *Sig is existentially unforgeable under a random message attack if the adversary is not allowed any signing queries but receives q message/signature pairs for uniform random messages at the beginning.*

Setup. $\mathcal{A}$ randomly picks a constant $0 \le \varepsilon \le 1$ and sends ε to $\mathcal{C}$. $\mathcal{C}$ creates a *blindset* $\mathsf{B}_\varepsilon^{\mathsf{S}} \subseteq \mathcal{M}_\lambda$ by putting each message $m \in \mathcal{M}_\lambda$ into $\mathsf{B}_\varepsilon^{\mathsf{S}}$ with probability ε, then generates a pair of keys $(pk, sk) \leftarrow \mathsf{S.Gen}(1^\lambda)$, and sends pk to $\mathcal{A}$.

Query. $\mathcal{A}$ can make a number of signing queries to $\mathcal{C}$.

- Signing Query: $\mathcal{A}$ sends a query $(\mathsf{sign}, \sum \psi_{m,t}|m,t\rangle)$ with superposition over m to $\mathcal{C}$, then $\mathcal{C}$ randomly choose a string r and responds as follows

$$\sum_{m,t} \psi_{m,t}|m,t\rangle \to \sum_{m,t} \psi_{m,t}|m, t \oplus \mathsf{B}_\varepsilon^{\mathsf{S}} f(m)\rangle,$$

where

$$\begin{cases} \mathsf{B}_\varepsilon^{\mathsf{S}} f(m) = \perp \text{ if } m \in \mathsf{B}_\varepsilon^{\mathsf{S}}, \\ \mathsf{B}_\varepsilon^{\mathsf{S}} f(m) = \mathsf{S.Sign}(m, sk; r) \text{ otherwise.} \end{cases}$$

Forge. $\mathcal{A}$ outputs (σ^*, m^*). $\mathcal{C}$ checks these following conditions:

$$\begin{cases} \mathsf{S.Verify}(pk, \sigma^*, m^*) = 1, \\ m^* \in \mathsf{B}_\varepsilon^{\mathsf{S}}. \end{cases}$$

If all conditions hold, $\mathcal{C}$ returns 1; otherwise, it returns 0.

Fig. 1. Blind-Unforgeability Experiment for Signatures

3.2 Construction

In this section, we recall the construction from [4]. We then prove that the construction generally converts any EUF-CMA secure signature into a BU secure signature. Let $\mathsf{H} = (\mathsf{Gen}, \mathsf{Eval}, \mathsf{Inv}, \mathsf{Sample})$ be a chameleon hash function, and $\mathsf{Sig} = (\mathsf{Gen}, \mathsf{Sign}, \mathsf{Verify})$ be a signature scheme. Let $\mathcal{Q}, \mathcal{R}$ be families of pairwise independent functions mapping messages to randomness used by H.Inv, Sig.Sign, respectively, we describe the construction below.

$\mathsf{Gen}(1^\lambda)$: On input a security parameter λ, one performs as follows:
1. Generate $(sk_h, pk_h) \leftarrow \mathsf{H.Gen}(1^\lambda)$.
2. Generate $(sk_s, pk_s) \leftarrow \mathsf{Sig.Gen}(1^\lambda)$.
3. Output $(sk, pk) = ((sk_h, sk_s), (pk_h, pk_s))$.

$\mathsf{Sign}(pk_h, sk_s, m)$: On input a public hashing key pk_h, a secret key sk_s and a message m, a signer performs as follows:
1. Sample $Q \leftarrow \mathcal{Q}, R \leftarrow \mathcal{R}$.
2. Compute $r \leftarrow \mathsf{H.Sample}(\lambda, R(m)), s \leftarrow Q(m), h \leftarrow \mathsf{H.Eval}(pk_h, m, r)$.
3. Compute $\sigma \leftarrow \mathsf{Sig.Sign}(sk_s, h; s)$.
4. Output (r, σ).

$\mathsf{Verify}(pk, m, (r, \sigma))$: On input a public key pk, a message m, and a signature (r, σ), a verifier performs as follows:
1. Parse $pk = (pk_h, pk_s)$.
2. Compute $h \leftarrow \mathsf{H}(pk_h, m, r)$.
3. Output $\mathsf{Sig.Verify}(pk_s, h, \sigma)$.

3.3 Security Proof

Theorem 1. *The signature described in section 3.2 is blind-unforgeable, assuming* Sig *is EUF-CMA secure and* H *is a secure chameleon hash function.*

Proof. Let W_t be the probability $\mathcal{A}_S$ wins the game G_t. We prove Theorem 1 via a set of games as follows:

Game G_0: This game is the original blind-unforgeability experiment between $\mathcal{A}_S$ and $\mathcal{C}_S$ described in Fig. 1. Let $q = \text{poly}(\lambda)$, suppose that $\mathcal{A}_S$ makes at most q signing queries in Query phase, we have $W_0 = \Pr\left[\text{Adv}_{\text{BU}}^{\lambda,Q}(\mathcal{A}_S) = 1\right] = \epsilon_s$.

Game G_1: This game is similar to G_0, except that, for the i-th signing query, instead of sampling Q_i, R_i from $\mathcal{Q}$, $\mathcal{R}$, respectively, $\mathcal{C}_S$ chooses Q_i, R_i as truly random functions. This also means $\mathcal{C}_S$ compute $r_i \leftarrow \text{H.Sample}(\lambda)$ and chooses s_i uniformly random. Based on Lemma 2, we have $W_1 = W_0 = \epsilon_s$.

Game G_2: This game is similar to G_1, except that, for the i-th signing query, instead of computing h_i using H.Eval, $\mathcal{C}_S$ samples h_i uniformly random, and computes $r_i \leftarrow \text{H.Inv}(sk_h, h_i, m_i; t_i)$, where t_i is a uniform randomness. Based on the property of H.Inv, we have $W_2 \approx_s W_1 = \epsilon_s$.

Game G_3: This game is similar to G_2, except let $\ell = 2C_0 qp$ where C_0 is a constant in Lemma 1, $\mathcal{C}_S$ samples a list of $q\ell$ values $\tilde{h}_{i,j}$ (where $i \in [q], j \in [\ell]$), and computes $\tilde{\sigma}_{i,j} = \text{Sig.Sign}(sk_s, \tilde{h}_{i,j})$ in Setup phase. $\mathcal{C}_S$ then uses $(\tilde{h}_{i,j}, \tilde{\sigma}_{i,j})$ to answer $\mathcal{A}_S$'s the i-th signing query in Query phase, and computes $t_i \leftarrow T_i(m)$ where T_i is a truly random function. Based on Lemma 1, we have $W_3 \geq \epsilon_s - 1/2p$.

Game G_4: This game is similar to G_3, except that, $\mathcal{C}_S$ chooses T_i as pairwise independent functions instead of truly random functions, G_4 now can be simulated efficiently. Based on Lemma 2, we have $W_4 = W_3 \geq \epsilon_s - 1/2p$.

Next, our idea is based on an adversary $\mathcal{A}_S$ winning G_4, we construct an adversary $\mathcal{A}_{\text{RMA}}$ winning the EUF-RMA game with a noticeable probability. The reduction is as follows. Phase Setup: $\mathcal{C}_{\text{RMA}}$ generates a key pair $(\hat{pk}, \hat{sk})$ and sends to $\mathcal{A}_{\text{RMA}}$. $\mathcal{C}_{\text{RMA}}$ samples $q\ell$ pairs of message/signature as described in G_4, then sets a list of signed messages Signed $= \{\tilde{h}_{i,j}\}$, where $i \in [q], j \in [\ell]$, and sends these pairs to $\mathcal{A}_{\text{RMA}}$. $\mathcal{A}_S$ randomly picks a constant $0 \leq \varepsilon \leq 1$ and sends ε to $\mathcal{A}_{\text{RMA}}$ who now is in a role of the challenger $\mathcal{C}_S$. $\mathcal{A}_{\text{RMA}}$ defines the set B_ε^S as in the BU game. $\mathcal{A}_{\text{RMA}}$ generates (pk_h, sk_h), sets $pk_s = \hat{pk}$, and sends $pk = (pk_h, pk_s)$ to $\mathcal{A}_S$. Phase Query: When $\mathcal{A}_S$ sends a query on message m. If $m \notin B_\varepsilon^S$, $\mathcal{A}_{\text{RMA}}$ returns valid signatures using the sets of $q\ell$ message/signature pairs. Note that, given m_i and h_i, $\mathcal{A}_{\text{RMA}}$ can compute $r_i \leftarrow \text{H.Inv}(sk_h, m_i, h_i; t_i)$ such that $\text{H.Eval}(pk_h, m_i, r_i) = h_i$. If $m \in B_\varepsilon^S$, $\mathcal{A}_{\text{RMA}}$ aborts. Phase Forge: $\mathcal{A}_S$ produces a forgery (m^*, r^*, σ^*) and sends to $\mathcal{A}_{\text{RMA}}$. $\mathcal{A}_{\text{RMA}}$ computes $h^* = \text{H.Eval}(pk_h, m^*, r^*)$, sends a forgery (h^*, σ^*) to $\mathcal{C}_{\text{RMA}}$. We have two cases: *Case 1:* There exists a h_k such that $h^* = h_k \in$ Signed, this means $\text{H.Eval}(pk_h, m^*, r^*) = \text{H.Eval}(pk_h, m_k, r_k)$, and $(m^*, r^*) \neq (m_k, r_k)$ (since $m^* \in B_\varepsilon^S$ never queried before), this happens with a negligible probability assuming H is collision-resistant. *Case 2:* $h^* \notin$ Signed, we have $h^* = \text{H.Eval}(pk_h, m^*, r^*)$, and $\text{Sig.Verify}(pk_s, h^*, \sigma^*) = 1$ (since (m^*, r^*, σ^*) is a valid forgery of $\mathcal{A}_S$). This means (h^*, σ^*) is a valid forgery of $\mathcal{A}_{\text{RMA}}$ in the EUF-RMA experiment. This event happens with probability ϵ_{RMA}, we have $\epsilon_{\mathsf{RMA}} = W_4 - \mathsf{negl}(\lambda) \geq \epsilon_s - 1/2p - \mathsf{negl}(\lambda)$. Since we assume Sig is EUF-RMA secure, ϵ_{RMA} is negligible which implies ϵ_s is negligible. $\qquad\square$

4 Compact Post-Quantum Ring Signatures

4.1 Ring Signatures

Definition 8 (Ring Signatures). *Given a security parameter λ, and $N = \mathsf{poly}(\lambda)$, a ring signature $\mathsf{RS} = (\mathsf{RS.Gen}, \mathsf{RS.Sign}, \mathsf{RS.Verify})$ is described as below.*
$(pk, sk) \leftarrow \mathsf{RS.Gen}(1^\lambda, Q)$: *Given a security parameter λ, and a super-polynomial $Q = 2^{log^2\lambda}$ presenting the maximum number of ring members, it returns a pair of public key and secret key (pk, sk).*
$\Sigma \leftarrow \mathsf{RS.Sign}(sk, \mathsf{R}, m)$: *Given a secret key sk, a ring $\mathsf{R} = \{pk_i\}_{i=1}^N$, and a message m, it returns a signature Σ.*
$0/1 \leftarrow \mathsf{RS.Verify}(\mathsf{R}, m, \Sigma)$: *Given a a ring $\mathsf{R} = \{pk_i\}_{i=1}^N$, a message m, and a signature Σ, the algorithms outputs 1/0 representing a valid/invalid signature.*

4.2 Security Model

We show the Post-Quantum Anonymity experiment [6] in Fig. 2.

Setup. $\mathcal{C}$ generates list of $(pk_i, sk_i) \leftarrow \mathsf{RS.Gen}(1^\lambda, Q; r_i)$ for each user $i \in [N]$, then forms a list of public keys $\mathsf{R} = \{pk_i\}_{i=1}^N$, and sends $\{(pk_i, sk_i, r_i)\}_{i=1}^N$ to $\mathcal{A}$.
Challenge. $\mathcal{A}$ picks two indices $i_0 \in [N], i_1 \in [N]$, and sends to $\mathcal{C}$. Upon receiving, $\mathcal{C}$ randomly chooses a bit $b \leftarrow_\$ \{0,1\}$, a string r, and responds as follows

$$\sum_{\mathsf{R},m,t} \psi_{\mathsf{R},m,t} |\mathsf{R}, m, t\rangle \to \sum_{\mathsf{R},m,t} \psi_{\mathsf{R},m,t} |\mathsf{R}, m, t \oplus f(\mathsf{R}, m)\rangle,$$

where

$$\begin{cases} f(\mathsf{R}, m) = \mathsf{RS.Sign}(\mathsf{R}, m, sk_{i_b}; r) \text{ if } pk_{i_0}, pk_{i_1} \in \mathsf{R}, \\ f(\mathsf{R}, m) = \perp \text{ otherwise.} \end{cases}$$

Guess. $\mathcal{A}$ guesses b'. If $b = b'$, $\mathcal{C}$ returns 1; otherwise, it returns 0.

Fig. 2. Post-Quantum Anonymity Experiment for Ring Signatures

Definition 9 (Post-Quantum Anonymity). *Given security parameter λ, and $N = \mathsf{poly}(\lambda)$, a ring signature RS is post-quantum anonymous if for any QPT adversary $\mathcal{A}$ in Experiment 2, we have*

$$\left| \Pr\left[\mathsf{Adv}_{\mathsf{RS,PQ\text{-}Anon}}^{\lambda, N}(\mathcal{A}) = 1 \right] - 1/2 \right| \leq \mathsf{negl}(\lambda).$$

We show the Post-Quantum Blind-Unforgeability experiment [6] in Fig. 3.

Setup. $\mathcal{A}$ randomly picks a constant $0 \le \varepsilon \le 1$ and sends ε to $\mathcal{C}$, then $\mathcal{C}$ initiates Corrupted $= \emptyset$. Next, $\mathcal{C}$ creates a *blindset* $\mathsf{B}_\varepsilon^{\mathsf{RS}} \subseteq 2^{\mathcal{R}_\lambda} \times \mathcal{M}_\lambda$ by putting each pair $(\mathsf{R}, m) \in 2^{\mathcal{R}_\lambda} \times \mathcal{M}_\lambda$ into $\mathsf{B}_\varepsilon^{\mathsf{RS}}$ with probability ε, where $\mathcal{R}_\lambda$ and $\mathcal{M}_\lambda$ are the ring and message space. It then generates a pair of keys $(pk_i, sk_i) \leftarrow \mathsf{RS.Gen}(1^\lambda)$ for each user. $\mathcal{C}$ Forms a list of public keys $\mathsf{R} = \{pk_i\}_{i=1}^N$ and sends R to $\mathcal{A}$.

Query. Adversary $\mathcal{A}$ can make two different types of queries to the challenger $\mathcal{C}$.

- Corrupted Query: $\mathcal{A}$ sends an index i to the secret key oracle $\mathcal{O}_{sk}$, $\mathcal{C}$ responds with $sk_i \leftarrow \mathcal{O}_{sk}(i)$ and sets Corrupted $\leftarrow$ Corrupted $\cup \{i\}$.
- Signing Query: $\mathcal{A}$ sends a query $(\mathsf{sign}, i, \sum \psi_{\mathsf{R},m,t} | \mathsf{R}, m, t\rangle)$ with superposition over R and m to $\mathcal{C}$, then $\mathcal{C}$ randomly choose a string r and responds as follows

$$\sum_{\mathsf{R},m,t} \psi_{\mathsf{R},m,t} | \mathsf{R}, m, t\rangle \rightarrow \sum_{\mathsf{R},m,t} \psi_{\mathsf{R},m,t} | \mathsf{R}, m, t \oplus \mathsf{B}_\varepsilon^{\mathsf{RS}} f(\mathsf{R}, m)\rangle,$$

where

$$\begin{cases} \mathsf{B}_\varepsilon^{\mathsf{RS}} f(\mathsf{R}, m) = \bot \text{ if } (\mathsf{R}, m) \in \mathsf{B}_\varepsilon^{\mathsf{RS}}, \\ \mathsf{B}_\varepsilon^{\mathsf{RS}} f(\mathsf{R}, m) = f(\mathsf{R}, m) \text{ otherwise}, \end{cases}$$

and

$$\begin{cases} f(\mathsf{R}, m) = \bot \text{ if } pk_i \notin \mathsf{R}, \\ f(\mathsf{R}, m) = \mathsf{RS.Sign}(\mathsf{R}, m, sk_i; r) \text{ otherwise}. \end{cases}$$

Forge. $\mathcal{A}$ outputs $(\sigma^*, m^*, \mathsf{R}^*)$. $\mathcal{C}$ checks these following conditions:

$$\begin{cases} \mathsf{R}^* \subseteq \mathsf{R} \setminus \mathsf{Corrupted}, \\ \mathsf{RS.Verify}(\sigma^*, \mathsf{R}^*, m^*) = 1, \\ (\mathsf{R}^*, m^*) \in \mathsf{B}_\varepsilon^{\mathsf{RS}}. \end{cases}$$

If all conditions hold, $\mathcal{C}$ returns 1; otherwise, it returns 0.

Fig. 3. Post-Quantum Blind-Unforgeability Experiment for Ring Signatures

Definition 10 (Post-Quantum Blind-Unforgeability). *Given security parameter λ, and $N = \mathsf{poly}(\lambda)$, a ring signature RS is post-quantum blind-unforgeable if for any QPT adversary $\mathcal{A}$ in Experiment 3, we have*

$$\Pr\left[\mathsf{Adv}_{\mathsf{RS},\mathsf{PQBU}}^{\lambda, N}(\mathcal{A}) = 1\right] \le \mathsf{negl}(\lambda).$$

4.3 Construction

We present a generic construction converting any BU secure signature into a compact PQRS with the following building blocks:

- A somewhere perfectly binding hash function SPB described in Sect. 2.3,
- A lossy public key encryption scheme LE described in Sect. 2.4,
- A ZAP for special super-complement languages described in Sect. 2.5,
- A BU signature scheme S describe in Definition 6.

- A collision-resistant hash function H. We assume H be a quantum ε_{col} collision-resistant hash function if any QPT quantum adversaries can efficiently find collisions of H with a negligible probability at most ε_{col}. One can construct such a hash function assuming the SIS problem is hard.

Let λ be the security parameter for SPB and LE, Q be the maximum number of ring members, $n = n(\lambda, \log Q)$ be the largest size of the statements of L, and $\tilde{D} = \tilde{D}(\lambda, Q)$ be the maximum depth of the NP verifier circuit for $\tilde{L}$, we describe the construction below.

KeyGen$(1^\lambda, Q)$: On input a security parameter λ, a number Q:
1. Generate a pair of signing and verification keys $(vk, sk) \leftarrow$ S.Gen(1^λ).
2. Sample an injective public key of LE : $pk \leftarrow$ LE.KSam(1^λ).
3. Compute the first message $\rho \leftarrow$ ZAP.V$(1^\lambda, 1^n, 1^{\tilde{l}}, 1^{\tilde{D}})$ for ZAP.
4. Set $VK = (vk, pk, \rho)$ and $SK = (sk, vk, pk, \rho)^1$, return (VK, SK).

Sign(SK_ℓ, R, m): Let the ℓ-th signer be the real signer, where $\ell \in [N]$. On input a secret key SK_ℓ, a ring R and a message m, the signer performs as follows:
1. Parse R $= (VK_1, ... VK_N)$.
2. Extract the secret key of the ℓ-th signer $SK_\ell = (sk_\ell, vk_\ell, pk_\ell, \rho_\ell)$.
3. Compute signature $\sigma \leftarrow$ S.Sign$(sk_\ell, H(R)\|m)$.
4. Generate $(hk_1, shk_1) \leftarrow$ SPB.Gen$(|R|, \ell)$, compute $h_1 \leftarrow$ SPB.Hash (hk_1, R).
5. Compute the witness $\tau \leftarrow$ SPB.Open(hk_1, shk_1, R, ℓ) to position ℓ.
6. Generate $(hk_2, shk_2) \leftarrow$ SPB.Gen$(|R|, \ell)$, compute $h_2 \leftarrow$ SPB.Hash (hk_2, R).
7. Sample pairwise-independent hash functions PH_1 and PH_2, compute $r_1 \leftarrow PH_1(H(R)\|m)$, $r_2 \leftarrow PH_2(H(R)\|m)$.
8. Compute ciphertext $c_1 \leftarrow$ LE.Enc$(pk_\ell, (\sigma, vk_\ell); r_1)$
9. Compute ciphertext $c_2 \leftarrow$ LE.Enc$(pk_\ell, 0^{|\sigma|+|vk_\ell|}; r_2)$
10. Let $VK_1 = (vk_1, pk_1, \rho_1)$ be the lexicographically smallest member of R, VK_1 must be unique.
11. Set statements $x_1 = (H(R), m, c_1, c_2, hk_1, hk_2, h_1, h_2)$, $x_2 = $ R, and witness $w = (vk_\ell, pk_\ell, \ell, \tau, \sigma, r_1)$.
12. Sample a pairwise-independent hash function PH_3, and compute $r_\pi \leftarrow PH_3(H(R)\|m)$.
13. Compute proof $\pi \leftarrow$ ZAP.P$(\rho_1, (x_1, x_2), w; r_\pi)$.
14. Output ring signature $\Sigma = (c_1, hk_1, c_2, hk_2, \pi)$.

Verify(Σ, m, R): On input the ring signature Σ on a message m, and a ring R, a verifier performs as follows:
1. Identify the lexicographically smallest verification key $VK_1 = (vk_1, pk_1, \rho_1)$ in R, and extract ρ_1.
2. Compute $h_1' \leftarrow$ SPB.Hash(hk_1, R), $h_2' \leftarrow$ SPB.Hash(hk_2, R).
3. Set $x_1 = (H(R), m, c_1, c_2, hk_1, hk_2, h_1', h_2')$, and $x_2 = $ R.
4. Return ZAP.Verify$(\rho_1, (x_1, x_2), \pi)$.

---

[1] We include verification key (vk, pk, ρ) in SK then Sign procedure can identify which verification key corresponding to the signing key.

We use ρ_1 instead of ρ_ℓ in Sign and Verify since if using ρ_ℓ to generate π then we also need ρ_ℓ to verify it; this means the verifier must know the index ℓ of the real signer in the ring R, which breaks the anonymity of ring signatures. Hence, the signer and the verifier initially agree to use ρ_1 to produce and verify π.

Theorem 2 (Completeness). *Our construction is complete assuming the correctness of* SPB, *the completeness of* LE *and* ZAP *hold.*

Theorem 3 (Efficiency). *Our construction is compact assuming the compactness property of* ZAP *and the efficiency property of* SPB *hold.*

Theorem 2 and Theorem 3 directly follow from properties of SPB, LE, and ZAP.

4.4   ZAP Super-Complement Language

We define $\tilde{L}$, a super-complement of L. Let statement $x_1 = (H(\mathsf{R}), m, c, hk, h)$, and witness $w = (VK_\ell = (vk_\ell, pk_\ell, \rho_\ell), \ell, \tau, \sigma, r_c)$, we define 3 relations as follows:

- $(x_1, w) \in R_1 \Leftrightarrow$ SPB.Verify$(hk, h, \ell, VK_\ell, \tau) = 1$,
- $(x_1, w) \in R_2 \Leftrightarrow$ LE.Enc$(pk_\ell, (\sigma, vk_\ell), r_c) = c$,
- $(x_1, w) \in R_3 \Leftrightarrow$ S.Verify$(vk_\ell, H(\mathsf{R})\|m, \sigma) = 1$.

We define the relation $R_{123} = R_1 \cap R_2 \cap R_3$. Let L_{123} be the language corresponding to R_{123}, we define $L = \{x = (H(\mathsf{R}), m, c_1, c_2, hk_1, hk_2, h_1, h_2)|(H(\mathsf{R}), m, c_1, hk_1, h_1) \in L_{123}) \vee (H(\mathsf{R}), m, c_2, hk_2, h_2) \in L_{123})\}$. Let $x_2 = \mathsf{R}, x = (x_1, x_2)$, and $\tilde{w} = msk$, we define the following relations:

- $(x, \tilde{w}) \in R_4 \Leftrightarrow \forall i \in [N]$:LE.Valid$(pk_i, \mathsf{LE.MSKExt}(msk, pk_i)) = 1) \wedge h = $ SPB.Hash(hk, R).
- $(x, \tilde{w}) \in R_5 \Leftrightarrow \exists VK = (vk, pk, \rho) \in \mathsf{R}$: LE.Valid$(pk, \mathsf{LE.MSKExt}(msk, pk)) = 1 \wedge$ LE.Dec$(\mathsf{LE.MSKExt}(msk, pk), c) = (\sigma, vk) \wedge$ S.Verify$(vk, H(\mathsf{R})\|m, \sigma) = 1$.

Next, we define the relation $R_{45} = R_4 \backslash R_5$, let L_{45} be the corresponding language, and let $\tilde{L} = \{x = (x_1 = (H(\mathsf{R}), m, c_1, c_2, hk_1, hk_2, h_1, h_2), x_2 = \mathsf{R})|(H(\mathsf{R}), m, c_1, hk_1, h_1, \mathsf{R}) \in L_{45} \wedge (H(\mathsf{R}), m, c_2, hk_2, h_2, \mathsf{R}) \in L_{45}\}$.

Lemma 6. *The language $\tilde{L}$ is a super-complement of L assuming the somewhere perfectly binding property of* SPB *and the completeness of the* LE *hold.*

Proof. Based on the definition of super-complement, to prove $\tilde{L}$ is a super-complement of L, we need to prove $x \in \tilde{L} \Rightarrow x_1 \notin L$. Our idea is to prove via a contrapositive such that $x_1 \in L \Rightarrow x \notin \tilde{L}$. Let $x_1' = (H(R), m, c_1, hk_1, h_1)$, $x_1'' = (H(R), m, c_2, hk_2, h_2)$, and $\tilde{w} = msk$. Note that $x \notin \tilde{L} \Rightarrow (x, \tilde{w}) \in R_5$. To prove $x_1 \in L \Rightarrow x \notin \tilde{L}$, for every $w = (VK_i = (vk_i, pk_i, \rho_i), i, \tau, \sigma, r_c)$ and $\tilde{w} = msk$, it suffices to show that $(x_1', w) \in R_{123} \wedge (x_1', \tilde{w}) \in R_4 \Rightarrow (x = (x_1', x_2), \tilde{w}) \in R_5$, and $(x_1'', w) \in R_{123} \wedge (x_1'', \tilde{w}) \in R_4 \Rightarrow (x = (x_1'', x_2), \tilde{w}) \in R_5$. We will only give the proof for the first condition, and the second one can be similarly followed. Since $(x_1', w) \in R_1 \wedge (x_1', \tilde{w}) \in R_4$, we have SPB.Verify$(hk_1, h_1, I, VK_i, \tau) = 1 \wedge h_1 = $ SPB.Hash(hk_1, R). Based on this and the somewhere perfectly binding property of SPB, we can conclude $VK_i \in$ R (1). Since $(x_1', \tilde{w}) \in R_4$, we also have LE.Valid$(pk_i,$ LE.MSKExt$(\tilde{w}, pk_i)) = 1$, which means we can efficiently extract a valid secret key for pk_i using LE.MSKExt. Assuming the completeness of LE holds, we can successfully decrypt the ciphertext c_1 to obtain the signature using the secret key (2). From (1), (2) and $(x_1', w) \in R_2 \cap R_3$, we have $VK_i \in$ R such that LE.Valid$(pk_i,$ LE.MSKExt$(\tilde{w}, pk_i)) = 1$, LE.Dec(LE.MSKExt$(\tilde{w}, pk_i), c_1) = (\sigma, vk_i)$, and S.Verify$(vk_i, H(\mathsf{R})||m, \sigma) = 1$, that implies $(x = (x_1', x_2), \tilde{w}) \in R_5$.

4.5 Security Proof

Theorem 4 (Post-Quantum Anonymity). *Our construction is post-quantum anonymous assuming the index hiding property of* SPB*, the lossiness of lossy public keys property of* LE*, the statistical witness indistinguishability of* ZAP *hold.*

Proof. We prove the post-quantum anonymity via a list of hybrids below.

Hybrid H_0: This is the original quantum anonymity experiment described in Fig. 2 in which the challenger $\mathcal{C}_{\mathsf{RS}}$ uses the signing key $SK_{i_0} = (sk_{i_0}, vk_{i_0}, pk_{i_0}, \rho_{i_0})$. $\mathcal{A}_{\mathsf{RS}}$ wins this game if it guesses $b' = 0$. Note that only one random r is used for the signing process of RS.Sign. Specifically, $\mathcal{C}_{\mathsf{RS}}$ only samples $\mathsf{PH}_1, \mathsf{PH}_2, \mathsf{PH}_3$ once which means for every signing query of superposition of the pair (R, m), these hash functions remain unchanged. This follows the logic that one can compute different random numbers by using a quantum pseudo-random function (used for the signing process) for all values in a superposition of messages, then de-randomize the signing procedure [4].

Hybrid H_1 is similar to H_0, except that $(hk_2, shk_2) \leftarrow$ SPB.Gen$(|\mathsf{R}|, i_1)$, denoted as (hk_2', shk_2'). Based on the index hiding property of the SPB, we have $H_1 \approx_c H_0$.

Hybrid H_2 is similar to H_1, except that $r_2 \leftarrow \mathsf{TRF}_2(H(\mathsf{R})||m)$, where TRF_2 is a truly random function. Based on Lemma 2, we have $H_2 = H_1$.

Hybrid H_3 is similar to H_2, except that $c_2 \leftarrow$ LE.Enc(pk_{i_1}, σ', r_2), denoted as c_2', where $\sigma' \leftarrow$ S.Sign$(sk_{i_1}, H(\mathsf{R}||m))$, note that σ' is a valid signature signed by sk_{i_1}. Let $\mathcal{O}_{sign}^{H_2}$ be the signing oracle of H_2 which outputs $\Sigma = (c_1, hk_1, c_2, hk_2, \pi)$, $\mathcal{O}_{sign}^{H_3}$ be the signing oracle of H_3 which outputs $\Sigma' = (c_1, hk_1, c_2', hk_2, \pi)$, the difference between Σ and Σ' is c_2 and c_2'. Based on the lossiness of lossy public keys property of LE, we have the distribution of c_2 and c_2' is statistically indistinguishable which implies that outputs of $\mathcal{O}_{sign}^{H_2}$ and $\mathcal{O}_{sign}^{H_3}$ is statistically indistinguishable. Let δ be the statistical distance of Σ and Σ', by Lemma 3, $\mathcal{A}_{\mathsf{RS}}$, making at most q queries to $\mathcal{O}_{sign}^{H_2}$ and $\mathcal{O}_{sign}^{H_3}$, can only distinguish these two by probability of $\sqrt{8C_0 q^3 \delta}$ which is negligible because δ is negligible. In other words, we have $H_3 \approx_s H_2$.

Hybrid H_4 is similar to H_3, except that we switch back to compute $r_2 \leftarrow \mathsf{PH}_2(H(\mathsf{R})||m)$. Based on Lemma 2, we have $H_4 = H_3$.

Hybrid H_5 is similar to H_4, except that $r_\pi \leftarrow \mathsf{TRF}_3(H(\mathsf{R})||m)$, where TRF_3 is a truly random function. Based on Lemma 2, we have $H_5 = H_4$.

Hybrid H_6 is similar to H_5, except that we compute $\tau' \leftarrow$ SPB.Open (hk_2', shk_2', R, i_1); then, we use a witness $w' \leftarrow (vk_{i_1}, pk_{i_1}, i_1, \tau', \sigma', r_2)$ to compute $\pi' \leftarrow$ ZAP.P$(\rho_1, (x_1, x_2), w')$. Note that w' is a valid witness of (R, m, c_2', hk_2'). Following argument for H_3, we have $H_6 \approx_s H_5$.

Hybrid H_7 is similar to H_6, except that we switch back to compute $r_\pi \leftarrow$ PH$_3(H(R)||m)$. Based on Lemma 2, we have $H_7 = H_6$.

Hybrid H_8 is similar to H_7, except that $r_1 \leftarrow$ TRF$_1(H(R)||m)$, denoted as r_1'. where TRF$_1$ is a truly random function. Based on Lemma 2, we have $H_8 = H_7$.

Hybrid H_9 is similar to H_8, except that $c_1 \leftarrow$ LE.Enc$(pk_{i_1}, (\sigma', vk_{i_1}), r_1')$. Following the argument for H_3, we have $H_9 \approx_s H_8$.

Hybrid H_{10} is similar to H_9, except that we switch back to compute $r_1 \leftarrow$ PH$_1(H(R)||m)$. Based on Lemma 2, we have $H_{10} = H_9$.

Hybrid H_{11} is similar to H_{10}, except that $(hk_1, shk_1) \leftarrow$ SPB.Gen$(|R|, i_1)$, denoted as (hk_1', shk_1'). Based on the index hiding property of the SPB, we have $H_{11} \approx_c H_{10}$.

Hybrid H_{12} is similar to H_{11}, except that $r_\pi \leftarrow$ TRF$_3(H(R)||m)$. where TRF$_3$ is a truly random function. Based on Lemma 2, we have $H_{12} = H_{11}$.

Hybrid H_{13} is similar to H_{12}, except that we set $w'' = (vk_{i_1}, pk_{i_1}, i_1, \tau'', \sigma', r_1)$, where $\tau'' =$ SPB.Open(hk_1', shk_1', R, i_1). Following the argument for H_6, we have $H_{13} \approx_s H_{12}$.

Hybrid H_{14} is similar to H_{13}, except that we switch back to compute $r_\pi \leftarrow$ PH$_3(H(R)||m)$. Based on Lemma 2, we have $H_{14} = H_{13}$.

Hybrid H_{15} is similar to H_{14}, except that $r_2 \leftarrow$ TRF$_2(H(R)||m)$. Based on Lemma 2, we have $H_{15} = H_{14}$.

Hybrid H_{16} is similar to H_{15}, except that $c_2 \leftarrow$ LE.Enc$(pk_{i_1}, 0^{|\sigma|+|vk_{i_1}|}, r_2)$. Following argument for H_3, we have $H_{16} \approx_s H_{15}$.

Hybrid H_{17} is similar to H_{16}, except that we switch back to compute $r_2 \leftarrow$ PH$_2(H(R)||m)$. Based on Lemma 2, we have $H_{17} = H_{16}$. This completes the proof. □

Theorem 5 (Post-Quantum Blind-Unforgeability). *Our construction is post-quantum blind-unforgeable assuming the completeness of master secret keys and almost-unique secret key properties of* LE, *the selective non-witness adaptive-statement soundness of* ZAP, *and the blind-unforgeability of* S *hold, and* H *is* ε_{col} *collision resistant.*

Proof. We prove the PQBU of our scheme via a sequence of hybrids as follows:

Hybrid H_0: This is the original PQBU experiment in 3 where all encryption keys pk_i are generated as $pk_i \leftarrow$ LE.KSam$(1^\lambda, r_i)$; $\mathcal{C}_{RS}$ sends $\{pk_i, r_i\}$ to $\mathcal{A}_{RS}$.

Hybrid H_1 is similar to H_0, but $\mathcal{C}_{RS}$ computes $(pk_i, msk) \leftarrow$ LE.MSKGen$(1^\lambda, N)$. $\mathcal{C}_{RS}$ stores msk and send list of public keys $\{pk_i,$ LE.RndExt$(pk_i)\}$ to $\mathcal{A}_{RS}$. Based on the indistinguishability property of the LE, we have $H_1 \approx_s H_0$.

Suppose that $\mathcal{A}_{RS}$ successfully outputs a forgery $\Sigma^* = (c_1^*, hk_1^*, c_2^*, hk_2^*, \pi^*)$ on (R^*, m^*), that means $(R^*, m^*) \in B_\varepsilon^{RS}$. Let $x^* = (x_1^* = (H(R^*), m^*, c_1^*, c_2^*, hk_1^*, hk_2^*, h_1^*, h_2^*), x_2^* = R^*)$, we will argue to show that

$$\Pr\left[x^* \in \tilde{L} \wedge \text{ZAP.Verify}(\rho_1^*, x^*, \pi^*) = 1\right] = \text{negl}(\lambda), \tag{1}$$

in which the condition for ZAP.Verify follows since the forgery is valid, and

$$\Pr\left[x^* \notin \tilde{L}\right] = \mathsf{negl}(\lambda). \tag{2}$$

If both of the above equations hold, we conclude that $\mathcal{A}_{\mathsf{RS}}$ can only produce a valid forgery with a negligible probability. Firstly, to argue Equation 1, for every user $i \in [N]$ in ring R, it suffices to prove

$$\Pr\left[x^* \in \tilde{L} \wedge \mathsf{ZAP.Verify}(\rho_i^*, x^*, \pi^*) = 1\right] = \mathsf{negl}(\lambda).$$

Because $x^* \in \tilde{L}$ means there exists a non-witness $\tilde{w}^*$ such that $(x^*, \tilde{w}^*) \in \tilde{R}$. However, based on the selective non-witness adaptive-statement soundness property of the ZAP, the case only happens with negligible probability. Our idea is to construct an adversary $\mathcal{A}_{\mathsf{ZAP}}$ from $\mathcal{A}_{\mathsf{RS}}$ to break the soundness with an overwhelming probability if $\mathcal{A}_{\mathsf{RS}}$ can successfully forge a valid forgery. $\mathcal{A}_{\mathsf{ZAP}}$ performs similarly to the challenger $\mathcal{C}_{\mathsf{RS}}$ in H_1 except that in the Phase Setup it randomly chooses a index $j \in [N]$ and sets $\rho^* = \rho_j^*$. Assume that $\mathcal{A}_{\mathsf{RS}}$ successfully forges a valid forgery (R^*, m^*, Σ^*), and sends it to $\mathcal{A}_{\mathsf{ZAP}}$. Using the forgery, $\mathcal{A}_{\mathsf{ZAP}}$ sets $x^* \leftarrow (x_1^*, x_2^*)$ and outputs (x^*, π^*). We can see that $\mathcal{A}_{\mathsf{ZAP}}$ can use the tuple (ρ^*, x^*, π^*) to break the soundness property of ZAP with a non-negligible probability which causes a contradiction. Then, Equation 1 must hold. Next, we prove Eq. 2. Suppose the adversary $\mathcal{A}_{\mathsf{RS}}$ wins the BU game, our idea is that we construct an adversary $\mathcal{A}_{\mathsf{S}}$ to break the BU game of the underlying signature Sig with an overwhelming probability. To do that, we reduce H_1 to the BU game of the underlying signature Sig as described below.

Phase Setup: $\mathcal{A}_{\mathsf{RS}}$ randomly picks a constant $0 \leq \varepsilon \leq 1$ and sends ε to the adversary $\mathcal{A}_{\mathsf{S}}$ who is in a role of the challenger $\mathcal{C}_{\mathsf{RS}}$. $\mathcal{A}_{\mathsf{S}}$ then computes ε' and forwards ε' to the challenger $\mathcal{C}_{\mathsf{S}}$ (we will discuss how $\mathcal{A}_{\mathsf{S}}$ computes ε' later). $\mathcal{A}_{\mathsf{S}}$ and $\mathcal{C}_{\mathsf{S}}$ defines two set $\mathsf{B}_\varepsilon^{\mathsf{RS}}$ and $\mathsf{B}_{\varepsilon'}^{\mathsf{S}}$ as in the BU game. $\mathcal{C}_{\mathsf{S}}$ generates a key pair $(\widehat{VK}, \widehat{SK}) \leftarrow \mathsf{Sig.Gen}(1^\lambda)$ and sends $\widehat{VK}$ to $\mathcal{A}_{\mathsf{S}}$. $\mathcal{A}_{\mathsf{S}}$ generates $(\{VK_i\}_{i=1}^N, \mathsf{msk}) \leftarrow \mathsf{LE.MSKGen}(1^\lambda, \mathsf{N})$, and randomly picks an index j and sets $(VK_j = \widehat{VK})$, and sends $\{VK_i\}_{i=1}^n$ to $\mathcal{A}_{\mathsf{RS}}$. $\mathcal{A}_{\mathsf{S}}$ also initiates $\mathsf{Corrupted} = \emptyset$. Phase Query: Corrupted Queries: $\mathcal{A}_{\mathsf{RS}}$ sends i to $\mathcal{A}_{\mathsf{S}}$, it computes $SK_i = \mathsf{LE.MSKExt}(\mathsf{msk}, VK_i)$ and responds with the corresponding secret key SK_i and sets $\mathsf{Corrupted} \leftarrow \mathsf{Corrupted} \cup \{i\}$ if $i \neq j$; otherwise, it aborts. Signing Queries: $\mathcal{A}_{\mathsf{RS}}$ sends $(\mathsf{sign}, i, \sum \psi_{\mathsf{R}, m, t} | \mathsf{R}, m, t)$ to $\mathcal{A}_{\mathsf{S}}$, $\mathcal{A}_{\mathsf{S}}$ performs:

- If $i \neq j$, $\mathcal{A}_{\mathsf{S}}$ computes $SK_i = \mathsf{LE.MSKExt}(\mathsf{msk}, VK_i)$, and using SK_i to produce the valid signatures in superposition $(\sum \psi_{\mathsf{R}, m, t} | \mathsf{R}, m, t \oplus \mathsf{B}_\varepsilon^{\mathsf{RS}} f(\mathsf{R}, m))$. $\mathcal{A}_{\mathsf{S}}$ responds with the signature.
- If $i = j$, $\mathcal{A}_{\mathsf{S}}$ asks $\mathcal{C}_{\mathsf{RS}}$ for a valid signature because it does not have the secret key SK_j. After receiving the valid signature, $\mathcal{A}_{\mathsf{S}}$ sends to $\mathcal{A}_{\mathsf{RS}}$.

Phase Forge: $\mathcal{A}_{\mathsf{RS}}$ outputs a valid forgery (σ^*, m^*, R^*) and sends to $\mathcal{A}_{\mathsf{S}}$. $\mathcal{A}_{\mathsf{S}}$ parses σ^* to get c_1^*, and decrypts c_1^* using $sk_j \leftarrow \mathsf{LE.MSKExt}(msk, pk_j)$ to recover σ_1^*.

$\mathcal{A}_S$ checks if S.Verify$(vk_j, H(\mathsf{R}^*)\|m^*, \sigma_1^*) = 1$, it sets $\sigma^* = \sigma_1^*$ and follows steps in RS.Sign to produce a valid signature Σ^*; otherwise it retries with c_2^*. $\mathcal{A}_S$ outputs $(\sigma^*, H(\mathsf{R}^*)\|m^*)$. Now, we will discuss how $\mathcal{A}_S$ compute the constant ε'. To ensure the reduction is correct, the following relations must hold:

$$\begin{cases} (\mathsf{R}, m) \in \mathsf{B}_\varepsilon^{\mathsf{RS}} \Rightarrow (H(\mathsf{R})\|m) \in \mathsf{B}_{\varepsilon'}^{\mathsf{S}}, \\ (\mathsf{R}, m) \notin \mathsf{B}_\varepsilon^{\mathsf{RS}} \Rightarrow (H(\mathsf{R})\|m) \notin \mathsf{B}_{\varepsilon'}^{\mathsf{S}}. \end{cases} \tag{3}$$

While the first equation is required in the Query phase to ensure $\mathcal{C}_{\mathsf{RS}}$ can correctly answer signing queries from $\mathcal{A}_{\mathsf{RS}}$, the second one is used to confirm that a forged signature of $\mathcal{A}_{\mathsf{RS}}$ is a valid forgery of $\mathcal{A}_S$. We define the reduction as follows:

– After defining the set $\mathsf{B}_\varepsilon^{\mathsf{RS}}$, with each pair (R, m), the challenger $\mathcal{C}_{\mathsf{RS}}$ computes a pair $(H(\mathsf{R}), m)$, and add $(H(\mathsf{R}), m)$ to the set B^{HRS}. We set two cases:
  • If $(\mathsf{R}, m) \in \mathsf{B}_\varepsilon^{\mathsf{RS}} \Rightarrow (H(\mathsf{R}), m)) \in B^{\mathsf{HRS}}$, this case is trivial.
  • If $(\mathsf{R}, m) \notin \mathsf{B}_\varepsilon^{\mathsf{RS}}$, we have either $(H(\mathsf{R}), m)) \in B^{\mathsf{HRS}}$, which happens with a negligible probability $\varepsilon_{\mathsf{col}}$ because H is collision resistant; or $(H(\mathsf{R}), m)) \notin B^{\mathsf{HRS}}$.

Therefore, we have:

$$\begin{cases} (\mathsf{R}, m) \in \mathsf{B}_\varepsilon^{\mathsf{RS}} \Rightarrow (H(\mathsf{R}), m) \in B^{\mathsf{HRS}}, \\ (\mathsf{R}, m) \notin \mathsf{B}_\varepsilon^{\mathsf{RS}} \Rightarrow (H(\mathsf{R}), m) \notin B^{\mathsf{HRS}}. \end{cases} \tag{4}$$

– From the set of $H(\mathsf{R})$ in B^{HRS}, $\mathcal{C}_{\mathsf{RS}}$ calculates a probability $\varepsilon' := \varepsilon - \varepsilon_{\mathsf{col}}$, and send ε' to $\mathcal{C}_S$. Note that this modification does not affect the view of $\mathcal{A}_{\mathsf{RS}}$ since the difference between ε and ε' is only $\varepsilon_{\mathsf{col}}$ which is negligible.
– After receiving ε', $\mathcal{C}_S$ forms the set $\mathsf{B}_{\varepsilon'}^{\mathsf{S}}$ by getting every pair $(H(\mathsf{R}), m)$ with probability ε', then concatenating them to $(H(\mathsf{R})\|m)$, and putting them in the set $\mathsf{B}_{\varepsilon'}^{\mathsf{S}}$. $\mathsf{B}_{\varepsilon'}^{\mathsf{S}}$ is identical to B^{HRS} since both of them are generated by putting each pair $(H(\mathsf{R}), m)$ in with the same probability ε'. We have:

$$\begin{cases} (\mathsf{R}, m) \in B^{\mathsf{HRS}} \Rightarrow (H(\mathsf{R})\|m) \in \mathsf{B}_{\varepsilon'}^{\mathsf{S}}, \\ (\mathsf{R}, m) \notin B^{\mathsf{HRS}} \Rightarrow (H(\mathsf{R})\|m) \notin \mathsf{B}_{\varepsilon'}^{\mathsf{S}}. \end{cases} \tag{5}$$

From Eqs. 4 and Eq. 5, we can conclude Eq. 3. Next, we need to prove that S.Verify$(\widehat{VK}, H(\mathsf{R}^*)\|m^*, \sigma^*) = 1$ happens with a non-negligible probability. We are assuming that $x^* \notin \tilde{L}$ which means either $(H(\mathsf{R}^*), m^*, c_1^*, hk_1^*, h_1^*, \mathsf{R}^*) \notin L_{45}$ or $(H(\mathsf{R}^*), m^*, c_2^*, hk_2^*, h_2^*, \mathsf{R}^*) \notin L_{45}$, or both happen. Without loss of generality, we assume $(H(\mathsf{R}^*), m^*, c_1^*, hk_1^*, h_1^*, \mathsf{R}^*) \notin L_{45}$. Note that in the reduction, public keys and the master secret key are generated using LE.MSKGen, and also $\mathsf{R}^* \subseteq \mathsf{R}$, we have $(x^*, msk) \in R_4$. Because $(x^*, msk) \in R_4$ and $x \notin L_{45}$, we can imply that there exists a string $\tilde{w}^*$ such that $(x^*, \tilde{w}^*) \in R_5$, that means there exist a $VK^* = (vk^*, pk^*, \rho^*)$ such that

$$\begin{cases} \mathsf{LE.Valid}(pk^*, \mathsf{LE.MSKExt}(\tilde{w}^*, pk^*)) = 1 \\ \mathsf{LE.Dec}(\mathsf{LE.MSKExt}(\tilde{w}^*, pk^*), c_1^*) = (\sigma^*, vk^*) \\ \mathsf{S.Verify}(vk^*, H(\mathsf{R}^*)\|m^*, \sigma^*) = 1. \end{cases} \tag{6}$$

Based on the almost-unique secret key property of LE, we have LE.MSKExt($\tilde{w}^*$, pk^*) = LE.MSKExt(msk, pk^*). Based on Eq. 6, we can see that c_1^* is a valid encryption of the message $H(R^*||m)$, and $(H(R^*||m), \sigma^*)$ is a valid forgery for the Sig using VK^*. Since $\mathcal{A}_S$ randomly picks an index j in the ring of N users, the probability that $VK^* = VK_j = \hat{VK}$ is $1/N$, we have $\text{Adv}_{BU}^{\lambda,N}(\mathcal{A}_S) \geq \frac{1}{N}\left(\Pr\left[x^* \notin \tilde{L}\right] - \text{negl}(\lambda)\right)$. As we assume the underlying S is blind-unforgeable, then $\text{Adv}_{BU}^{\lambda,N}(\mathcal{A}_S)$ is negligible, which implies $\Pr[x^* \notin \tilde{L}]$ is also negligible. This completes the proof.   □

Acknowledgement. We are grateful to the Inscrypt 2023 anonymous reviewers for their helpful comments. This work is partially supported by the Australian Research Council Linkage Project LP190100984. Dung Hoang Duong is partially supported by AEGiS 2023 grant from the University of Wollongong.

References

1. Alagic, G., Majenz, C., Russell, A., Song, F.: Quantum-Access-Secure Message Authentication via Blind-Unforgeability. In: Canteaut, A., Ishai, Y. (eds.) EURO-CRYPT 2020. LNCS, vol. 12107, pp. 788–817. Springer, Cham (2020). https://doi.org/10.1007/978-3-030-45727-3_27
2. Backes, M., Döttling, N., Hanzlik, L., Kluczniak, K., Schneider, J.: Ring signatures: Logarithmic-size, no setup–from standard assumptions. In: Ishai, Y., Rijmen, V. (eds.) Advances in Cryptology - EUROCRYPT 2019. pp, pp. 281–311. Springer International Publishing, Cham (2019)
3. Boneh, D., et al.: Random oracles in a quantum world. In: Lee, D.H., Wang, X. (eds.) ASIACRYPT 2011. LNCS, vol. 7073, pp. 41–69. Springer, Heidelberg (2011). https://doi.org/10.1007/978-3-642-25385-0_3
4. Boneh, D., Zhandry, M.: Secure signatures and chosen ciphertext security in a quantum computing world. In: Canetti, R., Garay, J.A. (eds.) CRYPTO 2013. LNCS, vol. 8043, pp. 361–379. Springer, Heidelberg (2013). https://doi.org/10.1007/978-3-642-40084-1_21
5. Cash, D., Hofheinz, D., Kiltz, E., Peikert, C.: Bonsai trees, or how to delegate a lattice basis. In: Gilbert, H. (ed.) EUROCRYPT 2010. LNCS, vol. 6110, pp. 523–552. Springer, Heidelberg (2010). https://doi.org/10.1007/978-3-642-13190-5_27
6. Chatterjee, R., Chung, K.M., Liang, X., Malavolta, G.: A note on the post-quantum security of (ring) signatures. In: Hanaoka, G., Shikata, J., Watanabe, Y. (eds.) Public-Key Cryptography - PKC 2022. pp, pp. 407–436. Springer International Publishing, Cham (2022)
7. Chatterjee, R., et al.: Compact ring signatures from learning with errors. In: Malkin, T., Peikert, C. (eds.) Advances in Cryptology - CRYPTO 2021. pp, pp. 282–312. Springer International Publishing, Cham (2021)
8. Barapatre, P., Pandu Rangan, C.: Anonymous identity-based identification scheme in Ad-Hoc groups without pairings. In: Gierlichs, B., Guilley, S., Mukhopadhyay, D. (eds.) SPACE 2013. LNCS, vol. 8204, pp. 130–146. Springer, Heidelberg (2013). https://doi.org/10.1007/978-3-642-41224-0_10

9. Don, J., Fehr, S., Majenz, C.: The measure-and-reprogram technique 2.0: multi-round fiat-shamir and more. In: Micciancio, D., Ristenpart, T. (eds.) CRYPTO 2020. LNCS, vol. 12172, pp. 602–631. Springer, Cham (2020). https://doi.org/10.1007/978-3-030-56877-1_21

10. Garg, S., Yuen, H., Zhandry, M.: New security notions and feasibility results for authentication of quantum data. In: Katz, J., Shacham, H. (eds.) Advances in Cryptology - CRYPTO 2017, pp. 342–371. Springer International Publishing, Cham (2017)

11. Don, J., Fehr, S., Majenz, C.: The Measure-and-Reprogram Technique 2.0: Multi-round Fiat-Shamir and More. In: Micciancio, D., Ristenpart, T. (eds.) CRYPTO 2020. LNCS, vol. 12172, pp. 602–631. Springer, Cham (2020). https://doi.org/10.1007/978-3-030-56877-1_21

12. Groth, J., Kohlweiss, M.: One-Out-of-Many Proofs: Or how to leak a secret and spend a coin. In: Oswald, E., Fischlin, M. (eds.) EUROCRYPT 2015. LNCS, vol. 9057, pp. 253–280. Springer, Heidelberg (2015). https://doi.org/10.1007/978-3-662-46803-6_9

13. Katz, J.:Digital signatures: Background and definitions. In Digital Signatures, pp. 3–33. Springer, 2010

14. Krawczyk, H. and Rabin, T.: Chameleon hashing and signatures. 1998

15. Liu, Q., Zhandry, M.: Revisiting post-quantum fiat-shamir. In: Boldyreva, A., Micciancio, D. (eds.) Advances in Cryptology - CRYPTO 2019. pp, pp. 326–355. Springer International Publishing, Cham (2019)

16. Nguyen, T.N., et al.: Efficient unique ring signatures from lattices. In: Atluri, V., Di Pietro, R., Jensen, C.D., Meng, W. (eds.) Computer Security - ESORICS 2022. pp, pp. 447–466. Springer Nature Switzerland, Cham (2022)

17. Rivest, R.L., Shamir, A., Tauman, Y.: How to leak a secret. In: Boyd, C. (ed.) ASIACRYPT 2001. LNCS, vol. 2248, pp. 552–565. Springer, Heidelberg (2001). https://doi.org/10.1007/3-540-45682-1_32

18. Ta, A.T., et al.: Efficient unique ring signature for blockchain privacy protection. In: Baek, J., Ruj, S. (eds.) Information Security and Privacy, pp. 391–407. Springer, Cham (2021)

19. Yuen, T.H., Esgin, M.F., Liu, J.K., Au, M.H., Ding, Z.: Dualring: generic construction of ring signatures with efficient instantiations. In: Malkin, T., Peikert, C. (eds.) Advances in Cryptology - CRYPTO 2021, pp. 251–281. Springer International Publishing, Cham (2021)

20. Zhandry, M.: How to construct quantum random functions. In: 2012 IEEE 53rd Annual Symposium on Foundations of Computer Science, pp. 679–687, 2012

21. Zhandry, M.: Secure identity-based encryption in the quantum random oracle model. In: Safavi-Naini, R., Canetti, R. (eds.) CRYPTO 2012. LNCS, vol. 7417, pp. 758–775. Springer, Heidelberg (2012). https://doi.org/10.1007/978-3-642-32009-5_44

Secure Multi-party SM2 Signature Based on SPDZ Protocol

Xiaotong Li[1], Hao Wang[1(✉)], Jiyang Chen[2], Shikuan Li[2], Yuxiang Sun[3], and Ye Su[1(✉)]

[1] School of Information Science and Engineering, Shandong Normal University, Jinan 250358, China
wanghao@sdnu.edu.cn, suye@sdnu.edu.cn
[2] Shandong Zhengzhong Information Technology Co., Ltd., Jinan 250101, China
chenjy@sdas.org lishik@sdas.org
[3] Qilu Bank Co., Ltd., Jinan 250014, China

Abstract. Nowadays, the demand for signing and verifying data in various fields is getting higher and higher, and digital signature schemes need to be adapted to two-party or even multi-party and multi-device scenarios. To meet the needs of multi-party signature scenarios, we propose a multi-party SM2 signature scheme based on SPDZ protocol. The basic signature scheme used in this paper is the SM2 digital signature algorithm in the standard "SM2 Elliptic Curve Public Key Cryptography" of ISO/IEC14888-3, which has the advantages of high security and reliability as well as efficient signature speeds. Our scheme allows multiple participants to jointly sign a message while resisting up to $n-1$ malicious corrupted parties in dishonest-majority settings. Compared to existing schemes against malicious adversaries, our scheme discards costly zero-knowledge proofs in favor of low-overhead MACs, which reduces the computational and communication complexity of multi-party signatures. We analyze the security and performance evaluation of the scheme, and the results show that the scheme has high efficiency while ensuring security.

Keywords: multi-party signature · multi-party computation · dishonest majority · SPDZ protocol

1 Introduction

With the rapid development of the Internet and communication systems as well as the increasing demand for signing and verifying data in various fields, digital signature technology has emerged. On the one hand, various contracts and agreements of electronic payment and online lending businesses in the financial field, electronic medical records and medical documents of medical insurance application businesses in the medical field, and various documents and data in governmental organizations, internal enterprises, and e-commerce all need to be signed and verified using multi-signature. On the other hand, with the proliferation of mobile devices such as smartphones, tablets, and smartwatches, as well as the development of the Internet of Things (IoT), the need to utilize multiple devices for collaborative signatures has emerged.

Researchers have worked on signature schemes that satisfy the above application scenarios. Two solution ideas, two-party co-signature schemes and threshold signature schemes based on Shamir's secret sharing, have been proposed. A two-party signature scheme is a co-signature scheme that involves only two entities: a mobile terminal and a secure trusted server. Representative ones are two-party ECDSA signature schemes [15,20] and two-party signature protocols based on the SM2 algorithm [17,27]. Obviously, two-party signature schemes are not flexible enough and have limited application scenarios. Threshold signature scheme [7] is to divide the private key into n slices, held by n participants, which are valid only when there are more than a threshold $t(t < n)$ number of participants collaborate to sign the key. However, such threshold signature schemes [16,18,23] generally require a trusted center and multiple encryption and decryption operations, as well as multiple multiplication and exponentiation operations, resulting in higher computational complexity and more computational resources.

In addition, in a multi-party signature scenario, the participants may not be honest; they may be semi-honest or even malicious. In order to resist malicious signature parties, researchers have used zero-knowledge proofs in the signing process, but this raises computational complexity and may reduce efficiency and usability.

Therefore, we need to design an efficient multi-party signature scheme that breaks the above limitations, can be flexibly applied to multiple signature scenarios, and has the security of resisting malicious signature parties. SM2, as the international standard ISO/IEC14888-3, has the advantages of high security, high reliability, high signature efficiency, etc., so we choose it as the basic signature algorithm.

In this paper, we combine a signature algorithm with secure multi-party computation to design a SPDZ-based multi-party SM2 signature scheme. The scheme can combine the above advantages and resist up to n-1 malicious corrupted parties in a dishonest majority setting. Our scheme can be applied to the scenario of jointly signing by multiple signature parties and co-signing between different devices. The specific contributions of this paper are as follows:

- We propose a multi-party signature scheme based on SPDZ protocol [5,6] that is resistant to malicious signature participants.
- We divide the scheme into two phases: an offline phase and a signing phase. We make the signing process efficient by using a semi-honest cloud server in the offline phase to prepare data for the signing phase.

The rest of the paper is organized as follows. Section 2 provides related works on signature schemes in multi-party settings. Section 3 introduces relevant background materials for this paper. Section 4 describes the system model, security model, communication model, and functionalities. Section 5 presents our proposed multi-party SM2 signature scheme in detail. Section 6 analyzes the security of our scheme. Section 7 analyzes the efficiency of our scheme. Finally, Sect. 8 concludes the paper and discusses future directions for research.

2 Related Work

In 1979, Shamir [22] proposed the theory of threshold secret sharing, which set off a flurry of research on threshold signature schemes, e.g. [9,11,12,24,25]. Gennaro et al. [12] formally defined interactive threshold signature, but their proposed scheme requires a large number of interactions. In 2016, Gennaro et al. [11] optimized the threshold signature scheme using the Paillier homomorphic encryption algorithm, and he improved his scheme again [9] in 2018. Lindell et al. [21] improved the efficiency of the ECDSA threshold signature scheme using an additive homomorphic encryption scheme. In 2020, Canetti et al. [8] and Gennaro et al. [10] constructed non-interactive threshold optimal schemes using homomorphic encryption and zero-knowledge proofs, respectively, but the efficiency was dragged down by the two primitives described above.

In 2010, SM2 was proposed and attracted many researchers to study it. Shang et al. [23] proposed an SM2 threshold signature scheme that resists $n/2$ eavesdropping attacks and $n/3$ suspension attacks. However, the inverse and multiplication sharing in its construction leads to the exponential expansion problem. Yang et al. [18] proposed an SM2 threshold signature scheme that eliminates the need for a trusted third party. However, the scheme still utilizes multiplication sharing. Zhang et al. [27] proposed an SM2 two-party signature scheme that is achieved through a single round of communication, but its use of the Paillier homomorphic encryption algorithm leads to inefficiency. Hou et al. [17] used zero-knowledge proof, homomorphic encryption, and bit commitment to construct a secure SM2 two-party signature scheme, whose efficiency is unsatisfactory due to the homomorphic encryption. Feng et al. [7] deformed the structure of SM2 and constructed a lightweight SM2 two-party signature scheme using zero-knowledge proof, whose efficiency is greatly improved. Su et al. [26] proposed a provably secure collaborative signature scheme. Han et al. [14] constructed an efficient two-party SM2 signature scheme using secret sharing.

3 Preliminaries

3.1 Secure Multi-party Computation

Secure Multi-Party Computation(MPC) [4] enables multiple data participants to execute a function jointly, where the participants do not know each other's inputs, and in the end, all participants can only get the result of the function execution without getting any intermediate outputs. The original inputs of all participants will not be leaked.

MPC can be abstracted into the following mathematical model. Let $\mathcal{P} = \mathcal{P}_1, \mathcal{P}_2, ..., \mathcal{P}_n$ be a set of n participants who want to cooperate in accomplishing secure computation on a given function $f(x_1, x_2, ..., x_n) = (y_1, y_2, ..., y_3)$ where the n inputs of the function $f(x_1, x_2, ..., x_n)$ are held privately by n participants $\mathcal{P}_1, \mathcal{P}_2, ..., \mathcal{P}_n$ without being known by others, and at the end of the computation $\mathcal{P}_1, \mathcal{P}_2, ..., \mathcal{P}_n$ get $(y_1, y_2, ..., y_3)$ respectively. During the computation process, the participant $\mathcal{P}_i(i = 1, 2, ..., n)$ can only get the output y_i according to his own input x_i, without getting any additional information about the other participants.

3.2   The SPDZ Protocol

The SPDZ protocol [5,6] is a general multiparty computation protocol utilizing an additive secret-sharing scheme to achieve secure computation and information-theoretic MACs to enable against malicious behaviors by dishonest participants. In addition, the SPDZ protocol is a two-phase protocol consisting of an input-independent preprocessing phase and an input-dependent online phase. In the preprocessing phase, participants generate "raw material" used in the online phase by performing computationally expensive asymmetric-key operations. In the online phase, participants only need to perform lightweight operations to achieve secure computation and gain high efficiency. The main idea behind the SPDZ protocol is that participants use a global key α to generate a MAC $\alpha \cdot a$ for each secret value a, and they secret-share both value a and MAC $\alpha \cdot a$ additively. The MACs protect secret values from being manipulated by an active adversary.

We now summarize the core operations for computation in SPDZ protocol.

- **Share representation:** $\langle a \rangle = ((a_1, ..., a_n), (\gamma(a)_1, ..., \gamma(a)_n))$, where $a = a_1 + \cdots + a_n$ is the secret value, $\gamma(a) = \gamma(a)_1 + \cdots + \gamma(a)_n$ is the MAC corresponding to a.
- **Input:** $\langle x \rangle \leftarrow \mathsf{Input}(x, \mathcal{P}_i)$, where $x \in \mathbb{F}_p$. Secret shares a private input x from party $\mathcal{P}_i$ and generates a MAC for x.
- **Linear operations:** $\langle x \rangle + \langle y \rangle = (x + y, \gamma(x) + \gamma(y))$;
  $e \cdot \langle a \rangle = (e \cdot a, e \cdot \gamma(a)) = \langle e \cdot a \rangle$;
  $e + \langle x \rangle = ((x_1 + e, x_2, ..., x_n), (\gamma(x)_1 + e \cdot \alpha_1, \gamma(x)_2 + e \cdot \alpha_2, ..., \gamma(x)_n + e \cdot \alpha_n))$.
  Linear operations or addition by a constant can be performed locally.
- **Secure multiplication:** Secure multiplication is implemented using beaver's triple [1]. To multiply $\langle x \rangle$ and $\langle y \rangle$, participants need to take a multiplication triple $(\langle a \rangle, \langle b \rangle, \langle c \rangle)$ generated in preprocessing phase and compute $\langle \epsilon \rangle \leftarrow \langle x \rangle - \langle a \rangle$, $\langle \delta \rangle \leftarrow \langle y \rangle - \langle b \rangle$ and open the results to get ϵ, δ. Then, the multiplication can be computed as $\langle x \rangle \cdot \langle y \rangle = \langle c \rangle + \epsilon \cdot \langle b \rangle + \delta \cdot \langle a \rangle + \epsilon \cdot \delta = \langle x \cdot y \rangle$.
- **Partially open:** Partially open means that participants only open the value without opening the MAC.

3.3   SM2 Signature Algorithm

SM2 is a set of elliptic curve cryptographic algorithms promulgated by the National Cryptography Administration of China as the standard algorithm for commercial public key cryptography in China. The SM2 digital signature scheme is defined as follows:

E is an elliptic curve over a finite field $\mathbb{F}_p$, G is a base point on the elliptic curve E (where G has a large order N). $H : \{0,1\}^* \to \mathbb{Z}_N$ is a hash function that outputs an integer, and $H_{256} : \{0,1\}^* \to \{0,1\}^{256}$ is a hash function that outputs a 256-bit string. $d \leftarrow_R \mathbb{Z}_N$ is the private key of the SM2 signature scheme. $P_A = d \cdot G$ is the corresponding public key.

The process of signing message M by SM2 elliptic curve digital signature algorithm is described as follows.

Signature Algorithm.

(1) Compute $Z = H_{256}(ENTL \parallel ID \parallel a \parallel b \parallel x_G \parallel y_G \parallel x_A \parallel y_A)$, where $ENTL$ is two bytes converted from the length information of the user's identification ID, a and b are elliptic curve parameters, (x_G, y_G) is the coordinate of the base point G, x_A, y_A are coordinates of the public key P_A.
(2) Compute $e = H(Z \parallel M)$.
(3) Choose a random number $k \leftarrow_R \mathbb{Z}_N$.
(4) Compute $(x_1, y_1) = k \cdot G$.
(5) Compute $r = (e + x_1) \bmod N$, if $r = 0$ or $r + k = N$, then return step (3).
(6) Compute $s = ((1 + d)^{-1} \cdot (k - r \cdot d)) \bmod N$, if $s = 0$,then return step (3).
(7) The signature result is (r, s).

When the verifier receives the message M' and signature (r', s'), the verification process of the SM2 signature algorithm is described as follows.

Signature Verification.

(1) Respectively check whether $r', s' \in [1, N-1]$ is established, if not, the verification fails.
(2) Compute $e' = H(Z \parallel M')$.
(3) Compute $(x_1', y_1') = s' \cdot G + (r' + s') \cdot P_A$.
(4) Check whether $(e' + x_1') \bmod N = r'$ established, if the verification passes, the signature is valid, else the signature is invalid.

In our construction, we use a deformed SM2 public key $P_A = (d^{-1} - 1) \cdot G$ and the signature becomes $s = d \cdot (k + r) - r \bmod N$ accordingly [7].

3.4   Secret Sharing

Secret sharing is a cryptographic technique. Its basic idea is to partition the secret message s into n parts and distribute these parts to n different participants to protect the security of the secret message. And as long as one share is not leaked, no information about the secret message s will be revealed even if all the other $n - 1$ shares are leaked. The secret message s can be reconstructed only when all the participants come together.

3.5   Message Authentication Code

Message Authentication Code (MAC) is a technique used to ensure the integrity of a message, which is based on the computation of a message application key to generate a fixed-length authentication tag. In the SPDZ protocol, the MAC is obtained by multiplying the global key with the message, and it is not possible to lie about the MAC values unless the malicious participants know the global key used to generate the MAC.

3.6   Notation

For the convenience of reading, we summarize the notations used in this paper in Table 1.

Table 1. Notations

Notation	Meaning
$\mathbb{F}_p$	Prime field, where p is a large prime number
$\mathcal{P}_i$	The signature party
$\mathcal{CS}$	The cloud server
$\langle \cdot \rangle$	The additive secret share with MAC
$\gamma(\cdot)$	The MAC value
α	The global key
d	The signature private key
pk	The signature public key
H	The hash function

4   Models and Functionalities

In this section, we formalize our system model and threat model and identify our design goals.

4.1   System Model

In the multi-party SM2 signature scheme of this paper, two types of entities are involved, which are n signature parties $\mathcal{P}$, and 1 cloud server $\mathcal{CS}$. As shown in Fig. 1.

- Cloud server: The cloud server $\mathcal{CS}$ is an honest but curious entity that generates "raw materials" needed for the signing phase during the preprocessing phase and sends the generated data to the signature parties.

– Signature parties: Signature parties are a group of entities that intend to sign a message jointly. They distrust each other, and even up to n-1 of them can be corrupted by a malicious adversary. Signature parties receive "raw materials" sent from $\mathcal{CS}$ and utilize these "raw materials" to perform the online signing phase. The signing phase contains the KeyGen protocol and the signature protocol. Each participant randomly selects a slice of the signature private key when executing the KeyGen protocol. All participants compute the joint signature private key, and then they compute the signature public key from the obtained private key. The KeyGen protocol needs to be executed only once, and then the signature public-private key pair can be utilized to execute the signature protocol for arbitrary times. When executing the signature protocol, the participants utilize the joint private key to generate a joint signature on the message to be signed.

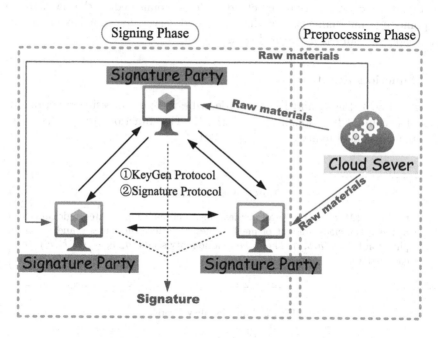

Fig. 1. System model

4.2 Security Model

We prove security according to the standard simulation-based security model with the ideal/real paradigm [3,13]. We assume that the probabilistic polynomial-time (PPT) adversary is malicious and static, i.e., it can arbitrarily deviate from the protocol setting during protocol execution and only determine which participants to corrupt before protocol execution. In the case of a dishonest majority, we follow the standard approach of considering security with abort, which means that the adversary can determine whether the honest party successfully obtains the output or not.

We prove the security of our protocol in a hybrid model, where participants execute the protocol using a real message and have access to a sub-functionality. When the sub-functionality is denoted as $\mathcal{F}$, we say the protocol works in the $\mathcal{F}$-hybrid model. Based on the definition of the Universal Composability (UC) framework, if all sub-protocols are UC-secure, then our protocol can also be proven secure within this framework.

4.3 Communication Model

We assume that the participants are connected via secure point-to-point channels and broadcast channels, that the cloud server is connected to the participants via point-to-point channels, and that the cloud server does not have access to the broadcast channels between the participants.

4.4 Functionalities

In Fig. 2, Fig. 3, Fig. 4, and Fig. 5, we describe the preprocessing functionality $\mathcal{F}_{\text{Prep}}$, the commit functionality $\mathcal{F}_{\text{Com}}$, the KeyGen functionality $\mathcal{F}_{\text{KeyGen}}$, and the signature functionality $\mathcal{F}_{\text{Sign}}$, respectively.

Functionality $\mathcal{F}_{\text{Prep}}$

On input ($Material$) from all parties, the functionality generates a global key α and a sufficient amount of mask values v, verificaton values e and multiplication triples (a, b, c). Then, the functionality sends $(\alpha_i, v_i, e_i, (a_i, b_i, c_i))$ to each party $\mathcal{P}_i$.

Fig. 2. Functionality Prep

5   Multi-party Signature Protocol

The multi-party signature protocol proposed in this paper is divided into two phases: a preprocessing phase performed by the cloud server and a signing phase performed by the signature participants.

Functionality $\mathcal{F}_{\text{Com}}$

- On input $(Commit, id, i, x)$ from party $\mathcal{P}_i$, if id has been recorded, the functionality stores (id, i, x) and sends (id, i) to all parties.
- On input $(Open, id, i)$ from party $\mathcal{P}_i$, if (id, i, x) has been recorded, the functionality retrieves (id, i, x) and outputs them to all parties.

Fig. 3. Functionality Com

Functionality $\mathcal{F}_{\text{KeyGen}}$

(1) On input $(KeyGen, (a, b, G, N, h))$ from all parties, the functionality generates a key pair (d, pk) and stores $((a, b, G, N, h), d, pk)$.
(2) On input $(Output)$ from all parties, if $((a, b, G, N, h), d, pk)$ has been recorded, the functionality retrieves (d, pk) and outputs them to the environment. Wait for "OK" from the environment, then send d_i to each party $\mathcal{P}_i$ and pk to all parties. Otherwise, $\bot$ is output to all parties.

Fig. 4. Functionality KeyGen

Functionality $\mathcal{F}_{\text{Sign}}$

(1) On input $(Signature, id, M)$ from all parties, if the $(Signature, id, M)$ is not present in memory, the functionality generates an SM2 signature $\sigma := (r, s)$ and stores (id, M, σ).
(2) On input $(Output, id)$ from all parties, if id has been recorded, the functionality retrieves (id, M, σ) and outputs them to the environment. Wait for "OK" from the environment, then send (σ) to all parties. Otherwise, $\bot$ is output to all parties.

Fig. 5. Functionality Sign

5.1 Preprocessing Phase

In the preprocessing phase, the cloud server $\mathcal{CS}$ is responsible for generating the "raw material" needed in the signing phase over $(\mathbb{F}_p)^s$. For $\mathbf{m} = (m_1, ..., m_s)$, we define $\langle \mathbf{m} \rangle = (\langle m_1 \rangle, ..., \langle m_s \rangle)$, and the operations on this type of share representation are componentwise. Specifically, the following four types of data are generated during the preprocessing phase:

- The global key α;
- The mask values $\langle \mathbf{v} \rangle$;
- The verification values $\langle \mathbf{e} \rangle$;
- The multiplication triples $(\langle \mathbf{a} \rangle, \langle \mathbf{b} \rangle, \langle \mathbf{c} \rangle)$.

where the global key α is the global checking parameter used to generate the MAC as well as to check the intermediate values and calculation results. The remaining three data types are used for sharing input, batch checking, and secure multiplication. The details of the preprocessing procedure are shown in Fig. 6.

Procedure Preprocessing

- **Global key**
  1. $\mathcal{CS}$ chooses $\alpha_1, ..., \alpha_n$ randomly and sets $\alpha = \alpha_1 + ... + \alpha_n$.
  2. $\mathcal{CS}$ sends α_i to signature party $\mathcal{P}_i$.
- **Mask values**
  1. $\mathcal{CS}$ chooses $\mathbf{v}_1^j, ..., \mathbf{v}_n^j$ randomly and sets $\mathbf{v}^j = \mathbf{v}_1^j + ... + \mathbf{v}_n^j$, where $j = 1, ..., n$.
  2. $\mathcal{CS}$ computes $\gamma(\mathbf{v}^j) = \alpha \cdot \mathbf{v}^j$.
  3. $\mathcal{CS}$ splits $\gamma(\mathbf{v}^j)$ into n shares to obtain $\gamma(\mathbf{v}^j)_1, ..., \gamma(\mathbf{v}^j)_n$.
  4. $\mathcal{CS}$ generates $\langle \mathbf{v}^j \rangle$, where $\langle \mathbf{v}^j \rangle := ((\mathbf{v}_1^j, ..., \mathbf{v}_n^j), (\gamma(\mathbf{v}^j)_1, ..., \gamma(\mathbf{v}^j)_n))$.
  5. $\mathcal{CS}$ sends $\langle \mathbf{v}^j \rangle_i = (\mathbf{v}_i^j, \gamma(\mathbf{v}^j)_i)$ to every signature party $\mathcal{P}_i$ and $\mathbf{v}^j$ to signature party $\mathcal{P}_j$.
- **Verification values**
  1. $\mathcal{CS}$ chooses $\mathbf{e}_1, ..., \mathbf{e}_n$ randomly and sets $\mathbf{e} = \mathbf{e}_1 + ... + \mathbf{e}_n$.
  2. $\mathcal{CS}$ computes $\gamma(\mathbf{e}) = \alpha \cdot \mathbf{e}$.
  3. $\mathcal{CS}$ splits $\gamma(\mathbf{e})$ into n shares to obtain $\gamma(\mathbf{e})_1, ..., \gamma(\mathbf{e})_n$.
  4. $\mathcal{CS}$ generates $\langle \mathbf{e} \rangle$, where $\langle \mathbf{e} \rangle := ((\mathbf{e}_1, ..., \mathbf{e}_n), (\gamma(\mathbf{e})_1, ..., \gamma(\mathbf{e})_n))$.
  5. $\mathcal{CS}$ sends $\langle \mathbf{e} \rangle_i = (\mathbf{e}_i, \gamma(\mathbf{e})_i)$ to signature party $\mathcal{P}_i$.
- **Multiplication triples**
  1. $\mathcal{CS}$ chooses $\mathbf{a}_1, ..., \mathbf{a}_n, \mathbf{b}_1, ..., \mathbf{b}_n$ randomly and sets $\mathbf{a} = \mathbf{a}_1 + ... + \mathbf{a}_n$, $\mathbf{b} = \mathbf{b}_1 + ... + \mathbf{b}_n$.
  2. $\mathcal{CS}$ computes $\mathbf{c} = \mathbf{a} \cdot \mathbf{b}$.
  3. $\mathcal{CS}$ computes $\gamma(\mathbf{a}) = \alpha \cdot \mathbf{a}$, $\gamma(\mathbf{b}) = \alpha \cdot \mathbf{b}$, $\gamma(\mathbf{c}) = \alpha \cdot \mathbf{c}$.
  4. $\mathcal{CS}$ splits $\gamma(\mathbf{a})$, $\gamma(\mathbf{b})$, $\gamma(\mathbf{c})$, $\mathbf{c}$ into n shares respectively to obtain $\gamma(\mathbf{a})_1, ..., \gamma(\mathbf{a})_n, \gamma(\mathbf{b})_1, ..., \gamma(\mathbf{b})_n, \gamma(\mathbf{c})_1, ..., \gamma(\mathbf{c})_n, \mathbf{c}_1, ..., \mathbf{c}_n$.
  5. $\mathcal{CS}$ generates $\langle \mathbf{a} \rangle$, $\langle \mathbf{b} \rangle$, $\langle \mathbf{c} \rangle$, where $\langle \mathbf{a} \rangle = ((\mathbf{a}_1, ..., \mathbf{a}_n), (\gamma(\mathbf{a})_1, ..., \gamma(\mathbf{a})_n))$, $\langle \mathbf{b} \rangle = ((\mathbf{b}_1, ..., \mathbf{b}_n), (\gamma(\mathbf{b})_1, ..., \gamma(\mathbf{b})_n))$, $\langle \mathbf{c} \rangle = ((\mathbf{c}_1, ..., \mathbf{c}_n), (\gamma(\mathbf{c})_1, ..., \gamma(\mathbf{c})_n))$.
  6. $\mathcal{CS}$ sends $\langle \mathbf{a} \rangle_i = (\mathbf{a}_i, \gamma(\mathbf{a})_i)$, $\langle \mathbf{b} \rangle_i = (\mathbf{b}_i, \gamma(\mathbf{b})_i)$, $\langle \mathbf{c} \rangle_i = (\mathbf{c}_i, \gamma(\mathbf{c})_i)$ to signature party $\mathcal{P}_i$.

Fig. 6. The Preprocessing Procedure

5.2 Signing Phase

In the signing phase, the signature parties sign the message jointly. The signing phase consists of four protocols which are Π_{MACCheck}, Π_{Share}, Π_{KeyGen} and $\Pi_{\text{Signature}}$.

MACCheck. The signature parties perform the MACCheck protocol to check the correctness of intermediate values and calculation results. Assuming that there is a set of values to be checked, all the signature participants need to do is to partially open a verification value generated in the preprocessing phase and utilize that value for batch checking, as well as checking the value itself. If it fails the check, the protocol aborts, or continues otherwise. The details of the MACCheck protocol are shown in Fig. 7.

Protocol Π_{MACCheck}

Input: A set of partially opened values $\{a_1, ..., a_T\}$, where T is the number of partially opened values; α_i, $(\gamma(a_j)_i)$ from each signature party $\mathcal{P}_i$, where $j = 1, ..., T$.

Output: Output "OK" if the check succeeds and "$\perp$" if the check fails.

MACCheck($a_1, ..., a_T$):
1. All signature parties partially open a verification value $\langle e \rangle$.
2. All signature parties compute $a \leftarrow \sum_j e^j \cdot a_j + e^{T+2}$.
3. Each signature party $\mathcal{P}_i$ computes $\gamma_i \leftarrow e^{T+1} \cdot \gamma(e)_i + \sum_{j=1}^T e^j \cdot \gamma(a_j)_i$, and $\sigma_i \leftarrow \gamma_i - \alpha_i \cdot a$.
4. Each signature party $\mathcal{P}_i$ calls $\mathcal{F}_{COM}$ to commit to σ_i and broadcast the commitment.
5. Each signature party $\mathcal{P}_i$ calls $\mathcal{F}_{COM}$ to open commitments from other signature parties, thus all signature parties obtain $\sigma_1, ..., \sigma_n$.
6. All signature parties check $\sigma \leftarrow \sigma_1 + \cdots + \sigma_n$: if $\sigma = 0$, output "OK"; if $\sigma \neq 0$, output "$\perp$".

Fig. 7. The MACCheck Protocol

Share. The share protocol is used to share the inputs of the signature parties. Suppose each party has an input of the same type (e.g., private key) u_i, and they want to get a share of the sum of all parties' inputs of that type (e.g., the joint private key) $u = \sum u_i$. So each party takes a mask value to blind his input and broadcasts the blinded result to all parties. Then each party uses the share of the blinded value he holds and adds it to the received value to get the share of input u_i of party $\mathcal{P}_i$. After all parties have shared their inputs, each party adds the shares of the inputs that it holds thus obtaining the share $\langle u \rangle$ of the sum of the input of that type. The details of the Share protocol are shown in Fig. 8.

KeyGen Protocol. In the KeyGen protocol, each signature party chooses a private key, and all parties call the share protocol to obtain the joint private key $\langle d \rangle$. After that, the parties get the public key $\langle pk \rangle$ through secure computation. The details are shown in Fig. 9.

Protocol Π_{Share}

Input: $\{u_1, ..., u_n\}$ from all signature parties.
Output: $\langle u \rangle$, where $u = u_1 + ... + u_n$.
Share$(u_1, ..., u_n)$:
  1. Each signature party $\mathcal{P}_i$ takes an available mask value $(v_{u_i}, \langle v_{u_i} \rangle)$.
  2. Each signature party $\mathcal{P}_i$ computes $\epsilon_{u_i} \leftarrow u_i - v_{u_i}$, and broadcasts ϵ_{u_i}.
  3. All signature parties compute $\langle u_i \rangle \leftarrow \langle v_{u_i} \rangle + \epsilon_{u_i}$.
  4. Let $\langle u_j \rangle_i$ denote the share that $\mathcal{P}_i$ holds of the value shared by $\mathcal{P}_j$.
  5. Each signature party $\mathcal{P}_i$ computes $\langle u \rangle_i \leftarrow \sum_j \langle u_j \rangle_i$.
  6. Output $\langle u \rangle$, and each signature party $\mathcal{P}_i$ holds $\langle u \rangle_i = (u_i, \gamma(u)_i)$.

Fig. 8. The Share Protocol

Protocol Π_{KeyGen}

Input: Elliptic curve parameters (a, b, G, N, h), where a and b are the coefficients of the elliptic curve equation, G is the base point of the elliptic curve, N is the order of the base point G, h is the cofactor of the elliptic curve.
Output: The public key pk and the private key $\langle d \rangle$.
KeyGen(a, b, G, N, h):
  1. Each signature party $\mathcal{P}_i$ chooses $d_i \in \mathbb{Z}_N$ as signature private key. Define $d := \sum_{i=1}^n d_i (mod\ N)$.
  2. Each signature party $\mathcal{P}_i$ chooses $R_i \in \mathbb{Z}_N$. Define $R := \sum_{i=1}^n R_i (mod\ N)$.
  3. The signatures parties call protocol Π_{Share} to share $\{d_1, ..., d_n\}$ and $\{R_1, ..., R_n\}$ thereby obtaining $\langle d \rangle$ and $\langle R \rangle$.
  4. The signature parties take a multiplication triple $(\langle a \rangle, \langle b \rangle, \langle c \rangle)$
  5. All signature parties compute $\langle \epsilon_{dR} \rangle \leftarrow \langle d \rangle - \langle a \rangle$, $\langle \delta_{dR} \rangle \leftarrow \langle R \rangle - \langle b \rangle$, and partially open $\langle \epsilon_{dR} \rangle$, $\langle \delta_{dR} \rangle$ to obtain ϵ_{dR}, δ_{dR}.
  6. All signature parties compute $\langle d \cdot R \rangle \leftarrow \langle c \rangle + \epsilon_{dR} \cdot \langle b \rangle + \delta_{dR} \cdot \langle a \rangle + \epsilon_{dR} \cdot \delta_{dR}$.
  7. All signature parties partially open $\langle dR \rangle$ to obtain dR, and compute the inverse of dR thereby getting $d^{-1} \cdot R^{-1}$.
  8. All signature parties compute $\langle pk \rangle \leftarrow (d^{-1} \cdot R^{-1} \cdot \langle R \rangle - 1) \cdot G$.
  9. The signature parties call the protocol Π_{MACCheck} to check all the values partially opened so far. If it succeeds, they continued. If it fails, they output "$\perp$" and abort.
  10. The signature parties open $\langle pk \rangle$ and call protocol Π_{MACCheck} to check its MAC. If it succeeds, they accept pk as a valid signature public key. If it fails, they output "$\perp$" and abort.

Fig. 9. The KeyGen Protocol

Note that under the premise of ensuring secure storage of private keys, the KeyGen protocol only needs to run once, and the generated public-private key pair can be reused in the Signature protocol.

Signature Protocol. Signature parties in this protocol utilize the key information generated by the KeyGen protocol to jointly generate the SM2 signature of message M and verify the correctness of the computed result using the MAC. The specific steps are shown in Fig. 10.

In Fig. 11 we show the invocation of the protocols and the flow of the main data as the entire architecture completes a signature.

6   Security Proof

Now, we state the theorem on the security of the KeyGen protocol and signature protocol.

Theorem 1. *In the* $\mathcal{F}_{\text{Prep}}, \mathcal{F}_{\text{Com}}$-*hybrid model, the protocol* Π_{KeyGen} *implements* $\mathcal{F}_{\text{KeyGen}}$ *with statistical security against any static active adversary corrupting up to n - 1 parties.*

Simulator $\mathcal{S}_{\text{KeyGen}}$

(1) The simulator calls $\mathcal{F}_{\text{Prep}}$ to get "raw material". The simulator will read all the data of the corrupted parties in the copy of $\mathcal{F}_{\text{Prep}}$.
(2) The simulator calls $\mathcal{F}_{\text{KeyGen}}$ to get pk.
(3) The protocol proceeds to the checking phase and aborts if the check fails in step 9, otherwise the simulator gets the result pk through $\mathcal{F}_{\text{KeyGen}}$. The simulator opens pk according to the protocol and sends "OK" to $\mathcal{F}_{\text{KeyGen}}$ if pk passes the check.

Proof. By observing the construction of the simulator $\mathcal{S}_{\text{KeyGen}}$, we can see that the environment view of an ideal Keygen process is statistically indistinguishable from the real Keygen process view. The private key d chosen by the honest parties as well as the random value R are uniformly random, as is the $\epsilon_d \leftarrow d - v$ they broadcast. Secondly, the partially opened intermediate values ϵ_{dR} and δ_{dR} have been subtracted from the shares of random values a and b in the computation of d times R, so they are also uniformly random. In addition, the shares of MAC values held by honest parties are also uniformly random, with the same distribution in the real and simulated processes. Finally, if the simulated process aborts, the simulator $\mathcal{S}_{\text{KeyGen}}$ also make $\mathcal{F}_{\text{KeyGen}}$ abort, so the environment will see no output from the honest parties, consistent with the real protocol abort.

When the real KeyGen or simulated KeyGen is in its MACCheck step, the output value pk and some shares from the honest parties will be the only new data seen by the environment. These random shares are consistent with pk and its MAC in both the simulated and real cases. That is, when pk is the same, the view of the environment at the last step has the same distribution in the real and simulated processes.

In the simulation, pk is of course the correct summation of $pk = (d^{-1} - 1) \cdot G$, where d matches the shares read from the corrupted parties at the beginning. Thus, the proof can be completed by showing that the same situation occurs with

---

Protocol $\Pi_{\text{Signature}}$

Input: Message M.
Output: Signature (r, s).
Signature:

1. All signature parties compute $E \leftarrow H(Z \parallel M)$.
2. Each signature party $\mathcal{P}_i$ chooses $k_i \in \mathbb{Z}_N$. Define $k := \sum_{i=1}^{n} k_i (mod\ N)$.
3. All signature parties call protocol Π_{Share} to share $\{k_1, ..., k_n\}$ thereby obtaining $\langle k \rangle$.
4. All signature parties compute $(\langle x_1 \rangle, \langle y_1 \rangle) \leftarrow \langle k \rangle \cdot G$ and partially open $\langle x_1 \rangle$.
5. All signature parties compute $r \leftarrow (E + x_1) mod\ n$.
6. All signature parties compute $\langle u \rangle \leftarrow \langle k \rangle + r$.
7. The signature parties take a multiplication triple $(\langle A \rangle, \langle B \rangle, \langle C \rangle)$
8. All signature parties compute $\langle \epsilon_{du} \rangle \leftarrow \langle d \rangle - \langle A \rangle$, $\langle \delta_{du} \rangle \leftarrow \langle u \rangle - \langle B \rangle$ and partially open $\langle \epsilon_{du} \rangle$, $\langle \delta_{du} \rangle$ to obtain ϵ_{du}, δ_{du}.
9. All signature parties compute $\langle d \cdot u \rangle \leftarrow \langle C \rangle + \epsilon_{du} \cdot \langle B \rangle + \delta_{du} \cdot \langle A \rangle + \epsilon_{du} \cdot \delta_{du}$.
10. All signature parties compute $\langle s \rangle \leftarrow \langle d \cdot u \rangle - r$.
11. The signature parties call the protocol Π_{MACCheck} to check all the values partially opened so far. If it succeeds, they continued. If it fails, they output " $\perp$ " and abort.
12. The signature parties open $\langle s \rangle$ and call protocol Π_{MACCheck} to check its MAC. If it succeeds, they accept s as a valid signature component. If it fails, they output " $\perp$ " and abort.
13. Output the signature (r, s).

Fig. 10. The Signature Protocol

overwhelming probability in the real process. That is, the probability of the event that the real protocol terminates but the output is incorrect is negligible.

Since the multiplication triples in our scheme are generated by the procedure preprocessing executed by the semi-honest cloud server, the correctness of their multiplicative relations can be guaranteed. The only remaining cause of incorrect output is the existence of corrupt parties that have successfully cheated their shares during the execution of the protocol. We check the intermediate values as well as the output in step 9 and step 10, and from the security game in [6], we can observe that the probability that a party is able to cheat in step 9 is $4/|\mathbb{F}_p|$. The probability of successful cheating in step 10 is $2/|\mathbb{F}_p|$. Both of the above probabilities are negligible.

In this paper, we do not describe the specific construction of the protocol that implements the $\mathcal{F}_{\text{Com}}$ and the security proof, please refer to [6] for more details.

Theorem 2. *In the $\mathcal{F}_{\text{Prep}}, \mathcal{F}_{\text{Com}}$-hybrid model, the protocol $\Pi_{\text{Signature}}$ implements $\mathcal{F}_{\text{Sign}}$ with statistical security against any static active adversary corrupting up to n - 1 parties.*

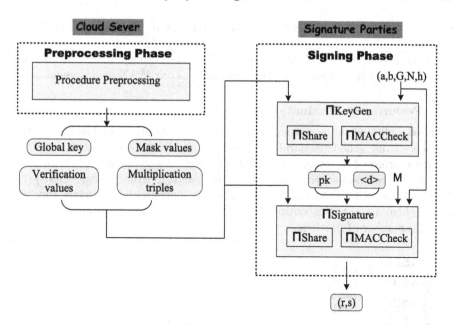

Fig. 11. Protocol and data flow

Simulator $\mathcal{S}_{\text{Sign}}$

(1) The simulator calls $\mathcal{F}_{\text{Prep}}$ to get "raw material". The simulator will read all the data of the corrupted parties in the copy of $\mathcal{F}_{\text{Prep}}$.

(2) The simulator calls $\mathcal{F}_{\text{Sign}}$ to get (r, s).

(3) The protocol proceeds to the checking phase and aborts if the check fails in step 9, otherwise the simulator gets the result s through $\mathcal{F}_{\text{Sign}}$. The simulator opens s according to the protocol and sends "OK" to $\mathcal{F}_{\text{Sign}}$ if s passes the check.

Proof. The security proof of Theorem 2 is along roughly the same lines as Theorem 1 and will not be repeated.

7 Performance Evaluation

In this section, we test the efficiency of the multi-party signature scheme proposed in this paper. We analyze the efficiency of completing signatures with different numbers of participants and compare it with signature schemes in other papers.

7.1 Experiment Setting

For the performance evaluation of our system, we use the MP-SPDZ library [19] and GMP 6.1.2. The hardware setup for our experiments is terminals with a

4-core 2.8Ghz Intel i7-7700HQ CPU and 16GB RAM. The average bandwidth is 10MB/s.

In the performance evaluation, we set 64-bit share length and different numbers of participants (from 2 to 10) respectively in our WAN environment.

7.2   Performance Evaluation

We have evaluated the performance of the signature protocol and key generation protocol of our scheme separately. Figure 12 shows the execution time of our signature protocol in settings with different numbers of signature parties (from 2 to 10). We compare it with the ECDSA threshold signature scheme [GGN] [11], [BGG] [2] and [GG] [10], which shows that our performance is better than the above schemes and the execution times of our protocol increases more smoothly with the number of participants.

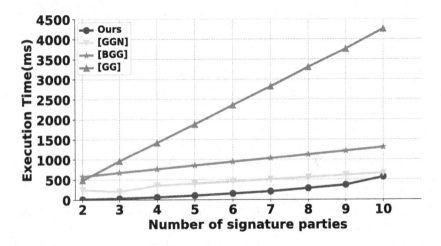

Fig. 12. Execution Times of Signature Protocol

Figure 13 shows the execution time of our KeyGen protocol in settings with different numbers of signature parties. We also tested the amount of data sent by each signature party in settings with different numbers of signature parties, shown in Fig. 14. We can see that as the number of parties increases, the amount of data sent per signature party increases linearly.

In addition, we compare our scheme with representative SM2-based two-party signature schemes. Since our scheme supports multi-party settings, and the schemes we are comparing only support two-party settings, we set the number of participants in our protocol to 2. In the signature protocol, we take the average execution times of the two participants for comparison. Table.2 shows that the execution time of our scheme is 27.26 ms for the KeyGen protocol and 15.56 ms for the Signature protocol, which is a decent performance among the schemes we listed. The efficiency of our protocol in a two-party setup is comparable to efficient two-party signature schemes.

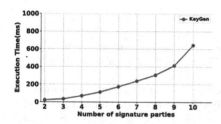

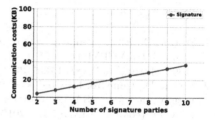

Fig. 14. Communication Costs of Signature Protocol

Fig. 13. Execution Times of KeyGen Protocol

Table 2. Efficiency comparison with two-party co-signature schemes(time in ms)

Scheme	KeyGen	Signature	Number of participants supported
Original SM2	9.74	11.72	⊘
ZHZC [27]	375.37	417.09	2
HYZZ [17]	375.85	342.28	2
ST [26]	27.40	19.37	2
FHLL [7]	26.65	14.42	2
HBGQ [14]	26.74	10.55	2
Ours	27.26	15.56	$n(n \geq 2)$

8   Conclusion

With the development of the Internet, communication systems, smart devices, and the Internet of Things (IoT), as well as cooperation and the division of rights in various scenarios make it necessary for digital signature schemes to be adapted to multi-party settings. Therefore, we propose a secure SM2 multi-party signature scheme based on SPDZ protocol, enabling multiple participants to sign messages jointly. We demonstrate that our scheme is UC secure through security analysis. Performance evaluation shows that the efficiency of our scheme is satisfactory. In future work, we will focus on improving the robustness of our scheme as well as further optimizing the efficiency.

Acknowledgment. This work was supported by the National Natural Science Foundation of China (No. 62071280, No. 62302280), the National Natural Science Foundation of Shandong Province (No. ZR2023QF133), the Major Scientific and Technological Innovation Project of Shandong Province (No. 2020CXGC010115), and the Science and Technology SMEs Innovation Ability Enhancement Project of Shandong Province (No. 2022TSGC1018).

References

1. Beaver, D.: Efficient multiparty protocols using circuit randomization. In: Feigenbaum, J. (ed.) CRYPTO 1991. LNCS, vol. 576, pp. 420–432. Springer, Heidelberg (1992). https://doi.org/10.1007/3-540-46766-1_34

2. Boneh, D., Gennaro, R., Goldfeder, S.: Using Level-1 homomorphic encryption to improve threshold DSA signatures for bitcoin wallet security. In: Lange, T., Dunkelman, O. (eds.) LATINCRYPT 2017. LNCS, vol. 11368, pp. 352–377. Springer, Cham (2019). https://doi.org/10.1007/978-3-030-25283-0_19

3. Canetti, R.: Security and composition of multiparty cryptographic protocols. J. Cryptol. **13**, 143–202 (2000)

4. Cramer, R., Damgård, I.B., et al.: Secure multiparty computation. Cambridge University Press (2015)

5. Damgård, I., Keller, M., Larraia, E., Pastro, V., Scholl, P., Smart, N.P.: Practical covertly secure MPC for dishonest majority – Or: breaking the SPDZ limits. In: Crampton, J., Jajodia, S., Mayes, K. (eds.) ESORICS 2013. LNCS, vol. 8134, pp. 1–18. Springer, Heidelberg (2013). https://doi.org/10.1007/978-3-642-40203-6_1

6. Damgård, I., Pastro, V., Smart, N., Zakarias, S.: Multiparty computation from somewhat homomorphic encryption. In: Safavi-Naini, R., Canetti, R. (eds.) CRYPTO 2012. LNCS, vol. 7417, pp. 643–662. Springer, Heidelberg (2012). https://doi.org/10.1007/978-3-642-32009-5_38

7. Feng, Q., Debiao, H., Min, L., Li, L.: Efficient two-party sm2 signing protocol for mobile internet. J. Comput. Res. Dev. 57(2020–10-2136), 2136 (2020). https://doi.org/10.7544/issn1000-1239.2020.20200401, https://crad.ict.ac.cn/en/article/doi/10.7544/issn1000-1239.2020.20200401

8. Gagol, A., Kula, J., Straszak, D., Swietek, M.: Threshold ECDSA for decentralized asset custody. Cryptology ePrint Archive (2020)

9. Gennaro, R., Goldfeder, S.: Fast multiparty threshold ECDSA with fast trustless setup. In: Proceedings of the 2018 ACM SIGSAC Conference on Computer and Communications Security, pp. 1179–1194 (2018)

10. Gennaro, R., Goldfeder, S.: One round threshold ECDSA with identifiable abort. Cryptology ePrint Archive (2020)

11. Gennaro, R., Goldfeder, S., Narayanan, A.: Threshold-Optimal DSA/ECDSA signatures and an application to bitcoin wallet security. In: Manulis, M., Sadeghi, A.R., Schneider, S. (eds.) ACNS 2016. LNCS, vol. 9696, pp. 156–174. Springer, Cham (2016). https://doi.org/10.1007/978-3-319-39555-5_9

12. Gennaro, R., Jarecki, S., Krawczyk, H., Rabin, T.: Robust threshold DSS signatures. In: Maurer, U. (ed.) EUROCRYPT 1996. LNCS, vol. 1070, pp. 354–371. Springer, Heidelberg (1996). https://doi.org/10.1007/3-540-68339-9_31

13. Goldreich, O.: Foundations of cryptography: Basic applications cambridge cambridge University Press 10.1017. CBO9780511721656 Google Scholar Google Scholar Cross Ref Cross Ref (2004)

14. Han, G., Bai, X., Geng, S., Qin, B.: Efficient two-party SM2 signing protocol based on secret sharing. J. Syst. Architect. **132**, 102738 (2022)

15. He, D., Zhang, Y., Wang, D., Choo, K.K.R.: Secure and efficient two-party signing protocol for the identity-based signature scheme in the IEEE p1363 standard for public key cryptography. IEEE Trans. Dependable Secure Comput. **17**(5), 1124–1132 (2018)

16. Hong, H., Sun, Z., Liu, X.: A key-insulated CP-ABE with key exposure accountability for secure data sharing in the cloud. KSII Trans. Internet Inf. Syst. **10**(5), 2394 (2016)

17. HOU, H.X., Yang, B., ZHANG, L.N., ZHANG, M.R.: Secure two-party SM2 signature algorithm. ACTA ELECTONICA SINICA 48(1), 1 (2020)
18. Jie, Y., Yu, L., Li-yun, C., Wei, N.: A SM2 elliptic curve threshold signature scheme without a trusted center. KSII Trans. Internet Inf. Syst. 10(2) (2016)
19. Keller, M.: MP-SPDZ: A versatile framework for multi-party computation. Cryptology ePrint Archive, Report 2020/521 (2020). https://eprint.iacr.org/2020/521
20. Lindell, Y.: Fast secure two-party ECDSA signing. J. Cryptology **34**(4), 1–38 (2021). https://doi.org/10.1007/s00145-021-09409-9
21. Lindell, Y., Nof, A.: Fast secure multiparty ECDSA with practical distributed key generation and applications to cryptocurrency custody. In: Proceedings of the 2018 ACM SIGSAC Conference on Computer and Communications Security, pp. 1837–1854 (2018)
22. Shamir, A.: How to share a secret. Commun. ACM **22**(11), 612–613 (1979)
23. Shang, M., Ma, Y., Lin, J., Jing, J.: A threshold scheme for SM2 elliptic curve cryptographic algorithm. J. Cryptologic Res. 1(2), 155 (2014). 10.13868/j.cnki.jcr.000015. https://www.jcr.cacrnet.org.cn/EN/10.13868/j.cnki.jcr.000015
24. Shoup, V.: Practical threshold signatures. In: Preneel, B. (ed.) EUROCRYPT 2000. LNCS, vol. 1807, pp. 207–220. Springer, Heidelberg (2000). https://doi.org/10.1007/3-540-45539-6_15
25. Wee, H.: Threshold and revocation cryptosystems via extractable hash proofs. In: Paterson, K.G. (ed.) EUROCRYPT 2011. LNCS, vol. 6632, pp. 589–609. Springer, Heidelberg (2011). https://doi.org/10.1007/978-3-642-20465-4_32
26. Yin-Xue, S.U., Hai-Bo, T.: A two-party SM2 signing protocol and its application
27. Zhang, Y., He, D., Zhang, M., Choo, K.K.R.: A provable-secure and practical two-party distributed signing protocol for SM2 signature algorithm. Front. Comp. Sci. **14**, 1–14 (2020)

Blockchain

Epoch: Enabling Path Concealing Payment Channel Hubs with Optimal Path Encryption

Ming Liu[1], Mingyue Zhang[1], Guangshun Li[1], Yuemei Hu[1], Tao Li[1], Yilei Wang[1], and Bo Lan[2(✉)]

[1] School of Computer Science, Qufu Normal University, Rizhao, China
[2] Beijing Shougang Automation Information Technology Co., Ltd., Beijing, China
lanbo@shougang.com.cn

Abstract. Payment channel path information includes node identity and balance. With this public information, an attacker can initiate a recurring transaction against the victim node, resulting in the victim node's available balance being fully locked in the recurring transaction, thereby increasing the cost of collateral due to the longer lock time. The current solution primarily focuses on hiding the balance. However, it is not resistant to LockDown attacks because the attacker, as a payment sender, subjectively chooses a looped payment path to initiate a circular transaction. Additionally, existing solutions suffer from high deposit costs due to long loop paths. In this paper, we propose Epoch, a payment channel scheme whose core component is a new cryptographic primitive–optimal path encryption (OPE) protocol, which enables the concealment of path information. Specifically, the administrator uses a homomorphic one-way function to encrypt a payment path that satisfies the sender's requirements, and the results in hiding path information such as the identity of the nodes in this path. This ensures that the sender does not steal information about the payment path in advance of adopting the payment path, and hence cannot initiate circular transactions. We give a security analysis of the OPE protocol in a universal composability (UC) framework, showing that the OPE protocol can hide path information and resist LockDown attacks. Furthermore, our scheme can process transactions in multiple hubs in parallel, which reduces the cost of collateralizing the deposit for transactions going through four Hubs by 75% compared to previous approaches.

Keywords: Payment Channel · Path Information Hiding · UC · Homomorphic One-way Function · LockDown Attack

1 Introduction

Blockchain technology is widely used as the underlying technology for cryptocurrencies such as Bitcoin and Ether due to its decentralization, data tamper-proofing, and data traceability. People believe that blockchain records data information that is fair, impartial, and open. Unfortunately, blockchain's inefficient

© The Author(s), under exclusive license to Springer Nature Singapore Pte Ltd. 2024
C. Ge and M. Yung (Eds.): Inscrypt 2023, LNCS 14526, pp. 107–125, 2024.
https://doi.org/10.1007/978-981-97-0942-7_6

transaction throughput has limited its overall growth. While off-chain payment channels [1] emerged immediately afterward, the openness and transparency of blockchain data allowed malicious users to utilize the data information to launch attacks on cryptocurrencies.

1.1   Related Works

Various solutions   [2–6] have been proposed, among which payment channels are widely used as an essential technical means to realize fast, secure, and low-cost peer-to-peer payments. The groundbreaking application of Lightning Network (LN)   [1] signifies that payment channel technology has become a widely deployed solution in practice. The core idea of LN is to move high-frequency, small transactions to an off-chain, two-way payment channel, thereby reducing the authentication burden on the blockchain, shortening transaction times, and addressing scalability issues. Fortunately, bi-directional payment channels have been developed into payment channel networks (PCNs). Transactions are only recorded in the blockchain when the channel is created and closed. In 2017, G Malavolta et al. [7] proposed a novel payment channel network model that allows for efficient transaction processing and a low-latency payment experience while ensuring concurrency and privacy. In 2018 G Malavolta et al. [8] put forward to utilize the anonymous multi-hop locking (AMHL) technique to increase the privacy and safety of transactions and enhance the scalability and interoperability of the blockchain. Although this technique can satisfy relational anonymity (intermediate nodes only know the information of front and back nodes), it cannot ensure the unlinkability of transaction names.

1.2   Motivations and Contributions

Although payment channel technology has been used successfully in all of the above solutions, there are still problems. For example, the public path information in the payment channel makes the node vulnerable to attacks and fails to ensure user data privacy and the security of the payment channel. This issue raises several challenges [9], such as selfish mining attacks [10,11], double-spending attacks [12], and other attacks against cryptocurrencies. In addition, there are still challenges to the confidentiality of payment path information, atomicity of payments, and the recent interest in attacks such as LockDown [13]. To address these challenges Auto-Tune solution [14] uses a method of hiding the capacity of the payment channel to avoid privacy breaches. However, attackers can still autonomously find paths containing victim nodes in PCNs to launch LockDown attacks, congestion attacks [15], *etc.*, resulting in undesirable conditions such as forced payment channel shutdown and network paralysis. Hence, how to solve the scalability of blockchain and ensure the data privacy of users has become one of the common concerns of cryptocurrency users nowadays.

Challenge 1: Resisting LockDown Attacks. A situation where a node in the path is subject to a LockDown attack when making payments through multiple nodes (multi-hop). Specifically, the LockDown attack focuses on the attacker Alice initiating a circular transaction based on the sum of all incoming (or outgoing) channel balances of the victim node Bob (the transaction value is equal to the sum of the balances in the incoming direction). This allows the attacker Alice to deplete all of Bob's channel balances in this direction (incoming/outgoing), compromising the security of the payment path and even bringing down part of the off-chain network.

Challenge 2: Confidentiality of Path Information. Increasing the confidentiality of transaction path information in blockchain is to protect the security of user privacy. Qiao Y et al. [16] analyzed that payment path information leakage can trigger attacks such as payment retrospect [15]. As long as the path information is compromised, malicious users can easily choose which nodes the payment path passes through to conduct LockDown attacks, phishing attacks [17] or replay attacks [18], compromising the safety of honest users' assets. For the two latter attacks, on the one hand, an attacker can use transaction path information to forge a seemingly legitimate transaction request and trick users into transferring assets to the attacker's account. On the other hand, an attacker can use the transaction path information to replay a previous transaction to obtain additional assets or conduct other illicit activities.

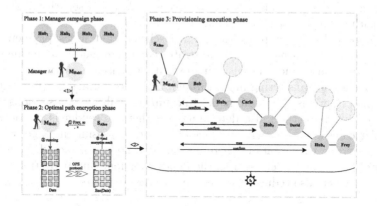

Fig. 1. Flow schematic of the Epoch scheme.

To address these challenges, we propose Epoch, a payment channel scheme that implements payment path information that can be hidden. The scheme consists of a manager campaign phase, an optimal path encryption phase, and a provisioning execution phase, for the main ideas, please refer to Fig. 1. Specifically, the hub node freely enters the first phase and returns an administrator M through an automatic election algorithm. M carries out the subsequent operations of this payment (<1>). The M then enters the second phase, invokes the

OPE protocol, encrypts the information of each node on the path with a homomorphic one-way function in the process of finding the optimal path according to the sender's selection criteria (sc), and generates a proof π_1 of the encryption result. M sends the encryption result, the proof π and the total cost paid together to the sender, who decides whether to choose this route or not. In this paper, we have chosen the shortest payment distance as the sc. Finally, we enter the provisioning execution phase (<2>), in which we focus on how to achieve atomicity in multi-channel payments. Firstly, the manager node sets a time t_1 within which all channel operations need to be completed, otherwise, the payment will be rolled back. When the other hub nodes (Hub_2, Hub_3, and Hub_4) have finished preparing the payment, completion of preparation message mes is sent to the manager. The manager node receives the full message mes and returns to each hub node to confirm the message and finally complete the payment. The introduction of the OPE protocol achieves the purpose of protecting user privacy and payment channel security by hiding the path information of the payment channel. Epoch with OPE as the core can improve the security and reliability of the payment channel, avoid the attacks brought by circular transactions and help the scalability problem of blockchain technology to be better solved.

The main contributions of this paper are as follows.

- We propose the optimal path encryption protocol, which is based on homomorphic one-way functions, non-interactive zero-knowledge proofs, and commitment schemes. We also comprehensively analyze the security of the optimal path encryption protocol in the UC framework.
- We propose Epoch, a payment channel scheme that hides payment path information, consisting of an administrator campaign phase, an optimal path encryption phase, and a provisioning execution phase.
- For the case of transferring funds through multiple hub nodes, Epoch utilizes a method of provisioning hub nodes to complete multiple transactions simultaneously. The method also determines whether the sender is performing a circular transaction through only one hub node by passing messages between hubs, avoiding the situation where a single hub node is attacked. Simulation results show that Epoch reduces the deposit for four hub node transactions by 75%, which also reduces the pressure on user deposits to be locked.

1.3   Roadmap

The rest of this paper is organized as follows. Section §2 introduces the basics, such as payment channel networks, homomorphic one-way functions, and commitment schemes. Section §3 first describes the security and privacy objectives to be achieved by the solution, followed by a description of the three phases of the solution. Section §4 provides a comprehensive analysis of the security of the OPE protocol. Section §5 simulates the interaction process of the protocol and analyses the changes in the deposit. Section §6 concludes the paper.

2   Preliminary

2.1   Payment Channel Network

PCN [1] is a distributed payment protocol based on blockchain technology that allows users to make fast and low-cost payments between them while avoiding the delays and high fees associated with traditional payments. Users in a PCN connect by creating and closing payment channels. The creation operation is openChannel($v_1, v_2, \beta_1, \beta_2, t$) $\rightarrow$ $\{1, 0\}$ and the closing operation is closeChannel($c(v_1, v_2)$) $\rightarrow$ $\{1, 0\}$. The v represents the user, β represents the user balance, t represents the timestamp, $c(v_i, v_{i+1})$ denotes the channel identifier between the two nodes, 1 means the channel is open and 0 means it is closed. The payment channel allows for iterative small transactions between two parties to a transaction by locking a certain amount of money on the blockchain and making payments as signed transactions off-chain, which are only submitted to the blockchain when there is a concern about malicious behavior. One of the update operations for both sides of the transaction is pay(v_i, v_{i+1}, Bal), with Bal denoting the number of amounts to be paid by user v_i to v_{i+1}.

2.2   Payment Channel Hub

PCH [19–22] usually has more liquidity and higher payout capacity than other nodes. PCH also has the above operations openChannel, closeChannel, and pay. The unique point is that the pay process involves the sender v_S, the hub node v_T and the receiver v_R. We denote the channel between v_S and v_T as $C(v_S, v_T)$ and the channel between v_T and v_R as $C(v_T, v_R)$. The two nodes agree on the transfer intention and record the latest balance allocation result while ensuring that the nodes have sufficient balance, i.e., if $cash_S >= Bal$ and $cash_T >= Bal$ is satisfied, update $cash_S -= Bal$ and $cash_T += Bal$ in $C(v_S, v_T)$ and update $cash_T -= Bal$ and $cash_R += Bal$ in $C(v_T, v_R)$, and add the updates to $C(v_S, v_T).state$ and $C(v_T, v_R).state$ respectively. PCH provides an efficient communication hub for other users to make real-time money transfers, by creating several payment channels that allow users to make bulk payments without having to execute transactions on the blockchain. PCH helps payments incur less cost and latency, and increases payment scalability and security.

2.3   Homomorphic One-Way Functions

Homomorphic one-way functions are often used in the field of cryptography to encrypt, decrypt, and compute without exposing data to others [23]. Specifically, a function f that satisfies the following conditions:

(1) For any input x, the corresponding output $y = f(x)$ can be computed by this function.
(2) Without knowing the key to the function f, it is difficult to invert x by y.
(3) For the domain of definition and the domain of value of a function f defined as two abelian groups, respectively, and for any pair (x_1, x_2), there is $g(x_1 \circ x_2)$ $= g(x_1) \circ g(x_2)$, where $\circ$ denotes the group operation.

2.4 Non-interactive Zero-Knowledge Proof

The non-interactive zero-knowledge proof (NIZK) scheme [24] consists of two algorithms $NIZK = (PNIZK, VNIZK)$ for proof and verification. The $PNIZK$ algorithm takes inputs x and witnesses w and outputs a proof π, i.e., $\pi \leftarrow PNIZK(x, w)$. The $VNIZK$ algorithm takes input x and proof π and outputs a proof $VNIZK(x, \pi) \in 0, 1$. The NIZK scheme allows the verifier to use the proof π to verify the truth of the statement x without needing to know any information other than the existence of the witness w.

2.5 Commitment Scheme

A commitment scheme consists of two phases, commitment, and validation, and its message space is M. The interactors of the scheme include the committer and the receiver [25]. During the first step, the commitment party computes the commitment value using the commitment algorithm $(com(m; r), decom) \leftarrow PCOM(m, r)$. The com represents the result of the commitment party's committing the message $m \in M$ and the random number r, and the $decom$ represents the unraveled commitment value. The promisor then sends $com(m; r)$ to the receiver. In the second step, the promising party sends the uncommitted value $decom = (m; r)$. The receiver then needs to verify that the value is correct, i.e., $VCOM(com, m, r) \in 0, 1$. The commitment scheme ensures that the information promised by the committer is always consistent and can be verified by the receiver. The commitment scheme used in this paper has perfectly binding and perfectly hiding features. Where perfectly binding [26] means that the commitment values must be different for different messages, i.e., for any different messages m_1 and m_2, their corresponding commitment values $com(m_1; r_1) \neq com(m_2; r_2)$, where r_1 and r_2 are different random numbers. Perfectly hiding [27] means that the adversary cannot distinguish what the messages m in them are by the commitment value com, respectively, i.e., for any message $m \in M$ and $m' \in M$, its corresponding commitment value $com(m; r)$ and $com(m'; r')$ are indistinguishable to the adversary, i.e., the adversary cannot infer anything about m or m' from the commitment values.

2.6 LockDown Attack

This attack is a new type of attack against the LN channel and focuses on the availability of balances in the channel. LN relies on payment channels between nodes to facilitate transactions. These channels have a specific capacity, which is determined by the amount of funds locked in the channel. The balance of the channel is the result of the distribution of these funds between the two nodes participating in the channel. The LockDown attack targets the channel balance's availability by creating a large number of low-value transactions that deplete the target channel's available balance. The attacker does this by opening multiple channels at the target node and then making a series of low-value payments through these channels. This results in the target node's available balance being locked in pending transactions, effectively making it unavailable for other legitimate transactions. As a result, the target node's ability to route payments through the LN is severely compromised, leading to an overall degradation of the network's performance. This attack is particularly damaging to nodes that are critical routing hubs in the network, as it can have a cascading effect on the overall connectivity and transaction throughput of the network.

3 Epoch

3.1 Security and Privacy Goals

We now define the security and privacy goals of our solution.

-**Confidentiality of path information.** Confidentiality of the path information is to prevent make known the details in the payment path to anyone to make certain the confidentiality of the information on the path.

-**Atomicity.** Atomicity is the concept that all transactions are either executed successfully in their entirety or not and that no partial transactions are allowed to succeed. If a transaction is not completed, all transactions need to be rolled back.

-**Resistant to LockDown attacks.** LockDown attack defense means that the scheme resists an attacker who initiates a recurring payment by exploiting specific information in the path, such as username and balance information, to eventually deplete the balance in the payment channel.

3.2 Our Solution

We propose an off-chain payment scheme called Epoch that hides payment path information. It is resistant to LockDown attacks, maintains the atomicity of transactions and the confidentiality of path information, in addition to being able to process transactions in parallel when transacting through multiple hubs.

In the following, we present our solution in a progressive description. First, we give a naive solution, then discuss the challenges it faces and show how to overcome them, and finally arrive at the final version of the solution.

Naive solution. Multi-hop payments are transformed into sequential payments via multiple hub nodes.

It is clear from the principle of the LockDown attack that we can avoid the attack by hiding the direction of user transactions in the channel. Fortunately, the transactions passing through the hub nodes cannot be detected by anyone as the sender and receiver of each transaction. This achieves the goal of hiding the direction of transactions, but there are two challenges. (1) LockDown attacks can only be suppressed due to the high economic cost and the serial efficiency is not ideal. (2) As the hub node is unable to determine whether a circular transaction exists, it is still possible for an attacker to launch an attack, which may pose a threat to the security of the PCN, the details of which can be seen in Fig. 2.

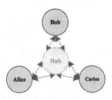

Fig. 2. Diagram of a recurring transaction through the same payment channel hub.

We then further optimize the idea. This paper uses multiple hubs for parallel transactions.

While this solves the first two problems, there are still two challenges: (i) an attacker can determine whether the attacked node is in a round-robin transaction based on the information of the payment path and thus execute a LockDown attack. (ii) How to ensure the atomicity of parallel execution of transactions. Specifically, most payments under the chain are multi-hop payments. Yet, the sender of a multi-hop path can choose which nodes the path passes through. At this point, if a malicious attacker is acting as a sender, a path with a ring is selected to launch a LockDown attack based on the balance information of the victim node. Eventually, the attacker exhausts the channel balance of the victim node in all input (or output) directions, causing a partial breakdown of the network and crippling the victim node's ability to become a critical hub in the network.

For the (i) problem, this paper prevents a malicious attacker from accurately selecting the path containing the victim node by hiding the identity of the user in the payment path. For the (ii) problem, this paper utilizes parallel provisioning of messages, so we require a manager M to execute.

Phase 1: Manager campaign phase. In this paper, four hub nodes are set to participate in this election. See Algorithm 1 for a description of the manager election algorithm. First, we define a function for randomly selecting a manager node. Since each one has an equal probability of being selected, we store the node names in a list and randomly select an element using the random.choice() function in Python.

Next, we want to simulate the entire election process. We a counter to keep track of how many times each person has been re-elected, and then use a while loop to simulate the process of having multiple rounds of elections in a row. In each round, we first select a random manager and then check whether the node has been re-elected three times (up to n-1 times, not the same person each time). If so, a new manager is selected at random until one is selected who has not been re-elected three times. Finally, we return the manager's name and the number of times he has been re-elected. In addition, given that the manager node is evil, we make it sign a deposit smart contract to guarantee that the payment path it chooses each time is the optimal path (the shortest payment distance), otherwise, the deposit will be deducted.

Algorithm 1: Manager Campaign Process

Input: The name of the participant.

Output: Return the name of the final manager and the number of times he has been re-elected.

1: **(1) Participant Names:**
2: ① people = [Hub_1, Hub_2, Hub_3, Hub_4];
3: ② def select-manager()
4:          return random.choice(people)
5: **(2) Simulate the election process:**
6: counts = person: 0 for person in people;
7: **while** True **do**   ▷ Simulate multiple rounds of the election process
8:      manager = selectManager()   ▷ Pick a manager
9:      **if** counts[manager] <2
10:          counts[manager] += 1   ▷ Check if he has been re-elected n-1 times
11:      **else:**
12:          continue   ▷ If he has been re-elected n-1 times, then re-elect him
13:      **if** max(counts.values()) == 2
14:          break
15: **end while**
16: **for** a person, count in counts. items() **do** ▷ Return the name of the final manager and the number of times he has been reelected
17:     **if** count <= 2
18:     **return** person, count.
19: **end for**

Phase 2: Optimal path encryption phase. In this paper, the payment path selection criterion sc defaults to the shortest payment distance. When paying through multiple hubs, we use the homomorphic one-way function property to encrypt the user information on the path one by one. Upon encrypted, the attacker node cannot access the private information of all the intermediary nodes in the payment path, and cannot select the circular transmission. We use homomorphic one-way function encryption to ensure that the protocol is applied to PCNs. The participants of the protocol are the manager M and the sender V_S. M constructs a homomorphic graph containing the topology of all hub nodes and their connected nodes in the first phase. The information about the optimal paths, such as node names and channel amounts, is encrypted using homomorphic encryption. At the same time, M provides a proof π to V_S using zero-knowledge proof techniques for proving that the encrypted path is indeed the optimal path from V_S to the receiver. Finally, the encryption result is sent to the sender together with the proof π. The protocol is shown in Protocol 1 and is described as follows:

Protocol 1: Optimal Path Encryption

Input: Manager M inputs the graph $G_2 = (V', E)$ and the homomorphic one-way function h. Sender V_S inputs the starting point, the endpoint, and the commitment values $com(V_S)$, $com(f)$, and $com(sc)$ of the selection criteria.

Auxiliary inputs: Start point V_S, endpoint f, and selection criterion sc for the shortest payout distance.

Output: V_S The shortest path encrypted-path, the total amount total-value and the proof π of the output encryption obtained by the sender.

1: V_S sends M a commitment $com(V_S)$, $com(f)$ and $com(sc)$ about the starting point V_S, the ending point f and the selection criterion sc of the payment path.
2: M performs the following steps:

    (1) M constructs an isomorphism $G_2 = (V', E)$ of the network topology graph $G_1 = (V, E)$ with respect to the nodes Hub_i $i \in \{1, n\}$.

    (2) M computes the shortest path from V_S to f using the algorithm that satisfies the shortest payout distance.

      i. Among the neighboring nodes of V_S, the nodes satisfying the shortest payment distance are searched in turn and their node names and their edge weights are homomorphically encrypted.

      ii. The encrypted nodes and edge weights will be added as a tuple $(h(u), h(w(u, v)))$ to the list encrypted-path.

    Repeat the above until the end f, adding the encrypted node $h(f)$ as tuple $(h(f), None)$ to the end of the list encrypted-path.

    (3) Meanwhile, generate a proof π for the encrypted result using the zero-knowledge proof technique.

    (4) Send the list of encrypted optimal paths encrypted-path, the total amount paid total-value and the generated proof π together to V_S.

    (5) V_S sends the decommitment $decom$ to the manager M.

First, a commitment value is sent by the sender V_S to the manager M regarding the starting point, the endpoint, and the selection criteria of the payment path (step 1 in the protocol). After receiving the message, M represents the payment channel connectivity of all nodes as a graph $G_1 = (V, E)$, where nodes and hub nodes are points of the graph, payment channels are edges of the graph, and the total channel balance is the weight of the edges. Then M constructs an isomorphic graph of $G_2 = (V', E)$, where V' refers to the randomization of the original names of the nodes to numbers (step 1. (1) in the protocol). Next, M finds the most suitable path. The node v_S is taken as the start point and the node f as the endpoint. M traverses the graph G_2 sequentially starting from V_S and encrypts its node name and its edge weights with a homomorphic one-way function whenever it finds a node that satisfies the shortest payment distance. The encrypted node and edge weights are added to the list encrypted-path as tuples $(h(u), h(w(u, v)))$. To the endpoint f, the encrypted node $h(f)$ is added as a tuple $(h(f), None)$ to the end of the list encrypted-path. None represents the endpoint with no successor nodes (step 1. (2) in the protocol). The manager

M generates a proof π of the encrypted result output by the algorithm using the zero-knowledge proof technique, which is used to prove that the encrypted shortest path is indeed the shortest path from V_S to f (step 1. (3) in the protocol). Finally, M sends V_S with the encrypted optimal path encrypted-path, the total amount paid total-value, and the generated proof π. The sender sends the uncommitment, i.e., the starting point V_S and the ending point f, to M (step 1. (4) in the protocol). This concludes the protocol.

The sender verifies the encryption result and, if successful, agrees to pay using the shortest path of this encryption. M then decrypts and transfers the money based on the multi-hop path obtained in the previous phase. In the second phase, on the one hand, the attacker cannot decrypt the user names and transmission margins of all nodes on the shortest payment path, and therefore cannot obtain the presence of the attacked node Bob in the path, and therefore cannot initiate a round-robin transaction against node Bob, when the attacker acts as the sender after this encryption. From the above operation, it follows that our protocol can effectively prevent the sender node from selecting a fixed node for transfer (it cannot see which nodes are included in this transfer until the payment is made).

Phase 3: Provisioning execution phase. Specifically, within the time t_1 set by M, each hub completes its transmission preparation and returns a message mes to M. After receiving mess from all the hubs, M returns a message confirm to each hub, which represents the start of parallel transfer (the process uses techniques such as hash time lock like traditional off-chain transfers). Finally, M returns a confirm message to each hub agreeing that the nodes in each group will broadcast their latest transmission balance to the blockchain to complete the multi-hop payment. The basic process can be seen in Fig. 3, in which phase① is when the Hub receives a request from the receiver and sends a puzzle. In the② phase, the sender uses the puzzle number sent by the receiver to transfer the solution of the puzzle to the Hub node in an oblivious puzzle transfer (OPT) protocol. Please refer to the specific literature [29] for details of each phase in Fig. 3.

In addition to ensuring the atomicity of the transaction process, this phase also ensures that the manager node can determine whether a round-robin attack as shown in Fig. 2 has occurred. When a circular transaction as in Fig. 2 occurs, the manager node does not receive the message mes from other hub nodes, so the manager node will refuse to return the confirm message and abort the transaction. To ensure the unlinkability of multi-hub transactions, we use an obfuscated transaction approach, specifically, each hub node needs to collect ten transaction requests before it can send a ready message mes to the manager node (① in Fig. 3).

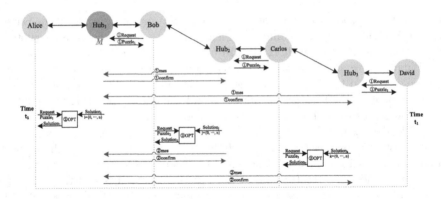

Fig. 3. Execution process of multichannel blending of atoms.

4   Security Analysis

In this section, we give the attacker model of this scheme and define UC [28]. Then, we describe the ideal operation of the OPE protocol. Yet, we analyze the security of the behaviors in OPE protocol.

Attacker model. In the security definition phase, we define the adversary's capabilities and goals and describe the security properties that the protocol should satisfy. We define the adversary as a static adversary A with the goal that A can control an arbitrary number of participants and can interact with the environment ϵ, but cannot break the homomorphic one-way function h. The security properties we wish the protocol should satisfy are correctness and privacy.

When the adversary A interacts with the manager M running the protocol, the set of outputs of the environment ϵ is represented as $EXEC_{OPE,A,\epsilon}$. We can write the set of outputs of environment ϵ as $EXEC_{F,S,\epsilon}$ when the simulator S interacts with the trusted functionality F. Then the UC implementation concerning the global function is defined as

Definition 1 *(Global Universal Composability.) There is a protocol ρ, UC implementing the ideal function F on global channels and global time, and if for any probabilistic polynomial time (PPT) adversary A, there exists a simulator S, then the output sets $EXEC_{\rho,A,\epsilon}$ and $EXEC_{F,S,\epsilon}$ are computationally indistinguishable for any environment ϵ.*

4.1   Ideal Functionality F_{OPE}

We define an ideal functionality F_{OPE} that represents the optimal path encryption process. F_{OPE} contains two participants, the sender V_S and the manager M, respectively. The ideal functional F_{OPE} is described as follows: When V_S enters the request message $(Request, M, com)$, F_{OPE} does the following:

(1) Forwards the message $(Request, M, com)$ to M and the simulator S.
(2) If receives the message $(Request\text{-}ok, b)$ from M and $b = \perp$ then abort, tell V_S to abort.
(3) Otherwise, receive a message $(Request\text{-}ok, b, f, G_2 = (V', E))$ from M.
(4) Find the optimal payment path according to the graph $G_2 = (V', E)$, encrypt the result (encrypted-path), and calculate the total value of the payment path (total-value).
(5) Finally sends encrypted-path, total-value to V_S and S.
(6) Receives the uncommitted message from V_S and forwards it to M and S.

4.2   Security Proof of the OPE Protocol

Initialization. At input, the public parameters include the homomorphic graph G_2 and the homomorphic one-way function h. In this whole process, we omit the role and function of the homomorphic one-way function h, since it is taken to be a standard function available to all participants. Since M uses homomorphic graphs, this allows hiding the true topology without destroying the network structure. Moreover, since h is a homomorphic one-way function, it is possible to securely encrypt information such as nodes in the graph without revealing any information.

Theorem 1 *Assuming that COM and NIZK are secure commitment schemes, OPE can be achieved under UC with ideal functionalities F_{OPE} in the (F_{COM}, F_{NIZK})-hybrid model.*

Proof Next, we discuss the security of the OPE protocol in the case that the sender and the manager M are corrupted respectively.

Hybrid h_0: The structure of h_0 is the same as that of the OPE protocol.

Hybrid h_1: Replaces the step of using the commitment scheme in h_0 with a call to functionality F_{COM} as shown in Fig. 4. We should note that commitment also has two important properties, perfectly binding and perfectly hiding. Perfectly binding can be understood as the probability of finding two different values x_1, x_2 (random number $r_1 \neq r_2$) satisfying $com_1 = com_2$ for any PPT adversary can be Perfectly hiding: adversaries as above, in for $x_1 \neq x_2$ the commitment com_1, com_2 is indistinguishable.

Hybrid h_2: All calls to the non-interactive zero-knowledge scheme NIZK are replaced with calls to the functionality F_{NIZK} in Fig. 5, which uses the relation R.

Hybrid h_3: In this hybrid model, the security of both step 1 and step (3)(4)(5) of the protocol is guaranteed. For the remaining steps, when M is corrupted, the optimal path from V_S to f may be replaced with a randomly chosen path. This will lead to the discovery that it is not the path from V_S to f when V_S verifies encrypted-path. Therefore the simulation will be aborted. Additionally, we have a deposit smart contract signed by the manager as a double guarantee that M performs an honest operation. Consequently, the operation of the simulator S_{OPE} is shown below.

Ideal Functionality F_{COM}

·Commit: P_0 and P_1 interact when P_0 sends a promise Com(x, *sid*) for message x. If the FCOM detects that a commitment to message x already exists, there is no feedback. Otherwise FCOM stores Com(x, *sid*, i) and returns it to P_0(receive, *sid*).

·Decommit: When P_1 enters (decommit, *sid*). If FCOM stores the message (x, *sid*, i) then send Decom(x, *sid*) to P_0. Otherwise no feedback.

Fig. 4. The ideal functionality of the commitment scheme is F_{COM}.

Ideal Functionality F_{NIZK}

The participants are P_0 and P_1. When P0 enters the request (proof, *sid*, x, w), there is no feedback if (x, w) $\notin$ R or if *sid* has been used before. Otherwise, the message (proof, *sid*, x) is sent to P_1. And vice versa.

Fig. 5. Ideal functional F_{NIZK} for the non-interactive zer knowledge scheme.

(1) When manager M is corrupted, S_{OPE} does the following:
 ① S computes a commitment to send to M for the auxiliary inputs starting point V_S, ending point f, and selection criterion sc in the protocol.
 ② S waits for a response from adversary A (representing M), and aborts if A does not respond. Otherwise S receives encrypted-path, total-value and π from A.
 ③ Finally, S verifies encrypted-path, and if successful, sends the decommitment $decom(V_S, f, sc)$ to A. Otherwise aborts.
(2) When the sender V_S is corrupted, S_{OPE} does the following:
 ①S receives the message (*Request*, M, *com*) from A then finds the optimal path based on the auxiliary input and sends the messages encrypted-path, total-value, and π to A respectively.
 ② Finally receives the decommitted decom from A.

Next, we proceed to prove the indistinguishability of the neighboring experiments for the environment ϵ.

Lemma 1 *For any environment ϵ, it holds that $EXEC_{h_0,A,\epsilon} \approx EXEC_{h_1,A,\epsilon}$.*

Proof We note that the difference between the two is in the invocation of the commitment scheme, and thus the security of the hybrid protocol depends on the security of the commitment scheme.

Lemma 2 *For any environment ϵ, it holds that $EXEC_{h_1,A,\epsilon} \approx EXEC_{h_2,A,\epsilon}$.*

Proof Based on the former, we note that the security of the non-interactive zero-knowledge proof scheme is sufficient to support the security of the hybrid protocol.

Lemma 3 *For an arbitrary environment* ϵ, *it holds that* $EXEC_{h_2,A,\epsilon} \approx EXEC_{h_3,A,\epsilon}$.

Proof As we have seen when the honest V_S interacts with the corrupted M, the operations of the M nodes in the two hybrids h_2 and h_3 differ. Thus, it is only necessary to limit the probability of such events occurring. In the h_2 model, the M node will intentionally output the wrong payment path, which will cause the simulation to terminate. And in the h_3 model when the M node outputs a payment path randomly leading to zero-knowledge proof and smart contract verification failure, it will also lead to the termination of the simulation. And in both models the probability that an adversary performs an evil act that results in an abort is limited to $1/2$, so for the environment the two models are indistinguishable.

Lemma 4 *For an arbitrary environment* ϵ, *it considers* $EXEC_{h_3,A,\epsilon} \approx EXEC_{F_{OPE},S,\epsilon}$.

Proof The simulation process and the final output of both hybrid models are the same, only the formulation is slightly different. Therefore, the distinguisher is indistinguishable.

4.3 Discussion

Privacy Proof. During the protocol execution, M encrypts the optimal payment path and its edge weights using a homomorphic one-way function h. Since h is a homomorphic one-way function, it also means that only the key holder can decrypt the ciphertext data. Hence, the protocol satisfies the private property.

Correctness Proof. In the protocol, we compute the optimal path from V_S to f using an algorithm that satisfies the selection criterion sc and add its encrypted node and edge weights to the list of encrypted-path. In the meantime, the proof π is generated using the zero-knowledge proof technique to prove that the encrypted optimal path is the shortest payment path from the start point to the endpoint in the auxiliary input. Specifically, after V_S receives the encrypted-path and the proof π, V_S verifies the correctness of the proof π to check if it is true. If the verification is successful, then V_S can select this payment path. The correctness of the protocol is guaranteed because the protocol uses zero-knowledge proof techniques to prove the correctness of the optimal path.

5 Performance Analysis

The simulation procedure is written in Python, which relies on the phe cryptographic library for cryptographic operations. We simulated the average interaction time of the nodes in the second phase, analyzing the variation of the deposits transacted through the PCH and the complexity of the local code.

Average Time. We simulated the Python code on a local inter CORE i7, Windows 10 computer for the manager campaign phase and the protocol interaction and give the average interaction time for the second phase in Fig. 6. Our simulation is set, as in previous literature, to have all nodes know the network topology, so we do not consider the time to construct the topology in our simulation. We can see that the average times in the graphs are all much smaller than the time it takes for a blockchain to complete a transaction (ten minutes).

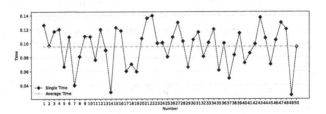

Fig. 6. Schematic of the average running time of the protocol.

Deposit. We also focus on the change in the number of deposits when users pay using the method in this paper, as shown in Fig. 7. The scheme reduces the cost of m transactions for four hub nodes from 8m*Q*t (=2m*Q*4t) deposits to 2m*Q*t deposits, where t denotes time and Q denotes the number of base deposits between two nodes. In other words, we reduce the deposit via the four hub nodes by 75%.

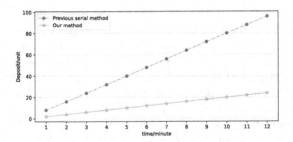

Fig. 7. Change in payment deposit after enabling the provisioning run phase.

Complexity Analysis. This paper is written in Python and the description has been given in the first phase, the main complexity analysis is in the second phase of the optimal path encryption protocol selected. The time complexity of this protocol comes from the selection criteria of the optimal path. Since we have selected the shortest path, Dijkstra's algorithm is chosen in the implementation and the total time complexity can be expressed as $O(ElogV)$, where E is the number of edges and V is the number of nodes. In addition, when encrypting the node and edge weights on the shortest path with homomorphic one-way functions, one exponential operation is required for each node and edge weight, so the time complexity is $O(n)$, where n is the shortest path length.

6   Conclusion

To enhance the confidentiality of off-chain payment paths in the context of solving the blockchain scalability problem, we propose a payment channel design scheme based on the nature of homomorphic one-way functions. Firstly, the scheme ensures that the attacker will not be informed of the payment path in advance. Secondly, due to the nature of our multi-hub transaction scenario, where the hub nodes set the amount of each transaction to a uniform size, the attacker cannot infer from the many nodes with changing balances whether they belong to the same transfer. Moreover, this scheme can reduce the locking time of the deposit and alleviate the pressure on the locking channel of each node. Finally, simulation experiments prove that the scheme has significant advantages in solving the confidentiality of path information and reducing the cost of deposits. In the future, we will further explore how to optimize the communication burden as well as the specific application aspects of this scheme, to better facilitate its application and development in cross-chain interoperability and digital asset circulation.

Acknowledgements. This study is supported by the Foundation of National Natural Science Foundation of China (Grant No.: 62072273, 61962009); The Major Basic Research Project of Natural Science Foundation of Shandong Province of China (ZR2019ZD10); Natural Science Foundation of Shandong Province (ZR2019MF062); Shandong University Science and Technology Program Project (J18A326); Guangxi Key Laboratory of Cryptography and Information Security (No: GCIS202112); Foundation of Guizhou Provincial Key Laboratory of Public Big Data (No. 2019BD-KFJJ009); This work was supported by the Key-Area Research and Development Program of Guangdong Province (No .2020B0101130015).

References

1. Poon, J., Dryja, T.: The bitcoin lightning network: Scalable off-chain instant payments, (2016)
2. Raiden Network. https://raiden.network/
3. Dziembowski, S., Eckey, L., Faust, S., Malinowski, D.: Perun: Virtual payment hubs over cryptocurrencies. In: 2019 IEEE Symposium on Security and Privacy SP, pp. 106–123. IEEE (2019)
4. Aumayr, L., Maffei, M., Ersoy, O., et al.: Bitcoin-compatible virtual channels. In: 2021 IEEE Symposium on Security and Privacy SP, pp. 901–918. IEEE (2021)
5. Egger, C., oreno-Sanchez, P., Maffei, M.: Atomic multi-channel updates with constant collateral in bitcoin-compatible payment-channel networks. In: Proceedings of the 2019 ACM SIGSAC Conference on Computer and Communications Security, pp. 801–815. ACM (2019)

6. Sivaraman, V., Venkatakrishnan, S, B., Ruan, K., et al.: High throughput cryptocurrency routing in payment channel networks. In: 17th USENIX Symposium on Networked Systems Design and Implementation, pp. 777–796. USENIX (2020)
7. Malavolta, G., Moreno-Sanchez, P., Kate, A., Maffei, M., Ravi, S.: Concurrency and privacy with payment-channel networks. In: Proceedings of the 2017 ACM SIGSAC Conference on Computer and Communications Security, pp. 455–471. ACM (2017)
8. Malavolta, G., Moreno-Sanchez, P., Schneidewind, C., et al.: anonymous multi-hop locks for blockchain scalability and interoperability. In: 26th Annual Network and Distributed System Security Symposium NDSS. The Internet Society (2019)
9. Kappos, G., et al.: An empirical analysis of privacy in the lightning network. In: Borisov, N., Diaz, C. (eds.) FC 2021. LNCS, vol. 12674, pp. 167–186. Springer, Heidelberg (2021). https://doi.org/10.1007/978-3-662-64322-8_8
10. Nayak, K., Kumar, S., Miller, A., et al.: Stubborn mining: generalizing selfish mining and combining with an eclipse attack. In: 2016 IEEE European Symposium on Security and Privacy EuroSP, pp. 305–320. IEEE (2016)
11. Zhang, Y., Zhao, M., Li, T., et al.: Achieving optimal rewards in cryptocurrency stubborn mining with state transition analysis. Inf. Sci. **625**, 299–313 (2023)
12. Zheng, J., Huang, H., Zheng, Z., et al.: Adaptive Double-Spending Attacks on PoW-based Blockchains, IEEE Transactions on Dependable and Secure Computing (2023)
13. Pérez-Solà, C., Ranchal-Pedrosa, A., Herrera-Joancomartí, J., Navarro-Arribas, G., Garcia-Alfaro, J.: LockDown: balance availability attack against lightning network channels. In: Bonneau, J., Heninger, N. (eds.) Financial Cryptography and Data Security: 24th International Conference, FC 2020 , Kota Kinabalu, Malaysia, February 10–14, 2020 Revised Selected Papers, pp. 245–263. Springer International Publishing, Cham (2020). https://doi.org/10.1007/978-3-030-51280-4_14
14. Hong, H, J., Chang, S, Y., Zhou, X.: Auto-Tune: efficient autonomous routing for payment channel networks. In: 2022 IEEE 47th Conference on Local Computer Networks LCN, pp. 347–350. IEEE, (2022)
15. Mizrahi, A., Zohar, A.: Congestion attacks in payment channel networks. In: Financial Cryptography and Data Security - 25th International Conference, pp. 170–188. Springer (2021). https://doi.org/10.1145/3433210.3453089
16. Qiao, Y., Wu, K., Khabbazian, M.: Non-intrusive and high-efficient balance tomography in the lightning network. In: Proceedings of the 2021 ACM Asia Conference on Computer and Communications Security, pp. 832–843. ACM (2021)
17. Chen, W., Guo, X., Chen, Z., et al.: Phishing scam detection on ethereum: towards financial security for blockchain ecosystem. In: Proceedings of the Twenty-Ninth International Joint Conference on Artificial Intelligence, pp. 4456–4462. ijcai.org, (2020)
18. Dasgupta, D., Shrein, J.M., Gupta, K.D.: A survey of blockchain from security perspective. J. Bank. Financial Technol. **3**(1), 1–17 (2019)
19. Green, M., Miers, I.: Bolt: Anonymous payment channels for decentralized currencies. In: Proceedings of the 2017 ACM SIGSAC Conference on Computer and Communications Security, pp. 473–489. ACM, (2017)
20. Tairi, E., Moreno-Sanchez, P., Maffei, M.: A 2 l: Anonymous atomic locks for scalability in payment channel hubs. In: 2021 IEEE Symposium on Security and Privacy SP, IEEE, pp. 1834–1851. IEEE (2021)
21. Heilman, E., Alshenibr, L., Baldimtsi, F., et al.: Tumblebit: An untrusted bitcoin-compatible anonymous payment hub. In: Network and Distributed System Security Symposium, pp. 473–489. The Internet Society (2017)

22. Qin, X., Pan, S., Mirzaei, A., et al.: BlindHub: Bitcoin-Compatible Privacy-Preserving Payment Channel Hubs Supporting Variable Amounts. In 2023 IEEE Symposium on Security and Privacy SP, IEEE Computer Society, pp. 2020–2038 (2023)

23. Liu, J., Yang, B.: Collusion-resistant multicast key distribution based on homomorphic one-way function trees. IEEE Trans. Inf. Forensics Secur. 6(3), 980–991 (2011)

24. Blum, M., Feldman, P., Micali, S.: Non-interactive zero-knowledge and its applications. Providing Sound Foundations for Cryptography: On the Work of Shafi Goldwasser and Silvio Micali, pp. 329–349 (2019)

25. Juels, A., Wattenberg, M.: A fuzzy commitment scheme. In: Proceedings of the 6th ACM Conference on Computer and Communications Security, pp. 28–36. ACM (1999)

26. Mayers, D.: Unconditionally secure quantum bit commitment is impossible **78**(17), 3414 (1997)

27. Damgård, I., Nielsen, J.B.: Perfect hiding and perfect binding universally composable commitment schemes with constant expansion factor. In: Annual International Cryptology Conference, vol. 2442, pp. 581–596. Springer (2002). https://doi.org/10.1007/3-540-45708-9_37

28. Canetti, R.: Universally composable security: a new paradigm for cryptographic protocols. In: Proceedings 42nd IEEE Symposium on Foundations of Computer Science, pp. 136–145. IEEE (2001)

29. Wang, Y., Liu, M., Ma, H., et al.: Enabling scalable and unlinkable payment channel hubs with oblivious puzzle transfer. Inf. Sci. **630**, 713–726 (2023)

A General Federated Learning Scheme with Blockchain on Non-IID Data

Hao Wu[1,2], Shengnan Zhao[2], Chuan Zhao[2(✉)], and Shan Jing[1,3(✉)]

[1] School of Information Science and Engineering, University of Jinan,
Jinan 250022, Shandong, China
jingshan@ujn.edu.cn
[2] Quancheng Laboratory, Jinan 250103, China
ise_zhaoc@ujn.edu.cn
[3] Shandong Provincial Key Laboratory of Network-based Intelligent Computing,
Jinan 250022, Shandong, China

Abstract. The security of machine learning has received a lot of attention from the community. Federated learning enables more secure training processes of models in machine learning via local training and parameter interactions of participants. However, participants' data usually shows significant differences, *i.e.*, the characteristics of non-IID, affecting the convergence speed and accuracy of models to a large extent. In this paper, we propose a general federated learning scheme with blockchain to cover the shortage of federated learning caused by non-IID data. Specifically, each participant trains a GAN via local data first and then shares the generator corresponding to the GAN with the assistance of the blockchain. Based on the generator parameters on the blockchain, each participant augments the local data and trains the local model, alleviating a series of problems caused by the non-IID data. The scheme achieves effective training of models while ensuring security. Experimental results show that the proposed scheme can speed up model convergence and improve the model's accuracy simultaneously. In the non-IID scenario, compared with the federated learning benchmark scheme, the accuracy in our scheme can be improved by up to 17%.

Keywords: Federated learning · Non-IID problem · Data augmentation · Data privacy

1 Introduction

With the constant maturity of artificial intelligence technology, more and more machine learning algorithms are applied to realistic technologies. As we all know,

This work is supported by the TaiShan Scholars Program (tsqn202211280), National Natural Science Foundation of China (No. 61702218, 62172258, 61972176), Shandong Provincial Natural Science Foundation (No. ZR2023LZH014, ZR2022ZD01, ZR2021LZH007, ZR2019LZH015), Shandong Provincial Key R&D Program of China (No. 2021SFGC0401, 2021CXGC010103), Department of Science&Technology of Shandong Province (No.SYS202201), and Quan Cheng Laboratory (Grant No. QCLZD202302).

machine learning is a typical data-driven task requiring plenty of high-quality samples to support training. Traditional methods are collecting data from various data providers and storing those data in a central server to carry out model training tasks. The collected data may contain sensitive information, and the abovementioned methods would cause privacy leakage [27]. On the other hand, the promulgation and implementation of new laws and regulations, such as the General Data Protection Regulation (GDPR) [23], California Consumer Privacy Act (CCPA), Personal Data Protection Act (PDPA), etc, put forward more stringent requirements towards data usage. Consequently, "data silos" have emerged across institutions or organizations, bringing significant challenges to joint training of machine learning models.

Federated learning (FL) provides a feasible solution to the abovementioned requirements. McMahan et al. [16] propose the FedAvg algorithm for the low-bandwidth environment of FL, where clients execute the stochastic gradient descent (SGD) algorithm [21] locally before interacting with the central server. Experiments show that FedAvg significantly reduces communication overhead when the data are independent and identically distributed (IID). However, it has little effect on non-independent and identically distributed (non-IID) data. Li et al. [13] analyze the convergence of the FedAvg and prove that the heterogeneity of the data would lead to a decrease in the convergence speed of FL.

The deterioration in the accuracy of FL is almost inevitable on non-IID or heterogeneous data [29]. Zhao et al. [28] show that the accuracy reduction of FL can be explained by the weight divergence and improve the training of non-IID data by sharing a small subset of data among all edge devices. Collins [4] regards FL tasks on heterogeneous data as n parallel learning tasks and works on learning shared data representations across clients. Tian et al. [22] propose a pre-shared data training strategy for non-IID data to avoid convergence divergence. Based on data sharing, these papers act on the data difference and can fundamentally solve the problem [15]. However, sharing raw data directly may bring the risk of privacy leakage. Jeong [10] proposes a data augmentation scheme named FAug, which uses a generative adversarial network (GAN) to rectify non-IID training datasets. Similar to [10], Li et al. [14] propose a novel framework SDA-FL to address the non-IID challenge. Specifically, each client trains a local GAN to generate synthetic data first and then uploads the data to the server to build a global shared synthetic dataset. Reference [18,26] train machine learning models through FL and use the trained models for data augmentation operations.

It effectively addresses the non-IID problem of sharing some data directly to balance data across institutions, but these methods take the risk of privacy leakage and may violate laws and regulations. On the other hand, it can reduce privacy leakage to a certain extent by providing a small amount of seed data to train a GAN for data augmentation. But privacy leakage is still unacceptable because it is still fatal to specific groups, such as patients with diseases. In addition, training GANs through FL to generate data has drawbacks. The communication in the network can be slower than local computation by many orders of magnitude [12].

Motivated by these limitations, we propose a general FL scheme called *Generative Models and Blockchain Aided Federated Learning* (GBA-FL) to alleviate the non-IID problem. The main contributions of this paper are as follows:

- We propose to perform data augmentation by directly sharing the generator parameters that satisfy the differential privacy to improve the data quality while ensuring data privacy.
- We design a scheme for the interaction of the generators of each participant via blockchain to ensure the transparency and traceability of the generators.
- We validate the scheme based on the MNIST and FashionMNIST datasets in the non-IID setting. Experiments show that the proposed scheme has significantly improved model convergence speed and accuracy.

2 Preliminaries

2.1 Differential Privacy

Differential privacy (DP) [7] ensures that, with a private dataset as input, the difference between the two outputs is difficult to detect whether a particular piece of data exists in the dataset or not. For any randomized algorithm $\mathcal{A}$, adjacent sets d and d' are the algorithm's input, and the output set is denoted by S. Algorithm $\mathcal{A}$ is said to satisfy (ϵ, δ) - DP if it satisfies:

$$Pr[\mathcal{A}(d) \in S] \leq e^\epsilon \cdot Pr[(\mathcal{A}(d') \in S] + \delta \tag{1}$$

Notably, adjacent sets mean that two datasets contain at most one different element. ϵ is a minimal value to measure the privacy budget. δ is a slack term.

Generally, the Laplace [6] or Gaussian [8] mechanism is usually used to realize DP protection in machine learning. The Gaussian noise mechanism $\mathcal{M}_\sigma$ parameterized by σ can be expressed by:

$$\mathcal{M}_\sigma = f(d) + \mathcal{N}(0, \sigma^2 I^2), \tag{2}$$

where I denotes the sensitivity of the random function f.

2.2 Generative Adversarial Network

To generate highly authentic samples, a GAN [9] contains two parts: a generator and a discriminator. The generator's input is a random vector z sampled from the prior distribution P_z, such as uniform distribution or Gaussian distribution, and the output is a virtual sample $G(z)$. The task of the generator is to generate samples $G(z)$ that are as realistic as possible to fool the discriminator. And the discriminator's task is to determine whether the input data is real or fake. The structure of GAN is shown in Fig. 1.

Mathematically, the objective function of GAN can be formulated via a min-max game with a value function $V(D, G)$ as:

$$\min_G \max_D V(D, G) = \mathbb{E}_{x \sim P_d} \log D(x) + \mathbb{E}_{z \sim P_z} \log(1 - D(G(z))), \tag{3}$$

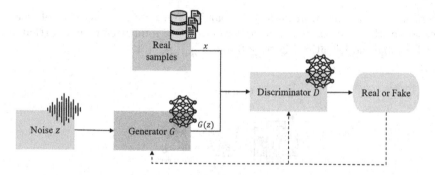

Fig. 1. Structure of GAN

where x is sampled from real data distribution P_d, z is sampled from the prior distribution P_z, $\mathbb{E}(\cdot)$ is the expectation, $D(\cdot)$ denotes the probability of x sampled from the real data.

2.3 Blockchain

Decentralization is an essential property of blockchain networks [1,17,19]. That is to say, blockchains do not store data centrally in a particular location. The distributed ledger makes the information more transparent and can be audited by the respective nodes at any time. A new block can be added to the chain only if most nodes in the network agree on the validity of the transaction and the validity of the block itself through a consensus mechanism [20].

In the blockchain, consensus mechanisms guarantee authenticity, reliability, and immutability. Based on a P2P network among the nodes, consensus mechanisms make blocks challenging to construct but easy to verify [5]. Proof of Work (PoW) is one of the most widely used consensus mechanisms in blockchain networks. Proof of Stake (PoS) avoids a large number of calculations in Pow and greatly shortens the calculation time. Therefore, PoS achieves higher network performance and better practicality.

2.4 Federated Learning

First proposed by Google [16], FL is a distributed machine learning framework that satisfies both privacy protection and data security. The architecture of FL is shown in Fig. 2. Each participant in FL does not need to share training samples, and the joint training of the model can be completed by interacting and aggregating the model parameters.

With increased attention paid to privacy protection, FL has become a very promising technology [24]. The task of FL can be described as the optimization of the following objective function:

$$\min \ F(\omega), \ where \ F(\omega) := \sum_{k=1}^{m} p_k F_k(\omega), \tag{4}$$

where m denotes the total number of participants, $F_k(\cdot)$ is the local objective function of the k-th participants, p_k is the relative influence of each participant on the global model satisfying $p_k \geq 0$ and $\sum_{k=1}^{m} p_k = 1$.

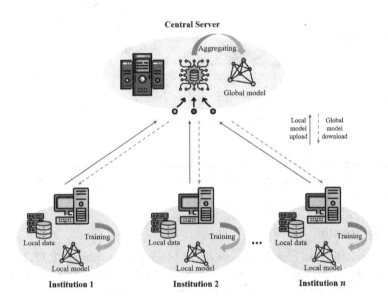

Fig. 2. Architecture of federated learning

3   Proposed GBA-FL Scheme

3.1   Overview

The scheme is suitable for FL scenarios with multiple institutions. We consider adding a preparation phase before the regular FL process. The main tasks in this phase include the training of GANs, the sharing of trained generator models, and the augmentation of the local data of each institution. None of the above tasks depends on the intermediate operations and outputs of subsequent FL and thus can exist independently of the FL process. Each institution trains a GAN based on local data and obtains a trained generator model to generate virtual samples representing the local data's characteristics. The generators trained by various institutions will be packaged into a block and uploaded to the blockchain. In this way, any institutions can download all generators' parameters from the blockchain and generate virtual samples for data augmentation, thereby alleviating the non-IID problem. The workflow of the GBA-FL framework is shown in Fig. 3. Now we introduce the scheme in detail.

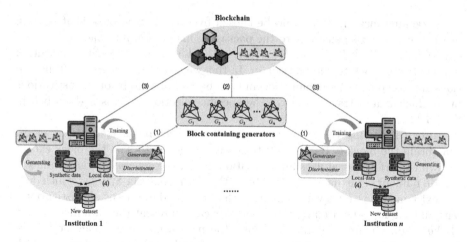

Fig. 3. Workflow diagram of GBA-FL

3.2 Non-IID Data Augmentation

In GBA-FL, multiple institutions jointly perform tasks related to model training and data interaction. These institutions come from the set K and are denoted by an index k. We assume that they have a local dataset S_k, and each dataset exhibits the characteristics of non-IID. The data owned by the institutions is sensitive and cannot be shared directly. All institutions participating in the training process are rigorously verified and non-malicious participants who expect to obtain higher-performance machine learning models and do not launch malicious attacks, such as poisoning attacks to damage the models or deliberate disruption of the training process.

To improve the effect of model training, institutions have to perform the training task with the assistance of the GBA-FL framework. First, each institution needs to initialize the generator parameter $\theta_{k,t=0}^{g}$ (t denotes the index of the round) and the discriminator parameter $\theta_{k,t=0}^{d}$ in the local GAN model, and iteratively train the GAN based on their local dataset S_k. The training process of GAN is a continuous game between the generator and the discriminator. The generator learns from local data and continuously generates virtual samples to fool the discriminator. The discriminator needs to judge the authenticity of the virtual samples. After T_k rounds of iterative updates, the discriminator cannot accurately judge the authenticity of the virtual samples. The resulting generator $\theta_{k,T_k}^{g} \to \theta_k^{g}$ can generate virtual samples similar to the original data. Now these samples can represent the characteristics of the local dataset. Considering the higher security of data privacy preservation, we use a GAN that satisfies DP for the above task. The detailed description is given in Sect. 3.3.

Now, each institution k prepares to share its trained generator θ_k^{g} for subsequent data augmentation tasks. To realize data sharing, it is necessary to select an institution to act the role of the packaging institution p, who is credible and performs tasks by rigorously following the protocol instructions. In this phase, the packaging institution p could be chosen from all institutions. That is, each institution sends its generator to the packaging institution p to package all generators into a block $b = block\{\theta_1^g, \theta_2^g, \ldots, \theta_K^g\}$. Then, the packaging institution p uploads the block to the blockchain. In this way, the generators of all institutions are stored in a blockchain node and can be downloaded by other institutions in an efficient and traceable way. The specific selection process is described in Sect. 3.4.

After completing the transaction on the blockchain, all institutions in FL can obtain the block b. Each institution uses the generators on the block except its own to perform local data augmentation. Next, the generators can produce a certain number of virtual samples to build the virtual dataset $S_k^{virtual}$, which does not exist in but is relatively similar to the original datasets of all institutions. Virtual samples generated by the generators can represent the data distribution of the original training data. Therefore, the institutions learn relevant feature information from training data. Finally, by assembling the local dataset S_k with the virtual dataset $S_k^{virtual}$, a new dataset $S_k' = S_k + S_k^{virtual}$ is constructed. The newly built dataset S_k' contains not only the local data characteristics of the current institution but also the data characteristics of other institutions.

So far, the local data augmentation task for each institution's non-IID data has been completed. Based on the dataset S_k', each participant can perform the subsequent FL training task.

3.3 Privacy-Preserving Training of GANs

All institutions must process the local data before GAN training. After that, each institution performs GAN training. By modelling the underlying data distribution, the ultimate goal of GAN is to generate virtual samples faithful to the original input distribution. However, study [3] finds that replacing the distribution of original data by publishing generators directly also suffers the risk of privacy leakage. Therefore, privacy-preserving methods must be taken to train the GAN.

In our GBA-FL scheme, we refer a novel gradient-sanitized Wasserstein GAN scheme (GS-WGAN) [2] to generate high-dimensional data with DP guarantees. The scheme trains all GANs in a privacy-preserving manner, ensuring that private information is protected after the generators are released. The discriminator keeps regular training during GAN training without privacy-preserving operations on its gradient information. Only the parameters passed by the discriminator to the generator will be sanitized. The generators trained in the above way can still satisfy the DP requirements. Meanwhile, the virtual samples generated by the generators have better usability. The training objectives are as follows:

$$\mathcal{L}_D = -\mathbb{E}_{x \sim P_d}[D(x)] + \mathbb{E}_{\tilde{x} \sim P_v}[D(\tilde{x})] + \lambda \mathbb{E}[(\|\nabla D(\alpha x + (1-\alpha)\tilde{x})\|_2 - 1)^2] \quad (5)$$

$$\mathcal{L}_G = -\mathbb{E}_{z \sim P_z}[D(G(z))] \quad (6)$$

where $\mathcal{L}_D$ and $\mathcal{L}_G$ denote training objectives for the discriminator and the generator, respectively. λ is the hyper-parameter used for the gradient penalty. P_v

denotes the distribution of generated samples. The variable α is sampled uniformly from $[0, 1]$ to adjust the proportional relationship between the real and generated samples.

3.4 Generators Decentralized Sharing

In our scheme, we introduce blockchain technology to realize the sharing of the generators through the way of distributed data storage. A blockchain is a distributed ledger consisting of a sequence of data blocks, and each data block contains a set of verifiable transactions [30]. Blocks contain the hash value of the previous block's header. One block is linked to the previous block by the hash value, which ensures the integrity and immutability of data on the blockchain.

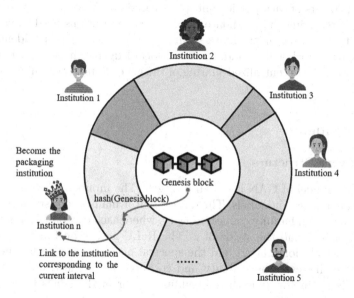

Fig. 4. Selection of the packaging institutions

Before carrying out the data-sharing task, a packaging institution must be selected in advance for the packaging of generators and the uploading of the block. In GBA-FL, we combine the PoS consensus and the consistent hashing protocol to select the packaging institution. Participants pledge currency as capital into smart contracts to campaign for the opportunity to be the packaging institution. The probability of the institution being selected as the packaging institution is directly proportional to the currency (stake) that they have in the system. The selection process for the packaging institution is as follows: (1) Input each institution's ID (*e.g.*, IP address) into a consistent hashing protocol to obtain a position on the ring space. (2) Select a certain number of positions in the ring and divide the ring into n intervals. The number of intervals is the same as the number of institutions, and the proportional relationship between intervals is the same as the stake ratio of each institution. (3) Associate each institution with the corresponding interval. The proportional relationship of the intervals is the same as the proportional relationship of the institutions' stake. All data values on the intervals can be indexed to the corresponding institutions. (4) Create a blockchain and hash the value of the Genesis block. (5) Map the hash value to the ring, and the institution associated with the interval where the hash value is located will be selected as the packaging institution. The selection of the packaging institution is shown in Fig. 4.

Once the packaging institution is selected, other institutions can send their generators. Each institution uses its private key to sign the generator. The packaging institution uses the corresponding public key to verify the generator, ensuring the credibility of the institution. Next, the packaging institution packages the verified generators of each participant into a candidate block and broadcasts the block. After receiving the candidate block, other institutions need to verify the legality of the transaction, the block's validity, and the participants' identity and stake. The new block will be added to their local ledger if the verification is correct. This way, the decentralized sharing of the generators among all institutions is realized.

4   Experiments

4.1   Network Structure

The network model of GAN is shown in Fig. 5. The inputs of the discriminator are grayscale images and labels. The discriminator mainly consists of three convolutional layers and a fully connected layer, where each convolutional layer uses the kernel of 5×5 and the stride of 2. The ReLU activation function is added after each convolutional layer, and the spectral normalization technique is also introduced to increase the stability and convergence of the training. In addition, the discriminator adds the embedding vector of the labels to the output for auxiliary classification.

The generator receives a random noise vector and a label as input. It mainly contains a fully connected layer, three residual blocks, and an output layer. The input random noise vector and the label are fed into the residual block after the concating operation and the processing of the fully connected layer. Each residual block contains two convolutional layers and a residual connection and uses spectral normalization technology for parameter normalization. Finally, the tensor is converted into an image of 28×28 through the convolutional layer and the Sigmoid activation function.

4.2   Datasets and Division Strategies

We implement the prototype of the GBA-FL system based on the MNIST [11] and FashionMNIST [25] datasets and analyze the performance. We design the

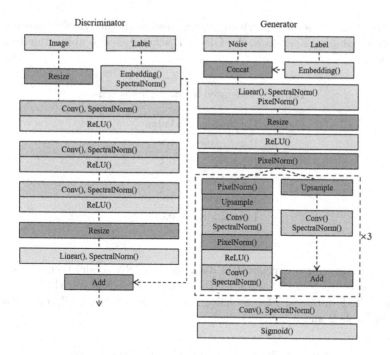

Fig. 5. Network Model of GAN

division strategies for the datasets in the IID and non-IID scenarios, respectively. In IID scenarios, the distribution of labels and the size of data owned by each institution should be the same. Therefore, we choose to construct 100 uniform datasets by random sampling from the whole dataset and assign them to institutions. Institutions can then perform local model training tasks based on their own dataset. In non-IID scenarios, the labels and distributions of local data vary significantly among institutions. Therefore, we consider sorting the training samples according to the labels of the training samples and gathering the samples with the same label together. Keeping the order after arrangement, we divide the dataset into 100 sub-datasets. According to the characteristics of the MNIST and FashionMNIST datasets, the labels in the above sub-datasets are single. Each institution can conduct local training based on one of the sub-datasets.

4.3   Model Accuracy Testing

We use the traditional FedAvg scheme as a benchmark to conduct related experiments to verify the effectiveness of the proposed GBA-FL scheme. We set the total number of institutions participating in the FL to 100 and select 10% of the institutions to participate in the training each round. The detailed parameter settings of FL are shown in Table 1. The GBA-FL scheme is mainly aimed at the preparation phase of FL, which is separated from the training process and has high scalability. Therefore, the GBA-FL scheme is also applicable to other FL schemes.

Table 1. Federated learning parameters

Parameter	Value
Participants	100
Fraction	0.1
Local Epochs	5
Batch Size	10
Learning Rate	0.01

To verify the impact of non-IID data on the CNN model training process, we test the accuracy in IID and non-IID scenarios based on the MNIST and the FashionMNIST datasets. The model's prediction accuracy in different rounds is shown in Table 2 and 3.

Table 2. Accuracy on MNIST in different rounds

Rounds	Accuracy/%		
	IID	*non-IID*	*GBA-FL*
10	96.57	34.68	68.78
25	97.69	65.86	79.40
50	98.53	75.46	88.72
75	98.74	81.61	90.73
100	98.91	85.73	91.36

Table 3. Accuracy on FashionMNIST in different rounds

Rounds	Accuracy/%		
	IID	*non-IID*	*GBA-FL*
10	89.94	35.26	72.68
25	91.29	47.43	83.21
50	92.55	62.47	85.37
75	93.28	65.32	84.62
100	93.75	68.81	86.59

Table 2 shows the accuracy results of the model based on the MNIST dataset in different scenarios. We can observe that in the IID scenario, the accuracy of the model reaches 96.57% in the 10th round, which is even higher than the result after 100 rounds of training in the non-IID scenario. This shows the great impact of non-IID data on the convergence speed of the model. After 100 rounds of training, the accuracy of the model under the non-IID setting finally reaches 85.73%. Compared with the model under the IID setting with the same number of rounds, the accuracy decreased by about 11%. These results show that non-IID data has a non-negligible impact on both the speed of model convergence and the accuracy of the model. The conclusions drawn from observing Table 3 are generally consistent with the above conclusions, but the difference is that the accuracy of the model in all three scenarios is almost lower than in Table 2 due to the higher complexity of the FashionMNIST dataset.

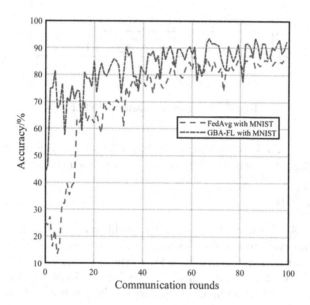

Fig. 6. Accuracy on MNIST

In addition, we can also clearly observe that after 10 rounds of training, the model in GBA-FL already has high accuracy. Meanwhile, comparing the data in the fourth column with the third column, we can find that the GBA-FL scheme has a significant improvement in accuracy and the convergence speed of the model. After 100 rounds of training, GBA-FL improves accuracy by 5.63% on the MNIST and 17.78% on the FashionMNIST.

Figure 6 and Fig. 7 show the variation of the model accuracy during the training process of the two schemes in the non-IID scenario with different datasets. We can see that the GBA-FL scheme can reduce the convergence time of the model and, at the same time, greatly improve the effects of the model. Especially for Fig. 7, the GBA-FL scheme shows a more noticeable effect. We speculate that it may be due to the fact that the FashionMNIST dataset contains more data

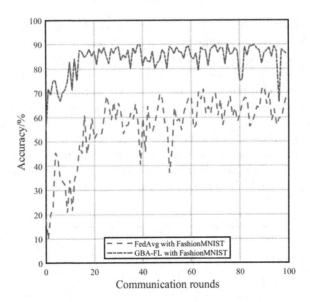

Fig. 7. Accuracy on FashionMNIST

features, and non-IID data has a more significant impact on this complex dataset, which also reflects the practicability of our scheme from the side.

5   Conclusion

We propose GBA-FL scheme to alleviate the problem caused by the non-IID data in FL. GANs are used to learn the local data characteristics of each participant, and the generator parameters are shared with the assistance of blockchain, which eventually achieves data augmentation for each participant. At the same time, the quality of the virtual samples generated by the generators has a particular impact on the overall effect of the scheme. In the future, we will conduct in-depth research on the processing strategy of virtual data and the access mechanism of the blockchain.

References

1. Ali, M., Karimipour, H., Tariq, M.: Integration of blockchain and federated learning for internet of things: recent advances and future challenges. Comput. Security **108**, 102355 (2021)
2. Chen, D., Orekondy, T., Fritz, M.: Gs-wgan: a gradient-sanitized approach for learning differentially private generators. Adv. Neural. Inf. Process. Syst. **33**, 12673–12684 (2020)
3. Chen, D., Yu, N., Zhang, Y., Fritz, M.: Gan-leaks: A taxonomy of membership inference attacks against generative models. In: Proceedings of the 2020 ACM SIGSAC Conference on Computer and Communications Security, pp. 343–362 (2020)

4. Collins, L., Hassani, H., Mokhtari, A., Shakkottai, S.: Exploiting shared representations for personalized federated learning. In: International Conference on Machine Learning, pp. 2089–2099. PMLR (2021)
5. Du, Y., et al.: Blockchain-aided edge computing market: smart contract and consensus mechanisms. IEEE Transactions on Mobile Computing (2022)
6. Dwork, C.: A firm foundation for private data analysis. Commun. ACM **54**(1), 86–95 (2011)
7. Dwork, C., McSherry, F., Nissim, K., Smith, A.: Calibrating noise to sensitivity in private data analysis. In: Theory of Cryptography: Third Theory of Cryptography Conference, TCC 2006, New York, NY, USA, March 4–7, 2006. Proceedings 3, pp. 265–284. Springer (2006)
8. Dwork, C., Roth, A., et al.: The algorithmic foundations of differential privacy. Found. Trends® in Theor. Comput. Sci. **9**(3–4), 211–407 (2014)
9. Goodfellow, I., et al.: Generative adversarial networks. Commun. ACM **63**(11), 139–144 (2020)
10. Jeong, E., Oh, S., Kim, H., Park, J., Bennis, M., Kim, S.L.: Communication-efficient on-device machine learning: Federated distillation and augmentation under non-iid private data. arXiv preprint arXiv:1811.11479 (2018)
11. LeCun, Y., Bottou, L., Bengio, Y., Haffner, P.: Gradient-based learning applied to document recognition. Proc. IEEE **86**(11), 2278–2324 (1998)
12. Li, T., Sahu, A.K., Talwalkar, A., Smith, V.: Federated learning: challenges, methods, and future directions. IEEE Signal Process. Mag. **37**(3), 50–60 (2020)
13. Li, X., Huang, K., Yang, W., Wang, S., Zhang, Z.: On the convergence of fedavg on non-iid data. arXiv preprint arXiv:1907.02189 (2019)
14. Li, Z., Shao, J., Mao, Y., Wang, J.H., Zhang, J.: Federated learning with gan-based data synthesis for non-iid clients. arXiv preprint arXiv:2206.05507 (2022)
15. Ma, X., Zhu, J., Lin, Z., Chen, S., Qin, Y.: A state-of-the-art survey on solving non-iid data in federated learning. Futur. Gener. Comput. Syst. **135**, 244–258 (2022)
16. McMahan, B., Moore, E., Ramage, D., Hampson, S., Arcas, B.A.: Communication-efficient learning of deep networks from decentralized data. In: Artificial intelligence and statistics, pp. 1273–1282. PMLR (2017)
17. Nakamoto, S.: Bitcoin: A peer-to-peer electronic cash system. Decentralized business review, p. 21260 (2008)
18. Nguyen, D.C., Ding, M., Pathirana, P.N., Seneviratne, A., Zomaya, A.Y.: Federated learning for Covid-19 detection with generative adversarial networks in edge cloud computing. IEEE Internet Things J. **9**(12), 10257–10271 (2021)
19. Nguyen, D.C., Pathirana, P.N., Ding, M., Seneviratne, A.: Blockchain for 5g and beyond networks: a state of the art survey. J. Netw. Comput. Appl. **166**, 102693 (2020)
20. Nofer, M., Gomber, P., Hinz, O., Schiereck, D.: Blockchain. business & information. Syst. Eng. **59**, 183–187 (2017)
21. Phuong, T.T., et al.: Distributed sgd with flexible gradient compression. IEEE Access **8**, 64707–64717 (2020)
22. Tian, P., Chen, Z., Yu, W., Liao, W.: Towards asynchronous federated learning based threat detection: a dc-adam approach. Comput. Security **108**, 102344 (2021)
23. Voigt, P., Von dem Bussche, A.: The eu general data protection regulation (gdpr). A Practical Guide, 1st Ed., Cham: Springer International Publishing **10**(3152676), 10–5555 (2017)
24. Wang, L., et al.: Privacy-preserving collaborative computation for human activity recognition. Security and Communication Networks 2022 (2022)

25. Xiao, H., Rasul, K., Vollgraf, R.: Fashion-mnist: a novel image dataset for bench-marking machine learning algorithms. arXiv preprint arXiv:1708.07747 (2017)
26. Zhang, L., Shen, B., Barnawi, A., Xi, S., Kumar, N., Wu, Y.: Feddpgan: federated differentially private generative adversarial networks framework for the detection of covid-19 pneumonia. Inf. Syst. Front. **23**(6), 1403–1415 (2021)
27. Zhao, C., et al.: Secure multi-party computation: theory, practice and applications. Inform. Sci. **476**, 357–372 (2019)
28. Zhao, Y., Li, M., Lai, L., Suda, N., Civin, D., Chandra, V.: Federated learning with non-iid data. arXiv preprint arXiv:1806.00582 (2018)
29. Zhu, H., Xu, J., Liu, S., Jin, Y.: Federated learning on non-iid data: a survey. Neurocomputing **465**, 371–390 (2021)
30. Zhu, J., Cao, J., Saxena, D., Jiang, S., Ferradi, H.: Blockchain-empowered federated learning: challenges, solutions, and future directions. ACM Comput. Surv. **55**(11), 1–31 (2023)

A Blockchain-Based Personal Health Record Sharing Scheme with Security and Privacy Preservation

Xuhao Li, Jiacheng Luo, Lu Zhou$^{(\boxtimes)}$, and Hao Wang

Nanjing University of Aeronautics and Astronautics, Nanjing 210000, China
lu.zhou@nuaa.edu.cn

Abstract. Personal health records (PHRs) have significant value for health management, accurate diagnosis, and disease research. However, PHR sharing may raise owners' concerns about security deficiency and privacy leakage. The current mainstream PHR sharing models rely on centralized systems with risks including data loss and tampering, unauthorized access, etc. Fortunately, blockchain possesses outstanding features such as decentralization, tamper-proof, and traceability, which endow it with great potential to solve sensitive data sharing issues. Based on this, we propose a blockchain-based PHR sharing scheme with security and privacy preservation. It utilizes a secure distributed storage system based on InterPlanetary File System (IPFS) and blockchain to avoid data tampering and single points of failure. We also design a decentralized attribute-based access control (ABAC) mechanism to achieve fine-grained controllable PHR sharing. In addition, the blockchain-based proxy re-encryption method can protect the confidentiality of PHR and prevent privacy leakage. Security analysis shows that our scheme achieves the expected security goals. Besides, we evaluated the proposed scheme on Hyperledger Fabric, and the results demonstrate that the scheme is feasible and efficient.

Keywords: Personal Health Record · Blockchain · Data security · Privacy preservation · IPFS · ABAC · Proxy re-encryption

1 Introduction

With the rapid advancement of digital health, people can collect their health data and create precise personal health records (PHRs). PHR is valuable for individuals, hospitals, and research institutions [1]. However, PHR sharing may raise owners' concerns about security deficiency and privacy leakage [2]. Many people rely on centralized third-party entities to store and share their PHRs, but these entities are not reliable or secure. Therefore, it is urgent to design a sound solution to enhance people's confidence in PHR sharing.

The increasing popularity of cloud services provides a flexible and efficient solution for sharing sensitive data [3]. Some studies have explored cloud-based

C. Ge and M. Yung (Eds.): Inscrypt 2023, LNCS 14526, pp. 141–159, 2024.
https://doi.org/10.1007/978-981-97-0942-7_8

methods to share PHR [4,5]. However, clouds are usually semi-trustworthy [6]. In real-world situations, the cloud may collude with other users to steal or tamper with the data. In addition, the single point of failure of the cloud server is common, threatening the integrity of PHRs [7].

Recently, blockchain-based data sharing schemes [8,9] have attracted widespread attention. Blockchain is a distributed and immutable database regarded as an ideal technology for solving data security issues [10]. Moreover, blockchain has the advantages of decentralization and transparency that can enhance trust in data sharing. However, there are still some challenges in applying blockchain to PHR sharing. First, PHR data is massive, while blockchain storage is limited [11]. Second, data requesters have different identities, but blockchain lacks effective access control mechanisms to manage their permissions. Third, since the on-chain information is publicly visible, protecting the privacy of PHR owners is another critical challenge.

To address these challenges, we propose a blockchain-based PHR sharing scheme with security and privacy preservation. In this work, the original PHR is encrypted and stored on the Interplanetary File System (IPFS). The corresponding index is stored on the blockchain, enabling other users can find the expected PHR. Furthermore, we design a decentralized attribute-based access control (ABAC) mechanism to achieve controllable PHR sharing with fine granularity. Moreover, the blockchain-based proxy re-encryption (PRE) method can protect the PHRs' confidentiality, avoiding privacy data leakage. The main contributions of this work can be summarized as follows.

1) We propose a secure distributed storage system based on IPFS and blockchain. PHR is encrypted and stored on IPFS in a decentralized way, avoiding the single point of failure. The corresponding index will be held on the blockchain, ensuring the integrity of shared PHR.
2) We designed a decentralized attribute-based access control mechanism. It uses smart contracts to manage user attributes and access policies and automatically verify access requests, achieving fine-grained, controllable PHR sharing.
3) We propose a blockchain-based proxy re-encryption (BPRE) method to protect the confidentiality of PHR. In this work, blockchain replaces the semi-trusted proxy to re-encrypt the PHR index. Only authorized users can decrypt the ciphertext and access the PHR, avoiding privacy data leakage.

2   Related Work

This section will introduce some existing applications of blockchain in data sharing from three aspects: secure storage, access control, and privacy protection.

Blockchain-Based Secure Storage. Liang et al. [12] proposed combining cloud and blockchain to permanently store the integrity proofs of shared data. Li et al. [13] designed a protocol that allows users to save proof of possession of data on the blockchain. These solutions ensure data integrity but rely on a centralized storage system that cannot avoid data abuse and privacy leakage.

Some studies [14,15] use permissioned blockchain as the storage platform. Unfortunately, permissioned blockchain faces problems such as ample storage overhead and data redundancy. Grabis et al. [16] proposed a data-sharing platform that combines blockchain and off-chain distributed storage systems. Naz et al. [17] adopted the InterPlanetary File System (IPFS) to store data but lacked a proper access control mechanism.

Blockchain-Based Access Control Mechanism. Zyskind et al. [18] proposed a decentralized personal data management system using blockchain as the automatic access controller. Yang et al. [19] stored the user permissions and access rules on the chain and used smart contracts to validate access requests. However, none of these schemes can achieve flexible and fine-grained access control. Liu et al. [20] presented a data sharing scheme based on attribute-based encryption (ABE) and blockchain to achieve attribute-based access control (ABAC). Moreover, Qin et al. [21] designed a multi-authority ABE algorithm. However, ABE-based ABAC mechanisms face attribute revocation and policy updating issues [22,23]. Zhang et al. [24] proposed a decentralized ABAC mechanism based on smart contracts. Unfortunately, their scheme fails to ensure the authenticity and integrity of user attributes. Furthermore, the scheme does not specify how to deal with complex access policies and rules, which poses scalability issues.

Blockchain-Based Privacy Preservation Method. Dubovitskaya et al. [25] designed a scheme based on blockchain and a hybrid encryption method involving symmetric and public key encryption. Zhang et al. [26] proposed an asymmetric searchable encryption (ASE) algorithm. However, these solutions require data owners to perform encryption and decryption operations frequently, which brings expensive computational overhead. ABE can achieve one-to-many encryption, but the computational overhead is large [22]. Manzoor et al. [27] adopt proxy re-encryption to encrypt data, and data owners only need to provide brief re-encryption keys to enable ciphertext transformation. Other studies [28–30] also used PRE algorithms, but none addressed the cheating problem or single point of failure of third-party proxies.

In summary, there are still limitations to blockchain-based data sharing, especially in terms of privacy preservation and efficiency. Therefore, we propose a secure and privacy-preserving PHR sharing scheme based on IPFS, decentralized ABAC, and blockchain-based PRE method. Compared with existing schemes, our method can ensure the security and flexibility of access control and the strong privacy of data transfer under lower overhead.

3   Preliminaries

3.1   Complexity Assumptions

Definition 1 (*Elliptic Curve Discrete Logarithm Problem, ECDLP*) Given an elliptic curve E, P is a primitive element, and its order is a large prime number n. For an element $Q \in E$, the *ECDLP* is solving for an integer k such that it satisfies: $kP = Q$, $1 < k < n$.

***ECDLP* Assumption.** There is no known polynomial time algorithm to solve the Elliptic Curve Discrete Logarithm Problem.

Definition 2 (*Elliptic Curve Computational Diffie-Hellman Problem, ECC-DHP*) Give an elliptic curve E, P is a primitive element, and its order is a large prime number n. For two points $S = aP$ and $Q = bP$ of the elliptic curve E, where a and b are unknown, the *ECCDHP* is to solve for another point R, which satisfies: $R = aQ = bS = abP$.

***ECCDHP* Assumption.** The advantage of any *PPT* adversary $\mathcal{A}$ of the Elliptic Curve Computational Diffie-Hellman Problem is defined as: $Adv = Pr\left[\mathcal{A}\left(P, aP, bP\right) = abP | a, b < n\right] \leq \varepsilon$, ε is negligible.

3.2   Blockchain and Smart Contract

Blockchain is a peer-to-peer distributed database with decentralization, tamper-resistance, and traceability features. The consortium blockchain is a semi-open blockchain run by multiple organizations, which can achieve faster transactions and higher privacy than public chains. All users must undergo identity verification before joining the consortium chain network. Moreover, different consortia can customize the consortium chain structure, consensus mechanism, etc., to adapt to different scenarios' characteristics and challenges.

The smart contract is a preset blockchain program that can execute automatically without human interference. Therefore, smart contracts can implement decentralized logic calculations and operation rules. Users can deploy contracts or invoke contract functions by sending transactions.

3.3   InterPlanetary File System

The InterPlanetary File System (IPFS) is an innovative network protocol designed to enable distributed storage, sharing, and persistence of files. IPFS is composed of peer-to-peer nodes rather than central servers, so the files stored inside will not be lost due to the failure of one node. In addition, IPFS uses a content addressing mechanism to locate and retrieve files. Each file has a hash value as its content identifier (CID), which is a hash address based on the content itself. Users can find files based on CID regardless of which nodes they are stored on, ensuring the security and integrity of the data.

3.4   Attribute-Based Access Control

Attribute-Based Access Control (ABAC) is a fine-grained access control method that grants or denies access based on attributes and access policies. The ABAC model has four attributes (AS, AO, AP, AE), representing the attributes of the subject, object, operation, and environment. The access policy is a set of rules specified by attributes. ABAC can determine access rights according to the access policy and the attributes in the access request. Therefore, the ABAC mechanism can achieve flexible and fine-grained access control to adapt to different environments and requirements.

3.5   Proxy Re-encryption

Proxy Re-encryption (PRE) is an encryption technology that supports secure transformation of ciphertexts. The authorizer only needs to give a simple re-encryption key to the proxy, and the proxy can transform the authorizer's ciphertext into the authorized party's ciphertext. Meanwhile, the proxy cannot obtain any plaintext information. A PRE algorithm consists of the following five functions.

- $PRE.KeyGen(pp) \rightarrow (sk, pk)$. Given a system public parameter pp, this algorithm outputs a public-private key pair (sk, pk) for the user.
- $PRE.ReKeyGen(sk_i, pk_j) \rightarrow rk_{i \rightarrow j}$. Input the private key sk_i of the data owner i and the public key of the data recipient j, this algorithm outputs the re-encryption key $rk_{i \rightarrow j}$.
- $PRE.Enc(pk_i, m) \rightarrow C$. Input the public key pk_i of the data owner i and the plaintext m, this algorithm outputs the initial ciphertext C.
- $PRE.ReEnc(C, rk_{i \rightarrow j}) \rightarrow C'$. Input the re-encryption key $rk_{i \rightarrow j}$, and the initial ciphertext C, this algorithm outputs the re-encrypted ciphertext C'.
- $PRE.ReDec(sk_j, C') \rightarrow m$. Input the private key sk_j of the data recipient j, and re-encrypted ciphertext C', this algorithm outputs the plaintext m.

4   The Proposed Scheme

4.1   System Model

In this section, we propose a PHR sharing system model based on consortium blockchain, as shown in Fig. 1. The model consists of five entities: 1) Data Owner, 2) Data Requester, 3) Blockchain Network, 4) InterPlanetary File System, 5) Attribute Authority. Each entity is described in detail as follows.

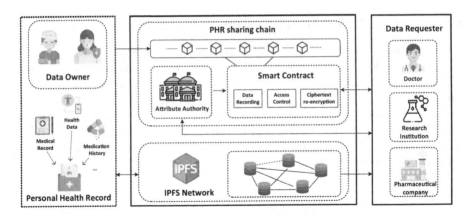

Fig. 1. System Model.

Data Owner (DO): DO is the owner of PHR and shares it as a data resource with other entities. Moreover, DO can set the access policy on the blockchain to control the sharing of his PHR.

Data Requester (DR): DR is a user who wants to obtain PHR, such as doctors, researchers, etc. We use attributes to describe the identity of DRs.

Blockchain Network (BN): BN is a consortium chain platform. It is responsible for recording PHRs and implementing decentralized access control.

InterPlanetary File System (IPFS): IPFS provides a distributed storage platform for PHRs. Users can upload or retrieve data through the IPFS client.

Attribute Authority (AA): AAs are a group of attribute authorities that grant attribute sets to DRs.

The descriptions of notations used in this article are shown in Table 1:

Table 1. Descriptions of the main notations

Notation	Description	Notation	Description
(sk, pk)	public/private key pair	$Attr()$	attribute set
m	PHR plaintext	P_m	access policy
k	symmetric key	RID	PHR resource identifier
I	PHR index	PID	policy identifier
l	the size of index	CID	the hash address
CI	the encrypted index	rk	re-encryption key

4.2   Threat Model and Security Goal

In our system, DOs are honest, and DRs are curious that may try to access PHRs beyond their permissions. AAs are the honest majority. Smart contracts are known and trusted programs. Malicious adversaries attempt to intercept, tamper and crack PHR during the sharing process. DR may collude with some AAs or other DRs to access unauthorized PHRs. Considering the above threat model, the security goals are as follows:

- *Data integrity and confidentiality:* If DO successfully submits a PHR, the authorized DR should have access to the complete and correct PHR data. Moreover, adversaries and DRs cannot infer the information of unauthorized PHRs, avoiding privacy data leakage.
- *Fine-grained access control:* DOs can set attribute-based access policies for shared PHRs according to their wishes. Only DRs who meet the access policy will be authorized.
- *Collusion resistance:* Even if DR colludes with some AAs, they cannot forge attributes to bypass the access control mechanism. In addition, DRs can only get authorized PHR even if they collude with each other.
- *Auditability:* The system can record and track the operations and accesses of PHRs, allowing DOs to see who and when accessed their PHR.

4.3 Scheme Construction

The PHR sharing protocol comprises six phases: system initialization, user registration, data storage and recording, policy setting, access control, and data access. The specific process is shown in Fig. 2.

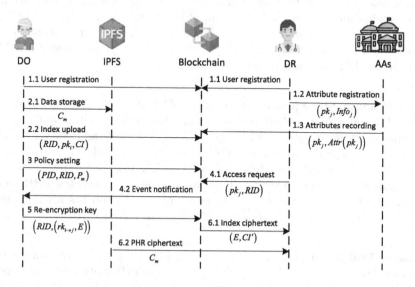

Fig. 2. Workflow of the proposed scheme.

Phase 1: System Initialization. Given a security parameter λ, the system generates two large prime numbers q and p of λ bits. Then, it chooses an elliptic curve E defined over F_p and finds a point P on E such that its order is q. G is an additive cyclic group generated by P. $Enc()$ and $Dec()$ are symmetric encryption and decryption algorithms, respectively. The size of the PHR index is set to l. Define three one-way collision-resistant hash functions: $H_1 : \{0,1\}^* \to \{0,1\}^l$, $H_2 : \{0,1\}^* \to Z_q^*$, $H_3 : \{0,1\}^l \times G^2 \to Z_q^*$. Finally, the public parameters are given by $pp = \{q, p, l, E, P, G, H_1, H_2, H_3\}$.

The organizations build a consortium chain BN and deploy relevant smart contracts. There are five contracts on the chain, namely Resource Management Contract (RMC), Attribute Management Contract (AMC), Policy Management Contract (PMC), Access Control Contract (ACC), and Ciphertext Re-encryption Contract (CRC). Among them, AMC, PMC, and ACC together constitute the decentralized access control system. In addition, organizations form an IPFS network and allow regular users to join.

Phase 2: User Registration. DO first chooses a random number $x_i \in Z_q^*$ as the address private key sk_i and calculates the corresponding address public key $pk_i = x_i P$. Then, he uses the address public key to register and obtains the corresponding certificate to join the blockchain network. Similarly, DR registers the address key pair (sk_j, pk_j).

Moreover, DR needs to apply to AAs for attribute registration. This step is skipped for DO to prevent identity leakage. Specifically, DR sends $(pk_j, Info_j)$ to AAs, where $Info_j$ is his true information. AAs jointly generate an attribute set $Attr(pk_j)$ for DR, which is saved in JSON format (e.g., $Attr = \{$ "Company": "hospital A", "Role": "doctor"$\}$). Then, AAs together sign and publish a transaction $Tx = AttrReg(pk_j, Attr(pk_j), \{\sigma_1, \sigma_2, .., \sigma_n\})$ to invoke the AMC to record the DR and his attribute set.

Phase 3: Data Storage and Recording. DO randomly selects a symmetric key k to encrypt the PHR m and obtains the ciphertext $C_m = Enc_k(m)$. The ciphertext is stored on IPFS, which returns a hash address CID. The symmetric key k and hash address CID form the PHR index $I = (k \| CID)$. Then, DO additionally generates an encryption key pair (sk_i^{enc}, pk_i^{enc}), a random number $r \in Z_q^*$, and execute Algorithm 1 to get the encrypted PHR index CI. Finally, DO selects a resource identifier RID and publishes a transaction $Tx = ResAdd(RID, pk_i, CI)$ to invoke the RMC to record PHR.

Phase 4: Policy Setting. To improve efficiency and privacy, we simplify the attribute structure in the ABAC model, ignoring the PHR's attributes and operation attributes. Each PHR has a corresponding access policy, and the access operation is defaulted to "read." The access policy defines the requirements for the DR and time. For example, an access policy $P = \{$ "Company": "hospital A", "Department": "surgery", "Role": ["doctor", "nurse"], "Time": "2023-12-31"$\}$. This

---

Algorithm 1 Encrypted Index Generation

Input: (sk_i^{enc}, pk_i^{enc}) ; $r \in Z_q^*$; $I = (k \| CID)$
Output: the encrypted index CI
1: $rpk_i^{enc} = (x_1 \| y_1)$;
2: $t = H_1(rpk_i^{enc}) = H_1(x_1 \| y_1)$;
3: $C_1 = rP = (x_0, y_0)$, $C_2 = I \oplus t$, $C_3 = H_2(I \| x_1 \| y_1)$, $C_4 = H_3(I \| C_1 \| C_3)$;
4: Outputs $CI = (C_1, C_2, C_3, C_4)$;

---

means that only the doctors or nurses in the surgery of hospital A can access PHR before 2023-12-31. Using the nesting of lists and dictionaries, P can express all the logical rules involving and/or.

Therefore, DO can set an access policy P_m for the PHR and save it in JSON format. Next, DO selects a policy identifier PID and publishes a transaction $Tx = PolicyAdd(PID, RID, P_m)$ to invoke the PMC for policy setting.

Phase 5: Access Control. DR can publish an access request transaction $Tx = CheckAccess(pk_j, RID)$ to invoke the ACC to apply for access authorization. According to the pk_j and RID in the access request, ACC will invoke the AMC and the PMC to obtain the attribute set $Attr(pk_j)$ of DR and the access policy P_m of PHR. If the attributes of DR and environment attributes meet the requirements, the access request will be accepted. Then, ACC notifies the DO to upload the re-encryption key for authorized DR by an *Event*.

Phase 6: Data Access. After receiving the notification, DO chooses a random number $e \in Z_q^*$ and executes Algorithm 2 to generate a random public key E and the re-encryption key $rk_{i \to j}$. Then, he publishes a transaction $Tx = RE(RID, (rk_{i \to j}, E))$ to invoke the CRC to complete the re-encryption of the index ciphertext CI. CRC will query the CI and execute Algorithm 3 to achieve ciphertext transformation.

Authorized DR can get E from the blockchain and calculate the decryption parameter $d' = (sk_j E, pk_j, E)$. Then, DR decrypts the re-encrypted index $CI' = (C_1', C_2', C_3', C_4')$ to get the index plaintext $I' = C_2' \oplus H_1(d')$. To ensure integrity, it is necessary to check whether $H_3(I' \| C_1' \| C_3')$ is equal to C_4'. Finally, DR retrieves and decrypts the PHR ciphertext from IPFS to get $m = Dec_k(C_m)$.

Algorithm 2 Re-encryption Key Generation

Input: $e \in Z_q^*$; $t = H_1(rpk_i^{enc})$; pk_j
Output: the re-encryption key $rk_{i \to j}$
1: $E = eP = (x_2, y_2)$;
2: $d = (epk_j, pk_j, E)$;
3: $rk_{i \to j} = t \oplus H_1(d) = H_1(rpk_i^{enc}) \oplus H_1(d)$;
4: **return** $rk_{i \to j}$;

Algorithm 3 Index Re-encryption

Input: $rk_{i \to j}$; $CI = (C_1, C_2, C_3, C_4)$
Output: the re-encrypted ciphertext CI'
1: $C_1' = C_1$;
2: $C_2' = C_2 \oplus rk_{i \to j}$;
3: $C_3' = C_3$; $C_4' = C_4$;
4: **return** $CI' = (C_1', C_2', C_3', C_4')$;

During the PHR sharing, the data recording, policy setting, access authorization, and ciphertext transformation operations are all recorded on the blockchain as transactions, allowing DO or regulatory agencies to audit.

Correctness: The correctness of the decryption process of the indexed ciphertext is verified as:

$$d' = (sk_j E, pk_j, E) = (epk_j, pk_j, E) = d,$$
$$I' = C_2' \oplus H_1(d') = I \oplus H_1(d) \oplus H_1(d') = I.$$

4.4 Smart Contract Design

This section focuses on analyzing the smart contracts in the system. Considering the space problem, some algorithms of smart contract functions will not be described in detail.

Resource Management Contract (RMC): The RMC implements the recording and querying of PHR. DO can invoke the *ResAdd()* function to record the PHR (RID, pk_i, CI), as shown in Algorithm 4. In addition, other users and contracts can invoke the *ResQry()* to query information of a PHR.

Attribute Management Contract (AMC): The AMC implements the management of the attribute sets. Only AAs can invoke the *AttrReg()* function to record the DR and his attribute set $(pk_j, Attr(pk_j))$. This function will check if the signatures $\{\sigma_1, \sigma_2, .., \sigma_n\}$ in the transaction are complete and valid. Other users and contracts can invoke the *AttrQry()* function to obtain DRs' attribute.

Policy Management Contract (PMC): The PMC implements the management of access policies. DO can invoke the *PolicyAdd()* function to set the access policy P_m for his PHR. The RID and PID are one-to-one matched. Other entities can query the access policy of a PHR according to the RID.

Access Control Contract (ACC): The ACC is responsible for verifying the access requests for PHR. As Algorithm 5 shows, the *CheckAccess()* function first calls the AMC and PMC to obtain the attributes of DR and the access policy of PHR based on the access request. Then, it checks the DR's attributes and environmental attributes against the access policy. If passed, ACC will notify the DO to upload the re-encryption key by an *Event*.

Ciphertext Re-encryption Contract (CRC): The CRC is responsible for the re-encryption of the index. The function *RE()* queries the index ciphertext CI of PHR, then transforms it according to the re-encryption key $rk_{i \to j}$, and outputs the re-encrypted ciphertext CI'.

Algorithm 4 RMC.ResAdd()

Input: RID ; pk_i ; CI
Output: *bool*
1: $err \leftarrow APIstub.GetState(RID)$;
2: **if** $err \mathrel{!=} null$ **then**
3:     **return** $Error$("Resource already exists");
4: **end if**
5: $Resource \leftarrow \{pk_i, CI\}$;
6: $APIstub.PutState(RID, [\,]byte(Resource))$;
7: **return** $shim.Success(\text{OK})$

Algorithm 5 ACC.CheckAccess()

Input: pk_j ; RID
Output: *bool*
1: $Attr \leftarrow AMC.AttrQry(pk_j)$;
2: $P \leftarrow PMC.PolicyQry(RID)$;
3: $time \leftarrow APIstub.GetTxTimestamp()$;
4: **for** $i = 0; i < P.length; i++$ **do**
5:     $item_i \leftarrow P[i]$;
6:     **if** $time > item_i[\text{"Time"}]$ **then**
7:         **return** $Error$("No permission")
8:     **end if**
9:     **for** $key, value := $ **range** $item_i$ && $key \mathrel{!=}$ "Time" **do**
10:         **if** $Attr[key] \notin value$ **then**
11:             **return** $Error$("No permission")
12:         **end if**
13:     **end for**
14: **end for**
15: $APIstub.SetEvent$ ("AccessGranted", $pk_j, RID, time$);
16: **return** $shim.Success(\text{OK})$

---

5   Security Analysis

5.1   Data Integrity and Confidentiality

Data Integrity. This work constructs a distributed storage system based on IPFS and blockchain. The PHR index is saved on the blockchain, which cannot be tampered with. Then, since the on-chain re-encryption calculation is reliable, authorized DR can get the correct index plaintext and access the expected PHR. Therefore, the integrity of shared PHRs is ensured in the sharing.

Data Confidentiality. To share PHR, DO first encrypts it with a random symmetric key and then encrypts this key with his public key to obtain the encrypted index. The private key is secure under the *ECDLP* assumption. Then, DO can generate a re-encrypted key for DR by BPRE, which allows him to obtain the decryptable index ciphertext. According to Theorem 1, the BPRE algorithm is

IND-CCA secure under the random oracle model. Therefore, adversaries and unauthorized DRs cannot break the security of the re-encrypted ciphertext, avoiding privacy data leakage.

Theorem 1. If the ECCDHP assumption holds under the cyclic group G, our proposed blockchain-based proxy re-encryption algorithm is IND-CCA secure under the random oracle model.

Proof. The proof process is shown in **Appendix**.

5.2   Fine-Grained Access Control

In the sharing, DOs can set up corresponding attribute-based access policies for their PHR on the blockchain. When receiving an access request, the ACC will automatically decide whether to authorize based on the DR's attributes and the PHR's access policy. This realizes fine-grained access control for PHRs without relying on centralized third-party institutions. In addition, we can flexibly update user attributes and access policies with low overhead

5.3   Collusion Resistance

To prevent collusion attacks between DR and AAs, our scheme requires that only attribute update transactions with signatures from all attribute authorities are valid. Since the identity of attribute authorities has been verified, it is hard for DR to collude with all of them to steal PHR. In addition, the BPRE algorithm is *IND-CCA* secure. Even if DRs collude with each other, they cannot break the unauthorized ciphertexts or DO's private key.

5.4   Auditability

In this work, a series of operations in the PHR sharing process, such as data recording, policy settings, access requests, and authorization, are recorded on the blockchain as immutable transactions. These transactions are attached with valid signatures of the operators, allowing DOs and regulators to audit.

6   Performance Evaluation

6.1   Scheme Comparison

Based on the security analysis, we compare the proposed scheme with other blockchain-based data sharing schemes [12,17,20,24,30] from six aspects of whether to use distributed storage, data integrity, data confidentiality, fine-grained access control, collusion resistance, auditability, as shown in Table 2.

Literature [12,17] lacks a flexible, fine-grained access control mechanism. Literature [20] suffers from the risk of key escrow and the threat of collusion attacks. Literature [24] lacks an effective encryption mechanism. Literature [30] relies on a centralized proxy to achieve ciphertext transformation, which leads to a lack of auditability. The comparison shows that our scheme can provide a more secure and private solution for PHR sharing.

Table 2. Comparison of the proposed scheme with other schemes

Properties	[12]	[17]	[20]	[24]	[30]	ours
Distributed storage	×	√	√	×	×	√
Data integrity	√	√	√	×	√	√
Data confidentiality	×	√	×	×	√	√
Fine-grained access control	×	×	√	√	×	√
Collusion resistance	×	×	×	√	√	√
Auditability	×	√	√	√	×	√

6.2 Experimental Setting

In the implementation, we built a PHR sharing system prototype to test the feasibility of the proposed scheme. The system security parameter is $\lambda = 256$. The 256-bit prime domain elliptic curve sm2p256v1 is adopted, which has the equation $y^2 = x^3 + ax + b$. The curve parameters can be found in [31]. The hybrid encryption mechanism is based on the AES-256 encryption and BPRE algorithm. Then, we implement the proposed cryptographic algorithm using Python 3.10 and GmSSL 3.2.2 on a computer with Intel(R) Core(TM) i7-1165G7 @ 2.80 GHz, 16 GB RAM, and OS Windows 10.

Moreover, we establish a consortium chain network using Hyperledger Fabric v2.0 on three machines with the same configuration as above. The consortium chain comprises an attribute authority organization, a data owner organization, and a hospital organization. Each organization configured three peer nodes with different roles. In addition, we built three ordering nodes to simulate a Raft ordering cluster and run the Raft consensus mechanism

6.3 Communication Overhead

Let $|M|$ denote the size of PHR, $|G|$ denote the size of the element in group G, $|Q|$ denote the size of the elements in Z_q^*, and $|P|$ denote the size of the key-value pair in the policy. The CID and the AES-256 key are both 32 bytes. Therefore, the index length l is 64 bytes.

The communication overhead of the PHR sharing process is shown in Table 3. We assume that all users have completed registration. In the data storage phase, DO uploads C_m to IPFS, which is $|M|$ bytes. Then, DO submits the CI and the pk_i to the blockchain, which is $2|G| + 2|Q| + 64$ bytes. In the policy setting phase, DO uploads the policy P_m, which is $n|P|$ bytes, and n is the number of key-value pairs. In the data access phase, DO submits $(rk_{i \to j}, E)$ to the blockchain, and then DR obtains E and CI' from the blockchain and downloads C_m from IPFS, with a total traffic of $3|G| + 2|Q| + |M| + 128$ bytes.

As we can see, the communication cost of data recording and policy setting is independent of the PHR. Since access policies are usually not complex, the cost of policy setting is negligible. In addition, the re-encryption key is brief.

Table 3. Communication overhead of our scheme

Phases	Communication overheads
Data storage	$|M|$
Data recording	$2|G| + 2|Q| + 64$
Policy setting	$n|P|$
Data access	$3|G| + 2|Q| + |M| + 128$

The communication cost mainly arises from data upload and download between users and IPFS, but this cost is inherent in data transfer. Therefore, the communication overhead of the scheme is acceptable for general users.

6.4 Computational Overhead

The computational overhead for users is mainly derived from the cryptographic algorithm. Therefore, we test the overhead of the hybrid encryption mechanism by setting different data sizes in Table 4. The *SystemInit* algorithm simulates the system setup and key generation. The *DataEnc* algorithm completes the data encryption. The *ReKeyGen* algorithm generates the re-encryption key. The ciphertext re-encryption is performed by the *CipReEnc* algorithm. The *DataDec* algorithm simulates the decryption of re-encrypted ciphertext.

Table 4. Computational overhead of the proposed scheme (ms)

Size	SystemInit	DataEnc	ReKeyGen	CipReEnc	DataDec
64KB	4.96	11.56	6.10	0.01	7.45
256KB	5.00	12.11	6.08	0.01	8.01
1024KB	5.07	14.37	6.13	0.01	9.56

From Table 4, we can see that only the time costs of *DataEnc* and *DataDec* change slightly with the data size. This is because we use a fast symmetric encryption algorithm to encrypt the original PHR data while using the complex BPRE algorithm to encrypt the fixed-length index. The time cost of the *CipReEnc* is negligible. The time cost of *ReKeyGen* is only half that of *DataEnc*, which is desirable for PHR sharers.

Moreover, we simulated other data sharing schemes with proxy re-encryption as a core component [29,30] for comparison. As shown in Fig. 3, our method has a relatively small computational overhead, which is not significantly affected by the change in data volume. The literature method [29] is similar to ours, but their PRE algorithm is based on RSA encryption, which incurs a relatively large computational overhead. The literature [30] uses a bilinear pairing technique, which has a high cost. The comparison results show that our scheme is friendly for resource-constrained users.

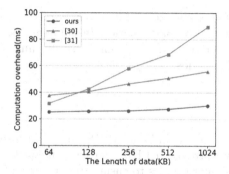

Fig. 3. Comparison of computational overhead in different schemes.

6.5 Performance of Smart Contracts

In the implementation, there are three organizations in the blockchain network, and they join a Channel together. The chaincodes (i.e., smart contract) deployed in the Channel are written in GO 1.12, including the five types described in Sect. 4.4, which can complete the entire PHR sharing process.

We tested the throughput of different smart contract functions, as shown in Fig. 4(a). The number of attributes in the user attribute set and the access policy is fixed. At different transaction sending rates, the throughput of query operations is significantly higher than write operations because they only involve queries to the state database. The on-chain encryption computation is efficient, and its throughput can reach over 600 tps. Moreover, the access request verification operation in ACC can achieve a maximum throughput of 400 tps, which is acceptable for realistic scenarios of PHR sharing.

Moreover, we simulated the literature scheme [24] and compared it with our work. As shown in Fig. 4(b), our decentralized access control mechanism has higher efficiency. We simplified the ABAC model's attribute structure, improving

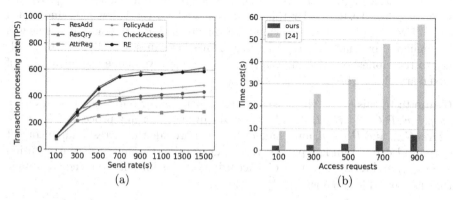

Fig. 4. (a) Throughput of different smart contract functions (b) Comparison of the access control efficiency of different schemes

the validation rate of access requests. Moreover, the PHR and the access policy are associated to avoid traversing queries. In summary, the above evaluation results show that our smart contract system is feasible and efficient, suitable for PHR sharing in real scenarios.

7 Conclusion

This work proposes a blockchain-based PHR scheme with security and privacy preservation. First, we propose a PHR sharing framework based on IPFS and blockchain among different entities to ensure the integrity of shared PHRs. Second, we design a decentralized attribute-based access control mechanism based on smart contracts, which realizes fine-grained and controllable PHR sharing. Moreover, we adopt a blockchain-based proxy re-encryption method to protect the PHRs' confidentiality without relying on semi-trusted proxies. Finally, we implement the proposed scheme on Hyperledger Fabric and evaluate the communication, computation overheads of users, and the performance of smart contracts. The results show that our scheme is efficient, cost-friendly, and able to satisfy the demands of real-world PHR sharing.

Acknowledgments. This work was supported by the National Key R&D Program of China (2021YFB2700503), the National Natural Science Foundation of China (62076125, 62032025, U20B2049, U20B2050, U21A20467, 62272228, U22B2029), the Shenzhen Science and Technology Program (JCYJ20210324134810028, JCYJ2021-0324134408023), the Key R&D Program of Guangdong Province (2020B0101090002), the Natural Science Foundation of Jiangsu Province (BK20200418), and the Shenzhen Virtual University Park Support Scheme (YFJGJS1.0).

Appendix

Our security model of indistinguishability under chosen ciphertext attacks (IND-CCA) is the same as [32]. We define a series of challenge games to prove the security of the BPRE under this security model. In the following games, each one differs slightly from the previous one. The behavior of the random oracle will be simulated by challenger C. Adversary $\mathcal{A}$ needs to guess $b \in \{0,1\}$ corresponding to the ciphertext C_{m_b} in each game. Therefore, we define the advantage of adversary $\mathcal{A}$ as: $Adv_{\mathcal{A}} = \left| Pr\left[b' = b \right] - \frac{1}{2} \right|$.

Game 0: In this game, challenger C first generates the public parameters $pp = \{q, p, l, E, P, G, H_1, H_2, H_3\}$. Adversary $\mathcal{A}$ can query for any process of $KeyGen$, $ReKeyGen$, and $Decrypt$, and challenger C will provide the corresponding correct output. $\mathcal{A}$ can obtain key pair (sk_i, pk_i), decryption parameter d, re-encryption key $rk_{i \to j}$ and data ciphertext C_i. According to this information, the advantage that he wins this game is: $Adv_{\mathcal{A}}^{G_0} = Adv_{\mathcal{A}}$.

Game 1: Challenger C plays the game with **Game 0**, except for the following content. When adversary $\mathcal{A}$ inputs x to query H_i ($i = 1, 2, 3$), C looks up the hash list for a matching y and returns it if found. Otherwise, C picks a random number y, and sets $H_i(x) = y$. When the challenger C receives the challenge of $\mathcal{A}$, if $\mathcal{A}$ inquires about H_1 with any input, C terminates the game. Otherwise, C returns the decrypted result. Since the hash function is a random process, Game 1 and Game 0 are indistinguishable based on the randomness of the hash functions. The advantage that adversary $\mathcal{A}$ wins this game is: $Adv_{\mathcal{A}}^{G_1} = Adv_{\mathcal{A}}^{G_0}$.

Game 2: Challenger C plays the game with **Game 1**, except there is a difference when calling *Decrypt*. When the input is (C_{m_b}, d'), and d' is a fake decryption parameter, if $\mathcal{A}$ does not inquire about H_1 with d', C terminates the game. Since the decryption algorithm is deterministic and H_1 is a random process, the success of $\mathcal{A}$ means that he has cracked the hash function. Therefore, the advantage that $\mathcal{A}$ wins this game is: $Adv_{\mathcal{A}}^{G_2} = Adv_{\mathcal{A}}^{G_0}$.

Game 3: Challenger C plays the game with **Game 2**, except there is a difference when calling *ReKeyGen* and *ReEnc*. In calling *ReKeyGen*, the input is d'. Challenger C queries the key list according to the input, and if the re-encryption key exists, returns it to adversary $\mathcal{A}$. If it does not exist, C generates the corresponding $rk'_{i \to j}$ for $\mathcal{A}$. Then, C checks whether the user's private key is leaked, and if so, terminates the game. In calling *ReEnc*, the input is $(C_i, rk'_{i \to j})$. C checks the key list, if $rk'_{i \to j}$ does not exist in the key list, terminate the game. In addition, if $\mathcal{A}$'s public key pk_i is illegally generated, C terminates the game. Considering that both *ReKeyGen* and *ReEnc* algorithms are deterministic, The difference between Game3 and Game2 is the possibility of cracking d. Based on the *ECCDHP* assumption, the advantage of $\mathcal{A}$ satisfies $\left| Adv_{\mathcal{A}}^{G_3} - Adv_{\mathcal{A}}^{G_2} \right| \leq Adv_{\mathcal{A}}^{ECCDH}$.

Game 4: Challenger C plays the game with **Game 3**, except for the following content. After receiving the challenge $\{m_0, m_1\}$ from $\mathcal{A}$, C computes the ciphertext $C_{m_b} = (C_1, C_2, C_3, C_4)$, $C_1 = rP$, $C_2 = m_b \oplus t = m_b \oplus rpk_C^{enc}$, $C_3 = H_2(m_b \| t)$, $C_4 = H_3(m_b \| C_1 \| C_3)$. Since r is a random number and H_1 is a random process, the re-encrypted ciphertext C'_{m_b} generated by C for $\mathcal{A}$ is indistinguishable from C_{m_b}. Therefore, Game 4 and Game 3 are indistinguishable, i.e., $Adv_{\mathcal{A}}^{G_4} = Adv_{\mathcal{A}}^{G_3}$. Moreover, in the case that r is not leaked, $\mathcal{A}$ can only randomly guess the value of b. The probability that $\mathcal{A}$ wins this game is equal to $1/2$. Therefore, we have the advantage of $\mathcal{A}$ is: $Adv_{\mathcal{A}}^{G_4} = \left| \frac{1}{2} - \frac{1}{2} \right| = 0$.

In summary, we can conclude that $Adv_{\mathcal{A}} \leq Adv_{\mathcal{A}}^{ECCDH}$. If the *ECCDHP* assumption holds, the advantage of adversary $\mathcal{A}$ is negligible, and our proposed BPRE algorithm is *IND-CCA* secure.

References

1. Tenforde, M., Jain, A., Hickner, J.: The value of personal health records for chronic disease management: what do we know? Family Medicine-Kansas City **43**(5), 351 (2011)
2. Keshta, I., Odeh, A.: Security and privacy of electronic health records: concerns and challenges. Egyptian Inform. J. **22**(2), 177–183 (2021)

3. Casola, V., Castiglione, A., Choo, K.K.R., et al.: Healthcare-related data in the cloud: challenges and opportunities. IEEE Cloud Comput. **3**(6), 10–14 (2016)
4. Xiong, H., Zhang, H., Sun, J.: Attribute-based privacy-preserving data sharing for dynamic groups in cloud computing. IEEE Syst. J. **13**(3), 2739–2750 (2018)
5. Mubarakali, A., Ashwin, M., Mavaluru, D., et al.: Design an attribute-based health record protection algorithm for healthcare services in cloud environment. Multimed. Tools Appl. **79**, 3943–3956 (2020)
6. Azeez, N.A., Van der Vyver, C.: Security and privacy issues in e-health cloud-based system: a comprehensive content analysis. Egyptian Inform. J. **20**(2), 97–108 (2019)
7. Jansen, W.A.: Cloud hooks: security and privacy issues in cloud computing. In: 2011 44th Hawaii International Conference on System Sciences, vol. 44, pp. 1–10. IEEE (2011). https://doi.org/10.1109/HICSS.2011.103
8. Guo, R., Shi, H., Zhao, Q., et al.: Secure attribute-based signature scheme with multiple authorities for blockchain in electronic health records systems. IEEE Access **6**, 11676–11686 (2018)
9. Cheng, X., Chen, F., Xie, D., et al.: Design of a secure medical data sharing scheme based on blockchain. J. Med. Syst. **44**(2), 52 (2020)
10. Deepa, N., Pham, Q.V., Nguyen, D.C., et al.: A survey on blockchain for big data: approaches, opportunities, and future directions. Future Generation Computer Systems (2022)
11. Hepp, T., Sharinghousen, M., Ehret, P., et al.: On-chain vs. off-chain storage for supply-and blockchain integration. it - Inf. Technol. **60**(5–6), 283–291 (2018). itit-2018-0014
12. Liang, X., Zhao, J., Shetty, S., et al.: Integrating blockchain for data sharing and collaboration in mobile healthcare applications. In: 2017 IEEE 28th Annual International Symposium on Personal, Indoor, and Mobile Radio Communications (PIMRC), vol. 28, pp. 1–5. IEEE (2017). PIMRC.2017.8292601
13. Li, H., Zhu, L., Shen, M., et al.: Blockchain-based data preservation system for medical data. J. Med. Syst. **42**(8), 141 (2018)
14. Zou, R., Lv, X., Zhao, J.: SPChain: blockchain-based medical data sharing and privacy-preserving eHealth system. Inform. Process. Manage. **58**(4), 102604 (2021)
15. Guo, R., Shi, H., Zhao, Q., et al.: Secure attribute-based signature scheme with multiple authorities for blockchain in electronic health records systems. IEEE Access **6**, 11676–11686 (2018)
16. Grabis, J., Stankovski, V., Zariņš, R.: Blockchain enabled distributed storage and sharing of personal data assets. In: 2020 IEEE 36th International Conference on Data Engineering Workshops (ICDEW), vol. 36, pp. 11–17. IEEE (2020). https://doi.org/10.1109/ICDEW49219.2020.00-13
17. Naz, M., Al-zahrani, F.A., Khalid, R., et al.: A secure data sharing platform using blockchain and interplanetary file system. Sustainability **11**(24), 7054 (2019). https://doi.org/10.3390/su11247054
18. Zyskind, G., Nathan, O.: Decentralizing privacy: Using blockchain to protect personal data. In: 2015 IEEE Security and Privacy Workshops, vol. 2015, pp. 180–184. IEEE (2015)
19. Yang, C., Tan, L., Shi, N., et al.: AuthPrivacyChain: a blockchain-based access control framework with privacy protection in cloud. IEEE Access **8**, 70604–70615 (2020)
20. Liu, J., Wu, M., Sun, R., et al.: BMDS: a blockchain-based medical data sharing scheme with attribute-based searchable encryption. In: ICC 2021 - IEEE

International Conference on Communications, vol. 2021, pp. 1–6. IEEE (2021). ICC42927.2021.9500573

21. Qin, X., Huang, Y., Yang, Z., et al.: A blockchain-based access control scheme with multiple attribute authorities for secure cloud data sharing. J. Syst. Architect. **112**, 101854 (2021)

22. Kumar, P., Alphonse, P.J.A.: Attribute based encryption in cloud computing: a survey, gap analysis, and future directions[J]. J. Netw. Comput. Appl. **108**, 37–52 (2018)

23. Fugkeaw, S.: A lightweight policy update scheme for outsourced personal health records sharing. IEEE Access **9**, 54862–54871 (2021)

24. Liu, H., Han, D., Li, D.: Fabric-IoT: a blockchain-based access control system in IoT. IEEE Access **8**, 18207–18218 (2020). ACCESS.2020.2968442

25. Dubovitskaya, A., Baig, F., Xu, Z., et al.: ACTION-EHR: patient-centric blockchain-based electronic health record data management for cancer care. J. Med. Internet Res. **22**(8), e13598 (2020)

26. Zhang, A., Lin, X.: Towards secure and privacy-preserving data sharing in e-health systems via consortium blockchain. J. Med. Syst. **42**(8), 140 (2018)

27. Manzoor, A., Braeken, A., Kanhere, S.S., et al.: Proxy re-encryption enabled secure and anonymous IoT data sharing platform based on blockchain. J. Netw. Comput. Appl. **176**, 102917 (2021)

28. Song, J., Yang, Y., Mei, J., et al.: Proxy re-encryption-based traceability and sharing mechanism of the power material data in blockchain environment. Energies **15**(7), 2570 (2022). https://doi.org/10.3390/en15072570

29. Chen, Z., Xu, W., Wang, B., et al.: A blockchain-based preserving and sharing system for medical data privacy. Futur. Gener. Comput. Syst. **124**, 338–350 (2021)

30. Agyekum, K.O.B.O., Xia, Q., Sifah, E.B., et al.: A proxy re-encryption approach to secure data sharing in the internet of things based on blockchain. IEEE Syst. J. **16**(1), 1685–1696 (2021)

31. Cryptopp Wiki: SM2. https://www.cryptopp.com/wiki/SM2. Accessed 12 Jun 2023

32. Keshta, I., Aoudni, Y., Sandhu, M., et al.: Blockchain aware proxy re-encryption algorithm-based data sharing scheme. Phys. Commun. **58**, 102048 (2023). https://doi.org/10.1016/j.phycom.2021.102048

Cryptography Primitive

General Constructions of Fuzzy Extractors for Continuous Sources

Yucheng Ma[1,2], Peisong Shen[1(✉)], Kewei Lv[1,2], Xue Tian[1,2], and Chi Chen[1,2]

[1] State Key Laboratory of Information Security, Institute of Information Engineering, Chinese Academy of Sciences, Beijing 100085, China
{mayucheng,shenpeisong,lvkewei,tianxue,chenchi}@iie.ac.cn
[2] School of Cyber Security, University of Chinese Academy of Sciences, Beijing 100049, China

Abstract. Fuzzy extractors are cryptographic primitives designed to generate cryptographic keys from noisy sources. While most existing fuzzy extractors are designed for discrete sources, our work focuses on fuzzy extractors for continuous sources. To evaluate the feasibility of key extraction from continuous sources, we introduce the notion of max-divergence, as classical entropy definitions are not directly applicable in this context. Building upon the concept of max-divergence, we extend the definition of fuzzy extractors to accommodate continuous sources. In addition, we introduce the notion of continuous-source fuzzy conductors, which generates strings with sufficient entropy from continuous noisy sources, and present a general approach for constructing continuous-source fuzzy extractors from continuous-source fuzzy conductors. Furthermore, we provide two constructions using lattice codes for error correction in the Euclidean space, and analyze the security of our constructions. Finally, we discuss the practical implementation of our proposed constructions.

Keywords: Fuzzy Extractor · Fuzzy Conductor · Max-divergence · Lattice Code · Euclidean Metric

1 Introduction

Uniformly distributed strings are essential in cryptographic applications, ensuring strong security and reliable encryption. In order to get uniformly distributed keys, a natural solution is to derive keys from physical sources that possess sufficiently large entropy, such as biometrics [5,19], physically unclonable functions [21] and quantum information generated from quantum devices [1]. Nevertheless, these physical sources inherently contain noise, which means different samples from the same source are close but not identical. This creates an obstacle when attempting to retrieve stable keys repeatedly from these noisy sources, as applying randomness extractors directly to noisy samples would yield different keys each time.

C. Ge and M. Yung (Eds.): Inscrypt 2023, LNCS 14526, pp. 163–182, 2024.
https://doi.org/10.1007/978-981-97-0942-7_9

Fuzzy Extractor. Dodis et al. [6] introduce the concept of *fuzzy extractors* with the aim of deriving stable keys from the same noisy sources. In general, a fuzzy extractor is comprised of two randomized algorithms: "generate" (Gen) and "reproduce" (Rep). The Gen algorithm takes an original reading w as input and generates a key r along with a corresponding public value p. On the other hand, the Rep algorithm takes the public value p and a fresh reading w' as input, and it reproduces the original key r. The correctness property of fuzzy extractors ensures that the Rep algorithm accurately reproduces the original key r if the distance between the readings w' and w is within the predefined error tolerance t. The security property of fuzzy extractors ensures that the statistical distance between the distribution of the key and a uniform distribution is negligible, even conditioned on the public value.

Fuzzy Conductor. The concept of *fuzzy conductor* was first proposed by Kanukurthi et al. [14]. A fuzzy conductor can be seen as a "weaker" version of a fuzzy extractor. It maintains the core functionality of a fuzzy extractor but imposes a security requirement on the average min-entropy of the output key conditioned on the public value. The term "fuzzy conductor" is derived from its role in conducting or transferring entropy from the source w to the resulting key k. By functioning as a conductor of entropy, the fuzzy conductor ensures that the resulting key possesses sufficient randomness.

Many noisy sources in various fields, including physics, biology, and signal processing, are best represented using continuous metric spaces. Continuous metric spaces offer a more accurate and precise representation of the underlying data, allowing for a more comprehensive analysis of the sources. Examples of such sources include human voice recordings, where the continuous variations in pitch, tone, and timing are critical for capturing the nuances of speech. Similarly, features extracted from images using deep convolutional neural network methods [19] rely on continuous representations to capture intricate details and variations in visual patterns.

In contrast to well-established results in discrete cases [6,9,11,16], the state of fuzzy extractors for continuous sources is still unclear. Some major challenges remain unsolved for continuous-source fuzzy extractor:

1. How to measure the unpredictability of continuous sources and its feasibility of key extraction?
2. Is there a general framework to construct continuous-source fuzzy extractor? While Dodis et al. [6] proposed so-called sketch-then-extract method to construct fuzzy extractor, can this method be extended to continuous case?

1.1 Related Work for Continuous-Source Fuzzy Extractors

There are only a few works [2,3,10,13,16,18,22–24] that specifically focus on extracting keys from continuous sources. Some of these works employ quantizers to convert continuous sources into discrete sources and then apply discrete fuzzy extractors [3,16,22]. This quantization process can result in the loss of entropy and introduce errors, particularly in the boundary regions of the source distribution. Buhan et al. [2] propose a generalized primitive called a fuzzy embedder, which is applicable to both continuous and discrete sources. Nevertheless, for continuous sources, the initial step of the fuzzy embedder involves quantization, which can introduce the aforementioned problems.

Other approaches utilize lattice-based structures to correct errors [13,18,24]. However, it should be pointed out that the constructions in [13,24] are fuzzy commitment schemes, and Gilkalaye et al. [13] primarily discuss security in the context of uniform distributions. Parente et al. [18] introduced a construction based on low-density lattice codes. Their construction imposes a requirement on the worst-case min-entropy of the output key and assumes that each position of the input is independently and identically distributed.

It is worth mentioning that some prior works [3,24] use False Reject Rate (FRR) to evaluate the correctness of their schemes. However, FRR is a statistic commonly used in identification systems to measure the likelihood of rejecting a valid user. As a cryptographic primitive, a fuzzy extractor should guarantee that the input values within a predefined distance yield the correct key, regardless of whether they come from the same source or not.

Verbitskiy et al. [23] pointed out that no universal optimal fuzzy extractor exists for continuous sources. They presented a generic construction specifically designed for one-dimensional probability distributions by using independent partitions. Nevertheless, it remains unclear how their technique can be extended to handle continuous sources in multiple dimensions. Fuller et al. [10] introduced the concept of distributional uncertainty, where the true underlying distribution is unknown or uncertain. In this context, they demonstrated that no fuzzy extractors can provide security guarantees for a family of continuous sources. Both of these results highlight the absence of universal continuous-source fuzzy extractors, as concepts like min-entropy are not well-defined unless the quantization process is explicitly specified.

The lack of precise methods to accurately measure the unpredictability of continuous sources has hindered the development of universal fuzzy extraction techniques from continuous sources. Classical methods used for discrete sources are inadequate in capturing the nuanced unpredictability and randomness of continuous sources.

1.2   Our Contributions

In this work, we first aim to address above challenges by proposing *max-divergence* as a new measure of unpredictability for continuous sources. This notion takes into account the unique characteristics of continuous sources and goes beyond the conventional approaches used for discrete sources. Building upon the notion of max-divergence, we make a significant contribution by demonstrating the existence of universal continuous-source fuzzy extractors (cs-fuzzy extractors) and continuous-source fuzzy conductors (cs-fuzzy conductors). Furthermore, we provide general techniques for constructing cs-fuzzy extractors and cs-fuzzy conductors.

Max-Divergence. Traditionally, the feasibility of extracting stable keys from discrete noisy sources is measured using the notion of *min-entropy* [6]. However, min-entropy is specific to discrete sources and cannot be directly applied to continuous sources. To address this limitation, we propose a new measure called max-divergence, which captures the unpredictability of continuous noisy sources.

Considering that min-entropy is defined as the Rényi entropy of order ∞, we begin by examining the differential Rényi entropy. Building upon the findings of Van and Harremos [8], we establish that the differential Rényi entropy of order ∞ is equivalent to the negative logarithm of the essential supremum of the probability density function $(-\log(\text{ess sup}_X f_X))$. We refer to this as the differential min-entropy. However, this notion lacks certain properties that would make it an appropriate measure of unpredictability for continuous sources.

In order to overcome this limitation, we propose a new notion called *max-divergence*, which is better suited for measuring the unpredictability of continuous sources. Max-divergence actually measures the deviation of the source distribution from the uniform distribution in the "worst-case". For a continuous random variable X defined over the space $\mathcal{S}$, the max-divergence of X is formally defined as

$$D_\infty(X) = \log\left(\text{ess} \sup_X \frac{f_X}{1/|\mathcal{S}|}\right).$$

Note that in our definition, we use the notion of essential supremum rather than maximum. The key distinction lies in the fact that the values of a function on a set of measure zero do not impact the essential supremum. Thus, the essential supremum serves as a more comprehensive measure than the maximum, particularly for functions defined on continuous spaces (such as probability density functions).

Continuous-Source Fuzzy Extractors and Fuzzy Conductors. Based on the notion of max-divergence, we extend the definitions of fuzzy extractors and fuzzy conductors to accommodate continuous sources. Similar to the sketch-then-extract paradigm (a secure sketch is used for reconstruction of noisy input and an extractor is used for deriving an almost uniform string from non-uniform input), we propose a general method to construct cs-fuzzy extractors using a combination of cs-fuzzy conductors and randomness extractors [17]. We call this approach "conduct-then-extract" approach, where the input w is first processed by a cs-fuzzy conductor to produce a string k, and then a randomness extractor is applied to k to obtain the output key r. The security of the output key r relies on the entropy of the output string k conditioned on the public value.

Furthermore, we present two constructions of cs-fuzzy conductors for Euclidean distance. Error correction for continuous input readings is achieved through the use of *nested lattice codes*. For code-offset construction, a lattice point k is randomly chosen as the secret string, and the shift from the lattice point k to the input w is stored as the public value s. The lattice point k can be recovered by decoding $w' - s$ to the closest lattice point. We also introduce the syndrome construction of cs-fuzzy conductors, which is a simplified version of code-offset construction.

Finally, we present a practical instantiation of our proposed constructions. In this instantiation, we use low-density lattice code (LDLC) to implement the nested lattice code, which achieves efficient and reliable error correction for continuous sources. Additionally, we employ some polynomial methods as the randomness extractor, ensuring efficient and reliable extraction of keys from the processed source.

2 Preliminaries

We use capital letters (e.g. X, Y) to denote random variables, lowercase letters (e.g. x, y) to denote samples and calligraphic letters (e.g. $\mathcal{S}$) to denote sets, and spaces. For a random variable X, we also denote by X the probability distribution of the variable. We use $U_{\mathcal{S}}$ to denote the uniform distribution over set or space $\mathcal{S}$. For a continuous random variable X, let $f_X(x)$ denote the probability density function (PDF) of X. In this work, we assume that the probability density function is always continuous.

For a vector $x \in \mathbb{R}^n$, let $\lfloor x \rceil$ denote the nearest integer vector. For any continuous random variable X, the *essential supremum* of probability density function f_X is

$$\operatorname*{ess\,sup}_{X} f_X = \sup \{M \in \mathbb{R} | f_X(x) \leq M \text{ almost everywhere}\}.$$

where "almost everywhere" means that for the set of points with measure zero, the inequality does not hold. In other words, the inequality holds for all $x \in X$ except for a set of points of measure zero. If $f_X(x)$ is a continuous function, then $\operatorname{ess\,sup}_X f_X = \sup \{f_X(x) | x \in X\}$. Let $|\mathcal{S}|$ denote the size of set or space $\mathcal{S}$. If $\mathcal{S}$ is countable, then $|\mathcal{S}|$ is equal to the number of elements in $\mathcal{S}$. Else if $\mathcal{S}$ is uncountable, then $|\mathcal{S}|$ is equal to the volume of $\mathcal{S}$. In this paper, the base of logarithm function is 2 except explicitly stated.

If an algorithm or a function is randomized, we use semicolon to separate the input and the internal randomness in order to make randomness explicit: $g(x;r)$ denotes running g on input x with randomness r. If X is a probability distribution, then $g(X)$ is the distribution induced on the image of g by applying the (possibly probabilistic) function g.

Metric Spaces. A metric space is a set $\mathcal{M}$ with a distance function dis: $\mathcal{M} \times \mathcal{M} \to \mathbb{R}^+$. In this work, we consider Euclidean norm, i.e., for a vector $x = (x_1, ..., x_n)$, $||x||_2 = \sqrt{\sum_i^n x_i^2}$. We usually ignore the subscript and denote it simply by $||x||$. The associated Euclidean distance between two vectors is defined as $\mathrm{dis}(x, y) = ||x - y|| = \sqrt{\sum_i^n (x_i - y_i)^2}$.

Statistical Distance. The *statistical distance* between two discrete random variables X and Y over countable set R is:

$$\Delta(X, Y) = \frac{1}{2} \sum_{r \in R} |\Pr(X = r) - \Pr(Y = r)|. \tag{1}$$

The statistical distance between two continuous random variables X and Y is:

$$\Delta(X, Y) = \frac{1}{2} \int |f_X(t) - f_Y(t)| \mathrm{d}t. \tag{2}$$

2.1   Min-Entropy, Secure Sketch and Extractor

Min-Entropy. For a discrete random variable X, the *min-entropy* of X is

$$H_\infty(X) = -\log\left(\max_x \Pr[X = x]\right). \tag{3}$$

The *average min-entropy* of X given another random variable Y is:

$$\tilde{H}_\infty(X|Y) = -\log\left(\mathbb{E}_{y\leftarrow Y}\left[\max_x \Pr[X = x|Y = y]\right]\right) \tag{4}$$

$$= -\log\left(\mathbb{E}_{y\leftarrow Y}\left[2^{-H_\infty(X|Y=y)}\right]\right). \tag{5}$$

Definition 1 (Secure Sketch [6]). *An* $(\mathcal{M}, m, \tilde{m}, t)$-*secure sketch with error* δ *is a pair of procedures* (SS, Rec). SS *on input* $w \in \mathcal{M}$ *outputs a bit string* $s \in \{0,1\}^*$. Rec *takes* $w' \in \mathcal{M}$ *and* $s \in \{0,1\}^*$ *as inputs, and outputs* $\tilde{w} \in \mathcal{M}$. (SS, Rec) *should have the following properties:*

1. Correctness: *if* $\mathrm{dis}(w, w') \leq t$ *then* $\mathsf{Rec}(w', \mathsf{SS}(w)) = w$. *If* $\mathrm{dis}(w, w') > t$, *then no guarantee is provided about the output of* Rec.
2. Security: *for any distribution* W *on* $\mathcal{M}$ *with* $H_\infty(W) \geq m$,

$$\tilde{H}_\infty(W|\mathsf{SS}(W)) \geq \tilde{m}.$$

A secure sketch is efficient if SS *and* Rec *run in expected polynomial time.*

Definition 2 (Average-case Extractors [6]). *A polynomial time probabilistic function* $\mathsf{Ext} : \mathcal{K} \to \mathcal{R}$ *with randomness space* $\mathcal{I}$ *is an average-case* $(\mathcal{K}, m, \mathcal{R}, \epsilon)$-*strong extractor if for any pairs of random variables* (K, S), *such that* K *is distributed over* $\mathcal{K}$ *and* $\tilde{H}_\infty(K|S) \geq m$, *we have:*

$$\Delta((\mathsf{Ext}(K; I), I, S), (U_\mathcal{R}, I, S)) \leq \epsilon,$$

where I *is uniform distributed over* $\mathcal{I}$.

Definition 3 (Universal Hash Functions [4]). *A family of hash functions* $\mathcal{H} = \{H_i : \mathcal{X} \to \mathcal{Y} \mid i \in \mathcal{I}\}$ *is universal if for all* $x_1 \neq x_2 \in \mathcal{X}$, *it satisfies:*

$$\Pr_{i \xleftarrow{\$} \mathcal{I}}[F_i(x_1) = F_i(x_2)] = \frac{1}{|\mathcal{Y}|}.$$

Lemma 1 (Generalized Leftover Hash Lemma [6, Lemma 2.4]). *If* $\mathcal{H} = \{H_i : \mathcal{X} \to \mathcal{Y} \mid i \in \mathcal{I}\}$ *is a family of universal hash functions. Then for any random variables* X *and* P,

$$\Delta((H_I(X), I, P), (U_\mathcal{Y}, I, P)) \leq \frac{1}{2}\sqrt{2^{-\tilde{H}_\infty(X|P)}|\mathcal{Y}|}.$$

In particular, universal hash functions are average-case $(\mathcal{X}, m, \mathcal{Y}, \epsilon)$-*strong extractors whenever* $|\mathcal{Y}| \leq 2^m \cdot (2\epsilon)^2$.

2.2 Lattice and Lattice Code

An n-dimensional lattice Λ is a subset of the real space $\mathbb{R}^m$ and is defined by basis vectors $(v_1, v_2, ..., v_n)$ where $v_i \in \mathbb{R}^m$. Every lattice point is a linear combination of the basis vectors scaled by integers $b_i \in \mathbb{Z}$:

$$x = \sum_{i=1}^{n} b_i v_i.$$

The $m \times n$ matrix G, whose columns are $v_1, v_2, ..., v_n$, is called the generator matrix of Λ. Then the lattice point can be formed as $x = Gb$ where $b \in \mathbb{Z}^n$. In this work, we only consider the lattice defined by square generator matrix, i.e., $m = n$. The results can be extended to non-square case easily. The minimum distance of a lattice Λ is given by:

$$d_{\min}(\Lambda) = \min_{x \in \Lambda \backslash 0} ||x||$$

The Voronoi cell of a lattice point x is the set of all points in $\mathbb{R}^n$ that are closer to this lattice point than to any other lattice points:

$$\mathcal{V}_\Lambda(x) = \{y \in \mathbb{R}^n : \forall x' \in \Lambda, \mathsf{dis}(x, y) \leq \mathsf{dis}(x', y)\}.$$

Specially, we use $\mathcal{V}(\Lambda)$ to denote the fundamental Voronoi cell (i.e., the origin-centered Voronoi cell, $\mathcal{V}_\Lambda(0)$) of lattice Λ. The volume of each Voronoi cell is equal to the determinant of G:

$$\mathrm{Vol}(\Lambda) = |\det(G)|.$$

For a lattice Λ with generator matrix G, the quantizer maps every points in $\mathbb{R}^n$ to the closest lattice point, which is also known as the *lattice decoder*. Formally, for every $x \in \mathbb{R}^n$,

$$Q_\Lambda(x) = \arg\min_{y \in \Lambda} ||x - y||.$$

The associated modulo operation is defined as:

$$y = x \bmod \Lambda = x - Q_\Lambda(x).$$

It is obvious that y is inside $\mathcal{V}(\Lambda)$.

In the case of real-valued metric space, if lattice Λ has the minimum distance d, then the error-correcting distance t of the lattice decoder should satisfy $t < d/2$. Note that t cannot be set as $d/2$. If $t = d/2$, the decoding of midpoint between two lattice points may cause an error, because the distances between the midpoint and both lattice points are equal. In this case, the decoder cannot determine with certainty which of the two lattice points was the original lattice point.

Like finite field codes, we consider the parity check matrix and the syndrome of lattice as defined in [20]. For a lattice Λ with generator matrix G, the check matrix is defined as $H = G^{-1}$. If Hx is an integer vector, then x is a lattice point. For any $y \in \mathbb{R}^n$, the syndrome then is defined as $\mathsf{syn}(y) = frac\{Hy\}$ where $frac\{x\}$ is defined as $frac\{x\} = x - \lfloor x \rfloor$. Observe that syndrome $\mathsf{syn}(y) = 0$ if and only if y is a lattice point. Hence, for a "noisy" lattice point $y = x + e$ (x is a lattice point and e is an additive error vector), the syndrome could be calculated as $\mathsf{syn}(y) = frac\{Hy\} = frac\{H(x+e)\} = frac\{He\} = \mathsf{syn}(e)$. This implies that the syndrome only depends on the error vector and remains unaffected by the lattice point. This property allows the decoder to determine and correct errors by focusing on the syndrome.

Different from the syndrome of linear code, we observe that the syndrome of lattice is not linear, i.e., $\mathsf{syn}(x+y) \neq \mathsf{syn}(x) + \mathsf{syn}(y)$. Suppose that $x = G(b_1 + \tilde{b}_1)$ and $y = G(b_2 + \tilde{b}_2)$ where b_1, b_2 are integer vectors and $\tilde{b}_1, \tilde{b}_2$ are fraction vectors, then $\mathsf{syn}(x) + \mathsf{syn}(y) = \tilde{b}_1 + \tilde{b}_2$, but $\mathsf{syn}(x+y) = \mathsf{frac}(\tilde{b}_1 + \tilde{b}_2) = \mathsf{frac}(\mathsf{syn}(x) + \mathsf{syn}(y))$.

A *lattice code* is typically the set of all lattice points within a shaping region. For lattices Λ_s and Λ_c, if $\Lambda_s \subset \Lambda_c$, we say Λ_s is nested in Λ_c. The lattice Λ_s is referred as coarse lattice (for shaping) and Λ_c as fine lattice (for coding). A *nested lattice code* [7] based on a nested lattice pair (Λ_c, Λ_s) is defined as $\mathcal{C} = \Lambda_c \cap \mathcal{V}(\Lambda_s)$. The information $m \in \mathbb{Z}^n$ is encoded to $c = Gm \bmod \Lambda_s$, where G is the generator matrix of Λ_c. The *nesting ratio* is defined as

$$\Gamma(\Lambda_c, \Lambda_s) = \left(\frac{\mathrm{Vol}(\Lambda_s)}{\mathrm{Vol}(\Lambda_c)} \right)^{1/n},$$

and the size of codebook $\mathcal{C}$ is

$$|\mathcal{C}| = \frac{\mathrm{Vol}(\Lambda_s)}{\mathrm{Vol}(\Lambda_c)}.$$

An example of nested lattice code is shown in Fig. 1.

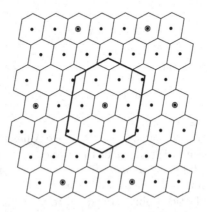

Fig. 1. Nested lattice code of ratio three in $\mathbb{R}^2$, the points of Λ_c are plotted in black dots and the points of Λ_s are plotted in black dots with circles.

3   New Measure of Unpredictability

In this section, we begin by introducing various notions of entropy. We highlight their limitations when applied to continuous sources. To address this issue and better capture the unpredictability of continuous sources, we propose a new notion called *max-divergence*. We demonstrate that the concept of max-divergence provides a more generalized and comprehensive measure of unpredictability.

Obviously, min-entropy is not suitable for continuous sources, as the probability of a single point is zero. We note that min-entropy is actually the Rényi entropy of order ∞, which can be applied to both discrete and continuous cases. In the context of continuous sources, we can consider the Rényi entropy and its differential version as alternative measures of entropy.

Rényi Entropy. The *differential Rényi entropy* of a continuous random variable X is:

$$h_\alpha(X) = \frac{1}{1-\alpha} \log \int (f_X(x))^\alpha dx. \tag{6}$$

Differential min-entropy refers to the differential Rényi entropy of order ∞. However, calculating the differential min-entropy directly from the formula can be challenging. To overcome this, we introduce the concept of differential Rényi divergence, which provides a practical approach for estimating the differential min-entropy of a continuous source.

Rényi Divergence. For the simple order $\alpha \in (0,1) \cup (1,\infty)$, the differential Rényi divergence of two continuous distributions X and Y is:

$$D_\alpha(X \parallel Y) = \frac{1}{\alpha-1} \log \int (f_X(r))^\alpha (f_Y(r))^{1-\alpha} dr. \tag{7}$$

If X has support in a space $\mathcal{S}$, then:

$$h_\alpha(X) = \log|\mathcal{S}| - D_\alpha(X \parallel U_\mathcal{S}). \tag{8}$$

Proof.

$$D_\alpha(X \parallel U_\mathcal{S}) = \frac{1}{\alpha-1} \log \int (f_X(r))^\alpha \cdot |\mathcal{S}|^{\alpha-1} dr$$

$$= \log|\mathcal{S}| + \frac{1}{\alpha-1} \log \int (f_X(r))^\alpha dr$$

$$= \log|\mathcal{S}| - h_\alpha(X).$$

The first equality follows from $f_{U_\mathcal{S}}(r) = \frac{1}{|\mathcal{S}|}$ and the final equality follows from the definition of differential Rényi entropy.

Proposition 1 ([8, Theorem 6]). *For* $\alpha = \infty$,

$$D_\infty(X\|Y) = \log\left(\operatorname*{ess\,sup}_X \frac{f_X}{f_Y}\right). \tag{9}$$

Proposition 2 (Differential Min-entropy). *For a continuous variable X, the differential min-entropy of X is:*

$$h_\infty(X) = -\log\left(\operatorname*{ess\ sup}_X f_X\right). \tag{10}$$

Proof. Combining 8 and 9, we can get above proposition easily.

However, the notion of differential min-entropy lacks certain properties that would make it a suitable measure of unpredictability for continuous sources. Firstly, it is not scaling invariant. If we consider a random variable Y that is obtained by scaling another random variable X as $Y = aX$, then $h_\infty(Y) = h_\infty(X) + \log|a|$. Besides, differential min-entropy can be negative. For instance, if X is a uniform distribution on the interval $[0, 0.5]$, then $h_\infty(X) = -\log 2 = -1$. Another limitation of the differential min-entropy is that it is not dimensionally correct. Since the probability density function f_X has units of $1/dx$, the argument inside the logarithm is not dimensionless.

In order to overcome these limitations, we adopt a divergence approach, which measures the deviation of the source distribution from the uniform distribution. This approach provides a relative measure of the unpredictability of a continuous source.

Definition 4 (Max-divergence). *For a continuous variable X over space $\mathcal{S}$, the max-divergence of X is defined as follows:*

$$D_\infty(X\|U_\mathcal{S}) = \log\left(\operatorname*{ess\ sup}_X \frac{f_X}{1/|\mathcal{S}|}\right) = \log(\operatorname*{ess\ sup}_X f_X) + \log|\mathcal{S}|. \tag{11}$$

For simplicity, we always omit the uniform distribution and denote max-divergence of X as $D_\infty(X)$. The max-divergence of X condition on another random variable Y is defined as

$$D_\infty(X|Y) = \log\left(\max_y(\operatorname*{ess\ sup}_{X|y} \frac{f_{X|y}}{1/|\mathcal{S}_{X|y}|})\right), \tag{12}$$

where $\mathcal{S}_{X|y}$ is the value space of the random variable $X|y$.

Comparing with differential min-entropy, max-divergence has following properties:

- *Non-negative.* Since ess $\sup_X f_X \geq 1/|\mathcal{S}|$, $D_\infty(X)$ equals zero if and only if X is uniform.
- *Dimensionless.* Both of f_X and $1/|\mathcal{S}|$ have units of $1/dx$, so the argument of the logarithm remains dimensionless.
- *Invariant under parameter transformations.* If variable x is transformed to $y(x)$, and the space $\mathcal{S}$ is transformed to $\mathcal{S}'$. Since $f_X(x)dx = f_Y(y)dy$ and $dx/|\mathcal{S}| = dy/|\mathcal{S}'|$, then max-divergence of Y can be rewritten as:

$$D_\infty(Y) = \log\left(\operatorname*{ess\ sup}_Y \frac{f_Y}{1/|\mathcal{S}'|}\right) = \log\left(\operatorname*{ess\ sup}_X \frac{f_X(x)\frac{dx}{dy}}{1/|\mathcal{S}|\frac{dx}{dy}}\right)$$

$$= \log\left(\operatorname*{ess\ sup}_X \frac{f_X}{1/|\mathcal{S}|}\right) = D_\infty(X)$$

Note that max-divergence is inversely proportional to the unpredictability. In other words, the smaller the max-divergence, the closer the distribution is to being uniform. Additionally, we provide a useful property that relates to the average min-entropy of a discrete variable given a continuous variable.

Lemma 2. *Let X be a discrete random variable and Y be a continuous variable. Then*

$$\tilde{H}_\infty(X|Y) \geq H_\infty(X) - D_\infty(Y|X). \tag{13}$$

Proof.

$$2^{-\tilde{H}_\infty(X|Y)} = \mathbb{E}_{y \leftarrow Y} \max_x \Pr[X = x | Y = y]$$

$$= \int \max_x \Pr[X = x | Y = y] \cdot f_Y(y) dy$$

$$= \int \max_x \Pr[X = x] \cdot f_{Y|X}(y|x) dy$$

$$\leq \int \max_x \Pr[X = x] \cdot \operatorname*{ess\,sup}_{Y|x} f_{Y|x} dy$$

$$\leq \int \max_{x_1} \Pr[X = x_1] \cdot \max_{x_2} (\operatorname*{ess\,sup}_{Y|x_2} f_{Y|x_2}) dy$$

$$= 2^{-H_\infty(X)} \cdot \int \max_x (\operatorname*{ess\,sup}_{Y|x} f_{Y|x}) dy$$

$$\leq 2^{-H_\infty(X)} \cdot \max_x \int \operatorname*{ess\,sup}_{Y|x} f_{Y|x} dy$$

$$= 2^{-H_\infty(X)} \cdot \max_x (|\mathcal{S}_{Y|x}| \cdot \operatorname*{ess\,sup}_{Y|x} f_{Y|x}),$$

where $\mathcal{S}_{Y|x}$ is the value space of the random variable $Y|x$. The first to third equality follows from the probability theory, the first inequality follows from the definition of essential supremum, the last inequality follows from the fact that when x is fixed, $\operatorname{ess\,sup}_{Y|x} f_{Y|x}$ is a constant. Then we can get:

$$\tilde{H}_\infty(X|Y) \geq H_\infty(X) - \log\left(\max_x(|\mathcal{S}_{Y|x}| \cdot \operatorname*{ess\,sup}_{Y|x} f_{Y|x})\right)$$

$$= H_\infty(X) - \log\left(\max_x(\operatorname*{ess\,sup}_{Y|x} \frac{f_{Y|x}}{1/|\mathcal{S}_{Y|x}|})\right)$$

$$= H_\infty(X) - D_\infty(Y|X).$$

Max-divergence can also be applied to discrete variables: for any discrete variable X over $\mathcal{M}$,

$$D_\infty(X) = \log\left(\max_x \frac{\Pr[X = x]}{1/|\mathcal{M}|}\right). \tag{14}$$

The following proposition establishes a relationship between min-entropy and max-divergence.

Proposition 3. *If $\mathcal{M}$ is countable, for any discrete variable X over $\mathcal{M}$, $\mathrm{H}_\infty(X) \geq m$ if and only if $D_\infty(X) \leq \log|\mathcal{M}| - m$.*

Proof. For any discrete variable X, we have:

$$D_\infty(X) = \log\left(\max_x \frac{\Pr[X = x]}{1/|\mathcal{M}|}\right) = \log|\mathcal{M}| + \log\left(\max_x \Pr[X = x]\right)$$
$$= \log|\mathcal{M}| - \mathrm{H}_\infty(X).$$

4   Fuzzy Extractors and Fuzzy Conductors

In this section, we begin by introducing the definition of fuzzy extractors designed for discrete sources. We then proceed to present our definitions of fuzzy extractors and fuzzy conductors specifically tailored for continuous sources. Finally, we demonstrate our general results on the relation between continuous-source fuzzy extractors and continuous-source fuzzy conductors, providing a comprehensive framework for secure key extraction from continuous sources.

Definition 5 (Fuzzy Extractor [6]). *An $(\mathcal{M}, m, \mathcal{R}, t, \epsilon)$-fuzzy extractor is a pair of procedures (Gen, Rep). Gen is a randomized function on input $w \in \mathcal{M}$ and outputs an extracted string $r \in \mathcal{R}$ with a public value $p \in \{0,1\}^*$. Rep is a possibly randomized function which takes $w' \in \mathcal{M}$ and $p \in \{0,1\}^*$ as inputs and outputs a string $r' \in \mathcal{R}$ or $\perp$. (Gen, Rep) should have the following properties:*

1. *Correctness: if $\mathsf{dis}(w, w') \leq t$ and r, p were generated by $(r,p) \leftarrow \mathsf{Gen}(w)$, then $\mathsf{Rep}(w', p) = r$. If $\mathsf{dis}(w, w') > t$, then no guarantee is provided about the output of Rep.*
2. *Security: for any distribution W on $\mathcal{M}$ with $\mathrm{H}_\infty(W) \geq m$, if $(R, P) \leftarrow \mathsf{Gen}(W)$, then $\Delta((R, P), (U_\mathcal{R}, P)) \leq \epsilon$.*

A fuzzy extractor is efficient if Gen and Rep run in expected polynomial time.

Traditionally, fuzzy extractors have been primarily designed for discrete sources, and the public value is defined over finite fields. In this context, the security property of fuzzy extractors is related to the min-entropy of the input distribution.

4.1   Fuzzy Extractors for Continuous Sources

In this section, we propose the definition of fuzzy extractors for continuous sources. We make slight modifications to the traditional definition by considering the max-divergence of the distribution instead of the min-entropy.

Definition 6 (Continuous-Source Fuzzy Extractor). *An $(\mathcal{M}, m, \mathcal{R}, t, \epsilon)$-continuous-source fuzzy extractor is a pair of procedures (Gen, Rep). Gen is a randomized function on input $w \in \mathcal{M}$ and outputs an extracted string $r \in \mathcal{R}$ with a public value $p \in \mathbb{R}^*$. Rep is a possibly randomized function which takes $w' \in \mathcal{M}$ and $p \in \mathbb{R}^*$ as inputs and outputs a string $r' \in \mathcal{R}$ or $\perp$. (Gen, Rep) should have the following properties:*

1. Correctness: *if* dis$(w, w') < t$ *and* r, p *were generated by* $(r, p) \leftarrow$ Gen(w), *then* Rep$(w', p) = r$. *If* dis$(w, w') \geq t$, *then no guarantee is provided about the output of* Rep.

2. Security: *for any distribution* W *on* $\mathcal{M}$ *with* $D_\infty(W) \leq m$, *if* $(R, P) \leftarrow$ Gen(W), *then* $\Delta((R, P), (U_\mathcal{R}, P)) \leq \epsilon$.

A continuous-source fuzzy extractor is efficient if Gen *and* Rep *run in expected polynomial time.*

Remark 1. The security property defined above could be generalized to include both discrete sources and continuous sources. According to Proposition 3, when the set of possible values $\mathcal{M}$ is countable and the input distribution W is discrete, the condition $D_\infty(W) \leq m$ is equivalent to $H_\infty(W) \geq \log|\mathcal{M}| - m$. This equivalence aligns with the definition of fuzzy extractors for discrete sources, where the security is based on the min-entropy of the input distribution. This ensures consistency between the security properties of fuzzy extractors for discrete and continuous sources.

4.2 Fuzzy Conductors for Continuous Sources

The concept of fuzzy conductors was introduced in [14]. Fuzzy conductors have similar functionalities as fuzzy extractors. However, instead of generating nearly uniformly distributed keys, fuzzy conductors produce strings with sufficient entropy. Similar to Definition 6, we propose the notion of continuous-source fuzzy conductors.

Definition 7 (Continuous-Source Fuzzy Conductor). *An* $(\mathcal{M}, m, \mathcal{K}, t, \tilde{m})$-*continuous-source fuzzy conductor is a pair of procedures* (Cnd, Rec). Cnd *on input* $w \in \mathcal{M}$ *outputs an extracted string* $k \in \mathcal{K}$ *with a public value* $s \in \mathbb{R}^*$. Rec *takes* $w' \in \mathcal{M}$ *and* $s \in \mathbb{R}^*$ *as inputs, and outputs a string* $k' \in \mathcal{K}$ *or* $\perp$. (Cnd, Rec) *should have the following properties:*

1. Correctness: *if* dis$(w, w') < t$ *and* (k, s) *were generated by* $(k, s) \leftarrow$ Cnd(w), *then* Rec$(w', s) = k$. *If* dis$(w, w') \geq t$, *then no guarantee is provided about the output of* Rec.

2. Security: *for any distribution* W *on* $\mathcal{M}$ *with* $D_\infty(W) \leq m$, *if* $(K, S) \leftarrow$ Cnd(W), *then* $\tilde{H}_\infty(K|S) \geq \tilde{m}$.

A continuous-source fuzzy conductor is efficient if Cnd *and* Rec *run in expected polynomial time.*

4.3 On the Relations Between CS-Fuzzy Extractors and CS-Fuzzy Conductors

In this section, we discuss the relations between cs-fuzzy extractors and cs-fuzzy conductors. Firstly, we demonstrate that a cs-fuzzy extractor implies a cs-fuzzy conductor. Secondly, we show that a cs-fuzzy extractor could be constructed from a cs-fuzzy conductor by incorporating a randomness extractor. These findings contribute to a better understanding of the interplay between cs-fuzzy extractors and cs-fuzzy conductors.

Verbitskiy et al. [23] pointed that for discrete sources, a fuzzy extractor implies a fuzzy conductor. We extend this result to the continuous case as shown in Lemma 3.

Lemma 3. *If* (Gen, Rep) *is an* $(\mathcal{M}, m, \mathcal{R}, t, \epsilon)$-*cs-fuzzy extractor, then the following* (Cnd, Rec) *is an* $(\mathcal{M}, m, \mathcal{R}, t, -\log\left(\frac{1}{|\mathcal{R}|} + \epsilon\right))$-*cs-fuzzy conductor:*

- Cnd(w): $(r, p) \leftarrow$ Gen(w), *set* $k = r$, $s = p$, *and output* (k, s).
- Rec(w', p): *reproduce* $r' \leftarrow$ Rep(w', p), *set* $k' = r'$, *and output* k'.

Proof. From the definition of cs-fuzzy extractors and the fact that $(K, S) \leftarrow$ Cnd(W), we have

$$\Delta((K, S), (U_{\mathcal{R}}, S)) = \frac{1}{2} \int \left(\sum_k |\Pr[K = k|S = s] - \frac{1}{|\mathcal{R}|}| \right) f_S(s) ds \leq \epsilon.$$

From probability theory, we know for any s,

$$\max_k \Pr[K = k|S = s] - \frac{1}{|\mathcal{R}|} \leq \frac{1}{2} \sum_k |\Pr[K = k|S = s] - \frac{1}{|\mathcal{R}|}|.$$

So we have

$$\begin{aligned}
\tilde{\mathrm{H}}_\infty(K|S) &= -\log\left(\mathbb{E}_s \max_k \Pr[K = k|S = s]\right) \\
&= -\log\left(\int \max_k \Pr[K = k|S = s] \cdot f_S(s) ds\right) \\
&\geq -\log\left(\int \left(\frac{1}{|\mathcal{R}|} + \frac{1}{2} \sum_k |\Pr[K = k|S = s] - \frac{1}{|\mathcal{R}|}|\right) f_S(s) ds\right) \\
&= -\log\left(\frac{1}{|\mathcal{R}|} + \frac{1}{2} \int \sum_k |\Pr[K = k|S = s] - \frac{1}{|\mathcal{R}|}| f_S(s) ds\right) \\
&\geq -\log\left(\frac{1}{|\mathcal{R}|} + \epsilon\right).
\end{aligned}$$

We then introduce our approach to construct cs-fuzzy extractors from cs-fuzzy conductors. In general, cs-fuzzy extractors can be constructed by applying average-case randomness extractors to the output strings of cs-fuzzy conductors. This method is specifically designed for continuous sources: the cs-fuzzy conductor transfers the "entropy" from a continuous source W to a random string K and then the randomness extractor extracts the final key from K.

Lemma 4. *Assume* (Cnd, Rec) *is an* $(\mathcal{M}, m, \mathcal{K}, t, \tilde{m})$-*cs-fuzzy conductor, let* Ext *be an average-case* $(\mathcal{K}, \tilde{m}, \mathcal{R}, \epsilon)$-*strong extractor. Then the following* (Gen, Rep) *is an* $(\mathcal{M}, m, \mathcal{R}, t, \epsilon)$-*cs-fuzzy extractor:*

– Gen(w): $(k, s) \leftarrow$ Cnd(w), set $r =$ Ext($k; i$), $p = (s, i)$, and output (r, p).
– Rep($w', (s, i)$) : recover $k' =$ Rec(w', s) and output $r' =$ Ext($k'; i$).

Proof. From the definition of fuzzy conductors (Definition 7), we have that $\tilde{H}_{\infty}(K|S) \geq \tilde{m}$. And since Ext is an average-case $(\mathcal{K}, \tilde{m}, \mathcal{R}, \epsilon)$-strong extractor, $\Delta((\text{Ext}(K; I), S, I), (U_{\mathcal{R}}, S, I)) = \Delta((R, P), (U_{\mathcal{R}}, P)) \leq \epsilon$.

5 Constructions for Euclidean Distance

In this section, we present two constructions of cs-fuzzy conductors for Euclidean distance. We also provide rigorous proofs to demonstrate that both schemes satisfy the requirements of cs-fuzzy conductors. By exploiting these results, cs-fuzzy extractors can be easily obtained from Lemma 4.

Both constructions use nested lattice codes. Suppose lattice $\Lambda_c \subset \mathbb{R}^n$ with $d_{\min}(\Lambda_c) = 2t$, G is the generator matrix of Λ_c and $H = G^{-1}$ is the parity check matrix of Λ_c. Given a nested lattice code $\mathcal{C} = \Lambda_c \cap \mathcal{V}(\Lambda_s)$ based on the nested lattice pair (Λ_c, Λ_s), our first construction involves selecting a random lattice point as the output string and storing the shift between w and the lattice point as the public value. To recover the string, we shift w' back to a nearby point and use the lattice code decoder to correct errors. Additionally, considering that communication channel in real-world is power-constrained, we use the image of w within $\mathcal{V}(\Lambda_s)$ instead of the original w. This is because we assume that $\mathcal{M} \subset \mathbb{R}^n$ and the space $\mathcal{M}$ may lie outside $\mathcal{V}(\Lambda_s)$. Further details are provided below and illustrated in Fig. 2(a).

Construction 1 (Code-offset Construction). *On input w, select a random lattice code c (this is equivalent to choosing a random $b \in \mathbb{Z}^n$ and computing $c = Gb \bmod \Lambda_s$). Set $k = Hc$ and $s = (w \bmod \Lambda_s) - c$. To compute Rec($w', s$), subtract the shift s from $(w' \bmod \Lambda_s)$ to get $c' = (w' \bmod \Lambda_s) - s$; decode c' to c by calculating $c = c' \bmod \Lambda_c$; and recover $k = Hc$.*

Since the distance between w and w' is less than t (dis(w, w') $< t$), it follows that the distance between c and c' is also less than t (dis(c, c') $< t$). As a result, c' will be successfully decoded to c, and the string will be recovered. It is worth noting that we choose the vector Hc as the output string instead of the lattice point c itself, as $Hc \in \mathbb{Z}^n$ while $c \in \mathbb{R}^n$.

Since the lattice code is linear, we can simplify Construction 1 as follows. This syndrome construction is also depicted in Fig. 2(b).

Construction 2 (Syndrome Construction). *Set $k = \lfloor H(w \bmod \Lambda_s) \rceil$, $s =$ syn(w). To compute Rec(w', s), compute $z =$ syn(w') $- s$ and $e = Gz \bmod \Lambda_c$; if $\|e\| \geq t$, output $\perp$, else output $k = \lfloor H((w' \bmod \Lambda_s) - e) \rceil$.*

As explained in Sect. 2.2, recover e is same as decoding the lattice code. Actually, the two constructions above are equivalent since for any lattice point c, syn(w) = syn($w - c$). We then show that the Rec can find the correct k. Observe that dis($w', w' - e$) $< t$ by the constraint on the length of e. In addition,

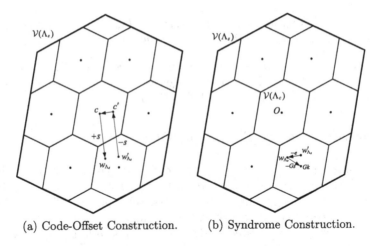

(a) Code-Offset Construction.   (b) Syndrome Construction.

Fig. 2. Constructions of CS-Fuzzy Conductor, $w_{\Lambda_s} = w \bmod \Lambda_s$ and $w'_{\Lambda_s} = w' \bmod \Lambda_s$.

$\mathsf{syn}(w'-e) = \mathsf{frac}\{\mathsf{syn}(w') - \mathsf{syn}(e)\} = \mathsf{frac}\{\mathsf{syn}(w') - (\mathsf{syn}(w') - s)\} = \mathsf{frac}\{s\} = s$. There is only one point less than distance t of w' whose syndrome is s. Otherwise, if there are two such point x_1 and x_2, we can get $x = x_1 - x_2 \in C$ and $\mathsf{dis}(x,0) < 2t$ which is contradicts to $d_{\min}(\Lambda_c) = 2t$. Therefore $w' - e$ must be equal to w.

Both of schemes are originally proposed by Dodis et al. [6] to construct secure sketches for Hamming metric based on linear code. In this work, we use lattice code instead to construct cs-fuzzy conductor for Euclidean metric. Since the lattice point c can be expressed as Gk, indicating a bijection between the space of k and C, we slightly abuse notation and refer to the space of output strings as C.

By intuition, we partition the input w into two components: the integer part and the fractional part. The fractional part is taken as public value, while the integer part serves as the secret string. The unpredictability of w ensures that even if the fractional part is revealed, the integer part remains difficult to guess (i.e., keep enough min-entropy). The formal theorem and proof are given below.

Theorem 1. *If lattice $\Lambda_c \subset \mathbb{R}^n$ with $d_{\min}(\Lambda_c) = 2t$ and $C = \Lambda_c \cap \mathcal{V}(\Lambda_s)$ is a nested lattice code based on the nested lattice pair (Λ_c, Λ_s), then the code-offset construction and syndrome construction are $(\mathcal{M}, m, \mathcal{C}, t, \log |\mathcal{C}| - m)$-cs-fuzzy conductors for $\mathcal{M} \subset \mathbb{R}^n$.*

Proof. For code-offset construction, we have:

$$\tilde{\mathsf{H}}_\infty(K|S) \geq \mathsf{H}_\infty(K) - D_\infty(S|K)$$
$$= \mathsf{H}_\infty(K) - D_\infty(W) \geq \log |\mathcal{C}| - m$$

The first inequality follows from Lemma 2, the equality follows from the fact that $S = W - C$ and C is determined by K.

For syndrome construction, let $W_{\Lambda_s} = W \bmod \Lambda_s$, we have

$$
\begin{aligned}
\tilde{H}_\infty(K|S) &= -\log\left(\mathbb{E}_s \max_k \Pr[K = k|S = s]\right) \\
&= -\log\left(\int \max_k \Pr[K = k|S = s] \cdot f_S(s) ds\right) \\
&\geq -\log\left(\int \operatorname*{ess\,sup}_{W_{\Lambda_s}} f_{W_{\Lambda_s}} ds\right) \\
&\geq -\log\left(\int \operatorname*{ess\,sup}_W f_W \cdot \frac{|\mathcal{M}|}{|\mathrm{Vol}(\Lambda_s)|} ds\right) \\
&= -\log\left(\operatorname*{ess\,sup}_W \frac{f_W}{1/|\mathcal{M}|} \cdot \frac{|\mathrm{Vol}(\Lambda_c)|}{|\mathrm{Vol}(\Lambda_s)|}\right) \\
&= \log \frac{|\mathrm{Vol}(\Lambda_s)|}{|\mathrm{Vol}(\Lambda_c)|} - \log\left(\operatorname*{ess\,sup}_W \frac{f_W}{1/|\mathcal{M}|}\right) \\
&= \log|\mathcal{C}| - D_\infty(W) \geq \log|\mathcal{C}| - m.
\end{aligned}
$$

The first inequality follows from the fact $w \bmod \Lambda_s$ is represented as a pair (k, s). The second inequality holds because we consider the entire space of w (i.e., the space $\mathcal{M}$) being mapped into $\mathcal{V}(\Lambda_s)$, and it satisfies

$$
\operatorname*{ess\,sup}_{W_{\Lambda_s}} f_{W_{\Lambda_s}} \leq \operatorname*{ess\,sup}_W f_W \cdot \frac{|\mathcal{M}|}{|\mathrm{Vol}(\Lambda_s)|}.
$$

These complete the proof of Theorem 1.

In general, combine the construction in Lemma 4 with Theorem 1, we obtain the following theorem.

Theorem 2. *If lattice $\Lambda_c \subset \mathbb{R}^n$ with $d_{\min}(\Lambda_c) = 2t$ and $\mathcal{C} = \Lambda_c \cap \mathcal{V}(\Lambda_s)$ is a nested lattice code based on the nested lattice pair (Λ_c, Λ_s), and there exist an average-case $(\mathcal{C}, \log|\mathcal{C}| - m, \mathcal{R}, \epsilon)$-strong extractor, then we can construct an $(\mathcal{M}, m, \mathcal{R}, t, \epsilon)$-cs-fuzzy extractors for $\mathcal{M} \subset \mathbb{R}^n$.*

If the randomness extractor is given by universal hash function, we have $|\mathcal{R}| \leq |\mathcal{C}| \cdot 2^{-m} \cdot (2\epsilon)^2$, which means the size of output key is limited by this upper bound.

6   Instantiation

Suppose lattice $\Lambda_c \subset \mathbb{R}^n$ with $d_{\min}(\Lambda_c) = 2t$, G is the generator matrix of Λ_c and $H = G^{-1}$ is the parity check matrix of Λ_c. Given the nested lattice code $\mathcal{C} = \Lambda_c \cap \mathcal{V}(\Lambda_s)$ based on the nested lattice pair (Λ_c, Λ_s) with nested ratio q, the size of codebook therefore is q^n. Observe that there is a bijection between $\mathbb{Z}_q^n$ and $\mathcal{C}$. The encoder maps the information $x \in \mathbb{Z}_q^n$ to a nested lattice codeword c by calculating $c = Gx \bmod \Lambda_s$ (this is equal to calculate $c = Gx - Q_{\Lambda_s}(Gx)$). An example of encoding is illustrated in Fig. 3.

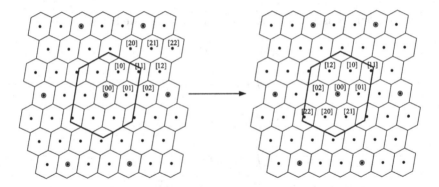

Fig. 3. Encoding $\mathbb{Z}_3^2$ to the nested lattice code.

Low-Density Lattice Codes (LDLC) [20] is a method of lattice code that draws upon the concept of Low-Density Parity Check Codes (LDPC) [12]. These codes are designed to have sparse and structured parity-check matrices, which enable efficient encoding and decoding processes.

To be specific, LDLC employs the lattice Λ_c with a square non-singular generator matrix G, where the parity check matrix $H = G^{-1}$ is sparse and has a determinant of $|\det(H)| = |\det(G)| = 1$. The message x is encoded to a lattice point with $c = Gx$, with encoding time complexity of $o(n)$ using the Jacobi method. For decoding, an iterative decoding algorithm, which is similar to those used in LDPC, is employed. The sparse structure of H allows for efficient decoding with computational complexity of $o(n)$.

LDLC is well-studied for unconstrained power channel (UPC) and the decoder will decode to the infinite lattice. For our constructions, the encoding and decoding process should be complemented by shaping. In nested lattice code, shaping is done by quantizing the lattice point of Λ_c onto the coarse lattice Λ_s. Kurkoski et al. [15] proposed a suboptimal quantizer for LDLC based on belief-propagation algorithm, which can be used for shaping.

Then we consider the randomness extractor. Let q be a prime, for $n > 1$, $x \in \mathbb{Z}_q^n$, $a \in \mathbb{Z}_q^{n-1}$, define $H_a(x) = \sum_{i=1}^{n-1} a_i x_i + x_n \bmod q$. It is easy to prove that $\mathcal{H} = \{H_a : \mathbb{Z}_q^n \to \mathbb{Z}_q | a \in \mathbb{Z}_q^{n-1}\}$ is a family of universal hash functions. By Lemma 1, we know that $H_a(x)$ is an average-case $(\mathbb{Z}_q^n, m, \mathbb{Z}_q, \epsilon)$-strong extractor with $q \leq 2^m \cdot (2\epsilon)^2$.

By applying LDLC with shaping algorithms and the randomness extractor above to our constructions, combine Lemma 1 with Theorem 2, we obtain the following theorem.

Theorem 3. *Let q be a prime and $\mathcal{M} \subset \mathbb{R}^n$. If lattice $\Lambda_c \subset \mathbb{R}^n$ with $d_{\min}(\Lambda_c) = 2t$ and $\mathcal{C} = \Lambda_c \cap \mathcal{V}(\Lambda_s)$ is a nested lattice code based on the nested lattice pair (Λ_c, Λ_s) with nested ratio q and is implied by LDLC, then we can construct an $(\mathcal{M}, m, \mathbb{Z}_q, t, \epsilon)$-cs-fuzzy extractors where $\epsilon = \frac{1}{2}\sqrt{2^m \cdot q^{1-n}}$. The generation and reproduction process are efficient, with computational complexity of $O(n)$.*

Remark 2. This is the first scheme of cs-fuzzy extractor applying max-divergence. Parente et al. [18] proposed a scheme using LDLC in the UPC with code-offset method, which is an instantiation of cs-fuzzy conductor. However, their approach relies on a specific quantization scheme to define the min-entropy of the distribution, making it less generalized [23]. Additionally, their construction cannot be extended to syndrome construction due to the absence of the shaping process.

7 Conclusion

In this paper, we focus on the key derivation from continuous sources. We first proposed the notion of max-divergence to measure the unpredictability of continuous sources and evaluate the feasibility of key extraction for continuous source. Then we presented the adapted definitions of fuzzy extractors and fuzzy conductors tailored for continuous sources, and we further explored the relation between these primitives. In addition, we proposed two generalized constructions using lattice code and analyzed the security of these constructions based on max-divergence. Finally, we demonstrated an implementation of a continuous-source fuzzy extractor using LDLC code. Many prior works focus on the reusability and robustness of fuzzy extractors. In the context of cs-fuzzy extractors, it is interesting to ask whether we can construct reusable and robust cs-fuzzy extractors. We leave these problems for future work.

References

1. Bennett, C.H., DiVincenzo, D.P.: Quantum information and computation. Nature **404**(6775), 247–255 (2000). https://doi.org/10.1038/35005001
2. Buhan, I., Doumen, J., Hartel, P., Tang, Q., Veldhuis, R.: Embedding renewable cryptographic keys into noisy data. Int. J. Inf. Secur. **9**(3), 193–208 (2010). https://doi.org/10.1007/s10207-010-0103-4
3. Buhan, I., Doumen, J., Hartel, P., Veldhuis, R.: Fuzzy extractors for continuous distributions. In: Proceedings of the 2nd ACM Symposium on Information, Computer and Communications Security. ACM (2007). https://doi.org/10.1145/1229285.1229325
4. Carter, J., Wegman, M.N.: Universal classes of hash functions. J. Comput. Syst. Sci. **18**(2), 143–154 (1979). https://doi.org/10.1016/0022-0000(79)90044-8
5. Daugman, J.: How iris recognition works. In: Proceedings of International Conference on Image Processing. IEEE (2009). https://doi.org/10.1109/icip.2002.1037952
6. Dodis, Y., Ostrovsky, R., Reyzin, L., Smith, A.: Fuzzy extractors: how to generate strong keys from biometrics and other noisy data. SIAM J. Comput. **38**(1), 97–139 (2008). https://doi.org/10.1137/060651380
7. Erez, U., Zamir, R.: Lattice decoding can achieve 1/2 log(1+SNR) on the AWGN channel using nested codes. In: Proceedings of 2001 IEEE International Symposium on Information Theory (IEEE Cat. No.01CH37252). IEEE (2004). https://doi.org/10.1109/isit.2001.935988

8. van Erven, T., Harremoes, P.: Rényi divergence and Kullback-Leibler divergence. IEEE Trans. Inf. Theory **60**(7), 3797–3820 (2014). https://doi.org/10.1109/tit. 2014.2320500

9. Fuller, B., Meng, X., Reyzin, L.: Computational fuzzy extractors. In: Sako, K., Sarkar, P. (eds.) ASIACRYPT 2013. LNCS, vol. 8269, pp. 174–193. Springer, Heidelberg (2013). https://doi.org/10.1007/978-3-642-42033-7_10

10. Fuller, B., Peng, L.: Continuous-source fuzzy extractors: source uncertainty and insecurity. In: 2019 IEEE International Symposium on Information Theory (ISIT). IEEE (2019). https://doi.org/10.1109/isit.2019.8849421

11. Fuller, B., Reyzin, L., Smith, A.: When are fuzzy extractors possible? In: Cheon, J.H., Takagi, T. (eds.) ASIACRYPT 2016. LNCS, vol. 10031, pp. 277–306. Springer, Heidelberg (2016). https://doi.org/10.1007/978-3-662-53887-6_10

12. Gallager, R.G.: Low-Density Parity-Check Codes. The MIT Press, Cambridge (1963). https://doi.org/10.7551/mitpress/4347.001.0001

13. Gilkalaye, B.P., Rattani, A., Derakhshani, R.: Euclidean-distance based fuzzy commitment scheme for biometric template security. In: 2019 7th International Workshop on Biometrics and Forensics (IWBF). IEEE (2019). https://doi.org/10.1109/iwbf.2019.8739177

14. Kanukurthi, B., Reyzin, L.: Key agreement from close secrets over unsecured channels. In: Joux, A. (ed.) EUROCRYPT 2009. LNCS, vol. 5479, pp. 206–223. Springer, Heidelberg (2009). https://doi.org/10.1007/978-3-642-01001-9_12

15. Kurkoski, B.M., Dauwels, J., Loeliger, H.A.: Power-constrained communications using LDLC lattices. In: 2009 IEEE International Symposium on Information Theory. IEEE (2009). https://doi.org/10.1109/isit.2009.5205635

16. Li, Q., Sutcu, Y., Memon, N.: Secure sketch for biometric templates. In: Lai, X., Chen, K. (eds.) ASIACRYPT 2006. LNCS, vol. 4284, pp. 99–113. Springer, Heidelberg (2006). https://doi.org/10.1007/11935230_7

17. Nisan, N., Zuckerman, D.: Randomness is linear in space. J. Comput. Syst. Sci. **52**(1), 43–52 (1996). https://doi.org/10.1006/jcss.1996.0004

18. Parente, V.P., van de Graaf, J.: A practical fuzzy extractor for continuous features. In: Nascimento, A.C.A., Barreto, P. (eds.) ICITS 2016. LNCS, vol. 10015, pp. 241–258. Springer, Cham (2016). https://doi.org/10.1007/978-3-319-49175-2_12

19. Schroff, F., Kalenichenko, D., Philbin, J.: FaceNet: a unified embedding for face recognition and clustering. In: 2015 IEEE Conference on Computer Vision and Pattern Recognition (CVPR). IEEE (2015). https://doi.org/10.1109/cvpr.2015.7298682

20. Sommer, N., Feder, M., Shalvi, O.: Low-density lattice codes. IEEE Trans. Inf. Theory **54**(4), 1561–1585 (2008). https://doi.org/10.1109/tit.2008.917684

21. Suh, G.E., Devadas, S.: Physical unclonable functions for device authentication and secret key generation. In: 2007 44th ACM/IEEE Design Automation Conference. IEEE (2007). https://doi.org/10.1109/dac.2007.375043

22. Sutcu, Y., Li, Q., Memon, N.: How to protect biometric templates. In: SPIE Proceedings. SPIE (2007). https://doi.org/10.1117/12.705896

23. Verbitskiy, E.A., Tuyls, P., Obi, C., Schoenmakers, B., Skoric, B.: Key extraction from general nondiscrete signals. IEEE Trans. Inf. Forensics Secur. **5**(2), 269–279 (2010). https://doi.org/10.1109/tifs.2010.2046965

24. Zheng, G., Li, W., Zhan, C.: Cryptographic key generation from biometric data using lattice mapping. In: 18th International Conference on Pattern Recognition (ICPR'06). IEEE (2006). https://doi.org/10.1109/icpr.2006.423

Geometry-Based Garbled Circuits Relying Solely on One Evaluation Algorithm Under Standard Assumption

Jingyu Ning and Zhenhua Tan(✉)

Software College, Northeastern University, Shenyang, China
{ningjy,tanzh}@mail.neu.edu.cn

Abstract. Garbled circuits are the leading cryptographic techniques for constant-round secure two-party computation (S2PC). Classical constructions of Garbled circuits (GC) utilize 4 ciphertexts per gate which have attracted great attention for optimizing the performance of communication. Under standard assumption, the best existing optimizations on GC have reduced the number of ciphertexts per gate to 2, while other more efficient optimizations rely on the very strict non-standard assumption. However, these optimizations are based on the different evaluation algorithms of different garbled gates, leading to the switching requirement of the evaluator between different types of binary gates. In this paper, we focus on the optimization under standard assumption, and propose a garbling method with two ciphertexts per gate. Our scheme requires only 1 evaluation algorithm to evaluate all the binary gates, inspired by the geometric theorems of "the distance from any point on the circle to the center of the circle is equal" and "the distance from any point on the perpendicular bisector of the line segment to the two ends of the line segment is equal". We transfer the four possible input options of each garbled gate into four binary coordinates in a two-dimensional surface, and construct garbled AND gates and garbled XOR gates with detailed garbling functions according to related geometric theorems. Finally, we proposed the geometry-based garbling scheme which could garble any circuits with AND gates, XOR gates and NOT gates by the proposed garbling algorithm, and the evaluation of all binary gates is to calculate the square of the distance between specific two-dimensional points, such that the number of evaluation algorithm is 1 during the whole garbling process. The security proof demonstrates that the proposed geometry-based garbling scheme satisfies the security requirements of privacy, obliviousness and authenticity. Related demo codes for our proposed Geometry-based GC is publicly available on Github: https://github.com/TAN-OpenLab/Geom-GC.

Keywords: Garbled circuit · Geometry-based gates · Secure two-party computation · Privacy-preserving

C. Ge and M. Yung (Eds.): Inscrypt 2023, LNCS 14526, pp. 183–202, 2024.
https://doi.org/10.1007/978-981-97-0942-7_10

1   Introduction

1.1   Background

Garbled circuits (GC), proposed by Yao in the 1980s firstly [32], are the leading cryptographic techniques for constant-round secure two-party computation (S2PC) in decades [10,15,18,22,24], and also applied into secure multi-party computation protocols (SMPC) [3,6,8,9,30]. How to optimize the performance of computation and communication of GC, has attracted extensive attention. Some focus on the reduction of size [2,11,16,17,23,25,26,33], some focus on the number of garbled circuits required to achieve malicious security [14,19,21,27,29], and some focus on the application of garbled circuits [1,31,34]. Nowadays, the computation of GC is not the bottleneck due to the extremely fast development of computing processor and the application of efficient symmetric-key operations [5,12,13,26], so that the optimization for the communication of GC attracts great interests.

There are two kinds of method to optimize the communication performance of GC. The first one is Garbled circuits with global offset under non-standard assumptions. The typical scheme is Free-XOR [17], where no garbled table is used and the garbling and evaluation of XOR gates are free during efficiently running [12,20,33]. However, they require non-standard assumptions which need a global offset Δ to set keys for each wire by $W_i^1 = W_i^0 \oplus \Delta$ after a related random W_i^0 is ready. The security of such optimization with global offset relies on the CCR (circular correlation robust hash function) assumption [7] and ciphertext is related to secret key by the offset [12].

The second communication optimization method rely only on a standard assumption (PRF, pseudorandom function) without global offset. Most of existing GC schemes belong to this kind. Each gate has four encryption keys as possible input for the two-input wire, and the output values are encrypted to be ciphertexts under these appropriate keys from the incoming wires [4,12,16,23,24,32]. As a result, each ciphertext usually corresponds to one input [4,16,23,32] or two inputs [24], so the number of ciphertexts per gate of existing schemes is between 2 to 4. Moreover, the evaluator calls the cryptographic primitive more than once. For example, when calculating the XOR gate, the method of [12] reduces the number of ciphertexts to 1 by setting the same offset between two input wires of a line. The method encrypts the two inputs separately, so the evaluator must call the encryption primitive twice to decrypt. Due to the above two bottlenecks, a new method is needed to reduce both the number of ciphertexts and the number of times that the evaluator calls the cryptographic primitive. A lightweight GC based on solid geometry transformation under standard PRF assumption was proposed by Tan et al. [28] recently. We improve Tan's protocol by substituting the three-dimensional space to the two-dimensional space in this paper.

Our Opinion and Observation. In this paper, we focus on the optimization of communication under standard assumption. In order to further reduce the number of ciphertexts for each gate in GC, we propose a novel scheme of Garbled Circuits based on geometric operation. We convert the computation in the garbled circuit to the geometric operation of finding the distance between two points on a two-dimensional plane so that only one ciphertext is required for any binary garbled gate. Our scheme is inspired by the following observations.

Observation 1 We consider the case of four nonconcyclic points on a two-dimensional plane, and any three of them are noncollinear. Then, any three noncollinear points uniquely determine a circle. The distance between any point of the circle and the center of the circle is equal to its radius, while the distance between the other point and the center of the circle is not equal to the radius. In this case, the distances between the four points to the center of the circle can be divided into two parts at a ratio of 3:1. In any AND gate, there are four input options, where three of them correspond to FALSE and one of them corresponds to TRUE, so the FALSE to TRUE ratio is also 3:1.

Observation 2 We consider the case of four nonconcyclic points on a two-dimensional plane divided into two pairs, and the line segment between each pair of points is not parallel to the other. The perpendicular bisectors of the two line segments intersect at a common point, so the distances between the intersection point and the points of the same line segment are equal, while the distances between the intersection point and the points of different line segments are not equal. In this case, the distances between the four points to the intersection point can be divided into two parts at a ratio of 2:2. In any XOR gate, there are four input options, where two of them correspond to FALSE and two of them correspond to TRUE, so the FALSE to TRUE ratio is also 2:2.

Based on the above two observations, we associate the four input options in the garbled gate with the four points on the two-dimensional plane and associate the distance between the points with the output of the garbled gate. Then, we implement the gate of the garbled circuit through geometric computation.

1.2 Overview of Our Approach

In a garbled circuit, each binary gate has two input wires and an output wire. Let (W_a^0, W_a^1), (W_b^0, W_b^1) denote the input wire labels and (W_i^0, W_i^1) denote the output wire labels, with W_a^0, W_b^0, and W_i^0 each encoding FALSE.

GeomAND. First, we convert the four options of input labels into coordinates of four points on a two-dimensional plane.

$$P_{00} \leftarrow F_{W_a^0 \oplus W_b^0}(W_a^0 || W_b^0); P_{01} \leftarrow F_{W_a^0 \oplus W_b^1}(W_a^0 || W_b^1);$$
$$P_{10} \leftarrow F_{W_a^1 \oplus W_b^0}(W_a^1 || W_b^0); P_{11} \leftarrow F_{W_a^1 \oplus W_b^1}(W_a^1 || W_b^1) \tag{1}$$

where $\oplus$ denotes bitwise XOR, and $||$ denotes connecting the two bit strings. F denotes a pseudorandom function instantiated as AES in this paper. Second, we create a circle with center C out of three points P_{00}, P_{01} and P_{10}. Let the square of the radius be W_i^0, and let the square of the distance between point P_{11} and C be W_i^1. Finally, let the coordinates of C be the ciphertexts.

GeomXOR. First, we convert the four options of input labels into four coordinates of points on a two-dimensional plane as Eq. 1. Second, let the intersection point of the perpendicular bisectors of the two line segments $P_{00}P_{11}$ and $P_{01}P_{10}$ be C. Let W_i^0 be the square of the distance between C and P_{00} (or P_{11}) and let W_i^1 be the square of the distance between C and P_{01} (or P_{10}). Finally, let let the coordinates of C be the ciphertexts.

Evaluation. The evaluation algorithms of GeomAND and GeomXOR gates are completely identical. The evaluator holds one out of the four input options, allowing the evaluator to obtain a point by the method in Eq. 1. Then, the evaluator calculates the square of the distance between the point and C, and takes the result as the output.

Consequently, we obtain a method to garble AND gates and XOR gates that requires 1 evaluation algorithm total. We call this method Geometry-AND, Geometry-XOR, or GeomAND, GeomXOR for short.

1.3 Our Contributions

This is the first time that the geometrical features have been utilized in garble circuits, providing a new idea about the construction of garble circuits.

We optimize the garbled circuit under a pseudorandom function assumption. In each AND gate, the ciphertexts correspond to the center of the circle. In each XOR gate, the ciphertexts correspond to the intersection point of the perpendicular bisectors. As a result, each gate requires storing two coordinates of a specific point as the two ciphertexts.

In addition, for any types of binary gates, the evaluator calculates the square of the distance between the point of input garbled values and the ciphertext point once. Consequently, the evaluator stores only one evaluation algorithm, eliminating the switches from different evaluation algorithms.

The remaining article is organized as follows. After discussing preliminaries in Sect. 2, we explicitly describe our circuit garbling scheme in Sect. 3, and analyse the performance of Geometry-based GC in Sect. 4. We provide a formal proof of security in Sect. 5 and the concluding remarks are presented in Sect. 6.

2 Preliminaries

Definition 1. *A garbling scheme consists of 4 algorithms, including* $Garble(1^\kappa, f) \rightarrow (C, e, d)$, $Encode(e, x) \rightarrow X$, $Eval(C, X) \rightarrow Y$ *and* $Decode(Y, d) \rightarrow y$, *where* 1^κ *is the security parameter,* f *is the input Boolean circuit,* e *and* d *represent the encoding and decoding information respectively.* C

is the garbled circuit, while Y is the garbled output during evaluation and y is the real output of the Boolean circuit. Figure 1 shows relations of the four algorithms.

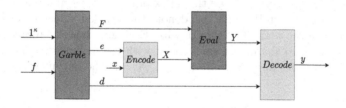

Fig. 1. Construction of the garbled circuit.

The correctness property is that, if $(C, e, d) \leftarrow Garble(1^\kappa, f)$, then for every x, it holds that $Decode(d, Eval(C, Encode(e, x))) = f(x)$.

Definition 2. *A garbling scheme must satisfy the following security properties:*

- *Privacy: Except for $f(x)$, (C, X, d) does not reveal any information about x and f. More formally, there exists a simulator S that takes the input $(1^\kappa, f, f(x))$ and the output (C, X, d) is indistinguishable from the real garbled circuit.*
- *Obliviousness: (C, X) does not reveal any information about x. More formally, there exists a simulator S that takes input $(1^\kappa, f)$ and the output (C, X) is indistinguishable from the real garbled circuit.*
- *Authenticity: Given input (C, X) alone, no adversary should be able to produce $\widetilde{Y} \neq Eval(C, X)$ such that $Decode\left(\widetilde{Y}, d\right) \notin \perp$, except with negligible probability.*

Definition 3. *Let $GF(p)$ be a finite field, where p is a prime. The garbled values, the coordinates and the squares of the distances in this paper are in the finite field $GF(p)$. Let the symbols "$+, \times$" in equations denote addition and multiplication in $GF(p)$, and let "$-x, \frac{1}{x}$" denote the additive and multiplicative inverse of x in $GF(p)$.*

Definition 4. *Let S be a distribution over $\{0,1\}^n$ and $F_s : \{0,1\}^k \to \{0,1\}^l$ be a family of functions indexed by strings s in the support of S. We say F_s is a (t, μ)-pseudorandom function family if for every Boolean valued oracle circuit $\mathcal{A}$ of size at most t,*

$$|Pr_S[\mathcal{A}^{F_s} accepts] - Pr_R[\mathcal{A}^R accepts]| \leq \mu(\kappa)c \qquad (2)$$

where s is distributed according to S, and R is a function sampled uniformly at random from the set of all functions from $\{0,1\}^k$ to $\{0,1\}^l$.

3   Our Garbling Scheme in Detail

3.1   Notation and Concepts.

Let $Inputs(f)$ and $Outputs(f)$ be the index of input wires and output wires in f. For each wire w_i, let W_i^0 and W_i^1 denote the garbled values of FALSE and TRUE. Let v_i be the real bit of the ith wire. Each gate has two input wires and one output wire, and shares the same index with the output wire. As shown in Fig. 2, the input wires of gate g_i are w_a and w_b, and the output wire is w_i.

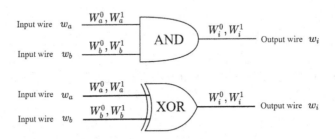

Fig. 2. Garbled AND gate g_i and XOR gate g_i.

Arbitrary Gates. Similar to [33], our geometry-based scheme can be used to garble any gate whose truth table contains an odd number of gates. All such gates can be denoted as,

$$g\left(v_a, v_b\right) = \left(\alpha_a \oplus v_a\right) \wedge \left(\alpha_b \oplus v_b\right) \oplus \alpha_c \tag{3}$$

where $\alpha_a, \alpha_b, \alpha_c \in \{0, 1\}$. We can construct different gates by changing α_a, α_b, and α_c in Table 1.

Table 1. Construction of different gates.

Gates	α_a	α_b	α_c	$g(\alpha_a, \alpha_b)$
AND	0	0	0	$\alpha_a \wedge \alpha_b$
NAND	0	0	1	$\neg(\alpha_a \wedge \alpha_b)$
OR	1	1	1	$\alpha_a \vee \alpha_b$
NOR	1	1	0	$\neg(\alpha_a \vee \alpha_b)$

Initialize$(1^\kappa, f)$:

   for each input wire $i \in Inputs(f)$:

     $W_i^0 \leftarrow \{0,1\}^\kappa$

     $W_i^1 \leftarrow \{0,1\}^\kappa$

     $e[i,0] \leftarrow W_i^0$

     $e[i,1] \leftarrow W_i^1$

     return $\left(W_{Inputs\ (f)}^0, W_{Inputs\ (f)}^1, e \right)$

Fig. 3. Initialization of garbling.

3.2 Garbling Procedure: Initialization.

For each input wire w_i of f, the generator samples two random garbled values $W_i^0 \leftarrow \{0,1\}^\kappa$ and $W_i^1 \leftarrow \{0,1\}^\kappa$, representing FALSE and TRUE. The correspondences between the truth values and the garbled values of the input wires are expressed as the encode information e, as shown in Fig. 3.

The core of this paper is the construction of garbled gates, and in the following, we will introduce the AND, XOR and NOT gates (Fig. 5, Fig. 7, Fig. 8).

3.3 Garbling Procedure: Geometry-AND Gates.

Each Geometry-AND gate with two input wires w_a and w_b takes W_a^0, W_a^1, W_b^0, W_b^1 as the input garbled values. The output of the Geometry-AND gate consists of the output garbled values W_i^0, W_i^1 and the two ciphertexts in C_i. There are four input options where only input option (W_a^1, W_b^1) will output W_i^1, and input options (W_a^0, W_b^0), (W_a^0, W_b^1) and (W_a^1, W_b^0) will output W_i^0. The procedure of the Geometry-AND gate is as follows.

1. For each option $(W_a^{v_a}, W_b^{v_b})$, we calculate the result of PRF, as $W_{ab} \leftarrow F_{W_a^{v_a} \oplus W_b^{v_b}}(W_a^{v_a} || W_b^{v_b})$ and convert W_{ab} into coordinates $(x_{v_a v_b}, y_{v_a v_b})$ of point $P_{v_a v_b}$ as $P_{v_a v_b} \leftarrow GetCoordinate(W_{ab})$ shown in Algorithm 1, where $a\ SHR\ b$ denotes the shift logical right instruction that shifts the bits of bit string a to the right by b bits and $length(a)$ denotes the length of bit string a. Firstly, we divide $W_{v_a v_b}$ into two blocks. Then, let the left half bits be $x_{v_a v_b}$, the right half bits be $y_{v_a v_b}$. Therefore, we obtain the coordinates of $P_{v_a v_b}$.
2. Let C_i be the center of the circle from the three points P_{00}, P_{01} and P_{10}.
3. As shown in Fig. 4, the distances between C_i and P_{00}, P_{01}, P_{10} are the radii. Let the square of the radius be the output value W_i^0, thereby we obtain the equation $W_i^0 = Dis^2(P_{00}, C_i) = Dis^2(P_{01}, C_i) = Dis^2(P_{10}, C_i)$. Let the distance between C_i and P_{11} be the output value $W_i^1 = Dis^2(P_{11}, C_i)$.
4. The ciphertexts are the coordinates of C_i.

Algorithm 1 GetCoordinate($W_{v_a v_b}$)

1: $x_{v_a v_b} \leftarrow (W_{temp} \leftarrow W_{v_a v_b})\, SHR\, (length(W_{v_a v_b})/2))$
2: $y_{v_a v_b} \leftarrow W_{v_a v_b}\, AND\, (2^{(length(W_{v_a v_b})/2)} - 1)$
3: $return\, <x_{v_a v_b}, y_{v_a v_b}>$

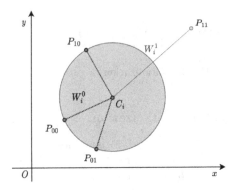

Fig. 4. Description of the Geometry-AND gate.

GeomAND$\left(W_a^0, W_a^1, W_b^0, W_b^1\right)$:

---

for $v_a, v_b \in \{0, 1\}$
  $W_{ab} \leftarrow F_{W_a^{v_a} \oplus W_b^{v_b}}\left(W_a^{v_a} \| W_b^{v_b}\right)$
  $P_{v_a v_b} \leftarrow GetCoordinate(W_{ab})$
$i \leftarrow NextIndex(a, b)$
calculate the center of circle C_i with (P_{00}, P_{01}, P_{10})
$W_i^0 \leftarrow Dis^2(P_{00}, C_i)$
$W_i^1 \leftarrow Dis^2(P_{11}, C_i)$
return $\left(W_i^0, W_i^1, C_i\right)$

Fig. 5. Garbling AND Gates.

3.4   Garbling Procedure: Geometry-XOR Gates.

As the Geometry-AND gate, each Geometry-XOR gate takes W_a^0, W_a^1, W_b^0, W_b^1 as the input garbled values and takes the output garbled values W_i^0, W_i^1 and the ciphertexts C_i as output. There are four input options where input options (W_a^0, W_b^0) and (W_a^1, W_b^1) will output W_i^0, and input options (W_a^0, W_b^1) and (W_a^1, W_b^0) will output W_i^1. The procedure of the Geometry-XOR gate is as follows.

1. Obtain the coordinates of $P_{v_a v_b}$ in the same method with Geometry-AND gates, where $v_a, v_b \in \{0, 1\}$.
2. Calculate the perpendicular bisectors l_1 and l_2 of the two line segments $P_{00}P_{11}$ and $P_{01}P_{10}$, respectively.
3. Calculate the intersection C_i of l_1 and l_2.

4. As shown in Fig. 6, the distance between C_i and P_{00} equals the distance between C_i and P_{11}. Let the square of the distance be the output value W_i^0 and we obtain the equation $W_i^0 = Dis^2(P_{00}, C_i) = Dis^2(P_{11}, C_i)$. The distance between C_i and P_{01} equals the distance between C_i and P_{10}. Let the square of the distance be the output value W_i^1 and we obtain the equation $W_i^1 = Dis^2(P_{01}, C_i) = Dis^2(P_{10}, C_i)$.
5. The ciphertexts are the coordinates of C_i.

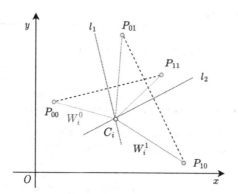

Fig. 6. Description of the Geometry-XOR gate.

GeomXOR$(W_a^0, W_a^1, W_b^0, W_b^1)$:

---

for $v_a, v_b \in \{0, 1\}$

$\quad W_{ab} \leftarrow F_{W_a^{v_a} \oplus W_b^{v_b}}(W_a^{v_a} \| W_b^{v_b})$

$\quad P_{v_a v_b} \leftarrow GetCoordinate(W_{ab})$

$i \leftarrow$ NextIndex(a, b)

calculate the perpendicular bisectors l_1 and l_2 of the two line segments $P_{00}P_{11}$ and $P_{01}P_{10}$

calculate the intersection C_i of l_1 and l_2

$W_i^0 \leftarrow Dis^2(P_{00}, C_i)$

$W_i^1 \leftarrow Dis^2(P_{01}, C_i)$

return (W_i^0, W_i^1, C_i)

Fig. 7. Garbling XOR Gates.

3.5   Garbling Procedure: Geometry-NOT Gates.

The NOT gate is a logical gate that produces a statement that is the inverse of an input statement. Therefore, in garbled circuits, we reverse the input garbled values to represent the output garbled values. Each Geometry-NOT gate with input wire w_a and output wire w_i takes W_a^0, W_a^1 as the input garbled values, thus the output garbled value W_i^0 equals W_a^1 and W_i^1 equals W_a^0, as shown in 8.

GeomNOT(W_a^0, W_a^1):

$i \leftarrow NextIndex(a)$

$W_i^0 \leftarrow W_a^1$

$W_i^1 \leftarrow W_a^0$

return (W_i^0, W_i^1)

Fig. 8. Garbling NOT Gates.

3.6   Algorithms of Proposed Geometry-Based GC

The Geometry-based GC algorithm is shown in Fig. 9 which consists of 4 algorithms: Garble(), Encode(), Eval() and Decode().

Garble:

1. Initialization. Generate the garbled values of input wires and encoding information.
2. For each gate g_i in the circuit, we invoke the gate function according to the type of gate and obtain the garbled output which can be the garbled input of the next gates. If the gate is a binary gate, we will get the ciphertexts C_i. When all gates have been built, let C be the set of all ciphertexts C_i.
3. For each output wire, prepare the decoding information with two garbled values from step 2.

Eval:

1. For each input wire w_i in the garbled circuit, set the garbled value W_i by the garbled input X.
2. For each binary gate g_i with input wires w_a and w_b, and output wire w_i. Let the input garbled values be W_a, W_b.
3. Convert (W_a, W_b) into a point P_i by GetCoordinate().
4. Obtain the coordinates of the point C_i from C.
5. Calculate the square of the distance between P_i and C_i as the output value W_i.
6. For each output wire w_i of f, assign the garbled value Y_i as W_i.

The Encode algorithm and the Decode algorithm are designed for basic functionality. The Encode algorithm maps the input plaintext bits x to the input garbled values X, and the Decode algorithm maps the output garbled values Y to the output plaintext bits y.

The above content is the description of our Geometry-based GC.

Correctness. If $(C, e, d) \leftarrow Garble(1^\kappa, f)$, then for every x, it holds that $Decode(d, Eval(C, Encode(e, x))) = f(x)$.

```
Garble(1ᴷ, f):
  (W⁰_Inputs(f), W¹_Inputs(f), e) ← Initialize(1ᴷ, f)
  for each gate gᵢ in circuit f
  if gᵢ is an AND gate with input wires wₐ, w_b and
  output wire wᵢ
      (W⁰ᵢ, W¹ᵢ, Cᵢ) ← GeomAND(W⁰ₐ, W¹ₐ, W⁰_b, W¹_b)
  if gᵢ is an XOR gate with input wires wₐ, w_b and
  output wire wᵢ
      (W⁰ᵢ, W¹ᵢ, Cᵢ) ← GeomXOR(W⁰ₐ, W¹ₐ, W⁰_b, W¹_b)
  if gᵢ is a NOT gate with input wire wₐ and output
  wire wᵢ
      (W⁰ᵢ, W¹ᵢ) ← GeomNOT(W⁰ₐ, W¹ₐ)
  for each wire i ∈ Outputs(f)
      d[i, 0] ← W⁰ᵢ
      d[i, 1] ← W¹ᵢ
  return (C, e, d)


Encode(e, x):
  for xᵢ ∈ x
      Xᵢ ← e[i, xᵢ]
  return X
```

```
Eval(C, X):
  for each wire i ∈ Inputs(C)
      Wᵢ ← Xᵢ
  for each binary gate gᵢ with input
  wires wₐ, w_b and output wire wᵢ:
      Wᵢ ← F_{Wₐ⊕W_b}(Wₐ‖W_b)
      Pᵢ ← GetCoordinate(Wᵢ)
      Wᵢ ← Dis²(Pᵢ, Cᵢ)
  for each wire i ∈ Outputs(C)
      Yᵢ ← Wᵢ
  return Y


Decode(d, Y):
  for Yᵢ ∈ Y
      if Yᵢ ← d[i, 0] then yᵢ ← 0
      else if Yᵢ ← d[i, 1] then yᵢ ← 1
      else return ⊥
  return Y
```

Fig. 9. Full GC algorithm.

Proof. In $Garble(1^\kappa, f)$, we first initialize the encoding information e. There-fore, each input wire of the circuit has two garbled values representing TRUE and FALSE, respectively. For each gate in the circuit with input wires w_a, w_b and output wire w_i. We obtain $P_{00} = (x_{00}, y_{00})$, $P_{01} = (x_{01}, y_{01})$, $P_{10} = (x_{10}, y_{10})$ and $P_{11} = (x_{11}, y_{11})$ to represent four possible input option.

Case 1. The gate is an AND gate. We construct a circle passing through the three points P_{00}, P_{01} and P_{10}. The equation of the circle is

$$Ax^2 + Ay^2 + Bx + Dy + E = 0 \qquad (4)$$

After substituting the three given points which lies on the circle, we get the system of equations that can be described by the determinant,

$$\begin{vmatrix} x^2 + y^2 & x & y & 1 \\ x_{00}^2 + y_{00}^2 & x_{00} & y_{00} & 1 \\ x_{01}^2 + y_{01}^2 & x_{01} & y_{01} & 1 \\ x_{10}^2 + y_{10}^2 & x_{10} & y_{10} & 1 \end{vmatrix} = 0 \qquad (5)$$

The coefficients A, B, D and E can be found by solving the following determi-nants,

$$A = \begin{vmatrix} x_{00} & y_{00} & 1 \\ x_{01} & y_{01} & 1 \\ x_{10} & y_{10} & 1 \end{vmatrix}, B = -\begin{vmatrix} x_{00}^2 + y_{00}^2 & y_{00} & 1 \\ x_{01}^2 + y_{01}^2 & y_{01} & 1 \\ x_{10}^2 + y_{10}^2 & y_{10} & 1 \end{vmatrix},$$

$$D = \begin{vmatrix} x_{00}^2 + y_{00}^2 & x_{00} & 1 \\ x_{01}^2 + y_{01}^2 & x_{01} & 1 \\ x_{10}^2 + y_{10}^2 & x_{10} & 1 \end{vmatrix}, E = - \begin{vmatrix} x_{00}^2 + y_{00}^2 & x_{00} & y_{00} \\ x_{01}^2 + y_{01}^2 & x_{01} & y_{01} \\ x_{10}^2 + y_{10}^2 & x_{10} & y_{10} \end{vmatrix} \qquad (6)$$

There will be an error if the points P_{00}, P_{01} and P_{10} are linearly dependent, namely $A = 0$. Since the security parameter is κ, the error probability

$$Pr[A = 0] = Pr[3 \text{ points coincide}] + Pr[2 \text{ points coincide}] + Pr[\text{only colinear}]$$
$$= 2^{-4\kappa} + 3 \times 2^{-2\kappa}(1 - 2^{-2\kappa}) + (1 - 2^{-2\kappa})(2^{-\kappa} - 2 \times 2^{-2\kappa}) \qquad (7)$$

is negligible for any probabilistic polynomial-time (PPT) algorithm $\mathcal{A}$.

Let $C_i = (x_o, y_o)$ be the center of the circle, and R be the radius.

$$x_o = -\frac{B}{2A}, \quad y_o = -\frac{D}{2A}, \quad R^2 = \frac{B^2 + D^2 - 4AE}{4A^2} \qquad (8)$$

Let $W_i^0 = R^2$, and let W_i^1 be the square of the distance between P_{11} and C_i, namely $W_i^1 = Dis^2(P_{11}, C_i) = (x_{11} - x_o)^2 + (y_{11} - y_o)^2$. Let the ciphertexts be the coordinates of C_i.

In summary, if the input $v_a \wedge v_b = 0$, then the garbled output $W_i^{v_i} = W_i^0$. If the input $v_a \wedge v_b = 1$, then the garbled output $W_i^{v_i} = W_i^1$. Consequently, we obtain $v_a \wedge v_b = v_i$.

Case 2. The gate is an XOR gate. The midpoint of the line segment $\overline{P_{00}P_{11}}$ are $(\frac{x_{00}+x_{11}}{2}, \frac{y_{00}+y_{11}}{2})$. The perpendicular bisector l_1 of the line segment $\overline{P_{00}P_{11}}$ is

$$(y_{00}-y_{11})(y - \frac{y_{00}+y_{11}}{2}) = -(x_{00}-x_{11})(x - \frac{x_{00}+x_{11}}{2}) \qquad (9)$$

In the same way, the perpendicular bisector l_2 of the line segment $\overline{P_{01}P_{10}}$ is

$$(y_{01}-y_{10})(y - \frac{y_{01}+y_{10}}{2}) = -(x_{01}-x_{10})(x - \frac{x_{01}+x_{10}}{2}) \qquad (10)$$

Let $C_i = (x_o, y_o)$ be the intersection of l_1 and l_2, then C_i is determined by solving the values of x_o and y_o from the equations of l_1 and l_2 by Cramer's rule,

$$\begin{cases} (y_{00} - y_{11})y_o = -(x_{00} - x_{11})x_o + \frac{x_{00}^2 - x_{11}^2 + y_{00}^2 - y_{11}^2}{2} \\ (y_{01} - y_{10})y_o = -(x_{01} - x_{10})x_o + \frac{x_{01}^2 - x_{10}^2 + y_{01}^2 - y_{10}^2}{2} \end{cases} \qquad (11)$$

We have

$$x_o = \frac{(x_{00}^2 - x_{11}^2 + y_{00}^2 - y_{11}^2)(y_{01}-y_{10}) - (x_{01}^2 - x_{10}^2 + y_{01}^2 - y_{10}^2)(y_{00}-y_{11})}{2(x_{00}-x_{11})(y_{01}-y_{10}) - 2(x_{01}-x_{10})(y_{00}-y_{11})}$$

$$y_o = \frac{(x_{01}^2 - x_{10}^2 + y_{01}^2 - y_{10}^2)(x_{00}-x_{11}) - (x_{00}^2 - x_{11}^2 + y_{00}^2 - y_{11}^2)(x_{01}-x_{10})}{2(x_{00}-x_{11})(y_{01}-y_{10}) - 2(x_{01}-x_{10})(y_{00}-y_{11})}$$

$$\qquad (12)$$

The error probability of $(x_{00}-x_{11})(y_{01}-y_{10}) = (x_{01}-x_{10})(y_{00}-y_{11})$ is

$$Pr[(x_{00}-x_{11})(y_{01}-y_{10}) = (x_{01}-x_{10})(y_{00}-y_{11})]$$
$$=Pr[\text{points coincide}] + Pr[\text{lines parallel}] \qquad (13)$$
$$=2^{-4\kappa} + 2 \times 2^{-2\kappa}(1 - 2^{-2\kappa}) + (1 - 2^{-2\kappa})2^{-\kappa}$$

is negligible for any PPT algorithm $\mathcal{A}$.

The square of the distance between C_i and P_{00} is equal to the square of the distance between C_i and P_{11}, and we set

$$W_i^0 = Dis^2(P_{00}, C_i) = Dis^2(P_{11}, C_i) = (x_{11} - x_o)^2 + (y_{11} - y_o)^2 \qquad (14)$$

In the same way, we set

$$W_i^1 = Dis^2(P_{01}, C_i) = Dis^2(P_{10}, C_i) = (x_{10} - x_o)^2 + (y_{10} - y_o)^2 \qquad (15)$$

The ciphertexts are the coordinates of C_i.

In summary, if the input $v_a \oplus v_b = 0$, the garbled output $W_i^{v_i} = W_i^0$. If the input $v_a \oplus v_b = 1$, the garbled output $W_i^{v_i} = W_i^1$. Therefore, we obtain $v_a \oplus v_b = v_i$.

After constructing all the gates in the circuit by the above method, we can obtain the decoding information d according to the garbled values of the output wires. Let $C = \{C_1, C_2, ...\}$ be the set of ciphertexts of all the gates.

Now we have (C, e, d), then for every $x = \{x_1, x_2, ...\}$, the function $Encode()$ outputs $X = \{X_1, X_2, ...\}$, where x denotes the plaintext input and X denotes the garbled input.

After obtaining C and X, the evaluator evaluates each gate of the circuit. For each gate with input wires a, b and output wire w_i, if wire w_a (or w_b) is an input wire of the circuit, then $W_a^{v_a} = X_a$ (or $W_b^{v_b} = X_b$). If wire w_a (or w_b) is an output wire of the previous gate, then $W_a^{v_a}$ (or $W_b^{v_b}$) equals the output garbled value of the previous gate.

Then $Eval()$ evaluates the circuit and outputs the garbled output Y. For each gate, the evaluator obtains $P_{v_a v_b} = (x_{v_a v_b}, y_{v_a v_b})$ by $GetCoordinate()$, and obtains $C_i = (x_0, y_0)$ from C. The evaluator calculates the square of the distance between $P_{v_a v_b}$ and C_i,

$$W_i^{v_i} = Dis^2(P_{v_a v_b}, C_i) = (x_{v_a v_b} - x_o)^2 + (y_{v_a v_b} - y_o)^2 \qquad (16)$$

According to Case 1 and Case 2, when the gate is an AND gate, if $v_a \wedge v_b = 0$, then $W_i^{v_i} = W_i^0$, and if $v_a \wedge v_b = 1$, then $W_i^{v_i} = W_i^1$. When the gate is an XOR gate, if $v_a \oplus v_b = 0$, then $W_i^{v_i} = W_i^0$, and if $v_a \oplus v_b = 1$, then $W_i^{v_i} = W_i^1$. After evaluating all gates, the evaluator obtains the garbled output $Y = \{W_i^{v_i} : i \in Output(f)\}$, where $Output(f)$ denotes the index of output wires. Then $Decode()$ decodes Y to output

$$y = \{v_i : i \in Output(f)\} \qquad (17)$$

Recall that we have $v_a \wedge v_b = v_i$ and $v_a \oplus v_b = v_i$ for every gate in f. Therefore, we can obtain the real output of the circuit

$$f(x) = \{v_i : i \in Output(f)\} \qquad (18)$$

Consequently, we have $Decode\,(d, Eval\,(F, Encode\,(e, x))) = f(x)$.

4   Performance Analysis

To demonstrate the performance of the proposed protocol, we report on it in comparison with the state-of-the-art GC protocols as shown in Table 2, where size per gate is the number of ciphertexts (multiples of the security parameter κ) and calls to H per gate is the number of calls to the pseudorandom function or hash function.

By utilizing free XOR technology, GC protocols under the CCR assumption need different evaluation algorithms to evaluate AND gates and XOR gates. It is evident that under PRF assumption, the early GC schemes [4,23,32] employed a sole evaluation algorithm. However, the size of ciphertexts was at least 3κ bits [23]. Recent GC schemes have decreased the size of each gate [12,24] yet this has resulted in an escalation of the number of evaluation algorithms utilized. Our geometry-based GC needs only one evaluation algorithm and reduces the number of ciphertexts per gate to two.

Table 2. Comparison of efficient garbling schemes (PRF = pseudorandom function, CCR = circular correlation robust hash function).

Technique	Ciphertexts		Calls to H per gate				Evaluation algorithms	Assump.
			Generator		Evaluator			
	XOR	AND	XOR	AND	XOR	AND		
Yao's [32]	4	4	4	4	2.5	2.5	1	PRF
Point-permute [4]	4	4	4	4	1	1	1	PRF
4-3GRR [23]	3	3	4	4	1	1	1	PRF
4-2GRR [24]	2	2	4	4	1	1	2	PRF
GLNP [12]	1	2	3	4	1.5	2	2	PRF
This work	2	2	4	4	1	1	1	**PRF**
Free XOR [17]	0	3	0	4	0	1	2	CCR
FleXOR [16]	0,1,2	2	0,2,4	4	0,1,2	1	2	CCR
Half gates [33]	0	2	0	4	0	2	2	CCR
Three half gates [26]	0	1.5	0	≤ 6	0	≤ 3	2	CCR

In order to evaluate the performance of our PSI protocol, we built and evaluated an implementation. Our complete implementation is available on Github: https://github.com/TAN-OpenLab/Geom-GC.

We implement our protocol in Python 3.8.10, and run our protocol on Ubuntu 20.04 with 8GB RAM and 4 cores over a localhost. We set the security parameter $\kappa = 31$, and the prime $p = 2147483647$ in the finite field $GF(p)$. The pseudorandom function is instantiated as AES. Table 3 shows the time it takes to run the Garble() algorithm, the Eval() algorithm, and the full Geometry-GC protocol on three different circuits of interest: AES-128, SHA1, DES and adder64. It is apparent from this table that the algorithms Garble() and Eval() consume the majority of the computational time in the overall GC protocol. The algorithm Garble() takes approximately four times longer than the algorithm Eval(), as each gate in Garble() invokes the PRF four times, while in Eval() it is invoked only once.

Table 3. Comparison of the size of the garbled circuit and the running time (in seconds)

Circuit	Number			Running time		
	AND	XOR	NOT	Garble()	Eval()	All GC
AES-128	6,800	25,124	18,175	20.774	5.124	26.597
SHA1	37,300	24,166	1,351	41.758	10.014	54.118
DES	18,175	1,351	10,875	12.987	3.132	17.83
adder64	63	313	0	0.263	0.061	0.438

5 Proof of Security

Theorem 1. The proposed protocol satisfies the security requirement of privacy. There exists a simulator S that takes the input $(1^\kappa, f, f(x))$ and the output (C, X, d) is indistinguishable from the real garbled circuit. More formally, we use the experiment in [12].

The privacy experiment $Expt^{priv(\kappa)}_{(G,\mathcal{A},S)}$:

1. Invoke adversary: $(f, x) \leftarrow \mathcal{A}(1^\kappa)$
2. Choose a random $\beta \in \{0, 1\}$.
3. If $\beta = 0$: compute $(C, e, d) \leftarrow Garble(1^\kappa, f)$ and $X \leftarrow Encode(e, x)$
   Else: compute $(C, X, d) \leftarrow S(1^\kappa, f, f(x))$
4. Give $\mathcal{A}$ the challenge (C, X, d), and obtain its guess: $\beta' \leftarrow \mathcal{A}(C, X, d)$
5. Output 1 if and only if $\beta' = \beta$

where $\mathcal{A}$ is a probabilistic polynomial time adversary and G denotes a garbling scheme. There are exists a probabilistic polynomial time simulator S and a negligible function μ such that for every $\kappa \in N$:

$$Pr[Expt^{priv(\kappa)}_{(G,\mathcal{A},S)} = 1] \leq 1/2 + \mu(\kappa) \tag{19}$$

Proof. A simulator S is invoked with input S and generates (C, X, d). Overall, S samples an active garbled value for each input wire of f and samples the ciphertexts C_i for each binary gate. Then S calculates the active garbled value for each other wire. As a result, all the garbled values that are used in evaluation are active garbled values. In detail, the simulator S works as follows.

1. For each input wire w_i in circuit f:
   (a) Choose an active garbled value: $W_i = \{0,1\}^\kappa$
   (b) Prepare the garbled input data: $X_i = W_i$
2. In topological order, for each gate g_i in f:
   (a) If g_i is a binary gate with input wires w_a, w_b and output wire w_i
       i. Choose a random ciphertext: $C_i = \{0,1\}^\kappa$
       ii. Compute the output wire active garbled value: $W_i = Dis^2(P_i, C_i)$, where $P_i = GetCoordinate\,(F_{W_a \oplus W_b}(W_a \| W_b))$
   (b) If g_i is a NOT gate with input wire w_a and output wire w_i: $W_i = W_a$
3. For each output wire w_i in circuit f, prepare the decoding information:
   $d\,[i, f\,(x)_i] = W_i$, $d\left[i, \overline{f\,(x)_i}\right] = \{0,1\}^\kappa$
4. Return (C, X, d)

Let n be the number of binary gates in a garbled circuit. The adversary $\mathcal{A}_j$ construct a hybrid circuit $M_j(f, x) \leftarrow (C, X, d)$, where $0 \leq j \leq n$. The first j gates in $M_j(f, x)$ are generated by the simulator $\mathcal{S}$, while gates $g_{j+1}, ..., g_n$ are generated by the real garbled circuit. It is evident that $M_0(x)$ is a real garbled circuit, while $M_n(x)$ is a simulated garbled circuit.

First, $\mathcal{A}_j$ samples an active garbled value for each input wire of f. Then generates the first j gates by the simulator $\mathcal{S}$. When calculates gates $g_{j+1}, ..., g_n$, $\mathcal{A}_j$ holds at least one garbled value on each input wire of w_a (or w_b), which is denoted by W_a^0 (or W_b^0), respectively. For each gate g_i in $M_j(f, x)$, let w_a, w_b be the input wires and w_i be the output wire. $\mathcal{A}_j$ constructs gate g_i as follows:

1. If there is only an active garbled value on each wire, then $\mathcal{A}_j$ chooses the other garbled value. By this method, $\mathcal{A}_j$ obtains W_a^0, W_b^0, W_a^1 and W_b^1.
2. Computes $F_0 = F_{W_a^0 \oplus W_b^0}(W_a^0 \| W_b^0)$, $F_1 = F_{W_a^0 \oplus W_b^1}(W_a^0 \| W_b^1)$, $F_2 = F_{W_a^1 \oplus W_b^0}(W_a^1 \| W_b^0)$, $F_3 = F_{W_a^1 \oplus W_b^1}(W_a^1 \| W_b^1)$.
3. Computes $P_{00} = GetCoordinate\,(F_0)$, $P_{01} = GetCoordinate\,(F_1)$, $P_{10} = GetCoordinate\,(F_2)$, $P_{11} = GetCoordinate\,(F_3)$.
4. Computes C_i, W_i^0 and W_i^1 from P_{00}, P_{01}, P_{10} and P_{11}. If g_i is an AND gate, then $(C_i, W_i^0, W_i^1) \leftarrow GeomAND()$. If g_i is an XOR gate, then $(C_i, W_i^0, W_i^1) \leftarrow GeomXOR()$.

$\mathcal{A}_j$ constructs the hybrid $M_{j-1}(x)$ and the hybrid $M_j(x)$. The difference between them is the way to generate the gate g_j. Now, there is adversary $\mathcal{A}$, who tries to distinguish $M_{j-1}(x)$ from $M_j(x)$. Thus $\mathcal{A}$ should distinguish whether gate g_j is generated by simulator or the real garbled circuit.

When constructing g_j of $M_j(x)$, the four points P_{00}, P_{01}, P_{10} and P_{11} are generates by PRF, and C_j is generated from P_{00}, P_{01}, P_{10} and P_{11}. Then we have

$$|Pr[\mathcal{A}^{C_j} accepts] - Pr[\mathcal{A}^{(f_1, f_2)} accepts]| \leq \mu(\kappa) \qquad (20)$$

where $f_1, f_2 \leftarrow F_S$. By Definition 4,

$$|Pr_S[\mathcal{A}^{F_s} accepts] - Pr_R[\mathcal{A}^R accepts]| \leq \mu(\kappa) \qquad (21)$$

we have that the coordinates of C_j are indistinguishable from random numbers. As P_{00} is generates by PRF, the distance between P_{00} and C_j, namely W_j^0, is indistinguishable from a PRF result.

$$|Pr_S[\mathcal{A}^{Dis} accepts] - Pr_S[\mathcal{A}^{Fs} accepts]| \leq \mu(\kappa) \tag{22}$$

By Definition 4, we have

$$|Pr_S[\mathcal{A}^{Dis} accepts] - Pr_R[\mathcal{A}^{R} accepts]| \leq \mu(\kappa) \tag{23}$$

We obtain that W_j^0, is indistinguishable from a random number. In the same vein, W_j^1, is indistinguishable from a random number.

When constructing g_j of $M_{j-1}(x)$, C_j and W_j^1 are sampled randomly, and $W_j^0 = Dis^2(P_{00}, C_j)$. When constructing g_j of $M_j(x)$, C_j and W_j^1 are calculated from the input garbled values. As C_j and W_j^1 of $M_j(x)$ are indistinguishable from random numbers, we have

$$M_{j-1}(x) \stackrel{c}{\equiv} M_j(x) \tag{24}$$

It can be shown that

$$M_0(x) \stackrel{c}{\equiv} ...M_{j-1}(x) \stackrel{c}{\equiv} M_j(x)... \stackrel{c}{\equiv} M_p(x) \tag{25}$$

Recall that $M_0(x)$ is a real garbled circuit, while $M_p(x)$ is a simulated garbled circuit. Then we have

$$|Pr_S[\mathcal{A}^{Fs} accepts] - Pr_R[\mathcal{A}^{R} accepts]| \leq \mu(\kappa) \tag{26}$$

Obliviousness. We generate (F, X) by a simulator and a real scheme at the same time and the proof method is the same as the private proof except we omit d.

Theorem 2. The proposed protocol satisfies the security requirement of authenticity. Given input (F, X) alone, no adversary should be able to produce $\widetilde{Y} \neq Eval(F, X)$ such that $Decode(\widetilde{Y}, d) \neq \bot$, except with negligible probability.

Proof. Suppose a probabilistic polynomial time adversary $\mathcal{A}$ outputs $\widetilde{Y} \neq Eval(F, X)$ such that $Decode(\widetilde{Y}, d) \neq \bot$. Therefore, there exists at least one output wire w_i that $\mathcal{A}$ knows both $d[i, 0]$ and $d[i, 1]$. However, $\mathcal{A}$ knows only one of them, because he does not have the decoding information d. $\mathcal{A}$ can succeed only with probability at most $2^{-\kappa}$. In conclusion, no adversary should be able to produce $\widetilde{Y} \neq Eval(F, X)$ such that $Decode(\widetilde{Y}, d) \neq \bot$, except with negligible probability.

6   Conclusions

This paper proposes a new method for garbling under standard assumptions, replacing traditional garbled construction with geometric computations. For each binary gate, we take the coordinates of a two-dimensional point as the ciphertexts, and let the output garbled values be the square of distance between specific points. Consequently, we achieve two ciphertexts per gate while the evaluator stores only one evaluation algorithm, avoiding the switching operation in evaluation.

Acknowledgments. This work is supported by the National Natural Science Foundation of China under Grants (61772125), the Fundamental Research Funds for the Central Universities (N2317004), and the National Key Research and Development Program of China under Grant No. 2019YFB1405803.

References

1. Alam, M., et al.: Secure policy execution using reusable garbled circuit in the cloud. Futur. Gener. Comput. Syst. **87**, 488–501 (2018). https://doi.org/10.1016/j.future.2017.12.067
2. Ashur, T., Cohen, E., Hazay, C., Yanai, A.: A new framework for garbled circuits. Cryptology ePrint Archive, Report 2021/739 (2021). https://ia.cr/2021/739
3. Baum, C., Orsini, E., Scholl, P., Soria-Vazquez, E.: Efficient constant-round MPC with identifiable abort and public verifiability. In: Micciancio, D., Ristenpart, T. (eds.) CRYPTO 2020. LNCS, vol. 12171, pp. 562–592. Springer, Cham (2020). https://doi.org/10.1007/978-3-030-56880-1_20
4. Beaver, D., Micali, S., Rogaway, P.: The round complexity of secure protocols. In: Proceedings of the Twenty-Second Annual ACM Symposium on Theory of Computing, pp. 503–513. STOC '90, Association for Computing Machinery, New York, NY, USA (1990). https://doi.org/10.1145/100216.100287
5. Bellare, M., Hoang, V.T., Keelveedhi, S., Rogaway, P.: Efficient garbling from a fixed-key blockcipher. In: 2013 IEEE Symposium on Security and Privacy, pp. 478–492 (2013). https://doi.org/10.1109/SP.2013.39
6. Ben-Efraim, A., Cong, K., Omri, E., Orsini, E., Smart, N.P., Soria-Vazquez, E.: Large scale, actively secure computation from LPN and Free-XOR garbled circuits. In: Canteaut, A., Standaert, F.-X. (eds.) EUROCRYPT 2021. LNCS, vol. 12698, pp. 33–63. Springer, Cham (2021). https://doi.org/10.1007/978-3-030-77883-5_2
7. Choi, S.G., Katz, J., Kumaresan, R., Zhou, H.-S.: On the security of the Free-XOR technique. In: Cramer, R. (ed.) TCC 2012. LNCS, vol. 7194, pp. 39–53. Springer, Heidelberg (2012). https://doi.org/10.1007/978-3-642-28914-9_3
8. Ciampi, M., Goyal, V., Ostrovsky, R.: Threshold garbled circuits and ad hoc secure computation. In: Canteaut, A., Standaert, F.-X. (eds.) EUROCRYPT 2021. LNCS, vol. 12698, pp. 64–93. Springer, Cham (2021). https://doi.org/10.1007/978-3-030-77883-5_3
9. Cohen, R., Garay, J., Zikas, V.: Broadcast-optimal two-round MPC. In: Canteaut, A., Ishai, Y. (eds.) EUROCRYPT 2020. LNCS, vol. 12106, pp. 828–858. Springer, Cham (2020). https://doi.org/10.1007/978-3-030-45724-2_28

10. Franz, M., Holzer, A., Katzenbeisser, S., Schallhart, C., Veith, H.: CBMC-GC: an ANSI C compiler for secure two-party computations. In: Cohen, A. (ed.) CC 2014. LNCS, vol. 8409, pp. 244–249. Springer, Heidelberg (2014). https://doi.org/10.1007/978-3-642-54807-9_15

11. Frederiksen, T.K., Nielsen, J.B., Orlandi, C.: Privacy-free garbled circuits with applications to efficient zero-knowledge. In: Oswald, E., Fischlin, M. (eds.) EUROCRYPT 2015. LNCS, vol. 9057, pp. 191–219. Springer, Heidelberg (2015). https://doi.org/10.1007/978-3-662-46803-6_7

12. Gueron, S., Lindell, Y., Nof, A., Pinkas, B.: Fast garbling of circuits under standard assumptions. J. Cryptol. 31(3), 798–844 (2018). https://doi.org/10.1007/s00145-017-9271-y

13. Guo, C., Katz, J., Wang, X., Weng, C., Yu, Yu.: Better concrete security for half-gates garbling (in the multi-instance setting). In: Micciancio, D., Ristenpart, T. (eds.) CRYPTO 2020. LNCS, vol. 12171, pp. 793–822. Springer, Cham (2020). https://doi.org/10.1007/978-3-030-56880-1_28

14. Heath, D., Kolesnikov, V.: Stacked garbling. In: Micciancio, D., Ristenpart, T. (eds.) CRYPTO 2020. LNCS, vol. 12171, pp. 763–792. Springer, Cham (2020). https://doi.org/10.1007/978-3-030-56880-1_27

15. Huang, Y., Evans, D., Katz, J., Malka, L.: Faster secure two-party computation using garbled circuits. In: Proceedings of the 20th USENIX Conference on Security, p. 35. SEC'11, USENIX Association, USA (2011). https://doi.org/10.5555/2028067.2028102

16. Kolesnikov, V., Mohassel, P., Rosulek, M.: FleXOR: flexible garbling for XOR gates that beats free-XOR. In: Garay, J.A., Gennaro, R. (eds.) CRYPTO 2014. LNCS, vol. 8617, pp. 440–457. Springer, Heidelberg (2014). https://doi.org/10.1007/978-3-662-44381-1_25

17. Kolesnikov, V., Schneider, T.: Improved garbled circuit: free XOR gates and applications. In: Aceto, L., Damgård, I., Goldberg, L.A., Halldórsson, M.M., Ingólfsdóttir, A., Walukiewicz, I. (eds.) ICALP 2008. LNCS, vol. 5126, pp. 486–498. Springer, Heidelberg (2008). https://doi.org/10.1007/978-3-540-70583-3_40

18. Kreuter, B., Shelat, A., Shen, C.H.: Towards billion-gate secure computation with malicious adversaries. IACR Cryptol. ePrint Arch. 2012, 179 (2012)

19. Lindell, Y.: Fast cut-and-choose-based protocols for malicious and covert adversaries. J. Cryptol. 29(2), 456–490 (2016). https://doi.org/10.1007/s00145-015-9198-0

20. Lindell, Y., Pinkas, B.: A proof of security of Yao's protocol for two-party computation. J. Cryptol. 22(2), 161–188 (2009). https://doi.org/10.1007/s00145-008-9036-8

21. Lindell, Y., Pinkas, B.: Secure two-party computation via cut-and-choose oblivious transfer. J. Cryptol. 25(4), 680–722 (2012). https://doi.org/10.1007/s00145-011-9107-0

22. Lindell, Y., Pinkas, B., Smart, N.P.: Implementing two-party computation efficiently with security against malicious adversaries. In: Ostrovsky, R., De Prisco, R., Visconti, I. (eds.) SCN 2008. LNCS, vol. 5229, pp. 2–20. Springer, Heidelberg (2008). https://doi.org/10.1007/978-3-540-85855-3_2

23. Naor, M., Pinkas, B., Sumner, R.: Privacy preserving auctions and mechanism design. In: Proceedings of the 1st ACM Conference on Electronic Commerce, pp. 129–139. EC '99, Association for Computing Machinery, New York, NY, USA (1999). https://doi.org/10.1145/336992.337028

24. Pinkas, B., Schneider, T., Smart, N.P., Williams, S.C.: Secure two-party computation is practical. In: Proceedings of the 15th International Conference on the Theory and Application of Cryptology and Information Security: Advances in Cryptology, pp. 250–267. ASIACRYPT '09, Springer-Verlag, Berlin, Heidelberg (2009). https://doi.org/10.1007/978-3-642-10366-7_15

25. Rosulek, M.: Improvements for gate-hiding garbled circuits. In: Patra, A., Smart, N.P. (eds.) INDOCRYPT 2017. LNCS, vol. 10698, pp. 325–345. Springer, Cham (2017). https://doi.org/10.1007/978-3-319-71667-1_17

26. Rosulek, M., Roy, L.: Three halves make a whole? Beating the half-gates lower bound for garbled circuits. In: Malkin, T., Peikert, C. (eds.) CRYPTO 2021. LNCS, vol. 12825, pp. 94–124. Springer, Cham (2021). https://doi.org/10.1007/978-3-030-84242-0_5

27. shelat, A., Shen, C.: Two-output secure computation with malicious adversaries. In: Paterson, K.G. (ed.) EUROCRYPT 2011. LNCS, vol. 6632, pp. 386–405. Springer, Heidelberg (2011). https://doi.org/10.1007/978-3-642-20465-4_22

28. Tan, Z., Ning, J.: Lightweight garbled circuit protocol based on solid geometry transformation under standard PRF assumption. Chinese J. Comput. **64**(10), 2240–2257 (2023). https://doi.org/10.11897/SP.J.1016.2023.02240

29. Huang, Y., Katz, J., Evans, D.: Efficient secure two-party computation using symmetric cut-and-choose. In: Canetti, R., Garay, J.A. (eds.) CRYPTO 2013. LNCS, vol. 8043, pp. 18–35. Springer, Heidelberg (2013). https://doi.org/10.1007/978-3-642-40084-1_2

30. Yang, K., Wang, X., Zhang, J.: More efficient MPC from improved triple generation and authenticated garbling. In: Proceedings of the 2020 ACM SIGSAC Conference on Computer and Communications Security, pp. 1627–1646. CCS '20, Association for Computing Machinery, New York, NY, USA (2020). https://doi.org/10.1145/3372297.3417285

31. Yang, Q., Peng, G., Gasti, P., Balagani, K.S., Li, Y., Zhou, G.: Meg: Memory and energy efficient garbled circuit evaluation on smartphones. IEEE Trans. Inf. Forensics Secur. **14**(4), 913–922 (2019). https://doi.org/10.1109/TIFS.2018.2868221

32. Yao, A.C.C.: How to generate and exchange secrets. In: 27th Annual Symposium on Foundations of Computer Science (SFCS 1986), pp. 162–167. IEEE (1986). https://doi.org/10.1109/SFCS.1986.25

33. Zahur, S., Rosulek, M., Evans, D.: Two halves make a whole. In: Oswald, E., Fischlin, M. (eds.) EUROCRYPT 2015. LNCS, vol. 9057, pp. 220–250. Springer, Heidelberg (2015). https://doi.org/10.1007/978-3-662-46803-6_8

34. Zhou, Z., Fu, Q., Wei, Q., Li, Q.: Lego: a hybrid toolkit for efficient 2PC-based privacy-preserving machine learning. Comput. Secur. **120**, 102782 (2022). https://doi.org/10.1016/j.cose.2022.102782

Full Domain Functional Bootstrapping with Least Significant Bit Encoding

Zhihao Li[1,2], Benqiang Wei[1,2], Ruida Wang[1,2], Xianhui Lu[1,2(✉)], and Kunpeng Wang[1,2]

[1] State Key Laboratory of Information Security, Institute of Information Engineering, Chinese Academy of Sciences, Beijing, China
luxianhui@iie.ac.cn
[2] School of Cyber Security, University of Chinese Academy of Sciences, Beijing, China

Abstract. Functional bootstrapping (FBS) is a powerful technique that evaluates a look-up table (LUT) while refreshing an LWE ciphertext in FHEW and TFHE schemes. However, the LUT evaluation over the message space is constrained by negacyclicity, which affects the practical application of functional bootstrapping. Existing methods require multiple FBS and some homomorphic operations to address this issue, which results in inferior performance compared with the original functional bootstrapping.

In this paper, we utilize the variant least significant bit (LSB) encoding method to efficiently achieve the full domain functional bootstrapping for message space in FHEW-like schemes. Specifically, the message space $\mathbb{Z}_t$ is embedded into the encoding space $\mathbb{Z}_N$ by setting the most significant bit of noise to zero. As a result, the encoding space is equal to the domain of the LUT and our functional bootstrapping can evaluate arbitrary functions. In addition, our technique can be applied to multi-value bootstrapping and tree-based bootstrapping. Thus, these algorithms only need one FBS to achieve the full domain property.

Finally, we implement our full domain functional bootstrapping in the OpenFHE cryptography library. Experiments demonstrate that up to 2 × performance improvement is achieved compared with the state-of-the-art work [27].

Keywords: Functional Bootstrapping · Full Domain · Least Significant Encoding · Multi-value Bootstrapping · Tree-based Bootstrapping

1 Introduction

Fully homomorphic encryption (FHE) is a promising technology for privacy-preserving scenarios (e.g., cloud computing) since it allows performing arbitrary computation on ciphertexts. In 2009, Gentry [17] constructed the first FHE scheme using ideal lattices. Especially, noise is introduced in the FHE schemes

C. Ge and M. Yung (Eds.): Inscrypt 2023, LNCS 14526, pp. 203–223, 2024.
https://doi.org/10.1007/978-981-97-0942-7_11

to ensure security, and it increases as the homomorphic operations proceed. Once the noise level reaches a certain threshold, the decryption function will no longer be able to recover the message.

To deal with this situation, Gentry proposed a technique named *bootstrapping*, which can evaluate the decryption circuit homomorphically to reduce the noise. By repeating this operation, an FHE scheme can evaluate circuits for arbitrary depth, which has been a significant component of FHE schemes and the main efficiency bottleneck in implementation. Subsequently, FHE schemes based on the assumptions of learning-with-errors (LWE) and Ring-LWE (RLWE) become prevalent and are divided into two types, namely, the word-wise and the bit-wise encryption schemes. The word-wise schemes support the so-called packed technique and focus on performing arithmetic circuits, represented by the BGV [6,21], BFV [5,16] and CKKS [8,9] schemes. The bit-wise schemes support bit-level operations and expertise in computing nonlinear operations such as comparisons, represented by the FHEW [15,28] and TFHE [10,11] schemes.

The bootstrapping of FHEW and TFHE schemes utilizes the structure of ring $\mathcal{R}_Q \simeq \mathbb{Z}_Q[X]/(X^N + 1)$, where the elements $\{1, X, ..., X^{N-1}, -1, ..., -X^{N-1}\}$ in $\mathcal{R}_Q$ form a multiplicative group of order $2N$. Given an LWE ciphertext $\mathsf{LWE}_s^n(m) = (\mathbf{a}, b)$ with modulus $2N$ and the bootstrapping key, one can homomorphically compute the RLWE ciphertext encrypting $\mathsf{testP} \cdot X^{b-\langle \mathbf{a},\mathbf{s}\rangle \bmod 2N} = \mathsf{testP} \cdot X^{\mathsf{Encode}(m) \bmod 2N}$. This procedure, known as functional bootstrapping (FBS), not only removes noise but also embeds a function with the polynomial testP as mentioned in [4]. The current schemes have used the most significant bit encoding (MSB) method as shown in Fig. 1, i.e., $\mathsf{Encode}(m) = \triangle \cdot m + e \in \mathbb{Z}_{2N}$. However, the polynomial testP contains N coefficients, which can only guarantee the correctness of LUT over $\mathbb{Z}_N$ rather than $\mathbb{Z}_{2N}$, unless the function satisfies the $F(x + N) = -F(x) \bmod Q$.

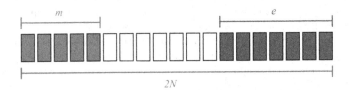

Fig. 1. The most significant bit (MSB) encoding

The negacyclicity severely weakens the power of FBS. A trivial method to resolve this issue is to set the MSB of the message to zero, but it would result in the linear homomorphism of LWE not being performed. Thus, a few zero bits must be padded in MSBs to correctly execute affine functions [12]. Subsequently, several efforts have focused on achieving full domain functional bootstrapping of FHEW and TFHE schemes without requiring padding bits. Unfortunately, these schemes are significantly slower than the original FBS. Furthermore, it is considered that using these methods directly for multi-value bootstrapping and tree-based bootstrapping is extremely inefficient, and even demands larger parameters. Therefore, the main challenge lies in developing an effective solution to address the aforementioned issue.

1.1 Our Contribution

We present an appropriate encoding method to address the negacyclicity of FBS and achieve full domain FBS for the message space. Here is a summary of our techniques and contributions.

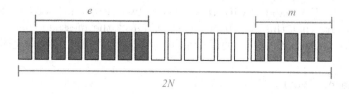

Fig. 2. The least significant bit(LSB) encoding. The message m is encoded in the LSB, whereas the noise e is encoded in the MSB. The leftmost bit is filled with gray, indicating that the most significant bit of the noise is set to zero. (Color figure online)

- **Cause for the negacyclicity.** Reviewing the negacyclicity for FBS, we regard the encoding form as the culprit. Specifically, in the original GSW encryption scheme [18], the message m is encoded in MSB associated with the gadget matrix $\mathbf{G}$, indicating that the encryption form is $2^i \cdot m$. As a result, the LUT is constrained by negacyclicity across the message space. We note that the RGSW encryption scheme with the least significant bit encoding also functions well during the FBS. Furthermore, noise growth and efficiency are identical to the MSB encoding form.
- **LSB message encoding.** We propose a variant of the least significant bit (LSB) encoding method as shown in Fig. 2. The encoding method prevents the noise generated by the affine functions in the LWE ciphertexts from spreading into the MSB before bootstrapping takes place. In this way, we can homomorphically compute an RLWE ciphertext of $\mathsf{testP} \cdot X^{b - \langle \mathbf{a}, \mathbf{s} \rangle \bmod 2N} = \mathsf{testP} \cdot X^{m + te \bmod 2N}$, where $m + te \in [-N/2, N/2)$. The definition domain of LUT is consistent with the encoding space and an arbitrary function $f : \mathbb{Z}_t \to \mathbb{Z}_t$ can be embedded in testP. Thus, we achieve the full domain FBS for the message space $\mathbb{Z}_t$ with just one bootstrapping procedure.
- **Transformation between LSB and MSB encodings.** We solve the full domain functional bootstrapping with MSB encoding by using the encoding transformation technique. To deal with the negacyclicity, we convert an LWE ciphertext with MSB encoding to the LSB encoding as the input of bootstrapping. It is worth mentioning that the inverse encoding transformation step can be avoided by simply modifying the test polynomial.

- **Scalability and implementation.** Our FBS technique is suitable for multi-value and tree-based functional bootstrapping. Finally, we implement the full domain functional bootstrapping algorithm within the OpenFHE open-source HE library. The results show that the proposed method is more efficient than state-of-the-art work.

We remark that the idea of using the LSB encoding method in the FHE scheme is not new. It has been employed in the BGV scheme and implemented in the HElib library [22]. However, our contribution lies in this encoding application to FHEW-like schemes and the solve the full domain functional bootstrapping, which is a novel aspect. Furthermore, Our approach does not change this fact $F(x + N) = -F(x) \bmod Q$ with the power-of-two cyclotomic setting. Nonetheless, we ensure that this condition does not affect the message space, thereby enabling us to evaluate arbitrary functions and achieve full domain FBS.

1.2 Related Work

In FHEW and TFHE schemes, gate bootstrapping is equivalent to performing a rounding function encapsulated in the test polynomial. After that, Boura et al. [4] showed that the rounding function can be substituted by more general (negacyclic) functions. Multi-value bootstrapping (MVBS) is an extension of functional bootstrapping that uses only one blind rotation to evaluate multiple functions, as noted in [7,13] schemes.

The full domain FBS is first presented by Chillotti et al. [13] for the TFHE scheme, which requires an MVBS and a BFV-like multiplication. However, the BFV-like multiplication introduces in more errors, while also lead to larger parameters. Subsequently, Kluczniak et al. [26] develop a PubMux gate by using GSW-like multiplication. But their approach requires an additional FBS.

The schemes [27,30] serve as the representation of the second method while the LWE modulus is set to N. During the bootstrapping process, $(\mathbf{a}, b)$ are viewed as elements with modulus $2N$, i.e., $b - \langle \mathbf{a}, \mathbf{s} \rangle = \frac{N}{t} \cdot m + e + kN$. The ciphertext $-kN$ is obtained by performing an FBS. Subsequently, by homomorphic addition, the ciphertext $\frac{N}{t} \cdot m + e$ with modulus $2N$ can be obtained in order to double the size of the message space by introducing the most significant bit. Finally, one can evaluate the $f(m)$ by another FBS on the new ciphertext.

The third method is based on the characteristics of odd-even functions. According to Clet et al. [14], any pseudo-odd or pseudo-even function can be evaluated by using at most two FBS, and any function can be expressed as the summation of a pseudo-even function and a pseudo-odd function. This indicates that an arbitrary function can be evaluated by using no more than four FBS, which can be lowered to three by utilizing the MVBS technique.

In Table 1, we compare above schemes in terms of message encoding, encoding space, and the number of FBS. Finally, the noise growth and experiment results are given in Sect. 5.

Table 1. Comparison of full domain FBS scheme. Here, N is the ring dimension, FBS is the functional bootstrapping, MVBS is the multi-valued bootstrapping, Mult is a homomorphic multiplication, ET is the encoding transformation.

Scheme	Encoding method	Encoding space	# Operations
Chillotti et al. [13]	MSB	$2N$	1 MVBS + 1 BFV Mutl
Kluczniak et al. [26]	MSB	$2N$	1 MVBS + 1 FBS
Liu et al. [27]	MSB	N	2 FBS
Yang et al. [30]	MSB	N	2 FBS
Clet et al. [14]	MSB	$2N$	2 FBS+ 1 MVBS
Our work I	LSB	N	1 FBS
Our work II	MSB	N	1 FBS +1 ET

1.3 Paper Organization

The rest of the paper is organized as follows. In Sect. 2, we provide the necessary background knowledge on functional bootstrapping in FHEW-like schemes. In Sect. 3, we describe our algorithm for full domain functional bootstrapping. In Sect. 4, we show how the algorithm can be used to perform functional extensions including multi-value bootstrapping and tree-based bootstrapping. In Sect. 5, we present some experimental results. In Sect. 6, we conclude the paper.

2 Preliminaries

2.1 Notation

We use lower-case bold letters for vectors and upper-case bold letters for matrices. For example, a vector $\mathbf{a}$ of n elements is described as $\mathbf{a} = (a_1, ..., a_n)$. $\langle \mathbf{a}, \mathbf{b} \rangle$ is the inner product between two vectors. For a real number r, $\lfloor r \rfloor$ $\lfloor r \rceil$ $\lceil r \rceil$ denote the floor round, nearest round, and upper round of r to integers, respectively. The parameter q is a positive integer and represents the modulus for the integers we are working with. We denote $\mathbb{Z}_q$ the ring $\mathbb{Z}/q\mathbb{Z}$ and the scope is $[-q/2, q/2) \cap \mathbb{Z}$.

We use $x \leftarrow D$ to denote the sampling of x according to distribution D. For a random variable $a \in \mathbb{Z}_q$, we denote $\mathsf{Var}(a)$ is the variance of a. Furthermore, we denote the ring of polynomials $\mathcal{R}_Q = \mathbb{Z}_Q/(X^N + 1)$ with coefficients in $\mathbb{Z}_Q$, where N is a power of 2 and $\phi(s) = (s_0, s_1, ..., s_{N-1}) \in \mathbb{Z}_Q^N$ is the vector of coefficients of the polynomial s. Similarly, given a ring element $a = a_0 + a_1 X + \cdots + a_{N-1}X^{N-1} \in \mathcal{R}$, we define $\mathsf{Var}(a)$ is the variance among the coefficients of the polynomial a. We denote $\|\mathbf{a}\|_p = \left(\sum_{i=1}^{n} |a_i|^p\right)^{1/p}$ the p -norm of a vector $\mathbf{a} \in \mathbb{Z}^n$ and compute the p-norm with a polynomial by taking its coefficient vector.

2.2 Learning with Errors

We recall the (Ring) learning with errors assumption raised by Regev et al. [29]. In LWE-based encryption schemes, there are two types of message encoding methods known as least significant bit (LSB) encoding and most significant bit (MSB) encoding, respectively. The basic LWE symmetric encryption scheme encrypts a message $m \in \mathbb{Z}_t$ under the secret key $\mathbf{s} \in \{-1, 0, 1\}^n$ as

$$\mathsf{LSB.LWE}_{\mathbf{s}}^n(m) = (\mathbf{a}, b = -\langle \mathbf{a}, \mathbf{s} \rangle + m + te) \in \mathbb{Z}_q^{n+1},$$

$$\mathsf{MSB.LWE}_{\mathbf{s}}^n(m) = (\mathbf{a}, b = -\langle \mathbf{a}, \mathbf{s} \rangle + \left\lfloor \frac{q}{t} \cdot m \right\rfloor + e) \in \mathbb{Z}_q^{n+1},$$

where $\mathbf{a} \leftarrow \mathbb{Z}_q^n$ is chosen uniformly at random, and the error $e \leftarrow \chi_\delta$. The message m is recovered only if the bound of the noise satisfies $|e| \leq \frac{q}{2t}$. The encryption scheme of RLWE [6] is defined as follows.

$$\mathsf{LSB.RLWE}_s(m) = (a, b = -as + m + te) \in \mathcal{R}_Q^2,$$

$$\mathsf{MSB.RLWE}_s(m) = (a, b = -as + \left\lfloor \frac{Q}{t} \cdot m \right\rfloor + e) \in \mathcal{R}_Q^2,$$

where $m \in \mathcal{R}_t, a \leftarrow \mathcal{R}_Q$ is chosen uniformly at random, and the error $e \leftarrow \chi_\delta^N$. In the following sections, if not specifically indicated, $\mathsf{LWE}_s(m)$ and $\mathsf{RLWE}_s(m)$ are used by default with the LSB encoding form.

2.3   Useful Algorithms

Sample Extraction. The Sample extraction technique extracts an LWE ciphertext for the constant term from an RLWE ciphertext without increasing the noise [11]. Input $\mathsf{ct} = \mathsf{RLWE}_s(m) = (a, b) \in \mathcal{R}_Q^2$, the $\mathsf{SampleExtraction}(\mathsf{ct})$ algorithm outputs a ciphertext $\mathsf{LWE}_{\phi(s)}^N(\phi(m)) = (a_0, -a_{N-1}, -a_{N-2}, ..., -a_1, b_0) \in \mathbb{Z}_Q^{N+1}$.

Key Switching The LWE-to-LWE key switching technique can change dimensions and secret keys in the ciphertext while keeping the message unchanged.

- The key switching key generation algorithm takes secret keys $z \in \mathbb{Z}^N$, $s \in \mathbb{Z}^n$ and a base B_{ks} as input, outputs $\mathsf{ksk}_{i,j,v} \in \mathsf{LWE}_{\mathbf{s}}^n \left(vz_i B_{ks}^j \right)$, for all $1 \leq i \leq N$, $0 \leq j \leq d_{ks} - 1$ and $v \in \{0, ..., B_{ks}\}$, where $d_{ks} = \lceil \log_{B_{ks}} q \rceil$.
- Given the key switching key $\{\mathsf{ksk}_{i,j,v}\}$ and a ciphertext $\mathsf{ct} = (\mathbf{a}, b) \in \mathsf{LWE}_{\mathbf{z}}^N(m)$, the key switching procedure computes the base B_{ks} expansion of each coefficient $a_i = \sum_j a_{i,j} B_{ks}^j$, and outputs

$$\mathsf{ct}' = \mathsf{LWE\text{-}to\text{-}LWE.KeySwitch}_{\mathbf{z} \to \mathbf{s}}(\mathsf{ct})$$

$$= (\mathbf{0}, b) - \sum_{i,j} \mathsf{ksk}_{i,j,a_{i,j}} \bmod q \in \mathsf{LWE}_{\mathbf{s}}^n(m).$$

The correctness is given in Appendix A.1. According to Theorem 6 of [15], the variance of the noise satisfies $\mathsf{Var}(e') \leq \mathsf{Var}(e) + Nd_{ks} \cdot \mathsf{Var}(e_{\mathsf{ksk}})$.

Modulus Switching. The modulus switching technique is used to reduce the magnitude of the noise by reducing the modulus of the ciphertext without changing the encrypted message [6]. For some integer $Q > q > t$, such that $Q \equiv 1 \bmod t, q \equiv 1 \bmod t$, it takes as input $\mathsf{ct} = (\mathbf{a}, b) \bmod Q \in \mathsf{LWE}_{\mathbf{s}}^n(m)$, outputs a ciphertext

$$\mathsf{ct}' = \mathsf{ModSwitch}_{Q \to q}(\mathsf{ct}) = (\mathbf{a}', b') \in \mathbb{Z}_q^{n+1},$$

where ct'_i is an integer satisfying closest to $\frac{q}{Q} \cdot \mathsf{ct}_i$ and $\mathsf{ct}'_i \equiv \mathsf{ct}_i \bmod t$, for $i \in [0, n]$. The correctness of the algorithm is given in Appendix A.2. According to Lemma 5 of [6], and the variance of noise satisfies $\mathsf{Var}(e') \leq (\frac{q}{Q})^2 \cdot \mathsf{Var}(e) + \frac{t}{2} \cdot \|\mathbf{s}\|_2^2$. Since we use the ternary secret key distribution that ensures that $\|s\|_2 \leq \sqrt{n/2}$. Thus, we can obtain that $\mathsf{Var}(e') \leq (\frac{q}{Q})^2 \cdot \mathsf{Var}(e) + \frac{tn}{4}$.

Encoding Transformation. Alperin-Sheriff et al. [2] proposed a transformation between the LSB and MSB message encodings for (Ring) LWE-based cryptosystems without increasing the noise provided that t and q are coprime. Input a ciphertext $\mathsf{ct} = \mathsf{MSB.LWE}_{\mathbf{s}}^n(m) = (\mathbf{a}, b = -\langle \mathbf{a}, \mathbf{s} \rangle + \lfloor \frac{q}{t} \cdot m \rceil + e) \in \mathbb{Z}_q^{n+1}$ for $q \equiv 1 \bmod t$, the encoding transformation algorithm outputs a ciphertext as

$$
\begin{aligned}
\mathsf{ct}' &= \mathsf{EncodeTrans}(\mathsf{ct}) \\
&= (t \cdot \mathbf{a}, t \cdot b) \bmod q \\
&= (\mathbf{a}', b' = -\langle \mathbf{a}', \mathbf{s} \rangle + (-m) + te) \bmod q \in \mathsf{LSB.LWE}_{\mathbf{s}}^n(-m)
\end{aligned}
$$

The correctness of the algorithm is given in Appendix A.3.

3   Full Domain Functional Bootstrapping

The full domain functional bootstrapping can evaluate an arbitrary function $f : \mathbb{Z}_t \to \mathbb{Z}_t$. We set the modulus of the input LWE ciphertext to satisfy $q = 2N$ by default. Firstly, we describe the RGSW encryption and external product with the least significant bit encoding in Sect. 3.1. Next, we present the full domain FBS with LSB encoding in Sects. 3.2 and 3.3. After that, we show a solution for MSB-based functional bootstrapping in Sect. 3.4.

3.1   RGSW Encryption

The RGSW cryptosystem [15,18] involves the gadget vector and gadget matrix. The gadget vector is typically represented as $\mathbf{g} = (1, B_g^1, \cdots, B_g^{d_g-1})$, where B_g is the decomposition base, and $d_g = \left\lfloor \log_{B_g} Q \right\rfloor + 1$. The gadget matrix, denoted as $\mathbf{G}$, can be expressed as $I_2 \otimes \mathbf{g}^T$, where $\otimes$ refers to the Kronecker product. The function $\mathbf{g}^{-1}$ takes the polynomial $a \in \mathcal{R}$ as an input and outputs a vector of the polynomial $(a_0, \cdots, a_{d_g-1}) \in \mathcal{R}^{d_g}$ that satisfies $a = \sum_{i=0}^{d_g-1} a_i \cdot B_g^i$. Some ciphertexts $\{ct_0, \cdots, ct_{2d_g-1}\} \in \mathsf{RLWE}_s^{2d_g}(0)$ are sampled and represented as the matrix $\mathbf{Z}$. The RGSW ciphertext of $m \in \mathcal{R}$ is of the form:

$$\mathsf{RGSW}_s(m) = \begin{pmatrix} ct_0 \\ \vdots \\ ct_{2d_g-1} \end{pmatrix} + m \cdot \mathbf{G} \in \mathcal{R}_Q^{2d_g \times 2}.$$

External Product. The external product operation $\odot$ with LSB encoding is the same as the MSB encoding, which can be performed between $\mathsf{RGSW}_s(m)$ and $\mathsf{RLWE}_s(\mu)$ ciphertexts. The result is an RLWE ciphertext as follows

$$\begin{aligned} ct' &= \mathsf{RLWE}_s(\mu) \odot \mathsf{RGSW}_s(m) \\ &= \mathbf{g}^{-1}(\mathsf{RLWE}_s(\mu)) \cdot \mathbf{Z} + m \cdot \mathsf{RLWE}_s(\mu) \\ &= \mathsf{RLWE}_s(0) + \mathsf{RLWE}_s(m \cdot \mu) \\ &= \mathsf{RLWE}_s(m \cdot \mu). \end{aligned}$$

Let $ct = \mathsf{RLWE}_s(\mu)$ with the error variance $\mathsf{Var}(e_1)$ and $\mathbf{g}^{-1}(ct) = (a_0, ..., a_{d_g-1}, b_0, ..., b_{d_g-1})$. Let $\mathsf{CT} = \mathsf{RGSW}_s(m)$, and $\{e_i\}_{i=0}^{2d_g-1}$ are the noise terms in CT, where $\mathsf{Var}(e_2)$ is the noise variance. Then, the noise of ct' is $e' = \sum_{i=0}^{d_g-1}(a_i \cdot e_i + b_i \cdot e_{i+d_g}) + m \cdot e$. For the message $m \in [0, 1]$, we have

$$\begin{aligned} \mathsf{Var}(e') &\leq \frac{2}{12} N d_g B_g^2 \cdot \mathsf{Var}(e_2) + \| m \|_2^2 \cdot \mathsf{Var}(e_1) \\ &\leq \frac{1}{6} N d_g B_g^2 \cdot \mathsf{Var}(e_2) + \mathsf{Var}(e_1). \end{aligned} \tag{1}$$

3.2   LUT Encoding

Before giving the formal analysis of the bootstrapping algorithm, let us briefly explain how to embed the LUT in the test polynomial testP. The test polynomial can be expressed as a composite function as

$$\mathsf{testP}(X) = \mathsf{Encode} \circ f \circ \mathsf{Decode}(X),$$

where the Encode and the Decode functions correspond to the message encoding form of the input and output LWE ciphertexts, respectively. In other words, the test polynomial has two purposes in our algorithm. On the one hand, it can remove the noise of the LWE ciphertext from the Decode function. For the LSB encoding form, the Decode function can be defined as

$$\mathsf{Decode}(X) = X \bmod t,$$

where t is the plaintext modulus. On the other hand, an arbitrary LUT function $f : \mathbb{Z}_t \to \mathbb{Z}_t$ is embedded in the coefficients of the test polynomial with a period

t. It should be noted that to guarantee the security of the LWE encryption with LSB encoding,

$$q \equiv 1 \bmod t \Rightarrow 2N \equiv 1 \bmod t$$

must be satisfied as mentioned in [25]. The condition leads to several coefficients in testP cannot be obtained, which are distributed around $N/2$, we set them to zero. Since we denote the range of $\mathbb{Z}_t$ as $[-\frac{t-1}{2}, \frac{t-1}{2}]$, the test polynomial testP can be set to

$$f(0) + f(-1)X + \cdots + f(-[t-1]/2)X^{\frac{t-1}{2}} + f([t-1]/2)X^{\frac{t+1}{2}} + \cdots + f(1)X^{t-1}$$

$$\vdots$$

$$+ f(0)X^{\lfloor \frac{N}{2t} - 1 \rfloor \cdot t} + \cdots + f(1)X^{\lfloor \frac{N}{2t} \rfloor \cdot t - 1}$$

$$+ 0 \cdot X^{\lfloor \frac{N}{2t} \rfloor \cdot t} + \cdots + 0 \cdot X^{N/2} + \cdots + 0 \cdot X^{N - \lfloor \frac{N}{2t} \rfloor \cdot t}$$

$$- f(-1)X^{N - \lfloor \frac{N}{2t} \rfloor \cdot t + 1} - \cdots - f(0)X^{N - \lfloor \frac{N}{2t} - 1 \rfloor \cdot t}$$

$$\vdots$$

$$- f(-1) \, X^{N-t+1} - \cdots - f(-[t-1]/2)X^{N - \frac{t+1}{2}} - f([t-1]/2)X^{N - \frac{t-1}{2}} \cdots - f(1)X^{N-1}.$$

We remark that this test polynomial can represents all values for $\mathbb{Z}_t$, whereas the test polynomial using MSB encoding can only represent the range of $[0, t/2]$.

3.3 Bootstrapping Key Generation Algorithm

The functional bootstrapping process requires the so-called bootstrapping keys. For a ternary LWE secret key $\mathbf{s} \in \{-1, 0, 1\}^n$, we generate $\mathsf{bsk}_{s'}(\mathbf{s})$ in RGSW ciphertext as shown in Algorithm 1 referring to [3].

Algorithm 1. Bootstrapping Key Generation

Input:
    A LWE secret key $\mathbf{s} \in \{-1, 0, 1\}^n$.
    A RLWE secret key $s' \in \mathcal{R}$.
Output:
    The bootstrapping key $\mathsf{bsk}_{s'}(\mathbf{s})$.
1: for $i = 0$ to $n - 1$ do;
2:       if $(s_i = -1)$, $\mathsf{bsk}_{i,0} = \mathrm{RGSW}_{s'}(0)$ and $\mathsf{bsk}_{i,1} = \mathrm{RGSW}_{s'}(1)$;
3:       if $(s_i = 0)$, $\mathsf{bsk}_{i,0} = \mathrm{RGSW}_{s'}(0)$ and $\mathsf{bsk}_{i,1} = \mathrm{RGSW}_{s'}(0)$;
4:       if $(s_i = 1)$, $\mathsf{bsk}_{i,0} = \mathrm{RGSW}_{s'}(1)$ and $\mathsf{bsk}_{i,1} = \mathrm{RGSW}_{s'}(0)$;
5: end for
6: **return** $\mathsf{bsk}_{s'}(\mathbf{s}) = \{\mathsf{bsk}_{i,0}, \mathsf{bsk}_{i,1}\}_{i \in [0, n-1]}$.

Algorithm 2. Full Domain Functional Bootstrapping with LSB Encoding

---

Input:

An LWE sample $\text{ct} = (\mathbf{a}, b = -\langle \mathbf{a}, \mathbf{s} \rangle + m + te) \in \text{LWE}_{\mathbf{s}}^n(m)$.

A bootstrapping key $\text{bsk}_{s'}(\mathbf{s})$, where noise is encoded in MSB and s' is the secret key of RLWE.

An LWE-to-LWE key switching key $\text{ksk}_{i,j,v}$ as shown in Section 2.3.

An arbitrary function $f : \mathbb{Z}_t \to \mathbb{Z}_t$.

Output:

An LWE sample $\text{ct}' = \text{LWE}_{\mathbf{s}}^n(f(m))$.

1: Set testP as shown in section 3.2.
2: Set $\text{acc} = (0, X^b \cdot \text{testP})$.
3: for $i = 0$ to $n - 1$ do;
4:     $\text{acc} = \text{acc} \odot ((X^{a_i} - 1) \cdot \text{bsk}_{i,0} + (X^{-a_i} - 1) \cdot \text{bsk}_{i,1}) + \text{acc}$;
5: end for
6: $\text{ct}' = \text{SampleExtract}(\text{acc})$.
7: $\text{ct}' = \text{ModSwitch}_{Q \to Q'}(\text{ct}')$.
8: $\text{ct}' = \text{KeySwitch}_{\phi(s') \to s}(\text{ct}')$.
9: $\text{ct}' = \text{ModSwitch}_{Q' \to q}(\text{ct}')$.
10: **return** ct'.

3.4 Full Domain FBS

Theorem 1. *Input an LWE ciphertext* $\text{ct} = \text{LWE}_{\mathbf{s}}^n(m)$ *with the LSB encoding, where error* $|e| \leq q/4t - 1$ *and let* $f : \mathbb{Z}_t \to \mathbb{Z}_t$ *be an arbitrary function, Algorithm 2 outputs a ciphertext* $\text{ct}' = \text{LWE}_{\mathbf{s}}^n(f(m))$ *with error variance* $\text{Var}(e_{\text{ct}'})$.

Proof. Firstly, we analyze line 4 of Algorithm 2

$$\text{acc}_i = \text{acc}_{i-1} \odot ((X^{a_i} - 1) \cdot \text{bsk}_{i,0} + (X^{-a_i} - 1) \cdot \text{bsk}_{i,1}) + \text{acc}_{i-1},$$

which can be seen as a ternary CMux gate by performing one external product operation. Given the ternary bootstrapping keys, it is easy to see that $\text{acc}_i = \text{RLWE}(X^{a_i \cdot s_i})$. Due to the fact that $(||X^{a_i} - 1||_2^2 + ||X^{-a_i} - 1||_2^2) \cdot \text{Var}(\text{err}(\text{bsk})) \leq 4 \cdot \text{Var}(\text{err}(\text{bsk}))$, we can obtain the variance as

$$\text{Var}(e_{\text{acc}_i}) \leq \frac{2Nd_gB_g^2}{3} \cdot \text{Var}(e_{\text{bsk}}) + \text{Var}(e_{\text{acc}_{i-1}})$$

by using Eq. 1, where $\text{Var}(e_{\text{bsk}})$ is the noise variance of bootstrapping keys $\text{bsk}_{i,0}$ and $\text{bsk}_{i,1}$.

From lines 3 to 5 of Algorithm 2, the accumulator acc performs n ternary CMux gate and this process is the so-called blind rotation. In addition, since the most significant bit of the noise is set to zero, i.e., $|e| \leq \frac{q}{4t} - 1$, we can get the fact that $m + te \in [-\frac{N+t}{2}, \frac{N-t}{2}) \subseteq (-\frac{N}{2}, \frac{N}{2})$, which is consistent with the domain of LUT. Based on the design of the test polynomial in Sect. 3.2, we can obtain that if $e \geq 0$, $X^{m+te} \cdot -f(m)X^{N-m-te} = f(m)$; otherwise, $X^{m+te} \cdot f(m)X^{-m-te} = f(m)$. Thus, the accumulator is

$$\begin{aligned} \mathsf{acc} &= \mathsf{RLWE}_s(\mathsf{testP} \cdot X^{b+\sum_{i=0}^{n-1} a_i s_i}) \\ &= \mathsf{RLWE}_s(\mathsf{testP} \cdot X^{m+te}) \\ &= \mathsf{RLWE}_s(f(m) + *X + \cdots + *X^{N-1}), \end{aligned}$$

where the constant term of the polynomial is $f(m)$, and $*$ represents terms that we don't care about. Since $\mathsf{Var}(e_{\mathsf{acc}_0}) = 0$, the variance of noise in blind rotation satisfies

$$\mathsf{Var}(e_{\mathsf{acc}}) \le \frac{2nNd_g B_g^2}{3} \cdot \mathsf{Var}(e_{\mathsf{bsk}}).$$

After that, in line 6 of the algorithm, the $\mathsf{LWE}_{\phi(s')}(f(m)) \in \mathbb{Z}_Q^{N+1}$ ciphertext is extracted by the sample extract operation without making the noise larger.

Then, before performing the key switching operation, we need to perform a modulus switching operation to a temporary modulus Q'. Then the LWE-to-LWE key switching operation is performed, which results in the ciphertext as $\mathsf{ct}' = \mathsf{LWE}_s(f(m)) \in \mathbb{Z}_{Q'}^{n+1}$, and the variance of the noise is

$$\mathsf{Var}(e_{\mathsf{ct}'}) \le (\frac{Q'}{Q})^2 \cdot \mathsf{Var}(e_{\mathsf{acc}}) + Nd_{\mathsf{ks}} \cdot \mathsf{Var}(e_{\mathsf{ksk}}) + \frac{tN}{4}.$$

Finally, the ciphertext $\mathsf{ct}' = \mathsf{LWE}_s(f(m)) \in \mathbb{Z}_q^{n+1}$ can be obtained by using modulus switching operation in LSB encoding form, and the noise in ct' has a variance as

$$\mathsf{Var}(e_{\mathsf{ct}'}) \le (\frac{q}{Q'})^2 \cdot \mathsf{Var}(e_{\mathsf{ct}'}) + \frac{tn}{4}. \tag{2}$$

In Sect. 5, we analyze in detail the effect of the variance of noise growth on the decryption failure rate for the output LWE ciphertext.

3.5 Full Domain FBS with MSB Encoding

In this subsection, we describe how to solve the full domain functional bootstrapping with MSB encoding in Algorithm 3.

Theorem 2. *Input an LWE ciphertext* $\mathsf{ct} = \mathsf{MSB.LWE}_{\mathsf{s}}^n(m)$ *with the MSB encoding, where with error* $|e| \le q/4t - 1$ *and let* $f : \mathbb{Z}_t \to \mathbb{Z}_t$ *be an arbitrary function, Algorithm 3 outputs a ciphertext* $\mathsf{ct}' = \mathsf{MSB.LWE}_{\phi(\mathsf{s}')}^N(f(m))$ *with error variance* $\mathsf{Var}(e_{\mathsf{ct}'})$.

Proof. Firstly, after performing the encoding transformation step, one can get a new LWE ciphertext $\mathsf{ct}' = \mathsf{LSB.LWE}_{\mathsf{s}}^n(-m) = (\mathbf{a}', b')$ with error $|e| \le q/4t - 1$. At this point, the LUT evaluation needs to be adjusted to $f(-m)$. Similar to Algorithm 2, after the blind rotation operation from lines 2 to 5 in Algorithm 3, the accumulator acc can be obtained as

$$\begin{aligned} \mathsf{acc} &= \mathsf{MSB.RLWE}_s(\mathsf{testP}_1 \cdot X^{b'+\sum_{i=0}^{n-1} a_i' s_i}) \\ &= \mathsf{MSB.RLWE}_s(\mathsf{testP}_1 \cdot X^{-m+te}). \end{aligned}$$

Algorithm 3. Full Domain Functional Bootstrapping with MSB Encoding

---

Input:

An LWE sample $ct = (\mathbf{a}, b = -\langle \mathbf{a}, \mathbf{s} \rangle + \lfloor \frac{q}{t} \cdot m \rceil + e) \in \mathsf{MSB.LWE}_\mathbf{s}^n(m)$.

A bootstrapping key $bsk_{s'}(\mathbf{s})$, where the noise is encoded in LSB and s' is the secret key of RLWE.

An arbitrary function $f : \mathbb{Z}_t \to \mathbb{Z}_t$.

Output:

An LWE sample $ct' = \mathsf{MSB.LWE}_{\phi(\mathbf{s'})}^N(f(m))$.

1: $ct' = \mathsf{EncodeTrans}(ct)$.

2: Let $\triangle = \lfloor \frac{Q}{t} \rceil$, and set $acc = (0, \triangle \cdot \mathsf{testP}_1 \cdot X^{b'})$.

3: **for** $i = 0$ to $n - 1$ **do**;

4:        $acc = acc \odot ((X^{a'_i} - 1) \cdot bsk_{i,0} + ((X^{-a'_i} - 1) \cdot bsk_{i,1}) + acc$;

5: **end for**

6: $ct' = \mathsf{SampleExtract}(acc)$.

7: **return** ct'.

Next, we set the test polynomial testP_1 in Eq. 3 so that $f(m)$ is fixed in the constant term of the polynomial with MSB encoding.

$$f(0) + f(1)X + \cdots + f([t-1]/2)X^{\frac{t-1}{2}} + f(-[t-1]/2)X^{\frac{t+1}{2}} + \cdots + f(-1)X^{t-1}$$

$$\vdots$$

$$+ f(0)X^{\lfloor \frac{N}{2t} \rfloor \cdot t} + \cdots + f(-1)X^{\lfloor \frac{N}{2t} \rfloor \cdot t - 1}$$

$$+ 0 \cdot X^{\lfloor \frac{N}{2t} \rfloor \cdot t} + \cdots + 0 \cdot X^{N/2} + \cdots + 0 \cdot X^{N - \lfloor \frac{N}{2t} \rfloor \cdot t}$$

$$- f(1)X^{N - \lfloor \frac{N}{2t} \rfloor \cdot t + 1} - \cdots - f(0)X^{N - \lfloor \frac{N}{2t} - 1 \rfloor \cdot t}$$

$$\vdots$$

$$- f(1) X^{N-t+1} - \cdots - f([t-1]/2)X^{N - \frac{t+1}{2}} - f(-[t-1]/2)X^{N - \frac{t-1}{2}} \cdots - f(-1)X^{N-1}. \tag{3}$$

By multiplying the factors $\triangle$ in the 2 line of the algorithm, we can get

$$acc = \mathsf{MSB.RLWE}_s(f(m) + *X + \cdots + *X^{N-1}).$$

Finally, the ciphertext $ct' = \mathsf{MSB.LWE}_{\phi(\mathbf{s'})}^N(f(m)) \in \mathbb{Z}_Q^{N+1}$ can be obtained by using sample extract operation, and the variance of noise $e_{ct'}$ is

$$\mathsf{Var}(e_{acc}) \leq \frac{2nNd_gB_g^2}{3} \cdot \mathsf{Var}(e_{bsk}).$$

In addition, the key switching and modulus switching operations can be performed with MSB encoding form if necessary. These steps are similar to that described in Sect. 3.4. We omit these details.

4 Multi-value and Tree-Based Functional Bootstrapping

We show that the proposed LSB encoding technique can be applied to multi-value and tree-based functional bootstrapping. We use the LSB encoding method by default in this section.

4.1 Multi-value Functional Bootstrapping

Carpov et al. [7] proposed a method for evaluating k different LUTs using one functional bootstrapping. Each LUT can be embedded in a test polynomial with the LSB encoding, as outlined in Sect. 3.3. For simplicity in analysis, we define these test polynomials as

$$\mathsf{testP}_i = \beta_0 + \beta_1 X + \cdots + \beta_{N-1}X^{N-1},$$

where $\beta_j \in [0, t)$ for all $0 \le i \le k - 1$ and $0 \le j \le N - 1$. These polynomials testP_i can be factored into the product of two polynomials v_0 and v_i, where v_0 is a common factor to all testP_i. In fact, As mentioned in [14], the polynomials v_0 and v_i can be set as

$$v_0 = \frac{1}{2} \cdot (1 + X + \cdots + X^{N-1}),$$

$$v_i = \beta_0 + \beta_{N-1} + (\beta_1 - \beta_0)X + \cdots + (\beta_{N-1} - \beta_{N-2})X^{N-1} \in \mathcal{R}_t.$$

Then we have

$$
\begin{aligned}
v_0 \cdot v_i &= (\beta_0 + \beta_{N-1} + (\beta_1 - \beta_0)X + \cdots + (\beta_{N-1} - \beta_{N-2})X^{N-1}) \cdot v_0 \bmod X^N + 1 \\
&= (\beta_0 + \beta_1 X + \cdots + \beta_{N-1}X^{N-1}) \cdot (1 - X) \cdot v_0 \bmod X^N + 1 \\
&= \beta_0 + \beta_1 X + \cdots + \beta_{N-1}X^{N-1} \bmod X^N + 1 \\
&= \mathsf{testP}_i.
\end{aligned}
$$

Note that the polynomial v_0 has fractional coefficients for $\frac{1}{2}$, which is indicated as $2^{-1} \pmod{Q}$ in practical operation. Algorithm 4 illustrates the full domain multi-value functional bootstrapping with LSB Encoding.

Theorem 3. *Input an LWE ciphertext* $\mathsf{ct} = \mathsf{LWE}_s^n(m)$ *with error* $|e| \le q/4t - 1$ *and let* $f_i : \mathbb{Z}_t \to \mathbb{Z}_t$ *be an arbitrary function, Algorithm 4 outputs k ciphertexts* $\mathsf{ct}_i' = \mathsf{LWE}_{\phi(s')}^N(f_i(m))$ *with error variance* $\mathsf{Var}(e_{\mathsf{ct}_i'})$.

Proof. The ciphertext $\mathsf{acc} = \mathsf{RLWE}_s(v_0 \cdot X^{b + \sum_{i=0}^{n-1} a_i s_i})$ can be obtained from lines 2 to 5 according to Algorithm 2. Then, we can compute

$$
\begin{aligned}
\mathsf{acc}_i &= \mathsf{RLWE}_s(v_0 \cdot X^{b + \sum_{i=0}^{n-1} a_i s_i}) \cdot v_i \\
&= \mathsf{RLWE}_s(\mathsf{testP}_i \cdot X^{b + \sum_{i=0}^{n-1} a_i s_i}) \\
&= \mathsf{RLWE}_s(\mathsf{testP}_i \cdot X^{m + te}) \\
&= \mathsf{RLWE}_s(f_i(m) + *X + \cdots + *X^{N-1})
\end{aligned}
$$

Algorithm 4. Multi-Value Functional Bootstrapping with LSB Encoding

---

Input:

An LWE sample $\mathsf{ct} = (\mathbf{a}, b = -\langle \mathbf{a}, \mathbf{s} \rangle + m + te) \in \mathsf{LWE}_\mathbf{s}^n(m)$.

A bootstrapping key $\mathsf{bsk}_{s'}(\mathbf{s})$, where noise is encoded in MSB and s' is the secret key of RLWE.

k arbitrary functions $f_i = v_0 \cdot v_i : \mathbb{Z}_t \to \mathbb{Z}_t$.

Output:

k LWE samples $\mathsf{ct}' = \mathsf{LWE}_{\phi(s')}^N(f_i(m))$.

1: Set $v_0 = (2^{-1} \mod Q) \cdot (1 + X + \cdots + X^{N-1})$

2: Set $\mathsf{acc} = (0, X^b \cdot v_0)$.

3: **for** $i = 0$ to $n - 1$ **do**;

4:         $\mathsf{acc} = \mathsf{acc} \odot ((X^{a_i} - 1) \cdot \mathsf{bsk}_{i,0} + (X^{-a_i} - 1) \cdot \mathsf{bsk}_{i,1}) + \mathsf{acc}$;

5: **end for**

6: **for** $i = 0$ to $k - 1$ **do**;

7:         $\mathsf{acc}_i = \mathsf{acc} \cdot v_i$;

8:         $\mathsf{ct}_i' = \mathsf{SampleExtract}(\mathsf{acc}_i)$.

9: **end for**

10: **return** $\{\mathsf{ct}_i'\}_{i \in [0, k-1]}$.

The correctness of the algorithm can be directly derived from blind rotation and factorization. Thus, these LUTs can be performed by using only one FBS. According to [19], the variance of the noise satisfies

$$\mathsf{Var}(e_{\mathsf{ct}_i}) \le t(t-1)^2 \cdot \frac{2nNd_g B_g^2}{3} \cdot \mathsf{Var}(e_{bsk}).$$

The operations for key switching and modulus switching can also be added if necessary.

4.2   Tree-Based Functional Bootstrapping

Guimarães et al. [19] proposed the tree-based lookup table technique to support functional bootstrapping for arbitrary large plaintext space. Let $m = \sum_{i=0}^{d-1} m_i B^i$, $\mathsf{ct}_i = \mathsf{LWE}^n(m_i)$ is the ciphertext in these blocks, where B is the decomposed base. The tree-based FBS is to use multiple functional bootstrapping associated with the ciphertext blocks to compose a tree that outputs new LUT.

However, the negacyclicity is further amplified in the tree-based bootstrapping process [19,20]. This means that the most significant bit of the message in each ciphertext block cannot be represented normally. It is possible that full domain tree-based FBS schemes are not universal since the current approaches to solving full domain FBS are far less effective than the original FBS.

Our technique can be directly applicable to tree-based bootstrapping as shown in Algorithm 5. The proposed method is a significant improvement for tree-based full domain FBS since each tree level only needs one FBS. In the line 3 of Algorithm 5, each iteration uses the ciphertext $\mathsf{ct}_i = \mathsf{LWE}_\mathbf{s}(m_i)$ as

---

Algorithm 5. Tree-based Functional Bootstrapping with LSB Encoding

---

Input:

A set of LWE samples $\mathsf{ct}_i = \mathsf{LWE}_{\mathbf{s}}^n(m_i)$, such that $m = \sum_{i=0}^{d-1} m_i B^i$ encodes the integer m in base B with d digits.

A set L of B^d polynomials encoding the lookup table of an arbitrary function f.

A bootstrapping key $\mathsf{bsk}_{s'}(\mathbf{s})$, where noise is encoded in MSB and s' is the secret key of RLWE.

An LWE-to-RLWE key switching key $\mathsf{ksk}_{i,j}$ as shown in Section 2.3.

Output:

An LWE sample $\mathsf{ct}' = \mathsf{LWE}_{\phi(\mathbf{s}')}^N(f(m))$.

1: Set $v_0 = L$
2: **for** $i = 0$ to $d - 1$ **do**;
3:      $\mathsf{ct}_k = \mathsf{MultiValueFBS}(\mathsf{ct}_i), k \in \{0, ..., B^{d-i-1}\}$;
4:      **for** $j = 1$ to B^{d-j-2} **do**;
5:          $\mathsf{testP}_{j-1} = \mathsf{LWE\text{-}to\text{-}RLWE.KeySwitch}_{\mathbf{s} \to \phi(\mathbf{s})}(\mathsf{ct}_{(j-1)\times B}, ..., \mathsf{ct}_{j \times B})$.
6:      **end for**
7: **end for**
8: **return** ct'.

---

a selector on each of the the B^{d-i-1} RLWE samples. This process results in B^{d-i-1} LWE samples by using the MultiValueFBS technique. After that, the LWE samples are packed into B^{d-i-2} RLWE samples by the LWE-to-RLWE key switching operation. The whole process ends after ct_0 is used. Finally, the ciphertext $\mathsf{ct}' = \mathsf{LWE}_{\phi(\mathbf{s}')}^N(f(m))$ can be obtained, where an arbitrary function f is encoded as B^d-sized LUT. The correctness of Algorithm 5 can refer to [19].

5 Comparative Analysis and Experimental Results

5.1 Security Analysis and Parameter Selection

We first briefly analyze the security of the proposed scheme. The conditions that $q \equiv 1 \bmod t$ need to be established to ensure the security of the LSB encoding for LWE and RLWE (RGSW) encryption as mentioned in [6] scheme. It has been instantiated by many schemes such as [23,25]. Additionally, our bootstrapping procedure follows the architecture of [15,28], which achieves IND-CPA security.

After that, the proposed algorithm in Sect. 3 works with the following parameters:

- λ, Security level ;
- t, LWE plaintext modulus;
- n, Lattice parameter of the LWE scheme;
- σ, Standard deviation of Gaussian distribution;
- Q, RLWE and RGSW modulus (used for NTTs);
- Q', Temporary modulus for RLWE that is used in the key switching;
- N, Ring dimension for RLWE/RGSW;
- q, LWE ciphertext modulus and $q = 2N$;

- B_g, Gadget base for RGSW encryption, which breaks integer Q into d_g digits;
- B_{ks}, Gadget base for key switching, which breaks integer Q into d_{ks} digits;

Table 2. Parameters for the functional bootstrapping

λ	n	N	t	σ	q	Q	Q'	B_g	d_g	B_{ks}	d_{ks}
128	512	1024	23	3.19	2048	$\approx 2^{27}$	2^{15}	2^7	4	2^5	3

Table 2 outlines a specific parameter set that provides us with a classic security parameter of 128-bit according to the HE standard [1]. The RLWE ciphertext modulus Q is a significant parameter that affects the efficiency of utilizing the fast NTT operation under the condition $Q \equiv 1 \bmod 2N$ as well as the capacity to tolerate noise growth. Furthermore, the noise growth will be able to achieve the desired effects with a smaller B_g for bootstrapping operations, but it would also increase the time of bootstrapping. Another option is to utilize a larger B_g, which will speed up the bootstrapping process at the cost of increasing noise. The plaintext modulus t in our scheme is subject to two constraints: the plaintext space in the FBS is constrained to around $4 \sim 5$ bits, and second, the condition $q \equiv 1 \bmod t$ must be met to ensure the underlying security.

5.2 Performance Comparison

Table 3. Noise growth and performance for full domain FBS scheme. Here, N is the ring dimension, t is the plaintext modulus, Q is the RLWE ciphertext modulus, d_g is the number of digits for gadget decomposition, TP is the RLWE tensor product, PM is defined in [26], ET is the encoding transformation.

Scheme	# Operations	Noise Growth	Times(ms)
Chillotti et al. [13]	1 BR + 1 TP + 2 KS + 1 MS	$\beta \cdot O(Nt)$	–
Kluczniak et al. [26]	2 BR + 1 PM +2 KS + 1 MS	$\beta \cdot O(\sqrt{Nd_g}Q^{1/d_g})$	–
Liu et al. [27]	2 BR + 2 KS + 2 MS	β	239.77
Our work I	1 BR + 1 KS + 1 MS	β	120.52
Our work II	1ET+ 1 BR + 1 KS + 1 MS	β	122.03

We display comparisons of noise growth, complexity, and run time of these full domain functional bootstrapping schemes in Table 3. To analyze the performance, we split the functional bootstrapping procedure into blind rotation (BR), key switching (KS), and modulus switching (MS) steps with the variance of noise $\beta^2 = (\frac{q}{Q})^2 \cdot (\sigma^2_{\mathsf{ACC}} + \sigma^2_{\mathsf{KS}}) + \sigma^2_{\mathsf{MS}}$, where the blind rotation is the main share for noise growth. Given the bound on the variance of the error, we can estimate the probability of decryption failure as $1 - \mathrm{erf}(\frac{q/t}{2\sqrt{2}\beta})$. By taking the noise result 2 of Sect. 3.4 into the equation of decryption failure, we can obtain the probability of success for Algorithm 2 is at least $1 - 2^{53}$ under the parameters in Table 2. In addition, in order to have a better comparison with other methods, we use the multi-valued bootstrapping technique to optimize the Chillotti et al. [13] and Kluczniak et al. [26] schemes. We implement methods of Algorithm 2, 3 and [27] in the OpenFHE library. The ternary secret key [3] is utilized in our comparison and each blind rotation step requires $2n(d_g + 1)$ NTT operations, where the complexity of each NTT operation is $O(N \log N)$. Table 3 presents the single-threaded timing results using the listed parameters. The experiments are run 1000 times on a machine with Intel(R) Core(TM) i5-12500 @ 3.00 GHz, 64 GB RAM running Ubuntu 22.04.2. The compiler was clang++ 9.0.0. We take the average time, which demonstrates that our method I is roughly twice as quick as the method from [27].

5.3 Practicability

We note that the instantiations of the FHEW and TFHE schemes do not use the LSB encoding form. In addition, the security requirement that t is a prime number, instead of a power-of-two, may limit the choice of the plaintext modulus in the proposed scheme. But the linear homomorphism transformation for the LWE ciphertext and functional bootstrapping are unaffected by the prime modulus. We remark that the LSB technique can apply to most of the homomorphic evaluation scenarios for the FHEW and TFHE schemes.

On the other hand, we have considered a technique known as homomorphic digit decomposition [27], which breaks a large-precision ciphertext into blocks, each of which contains the encrypted ciphertext following the message's digital decomposition. The proposed algorithms in Sect. 3 do not support this operation due to the prime modulus. We can replace the cyclotomic polynomial from $X^N + 1$ with some other cyclotomic polynomial of prime order. In this way, the plaintext modulus t can be set to the power of two. [24] provides some optional cyclotomic polynomials and analyzes the efficiency of the underlying NTT operation. One of our future works is to further investigate the combination of these polynomials with the LSB encoding method.

6 Conclusion

We propose a faster full domain functional bootstrapping scheme that utilizes the least significant bit encoding technique. Unlike previous methods, which either involve RLWE multiplication or require at least two FBS, our scheme only requires an FBS. Furthermore, as an extension of the technique, we can utilize the encoding transformation technique to solve the full domain FBS with the most significant bit encoding. The experiments demonstrate that our method is 2 times faster than [27]. Finally, our technique can be extended to full domain multi-valued FBS and tree-based FBS.

Acknowledgments. We are grateful for the helpful comments from the anonymous reviewers of Inscrypt 2023. This work was supported by CAS Project for Young Scientists in Basic Research (Grant No. YSBR-035).

A   Algorithms of functions presented in Section 2.4

A.1   Correctness of the Key Switching

Lemma 1. *Input an LWE ciphertext* $\mathsf{ct} = \mathsf{LWE}_{\mathbf{z}}^{N}(m)$ *with error variance* $\mathsf{Var}(e)$, *and the switching keys* $\mathsf{ksk}_{i,j,v}$ *with error variance* $\mathsf{Var}(e_{\mathsf{ksk}})$, *the key switching algorithm outputs a new LWE ciphertext* $\mathsf{ct}' = \mathsf{KeySwitch}_{\mathbf{z} \rightarrow \mathbf{s}}(\mathsf{ct})$ *with error variance* $\mathsf{Var}(e')$.

Proof. Let $\mathsf{ksk}_{i,j,v} = (\mathbf{a}'_{i,j,v}, \mathbf{a}'_{i,j,v} \cdot \mathbf{s} + v z_i B_{ks}^j + e_{i,j,v})$ *for some* $\mathbf{a}'_{i,j,v} \in \mathbb{Z}_q^n$ *and* $e_{i,j,v} \in \chi_\delta$, *the output ciphertext is*

$$\mathsf{ct}' = \mathsf{KeySwitch}_{\mathbf{z} \rightarrow \mathbf{s}}(\mathsf{ct})$$
$$= (\mathbf{0}, b) - \sum_{i,j} \mathsf{ksk}_{i,j,a_{i,j}}$$
$$= (\mathbf{a}', b') \bmod q \in \mathsf{LWE}_{\mathbf{s}}^n(m),$$

where $\mathbf{a}' = -\sum_{i,j} \mathbf{a}'_{i,j,a_{i,j}}$ *and* $b' = b - \mathbf{a} \cdot \mathbf{z} + \mathbf{a}' \cdot \mathbf{s} - \sum_{i,j} e_{i,j,a_{i,j}}$. *According to Theorem 6 of [15], the variance of the noise satisfies* $\mathsf{Var}(e') \leq \mathsf{Var}(e) + N d_{ks} \cdot \mathsf{Var}(e_{\mathsf{ksk}})$.

A.2   Correctness of the Modulus Switching

Lemma 2. *Input an LWE ciphertext* $\mathsf{ct} = (\mathbf{a}, b) \in \mathsf{LWE}_{\mathbf{s}}^n(m)$ *with error variance* $\mathsf{Var}(e)$ *modulo* Q, *the modulus switching algorithm outputs a new LWE ciphertext* $\mathsf{ct}' = \mathsf{ModSwitch}_{Q \rightarrow q}(\mathsf{ct})$ *with error variance* $\mathsf{Var}(e')$ *modulo* q.

Proof. Let the integers $Q > q > t$ *and* $Q \equiv 1 \bmod t, q \equiv 1 \bmod t$, *the output ciphertext is*

$$\mathsf{ct}' = \mathsf{ModSwitch}_{Q \rightarrow q}(\mathsf{ct})$$
$$= (\lfloor \frac{q}{Q} \cdot \mathbf{a} \rceil, \lfloor \frac{q}{Q} \cdot b \rceil)$$
$$= (\mathbf{a}', b') \in \mathbb{Z}_q^{n+1},$$

and satisfies the requirement that $a'_i \equiv a_i \bmod t, b' \equiv b \bmod t$. It is straightforward to conclude that $b + \langle \mathbf{a}, \mathbf{s} \rangle \bmod Q \bmod t = b' + \langle \mathbf{a}', \mathbf{s} \rangle \bmod q \bmod t$ according to Lemma 5 of [6], and the variance of noise satisfies $\mathsf{Var}(e') \leq (\frac{q}{Q})^2 \cdot \mathsf{Var}(e) + \frac{t}{2} \cdot \|\mathbf{s}\|_2^2$.

A.3   Correctness of the Encoding Transformation

Lemma 3. *Input an LWE ciphertext* $\mathsf{ct} \in \mathsf{MSB.LWE}_\mathbf{s}^n(m)$ *with error variance* $\mathsf{Var}(e)$, *the encoding transformation algorithm outputs a new LWE ciphertext* $\mathsf{ct}' = \mathsf{EncodeTrans}(\mathsf{ct}) \in \mathsf{LSB.LWE}_\mathbf{s}^n(-m)$ *with error variance* $\mathsf{Var}(e)$.

Proof. Let $\mathsf{ct} = (\mathbf{a}, b = -\langle \mathbf{a}, \mathbf{s} \rangle + \omega) \in \mathbb{Z}_q^{n+1}$ with $q \equiv 1 \bmod t$, where $\omega = \lfloor \frac{q}{t} \cdot m \rceil + e$. The decoding procedure of MSB encoding is

$$\left\lfloor \omega \cdot \frac{t}{q} \right\rceil = \omega \cdot \frac{t}{q} - f = m \bmod t$$

for some $f \in \frac{1}{q}\mathbb{Z} \cap [-1/2, 1/2)$. By multiplying by q and let $\mu = q \cdot f \in \mathbb{Z} \cap [-q/2, q/2)$, one can get $\omega \cdot t - \mu = q \cdot m \bmod tq$. Then $\mathsf{ct}' = \mathsf{EncodeTrans}(\mathsf{ct}) = (t \cdot \mathbf{a}, t \cdot b) \bmod q$ is a ciphertext with the LSB encoding since the decryption step is $\omega \cdot t = \mu \bmod q$ and

$$\mu = -q \cdot m \bmod t = -m \bmod t.$$

References

1. Albrecht, M., et al.: Homomorphic encryption security standard. Homomorphic Encryption. org, Toronto, Canada, Technical Report 11 (2018)
2. Alperin-Sheriff, J., Peikert, C.: Practical bootstrapping in quasilinear time. In: Canetti, R., Garay, J.A. (eds.) Annual Cryptology Conference, pp. 1–20. Springer, Heidelberg (2013). https://doi.org/10.1007/978-3-642-40041-4_1
3. Bonte, C., Iliashenko, I., Park, J., Pereira, H.V., Smart, N.P.: Final: faster FHE instantiated with NTRU and LWE. Cryptology ePrint Archive (2022)
4. Boura, C., Gama, N., Georgieva, M., Jetchev, D.: Simulating homomorphic evaluation of deep learning predictions. In: Dolev, S., Hendler, D., Lodha, S., Yung, M. (eds.) International Symposium on Cyber Security Cryptography and Machine Learning, pp. 212–230. Springer, Heidelberg (2019). https://doi.org/10.1007/978-3-030-20951-3_20
5. Brakerski, Z.: Fully homomorphic encryption without modulus switching from classical GapSVP. In: Safavi-Naini, R., Canetti, R. (eds.) Annual Cryptology Conference, pp. 868–886. Springer, Heidelberg (2012). https://doi.org/10.1007/978-3-642-32009-5_50
6. Brakerski, Z., Gentry, C., Vaikuntanathan, V.: (leveled) fully homomorphic encryption without bootstrapping. ACM Trans. Comput. Theory (TOCT) **6**(3), 1–36 (2014)
7. Carpov, S., Izabachène, M., Mollimard, V.: New techniques for multi-value input homomorphic evaluation and applications. In: Matsui, M. (ed.) Cryptographers' Track at the RSA Conference, pp. 106–126. Springer, Heidelberg (2019). https://doi.org/10.1007/978-3-030-12612-4_6
8. Cheon, J.H., Han, K., Kim, A., Kim, M., Song, Y.: Bootstrapping for approximate homomorphic encryption. In: Nielsen, J., Rijmen, V. (eds.) Annual International Conference on the Theory and Applications of Cryptographic Techniques, pp. 360–384. Springer (2018). https://doi.org/10.1007/978-3-319-78381-9_14

9. Cheon, J.H., Kim, A., Kim, M., Song, Y.: Homomorphic encryption for arithmetic of approximate numbers. In: Takagi, T., Peyrin, T. (eds.) International Conference on the Theory and Application of Cryptology and Information Security, pp. 409–437. Springer, Heidelberg (2017). https://doi.org/10.1007/978-3-319-70694-8_15

10. Chillotti, I., Gama, N., Georgieva, M., Izabachene, M.: Faster fully homomorphic encryption: bootstrapping in less than 0.1 seconds. In: Cheon, J., Takagi, T. (eds.) International Conference on the Theory and Application of Cryptology and Information Security, pp. 3–33. Springer, Heidelberg (2016). https://doi.org/10.1007/978-3-662-53887-6_1

11. Chillotti, I., Gama, N., Georgieva, M., Izabachène, M.: TFHE: fast fully homomorphic encryption over the torus. J. Cryptol. **33**(1), 34–91 (2020)

12. Chillotti, I., Joye, M., Paillier, P.: Programmable bootstrapping enables efficient homomorphic inference of deep neural networks. In: Dolev, S., Margalit, O., Pinkas, B., Schwarzmann, A. (eds.) International Symposium on Cyber Security Cryptography and Machine Learning, pp. 1–19. Springer, Heidelberg (2021). https://doi.org/10.1007/978-3-030-78086-9_1

13. Chillotti, I., Ligier, D., Orfila, J.B., Tap, S.: Improved programmable bootstrapping with larger precision and efficient arithmetic circuits for TFHE. In: Tibouchi, M., Wang, H. (eds.) International Conference on the Theory and Application of Cryptology and Information Security, pp. 670–699. Springer, Heidelberg (2021). https://doi.org/10.1007/978-3-030-92078-4_23

14. Clet, P.E., Zuber, M., Boudguiga, A., Sirdey, R., Gouy-Pailler, C.: Putting up the swiss army knife of homomorphic calculations by means of tfhe functional bootstrapping. Cryptology ePrint Archive (2022)

15. Ducas, L., Micciancio, D.: FHEW: bootstrapping homomorphic encryption in less than a second. In: Oswald, E., Fischlin, M. (eds.) Advances in Cryptology - EUROCRYPT 2015–34th Annual International Conference on the Theory and Applications of Cryptographic Techniques, Sofia, Bulgaria, 26–30 April 2015, Proceedings, Part I. Lecture Notes in Computer Science, vol. 9056, pp. 617–640. Springer, Heidelberg (2015). https://doi.org/10.1007/978-3-662-46800-5_24

16. Fan, J., Vercauteren, F.: Somewhat practical fully homomorphic encryption. Cryptology ePrint Archive (2012)

17. Gentry, C.: Fully homomorphic encryption using ideal lattices. In: Proceedings of the Forty-First Annual ACM Symposium on Theory of Computing, pp. 169–178 (2009)

18. Gentry, C., Sahai, A., Waters, B.: Homomorphic encryption from learning with errors: conceptually-simpler, asymptotically-faster, attribute-based. In: Canetti, R., Garay, J.A. (eds.) Annual Cryptology Conference, pp. 75–92. Springer, Heidelberg (2013). https://doi.org/10.1007/978-3-642-40041-4_5

19. Guimarães, A., Borin, E., Aranha, D.F.: Revisiting the functional bootstrap in TFHE. IACR Trans. Cryptogr. Hardware Embed. Syst. 229–253 (2021)

20. Guimarães, A., Borin, E., Aranha, D.F.: Mosfhet: optimized software for FHE over the torus. Cryptology ePrint Archive (2022)

21. Halevi, S., Shoup, V.: Algorithms in helib. In: Garay, J.A., Gennaro, R. (eds.) Annual Cryptology Conference, pp. 554–571. Springer, Heidelberg (2014). https://doi.org/10.1007/978-3-662-44371-2_31

22. Halevi, S., Shoup, V.: Design and implementation of helib: a homomorphic encryption library. Cryptology ePrint Archive (2020)

23. Halevi, S., Shoup, V.: Bootstrapping for helib. J. Cryptol. **34** (2021). https://doi.org/10.1007/s00145-020-09368-7

24. Joye, M., Walter, M.: Liberating TFHE: programmable bootstrapping with general quotient polynomials. Cryptology ePrint Archive, Paper 2022/1177 (2022). https://eprint.iacr.org/2022/1177
25. Kim, A., Polyakov, Y., Zucca, V.: Revisiting homomorphic encryption schemes for finite fields. In: Tibouchi, M., Wang, H. (eds.) International Conference on the Theory and Application of Cryptology and Information Security. pp. 608–639. Springer, Heidelberg (2021). https://doi.org/10.1007/978-3-030-92078-4_21
26. Kluczniak, K., Schild, L.: FDFB: full domain functional bootstrapping towards practical fully homomorphic encryption. IACR Trans. Cryptogr. Hardware Embed. Syst. **2023**(1), 501–537 (2022). https://doi.org/10.46586/tches.v2023.i1.501-537
27. Liu, Z., Micciancio, D., Polyakov, Y.: Large-precision homomorphic sign evaluation using FHEW/TFHE bootstrapping. In: Agrawal, S., Lin, D. (eds.) International Conference on the Theory and Application of Cryptology and Information Security, pp. 130–160. Springer, Heidelberg (2022). https://doi.org/10.1007/978-3-031-22966-4_5
28. Micciancio, D., Polyakov, Y.: Bootstrapping in FHEW-like cryptosystems. In: Proceedings of the 9th on Workshop on Encrypted Computing & Applied Homomorphic Cryptography, pp. 17–28 (2021)
29. Regev, O.: On lattices, learning with errors, random linear codes, and cryptography. J. ACM (JACM) **56**(6), 1–40 (2009)
30. Yang, Z., Xie, X., Shen, H., Chen, S., Zhou, J.: TOTA: fully homomorphic encryption with smaller parameters and stronger security. Cryptology ePrint Archive (2021)

Public Key Cryptography

PFE: Linear Active Security, Double-Shuffle Proofs, and Low-Complexity Communication

Hanyu Jia and Xiangxue Li$^{(\boxtimes)}$

Shanghai Key Laboratory of Trustworthy Computing, School of Software Engineering, East China Normal University, Shanghai, China
xxli@cs.ecnu.edu.cn

Abstract. We consider the private function evaluation (PFE) problem in the malicious adversary model. Current state-of-the-art in PFE based on Valiant's universal circuits (Liu, Yu, etc., CRYPTO 2021) seems to reach a theoretical optimum ($13g \cdot \log g$) (g is the number of the gates in the circuit), but still does not avoid the logarithmic factor in circuit size.

In constructing PFE with linear active security, one essential building block is to prove the correctness of an extended permutation (EP, Mohassel and Sadeghian at EUROCRYPT 2013) by a zero-knowledge (ZK) protocol with linear complexity. Mohassel, Sadeghian, and Smart (ASIACRYPT 2014) presented a three-phase instantiation $\mathcal{ZK}_{EP}$, which is supposed to validate that the function owner has done his local computation in the right way. In particular, $\mathcal{ZK}_{EP}$ consists of a dummy placement phase, a replication phase, and a permutation phase, and each of the phases is of size $2g$. The overhead required by $\mathcal{ZK}_{EP}$ thus seems really heavy, reducing its practicability. We present in this paper a novel and efficient framework $\mathcal{ZK}_{DS}$ for proving the correct EP. We show that double shuffles (DS) suffice in $\mathcal{ZK}_{DS}$: one shuffle is of size $u + g - o$ (u is the number of input wires in the circuit and o the number of output wires, and we have generally $g \gg u, u \approx o$), another is of size $2g$, and no replication phase is required. The verifier generates the randomness for the first shuffle whose outputs determine the outgoing wires. The second shuffle reuses and extends the randomness and determines the incoming wires. Besides its linear complexity and succinct double-shuffle structure, $\mathcal{ZK}_{DS}$ reduces the communication overhead by more than 50% (including the ciphertexts and corresponding proofs), compared to $\mathcal{ZK}_{EP}$.

From $\mathcal{ZK}_{DS}$, we can build an actively secure online/offline PFE framework with linear complexity. The online phase could be instantiated by any well-studied secure function evaluation (SFE) with linear active security (e.g., Tiny-OT at CRYPTO 2012). The offline phase depends only on the function and uses $\mathcal{ZK}_{DS}$ to prove the EP relationship between $u + g - o$ outgoing wires and $2g$ incoming wires in the topological circuit $\mathcal{C}_f$ derived from the private function f. The design pushes actively secure PFE to be more compact in practice.

Keywords: Private Function Evaluation · Active Security · Zero-Knowledge Proof · Extended Permutation · Shuffle

© The Author(s), under exclusive license to Springer Nature Singapore Pte Ltd. 2024
C. Ge and M. Yung (Eds.): Inscrypt 2023, LNCS 14526, pp. 227–252, 2024.
https://doi.org/10.1007/978-981-97-0942-7_12

1   Introduction

1.1   Secure Multi-party Computation

A BRIEF DESCRIPTION. Computations performed on a local computer are not subject to malicious eavesdropping, whereas computations performed on two or more devices generally rely on the trustworthiness of the entire remote system. This carries the risk of leaking private data provided by the participants. Secure Multi-Party Computation (MPC) protocols can effectively provide the privacy-preserving functionality [13,50]. Through cryptographic methods, it no longer relies on the presence of trusted third parties, ensuring that remote computing can operate correctly while preserving the privacy of private data. One can find readily extensive and significant applications of MPC protocols in the era of increasing obsession with data insights [12,39].

SFE AND PFE. There are two cases of MPC protocols according to the public or private function to be computed. Secure Function Evaluation (SFE) is a common case in MPC that allows two or more parties $P_1, \cdots, P_w$ to jointly compute a publicly known function f on the private input data x_i of P_i ($i = 1, \cdots, w$). SFE guarantees that each party can get the result $f(x_1, \cdots, x_w)$ without revealing their private inputs x_i. Many SFE protocols have been proposed so far, and most of them rely on compiling the publicly known function into Boolean circuit, such as Yao's Garbled Circuit protocol [35,51], BGW protocol [4], and GMW protocol [22]. Private Function Evaluation (PFE) is a special case of MPC protocols, where the function is a private input for one of the parties. In PFE, the function owner compiles his private function into a circuit $\mathcal{C}_f$ (boolean circuit or arithmetic circuit) and opens some parameters of the circuit to other parties [6,28,30,32,40,41], such as the number of gates (g), the number of input wires (u), the number of output wires (o), or some auxiliary parameters. Though these parameters of $\mathcal{C}_f$ depend on the specific protocols, they should not enable other parties to learn the function in polynomial time.

APPLICATION SCENARIOS OF PFE. There are various application scenarios for PFE, and we give several examples here. In privacy-protected car insurance rate calculation [25], the customer data and the details of the rate calculation are kept private. In privacy-preserving intrusion detection systems [44], the server cannot learn the data of the client and the client cannot learn the signature on the server side. In the credit check [17], it is required that neither private financial data of the customers nor private criteria of the lenders might be revealed. Attribute-based access control can be enhanced to protect both sensitive credentials and sensitive policies by using PFE [16]. There are also applications in medicine [2] and in software diagnostics [7].

GENERAL DESIGNS OF PFE. There are two main design approaches for PFE protocols. One of the most common approaches is to reduce PFE protocols to typical SFE protocols [1,26,31,32,37,38,48,52] by safely evaluating an open Universal Circuit (UC). This series of methods focus on optimizing the number of gates in the UC. The smaller the number of gates in the circuits, the smaller the total overhead spent on protocols. However, current state-of-the-art in PFE based on Valiant's universal circuits [38] seems to reach a theoretical optimum $13g \cdot \log g$ (g is the number of the gates in the circuit), but still does not avoid the logarithmic factor in circuit size. Despite the amazing versatility of universal circuits, independent techniques (free of the family of universal circuits) need to be investigated to create actively secure PFE protocols with linear complexity in circuit size. In a general framework proposed by Mohassel and Sadeghian [40], the task of the hidden circuit is done by the *oblivious expansion permutation* (OEP) and one additional task of securely evaluating its gates is done by the *private gate evaluation* (PGE). Both tasks are handled independently and then combined naturally to form a more efficient PFE protocol. The second approach can construct PFE protocols with linear complexity in circuit size in both two-party and multi-party cases. For large circuits, the second method is more efficient than the first one based on UC. In addition to these two approaches for constructing general PFE protocols, there are many purpose-specific PFE protocols, e.g., Katz and Malka [30] proposed a two-party PFE protocol combining Yao's garbled circuit protocol and a single homomorphic encryption (HE) scheme.

TWO SECURITY MODELS IN MPC. Security models in MPC include semi-honest adversary model and malicious adversary model. The semi-honest adversary is the corrupt party, but he follows the specified protocol. In other words, the corrupt party runs the protocol honestly, but he tries to learn as much as possible from the messages sent by other parties. Semi-honest adversaries are often referred to as honest-but-curious adversaries as well. A malicious adversary (often referred to as active adversary) is the corrupt party who can violate the specified protocol at will. Namely, a malicious adversary has all the capabilities of semi-honest adversary and can take any action he wants during the execution of the protocol in an attempt to learn more. In the work, we are concerned particularly about the malicious adversary model. SFE protocols in the malicious model are well studied [15,29,33,34,36,46], and they can be combined with UC to readily construct PFE protocols in the malicious adversary model [1,38]. We mention that there exists logarithmic factor in circuit size even in the optimal UC constructions, so do the PFE protocols derived in this way. Mohassel, Sadeghian and Smart [42] propose a novel framework (MSS framework) for PFE protocols in the malicious adversary model. Therein the idea of switching network is used to construct extended permutation (EP) in [40] (e.g. CTH in Fig. 3), and other primitives include actively secure SFE protocol, one-time MACs, and linear zero-knowledge proof ($\mathcal{ZK}_{EP}$) protocol of "correct extended permutation" of ElGamal ciphertexts. MSS framework has the advantage of linear complexity in circuit size (there are a host of exponentiations in the protocol $\mathcal{ZK}_{EP}$, however). Although application scenarios of MPC protocols with active security are more realistic, their designing is more difficult than those in the semi-honest adversary model. Fortunately, we do have several general PFE protocol constructions against malicious adversary (besides those based on UC).

$\mathcal{ZK}_{EP}$ PROTOCOL WITH LINEAR COMPLEXITY IN CIRCUIT SIZE. $\mathcal{ZK}_{EP}$, the zero-knowledge proof protocol for "correct extended permutation", was proposed in [42] to prove the correctness of the extended permutation of ElGamal ciphertexts, i.e., m ciphertexts are extended to n ciphertexts ($m \leq n$). With the best knowledge we have learned, it is an open problem to build a zero-knowledge protocol of extended permutation in one single component with the cost of linear complexity. The solution by Mohassel, Sadeghian, and Smart [42] is to decouple $\mathcal{ZK}_{EP}$ protocol into a composition of three well-designed components. The original construction of EP is based on a switching network [32,49], but in this case, to construct a scheme with linear overhead in circuit size, a singly homomorphic encryption (instead of using a switching network) is used to compute each component and re-randomize the ciphertexts. Both the first and the third components are shuffle operation, and to hide the permutation relation, P_1 (prover) chooses uniform random value a_i for each of the n ciphertexts provided by the verifiers for re-randomization, where the computation uses HE property. Linear ZK proofs of shuffle [20], $\mathcal{ZK}_{shuffle}$, is used to prove the correctness of these two components. The second component is a replication phase and it requires a separate ZK protocol ($\mathcal{ZK}_{rep}$) to justify the action of the phase. The input ciphertexts of the first component include m real ciphertexts provided by the verifiers and n - m identical dummy values encrypted with a homomorphic encryption scheme (where the public key is public and the private key is shared secretly among verifiers). The inputs of the second component are the outputs of the first component, and the inputs of the third component are the outputs of the second component. We illustrate $\mathcal{ZK}_{EP}$ in relation to the parameters in the circuit $\mathcal{C}_f$, i.e., $m = g + u - o$ and $n = 2g$, usually $g \gg u$ and $g \gg o$. To facilitate the reader's understanding, we recall the construction of $\mathcal{ZK}_{EP}$ in Fig. 1.

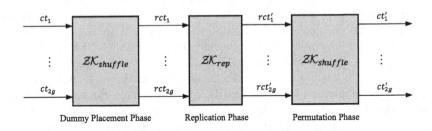

Fig. 1. The $\mathcal{ZK}_{EP}$ protocol construction for [42].

- The first component (with n inputs and n outputs) is a shuffle operation. Its inputs contain n ElGamal ciphertexts fed by the verifiers, including m ciphertexts corresponding to real values and $n - m$ ciphertexts corresponding to the identical dummy values. Assume that some real ciphertext needs to be used k times in the circuit (i.e., it will be copied $k - 1$ times). Then in the outputs of the component, this real ciphertext would be immediately followed by $k - 1$ dummy ciphertexts. The output ciphertexts of the permutation are re-randomized, $rct_i = ct_{\pi(i)} + \text{Enc}_{pk}(a_i)$ (a_i is chosen uniformly at random), in order to hide the permuting relation in the component. This indeed gets a permutation and the component can be regarded as a shuffling of the input ciphertexts. Mohassel, Sadeghian, and Smart argue that the correctness of the first component can be verified by correct shuffle proof $\mathcal{ZK}_{shuffle}$ [20], which takes $18 * n$ exponentiations in proving the correctness.

- The next one is a replication phase of the real ciphertexts, taking the outputs of the first component as its inputs. In the outputs of the component, each ciphertext corresponding to dummy value would be replaced by the last ciphertext (before it) corresponding to the real value directly. Naturally, all ciphertexts are re-randomized. To verify the correctness of the component's action, the protocol $\mathcal{ZK}_{rep}$ is used. More Precisely, $\mathcal{ZK}_{rep}$ is equipped with three zero-knowledge protocols, two of which are $\mathcal{ZK}_{eq}$ [8] and the third one is $\mathcal{ZK}_{no}$ [27]. These two $\mathcal{ZK}_{eq}$ protocols are used to verify whether the i-th output of the component is equal to its i-th input ($2 \leq i \leq n$) or its $(i-1)$-th output. For the first output result, we simply verify whether it is equal to the first input. $\mathcal{ZK}_{no}$ is used to verify that each output ciphertext is not the dummy-valued ciphertext. We write $\mathcal{ZK}_{rep}(\{rct_i, rct_i'\})$ as below:

$$\mathcal{ZK}_{rep}^1 = \mathcal{ZK}_{no}(rct_1') \wedge \mathcal{ZK}_{eq}(rct_1, rct_1') \ : \ i = 1 \tag{1}$$

$$\mathcal{ZK}_{rep}^i = \left(\mathcal{ZK}_{eq}(rct_i, rct_i') \vee \mathcal{ZK}_{eq}(rct_{i-1}', rct_i')\right) \wedge \mathcal{ZK}_{no}(rct_i') : 2 \leq i \leq n \tag{2}$$

$$\mathcal{ZK}_{rep} = \wedge_{i=1,\cdots,n}(\mathcal{ZK}_{rep}^i). \tag{3}$$

If Eq. (3) is correct, the component is justified. From [8] and [27], we have that the component takes at least $36 * n$ exponentiations.

- Last component is also a shuffle operation, taking the outputs of the second component as its inputs. This component needs to permute the copied real ciphertexts to their appropriate positions. To hide the knowledge of the mapping, all the input ciphertexts should be re-randomized. $\mathcal{ZK}_{shuffle}$ is used once more to verify the correctness of the component.

The protocol $\mathcal{ZK}_{shuffle}$ used in [41] was proposed by Furukawa and Sako [20], where the exponentiations required for shuffling n ciphertexts are about $18 \cdot n$ and the proof is of length $2^{11} \cdot n$ bits. In recent years, there are some optimizations on $\mathcal{ZK}_{shuffle}$ so that the resulting proofs require less overhead [3,18–20,23,24,47]. Replacing a better $\mathcal{ZK}_{shuffle}$ directly makes $\mathcal{ZK}_{EP}$ less overhead. Similarly, replacing a better $\mathcal{ZK}_{rep}$ could also make the overhead of $\mathcal{ZK}_{EP}$ less. Rather than such trivial replacement, we attempt to optimize the proof framework of $\mathcal{ZK}_{EP}$. It is surely feasible that above-mentioned replacements can be taken in our proposed framework (if any).

1.2 Motivation and Contributions

This paper focuses on constructing actively secure PFE protocols. Our main observation from current state-of-the-art [42] is that the framework for constructing $\mathcal{ZK}_{EP}$ might exist redundant components, resulting in excessive exponentiations and communication overhead. In particular, $\mathcal{ZK}_{EP}$ consists of a dummy placement phase, a replication phase, and a permutation phase, and each of the phases is of size $2g$. The overhead required by $\mathcal{ZK}_{EP}$ protocol thus seems really outrageous, resulting in a reduction in the practicability of the protocol. If we could remove the redundant components or reduce the size of the components, $\mathcal{ZK}_{EP}$ would be improved in terms of less exponentiations and communication overhead, and the resulting actively secure PFE framework could thereby be more practical. We present in this paper a novel and efficient framework $\mathcal{ZK}_{DS}$ to verify the "correct extended permutation" of the ElGamal ciphertexts. We show that double shuffles suffice in $\mathcal{ZK}_{DS}$: one shuffle is of size $u + g - o$ (u is the number of input wires in the circuit and o the number of output wires, and we have generally $g \gg u, u \approx o$), another is of size $2g$, and no replication phase is required. Besides its linear complexity and succinct double-shuffle structure, $\mathcal{ZK}_{DS}$ protocol reduces the communication overhead by more than 50% (including the ciphertexts and corresponding proofs), compared to $\mathcal{ZK}_{EP}$.

We can feed $\mathcal{ZK}_{DS}$ into actively secure PFE framework [42], making the resulting PFE more compact. This would lead to a PFE with the least overhead in the literature. In addition, $\mathcal{ZK}_{DS}$ (equipped with Yao's garbled circuit [30]) can also find its position in constructing fully secure two-party PFE with constant rounds. This would produce a more substantial solution to the open problem of constructing fully secure constant-round PFE with linear complexity [30], compared to the straight combination of the PFE by Katz and Malka [30] and $\mathcal{ZK}_{EP}$ by Mohassel, Sadeghian, and Smart [42].

THE PROTOCOL $\mathcal{ZK}_{DS}$. In $\mathcal{ZK}_{EP}$, the essential trick is to verify the correctness of extending m ciphertexts into n ciphertexts using the linear ZK protocol. Proving the correct shuffle by a linear zero-knowledge protocol is already well-studied. Note that the input size of the permutation is equal to its output size in the shuffle. It is known [41] that there exist some obstacles in applying the method of Furukawa and Sako [20] to extended permutations. The community does not know so far how to apply directly the zero-knowledge protocol on shuffling in the extended permutation with linear complexity. $\mathcal{ZK}_{EP}$ takes extra $n - m$ dummy values to convert the "extended permutation" problem into a "permutation" problem. This approach increases the input size of the permutation and requires a separate $\mathcal{ZK}_{rep}$ protocol to justify the copy operation and the zero dummy value, which definitely introduces a lot of extra exponentiations. As far as we know, $\mathcal{ZK}_{EP}$ is the only linear protocol that validates extended permutations. If the input size of the permutation could be reduced and unnecessary ZK protocols could be removed, it will save a lot of computation and communication overhead, making the actively secure PFE more practical. Inspired by above-mentioned optimization purpose, we propose the design $\mathcal{ZK}_{DS}$. One interesting trick behind $\mathcal{ZK}_{DS}$ is that we let the prover initialize the protocol by sending a set $\boldsymbol{C} := \{c_1, \cdots, c_m\}$ to the verifier. This tells the verifier that the i-th ciphertext (to be generated by the verifier and sent to the prover) would be used c_i times, $i = 1, \cdots, m$. We argue that this special set $\boldsymbol{C}$ does not leak the private knowledge of the prover. In fact, this set $\boldsymbol{C}$ also appears in the second component of $\mathcal{ZK}_{EP}$ (see Sect. 3 for more details). The protocol $\mathcal{ZK}_{DS}$ consists of just two independent shuffles: one is of size m and another of size n. The prover only needs to prove to the verifier that the two shuffles are correct, i.e., he has made correct extended permutations. Succinct $\mathcal{ZK}_{DS}$ of double-shuffle structure does not require the protocol $\mathcal{ZK}_{rep}$ which is indispensable to $\mathcal{ZK}_{EP}$. Both $\mathcal{ZK}_{DS}$ and $\mathcal{ZK}_{EP}$ call shuffle operation twice. In the context of PFE from $\mathcal{ZK}_{DS}$ and $\mathcal{ZK}_{EP}$: each of the two shuffles in $\mathcal{ZK}_{EP}$ is of size $2g$; in $\mathcal{ZK}_{DS}$ however, one shuffle is of size g and another is of size $2g$, which makes the double-shuffle structure in $\mathcal{ZK}_{DS}$ approximately 25% "smaller than" that in $\mathcal{ZK}_{EP}$. The total gain ($\mathcal{ZK}_{DS}$ vs. $\mathcal{ZK}_{EP}$) in communication overhead is greater than 50%. On the one hand, there are many ZK proofs required in $\mathcal{ZK}_{EP}$ but not required in $\mathcal{ZK}_{DS}$. On the other hand, the consumption of the ciphertext communication in $\mathcal{ZK}_{DS}$ is about a half of that in $\mathcal{ZK}_{EP}$. One might thereby obtain a more compact PFE from $\mathcal{ZK}_{DS}$ (than from $\mathcal{ZK}_{EP}$). Section 3 presents detailed performance comparison.

GENERAL FRAMEWORK OF ACTIVELY SECURE PFE WITH LINEAR COMPLEXITY. Our linear-complexity framework for actively secure PFE is decoupled into two phases, online and offline, aiming at the players jointly computing $f(x_1, \cdots, x_u)$. At the end of the framework, the function owner cannot learn valid knowledge of the private input data, and the data owner cannot learn valid knowledge of the private function. The offline phase is independent of the input data, but depends on the function. The function owner evaluates his private function f into a topological circuit $\mathcal{C}_f$ before the protocol starts. There are $g + u - o$ outgoing wires and $2g$ incoming wires in $\mathcal{C}_f$. These two types of wires make an extended permutation relationship and this is the exact knowledge that we should protect about the circuit (see Sect. 2 for details). The online phase could be instantiated by any well-studied SFE protocol with linear active security [41]. The offline phase is a bit tricky, and it appears not easy to verify the relationship of extended permutation between outgoing wires and incoming wires through some primitive with linear complexity. If both the online and offline phases have linear complexity in the circuit size, we can then naturally get a linear PFE. The protocol $\mathcal{ZK}_{EP}$ proposed by [41] seems to be a feasible solution to the tricky problem, but complicated and not practically efficient due to its relatively high overhead. Our $\mathcal{ZK}_{DS}$ protocol is a better candidate to solving the problem and the resulting PFE from $\mathcal{ZK}_{DS}$ has the advantage of smaller communication overhead and computation overhead. This will practically push actively secure PFE with linear complexity in the circuit size. Note that the correct extended permutation protocol would be invoked two times in this general framework, meaning that more efficient ZK protocols for the correctness of EP are more desirable for practical PFE. We describe more details of the general PFE framework with linear active security in Sect. 4.

2   Notations and Definitions

$[a]$ indicates that the value a is shared by a secret sharing scheme. We use bold (lower-case or capital) letters to denote sets (e.g., $\boldsymbol{ct}$, $\boldsymbol{C}$, $\boldsymbol{C'}$, $\boldsymbol{l}$, etc.) and standard letters (e.g., a_i, ct_i, c_i, ow_i, l_i, etc.) for values or elements of a set. For a set $\boldsymbol{D}$, $|\boldsymbol{D}|$ denotes the size of the set, and we write $\boldsymbol{D} = \{D_1, \cdots, D_{|\boldsymbol{D}|}\}$ or $\boldsymbol{D} = \{D_i\}_{i=1}^{|\boldsymbol{D}|}$. We use π to denote a map from a set to another set, e.g., i is a preimage and j is the corresponding image, then we have $j = \pi(i)$. The abstract diagram (see Fig. 2) could enable the readers to better understand the mapping relationship between incoming wires and outgoing wires. Hereafter we suppose P_1 to be the function owner (and P_1 can also keep input data x_1 in multi-party PFE).

We use a singly homomorphic encryption scheme (Gen, Enc, Dec). We view its plaintext space as a cyclic group $\mathbb{G}$ of prime order p. Let k be a system parameter and $r \leftarrow_R \{0,1\}^k$ denote sampling r uniformly at random from $\{0,1\}^k$. Given n the security parameter of the homomorphic scheme, key generation algorithm outputs a pair of public and private keys $(pk, sk) \leftarrow \mathrm{Gen}(1^n)$. Single homomorphism says that we have $\mathrm{Dec}_{sk}(c_1 + c_2) = \mathrm{Dec}_{sk}(c_1) + \mathrm{Dec}_{sk}(c_2)$, given ciphertexts $c_1 = \mathrm{Enc}_{pk}(m)$ and $c_2 = \mathrm{Enc}_{pk}(r)$, m and $r \in \mathbb{G}$. For this kind of homomorphic property, some public key encryption schemes are available, such as ElGamal [21], BFV [14], and Paillier [45] etc. Therein, ElGamal encryption scheme (whose security is based on the Diffie-Hellman assumption) can provide efficient implementation with no decryption error and has been used in some known FFE [30] and GC designs [28]. In our protocols, we use ElGamal encryption scheme as well. We also mention that in some homomorphic encryption schemes the homomorphic operations would generate noise. For our concern, the noise grows as we perform homomorphic addition on the ciphertext, and decryption failure would occur when the noise exceeds some threshold and the ciphertext turn out to be meaningless. This is at a not-so-bad position however, as noise generally increase slowly in homomorphic additions.

We also need a symmetric cipher (sEnc, sDec) whose key space is a group $\mathbb{G}(k)$ of order $p = p(k)$, and similarly, the plaintext space is the same as used in the public key encryption. In practice, this can be achieved for any desired $\mathbb{G}$ by using AES with key SHA-1(τ) (truncated to 128 bits [30]), $\tau \in \mathbb{G}$. Given a ciphertext $c_3 = \mathrm{sEnc}(sk, m)$ (sk is the secret key in the symmetric cipher), we have $m = \mathrm{sDec}(sk, c_3)$. The symmetric cipher would be used in our protocols

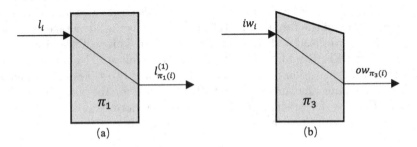

Fig. 2. l maps to $l^{(1)}$ and $\boldsymbol{iw}$ maps to $\boldsymbol{ow}$. Two kinds of mapping functions are used in our protocols: π_1 and π_3. The former is a bijective function and the latter is surjective (not injective).

to create standard Yao's garbled circuit (GC) for each garbled table (GT) and decrypt each GT. It is required [35] for (sEnc, sDec) that it has elusive and efficiently verifiable range. AES-128 is one known symmetric cipher, as used in the linear PFE by Holz, Nissim, etc [28, Sect. 5.1].

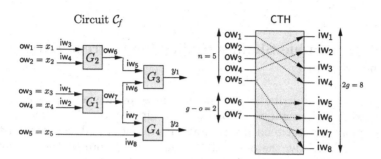

Fig. 3. An example circuit and the corresponding mapping [40]. The circuit topology hidden (CTH) indicates an extended permutation (EP).

In our protocol, the function owner P_1 compiles his private function f into a Boolean or Arithmetic circuit $\mathcal{C}_f$. $\mathcal{C}_f$ has u inputs, g gates, and o outputs (usually $g \gg u$ and $u \approx o$). We write $N := u+g$. The $\mathcal{C}_f$ is like a directed acyclic graph in which the gates have topological order, namely, g gates has been numbered from smallest to largest P_1 according to the topology of $\mathcal{C}_f$, denoted as $\{G_1, \cdots, G_g\}$. If $\mathcal{C}_f$ is an arithmetic circuit, it is composed of additive and multiplicative gates, with the bit value of 0 for additive gates and 1 for multiplicative gates. If $\mathcal{C}_f$ is a Boolean circuit, each of the gayes is only a two fan-in NAND gate and its functionality does not need to be hidden. We divide all g gates in $\mathcal{C}_f$ into output gates and non-output gates according to the destination of the output wires. We suppose that the last o gates in the gate sequence of the circuit are output gates and the first $g - o$ are non-output gates, i.e., $\{G_1, \cdots, G_{g-o}\}$ is non-output gate sequence, and $\{G_{g-o+1}, \cdots, G_g\}$ is o output gate sequence.

In this already topologically ordered Boolean circuit, we collect all the input wires of the circuit $\mathcal{C}_f$ and all the outputs of the non-output gates and define the collection as a set of outgoing wires, denoted as $\boldsymbol{ow}$. We have $|\boldsymbol{ow}| = N - o$. Similarly, we get the set $\boldsymbol{iw}$ of incoming wires from all the input wires of all gates, and $|\boldsymbol{iw}| = 2g$. Obviously, $|\boldsymbol{ow}| \leq |\boldsymbol{iw}|$. Both $\boldsymbol{ow}$ and $\boldsymbol{iw}$ are topologically ordered sets for the circuit $\mathcal{C}_f$ and correspond to the topologically ordered g gates. We suppose w.l.o.g. that $\boldsymbol{ow} = \{ow_1, \cdots, ow_{N-o}\}$ and $\boldsymbol{iw} = \{iw_1, \cdots, iw_{2g}\}$. We provide Fig. 3 for better reader-friendliness. To fully capture the topology of the circuit, we give each of the outgoing wires and incoming wires in the circuit a unique label. Each gate in $\mathcal{C}_f$ is arbitrary fan-out and any outgoing wire ow_i could used multiple times (and at least once), $i \in \{1, \cdots, |\boldsymbol{ow}|\}$. If ow_i is used c_i' times, we also say it has $c_i' - 1$ copies. As P_1 knows all the knowledge of $\mathcal{C}_f$, he can first generate a set $\boldsymbol{C'} = \{c_1', \cdots, c_{|\boldsymbol{ow}|}'\}$, $\sum_{i=1}^{|\boldsymbol{ow}|} c_i' = 2g$ and then perform a random permutation on C' to get the set $C = \{c_1, \cdots, c_{|ow|}\}$. In other words, P_1 chooses a random map π such that $c_i' = c_{\pi(i)}$, $i = 1, \ldots, |ow|$. π is P_1's private knowledge. Data owner (say P_2) compiles his secret data x into binary form, i.e., $x = \{0,1\}^u$. P_1 sends P_2 u, g, o and C. This move does not leak the knowledge of C_f, which is hidden in the extended permutation relationship between ow and iw in the circuit.

3 $\mathcal{ZK}_{DS}$: Double Shuffles Suffice for Correct Extended Permutation

In this section, we describe $\mathcal{ZK}_{DS}$, an efficient zero-knowledge protocol for the "correct extended permutation" of ElGamal ciphertexts. The linear proof in circuit size for correct extended permutation is essential to design linear actively secure PFE. Currently, the only theoretically feasible protocol is $\mathcal{ZK}_{EP}$ [42], but it requires a large number of exponentiations. To make linear actively secure PFE protocols more practical, it is of significance to investigate more efficient protocols for verifying extended permutations.

3.1   Ideation and Observation

For the extended permutation relation of ow and iw in the circuit, Katz and Malka [30], and Mohassel and Sadeghian [40] present linear complexity solutions in the semi-honest adversary model by applying singly homomorphic encryption schemes. Therein, function owner P_1 follows the protocol in an honest-but-curious manner to make a valid extended permutation of the $|ow|$ ciphertexts. In the malicious adversary model however, P_1 may not follow the specification of the protocol when extending the permutation of the $|ow|$ ciphertexts, i.e., he does not perform the exact valid extended permutation. Now we need some validation mechanism on P_1's local work (to make sure that P_1 has done the exact EP). For actively secure SFE protocols, the cut-and-choose method is available for this kind of validation [33,53]. For PFE protocols however, it is not clear yet how to apply this method in checking EP's correctness [42]. The takeaway herein is that the EP is P_1's private knowledge now and cannot be revealed to the verifier even in checking its correctness. As an open problem, more attempts need to be made in applying the cut-and-choose approach to PFE. In the literature, one (and the only one) feasible validation mechanism is the linear complexity $\mathcal{ZK}_{EP}$ protocol proposed by Mohassel, Sadeghian, and Smart [42]. $\mathcal{ZK}_{EP}$ consists of three components (see Fig. 1) that have been well studied (with relatively high computation and communication however). We revisit $\mathcal{ZK}_{EP}$ and propose a more efficient $\mathcal{ZK}_{DS}$ which could facilitate actively secure PFE as well.

In the protocol $\mathcal{ZK}_{EP}$, data owner (verifier) provides $|ow|$ ciphertexts as input. Given these ciphertexts, function owner P_1 (prover) extends them to $|iw|$ ciphertexts. In the first component (i.e., dummy placement phase) of $\mathcal{ZK}_{EP}$, P_1 promotes $|iw| - |ow| \approx g$ dummy-valued ciphertexts as a supplement and thus converts the extended permutation problem into a permutation problem.

This approach obviously increases the size of the input ciphertexts and requires an additional protocol ($\mathcal{ZK}_{rep}$) to ensure that P_1 has performed the correct copy work. The purpose of extending the $|ow|$ ciphertexts to $|iw|$ ciphertexts is to obtain the $2g$ input labels of topologically sorted g gates and maintain the relationship between the plaintexts corresponding to the $|iw|$ ciphertexts and the plaintexts corresponding to the $|ow|$ ciphertexts. To be more succinct, one heuristic motivation is to let P_1 tell the data owners in advance how many times each of the $|ow|$ ciphertexts would be copied, i.e., $C' = \{c'_1, \cdots, c'_{|ow|}\}$. Now there is no need to verify the correctness of the copying phase, i.e., the $\mathcal{ZK}_{rep}$ protocol could be removed. Unfortunately, this might also give away the valid knowledge of C_f. For example, the data owner knows how many times the $|ow|$-th ciphertext has been copied, and further knows where the output of the $(g-o)$-th gate in the topological order goes, i.e., we cannot rule out the possibility of leaking the valid knowledge of C_f. This is mainly due to the fact that the $|ow|$ ciphertexts sent by data owner correspond one by one to the u inputs of the circuit and the g - o outputs of the non-output gates (i.e., ow). However, this gap can be fixed by making the requirement that there exist a random mapping relation between ow and $|ow|$ ciphertexts provided by the data owner. In other words, we require that data owner provides $|ow|$ ciphertexts according to $C = \{c_1, \cdots, c_{|ow|}\}$, and this will remedy the flaw of leaking the knowledge of C_f that occurs in the first try. There is also no need to introduce almost g additional dummy-valued ciphertexts to 1st component of $\mathcal{Z}_{EP}$.

We mention that letting P_1 open the set C and reveal to data owner does not sacrifice the security of $\mathcal{ZK}_{DS}$. A simple rethinking of the $\mathcal{ZK}_{EP}$ protocol may find that it also reveals the set C. In the replication phase (second component) of the $\mathcal{ZK}_{EP}$ protocol, P_1 uses the $\mathcal{ZK}_{rep}$ protocol to prove the correctness of his replication work. $\mathcal{ZK}_{rep}$ contains three zero-knowledge protocols, two of which are $\mathcal{ZK}_{eq}$ [8] and the last one is $\mathcal{ZK}_{no}$ [27]. We have the detailed description in Sect. 1. In this component, the data owner can learn how many times a particular ciphertext among the $g + u - o$ shuffled ciphertexts has been copied. This knowledge does not reveal the topology of the circuit, as the data owner cannot learn the index of the ciphertext corresponding to the input ciphertext of the first component. In addition, the data owner cannot know to which final location the ciphertext is mapped in the next component.

To ease the readers' understanding, we summarize in Table 1 some symbols representing ciphertexts and plaintexts/random values. For the last 6 lines in Table 1, similar to l_i in l, we have $ctp_i^{(1)}$, $l_i^{(1)}$, $ct_i^{(2)}$, l_i', $ctp_i^{(2)}$, and $l_i^{(2)}$ in $ctp^{(1)}$, $l^{(1)}$, $ct^{(2)}$, l', $ctp^{(2)}$, and $l^{(2)}$ resp., and we omit these from the table. Other symbols can thus be defined in the same way and would be used in Sect. 4.

3.2 Constructing $\mathcal{ZK}_{DS}$

Above-mentioned observations would lead to a particular design that differs from $\mathcal{ZK}_{EP}$. In the $\mathcal{ZK}_{EP}$ protocol, P_1 privately computes the function f as C_f from which the mapping relation of the extended permutation is extracted. In

Table 1. Symbols.

Symbols	Annotations
l_i	random value generated by the verifier
l	a set of random values l_i
$ct_i^{(1)}$	the ciphertext of the plaintext l_i
$\boldsymbol{ct}^{(1)}$	the ciphertext set corresponding to the plaintext set l
$\boldsymbol{ctp}^{(1)}$	the ciphertext set obtained from permutation and re-randomization on $\boldsymbol{ct}^{(1)}$
$l^{(1)}$	the plaintext set corresponding to the ciphertext set $\boldsymbol{ctp}^{(1)}$
$\boldsymbol{ct}^{(2)}$	the ciphertext set extended from $\boldsymbol{ct}^{(1)}$
l'	the plaintext set corresponding to the ciphertext set $\boldsymbol{ct}^{(2)}$
$\boldsymbol{ctp}^{(2)}$	the ciphertext set obtained from permutation and re-randomization on $\boldsymbol{ct}^{(2)}$
$l^{(2)}$	the plaintext set corresponding to the ciphertext set $\boldsymbol{ctp}^{(2)}$

our design, what P_1 needs to extract include the mapping relationship between the $|\boldsymbol{ow}|$ ciphertexts sent by the data owner and $\boldsymbol{ow}$, and that between the $|\boldsymbol{iw}|$ ciphertexts (after copying the $|\boldsymbol{ow}|$ ciphertexts) and $\boldsymbol{iw}$, represented by the maps π_1 and π_2, respectively. Both π_1 and π_2 are bijective.

Our design $\mathcal{ZK}_{DS}$ only includes one permutation of size $N-o$ and one permutation of size $2g$. There is no need to perform the $\mathcal{ZK}_{rep}$ protocol or to generate the ciphertexts with about g dummy values. P_1 should re-randomize the ciphertexts he received in the interactive session to hide the knowledge of maps (i.e., π_1 and π_2 below). We give an abstract description in Fig. 4. From Fig. 4, one can see that $\mathcal{ZK}_{DS}$ is decoupled into two phases: the component of randomness-generating & outgoing-wires-determining, and the component of randomness-reusing & incoming-wires-determining. Both components can be proved correct by using $\mathcal{ZK}_{shuffle}$. We use π_1 to denote the permutation mapping in $\mathcal{ZK}_{shuffle_1}$, and π_2 to denote that in $\mathcal{ZK}_{shuffle_2}$. To facilitate the comparison with the $\mathcal{ZK}_{EP}$ protocol, we also apply the scheme for proving a shuffle in [20]. Table 2 lists the zero-knowledge proof protocols for the black-boxes of Fig. 4 used in our $\mathcal{ZK}_{DS}$ protocol. We mention that it is only for instantiation purpose and more efficient schemes (to prove shuffle, if any) are surely applicable to $\mathcal{ZK}_{DS}$ for better performance.

Our aim is to turn the $|\boldsymbol{ow}|$ ciphertexts corresponding to the set of random values $l^{(1)}$ into the $|\boldsymbol{iw}|$ ciphertexts corresponding to the set $l^{(2)}$ by "extended permutation". In both components, these ciphertexts are then re-randomized to hide the knowledge of permutation relation, and the final resulting ciphertexts are later open to the verifier. We use the set $C = \{c_1, \cdots, c_{|\boldsymbol{ow}|}\}$, $\sum_{i=1}^{|\boldsymbol{ow}|} c_i = 2g$.

We take the set C as one of system inputs of P_1, i.e., P_1 sends the set C to the verifier to initialize the interaction. The verifier then generates a set l of random values ($|l| = |\boldsymbol{ow}|$) and a public/private key pair (pk, sk) of ElGamal encryption scheme. The verifier encrypts each entry l_i in l with pk and obtains the set of ciphertexts $\boldsymbol{ct}^{(1)}$, $ct_i^{(1)} = \text{Enc}_{pk}(l_i)$. Our $\mathcal{ZK}_{DS}$ protocol consists of two parts: the first part is the $\mathcal{ZK}_{shuffle_1}$ with $|\boldsymbol{ow}|$ inputs and the second one

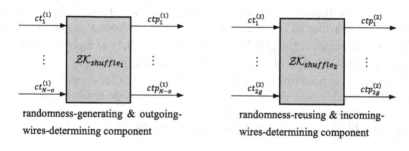

Fig. 4. $\mathcal{ZK}_{DS}$ construction consisting of two $\mathcal{ZK}_{shuffle}$ protocols.

is the $\mathcal{ZK}_{shuffle_2}$ with $|iw|$ inputs. The verifier sends the set of ciphertexts $ct^{(1)}$ and pk to P_1. The set $ct^{(1)}$ is directly used as the input of the first component. Next, we describe the two components in detail.

3.2.1 Randomness-Generating and Outgoing-Wires-Determining

Once the verifier gets the sets $l^{(1)}$ ($|l^{(1)}| = N - o$) and $l^{(2)}$ ($|l^{(2)}| = 2g$) [42], he would easily compute on each of the g gates determined by incoming wires and outgoing wires. If $l^{(1)}$ is generated by the verifier himself (as in [42]), then it seems that a replication phase is necessary. Unlike prior trick, we let $l^{(1)}$ be jointly decided by the verifier and the prover. As the verifier wants P_1 to extend and permute the set $l^{(1)}$ into the set $l^{(2)}$ as well as prevents P_1 from learning $l^{(1)}$, we equip the prover the capability of generating the encryption $ctp_i^{(1)} = \text{Enc}_{pk}(l_i^{(1)})$ even without the exact knowledge $l_i^{(1)}$. Instead of generating the set $l^{(1)}$ directly, the verifier generates a set of $l = \{l_i\}_{i=1}^{N-o}$, and encrypts them (under pk) into a set of ciphertexts $ct^{(1)} = \{ct_i^{(1)}\}_{i=1}^{N-o}$, where $ct_i^{(1)} = \text{Enc}_{pk}(l_i)$. The set l has a shuffle (and re-randomization) relation with the set $l^{(1)}$ (to be determined by P_1). The verifier sends the set $ct^{(1)}$ to P_1. P_1 takes the set of ciphertexts $ct^{(1)}$ as the input to this component, and the size of the input is $|ow|$. The i-th value c_i in the set C says that the i-th ciphertext in the set $ct^{(1)}$ would be used c_i times. We have thereby that there are c_i ciphertexts in the following set $ctp^{(2)}$ corresponding to the same plaintext l_i, but due to the shuffle, the verifier does not know which specific plaintext value in $l^{(1)}$ corresponds to. The probability that the verifier correctly guesses this shuffle relationship is negligible. We denote the permutation function of this component by the function

Table 2. Zero-knowledge protocol used in our $\mathcal{ZK}_{DS}$. Generator g, public key $h = g^{sk}$, $ct_i = (\alpha_i, \beta_i)$ and $ctp_i = (\alpha_i', \beta_i')$.

ZK Protocol	Relation/Language	Ref.
$\mathcal{ZK}_{shuffle}(ct, ctp)$	$\mathcal{R}_{shuffle} = \{(G, g, h, ct, ctp) \mid \exists \pi, \text{ s.t.}$ $\alpha_i' = g^{r_i}\alpha_{\pi(i)} \wedge \beta_i' = h^{r_i}\beta_{\pi(i)} \wedge \pi \text{ is perm.}\}$	[20]

π_1. P_1 knows the topology of the circuit and gets the set $\boldsymbol{ctp}^{(1)}$ by permuting the set $\boldsymbol{ct}^{(1)}$ according to the function π_1. To hide the knowledge of π_1, P_1 also does a re-randomization $\mathrm{Enc}_{pk}(l_i^{(1)}) = \mathrm{Enc}_{pk}(l_{\pi_1^{-1}(i)} + a_i)$ (a_i is chosen uniformly at random). All the steps of permutation and re-randomization are performed locally by P_1, who needs to prove the correctness of his local operations to the verifier. The randomness-generating & outgoing-wires-determining component can be seen as a shuffle of the input ciphertexts, and we use the $\mathcal{ZK}_{shuffle}$ protocol as a black box to justify this component [42].

3.2.2   Randomness-Reusing and Incoming-Wires-Determining

In the previous component, the verifier gets the set of ciphertexts $\boldsymbol{ct}^{(1)}$. In the current component, the ciphertexts in $\boldsymbol{ct}^{(1)}$ generated by P_2 and sent to P_1 in the first component are reused. In particular, P_1 copies $\boldsymbol{ct}^{(1)}$ to produce a new set $\boldsymbol{ct}^{(2)}$ of ciphertexts according to the values in the set $\boldsymbol{C}$. We take as an example the i-th ciphertext $ct_i^{(1)}$ in the set $\boldsymbol{ct}^{(1)}$ which corresponds to the value c_i in $\boldsymbol{C}$. Then in the inputs of this component, the subsequent $c_i - 1$ ciphertexts after this ciphertext are all set as the exact $ct_i^{(1)}$. Since the sum of the values in $\boldsymbol{C}$ is $2g$, we have exactly $2g$ ciphertexts after the copy step. The verifier also knows $\boldsymbol{C}$ and the set $\boldsymbol{ct}^{(1)}$ is generated by himself, thus one may view that the input of the $2g$ ciphertexts in the second component are also provided by the verifier (but without the cost of communication). We use l' to denote the plaintext set corresponding to the ciphertext set $\boldsymbol{ct}^{(2)}$, i.e., $ct_i^{(2)} = \mathrm{Enc}_{pk}(l_i')$, $1 \le i \le 2g$. P_1 knows how many times each ciphertext in $\boldsymbol{ct}^{(1)}$ has been copied separately and knows the topology of the circuit, so he can permute them to get the ciphertext set corresponding to $l^{(2)}$. We denote the permutation map of this component by π_2. Naturally, all permuted ciphertexts are re-randomized: $\mathrm{Enc}_{pk}(l_i^{(2)}) = \mathrm{Enc}_{pk}(l'_{\pi_2^{-1}(i)} + b_i)$, where b_is are chosen uniformly at random. We write the result of the second component by the permutation and re-randomization as $\boldsymbol{ctp}^{(2)} = \{ctp_i^{(2)}\}_{i=1}^{2g}$, where $ctp_i^{(2)} = \mathrm{Enc}_{pk}(l_i^{(2)})$. Again, the permutation and re-randomization of this component is performed locally by P_1, who needs to prove the correctness of his local operations to the verifier. This randomness-reusing & incoming-wires-determining component can be seen as a shuffle of $2g$ input ciphertexts and the correctness of this phase can be checked via the $\mathcal{ZK}_{shuffle}$ protocol.

3.2.3   Performance Improvement

$\mathcal{ZK}_{DS}$ needs only two independent shuffles in the two components of randomness-generating & outgoing-wires-determining and randomness-reusing & incoming-wires-determining. In contrast, $\mathcal{ZK}_{EP}$ requires three components, i.e., the dummy placement phase, the replication phase and the permutation phase, the first and third of which are also shuffle structure. We first compare only the two shuffles in $\mathcal{ZK}_{DS}$ and $\mathcal{ZK}_{EP}$. $\mathcal{ZK}_{DS}$ has "smaller" shuffle than $\mathcal{ZK}_{EP}$. In fact, the sizes of the shuffles in $\mathcal{ZK}_{DS}$ are g and $2g$, respectively. However, each of the sizes is $2g$ in $\mathcal{ZK}_{EP}$. Therefore, $\mathcal{ZK}_{DS}$ saves approximately 25%

of the size over $\mathcal{ZK}_{EP}$ in the double-shuffle structure. In addition, $\mathcal{ZK}_{DS}$ does not use the Replication phase which is indispensable in $\mathcal{ZK}_{EP}$. Table 3 lists the input/output sizes for each component of $\mathcal{ZK}_{EP}$ and $\mathcal{ZK}_{DS}$. For more explicit efficiency comparison with $\mathcal{ZK}_{EP}$, we also use the scheme of [20] here (same as that in [42]).

Consider the computation overhead. For the randomness-generating & outgoing-wires-determining component in $\mathcal{ZK}_{DS}$, the $\mathcal{ZK}_{shuffle_1}$ protocol takes $|ow| * 18$ (i.e., $(N - o) * 18$) exponentiations; for the randomness-reusing & incoming-wires-determining component, the $\mathcal{ZK}_{shuffle_2}$ protocol takes $|iw| * 18$ (i.e., $2g * 18$) exponentiations. Comparatively, each size of the shuffles in $\mathcal{ZK}_{EP}$ is $2g$ and thus a total of $2 * 2g * 18$ exponentiations are required. In addition, the overhead of the Replication phase includes $2g$ re-randomizations and the $\mathcal{ZK}_{rep}$ protocol. The computational overhead of $2g$ re-randomizations consists of $2g$ encryptions of random values and $2g$ homomorphic addition operations. The $\mathcal{ZK}_{rep}$ protocol is described in Eq. 3 and further includes the $\mathcal{ZK}_{no}$ protocol [27] and the $\mathcal{ZK}_{eq}$ protocol [8]. It turns out that at least $2g * 36$ exponentiations are required for Eq. 3. For total computational overhead, $\mathcal{ZK}_{DS}$ saves approximately 64.5% of exponentiations compared to $\mathcal{ZK}_{EP}$. We mention that there are different proposals for $\mathcal{ZK}_{rep}$ with different overheads. There is surely not a surprise that more efficient $\mathcal{ZK}_{shuffle}$ will make $\mathcal{ZK}_{DS}$ even better performance. For example, it is reported that the protocol of [3] is 3.4× faster than the protocol of [20]. To sum up, $\mathcal{ZK}_{DS}$ shows great advantages over $\mathcal{ZK}_{EP}$ in terms of computational overhead.

Consider the communication overhead. $\mathcal{ZK}_{DS}$ gains communication overhead advantages over $\mathcal{ZK}_{EP}$ from three facets. The first saving is the proof communication about the $\mathcal{ZK}_{shuffle}$ protocol of approximate g ciphertexts. The second saving is the proof communication of the $\mathcal{ZK}_{rep}$ protocol. The third saving is approximate $4g$ of ciphertexts communication (only 50% of $\mathcal{ZK}_{EP}$). We emphasize that the communication overhead of the proofs is generally far larger than that of the ciphertexts themselves, e.g., the proof size of the shuffle about g ciphertexts has $2^{11} * g$ bits in [20].

Table 3. The sizes of each component in the $\mathcal{ZK}_{EP}$ and $\mathcal{ZK}_{DS}$ protocols. Usually $g \gg u$ and $u \approx o$.

name	component name	input/output sizes	ZK protocol
$\mathcal{ZK}_{EP}$	Dummy Placement Phase	$2g$	$\mathcal{ZK}_{shuffle}$
	Replication Phase	$2g$	$\mathcal{ZK}_{rep}$
	Permutation Phase	$2g$	$\mathcal{ZK}_{shuffle}$
$\mathcal{ZK}_{DS}$	randomness-generating & outgoing-wires-determining	$g+u-o$	$\mathcal{ZK}_{shuffle}$
	randomness-reusing & incoming-wires-determining	$2g$	$\mathcal{ZK}_{shuffle}$

3.2.4 $\mathcal{ZK}_{DS}$ Protocol Description

The real inputs of the verifier in $\mathcal{ZK}_{DS}$ are the ElGamal ciphertexts corresponding to l of length $|ow|$, and in addition he knows C. The prover first applies one shuffle to the ciphertexts $\{ct_1^{(1)}, \cdots, ct_{|ow|}^{(1)}\}$ and another shuffle to the ciphertexts $\{ct_1^{(2)}, \cdots, ct_{|iw|}^{(2)}\}$, where $ct_i = (\alpha_i, \beta_i)$ (of ElGamal encryption). The prover obtains two sets of re-randomized ciphertexts as $\{ctp_1^{(1)}, \cdots, ctp_{|ow|}^{(1)}\}$ and $\{ctp_1^{(2)}, \cdots, ctp_{|iw|}^{(2)}\}$, where $ctp_i = (\alpha_i', \beta_i')$. The prover needs only two correct shuffle proofs to show the correctness of his local computations. Table 4 shows the full description of the $\mathcal{ZK}_{DS}$ protocol.

We employ the techniques of Cramer et al. [9], to combine honest verifier zero-knowledge (HVZK) proof systems corresponding to each component, at no extra cost, into HVZK proof systems of the same class [41].

Theorem 1. *The protocol in Table 4 is HVZK proof of the extended permutation.*

Proof. Below is a description of the proof. We describe our $\mathcal{ZK}_{DS}$ protocol as an HVZK proof of the extended permutation if our construction can achieve the extended permutation effect. In our framework, the verifier is given the C. The goal of the first component of our construction is to let P_1 helps the verifier determine the labels of outgoing wires. This component really acts the permutation and re-randomization, and it corresponds to the permutation map π_1. It needs to ensure that all the input $|ow|$ ciphertexts come from the verifier and no other new elements are introduced. $\mathcal{ZK}_{shuffle_1}$ guarantees the correctness of the first component. $\mathcal{ZK}_{shuffle}$ has two features: one is that the inputs are provided by the verifier, another is that the inputs and the outputs are of the same size. The goal of the second component of our construction is to determine the labels of the incoming wires. This component also performs the permutation and re-randomizataion, and it corresponds to the permutation map π_2. The inputs to this component can be viewed as provided by the verifier who also knows C. $\mathcal{ZK}_{shuffle_2}$ is used to check the correctness of this component. The outputs of the first component $ctp^{(1)}$ represent the knowledge about ow and the outputs of the second component $ctp^{(2)}$ represent the knowledge about iw. The verifier receives $ctp^{(1)}$ and $ctp^{(2)}$ and can decrypt them to recover their plaintexts ($l^{(1)}$ and $l^{(2)}$). The ow to iw conversion is the mapping knowledge of the extended permutation, i.e., $l^{(1)}$ to $l^{(2)}$ conversion is the extended permutation relationship. Due to the property of homomorphic encryption, P_1 does not see $l^{(1)}$ and $l^{(2)}$. Due to two different permutations and re-randomization, the verifier does not know the mapping relationship between the set $l^{(1)}$ and the set $l^{(2)}$. To summarize, our solution achieves the EP effect. Once both the first component and the second component pass the verification, one can believe that the prover performs a valid EP, and also a valid circuit topology. The proofs of above two components make up the proof of $\mathcal{ZK}_{DS}$ protocol. Finally we employ the techniques of Cramer et al. [9], to combine HVZK proof systems corresponding to each component, at no extra cost, into HVZK proof systems of the same class. Note that we make a black-box call to the underlying ZK proof system.

Table 4. The protocol for zero-knowledge proof of $\mathcal{ZK}_{DS}$

Protocol $\mathcal{ZK}_{DS}$

Verifier's Input: Ciphertexts $ct^{(1)} = \{ct_1^{(1)}, \cdots, ct_{|ow|}^{(1)}\}$.

P_1's **Input:** The permutation maps π_1, π_2 and set C (random permutation of C').

P_1 sends the set C and $u + g - o$ to **Verifier.**

Verifier sends the ciphertext set $ct^{(1)} = \{ct_1^{(1)}, \cdots, ct_{|ow|}^{(1)}\}$ and pk to P_1.

P_1 **evaluates the components.**

- P_1 finds the corresponding permutation π_1 for randomness-generating & outgoing-wires-determining component and π_2 for randomness-reusing & incoming-wires-determining component, respectively.
- P_1 produces ciphertexts $ct^{(2)} = \{ct_1^{(2)}, \cdots, ct_{|iw|}^{(2)}\}$ from ciphertexts $ct^{(1)} = \{ct_1^{(1)}, \cdots, ct_{|ow|}^{(1)}\}$ according to C.
- P_1 applies the randomness-generating & outgoing-wires-determining component to $\{ct_1^{(1)}, \cdots, ct_{|ow|}^{(1)}\}$, and finds $ctp^{(1)} = \{ctp_1^{(1)}, \cdots, ctp_{|ow|}^{(1)}\}$.
- P_1 applies the randomness-reusing & incoming-wires-determining component to $\{ct_1^{(2)}, \cdots, ct_{|iw|}^{(2)}\}$, and finds $ctp^{(2)} = \{ctp_1^{(2)}, \cdots, ctp_{|iw|}^{(2)}\}$.

P_1 **computes the ZK proofs and sends out the outputs of two components and the proofs.**

- Player P_1 uses the $\mathcal{ZK}_{shuffle_1}(ct^{(1)}, ctp^{(1)})$ and $\mathcal{ZK}_{shuffle_2}(ct^{(2)}, ctp^{(2)})$ protocols to produce proof of correctness for his evaluation of randomness-generating & outgoing-wires-determining component and randomness-reusing & incoming-wires-determining component.
- Player P_1 sends $\{ctp_1^{(1)}, \cdots, ctp_{|ow|}^{(1)}\}$, $\{ctp_1^{(2)}, \cdots, ctp_{|iw|}^{(2)}\}$ and all proofs to verifier.

Verifier verifies P_1 **operations.**

- Verifier verifies P_1's operations by checking the the proofs sent by P_1.

4 General Linear-Complexity PFE Framework with Active Security

This section describes a general actively secure PFE framework with linear complexity in circuit size. Our $\mathcal{ZK}_{DS}$ protocol can be used in PFE framework with active security [41]. We suppose u parties whose joint task is to compute $f(x_1, \cdots, x_u)$. In many PFE application scenarios, the function owner is not the recipient of the final computed result. In the malicious model, whether PFE protocol is robust or aborted is related to the underlying SFE protocol [5,10,11,43].

4.1 Description of the General Actively Secure PFE Framework

Our framework is not based on the universal circuit, but consists of an offline phase and an online phase. The offline phase is independent of data owners' private data, but depends on function owner's private function. This framework can turn any actively secure SFE protocol (with the following features) into an actively secure PFE protocol. The features of the underlying SFE protocol include: its construction is based on secret sharing, it is actively secure (either robust or with aborts), and it has the abilities of implementing reactive functionalities [13], of opening various shares securely, and of efficiently generating random values for sharing. Some candidate SFE protocols include BDOZ [5], SPDZ [11], Tiny-OT [43] or VIFF [10]. We declare that we do not specify which specific SFE protocol to use, as long as the above conditions are met, it can be turned into an actively secure PFE protocol through our framework.

In our protocol, P_1 is the function owner who privately evaluates the function f as a topological circuit $\mathcal{C}_f$. Each data owner provides his private data as input. The online phase in our framework is linear in circuit size and it can be implemented by the actively secure SFE protocol that satisfies the conditions. If the offline phase is also linear in circuit size, then we obtain a linear-complexity, actively secure PFE. The tricky problem herein is how to extend and permute two sets of random values of length $|ow|$ ($[\boldsymbol{l}^{(1)}]$ and $[\boldsymbol{t}^{(1)}]$) into two sets of random values of length $|iw|$ ($[\boldsymbol{l}^{(2)}]$ and $[\boldsymbol{t}^{(2)}]$) using a linear method in the offline phase. $[\boldsymbol{l}^{(1)}]$ and $[\boldsymbol{t}^{(1)}]$ are two sets of shared random values generated by the data owners through the underlying SFE, where those secret shares cannot be learned by P_1. The data owners then jointly encrypt the two sets of shared values using a singly homomorphic encryption, and P_1 transforms the resulting ciphertext sets ($\boldsymbol{ctp}^{(1)}$ and $\boldsymbol{ctp}'^{(1)}$) into two sets of ciphertext ($\boldsymbol{ctp}^{(2)}$ and $\boldsymbol{ctp}'^{(2)}$) by applying extended permutation and re-randomization. The data owners jointly decrypt $\boldsymbol{ctp}^{(2)}$ and $\boldsymbol{ctp}'^{(2)}$ to obtain shares of the resulting plaintexts.

In our scheme, instead of generating $[\boldsymbol{l}^{(1)}]$ and $[\boldsymbol{t}^{(1)}]$ directly, the data owners generate two sets of shared random values $[\boldsymbol{l}]$ and $[\boldsymbol{t}]$ of length $|ow|$ through the underlying SFE protocol. P_1 helps data owners to evaluate $[\boldsymbol{l}]$ and $[\boldsymbol{t}]$ into $[\boldsymbol{l}^{(1)}]$ and $[\boldsymbol{t}^{(1)}]$, respectively. P_1 knows the topology of $\mathcal{C}_f$ and can apply the extended permutation to turn $[\boldsymbol{l}^{(1)}]$ and $[\boldsymbol{t}^{(1)}]$ into $[\boldsymbol{l}^{(2)}]$ and $[\boldsymbol{t}^{(2)}]$, respectively. In order to obtain active security of the offline phase, the following three calculation steps are required to be actively secure.

1. Two sets of random values $[\boldsymbol{l}]$ and $[\boldsymbol{t}]$ are shared among data owners, and they need to be encrypted jointly by the parties involved through the underlying SFE protocol to obtain the ciphertext sets $\boldsymbol{ct}^{(1)}$ and $\boldsymbol{ct}'^{(1)}$, i.e., $ct_i^{(1)} = \mathrm{Enc}_{pk}(l_i)$ and $ct_i'^{(1)} = \mathrm{Enc}_{pk}(t_i)$. The encryption scheme herein needs to be singly homomorphic (e.g., ElGamal encryption), where the secret key is secretly shared among the parties. The resulting ciphertexts are sent to P_1.

2. P_1 applies the $\mathcal{ZK}_{DS}$ protocol to convert the ciphertexts $\boldsymbol{ct}^{(1)}$ (resp., $\boldsymbol{ct}'^{(1)}$) into $\boldsymbol{ctp}^{(1)}$ (resp., $\boldsymbol{ctp}'^{(1)}$) and $\boldsymbol{ctp}^{(2)}$ (resp., $\boldsymbol{ctp}'^{(2)}$), respectively. P_1 sends them to the data owners where $ctp_i^{(1)} = \mathrm{Enc}_{pk}(l_i^{(1)})$, $ctp_i^{(2)} = \mathrm{Enc}_{pk}(l_i^{(2)})$, $ctp_i'^{(1)} = \mathrm{Enc}_{pk}(t_i^{(1)})$ and $ctp_i'^{(2)} = \mathrm{Enc}_{pk}(t_i^{(2)})$. The $\mathcal{ZK}_{DS}$ protocol proves that P_1's local work is correct.

3. Data owners jointly decrypt the two sets of ciphertexts $\boldsymbol{ctp}^{(1)}$ (resp., $\boldsymbol{ctp}'^{(1)}$) and $\boldsymbol{ctp}^{(2)}$ (resp., $\boldsymbol{ctp}'^{(2)}$) by the underlying SFE protocol and get the shares of the recovered plaintexts $[\boldsymbol{l}^{(1)}]$ (resp., $[\boldsymbol{t}^{(1)}]$) and $[\boldsymbol{l}^{(2)}]$ (resp., $[\boldsymbol{t}^{(2)}]$).

In our construction, we use ElGamal encryption as the singly homomorphic encryption to generate public key and shared secret key through the underlying SFE protocol [41, Fig. 11]. We assume secret key is in the form of shared bits, i.e., $[sk] = \sum [sk_i] * 2^i$. In the first step, all parties jointly encrypt some plaintext γ

(each one has a share of γ in $[\gamma]$) and then output an ElGamal ciphertext (α_i, β_i). The two sets of shared random values are jointly encrypted as $\boldsymbol{ct}^{(1)}$ and $\boldsymbol{ct}'^{(1)}$, which are used as inputs for the two extended permutations, respectively. In the second step, this tricky problem can be solved using twice our $\mathcal{ZK}_{DS}$ protocol. At the end of the second step, the data owners have the ciphertexts $\boldsymbol{ctp}^{(1)}$ (resp., $\boldsymbol{ctp}'^{(1)}$) and $\boldsymbol{ctp}^{(2)}$ (resp., $\boldsymbol{ctp}'^{(2)}$). In the third step, the data owners jointly decrypt four sets of ciphertexts to obtain the shares of the plaintexts. With all these three steps, one can readily combine them into an actively secure PFE.

4.2 The Offline Phase

Next, we describe the offline phase of the actively secure PFE framework. The function owner evaluates the private function f as a topological circuit $\mathcal{C}_f$, which is like a directed acyclic graph with g gates, u inputs and o outputs. These g gates are only two fan-in and could be any fan-out. For gates with fan-out greater than 1, we count each of their output wires as a different wire. This differs from the gates in the universal circuit, where all gates are with fan-out smaller than or equal to two. Suppose we have an arithmetic circuit and g gates in $\mathcal{C}_f$ are additive or multiplicative gates. We use bit 0 to represent that a gate is additive gate, i.e., $G_i = 0$, and 1 to represent a multiplicative gate, i.e., $G_i = 1$. P_1 secretly shares the bit string of the g gates with the data owners. P_1 also broadcasts $\boldsymbol{C}$.

Each data owner has his private input data, say $x_i \in \mathbf{F}_{p^k}$. All data owners need to jointly prepare two pairs of random value sets $([\boldsymbol{l}],[\boldsymbol{r}])$ and $([\boldsymbol{t}],[\boldsymbol{s}])$ through the underlying SFE protocol, $|\boldsymbol{l}| = |\boldsymbol{t}| = |\boldsymbol{ow}|$ and $|\boldsymbol{r}| = |\boldsymbol{s}| = |\boldsymbol{iw}|$. The two sets of shared random values $[\boldsymbol{l}]$ and $[\boldsymbol{t}]$ are jointly encrypted into $\boldsymbol{ct}^{(1)}$ and $\boldsymbol{ct}'^{(1)}$. The data owners send the public key pk, $\boldsymbol{ct}^{(1)}$ and $\boldsymbol{ct}'^{(1)}$ to P_1. Through the $\mathcal{ZK}_{DS}$ protocol, the two sets of ciphertexts are permuted and re-randomized by P_1 into $\boldsymbol{ctp}^{(1)}$ and $\boldsymbol{ctp}'^{(1)}$ ($|\boldsymbol{ctp}^{(1)}| = |\boldsymbol{ctp}'^{(1)}| = |\boldsymbol{ow}|$), and $\boldsymbol{ctp}^{(2)}$ and $\boldsymbol{ctp}'^{(2)}$ ($|\boldsymbol{ctp}^{(2)}| = |\boldsymbol{ctp}'^{(2)}| = |\boldsymbol{iw}|$), respectively. We take $[\boldsymbol{l}]$ as an example, which corresponds to the ciphertext set $\boldsymbol{ct}^{(1)}$ sent to P_1 by the data owners. P_1 applies the first permutation π_1 and re-randomization and gets $ctp_i^{(1)} = \text{Enc}_{pk}(l_i^{(1)}) = \text{Enc}_{pk}(l_{\pi_1(i)} + a_i)$, with a_i being a random value chosen uniformly by P_1. P_1 copies the ciphertexts $\boldsymbol{ct}^{(1)}$ according to $\boldsymbol{C}$ and obtains a set of ciphertexts $\boldsymbol{ct}^{(2)}$ ($|\boldsymbol{ct}^{(2)}| = |\boldsymbol{iw}|$). Then P_1 applies the second permutation π_2 and re-randomization and gets $ctp_i^{(2)} = \text{Enc}_{pk}(l_i^{(2)}) = \text{Enc}_{pk}(l'_{\pi_2(i)} + b_i)$, with b_i being a random value chosen uniformly by P_1. P_1 proves the correctness of his local work with the $\mathcal{ZK}_{DS}$ protocol. The transformation of the set $\boldsymbol{t}$ is the same as that of $\boldsymbol{l}$. The data owners jointly decrypt $\boldsymbol{ctp}^{(1)}$ and $\boldsymbol{ctp}^{(2)}$ to obtain $[\boldsymbol{l}^{(1)}]$ and $[\boldsymbol{l}^{(2)}]$, and decrypt $\boldsymbol{ctp}'^{(1)}$ and $\boldsymbol{ctp}'^{(2)}$ to obtain $[\boldsymbol{t}^{(1)}]$ and $[\boldsymbol{t}^{(2)}]$.

Each of the above-mentioned sets with $|\boldsymbol{iw}|$ entries is fresh for the inputs to the g gates. Each of the sets with $|\boldsymbol{ow}|$ entries is fresh for the outputs of the $g - o$ non-output gates and the u inputs of the circuit. The data owners have the shares of the random value r_i and the shares of $l_i^{(2)}$, respectively, and then compute $[p_i] = [r_i - l_i^{(2)}]$ through the underlying SFE protocol. The data owners generate a global MAC key K through the underlying SFE protocol, which is shared among the parties and no one can forge the MACs. Also the data owners have the shares of the random value s_i and the shares of $t_i^{(2)}$, respectively, and then compute $[q_i] = [s_i - t_i^{(2)}] + p_i * [K]$ through the underlying SFE protocol. The data owners broadcast the sets $\boldsymbol{p}$ and $\boldsymbol{q}$ to P_1. We give the protocols for specific offline phases in Table 5. The set $\boldsymbol{l}^{(1)}$ is used for one-time pad (OTP) encryption of the data in the online phase. The set $\boldsymbol{t}^{(1)}$ is used for MAC verification of the data after OTP encryption in the online phase. These MACs will be used to check if P_1 is working correctly locally during the online phase below.

4.3 The Online Phase

Next, we describe the online phase of the actively secure PFE framework. Each data owner has private input data (say x_j of P_j, $1 \leq j \leq u$), and needs to share his data secretly with other data owners (denoted as $[x_j]$). For example, P_j shares his private data x_j with other data owners through Shamir's secret sharing scheme. We do not emphasize here the exact threshold and this should be considered according to the actual application scenario.

There are $|\boldsymbol{ow}|$ outgoing wires and $|\boldsymbol{iw}|$ incoming wires ($|\boldsymbol{ow}| \leq |\boldsymbol{iw}|$). The outgoing wires would be extended and permuted to obtain the incoming wires. In other words, one certain outgoing wire might have several copies in the incoming wires and thus we get an extended permutation from the outgoing wires to the incoming wires. To facilitate the representation, we consider its "reverse" relationship from the incoming wires to the outgoing wires (as shown in Fig. 2), which is really a surjection map (denoted as π_3).

Now each data owner owns a share in $[x_j]$. All data owners need to do preparatory computations on the data in the input circuit. They do OTP encryption for x_j with $\boldsymbol{l}^{(1)}$ generated in the offline phase, denote as $[u_j] = [x_j] + [l_j^{(1)}]$, and additionally compute $[v_j] = [t_j^{(1)}] + ([x_j] + [l_j^{(1)}]) * [K]$, where j is the outgoing wire's index corresponding to that input wire of the circuit, and both $\boldsymbol{u}$ and $\boldsymbol{v}$ are recovered via the underlying SFE protocol. At the beginning of the online phase, the data owners send $\boldsymbol{u}$ and $\boldsymbol{v}$ to P_1. For ease of explanation, we set $y_k = x_{\pi_3(k)}$ for $k \in \{1, \cdots, |\boldsymbol{iw}|\}$, i.e., if a wire has input $[x_j]$ as outgoing wire then it has the same value $[y_k]$ as incoming wire where $j = \pi_3(k)$. P_1 has all the knowledge of circuits and re-randomization, and he can compute $\boldsymbol{u}$ and $\boldsymbol{v}$ as

$$u_k' = u_{\pi_3(k)} = [y_k] + [l_k^{(2)}], \text{ and } v_k' = v_{\pi_3(k)} = [t_k^{(2)}] + (y_k + l_k^{(2)}) * [K], \quad (4)$$

P_1 knows $\boldsymbol{p}$ and $\boldsymbol{q}$ generated in the offline phase, and next P_1 computes

$$d_k = u_k' + p_k = y_k + r_k \text{ and } m_k = v_k' + q_k = s_k + (y_k + r_k) * K, \quad (5)$$

respectively, and broadcasts $\boldsymbol{d}$ and $\boldsymbol{m}$ to all data owners. Data owners calculate $[n_k] = [s_k] + (y_k + r_k) * [K]$ via the underlying SFE protocol and check whether n_k is equal to m_k. If $n_k \neq m_k$, it means that P_1 has cheated during his local computation. At this point, the other parties decide whether to abort the protocol based on the properties of the underlying SFE protocol, or return P_1's input to

Table 5. Linear implementation of the Offline Phase by $\mathcal{ZK}_{DS}$.

Linear Implementation of The Offline Phase from $\mathcal{ZK}_{DS}$ Protocol

This protocol invokes the underlying SFE protocol, so we only describe the operations related to the private function.

Input Function:

P_1 **shares his circuit/function.**

- P_1 secretly shares G_i with the other players, $i \in \{1, \cdots, g\}$.
- Players evaluate and open $[G_i] \cdot (1 - [G_i])$ for $i \in \{1, \cdots, g\}$. If any of them is not 0, it means that P_1 has not entered a valid function and the players have to abort the protocol.

Players generate randomness for inputs and outputs of two shuffles.

- Data owners jointly generate the secretly shared random values $[l] = \{[l_1], \cdots, [l_{|ow|}]\}$ and $[r] = \{[r_1], \cdots, [r_{|iw|}]\}$ through the underlying SFE protocol. l is for the input of the randomness-generating & outgoing-wires-determining component, and the l' transformed according to C is for the input of the randomness-reusing & incoming-wires-determining component. r is prepared for the output of the randomness-reusing & incoming-wires-determining component.
- Data owners jointly generate the secret shared the MAC key K, shared random values $[t] = \{[t_1], \cdots, [t_{|ow|}]\}$ and $[s] = \{[s_1], \cdots, [s_{|iw|}]\}$ by the underlying SFE protocol. t is for the input of the randomness-generating & outgoing-wires-determining component, and t' transformed according to C is for the input of the randomness-reusing & incoming-wires-determining component. s is prepared for the output of the randomness-reusing & incoming-wires-determining component.

P_1 **applies** (l, t) **and** (l', t') **to the two shuffles.**

- Data owners call joint key generate algorithm. This generates public key for ElGamal encryption and shared secret key, i.e., $[sk] = \sum_{i=1}^{n}[sk_i] * 2^i$, where n is the total number of the data owners.
- Data owners call joint encryption algorithm. From the plaintext shares $\{[l_1], \cdots, [l_{|ow|}]\}$ and $\{[t_1], \cdots, [t_{|ow|}]\}$, they get ciphertexts $\{ct_1^{(1)}, \cdots, ct_{|ow|}^{(1)}\}$ and $\{ct_1'^{(1)}, \cdots, ct_{|ow|}'^{(1)}\}$ which are then sent to P_1.
- P_1 applies π_1 and re-randomization to $\{ct_1^{(1)}, \cdots, ct_{|ow|}^{(1)}\}$ to obtain $\{ctp_1^{(1)}, \cdots, ctp_{|ow|}^{(1)}\}$. Transforms $\{ct_1^{(1)}, \cdots, ct_{|ow|}^{(1)}\}$ into $\{ct_1^{(2)}, \cdots, ct_{|iw|}^{(2)}\}$ according to C. Applies π_2 and re-randomization to $\{ct_1^{(2)}, \cdots, ct_{|iw|}^{(2)}\}$ and obtains $\{ctp_1^{(2)}, \cdots, ctp_{|iw|}^{(2)}\}$. Similarly, from $\{ct_1'^{(1)}, \cdots, ct_{|ow|}'^{(1)}\}$, gets $\{ctp_1'^{(1)}, \cdots, ctp_{|ow|}'^{(1)}\}$ and $\{ctp_1'^{(2)}, \cdots, ctp_{|iw|}'^{(2)}\}$.
- P_1 applies the $\mathcal{ZK}_{DS}$ protocol to prove that he already uses two valid "extended permutations".
- Data owners call joint decryption algorithm. From $\{ctp_1^{(1)}, \cdots, ctp_{|ow|}^{(1)}\}$ and $\{ctp_1^{(2)}, \cdots, ctp_{|iw|}^{(2)}\}$, they obtain $\{[l_1^{(1)}], \cdots, [l_{|ow|}^{(1)}]\}$ and $\{[l_1^{(2)}], \cdots, [l_{|iw|}^{(2)}]\}$. Similarly, from $\{ctp_1'^{(1)}, \cdots, ctp_{|ow|}'^{(1)}\}$ and $\{ctp_1'^{(2)}, \cdots, ctp_{|iw|}'^{(2)}\}$, they get the shares $\{[t_1^{(1)}], \cdots, [t_{|ow|}^{(1)}]\}$ and $\{[t_1^{(2)}], \cdots, [t_{|iw|}^{(2)}]\}$.

Data owners calculate and broadcast p **and** q.

- Data owners calculate $[p_k] = [r_k] - [l_k^{(2)}]$ and $[q_k] = [s_k] - [t_k^{(2)}] + p_k * [K]$ by the underlying SFE protocol, $k \in \{1, \cdots, |iw|\}$.

---

and X. Li

continue the protocol without P_1's involvement. If $n_k = m_k$, P_1 is uncorrupted, then the data owner computes $[y_k] = d_k - [r_k]$ by the underlying SFE protocol. For g gates that are topologically ordered, the data owners can then compute

$$[z_i] = (1 - [G_i]) * ([y_{2i-1}] + [y_{2i}]) + [G_i] * [y_{2i-1}] * [y_{2i}], i \in \{1, \cdots, g\} \qquad (6)$$

Each data owner now has a share of $[z_i]$. The corresponding outgoing wire's index of $[z_i]$ is $w = u + i$. Data owners then continue to compute $[u_w]$ and $[v_w]$ and repeat the operations until all g gates have been computed. The outputs of the last o gates constitute the computation result of the function on the inputs.

Informally speaking, the function owner P_1 uses the difference set generated in the offline phase to convert the encrypted output of one gate to the encrypted input of the upcoming gate, while maintaining a one-time MAC of all values. Once all g gates have been computed, it completes the entire computation of the function. This passing phase of P_1 neither learns the private inputs of data owners nor reveals the knowledge of the circuit topology. Data owners can go through the MACs to check whether the local operation of P_1 is correct without sacrificing the topology of the circuit. If some MAC authentication fails, then there exist incorrectness in P_1's local computations. The above operations between multiple parties are performed securely via the underlying SFE protocol.

4.4 Proof of Offline Protocol

We construct a simulator $\mathcal{S}_{offline}$ such that a poly-time environment $\mathcal{Z}$ cannot distinguish between a real protocol system and an ideal protocol system. We assume here a static, active corrupted adversary. $\mathcal{S}_{offline}$ runs a copy of the protocol given in Fig. 5, which relays messages between the parties and $\mathcal{Z}$ so that $\mathcal{Z}$ will see the same interface as when the actual protocol is interacted with.

To see that the simulated process is indistinguishable from the real process, we will show that the view of the environment in the ideal process is statistically indistinguishable from the view in the real process. This view includes the corrupt player's view of the protocol execution as well as the honest player's inputs and outputs. Let's denote the set of corrupted parties by $\mathcal{A} \subset \{P_1, \cdots, P_u\}$.

The view of adversaries $\mathcal{A} - \{P_1\}$, includes the share of G_i, the share of random values for inputs and outputs of EP, $\{l_i\}_{i=1}^{|ow|}$, $\{r_i\}_{i=1}^{|iw|}$, $\{t_i\}_{i=1}^{|ow|}$, $\{s_i\}_{i=1}^{|iw|}$, $\{l_i^{(1)}\}_{i=1}^{|ow|}$, $\{l_i^{(2)}\}_{i=1}^{|iw|}$, $\{t_i^{(1)}\}_{i=1}^{|ow|}$, $\{t_i^{(2)}\}_{i=1}^{|iw|}$, $\{ct_i^{(1)}\}_{i=1}^{|ow|}$, $\{ctp_i^{(1)}\}_{i=1}^{|ow|}$, $\{ct_i^{(2)}\}_{i=1}^{|iw|}$, $\{ctp_i^{(2)}\}_{i=1}^{|iw|}$, $\{ct_i^{'(1)}\}_{i=1}^{|ow|}$, $\{ctp_i^{'(1)}\}_{i=1}^{|ow|}$, $\{ct_i^{'(2)}\}_{i=1}^{|iw|}$, $\{ctp_i^{'(2)}\}_{i=1}^{|iw|}$, and finally, $\{p_i\}_{i=1}^{|iw|}$, $\{q_i\}_{i=1}^{|iw|}$. The shared values all look random and therefore are indistinguishable between ideal and real execution. $\{ct_i^{(1)}\}_{i=1}^{|ow|}$, $\{ct_i^{(2)}\}_{i=1}^{|iw|}$, $\{ct_i^{'(1)}\}_{i=1}^{|ow|}$ and $\{ct_i^{'(2)}\}_{i=1}^{|iw|}$ are ElGamal encryptions under shared secret key, and therefore are indistinguishable between ideal and real execution. $\{ctp_i^{(1)}\}_{i=1}^{|ow|}$, $\{ctp_i^{(2)}\}_{i=1}^{|iw|}$, $\{ctp_i^{'(1)}\}_{i=1}^{|ow|}$ and $\{ctp_i^{'(2)}\}_{i=1}^{|iw|}$ are valid re-randomization of ElGamal ciphertexts if protocol does not abort due to $\mathcal{ZK}_{DS}$ verication. $\{l_i^{(1)}\}_{i=1}^{|ow|}$, $\{l_i^{(2)}\}_{i=1}^{|iw|}$, $\{t_i^{(1)}\}_{i=1}^{|ow|}$ and $\{t_i^{(2)}\}_{i=1}^{|iw|}$ are obtained by permutation and re-randomization. The final result

$\{p_i\}_{i=1}^{|iw|}$ and $\{q_i\}_{i=1}^{|iw|}$ are computed as a result of two shared random values, and therefore has a uniform distribution in both ideal and real execution.

The adversary P_1 has the same view as the other malicious players, except for the uniform random value set $\{a_i\}_{i=1}^{|ow|}$ and $\{b_i\}_{i=1}^{|iw|}$ that he alone has. The shared values all have uniform distribution. In the ideal functionality we also have a uniform distribution, and as a result ideal and real executions are indistinguishable to the environment $\mathcal{Z}$.

4.5 Proof of Online Protocol

We construct a simulator $\mathcal{S}_{online}$ such that a poly-time environment $\mathcal{Z}$ cannot distinguish between a real protocol system and an ideal protocol system. We assume here a static, active corrupted adversary. $\mathcal{S}_{online}$ runs a copy of the protocol given in Sect. 4.3, which relays messages between the parties and $\mathcal{Z}$ so that $\mathcal{Z}$ will see the same interface as when the actual protocol is interacted with.

To see that the simulated and real processes cannot be distinguished, we will show that the view of the environment in the ideal process is statistically indistinguishable from the view in the real process. This view consists of the corrupt players' view of the protocol execution as well as the inputs and outputs of honest players. The view of adversary includes $\{u_i\}_{i=1}^{|ow|}$, $\{v_i\}_{i=1}^{|ow|}$, $\{d_i\}_{i=1}^{|iw|}$, $\{m_i\}_{i=1}^{|iw|}$, $\{n_i\}_{i=1}^{|iw|}$ and $\{z_i\}_{i=1}^{g}$. The shared values all look random and therefore are indistinguishable between ideal and real execution.

We next show that $\{d_i\}_{i=1}^{|iw|}$ and $\{m_i\}_{i=1}^{|iw|}$ have uniform distribution. Observe that u_i is blinded using the random value of input wires which is shared and therefore acts as a one-time pad, and as P_1 prepares the two inputs, it maintains the uniform distribution. Furthermore, p_i also has uniform distribution from the security offline protocol. The value s_i acts as a one-time pad which is shared between the players and therefore, m_i has a uniform distribution. In the ideal functionality we also have a uniform distribution, and as a result ideal and real are indistinguishable to the environment $\mathcal{Z}$. For a malicious P_1, the distributions are the same, but we have to make sure that he has performed the input preparation correctly. In the next phase players check the P_1's computation. Player P_1 cheating means he has not calculated d_i and m_i correctly. For him to be successful, he has to somehow adjust n_i and m_i to be equal. He only has a option to adjust d_i and his share of s_i to make the equality hold. Since he does not know K, the value $d_i \cdot K$ has a uniform distribution, and therefore the probability of him modifying s_i to make the equality hold is equivalent to guessing K and hence exponentially small in length of K. It follows that with overwhelming probability after the check the P_1's computation has been done correctly. If any check fails the simulator aborts and stop.

The final result z_i is secret shared and as result has a uniform distribution. For the output wires, players open their share, and z_i is learnt by all parties. In order to make the distribution of outputs indistinguishable, the simulator has to modify his share of z_i in the ideal execution. He is able to do so and produce the exact same output for the ideal execution. This completes the proof.

5   Conclusions and Future Work

We propose a novel framework $\mathcal{ZK}_{DS}$ for proving "correct extended permutation". Compared with the only existing solution $\mathcal{ZK}_{EP}$, $\mathcal{ZK}_{DS}$ is more succinct and efficient in the sense that it removes the replication component $\mathcal{ZK}_{rep}$ and that its double shuffles are "smaller". Significant gains on computation and communication complexities are thereby obtained. $\mathcal{ZK}_{DS}$ seems to be optimal from the perspective of double-shuffle structure. It is still an open problem (at least it is unlikely to us) to design a linear ZK protocol for the "correct extended permutation" with exact one single shuffle. We are also interested in other efficient methods (rather than ZK proofs) in verifying extended permutations.

From $\mathcal{ZK}_{DS}$, we construct more compact PFE with linear active security for general purpose setting. The general PFE framework needs two invocations of $\mathcal{ZK}_{DS}$ for "correct extended permutation". We are further interested in more attempts to construct actively secure two-party PFE that is as (almost) "lightweight" as semi-honest secure PFE for some particular scenarios. For example, in all steps of some two-party PFE construction, can we re-use some steps for the same function f and different data x while preserving the active security of the PFE? We leave the constructions with steps-reusing feature as an open problem.

Acknowledgement. The work is supported by National Natural Science Foundation of China (61971192), Shanghai Municipal Education Commission (2021-01-07-00-08-E00101), and Shanghai Trusted Industry Internet Software Collaborative Innovation Center.

References

1. Alhassan, M.Y., Günther, D., Kiss, Á., Schneider, T.: Efficient and scalable universal circuits. J. Cryptol. 33(3), 1216–1271 (2020)
2. Barni, M., Failla, P., Kolesnikov, V., Lazzeretti, R., Sadeghi, A., Schneider, T.: Secure evaluation of private linear branching programs with medical applications. In: ESORICS 2009 (2009)
3. Bayer, S., Groth, J.: Efficient zero-knowledge argument for correctness of a shuffle. In: EUROCRYPT 2012 (2012)
4. Ben-Or, M., Goldwasser, S., Wigderson, A.: Completeness theorems for non-cryptographic fault-tolerant distributed computation (extended abstract). In: STOC (1988)
5. Bendlin, R., Damgård, I., Orlandi, C., Zakarias, S.: Semi-homomorphic encryption and multiparty computation. In: EUROCRYPT (2011)
6. Bicer, O., Bingol, M.A., Kiraz, M.S., Levi, A.: Highly efficient and re-executable private function evaluation with linear complexity. IEEE Trans. Dependable Secure Comput. 19(2), 835–847 (2020)
7. Brickell, J., Porter, D.E., Shmatikov, V., Witchel, E.: Privacy-preserving remote diagnostics. In: ACM CCS (2007)
8. Chaum, D., Pedersen, T.P.: Wallet databases with observers. In: CRYPTO (1992)
9. Cramer, R., Damgård, I., Schoenmakers, B.: Proofs of partial knowledge and simplified design of witness hiding protocols. In: CRYPTO (1994)

10. Damgård, I., Geisler, M., Krøigaard, M., Nielsen, J.B.: Asynchronous multiparty computation: theory and implementation. In: PKC (2009)
11. Damgård, I., Pastro, V., Smart, N.P., Zakarias, S.: Multiparty computation from somewhat homomorphic encryption. In: CRYPTO (2012)
12. Demmler, D., Schneider, T., Zohner, M.: ABY - a framework for efficient mixed-protocol secure two-party computation. In: NDSS (2015)
13. Evans, D., Kolesnikov, V., Rosulek, M.: A pragmatic introduction to secure multi-party computation. Found. Trends Priv. Secur. **2**(2–3), 70–246 (2018)
14. Fan, J., Vercauteren, F.: Somewhat practical fully homomorphic encryption. http://eprint.iacr.org/2012/144
15. Frederiksen, T.K., Jakobsen, T.P., Nielsen, J.B., Nordholt, P.S., Orlandi, C.: Minilego: efficient secure two-party computation from general assumptions. In: EUROCRYPT (2013)
16. Frikken, K.B., Atallah, M.J., Li, J.: Attribute-based access control with hidden policies and hidden credentials. IEEE Trans. Comput. **55**(10), 1259–1270 (2006)
17. Frikken, K.B., Atallah, M.J., Zhang, C.: Privacy-preserving credit checking. In: EC (2005)
18. Furukawa, J.: Efficient and verifiable shuffling and shuffle-decryption. IEICE Trans. Fundam. Electron. Commun. Comput. Sci. **88-A**(1), 172–188 (2005)
19. Furukawa, J., Miyauchi, H., Mori, K., Obana, S., Sako, K.: An implementation of a universally verifiable electronic voting scheme based on shuffling. In: FC (2002)
20. Furukawa, J., Sako, K.: An efficient scheme for proving a shuffle. In: CRYPTO (2001)
21. Gamal, T.E.: A public key cryptosystem and a signature scheme based on discrete logarithms. In: CRYPTO (1984)
22. Goldreich, O., Micali, S., Wigderson, A.: How to play any mental game. In: STOC (1987)
23. Groth, J.: A verifiable secret shuffle of homomorphic encryptions. J. Cryptol. **23**(4), 546–579 (2010)
24. Groth, J., Ishai, Y.: Sub-linear zero-knowledge argument for correctness of a shuffle. In: EUROCRYPT (2008)
25. Günther, D., Kiss, Á., Scheidel, L., Schneider, T.: Poster: framework for semi-private function evaluation with application to secure insurance rate calculation. In: ACM CCS (2019)
26. Günther, D., Kiss, Á., Schneider, T.: More efficient universal circuit constructions. In: ASIACRYPT (2017)
27. Hazay, C., Nissim, K.: Efficient set operations in the presence of malicious adversaries. In: PKC (2010)
28. Holz, M., Kiss, Á., Rathee, D., Schneider, T.: Linear-complexity private function evaluation is practical. In: ESORICS (2020)
29. Jawurek, M., Kerschbaum, F., Orlandi, C.: Zero-knowledge using garbled circuits: how to prove non-algebraic statements efficiently. In: ACM CCS (2013)
30. Katz, J., Malka, L.: Constant-round private function evaluation with linear complexity. In: ASIACRYPT (2011)
31. Kiss, Á., Schneider, T.: Valiant's universal circuit is practical. In: EUROCRYPT (2016)
32. Kolesnikov, V., Schneider, T.: A practical universal circuit construction and secure evaluation of private functions. In: FC (2008)
33. Lindell, Y.: Fast cut-and-choose based protocols for malicious and covert adversaries. In: CRYPTO (2013)

34. Lindell, Y., Pinkas, B.: An efficient protocol for secure two-party computation in the presence of malicious adversaries. In: EUROCRYPT (2007)
35. Lindell, Y., Pinkas, B.: A proof of security of yao's protocol for two-party computation. J. Cryptol. **22**(2), 161–188 (2009)
36. Lindell, Y., Riva, B.: Blazing fast 2PC in the offline/online setting with security for malicious adversaries. In: ACM CCS (2015)
37. Lipmaa, H., Mohassel, P., Sadeghian, S.: Valiant's universal circuit: improvements, implementation, and applications, iACR Eprint 2016/017 (2016)
38. Liu, H., Yu, Y., Zhao, S., Zhang, J., Liu, W.: Pushing the limits of valiant's universal circuits: simpler, tighter and more compact. In: CRYPTO (2021)
39. Malkhi, D., Nisan, N., Pinkas, B., Sella, Y.: Fairplay - secure two-party computation system. In: USENIX Security (2004)
40. Mohassel, P., Sadeghian, S.S.: How to hide circuits in MPC an efficient framework for private function evaluation. In: EUROCRYPT (2013)
41. Mohassel, P., Sadeghian, S.S., Smart, N.P.: Actively secure private function evaluation. http://eprint.iacr.org/2014/102
42. Mohassel, P., Sadeghian, S.S., Smart, N.P.: Actively secure private function evaluation. In: ASIACRYPT (2014)
43. Nielsen, J.B., Nordholt, P.S., Orlandi, C., Burra, S.S.: A new approach to practical active-secure two-party computation. In: CRYPTO (2012)
44. Niksefat, S., Sadeghiyan, B., Mohassel, P., Sadeghian, S.S.: ZIDS: a privacy-preserving intrusion detection system using secure two-party computation protocols. Comput. J. **57**(4), 494–509 (2014)
45. Paillier, P.: Public-key cryptosystems based on composite degree residuosity classes. In: EUROCRYPT (1999)
46. Shelat, A., Shen, C.: Two-output secure computation with malicious adversaries. In: EUROCRYPT (2011)
47. Terelius, B., Wikström, D.: Proofs of restricted shuffles. In: AFRICACRYPT (2010)
48. Valiant, L.G.: Universal circuits (preliminary report). In: STOC (1976)
49. Waksman, A.: A permutation network. J. ACM **15**(1), 159–163 (1968)
50. Yao, A.C.: Protocols for secure computations. In: FOCS (1982)
51. Yao, A.C.C.: How to generate and exchange secrets. In: FOCS (1986)
52. Zhao, S., Yu, Y., Zhang, J., Liu, H.: Valiant's universal circuits revisited: an overall improvement and a lower bound. In: ASIACRYPT (2019)
53. Zhu, R., Huang, Y., Katz, J., Shelat, A.: The cut-and-choose game and its application to cryptographic protocols. In: USENIX Security (2016)

CCA-Secure Identity-Based Matchmaking Encryption from Standard Assumptions

Shen Lin[1], Yu Li[1,2], and Jie Chen[1]($\boxtimes$)

[1] Shanghai Key Laboratory of Trustworthy Computing, Software Engineering
Institute, East China Normal University, Shanghai 200062, China
{slin,yli}@stu.ecnu.edu.cn, s080001@e.ntu.edu.sg
[2] University of Wollongong, Wollongong, NSW 2522, Australia

Abstract. Identity-based Matchmaking Encryption (IB-ME) is a new form of encryption that enables anonymous communication by specifying identities for both sender and receiver. Its applications in network services put forward higher requirements for the security of IB-ME. According to existing research, the security definition of IB-ME against chosen-plaintext attacks or chosen-ciphertext attacks is still vague.

In this paper, we give the first clear definition of CCA-security of IB-ME and propose the first CCA-secure IB-ME scheme under the standard assumptions in the standard model. We first construct a CCA-secure anonymous IBE scheme by combining anonymous hierarchical IBE with CHK CPA-CCA conversion at EUROCRYPT'04. Our proposed IB-ME scheme is a variant of two-level IBE, whose first level is this CCA-secure anonymous IBE, and the second level is a signature derived from this IBE. And its security is proven under standard assumptions and standard model.

Keywords: Identity-Based Matchmaking Encryption ·
Chosen-ciphertext attack · Identity-based encryption · Standard Model

1 Introduction

Matchmaking encryption (ME) is a new form of encryption primitive that allows both sender and receiver to specify access policies that the other part should satisfy to get plaintext message revealed [2]. In ME, a sender can specify an access policy $\mathbb{R}$ for the receiver and encrypt a message using the encryption key ek_σ with identity σ; the receiver can obtain a decryption key $dk_\mathbb{S}$ from an authority which embeds the access policy $\mathbb{S}$ for the sender. The receiver can

Supported by National Natural Science Foundation of China (61972156, 62372180), NSFC-ISF Joint Scientific Research Program (61961146004), Innovation Program of ShanghaiMunicipal Education Commission (2021-01-07-00-08-E00101) and the "Digital Silk Road" Shanghai International Joint Lab of Trustworthy Intelligent Software (22510750100).

C. Ge and M. Yung (Eds.): Inscrypt 2023, LNCS 14526, pp. 253–273, 2024.
https://doi.org/10.1007/978-981-97-0942-7_13

decrypt the ciphertext if and only if $\sigma \in \mathbb{S}$ and $\rho \in \mathbb{R}$. It also can be seen as a non-interactive Secret Handshake [3] with enhanced functionality.

Identity-based matchmaking encryption (IB-ME) is a special case of ME under restricted identity-based settings. In IB-ME, the matching condition can be simplified to $\sigma = \mathsf{snd}$ and $\rho = \mathsf{rcv}$ which is similar to standard identity-based encryption (IBE). IB-ME is more efficient than ME for general functions and more feasible to implement. From another point of view, IB-ME can also be seen as a generalization of anonymous IBE.

More Strict Security Requirements for IB-ME. IB-ME can be used in network services for communication from anonymous but authentic sources, such as social matchmaking confidentiality, encrypting bids, and even marginalized and dissident communities in authoritarian countries [2,19], putting forward higher requirements for the security of IB-ME.

Ateniese et al. [2] give the definition of security of IB-ME from two aspects: privacy and authenticity. Privacy property captures the secrecy of the sender's inputs $(\sigma, \mathsf{rcv}, m)$. The adversary limited in the definition of privacy can access key generation oracles in the query phase. It covers a wide range of adversaries, but it is somewhat vague and one-sided about the ability of the adversary's attacks. According to the threat model of classic public-key encryption, an adversary's attack can be classified as chosen-plaintext attack (CPA) and chosen-ciphertext attack (CCA). The current privacy definition only implies against chosen-plaintext attacks. The privacy definition against chosen-ciphertext attacks still remains blank. When the adversary's ability is enhanced to perform chosen-ciphertext attacks, the security of current IB-ME schemes [2,8,12,26] will be weakened.

Therefore, here comes the question: Can we construct an IB-ME scheme against chosen ciphertext attack? This can go further: Can we construct **a CCA-secure scheme under standard assumptions** without using random oracles?

Our Contributions. This work gives a positive answer to the questions above.

- *Formal definition of CCA-security of IB-ME.* We give a formal definition of privacy against chosen-ciphertext attacks in IB-ME. We claim that the former security definition of IB-ME is against chosen-plaintext attacks (CPA). The adversary with the ability of chosen-ciphertext attacks in the IB-ME setting can adaptively query key generation oracles and decryption oracles in the privacy security game. The authenticity security game remains the same. It is the first clear definition of CCA-security in IB-ME.
- *CCA-Secure IB-ME Scheme.* We use CHK conversion technique [7] to construct a CCA-secure anonymous IBE scheme. This scheme is based on an adaptively secure anonymous HIBE scheme and a strong one-time signature (OTS) scheme. Its CCA-security is implied by the CPA-security of the underlying anonymous HIBE and the unforgeability of the underlying OTS. After that, we build a CCA-secure IB-ME scheme which is a variant of two-level IBE we have proposed, and the second level serves as a signature scheme to

provide authenticity. It is the first CCA-secure IB-ME scheme under SXDH assumption in the standard model.

1.1 Technical Overview

To achieve the above results, we divide the process into two steps. First, we obtain a CCA-security IBE scheme, and then we use this to build a CCA-security IB-ME scheme.

CCA-Secure IBE from 2-Level HIBE. We use generic conversion frameworks to construct a CCA-secure IBE from 2-level HIBE. There are three generic CCA conversion techniques [7,13,18]. In this paper, we use the CHK technique [7] to achieve our results, which treats the verification key vk in one-time signature [6,30] as a part of identity and embeds it into the ciphertext and secret key. Precisely, the identity in CCA-secure HIBE is encoded into (id, vk) embedded in ciphertext, and the secret key for id can be delegated into a secret key for (id, vk). The one-time signature scheme will sign the ciphertext after it is generated. A $l+1$-level CPA-secure HIBE can be used to construct a l-level CCA-secure HIBE as claimed in [7], so we use 2-level CPA-secure HIBE to construct a CCA-secure 1-level HIBE, i.e., IBE.

CCA-Secure IB-ME from Anonymous CCA-Secure IBE. The proposed IB-ME scheme is a variant of 2-level IBE with anonymity and unforgeability where the first level is this CCA-secure IBE, and the second level is similar to signature scheme derived from the IBE as in [8]. The secret key in CCA-secure IBE is treated as dk_ρ in IB-ME and both receiver's identity rcv and vk are embedded in the ciphertext. We prove the privacy property against chosen-ciphertext attacks and the authenticity property of our IB-ME scheme, thus achieving the CCA-secure IB-ME scheme.

1.2 Related Works

IBE and HIBE. Identity-based encryption is proposed by Shamir in 1984 [24] where the ciphertext can only be decrypted by a receiver who has this identity. According to the security models, the IBE can be classified into schemes in the standard model and in the random oracle model [4]. According to the hardness assumptions schemes' security based on, it can be classified into schemes under pairings [9,10], quadratic residuosity [11,16] and lattices [1,17].

Hierarchical IBE is an extension of typical IBE which supports multi-level secret key delegation with an existing secret key, first proposed by Horwitz [14]. In 2006, Boyen and Waters proposed the first anonymous HIBE scheme [5], with a proof of security in the selective identity model. Then, Waters introduces an effective technique called dual system encryption in [27] to achieve fully secure IBE and HIBE schemes in simple assumptions. From 2008 to 2012, Okamoto and Takashima published a sequence of works about Dual Pairing Vector Space (DPVS) [20–22], which provides a new method to achieve fully secure IBE and HIBE under bilinear pairing groups. Chen et al. [10] combined DPVS and dual system encryption together to give an IBE scheme with better performance and lays the framework for follow-up constructions. Following their work, Ramanna et al. [23] construct an efficient anonymous compact HIBE scheme under asymmetric pairings. This scheme is a practical building block of our work.

ME and IB-ME. Matchmaking encryption is first introduced by Ateniese et al. [2] in 2019 and IB-ME is a restricted identity-based setting of ME. They also provided the first IB-ME from the bilinear Diffie-Hellman assumption in the random oracle model. The following-up work proposed by Francati et al. [12] gave the first IB-ME scheme without random oracles, but under q-ABDHE assumption and non-interactive zero-knowledge (NIZK) proof systems. In 2021, Xu et al. [28] extended IB-ME to a matchmaking attribute-based encryption scheme and used it in cloud-fog computation [29]. In 2022, Chen et al. [8] introduced the first IB-ME scheme from standard assumption. In the same year, Wang et al. [26] construct an IB-ME scheme based on a 2-level anonymous HIBE and lattice-based identity-based signature (IBS) and it is the first lattice-based IB-ME scheme. Recently, Jiang et al. [15] introduced a revocable IB-ME scheme from standard assumptions, which extends IB-ME's functionality. In 2023, Sun et al. [25] proposed a CCA-secure ME scheme from identity-based broadcast matchmaking encryption for one-to-many data sharing.

2   Preliminaries

2.1   Notations

We denote $\mathbb{Z}$ as integer numbers, $\mathbb{N}$ as natural numbers and $\mathbb{Z}_q$ as $\mathbb{Z}/(q\mathbb{Z})$. We write $x \xleftarrow{R} D$ to denote x is sampled uniformly random from set D. $c \leftarrow f(x)$ denotes c is the output of the algorithm with input x, when f is a function or an algorithm. $c := x$ denotes c is defined by x. Let $[h]_1$ denote g_1^h and $[h]_2$ denote g_2^h, where g_1 / g_2 is the generator of a cyclic group G_1 / G_2.

We use lowercase letters (x, y, z) to denote elements in vectors or matrices. We use bold lowercase letters $(\mathbf{x}, \mathbf{y}, \mathbf{z})$ to denote vectors and bold uppercase letters $(\mathbf{X})$ to denote matrices. And $\langle \mathbf{x}, \mathbf{y} \rangle$ denotes the inner product of vector $\mathbf{x}$ and $\mathbf{y}$. Let $\mathbb{B}, \mathbb{B}^*$ be vector spaces over $\mathbb{Z}_q$. The security parameter λ occurs throughout scheme algorithms. Algorithms implicitly take λ as input. We define a negligible function in λ as $\mathsf{negl}(\lambda)$.

2.2   Dual Vector Pairing Space Generation

The construction of our CCA-secure IBE and IB-ME scheme is based on Dual Pairing Vector Spaces (DPVS) from asymmetric pairing proposed by Okamoto and Takashima [20–22]. Here we will review the generation of DPVS.

Definition 1 (Asymmetric bilinear pairings). *Let G_1, G_2 and G_T be cyclic groups of prime order q. A pairing is a tuple $(q, G_1, G_2, G_T, e, g_1, g_2)$, where $g_1 \neq 1$ is a generator of group G_1 and $g_2 \neq 1$ is a generator of group G_2. $e : G_1 \times G_2 \to G_T$ is a polynomial-time computable non-degenerate bilinear map. For $g_1^x \in G_1$ and $g_2^y \in G_2$, we have $e(g_1^x, g_2^y) \neq 1$ and $e(g_1^x, g_2^y) = e(g_1, g_2)^{xy}$.*

We also consider vectors of group elements from individual elements. For $\mathbf{v} = (v_1, \ldots, v_n) \in \mathbb{Z}_q^n$ and $g_\beta \in G_\beta$ for $\beta \in \{1, 2\}$, $g_\beta^{\mathbf{v}} := (g_\beta^{v_1}, \ldots, g_\beta^{v_n})$. For $\mathbf{v}, \mathbf{w} \in \mathbb{Z}_q^n$, we define $e(g_1^{\mathbf{v}}, g_2^{\mathbf{w}}) := \prod_{i=1}^n e(g_1^{v_i}, g_2^{w_i}) = e(g_1, g_2)^{\mathbf{v} \cdot \mathbf{w}}$.

Dual Pairing Vector Spaces: For a fixed dimension n, we will choose two random bases $\mathbb{B} := (\mathbf{b}_1, \ldots, \mathbf{b}_n)$ and $\mathbb{B}^* := (\mathbf{b}_1^*, \ldots, \mathbf{b}_n^*)$ of $\mathbb{Z}_q^n$. These bases should satisfy dual orthonormal, namely

$$\mathbf{b}_i \cdot \mathbf{b}_j^* \equiv 0 \ (mod \ q), \forall i \neq j \in [n], \quad \mathbf{b}_j \cdot \mathbf{b}_j^* \equiv \Psi \ (mod \ q), \forall j \in [n], \Psi \in \mathbb{Z}_q,$$

where Ψ is a random non-zero element in $\mathbb{Z}_q$. We denote such dual orthonormal bases generating algorithm as $\mathsf{Dual}(\mathbb{Z}_q^n)$. As for the vectors of G_1 and G_2, we have

$$e(g_1^{\mathbf{b}_i}, g_2^{\mathbf{b}_j^*}) = 1, \forall i \neq j$$

In the subsequent constructions and proofs, we will make use of this property of DPVS.

Definition 2 (DDH1: Decisional Diffie-Hellman Assumption in G_1). *Given a group generator $\mathcal{G}$, we define a distribution as follows:*

$$\mathbb{G} := (q, G_1, G_2, G_T, g_1, g_2, e) \xleftarrow{R} \mathcal{G},$$
$$a, b, c \xleftarrow{R} \mathbb{Z}_q, \ D := (\mathbb{G}; g_1, g_2, g_1^a, g_1^b).$$

We suppose that for any PPT algorithm $\mathcal{A}$ (outputs 0 or 1),

$$\mathsf{Adv}_{\mathcal{A}}^{DDH1}(\lambda) := |\Pr[\mathcal{A}(D, g_1^{ab}) = 1] - \Pr[\mathcal{A}(D, g_1^{ab+c}) = 1]|$$

is negligible in the security parameter λ.

The dual assumption in G_2 is denoted as DDH2, and its definition is the same as Def. 2 where G_1 is replaced by G_2.

Definition 3. *The Symmetric External Diffie-Hellman assumption holds if DDH problems are intractable in both G_1 and G_2.*

Now we will introduce some hardness assumptions derived from SXDH assumption, which are mainly used in privacy proof.

Definition 4 (DS1:Decisional Subspace Assumption in G_1). *Given a group generator $\mathcal{G}$, we define a distribution as follows:*

$$\mathbb{G} := (q, G_1, G_2, G_T, g_1, g_2, e) \xleftarrow{R} \mathcal{G}, \ (\mathbb{B}, \mathbb{B}^*) \xleftarrow{R} \mathsf{Dual}(\mathbb{Z}_q^n), \tau_1, \tau_2, \mu_1, \mu_2 \xleftarrow{R} \mathbb{Z}_q,$$
$$U_1 := g_2^{\mu_1 \mathbf{b}_1^* + \mu_2 \mathbf{b}_{K+1}^*}, \ldots, U_K := g_2^{\mu_1 \mathbf{b}_K^* + \mu_2 \mathbf{b}_{2K}^*}, \ V_1 := g_1^{\tau_1 \mathbf{b}_1}, \ldots, V_K := g_1^{\tau_1 \mathbf{b}_K},$$
$$W_1 := g_1^{\tau_1 \mathbf{b}_1 + \tau_2 \mathbf{b}_{K+1}}, \ldots, V_K := g_1^{\tau_1 \mathbf{b}_K + \tau_2 \mathbf{b}_{2K}},$$
$$D := (\mathbb{G}; g_2^{\mathbf{b}_1^*}, \ldots, g_2^{\mathbf{b}_K^*}, g_2^{\mathbf{b}_{2K+1}^*}, g_2^{\mathbf{b}_N^*}, g_2^{\mathbf{b}_1}, g_1^{\mathbf{b}_1}, \ldots, g_1^{\mathbf{b}_1}, U_1, \ldots, U_K, \mu_2)$$

where K, N are fixed integers such that $2K \leq N$. We suppose that for any PPT algorithm $\mathcal{A}$ (outputs 0 or 1),

$$\mathsf{Adv}_{\mathcal{A}}^{DS1}(\lambda) := |\Pr[\mathcal{A}(D, V_1, \ldots, V_K) = 1] - \Pr[\mathcal{A}(D, W_1, \ldots, W_K) = 1]|$$

is negligible in the security parameter λ.

Lemma 1. *If the DDH assumption in G_1 holds, then the Subspace assumption in G_1 stated in Definition 4 also holds. More precisely, for any adversary $\mathcal{A}$ against the Subspace assumption in G_1, there exist probabilistic algorithms $\mathcal{B}$ whose running times are essentially the same as that of $\mathcal{A}$, such that*

$$\mathsf{Adv}_{\mathcal{A}}^{\mathsf{DS1}}(\lambda) \leq \mathsf{Adv}_{\mathcal{B}}^{\mathsf{DDH1}}(\lambda).$$

Proof. Detailed proofs can be found in [9]. ∎

The dual assumption in G_2 is denoted as DS2, and its definition is the same as Def. 4 where G_1 is replaced by G_2. Similarly, we can prove the Subspace assumption holds in G_2 if the DDH assumption in G_2 holds.

We will use the statistical indistinguishability lemma from [22] to calculate the adversary's advantage in the security analysis phase.

Lemma 2. *For $p \in \mathbb{Z}_q$, let $C_p := \{(\mathbf{x}, \mathbf{v} | \mathbf{x}, \mathbf{v} = p, \mathbf{0} \neq \mathbf{x}, \mathbf{0} \neq \mathbf{v} \in \mathbb{Z}_q^n)\}$. $\forall (\mathbf{z}, \mathbf{w}) \in C_p$, and $\mathbf{A} \xleftarrow{R} \mathbb{Z}_q^{n \times n}$ (and is invertible with great probability,*

$$\mathsf{Pr}[\mathsf{x}\mathbf{A}^\top = \mathbf{z} \wedge \mathbf{v}\mathbf{A}^{-1} = \mathbf{w}] = \frac{1}{\#C_p}$$

where $\#C_p$ means the number of elements in C_p.

2.3 (Hierarchical) Identity-Based Encryption

An Identity-Based Encryption (IBE) scheme consists of the following four algorithms, namely Setup, KeyGen, Enc and Dec.

- Setup(1^λ) $\rightarrow$ (mpk, msk): It takes as input the security parameter 1^λ. It outputs public parameter pp, master public key mpk and master secret key msk.
- KeyGen(mpk, msk, id) $\rightarrow$ $\mathsf{SK}_{\mathsf{id}}$: It takes as input the master public key mpk, the master secret key msk and an identity id. It generates decryption key $\mathsf{SK}_{\mathsf{id}}$.
- Enc(mpk, M, id) $\rightarrow$ C: It takes as input the master public key mpk, the message M and an identity id. It outputs a ciphertext C.
- Dec($mpk, \mathsf{SK}_{\mathsf{id}}, C$) $\rightarrow$ M' or $\perp$: It takes as input the master public key mpk, the decryption key $\mathsf{SK}_{\mathsf{id}}$ and the ciphertext C. If the decryption succeeds, the algorithm outputs message M'. Otherwise, it outputs $\perp$.

The chosen-ciphertext security of IBE is defined by the following game played by an adversary $\mathcal{A}$ and a challenger $\mathcal{C}$.

- Setup: $\mathcal{C}$ runs the algorithm Setup to obtain mpk and msk. Then it gives mpk to $\mathcal{A}$.
- Query 1: $\mathcal{A}$ can repeatedly make queries to oracles:
  - KeyGen($\cdot$) to request decryption key $\mathsf{SK}_{\mathsf{id}}$ for identity id;

- Dec($\cdot$) to request message m for identity id and ciphertext ct.
- Challenge: The adversary $\mathcal{A}$ chooses two challenge message-identity pairs (m_0, id_0^*) and (m_1, id_1^*). $\mathcal{C}$ randomly choose $b \leftarrow \{0, 1\}$, encrypts m_b and sends the ciphertext C_b back to $\mathcal{A}$. Note that both the identities and messages cannot be queried in Query 1.
- Query 2: This phase is almost the same as Query 1 except C_b and the secret keys for id_0^* and id_1^* cannot be queried.
- Guess: $\mathcal{C}$ outputs a guess b' for b.

If $b' = b$, then $\mathcal{A}$ succeeds. The advantage of the adversary $\mathcal{A}$ is defined as $\mathsf{Adv}_{\mathcal{A}}^{\mathsf{IBE}} = |\Pr[b = b'] - 1/2|$.

Definition 5. *An IBE scheme is CCA-secure and anonymous if the advantage of any PPT adversary $\mathcal{A}$ is negligible in the above game.*

A Hierarchical Identity-Based Encryption (HIBE) scheme consists of the following five algorithms, namely Setup, KeyGen, Enc, Delegate and Dec.

- Setup(1^λ) $\rightarrow$ (mpk, msk): It takes as input the security parameter 1^λ. It outputs the master public key mpk and the master secret key msk.
- KeyGen($mpk, msk, \mathbf{id}$) $\rightarrow$ SK$_{\mathbf{id}}$: It takes as input the master public key mpk, the master secret key msk and an identity vector $\mathbf{id}$. It generates secret key SK$_{\mathbf{id}}$.
- Enc(mpk, M, id) $\rightarrow$ C: It takes as input the master public key mpk, the message M and the identity id. It outputs a ciphertext C.
- Delegate(mpk): It takes as input the master public key mpk, a l-depth identity vector $\mathbf{id}_l = (\mathsf{id}_1, \ldots, \mathsf{id}_l)$ and a secret key for a $(l-1)$-depth identity SK$_{\mathbf{id}_{l-1}}$ and outputs the secret key SK$_{\mathbf{id}_l}$ for identity $\mathbf{id}_l = (\mathsf{id}_1, \ldots, \mathsf{id}_l)$.
- Dec($mpk, \mathsf{SK}_{\mathsf{id}}, C$) $\rightarrow$ M' or $\perp$: It takes as input the master public key mpk, the decryption key SK$_{\mathsf{id}}$ and the ciphertext C. If the decryption succeeds, the algorithm outputs message M'. Otherwise, it outputs $\perp$.

3   CCA-Security of IB-ME

3.1   Identity-Based Matchmaking Encryption

An Identity-based Matchmaking Encryption (IB-ME) scheme consists of the following five algorithms, namely Setup, SKGen, RKGen, Enc and Dec.

- Setup(1^λ) $\rightarrow$ (mpk, msk) : It takes as input the security parameter 1^λ. It outputs master public key mpk and master secret key msk.
- SKGen(mpk, msk, σ) $\rightarrow$ ek_σ : It takes as input the master public key mpk, master secret key msk and identity σ. It outputs the encryption key ek_σ for σ.
- RKGen(mpk, msk, ρ) $\rightarrow$ dk_ρ : It takes as input the master public key mpk, master secret key msk and identity ρ. It outputs the decryption key dk_ρ for ρ.

- $\mathsf{Enc}(mpk, ek_\sigma, \mathsf{rcv}, m) \to ct$: It takes as input the master public key mpk, the encryption key ek_σ, receiver's identity rcv and a message m. It ouputs a ciphertext ct for m linked to σ and rcv.
- $\mathsf{Dec}(mpk, dk_\rho, \mathsf{snd}, ct) \to m'$: It takes as input the master public key mpk, decryption key dk_ρ, sender's identity snd and ciphertext ct. It outputs either a valid message m' or $\bot$.

3.2 Privacy of IB-ME Against Chosen-Ciphertext Attacks

The notion of privacy of IB-ME against chosen-ciphertext attacks refers to IND-CCA security of HIBE [14] and IND-CCA-security of IBE [7]. The security game $\mathsf{Game}_{\mathcal{A},\Pi}^{\mathsf{cca\text{-}priv}}$ is described as below:

1. Setup: The challenger $\mathcal{C}$ runs $\mathsf{Setup}(1^\lambda)$ to get (mpk, msk). The adversary $\mathcal{A}$ is given mpk.
2. Query 1: The adversary $\mathcal{A}$ can make queries to three oracles:
    - $\mathsf{SKGen}(\cdot)$ to request encryption key ek_σ for identities σ;
    - $\mathsf{RKGen}(\cdot)$ to request decryption key dk_ρ for identities ρ;
    - $\mathsf{Dec}(\cdot)$ to request message m for identity ρ and snd, and ciphertext ct;
3. Challenge: The adversary $\mathcal{A}$ chooses two challenge message-identity pairs $(m_0, \mathsf{rcv}_0, \sigma_0)$ and $(m_1, \mathsf{rcv}_1, \sigma_1)$, and sends them to the challenger $\mathcal{C}$. The challenge messages and identities cannot be queried in Query 1 phase. The challenger randomly picks $b \in \{0,1\}$ and encrypts m_b to obtain $ct_b \leftarrow \mathsf{Enc}(mpk, ek_{\sigma_b}, \mathsf{rcv}_b, m_b)$. Then $\mathcal{C}$ sends ct_b back to $\mathcal{A}$.
4. Query 2: The adversary $\mathcal{A}$ can query the same three oracles in this phase, except that it may not query about the challenge ciphertext ct_b and identities $\mathsf{rcv}_0, \mathsf{rcv}_1, \sigma_0, \sigma_1$.
5. Guess: The adversary $\mathcal{A}$ outputs $b' \in \{0,1\}$. If $b = b'$, $\mathcal{A}$ wins the game and it returns 1. Otherwise, it returns 0.

Definition 6 (Privacy of IB-ME against chosen-ciphertext attacks). *An IB-ME scheme Π satisfies privacy against chosen-ciphertext attacks if for any valid PPT adversary $\mathcal{A}$,*

$$|\Pr[\mathsf{Game}_{\mathcal{A},\Pi}^{\mathsf{cca\text{-}priv}}(\lambda) = 1] - \frac{1}{2}|$$

is negligible in security parameter λ.

3.3 Authenticity of IB-ME

The definition of authenticity of IB-ME remains the same as in [2]. The security game $\mathsf{Game}_{\mathcal{A},\Pi}^{\mathsf{ib\text{-}auth}}$ is described below:

1. Setup: The challenger $\mathcal{C}$ runs $\mathsf{Setup}(1^\lambda)$ to get (mpk, msk). The adversary $\mathcal{A}$ is given mpk.
2. Query: The adversary $\mathcal{A}$ can make queries to two oracles:

- SKGen($\cdot$) to request encryption key ek_σ for identities σ;
- RKGen($\cdot$) to request decryption key dk_ρ for identities ρ;

3. Challenge: The adversary $\mathcal{A}$ forges a challenge ciphertext and identities tuple (ct, snd, ρ), then sends them to the challenger $\mathcal{C}$. The challenge ciphertexts and identities cannot be queried in the Query phase. The challenger obtains decryption key $dk_\rho \leftarrow \mathsf{RKGen}(mpk, msk, \rho)$ and decrypts ct to obtain $\mu \leftarrow \mathsf{Dec}(mpk, dk_\rho, \mathsf{snd}, ct)$.

4. Verify: If $\forall \sigma \in \mathcal{Q}_S$, $(\sigma \neq \mathsf{snd}) \wedge (\mu \neq \perp)$ holds, then $\mathcal{A}$ wins the game.

Definition 7 (Authenticity of IB-ME). *An IB-ME scheme Π satisfies authenticity if for any valid PPT adversary $\mathcal{A}$,*

$$|\Pr[\mathsf{Game}_{\mathcal{A},\Pi}^{\mathsf{ib\text{-}auth}}(\lambda) = 1] - \frac{1}{2}|$$

is negligible in security parameter λ.

Definition 8 (CCA-secure IB-ME). *If an IB-ME scheme Π satisfies both CCA privacy (Def.6) and authenticity (Def.7), it is a CCA-secure IB-ME scheme.*

4   CCA-Secure IBE from 2-Level HIBE

4.1   CCA-Secure IBE Construction

Here we use the anonymous CPA-secure HIBE scheme based on DPVS proposed by [23] (denoted as AHIBE) to start our construction. By combining the CPA-secure 2-level HIBE with strong one-time signature $\mathsf{OTS} = (\mathsf{Setup}, \mathsf{Sign}, \mathsf{Vrfy})$ (where this signature query can only be asked for less than once), a CCA-secure IBE scheme Π can be constructed as follows:

- Setup(1^λ): Run AHIBE.Setup(1^λ) to obtain $\mathbb{G} := (G_1, G_2, G_T, g_1, g_2, e)$, $(\mathbb{D}, \mathbb{D}^*) \leftarrow \mathsf{Dual}(\mathbb{Z}_q^6)$, master public key mpk and master secret key msk, where

$$mpk := \{\mathbb{G}; [\mathbf{d}_2 + \mathbf{d}_3]_1, [\theta_1 \mathbf{d}_1]_1, [\theta_2 \mathbf{d}_1]_1, g_T^\alpha\}, \quad g_T := e(g_1, g_2)^{\mathbf{d}_1 \cdot \mathbf{d}_1^*},$$
$$msk := \{[\alpha \mathbf{d}_2^*]_2, [\mathbf{d}_1^*]_2, [\theta_1 \mathbf{d}_2^*]_2, [\theta_2 \mathbf{d}_3^*]_2\}, \quad \theta_1, \theta_2, \alpha \xleftarrow{R} \mathbb{Z}_q.$$

- KeyGen(mpk, msk, id): Run AHIBE.KeyGen(mpk, msk, id) to obtain $\mathsf{SK}_{\mathsf{id}} = (k_1, k_2, (b_1, b_2))$, where k_1 is used in decryption and k_2, b_1 and b_2 are auxiliary variables used to generate new SK in key delegation. The construction is as follows:

$$k_1 := [\alpha \mathbf{d}_2^* + r_1(\mathsf{id}\theta_1 \mathbf{d}_2^* - \mathbf{d}_1^*)]_2, \quad k_2 := [r_2(\mathsf{id}\theta_1 \mathbf{d}_2^* - \mathbf{d}_1^*)]_2,$$
$$b_1 := [r_1 \theta_2 \mathbf{d}_3^*]_2, \quad b_2 := [r_2 \theta_2 \mathbf{d}_3^*]_2, \quad r_1, r_2 \xleftarrow{R} \mathbb{Z}_q.$$

- Enc(mpk, M, id): Run OTS.Setup(1^k) to obtain verification key and signing key (vk, sk), where $|vk| = n = n(k)$. Let id$' = (\text{id}, vk)$.
  Run AHIBE.Enc(mpk, M, id') to obtain ct $= (C_0, C_1)$, where

$$C_0 := M \cdot (g_T^\alpha)^z, C_1 := [z(\mathbf{d}_2 + \mathbf{d}_3 + (\text{id}\theta_1 + vk\theta_2)\mathbf{d}_1)]_1, z \xleftarrow{R} \mathbb{Z}_q.$$

  Then sign the ciphertext ct to obtain the signature sig $\leftarrow$ OTS.Sign(sk, ct).
  The final ciphertext is C $= \{vk, \text{ct}, \text{sig}\}$.
- Decrypt($mpk, \text{SK}_{\text{id}^*}, C$): First check whether OTS.Vrfy(vk, ct, sig) $\overset{?}{=} 1$. If not, output $\bot$. Otherwise, run AHIBE.Delegate($mpk, \text{SK}_{\text{id}^*}, vk$) to generate the key SK$_{(\text{id}^*, vk)} = k_1'$, where

$$k_1' := k_1 \cdot b_1^{vk} \cdot (k_2 \cdot b_2^{vk})^{r_1'} = [\alpha \mathbf{d}_2^* + (r_1 + r_1' r_2)(\text{id}^* \theta_1 \mathbf{d}_2^* + vk\theta_2 \mathbf{d}_3^* - \mathbf{d}_1^*)]_2.$$

  Output $M := $ AHIBE.Dec($mpk, \text{SK}_{(\text{id}^*, vk)}, \text{ct}$).

Correctness. Correctness holds if and only if id $=$ id*:

$$
\begin{aligned}
C_0/e(C_1, k_1') &= \frac{M \cdot (g_T^\alpha)}{e(g_1, g_2)^{(z(\mathbf{d}_2 + \mathbf{d}_3 + (\text{id} \cdot \theta_1 + vk \cdot \theta_2)\mathbf{d}_1)) \cdot (\alpha \mathbf{d}_2^* + (r_1 + r_1' r_2)(\text{id}^* \cdot \theta_1 \mathbf{d}_2^* + vk \cdot \theta_2 \mathbf{d}_3^* - \mathbf{d}_1^*))}} \\
&= \frac{M \cdot (g_T^\alpha)}{e(g_1, g_2)^{z\alpha \cdot \mathbf{d}_2 \cdot \mathbf{d}_2^* + (zr_1 + zr_1' r_2)(\text{id}^* \theta_1 \mathbf{d}_2 \cdot \mathbf{d}_2^* + vk \cdot \theta_2 \mathbf{d}_3 \cdot \mathbf{d}_3^* - (\text{id}\theta_1 + vk \cdot \theta_2)\mathbf{d}_1 \cdot \mathbf{d}_1^*)}} \\
&= \frac{M \cdot (g_T^\alpha)}{e(g_1, g_2)^{z\alpha \cdot \mathbf{d}_2 \cdot \mathbf{d}_2^*}} = \frac{M \cdot (g_T^\alpha)^z}{g_T^{z\alpha}} = M.
\end{aligned}
$$

4.2   Security Analysis

The generic proof of this CCA-secure IBE (1-level HIBE) scheme from 2-level HIBE is similar to the security proof in paper [7]. Here we only give the theorem.

Theorem 1. *Suppose the probability of breaking* AHIBE *is* ϵ_1 *and the probability of forging a valid signature in* OTS *is* ϵ_2. *If* AHIBE *is adaptive-ID secure against chosen plaintext attack and* OTS *is a strong one-time signature scheme, then scheme* Π *is adaptive-ID secure against chosen-ciphertext attack. The advantage of a PPT adversary* $\mathcal{A}$ *attacking* Π *can be defined as follows:*

$$|\Pr[\text{Succ}] - \frac{1}{2}| \le \frac{1}{2}\Pr[\text{Forge}] + |\Pr[\text{Succ} \wedge \overline{\text{Forge}}] + \frac{1}{2}\Pr[\text{Forge}] - \frac{1}{2}|$$

$$\le \epsilon_1 + \frac{1}{2}\epsilon_2 = \text{negl}(\lambda)$$

5   CCA-Secure IB-ME Construction

Finally, we construct a CCA-secure IB-ME scheme from the CCA-secure IBE proposed in the above section.

5.1   Construction

- Setup(1^λ): Randomly pick $\eta, \theta_1, \theta_2, \alpha \xleftarrow{R} \mathbb{Z}_q$ to obtain parameters $\mathbb{G} := (G_1, G_2, G_T, g_1, g_2, e)$, $(\mathbb{D}, \mathbb{D}^*) \leftarrow \mathsf{Dual}(\mathbb{Z}_q^{10})$, master public key mpk and master secret key msk, where

$$mpk := \{\mathbb{G}; [\mathbf{d}_2 + \mathbf{d}_3]_1, [\theta_1 \mathbf{d}_1]_1, [\theta_2 \mathbf{d}_1]_1, g_T^\alpha\}, \quad g_T := e(g_1, g_2)^{\mathbf{d}_1 \cdot \mathbf{d}_1^*},$$
$$msk := \{\eta, [\mathbf{d}_4]_1, [\mathbf{d}_5]_1, [\alpha \mathbf{d}_2^*]_2, [\mathbf{d}_1^*]_2, [\mathbf{d}_4^*]_2, [\mathbf{d}_5^*]_2, [\theta_1 \mathbf{d}_2^*]_2, [\theta_2 \mathbf{d}_3^*]_2\}.$$

- RKGen(mpk, msk, ρ): Pick $s, r_1, r_2, r_3 \xleftarrow{R} \mathbb{Z}_q$ to obtain $dk_\rho := (k_1, k_2, k_3, k_4, (b_1, b_2))$. k_1, k_3, k_4 are used in decryption, and k_2, b_1, b_2 are auxiliary variables.

$$k_1 := [\alpha \mathbf{d}_2^* + r_1(\rho \theta_1 \mathbf{d}_2^* - \mathbf{d}_1^*) + s \mathbf{d}_4^*]_2, \ k_2 := [r_2(\rho \theta_1 \mathbf{d}_2^* - \mathbf{d}_1^*)]_2, \ k_3 := (g_T^\eta)^s,$$
$$k_4 := [r_3(\mathbf{d}_2^* - \mathbf{d}_3^*) + s \mathbf{d}_5^*]_2, \ b_1 := [r_1 \theta_2 \mathbf{d}_3^*]_2, \ b_2 := [r_2 \theta_2 \mathbf{d}_3^*]_2.$$

- SKGen(mpk, msk, σ): Pick $r \xleftarrow{R} \mathbb{Z}_q$ and the encryption key is computed as

$$ek_\sigma := [\eta \mathbf{d}_4 + r(\sigma \mathbf{d}_4 - \mathbf{d}_5)]_1.$$

- Enc($mpk, M, \mathsf{rcv}, ek_\sigma$): Run OTS.Setup($1^k$) to obtain verification key and signing key (vk, sk), where $|vk| = n = n(k)$. Let $\hat{id} = (\mathsf{rcv}, vk)$.
Then we can pick $z \xleftarrow{R} \mathbb{Z}_q$ and obtain $\mathsf{ct} = (C_0, C_1)$ for $\hat{id}$, where

$$C_0 := M \cdot (g_T^\alpha)^z, \ C_1 := ek_\sigma \cdot [z(\mathbf{d}_2 + \mathbf{d}_3 + (\mathsf{rcv} \cdot \theta_1 + vk \cdot \theta_2)\mathbf{d}_1)]_1.$$

Then sign the ciphertext ct to obtain the signature $\mathsf{sig} \leftarrow$ OTS.Sign(sk, ct). The final ciphertext is $C = \{vk, \mathsf{ct}, \mathsf{sig}\}$.

- Dec($mpk, dk_\rho, \mathsf{snd}, C$): Check whether OTS.Vrfy($vk, \mathsf{ct}, \mathsf{sig}) \stackrel{?}{=} 1$. If not, output $\perp$. Otherwise, pick $r_1', r_2' \xleftarrow{R} \mathbb{Z}_q$ to generate $\mathsf{SK}_{(\rho, vk)} = (k_1', k_3, k_4)$, where

$$k_1' := k_1 \cdot (b_1)^{vk} \cdot (k_2 \cdot (b_2)^{vk})^{r_1'}$$
$$= [\alpha \mathbf{d}_2^* + (r_1 + r_1' r_2)(\rho \theta_1 \mathbf{d}_2^* + vk \cdot \theta_2 \mathbf{d}_3^* - \mathbf{d}_1^*) + s \mathbf{d}_4^*]_2,$$

k_3 and k_4 remains the same. Compute $M := \dfrac{C_0}{e(C_1, k_1' \cdot k_4^{\mathsf{snd}}) \cdot k_3^{-1}}$

Correctness. Correctness holds when $\mathsf{rcv} = \rho$ and $\mathsf{snd} = \sigma$, let

$$k_{\mathsf{cca}} = [\alpha \mathbf{d}_2^* + (r_1 + r_1' r_2)(\rho \theta_1 \mathbf{d}_2^* + vk \theta_2 \mathbf{d}_3^* - \mathbf{d}_1^*)]_2,$$
$$k_{\mathsf{auth}} = [s \mathbf{d}_4^* + r_3 \cdot \mathsf{snd}(\mathbf{d}_2^* - \mathbf{d}_3^*) + s \cdot \mathsf{snd} \mathbf{d}_5^*]_2,$$
$$k_1' \cdot k_4 = k_{\mathsf{cca}} \cdot k_{\mathsf{auth}}, \ e(C_1, k_1' \cdot k_4^{\mathsf{snd}}) = e(C_1, k_{\mathsf{cca}}) \cdot e(C_1, k_{\mathsf{auth}}).$$

The calculation of $e(C_1, k_{\mathsf{cca}})$ is the same as the correctness of CCA-secure IBE, replacing id with rcv and id* with ρ.

$$e(C_1, k_{\mathsf{cca}}) = e(g_1, g_2)^{(z(\mathbf{d}_2 + \mathbf{d}_3 + (\mathsf{rcv} \cdot \theta_1 + vk \cdot \theta_2)\mathbf{d}_1)) \cdot (\alpha \mathbf{d}_2^* + (r_1 + r_1' r_2)(\rho \theta_1 \mathbf{d}_2^* + vk \cdot \theta_2 \mathbf{d}_3^* - \mathbf{d}_1^*))}$$
$$= e(g_1, g_2)^{z\alpha \cdot \mathbf{d}_2 \cdot \mathbf{d}_2^* + (zr_1 + zr_1' r_2)(id^* \theta_1 \mathbf{d}_2 \cdot \mathbf{d}_2^* + vk \cdot \theta_2 \mathbf{d}_3 \cdot \mathbf{d}_3^* - (id \cdot \theta_1 + vk \cdot \theta_2)\mathbf{d}_1 \cdot \mathbf{d}_1^*)}$$
$$= e(g_1, g_2)^{z\alpha \cdot \mathbf{d}_2 \cdot \mathbf{d}_2^*} = (g_T)^{z\alpha}.$$

As for $e(C_1, k_{\mathsf{auth}})$,

$$e(C_1, k_{\mathsf{auth}}) = e(g_1, g_2)^{(z(\mathbf{d}_2 + \mathbf{d}_3 + \eta\mathbf{d}_4 + r(\sigma\mathbf{d}_4 - \mathbf{d}_5))) \cdot (s\mathbf{d}_4^* + r_3 \cdot \mathsf{snd}(\mathbf{d}_2^* - \mathbf{d}_3^*) + s \cdot \mathsf{snd}\mathbf{d}_5^*)}$$

$$= e(g_1, g_2)^{\eta s\mathbf{d}_4 \cdot \mathbf{d}_4^* + rs(\sigma\mathbf{d}_4 \cdot \mathbf{d}_4^* - \mathsf{snd} \cdot \mathbf{d}_5 \cdot \mathbf{d}_5^*) + zr_3 \cdot \mathsf{snd}(\mathbf{d}_2 \cdot \mathbf{d}_2^* - \mathbf{d}_3 \cdot \mathbf{d}_3^*)}$$

$$= e(g_1, g_2)^{\eta s\mathbf{d}_4 \cdot \mathbf{d}_4^* + rs(\sigma\mathbf{d}_4 \cdot \mathbf{d}_4^* - \mathsf{snd} \cdot \mathbf{d}_5 \cdot \mathbf{d}_5^*)} = (g_T)^{\eta s}$$

$$\frac{C_0}{e(C_1, k_1' \cdot k_4^{\mathbf{snd}}) \cdot k_3^{-1}} = \frac{M \cdot (g_T)^{\alpha z}}{(g_T)^{\alpha z} \cdot (g_T)^{\eta s} \cdot (g_T)^{-\eta s}} = M.$$

5.2 Security Analysis

As for security, it can be proved that our proposed IB-ME scheme is CCA-security (Def. 8) according to the Theorem 2 and Theorem 3, namely satisfies privacy (Def. 6) and authenticity (Def. 7) simultaneously.

Theorem 2. *The proposed IB-ME scheme satisfies privacy with CCA-security under the SXDH assumption. Suppose the probability of forging a valid signature in* OTS *is* ϵ_2. *For any PPT adversary* $\mathcal{A}$, *there exists PPT algorithms* $\mathcal{A}_0, \mathcal{A}_{1,1}, \mathcal{A}_{1,2}, \ldots, \mathcal{A}_{Q,1}, \mathcal{A}_{Q,2}$, *such that:*

$$\mathsf{Adv}_{\mathcal{A}}^{\mathsf{IB\text{-}ME}}(\lambda) \le \mathsf{Adv}_{\mathcal{A}_0}^{\mathsf{DDH1}}(\lambda) + \sum_{j=1}^{Q}(\mathsf{Adv}_{\mathcal{A}_{j,1}}^{\mathsf{DDH2}} + \mathsf{Adv}_{\mathcal{A}_{j,2}}^{\mathsf{DDH2}}) + (12Q + 3)/q + \frac{1}{2}(Q + 2)\epsilon_2$$

where Q *is the maximum number of* $\mathcal{A}$'s *key queries.*

The proof of CCA-security follows dual system encryption methodology. We use hybrid games to prove the negligible gap between different forms of dk_ρ and ct. In a hybrid game sequence, C_1, k_1, k_2, k_4 are transformed into semi-functional form and C_0 and k_3 remain the same. **KeyGenSF** algorithm is used to generate semi-functional dk_ρ and ek_σ remains the same. **EncryptSF** algorithm is used to generate semi-functional ciphertext. The detailed algorithm descriptions are shown below.

EncryptSF: The algorithm picks $z, r, r_6, r_7, r_8, r_9, r_{10} \xleftarrow{R} \mathbb{Z}_q$ and form a semi-functional ciphertext as

$$ek_\sigma := [\,\eta\mathbf{d}_4 + r(\sigma\mathbf{d}_4 - \mathbf{d}_5)]_1,$$
$$\mathsf{ct}^{(\mathsf{SF})} := \{\, C_0 := M \cdot (g_T^\alpha)^z,$$
$$C_1 := ek_\sigma \cdot [z(\mathbf{d}_2 + \mathbf{d}_3 + \mathbf{d}_1(\mathsf{rcv}\theta_1 + vk\theta_2))$$
$$+ r_6\mathbf{d}_6 + r_7\mathbf{d}_7 + r_8\mathbf{d}_8 + r_9\mathbf{d}_9 + r_{10}\mathbf{d}_{10}]_1\}$$

Hereafter we ignore C_0 since it is always correctly generated.

KeyGenSF: There are two types of semi-functional keys used in the security proof, namely dk_ρ^{SF1} and dk_ρ^{SF2}. We denote the former as keys of SF1 type and the latter as keys of SF2 type.

– $dk_\rho^{SF1} := \{k_1^{SF1}, k_2, k_3, k_4, b_1^{SF1}, b_2\}$. The algorithm picks $s, s_{1,6}, s_{2,6}, z_{1,6}, z_{2,6} \xleftarrow{R} \mathbb{Z}_q$ and forms

$$k_1^{SF1} := [\alpha \mathbf{d}_2^* + r_1(\rho\theta_1\mathbf{d}_2^* - \mathbf{d}_1^*) + s\mathbf{d}_4^* + s_{1,6}\mathbf{d}_6^* + s_{1,7}\mathbf{d}_7^* + s_{1,9}\mathbf{d}_9^*]_2,$$
$$k_2 := [r_2(\rho\theta_1\mathbf{d}_2^* - \mathbf{d}_1^*)]_2, \quad k_3 := (g_T^\eta)^s, \quad k_4 := [r_3(\mathbf{d}_2^* - \mathbf{d}_3^*) + s\mathbf{d}_5^*]_2,$$
$$b_1^{SF1} := [r_1\theta_2\mathbf{d}_3^* + \underline{z_{1,8}\mathbf{d}_8^*}]_2, b_2 := [r_2\theta_2\mathbf{d}_3^*]_2.$$

– $dk_\rho^{SF2} := \{k_1^{SF2}, k_2^{SF2}, k_3, k_4^{SF2}, b_1^{SF2}, b_2^{SF2}\}$. The algorithm picks $s, \{s_{1,i}, s_{2,i}, z_{1,i}, z_{2,i}\}_{i=6,7,8} \xleftarrow{R} \mathbb{Z}_q$ and forms

$$k_1^{SF2} := k_1^{SF1}, k_2^{SF2} := [r_2(\rho\theta_1\mathbf{d}_2^* - \mathbf{d}_1^*) + s_{2,6}\mathbf{d}_6^* + s_{2,7}\mathbf{d}_7^*]_2,$$
$$k_3 := (g_T^\eta)^s, k_4^{SF2} := [r_3(\mathbf{d}_2^* - \mathbf{d}_3^*) + s\mathbf{d}_5^* + \underline{s_{4,7}\mathbf{d}_7^* + s_{4,8}\mathbf{d}_8^* + s_{4,10}\mathbf{d}_{10}^*}]_2,$$
$$b_1^{SF2} := b_1^{SF1}, b_2^{SF2} := [r_2\theta_2\mathbf{d}_3^* + \underline{z_{2,8}\mathbf{d}_8^*}]_2.$$

Hereafter we ignore k_3 since it is always correctly generated.

If one uses a semi-functional key to decrypt a normal ciphertext, the decryption will succeed since $(\mathbf{d}_6^*, \mathbf{d}_7^*, \mathbf{d}_8^*, \mathbf{d}_9^*, \mathbf{d}_{10}^*)$ are orthogonal to the vector space of C_1 and don't affect the decryption. Similarly, if one uses a normal key to decryption a semi-functional ciphertext, the decryption will succeed as well. However, if both the ciphertext and the key are semi-functional (without much loss of generality, taking SF2 key as example), the decryption will fail. $e(C_1, k_1'k_4^{snd})k_3^{-1}$ will produce an additional term. Decryption will fail unless $r_6(s_{1,6} + vkz_{1,6} + r_1'(s_{2,6} + vkz_{2,6})) + r_7(s_{1,7} + vkz_{1,7} + r_1'(s_{2,7} + vkz_{2,7})) + r_8(s_{1,8} + vkz_{1,8} + r_1'(vkz_{2,8})) + r_9s_{1,9} \equiv 0 \pmod{q}$, and $r_7s_{4,7} + r_8s_{4,8} + r_{10}s_{1,10} \equiv 0 \pmod{q}$. If these two equations hold, the key-ciphertext pair is *nominally semi-functional*.

Suppose the PPT adversary $\mathcal{A}$ can make Q decryption key queries. The proof of security consists of the following hybrid games:

– Game_{real}: the real security game described in the security model definition.
– Game_0: is the same as Game_{real} except that the challenge ciphertext is semi-functional.
– $\mathsf{Game}_{j,1}$: for j from 1 to Q, $\mathsf{Game}_{j,1}$ is the same as Game_0 except the first $j-1$ decryption keys are type SF2, the j-th decryption key is type SF1 and the remaining keys are normal.
– $\mathsf{Game}_{j,2}$: for j from 1 to Q, $\mathsf{Game}_{j,2}$ is the same as Game_0 except the first j decryption keys are type SF2 and the remaining keys are normal.
– Game_{final}: the same as $\mathsf{Game}_{Q,2}$ except the challenge ciphertext is a semi-functional encryption of a random message in G_T and two random identities in $\mathbb{Z}_q$.

The above sequence of games can be proved indistinguishable by the following lemmas.

Lemma 3. *Suppose an adversary $\mathcal{A}$ where $|\mathsf{Adv}_{\mathcal{A}}^{\mathsf{Game}_{real}} - \mathsf{Adv}_{\mathcal{A}}^{\mathsf{Game}_0}| = \epsilon$. Then there exists a PPT algorithm $\mathcal{A}_0$ where $\mathsf{Adv}_{\mathcal{A}_0}^{DS1} = \epsilon - 2/q - \frac{1}{2}\epsilon_2$, with $K = 5$ and $N = 10$.*

Proof. $\mathcal{A}_0$ is given

$$D := (\mathbb{G}; [\mathbf{b}_1^*]_2, [\mathbf{b}_2^*]_2, \ldots, [\mathbf{b}_5^*]_2, [\mathbf{b}_1]_1, \ldots, [\mathbf{b}_{10}]_1, U_1, U_2, U_3, U_4, U_5, \mu_2)$$

and $(T_1, T_2, T_3, T_4, T_5)$. $U_1 = [\mu_1 \mathbf{b}_1^* + \mu_2 \mathbf{b}_6^*]_2, U_2 = [\mu_1 \mathbf{b}_2^* + \mu_2 \mathbf{b}_7^*]_2, U_3 = [\mu_1 \mathbf{b}_3^* + \mu_2 \mathbf{b}_8^*]_2, U_4 = [\mu_1 \mathbf{b}_4^* + \mu_2 \mathbf{b}_9^*]_2, U_5 = [\mu_1 \mathbf{b}_5^* + \mu_2 \mathbf{b}_{10}^*]_2$. $\mathcal{A}_0$ is required to decide whether $(T_1, T_2, T_3, T_4, T_5)$ is distributed as $\mathsf{Dist}_1 = ([\tau_1 \mathbf{b}_1 + \tau_2 \mathbf{b}_6]_1, [\tau_1 \mathbf{b}_2 + \tau_2 \mathbf{b}_7]_1, [\tau_1 \mathbf{b}_3 + \tau_2 \mathbf{b}_8]_1, [\tau_1 \mathbf{b}_4 + \tau_2 \mathbf{b}_9]_1, [\tau_1 \mathbf{b}_5 + \tau_2 \mathbf{b}_{10}]_1)$ or $\mathsf{Dist}_2 = ([\tau_1 \mathbf{b}_1]_1, [\tau_1 \mathbf{b}_2]_1, [\tau_1 \mathbf{b}_3]_1, [\tau_1 \mathbf{b}_4]_1, [\tau_1 \mathbf{b}_5]_1)$.

The adversary $\mathcal{A}_0$ simulate Game_{real} or Game_0 with $\mathcal{A}$ depending on the distribution of $(T_1, T_2, T_3, T_4, T_5)$. It simulates the game in the following steps:

1. Setup : $\mathcal{A}_0$ chooses a random invertible matrix $\mathbf{A} \xleftarrow{R} \mathbb{Z}_q^{5 \times 5}$. And we have a pair of orthonormal basis $\mathbb{D} := (\mathbf{d}_1, \mathbf{d}_2, \ldots, \mathbf{d}_{10})$ and $\mathbb{D}^* := (\mathbf{d}_1^*, \mathbf{d}_2^*, \ldots, \mathbf{d}_{10}^*)$, where

$$\mathbf{d}_1 := \mathbf{b}_1, \ldots, \mathbf{d}_5 := \mathbf{b}_5, \quad (\mathbf{d}_6, \ldots, \mathbf{d}_{10}) := (\mathbf{b}_6, \ldots, \mathbf{b}_{10})\mathbf{A} \quad (1)$$

$$\mathbf{d}_1^* := \mathbf{b}_1^*, \ldots, \mathbf{d}_5^* := \mathbf{b}_5^*, \quad (\mathbf{d}_6^*, \ldots, \mathbf{d}_{10}^*) := (\mathbf{b}_6^*, \ldots, \mathbf{b}_{10}^*)(\mathbf{A}^{-1})^T. \quad (2)$$

   Then $\mathcal{A}_0$ pick $\eta \xleftarrow{R} \mathbb{Z}_q$ and runs $\mathsf{AHIBE.Setup}(1^\lambda)$ and $\mathsf{OTS.Setup}(1^\lambda)$ to get (mpk, msk) and (vk^*, sk^*). $\mathcal{A}_0$ sends mpk back to $\mathcal{A}$.
2. Query 1: Since $\mathcal{A}_0$ knows master secret key msk and the verify algorithm is public, $\mathcal{A}_0$ can properly run $\mathsf{SKGen}, \mathsf{RKGen}, \mathsf{Dec}$ to answer oracle queries.
   - $\mathsf{RKGen}(\cdot)$: If $\mathcal{A}$ queries a decryption key for identity ρ, $\mathcal{A}_0$ can get dk_ρ by running normal RKGen algorithm and sends it back to $\mathcal{A}$.
   - $\mathsf{SKGen}(\cdot)$: If $\mathcal{A}$ queries an encryption key for identity σ, $\mathcal{A}_0$ runs normal SKGen algorithm to get ek_σ and sends it back to $\mathcal{A}$.
   - $\mathsf{Dec}(\cdot)$: If $\mathcal{A}$ makes a decryption query on $\{\rho', \mathsf{snd}, \mathsf{C} = \{vk, \mathsf{sig}, \mathsf{ct}\}\}$, $\mathcal{A}_0$ responds as follows:
     (a) If $vk = vk^*$, $\mathcal{A}_0$ checks whether $\mathsf{Vrfy}_{vk}(\mathsf{ct}, \mathsf{sig}) = 1$. If so, $\mathcal{A}_0$ aborts and outputs a random bit. Otherwise, $\mathcal{A}_0$ returns $\perp$.
     (b) If $vk \neq vk^*$ and $\mathsf{Vrfy}_{vk}(\mathsf{C}, \mathsf{sig}) = 0$, $\mathcal{A}_0$ returns $\perp$.
     (c) If $vk \neq vk^*$ and $\mathsf{Vrfy}_{vk}(\mathsf{C}, \mathsf{sig}) = 1$, $\mathcal{A}_0$ encode $\mathsf{id}' = \rho'$ and queries a secret key for identity vector (vk, ρ') by running AHIBE's KeyGen algorithm. It then honestly decrypts the ciphertext and sends the plaintext to $\mathcal{A}$.
3. Challenge : $\mathcal{A}$ sends $\mathcal{A}_0$ two pairs $(m_0, \mathsf{rcv}_0^*, \sigma_0^*)$ and $(m_1, \mathsf{rcv}_1^*, \sigma_1^*)$. $\mathcal{A}_0$ chooses a random bit $\beta \in \{0, 1\}$ and picks $r' \xleftarrow{R} \mathbb{Z}_q$. Then $\mathcal{A}_0$ encrypts m_β under $\mathsf{rcv}_\beta^*, \sigma_\beta^*$ as follows:

$$ek_{\sigma_\beta^*} := g_1^{\eta \mathbf{b}_4}(T_4^{\sigma_\beta^*}T_5^{-1})^{r'}, C_0 := m_\beta \cdot (e(T_2, g_2^{b_2^*}))^\alpha = m_\beta \cdot (g_T^\alpha)^z,$$
$$C_1 := ek_{\sigma_\beta^*} \cdot T_1^{(\mathsf{rcv}_\beta^*) \cdot \theta_1 + (vk^*) \cdot \theta_2} \cdot T_2 \cdot T_3.$$

We have $z := \tau_1$ and $r := r'\tau_1$ implicitly. $\mathcal{A}_0$ signs (C_0, C_1) to get sig and finally sends $\mathsf{ct}_\beta = \{vk^*, \mathsf{sig}, (C_0, C_1)\}$ to $\mathcal{A}$.

4. Query 2 : Same as Query 1, except that it may not query about $(m_0, \mathrm{rcv}_0^*, \sigma_0^*)$, $(m_1, \mathrm{rcv}_1^*, \sigma_1^*)$ and ct_β.

If $(T_1, T_2, T_3, T_4, T_5)$ is distributed as Dist_1, then the ciphertext is semi-functional. The exponent part of C_1 has an additional term whose coefficients in basis $(\mathbf{d}_6, \mathbf{d}_7, \mathbf{d}_8, \mathbf{d}_9, \mathbf{d}_{10})$ can be written as

$$\tau_2 \mathbf{A}^{-1} (\mathrm{rcv}_\beta^* \theta_1 + (vk^*) \cdot \theta_2, 1, 1, r'\sigma_\beta^*, -r')^\top.$$

Since matrix $\mathbf{A}$ is randomly sampled, the coefficients are uniformly random except with probability $2/q$ according to Lemma 2 (when $\tau_2 = 0$ in Subspace problem or $(r_6, r_7, r_8, r_9, r_{10}) = (0, 0, 0, 0, 0)$ in SF ciphertext). If $(T_1, T_2, T_3, T_4, T_5)$ is distributed as Dist_2, this is a properly distributed normal encryption of m_β. Therefore, $\mathcal{A}_0$ can properly simulate Game_{real} and Game_0.

As claimed in Theorem 1, the advantage of $\mathcal{A}$ can be divided into two parts, namely $|\Pr[\mathrm{Succ} \wedge \mathrm{Forge}] - \frac{1}{2}\Pr[\mathrm{Forge}]| = \epsilon_2$ and $|\Pr[\mathrm{Succ} \wedge \overline{\mathrm{Forge}}] + \frac{1}{2}\Pr[\mathrm{Forge}] - \frac{1}{2}| = 2/q$. Therefore, $\mathrm{Adv}_{\mathcal{A}_0}^{\mathrm{DS1}} = \epsilon - 2/q - \frac{1}{2}\epsilon_2$.

Lemma 4. *Suppose an adversary $\mathcal{A}$ where $|\mathrm{Adv}_{\mathcal{A}}^{\mathrm{Game}_{j,1}} - \mathrm{Adv}_{\mathcal{A}}^{\mathrm{Game}_{j-1,2}}| = \epsilon$. Then there exists a PPT algorithm $\mathcal{A}_{j,1}$ where $\mathrm{Adv}_{\mathcal{A}_{j,1}}^{\mathrm{DS2}} = \epsilon - 6/q - \frac{1}{2}\epsilon_2$, with $K = 5$ and $N = 10$.*

Proof. $\mathcal{A}_{j,1}$ is given

$$D := (\mathbb{G}; [\mathbf{b}_1]_1, [\mathbf{b}_2]_1, \ldots, [\mathbf{b}_5]_1, [\mathbf{b}_1^*]_2, \ldots, [\mathbf{b}_{10}^*]_2, U_1, U_2, U_3, U_4, U_5, \mu_2) \quad (3)$$

and $(T_1, T_2, T_3, T_4, T_5)$. $U_1 = [\mu_1 \mathbf{b}_1 + \mu_2 \mathbf{b}_6]_1, U_2 = [\mu_1 \mathbf{b}_2 + \mu_2 \mathbf{b}_7]_1, U_3 = [\mu_1 \mathbf{b}_3 + \mu_2 \mathbf{b}_8]_1, U_4 = [\mu_1 \mathbf{b}_4 + \mu_2 \mathbf{b}_9]_1, U_5 = [\mu_1 \mathbf{b}_5 + \mu_2 \mathbf{b}_{10}]_1$. $\mathcal{A}_{j,1}$ is required to decide whether $(T_1, T_2, T_3, T_4, T_5)$ is distributed as $\mathrm{Dist}_1 = ([\tau_1 \mathbf{b}_1^* + \tau_2 \mathbf{b}_6^*]_2, [\tau_1 \mathbf{b}_2^* + \tau_2 \mathbf{b}_7^*]_2, [\tau_1 \mathbf{b}_3^* + \tau_2 \mathbf{b}_8^*]_2, [\tau_1 \mathbf{b}_4^* + \tau_2 \mathbf{b}_9^*]_2, [\tau_1 \mathbf{b}_5^* + \tau_2 \mathbf{b}_{10}^*]_2)$ or $\mathrm{Dist}_2 = ([\tau_1 \mathbf{b}_1^*]_2, [\tau_1 \mathbf{b}_2^*]_2, [\tau_1 \mathbf{b}_3^*]_2, [\tau_1 \mathbf{b}_4^*]_2, [\tau_1 \mathbf{b}_5^*]_2)$.

The adversary $\mathcal{A}_{j,1}$ simulate $\mathrm{Game}_{j,1}$ or $\mathrm{Game}_{j-1,2}$ with $\mathcal{A}$ depending on the distribution of $(T_1, T_2, T_3, T_4, T_5)$. It simulates the game in the following steps:

1. Setup : $\mathcal{A}_{j,1}$ chooses a random invertible matrix $\mathbf{A} \xleftarrow{R} \mathbb{Z}_q^{5 \times 5}$. The generation of $\mathbb{D}^*$ from $\mathbb{B}^*$ is the same as Eq. 1 and Eq. 2 in Lemma 3. The setup of (mpk, msk) and (vk^*, sk^*) is also the same as the real scheme Setup.
2. Query 1: Since $\mathcal{A}_{j,1}$ knows master secret key msk and the verify algorithm is public, $\mathcal{A}_{j,1}$ can properly run SKGen, RKGen, Dec to answer oracle queries.
   - RKGen$(\cdot)$: To answer first $j{-}1$ keys, $\mathcal{A}_{j,1}$ runs KeyGenSF to generate SF2 keys and sends back to $\mathcal{A}$. To answer the j-th key query for ρ_j, $\mathcal{A}_{j,1}$ can calculate dk_{ρ_j} by picking $s, r_2 \xleftarrow{R} \mathbb{Z}_q$ and calculating

$$k_1 := g_2^{\alpha \mathbf{b}_2^* + s\mathbf{b}_4^*} \cdot T_1^{-1} \cdot T_2^{\rho_j \theta_1}, k_2 := g_2^{r_2(\rho_j \theta_1 \mathbf{b}_2^* - \mathbf{b}_1^*)}, k_3 := (g_T^\eta)^s,$$
$$k_4 := g_2^{r_3(\mathbf{b}_2^* - \mathbf{b}_3^*) + s\mathbf{b}_5^*}, b_1 := T_3^{\theta_2}, b_2 := g_2^{r_2 \theta_2 \mathbf{b}_3^*}$$

We have $\tau_1 = r_1$ implicitly. If $(T_1, T_2, T_3, T_4, T_5)$ is distributed as Dist_2, dk_{ρ_j} is a normal decryption key. If $(T_1, T_2, T_3, T_4, T_5)$ is distributed as Dist_1, dk_{ρ_j} is a $\mathsf{SF1}$ decryption key, whose k_1 exponent has an additional part equal to $\tau_2(-\mathbf{b}_6^* + \rho_j\theta_1\mathbf{b}_7^* + 0 \cdot \mathbf{b}_8^* + 0 \cdot \mathbf{b}_9^* + 0 \cdot \mathbf{b}_{10}^*)$. The coefficients in the basis $(\mathbf{b}_6^*, \mathbf{b}_7^*, \mathbf{b}_8^*, \mathbf{b}_9^*, \mathbf{b}_{10}^*)$ form the vector $\tau_2(-1, \rho_j\theta_1, 0, 0, 0)$. To respond to the remaining decryption key queries, $\mathcal{A}_{j,1}$ simply runs the normal key generation algorithm.

  – $\mathsf{SKGen}(\cdot)$ and $\mathsf{Dec}(\cdot)$: The simulation of encryption key generation and decryption behave the same as in the Lemma 3.

3. Challenge : $\mathcal{A}$ sends $\mathcal{A}_{j,1}$ two pairs $(m_0, \mathsf{rcv}_0^*, \sigma_0^*)$ and $(m_1, \mathsf{rcv}_1^*, \sigma_1^*)$. $\mathcal{A}_{j,1}$ chooses a random bit $\beta \in \{0, 1\}$ and picks $r' \xleftarrow{R} \mathbb{Z}_q$. Then $\mathcal{A}_{j,1}$ encrypts m_β under $\mathsf{rcv}_\beta^*, \sigma_\beta^*$ as follows:

$$ek_{\sigma_\beta^*} := g_1^{\eta \mathbf{b}_4}(U_4^{\sigma_\beta^*} U_5^{-1})^{r'}, C_0 := m_\beta \cdot (e(U_2, g_2^{\mathbf{b}_2^*}))^\alpha = m_\beta \cdot (g_T^\alpha)^z,$$
$$C_1 := ek_{\sigma_\beta^*} \cdot U_1^{(\mathsf{rcv}_\beta^*) \cdot \theta_1 + (vk^*) \cdot \theta_2} \cdot U_2 \cdot U_3.$$

We have $z := \mu_1$ and $r := r'\mu_1$ implicitly. $\mathcal{A}_{j,1}$ signs (C_0, C_1) to get sig and finally sends $\mathsf{ct}_\beta = \{vk, \mathsf{sig}, (C_0, C_1)\}$ to $\mathcal{A}$. Similar as the proof of Lemma 3, the exponent of C_1 has an additional part, whose coefficients in the basis $(\mathbf{b}_6, \mathbf{b}_7, \mathbf{b}_8, \mathbf{b}_9, \mathbf{b}_{10})$ form the vector

$$\mathbf{x} = \mu_2((\mathsf{rcv}_\beta^*) \cdot \theta_1 + vk^*\theta_2, 1, 1, r'\sigma_\beta^*, -r') \tag{4}$$

4. Query 2 : Same as Query 1, except that it may not query about $(m_0, \mathsf{rcv}_0^*, \sigma_0^*)$, $(m_1, \mathsf{rcv}_1^*, \sigma_1^*)$ and ct_β.

If adversary $\mathcal{A}$ use $\mathsf{SF1}$ key dk_{ρ_j} to delegate a dk'_{ρ_j} for decryption, the additional exponent vector will be

$$\mathbf{y} = \tau_2(-1, \rho_j\theta_1, vk\theta_2, 0, 0) \tag{5}$$

If $\mathsf{rcv}_\beta^* = \rho_j$ (which is not allowed) and the decryption algorithm gives $\mathsf{snd}_\beta^* = \sigma_\beta^*$, then the vector $\mathbf{x}$ and $\mathbf{y}$ in Eq. 4 and Eq. 5 is orthogonal, e.g. $\langle \mathbf{x}, \mathbf{y} \rangle = 0$, resulting in a nominally semi-functional ciphertext and key pair. Then translate $\mathbf{x}$ and $\mathbf{y}$ into $\mathbf{x}'$ and $\mathbf{y}'$ in space $\mathbb{D}$ and $\mathbb{D}^*$, where $\mathbf{x}' = \mathbf{A}^{-1}\mathbf{x}^\top, \mathbf{y}' = \mathbf{A}^\top\mathbf{y}^\top$. In $\mathcal{A}$'s view, $\mathbf{x}$ and $\mathbf{y}$ are distributed as random vectors in the spans of $(\mathbf{d}_6, \ldots, \mathbf{d}_{10})$ and $(\mathbf{d}_6^*, \ldots, \mathbf{d}_{10}^*)$ except with a probability of $4/q$ according to Lemma 2 (when $\tau_2 = 0$ or $\mu_2 = 0$ in Subspace problem, or $\{s_{i,1}\}_{i=6,\ldots,10} = 0$, or $(r_6, \ldots, r_{10}) = (0, \ldots, 0)$). $\mathcal{A}_{j,1}$ properly simulates $\mathsf{Game}_{j,1}$.

If $(T_1, T_2, T_3, T_4, T_5)$ is distributed as Dist_2, $\mathbf{x}'$ is uniformly random except with probability $2/q$ proved in Lemma 3. $\mathcal{A}_{j,1}$ properly simulates $\mathsf{Game}_{j-1,2}$.

As claimed in Theorem 1, the advantage of $\mathcal{A}$ is $\mathsf{Adv}_{\mathcal{A}_{j,1}}^{\mathsf{DS2}} = \epsilon - 6/q - \frac{1}{2}\epsilon_2$.

Lemma 5. *Suppose an adversary $\mathcal{A}$ where $|\mathsf{Adv}_{\mathcal{A}}^{\mathsf{Game}_{j,1}} - \mathsf{Adv}_{\mathcal{A}}^{\mathsf{Game}_{j,2}}| = \epsilon$. Then there exists an adversary $\mathcal{A}_{j,2}$ where $\mathsf{Adv}_{\mathcal{A}_{j,2}}^{\mathsf{DS2}} = \epsilon - 6/q - \frac{1}{2}\epsilon_2$, with $K = 5$ and $N = 10$.*

Proof. $\mathcal{A}_{j,2}$ is given the distribution D and $(T_1, T_2, T_3, T_4, T_5)$ as the Eq. 3. $\mathcal{A}_{j,2}$ is required to decide whether $(T_1, T_2, T_3, T_4, T_5)$ is distributed as $\mathsf{Dist}_1 = ([\tau_1 \mathbf{b}_1^* + \tau_2 \mathbf{b}_6^*]_2, [\tau_1 \mathbf{b}_2^* + \tau_2 \mathbf{b}_7^*]_2, [\tau_1 \mathbf{b}_3^* + \tau_2 \mathbf{b}_8^*]_2, [\tau_1 \mathbf{b}_4^* + \tau_2 \mathbf{b}_9^*]_2, [\tau_1 \mathbf{b}_5^* + \tau_2 \mathbf{b}_{10}^*]_2)$ or $\mathsf{Dist}_2 = ([\tau_1 \mathbf{b}_1^*]_2, [\tau_1 \mathbf{b}_2^*]_2, [\tau_1 \mathbf{b}_3^*]_2, [\tau_1 \mathbf{b}_4^*]_2, [\tau_1 \mathbf{b}_5^*]_2)$.

Adversary $\mathcal{A}_{j,2}$ simulate $\mathsf{Game}_{j,1}$ or $\mathsf{Game}_{j,2}$ with $\mathcal{A}$ depending on the distribution of $(T_1, T_2, T_3, T_4, T_5)$. It simulates the game in the following steps:

1. Setup : $\mathcal{A}_{j,2}$ chooses a random invertible matrix $\mathbf{A} \xleftarrow{R} \mathbb{Z}_q^{5 \times 5}$. The generation of $\mathbb{D}^*$ from $\mathbb{B}^*$ is the same as Eq. 1 and Eq. 2 in Lemma 3. The setup of (mpk, msk) and (vk, sk) is also the same as the real scheme Setup.

2. Query 1: Since $\mathcal{A}_{j,2}$ knows master secret key msk and the verify algorithm is public, $\mathcal{A}_{j,2}$ can properly run $\mathsf{SKGen}, \mathsf{RKGen}, \mathsf{Dec}$ to answer oracle queries.
   - $\mathsf{RKGen}(\cdot)$: To answer the first j-1 keys, $\mathcal{A}_{j,2}$ runs $\mathsf{KeyGenSF}$ to generate SF2 keys and sends back to $\mathcal{A}$. To answer the j-th key query for ρ_j, $\mathcal{A}_{j,2}$ can get dk_{ρ_j} by picking $s, r_1, \{s_{i,1}\}_{i=6,\ldots,10}, z_{1,8}, k' \xleftarrow{R} \mathbb{Z}_q$ and computing

$$k_1 := [\alpha \mathbf{d}_2^* + r_1(\rho \theta_1 \mathbf{d}_2^* - \mathbf{d}_1^*) + s \mathbf{d}_4^* + s_{1,6} \mathbf{d}_6^* + s_{1,7} \mathbf{d}_7^* + s_{1,9} \mathbf{d}_9^*]_2,$$
$$k_2 := T_1^{-1} \cdot T_2^{\rho_j \theta_1}, k_3 := (g_T^\eta)^s, k_4 := g_2^{s \mathbf{b}_5^*} (T_2 T_3^{-1})^{k'},$$
$$b_1 := g_2^{r_1 \theta_2 \mathbf{b}_3^* + z_{1,8} \mathbf{b}_8^*}, b_2 := T_3^{\theta_2}.$$

We have $\tau_1 = r_2$ and $\tau_2 k' = r_3$ implicitly. If $(T_1, T_2, T_3, T_4, T_5)$ is distributed as Dist_2, dk_{ρ_j} is a normal decryption key. If it is distributed as Dist_1, dk_{ρ_j} is a SF2 decryption key, whose k_2 and k_4 exponent has an additional part, and the coefficients in the basis $(\mathbf{b}_6^*, \mathbf{b}_7^*, \mathbf{b}_8^*, \mathbf{b}_9^*, \mathbf{b}_{10}^*)$ form the vector $\tau_2(-1, \rho_j \theta_1, 0, 0, 0)$ and the vector $\tau_2(0, k', -k', 0, 0)$ respectively. To respond to the remaining decryption key queries, adversary $\mathcal{A}_{j,2}$ simply runs the normal key generation algorithm.
   - $\mathsf{SKGen}(\cdot)$ and $\mathsf{Dec}(\cdot)$: The simulation of encryption key generation and decryption behave the same as in the Lemma 3.

3. Challenge : The ciphertext simulation is the same as the Challenge phase in the Lemma 4. Similar as the proof of Lemma 4, the exponent of C_1 has an additional part whose coefficients in the basis $(\mathbf{b}_6, \mathbf{b}_7, \mathbf{b}_8, \mathbf{b}_9, \mathbf{b}_{10})$ form the vector

$$\mathbf{x} = \mu_2(\mathsf{rcv}_\beta^* \theta_1 + vk^* \theta_2, 1, 1, r' \sigma_\beta^*, -r') \tag{6}$$

4. Query 2 : Same as Query 1, except that it may not query about $(m_0, \mathsf{rcv}_0^*, \sigma_0^*)$, $(m_1, \mathsf{rcv}_1^*, \sigma_1^*)$ and ct_β.

If adversary $\mathcal{A}$ use SF2 key dk_{ρ_j} to delegate a dk'_{ρ_j} for decryption, the additional exponent vector of $k'_1 \cdot k_4^{\mathsf{snd}}$ will be

$$\mathbf{y} = \tau_2(-r'_1, \rho_j \theta_1 r'_1 + k'\mathsf{snd}, vk \theta_2 r'_1 - k'\mathsf{snd}, 0, 0). \tag{7}$$

If $\mathsf{rcv}_\beta^* = \rho_j$ (which is not allowed) and the decryption algorithm gives $\mathsf{snd}_\beta^* = \sigma_\beta^*$, then the vector $\mathbf{x}$ and $\mathbf{y}$ in Eq. 6 and Eq. 7 is orthogonal, e.g. $\langle \mathbf{x}, \mathbf{y} \rangle = 0$, resulting in a nominally semi-functional ciphertext and key pair. We now translate $\mathbf{x}$ and $\mathbf{y}$ into $\mathbf{x}'$ and $\mathbf{y}'$ in space $\mathbb{D}$ and $\mathbb{D}^*$. We have $\mathbf{x}' = \mathbf{A}^{-1}\mathbf{x}^\top, \mathbf{y}' = \mathbf{A}^\top \mathbf{y}^\top$. In $\mathcal{A}$'s view, $\mathbf{x}$ and $\mathbf{y}$ are distributed as random vectors in the spans of $(\mathbf{d}_6, \ldots, \mathbf{d}_{10})$ and $(\mathbf{d}_6^*, \ldots, \mathbf{d}_{10}^*)$ except with a probability of $4/q$ according to the Lemma 2. $\mathcal{A}_{j,2}$ properly simulates $\mathsf{Game}_{j,2}$.

If $(T_1, T_2, T_3, T_4, T_5)$ is distributed as Dist_2, $\mathbf{x}'$ is uniformly random except with probability $2/q$ proved in the Lemma 3. $\mathcal{A}_{j,2}$ properly simulates $\mathsf{Game}_{j,1}$.

As claimed in the Theorem 1, the advantage of $\mathcal{A}$ is $\mathsf{Adv}_{\mathcal{A}_{j,2}}^{\mathsf{DS2}} = \epsilon - 6/q - \frac{1}{2}\epsilon_2$.

Lemma 6. *The advantage of $\mathcal{A}$ in Game_{final} is $\mathsf{Adv}_{\mathcal{A}}^{final}(\lambda) \leq \mathsf{Adv}_{\mathcal{A}}^{Q,2}(\lambda) + 1/q + \frac{1}{2}\epsilon_2$.*

Proof. We introduce dual bases $\mathbb{F} := (\mathbf{f}_1, \ldots, \mathbf{f}_{10})$ and $\mathbb{F}^* := (\mathbf{f}_1^*, \ldots, \mathbf{f}_{10}^*)$ to prove the lemma. First pick $\mathbf{A} \xleftarrow{R} \mathbb{Z}_q^{5 \times 5}$. $\mathbf{A}_i$ denotes the i-th row of $\mathbf{A}$ and $a_{i,j}$ denotes the element in $\mathbf{A}$'s i-th row, j-th column. Define $\mathbb{F}$ and $\mathbb{F}^*$ as:

$$(\mathbf{f}_1, \ldots, \mathbf{f}_5) := (\mathbf{d}_1, \ldots, \mathbf{d}_5), \quad (\mathbf{f}_6, \ldots, \mathbf{f}_{10}) := \mathbf{A} \cdot (\mathbf{d}_1, \ldots, \mathbf{d}_5)^\top + (\mathbf{d}_6, \ldots, \mathbf{d}_{10}).$$
$$(\mathbf{f}_1^*, \ldots, \mathbf{f}_5^*) := -\mathbf{A} \cdot (\mathbf{d}_6^*, \ldots, \mathbf{d}_{10}^*)^\top + (\mathbf{d}_1^*, \ldots, \mathbf{d}_5^*), \quad (\mathbf{f}_6^*, \ldots, \mathbf{f}_{10}^*) := (\mathbf{d}_6^*, \ldots, \mathbf{d}_{10}^*).$$

Apparently, $(\mathbb{F}, \mathbb{F}^*)$ are also dual bases and just the linear transformation of $(\mathbb{D}, \mathbb{D}^*)$, so $(\mathbb{F}, \mathbb{F}^*)$ has the same distribution as $(\mathbb{D}, \mathbb{D}^*)$.

In $\mathsf{Game}_{j,2}$, $(C_1)_{\sigma_\beta^*}^{\mathsf{SF2}}$ and k_1, k_2, k_4 components in $\{dk_{\rho_j}^{\mathsf{SF2}}\}_{j \in [Q]}$ can be expressed over bases $(\mathbb{D}, \mathbb{D}^*)$ and $(\mathbb{F}, \mathbb{F}^*)$ as following (k_3, b_1 and b_2 remain the same):

$$(C_1)_{\sigma_\beta^*}^{\mathsf{SF2}} := [\eta\mathbf{d}_4 + r(\sigma_\beta^*\mathbf{d}_4 - \mathbf{d}_5) + z(\mathbf{d}_2 + \mathbf{d}_3 + \mathbf{d}_1((\mathsf{rcv}_\beta^*)\theta_1 + vk\theta_2)) +$$
$$r_6\mathbf{d}_6 + r_7\mathbf{d}_7 + r_8\mathbf{d}_8 + r_9\mathbf{d}_9 + r_{10}\mathbf{d}_{10}]_1 = [\eta\mathbf{f}_4 + \sum_{l=1}^{10}(r_l\mathbf{f}_l)]_1,$$

$$k_1^{\mathsf{SF2}} := [\alpha\mathbf{d}_2^* + r_{1,j}(\rho_j\theta_1\mathbf{d}_2^* - \mathbf{d}_1^*) + s_j\mathbf{d}_4^* + s_{1,6,j}\mathbf{d}_6^* + s_{1,7,j}\mathbf{d}_7^* + s_{1,9,j}\mathbf{d}_9^*]_2$$
$$= [\alpha\mathbf{f}_2^* + r_{1,j}(\rho_j\theta_1\mathbf{f}_2^* - \mathbf{f}_1^*) + s_j\mathbf{f}_4^* + \sum_{l=6}^{10}(t_{1,l,j}\mathbf{f}_l^*)]_2,$$

$$k_2^{\mathsf{SF2}} := [r_{2,j}(\rho_j\theta_1\mathbf{d}_2^* - \mathbf{d}_1^*) + s_{2,6,j}\mathbf{d}_6^* + s_{2,7,j}\mathbf{d}_7^*]_2$$
$$= [r_{2,j}(\rho_j\theta_1\mathbf{f}_2^* - \mathbf{f}_1^*) + \sum_{l=6}^{10}(t_{2,l,j}\mathbf{f}_l^*)]_2,$$

$$k_4^{\mathsf{SF2}} := [r_{3,j}(\mathbf{d}_2^* - \mathbf{d}_3^*) + s_j\mathbf{d}_5^* + s_{4,7,j}\mathbf{d}_7^* + s_{4,8,j}\mathbf{d}_8^* + s_{4,10,j}\mathbf{d}_{10}^*]_2$$
$$= [r_{3,j}(\mathbf{f}_2^* - \mathbf{f}_3^*) + s_j\mathbf{f}_5^* + \sum_{l=6}^{10}(t_{4,l,j}\mathbf{f}_l^*)]_2.$$

where

$$(r_1, r_2, r_3, r_4, r_5) := (z((\mathsf{rcv}_\beta^*)\theta_1 + vk\theta_2), z, z, r\sigma_\beta^*, -r) - (r_6, r_7, r_8, r_9, r_{10}) \cdot \mathbf{A}$$

$$(t_{1,6,j}, \ldots, t_{1,10,j}) := (-r_{1,j}, \alpha + \rho_j\theta_1 r_{1,j}, 0, s_j, 0) \cdot \mathbf{A} + (s_{1,6,j}, s_{1,7,j}, 0, s_{1,9,j}, 0)$$

$$(t_{2,6,j}, \ldots, t_{2,10,j}) := (-r_{2,j}, \rho_j \theta_1 r_{1,j}, 0, 0, 0) \cdot \mathbf{A} + (s_{2,6,j}, s_{2,7,j}, 0, 0, 0)$$

$$(t_{4,6,j}, \ldots, t_{4,10,j}) := (0, r_{3,j}, -r_{3,j}, 0, s_j) \cdot \mathbf{A} + (0, s_{2,7,j}, s_{2,8,j}, 0, s_{2,10,j})$$

Since $z, r, r_{1,j}, r_{2,j}, r_{3,j}, z_{8,j}, \{s_{m,n,j}\}_{m=1,2,4,n=6,\ldots,10}$ and $\mathbf{A}$ are randomly picked, the SF2 $\{dk_{\rho_j}\}$ components are uniformly distributed. Further, the delegated keys used in decryption for SF2 key are uniformly distributed. The SF2 component of $\{C_{ek_{\sigma_\beta^*}, rcv_\beta^*}\}$ is uniformly distributed unless $(r_6, \ldots, r_{10}) = (0, 0, 0, 0, 0)$.

The coefficient $(z((rcv_\beta^*)\theta_1 + vk\theta_2), z, z, r\sigma_\beta^*, -r)$ of $(\mathbf{d}_1, \ldots, \mathbf{d}_5)$ can change into a random coefficient $(r_1, r_2, r_3, r_4, r_5)$ of $(\mathbf{f}_1, \ldots, \mathbf{f}_5)$. In conclusion, $\mathsf{Game}_{Q,2}$ and Game_{final} are statistically indistinguishable in $\mathcal{A}$'s view except with a probability of $1/q$ (when $(r_6, \ldots, r_{10}) = (0, 0, 0, 0, 0)$).

As claimed in the Theorem 1, the advantage of $\mathcal{A}$ is given that $\mathsf{Adv}_{\mathcal{A}}^{final} \leq \mathsf{Adv}_{\mathcal{A}}^{Q,2}(\lambda) + 1/q + \frac{1}{2}\epsilon_2$.

Lemma 7. *For any adversary,* $\mathsf{Adv}_{\mathcal{A}}^{\mathsf{Game}_{final}}(\lambda) = 0$.

Proof. In Game_{final}, random bit β is independent from adversary's view. Therefore, $\mathsf{Adv}_{\mathcal{A}}^{\mathsf{Game}_{final}}(\lambda) = 0$.

From the Lemma 3 to the Lemma 7, we prove the privacy against chosen-ciphertext attacks of our IB-ME scheme under the SXDH assumption.

Theorem 3. *The proposed IB-ME scheme satisfied authenticity under the Symmetric External Diffie-Hellman assumption.*

Proof. The proof outline of authenticity is similar to [8], since the authenticity level of IB-ME and the ek_σ have the same structure to [8].

References

1. Agrawal, S., Boneh, D., Boyen, X.: Efficient lattice (h)ibe in the standard model. In: Gilbert, H. (ed.) EUROCRYPT 2010. LNCS, vol. 6110, pp. 553–572. Springer, Heidelberg (2010). https://doi.org/10.1007/978-3-642-13190-5_28
2. Ateniese, G., Francati, D., Nuñez, D., Venturi, D.: Match me if you can: matchmaking encryption and its applications. J. Cryptol. 34(3), 1–50 (2021). https://doi.org/10.1007/s00145-021-09381-4
3. Balfanz, D., Durfee, G., Shankar, N., Smetters, D., Staddon, J., Wong, H.C.: Secret handshakes from pairing-based key agreements. In: 2003 Symposium on Security and Privacy, 2003. pp. 180–196. IEEE (2003)
4. Boneh, D., Franklin, M.: Identity-based encryption from the weil pairing. In: Kilian, J. (ed.) CRYPTO 2001. LNCS, vol. 2139, pp. 213–229. Springer, Heidelberg (2001). https://doi.org/10.1007/3-540-44647-8_13
5. Boyen, X., Waters, B.: Anonymous hierarchical identity-based encryption (without random oracles). In: Dwork, C. (ed.) CRYPTO 2006. LNCS, vol. 4117, pp. 290–307. Springer, Heidelberg (2006). https://doi.org/10.1007/11818175_17
6. Buchmann, J., Dahmen, E., Ereth, S., Hülsing, A., Rückert, M.: On the security of the winternitz one-time signature scheme. In: Nitaj, A., Pointcheval, D. (eds.) AFRICACRYPT 2011. LNCS, vol. 6737, pp. 363–378. Springer, Heidelberg (2011). https://doi.org/10.1007/978-3-642-21969-6_23

7. Canetti, R., Halevi, S., Katz, J.: Chosen-ciphertext security from identity-based encryption. In: Cachin, C., Camenisch, J.L. (eds.) EUROCRYPT 2004. LNCS, vol. 3027, pp. 207–222. Springer, Heidelberg (2004). https://doi.org/10.1007/978-3-540-24676-3_13

8. Chen, J., Li, Y., Wen, J., Weng, J.: Identity-based matchmaking encryption from standard assumptions. In: International Conference on the Theory and Application of Cryptology and Information Security, pp. 394–422. Springer (2022). https://doi.org/10.1007/978-3-031-22969-5_14

9. Chen, J., Lim, H.W., Ling, S., Wang, H., Wee, H.: Shorter IBE and signatures via asymmetric pairings. In: Abdalla, M., Lange, T. (eds.) Pairing 2012. LNCS, vol. 7708, pp. 122–140. Springer, Heidelberg (2013). https://doi.org/10.1007/978-3-642-36334-4_8

10. Chen, J., Wee, H.: Fully, (almost) tightly secure ibe and dual system groups. In: Canetti, R., Garay, J.A. (eds.) CRYPTO 2013. LNCS, vol. 8043, pp. 435–460. Springer, Heidelberg (2013). https://doi.org/10.1007/978-3-642-40084-1_25

11. Cocks, C.: An identity based encryption scheme based on quadratic residues. In: Honary, B. (ed.) Cryptography and Coding 2001. LNCS, vol. 2260, pp. 360–363. Springer, Heidelberg (2001). https://doi.org/10.1007/3-540-45325-3_32

12. Francati, D., Guidi, A., Russo, L., Venturi, D.: Identity-based matchmaking encryption without random oracles. In: Adhikari, A., Küsters, R., Preneel, B. (eds.) INDOCRYPT 2021. LNCS, vol. 13143, pp. 415–435. Springer, Cham (2021). https://doi.org/10.1007/978-3-030-92518-5_19

13. Fujisaki, E., Okamoto, T.: Secure integration of asymmetric and symmetric encryption schemes. In: Wiener, M. (ed.) CRYPTO 1999. LNCS, vol. 1666, pp. 537–554. Springer, Heidelberg (1999). https://doi.org/10.1007/3-540-48405-1_34

14. Horwitz, J., Lynn, B.: Toward hierarchical identity-based encryption. In: Knudsen, L.R. (ed.) EUROCRYPT 2002. LNCS, vol. 2332, pp. 466–481. Springer, Heidelberg (2002). https://doi.org/10.1007/3-540-46035-7_31

15. Jiang, Z., Wang, X., Zhang, K., Gong, J., Chen, J., Qian, H.: Revocable identity-based matchmaking encryption in the standard model. IET Information Security (2023)

16. Joye, M.: Identity-based cryptosystems and quadratic residuosity. In: Cheng, C.-M., Chung, K.-M., Persiano, G., Yang, B.-Y. (eds.) PKC 2016. LNCS, vol. 9614, pp. 225–254. Springer, Heidelberg (2016). https://doi.org/10.1007/978-3-662-49384-7_9

17. Katsumata, S., Matsuda, T., Takayasu, A.: Lattice-based revocable (hierarchical) ibe with decryption key exposure resistance. Theoret. Comput. Sci. **809**, 103–136 (2020)

18. Naor, M., Yung, M.: Public-key cryptosystems provably secure against chosen ciphertext attacks. In: Proceedings of the Twenty-Second Annual ACM Symposium on Theory of Computing, pp. 427–437 (1990)

19. Nekrasov, M., Iland, D., Metzger, M., Parks, L., Belding, E.: A user-driven free speech application for anonymous and verified online, public group discourse. J. Internet Serv. Appl. **9**(1), 1–23 (2018)

20. Okamoto, T., Takashima, K.: Homomorphic encryption and signatures from vector decomposition. In: Galbraith, S.D., Paterson, K.G. (eds.) Pairing 2008. LNCS, vol. 5209, pp. 57–74. Springer, Heidelberg (2008). https://doi.org/10.1007/978-3-540-85538-5_4

21. Okamoto, T., Takashima, K.: Hierarchical predicate encryption for inner-products. In: Matsui, M. (ed.) ASIACRYPT 2009. LNCS, vol. 5912, pp. 214–231. Springer, Heidelberg (2009). https://doi.org/10.1007/978-3-642-10366-7_13

22. Okamoto, T., Takashima, K.: Fully secure functional encryption with general relations from the decisional linear assumption. In: Rabin, T. (ed.) CRYPTO 2010. LNCS, vol. 6223, pp. 191–208. Springer, Heidelberg (2010). https://doi.org/10.1007/978-3-642-14623-7_11
23. Ramanna, S.C., Sarkar, P.: Anonymous hibe from standard assumptions over type-3 pairings using dual system encryption. Cryptology ePrint Archive, Paper 2013/528 (2013)
24. Shamir, A.: Identity-Based Cryptosystems and Signature Schemes. In: Blakley, G.R., Chaum, D. (eds.) CRYPTO 1984. LNCS, vol. 196, pp. 47–53. Springer, Heidelberg (1985). https://doi.org/10.1007/3-540-39568-7_5
25. Sun, J., Xu, G., Zhang, T., Yang, X., Alazab, M., Deng, R.H.: Privacy-aware and security-enhanced efficient matchmaking encryption. IEEE Trans. Inf. Forensics Secur. 18, 4345–4360 (2023)
26. Wang, Y., Wang, B., Lai, Q., Zhan, Y.: Identity-based matchmaking encryption with stronger security and instantiation on lattices. Cryptology ePrint Archive, Paper 2022/1718 (2022)
27. Waters, B.: Dual system encryption: realizing fully secure ibe and hibe under simple assumptions. In: Halevi, S. (ed.) CRYPTO 2009. LNCS, vol. 5677, pp. 619–636. Springer, Heidelberg (2009). https://doi.org/10.1007/978-3-642-03356-8_36
28. Xu, S., et al.: Match in my way: fine-grained bilateral access control for secure cloud-fog computing. IEEE Trans. Dependable Secure Comput. 19(2), 1064–1077 (2020)
29. Xu, S., Ning, J., Ma, J., Huang, X., Pang, H.H., Deng, R.H.: Expressive bilateral access control for internet-of-things in cloud-fog computing. In: Proceedings of the 26th ACM Symposium on Access Control Models and Technologies, pp. 143–154 (2021)
30. Zaverucha, G.M., Stinson, D.R.: Short one-time signatures. Cryptology ePrint Archive, Paper 2010/446 (2010)

Post-Quantum Public-Key Authenticated Searchable Encryption with Forward Security: General Construction, and Applications

Shiyuan Xu[1]([⊠]), Yibo Cao[2], Xue Chen[1,3]([⊠]), Yanmin Zhao[1], and Siu-Ming Yiu[1]([⊠])

[1] Department of Computer Science, The University of Hong Kong, Pok Fu Lam, Hong Kong
{syxu2,ymzhao,smyiu}@cs.hku.hk
[2] School of Cyberspace Security, Beijing University of Posts and Telecommunications, Beijing, China
[3] Department of Computing, The Hong Kong Polytechnic University, Hung Hom, Hong Kong
xue-serena.chen@connect.polyu.hk

Abstract. Public-key encryption with keyword search (PEKS) was first proposed by Boneh et al. (EUROCRYPT 2004), achieving the ability to search for ciphertext files. Nevertheless, it is vulnerable to *inside keyword guessing attacks* (IKGA). Public-key authenticated encryption with keyword search (PAEKS), introduced by Huang et al. (Inf. Sci. 2017), on the other hand, is secure against IKGA. Nonetheless, it is susceptible to *quantum computing attacks*. Liu et al. and Cheng et al. addressed this problem by reducing to the lattice hardness (AsiaCCS 2022, ESORICS 2022). Furthermore, several scholars pointed out that the threat of secret key exposure delegates a severe and realistic concern, potentially leading to *privacy disclosure* (EUROCRYPT 2003, Compt. J. 2022). As a result, research focusing on mitigating key exposure and resisting quantum attacks for the PAEKS primitive is far-reaching.

In this work, we present the *first* generic construction and instantiation of forward-secure PAEKS primitive based on lattice hardness without trusted authorities, mitigating the secret key exposure while ensuring quantum-safe properties. We extend the scheme of Liu et al. (AsiaCCS 2022), and formalize a novel post-quantum PAEKS construction, namely FS-PAEKS. To begin with, we introduce the binary tree structure to represent the time periods, along with a lattice basis extension algorithm, and SamplePre algorithm to obtain the post-quantum one-way secret key evolution, allowing users to update their secret keys periodically. Furthermore, our scheme is proven to be IND-CKA and IND-IKGA secure in a quantum setting. In addition, we also compare the security of our primitive in terms of computational complexity and communication overhead with other top-tier schemes. Ultimately, we demonstrate two potential applications of FS-PAEKS.

C. Ge and M. Yung (Eds.): Inscrypt 2023, LNCS 14526, pp. 274–298, 2024.
https://doi.org/10.1007/978-981-97-0942-7_14

Keywords: Public-key authenticated encryption with keyword
search · Lattice · Forward security · Multi-ciphertext
indistinguishability · Trapdoor privacy · Generic construction

1 Introduction

Traditional PEKS primitive contains three entities, that is, data owner, data
user, and cloud server [1]. PEKS scheme realizes that encrypted data can easily
be retrieved by the specific user through a specific trapdoor, which not only
protects the data privacy but also realizes the searchability [2]. A fundamental
security criterion for PEKS is to against the chosen keyword attacks (CKA)
[3]. Nevertheless, Byun et al. formalized the notation of trapdoor privacy (TP)
for the PEKS scheme since if it only considers the CKA, the protocol may
be threatened by the inside keyword guessing attacks (IKGA) [4]. To circum-
vent this problem, Huang et al. initialized a novel variant of PEKS, namely,
public-key authenticated encryption with keyword search (PAEKS), combining
the message authentication technique into a ciphertext generation algorithm [5].
In this way, the trapdoor can merely be valid to the authenticated ciphertext
for a specific sender. Numerous scholars commenced their research works on the
PAEKS primitive due to its high security [6–11].

However, the above-mentioned PAEKS protocols are totally on the basis
of the discrete logarithm assumption, which is vulnerable to quantum computing attacks. Liu et al. constructed a lattice-based PAEKS primitive that offers
both CKA and IKGA security while also being resistant to quantum computing
attacks [12]. Unfortunately, the security of ciphertext may be compromised if the
secret key of a receiver is leaked due to inadequate storage or malicious actions
by adversaries. To address this issue, several scholars introduced the notation
of forward security in digital signatures [13–15], which was later adapted by
Canetti et al. for use in a forward secure public key encryption scheme [16]. This
protocol periodically updates the secret key, therefore even if it is compromised
in one period, the security of other periods remains intact.

1.1 Motivation

As inappropriate storage of secret keys may lead to their compromise by malicious attackers [17,18], it is essential to update them within a certain period to
ensure forward security. Zhang et al. formalized the FS-PEKS scheme, achieving
forward security, nevertheless, one disadvantage of this scheme is that a malicious attacker may acquire the keyword from the trapdoor [19]. In contrast,
Jiang et al. presented a forward secure scheme for PAEKS, without considering
quantum computing attacks [20]. Among that, their constructions still need a
trusted authority to calculate secret keys, which will result in additional storage
overhead.

Huang et al. subsequently presented a PAEKS primitive, which was reduced
to be secure under the discrete logarithm assumption [5]. However, with the

advancement of quantum computers, Shor generalized a quantum algorithm, demonstrating the feasibility of solving classical cryptographic primitives in probabilistic polynomial times [21,22]. Consequently, classical PAEKS schemes are now vulnerable. Hence, several scholars transformed the traditional PAEKS primitive into the quantum-resistant PAEKS protocol and formalized the generic constructions based on lattice hardness [12,23]. Nevertheless, their schemes contain flaws due to the secret key leakage problem.

Therefore, the aforementioned issues motivate the following question:

Can we construct and instantiate a generic post-quantum forward-secure PAEKS satisfied CI, TP, MCI security without trusted settings to mitigate the secret key leakage problem?

1.2   Our Contributions

We resolve the above question affirmatively and summarize our contributions as follows.

- We generalize the first PAEKS with forward security instantiation in lattice without trusted authorities, mitigating the secret key exposure while enjoying quantum safety. Our primitive extends Liu et al.'s scheme [12], and proposes a novel post-quantum forward secure PAEKS construction, namely FS-PAEKS. In addition, we formalize the CI, TP, and MCI security of the proposed FS-PAEKS primitive.
- The proposed FS-PAEKS scheme enjoys quantum-safe forward security. We introduce a binary tree structure to update the receiver's secret key with different time periods. It ensures that exposing the secret key corresponding to a specific time period does not enable an adversary to "crack" the primitive for any previous time period due to its one-way nature. Additionally, we further employ the minimal cover set to achieve secret key updating periodically for the receiver based on the key evolution mechanism. Finally, we utilize the lattice basis extension technique to maintain quantum-safe for updating secret keys.
- The proposed FS-PAEKS scheme can be proven secure in strong security models. Firstly, the initial phase does not need a trusted setup assumption and the ciphertext can only be obtained by a valid sender. In this way, the trapdoor is valid from a receiver, which avoids adversaries adaptively accessing oracles to obtain the ciphertext for any keyword. Consequently, we introduce a pseudo-random smooth projective hash function to achieve the above property and forward-secure trapdoor privacy under IND-IKGA. In addition, our scheme has also proven to be IND-CKA and IND-Multi-CKA secure in a quantum setting.
- Eventually, we give a security properties comparison with the other eight PEKS and PAEKS primitives. Besides, we compare with Behnia et al.'s scheme [24], Zhang et al.'s scheme [19], and Liu et al.'s scheme [12] in terms of computational complexity and communication overhead theoretically.

1.3 Overview of Technique

Technical Roadmap. Informally speaking, constructing a forward-secure PAEKS primitive in the context of the lattice is a combination of PEKS, public key encryption, smooth projective hash functions (SPHF), binary tree structure, and lattice basis extension algorithm. More concretely, we begin by revisiting the post-quantum PAEKS primitive as the basic structure [12]. Next, we employ the SPHF technique to transform the primitive into IND-CCA secure. We then take advantage of the hierarchical structure of the binary tree to represent time periods and utilize $\mathsf{node}(t)$ to represent the smallest minimal cover set for secret key update periodically, following the approach outlined in Cash et al. [25]. To the best of our knowledge, it is the most efficient mechanism to realize key updates and it serves as a stepping stone toward our goal. Finally, we introduce the ExtBasis and SamplePre algorithms to facilitate the post-quantum one-way secret key evolution.

Smooth Projective Hash Functions. Smooth projective hash functions, initially proposed by Cramer et al. [26], are utilized to transform one encryption primitive from IND-CPA to IND-CCA. Moreover, numerous scholars extended the SPHF tool to realize password-authenticated key exchange protocols [27–32]. We use a variant kind of SPHF, say "word-independent" SPHF, proposed by Katz et al. [33] for primitive construction. Generally speaking, the "word-independent" SPHF scheme includes five algorithms defined for the NP language $\mathcal{L}$ over a domain $\mathcal{X}$.

We define a language family $(\mathcal{L}_{Para_l, Trap_l})$ indexed by the language parameter $Para_l$ and language trapdoor $Trap_l$. Besides, we consider an NP language family $(\tilde{\mathcal{L}}_{Para_l})$ with witness relation $\tilde{\mathcal{K}}_{Para_l}$, s.t. $\tilde{\mathcal{L}}_{Para_l} := \{\chi \in \mathcal{X}_{Para_l} | \exists \omega, \tilde{\mathcal{K}}_{Para_l}(\chi, \omega) = 1\} \subseteq \mathcal{L}_{Para_l, Trap_l} \subseteq \mathcal{X}_{Para_l}$, where $\mathcal{X}_{Para_l}$ is a family of sets. In addition, the membership in $\mathcal{X}_{Para_l}$ and $\tilde{\mathcal{K}}_{Para_l}$ can be checked in polynomial time with $Para_l$, and $\mathcal{L}_{Para_l, Trap_l}$ can be checked in polynomial time with $Para_l, Trap_l$. We describe the approximate "word-independent" SPHF scheme below.

- Setup(λ): Given a security parameter λ, this PPT algorithm outputs a language parameter $Para_l$.
- KeyGen$_{\mathsf{Hash}}$($Para_l$): Given $Para_l$, this PPT algorithm outputs outputs hk as the hashing key.
- KeyGen$_{\mathsf{Proj}}$(hk, $Para_l$): Given hk and $Para_l$, this PPT algorithm outputs outputs the projection key pk.
- Hash(hk, $Para_l$, χ): Given hk, $Para_l$ and a word $\chi \in \mathcal{X}_{Para_l}$, this deterministic algorithm outputs Hash $\in \{0,1\}^\delta$ as a hash value, where $\delta \in \mathbb{N}$.
- ProjHash(pk, $Para_l$, χ, ω): Given pk, $Para_l$, $\chi \in \tilde{\mathcal{L}}_{Para_l}$ and a witness ω, this deterministic algorithm outputs ProjHash $\in \{0,1\}^\delta$ as a projected hash value, where $\delta \in \mathbb{N}$.

Informally speaking, an approximate "word-independent" SPHF protocol satisfies two attributes:

278   S. Xu et al.

(1) ϵ-approximate correctness: Given a word $\chi \in \tilde{\mathcal{L}}_{Para_l}$, and the corresponding witness ω, the SPHF scheme is ϵ-approximate correct when: $\Pr[\mathsf{HD}(\mathsf{Hash}(\mathsf{hk}, Para_l, \chi), \mathsf{ProjHash}(\mathsf{pk}, Para_l, \chi, \omega)) > \epsilon \cdot \delta] \approx 0$, where $\mathsf{HD}(a, b)$ means the hamming distance between two elements a and b.

(2) Pseudo-randomness: For some $\delta \in \mathbb{N}$, if a word $\chi \in \tilde{\mathcal{L}}_{Para_l}$, its hash value Hash is indistinguishable from a random element in $\{0, 1\}^\delta$; Otherwise, Hash is statistically indistinguishable from a random element chosen in $\{0, 1\}^\delta$.

Binary Tree for Representing Time Periods. We use binary tree encryption primitive for enrolling time periods [16]. Informally, we define numerous time periods $t \in \{0, 1, \cdots, 2^d - 1\}$, where d is the depth of the binary from the root node to the deepest leaf. In this paper, the time period t will be described in binary expression $t = (t_1 t_2 \cdots t_d)$. For example, if the depth is four and the last leaf can be described as $t = (1111)$. On each time period, it only has one path from the root node to the current leaf node and we define $\Theta^{(i)} = (\theta^{(1)} \theta^{(2)} \cdots \theta^{(i)})$, $i \in [1, d]$ as the path, where $\theta^{(i)} = 0$ if the i-th level node is the left leaf and $\theta^{(i)} = 1$ if the i-th level node is the right leaf. We also define $\mathsf{node}(t)$ to represent the smallest minimal cover set containing one ancestor of all leaves on the time period t and after the time period t, say including $\{t, t+1, \cdots, 2^d - 1\}$.

For simple understanding, we give an example in Fig. 1, describing a $d = 4$ binary tree with 16 time periods in total. In this figure, we show the meaning of $\mathsf{node}(t)$ as: $\mathsf{node}(0000) = \{\text{root}\}, \mathsf{node}(0001) = \{0001, 001, 01, 1\}, \mathsf{node}(0010) = \{001, 01, 1\}, \mathsf{node}(0011) = \{0011, 01, 1\}, \mathsf{node}(0100) = \{01, 1\}, \text{node } (0101) = \{0101, 011, 1\}, \mathsf{node}(0110) = \{011, 1\}, \mathsf{node}(0111) = \{0111, 1\}, \mathsf{node}(1000) = \{1\}, \mathsf{node}(1001) = \{1001, 101, 11\}, \mathsf{node}(1010) = \{101, 11\}, \mathsf{node}(1011) = \{1011, 11\}, \mathsf{node}(1100) = \{11\}, \mathsf{node}(1101) = \{1101, 111\}, \mathsf{node}(1110) = \{111\}, \mathsf{node}(1111) = \{1111\}$.

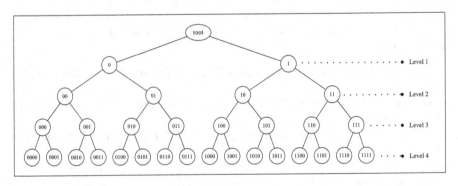

Fig. 1. Binary tree of depth $d = 4$ with binary expression time period (node).

Lattice Basis Extension. We use the lattice basis extension algorithm to construct a secret key one-way evolutionary mechanism (See Lemma 5 in Sect. 2.3). More concretely, we discretize the time period to 2^d segments, where d means the total depth of a binary tree. The matrix $\mathbf{M}_R$ is the public key for receiver and the matrix $\mathbf{S}_{\Theta^{(i)}}$ is the trapdoor, where $\Theta^{(i)} := (\theta_1, \theta_2, \cdots, \theta_j, \theta_{j+1}, \cdots, \theta_i)$. Consequently, the updated trapdoor can be calculated by any ancestor's trapdoor, and root node is the trapdoor of the original ancestor.

We first define $F_{\Theta^{(i)}} := [\mathbf{M}_R \parallel A_1^{(\theta_1)} \parallel A_2^{(\theta_2)} \parallel \cdots \parallel A_i^{(\theta_i)}]$ as the corresponding matrix of $\Theta^{(i)}$. For any depth $j < i$, where $j, i \in [1, d]$, given the trapdoor $\mathbf{S}_{\Theta^{(j)}}$ on time j, we have: $\mathbf{S}_{\Theta^{(i)}} \leftarrow \mathsf{ExtBasis}(F_{\Theta^{(i)}}, \mathbf{S}_{\Theta^{(j)}})$. After that, we specify the secret key update process as below.

$$sk_R(t) := (\mathbf{h}_R, \{\mathbf{r}_{R,1}\}, \{\mathbf{r}_{R,2}\}, \cdots, \{\mathbf{r}_{R,\kappa}\}, \mathbf{S}_{\Theta^{(i)}}),$$

where $\Theta^{(i)} \in \mathsf{node}(t)$ as the receiver's secret key on time t. Each node has the corresponding secret key in a binary tree. Receiver will update $sk_R(t)$ to $sk_R(t+1)$ through processing

$$sk_R(t+1) := (\mathbf{h}_R, \{\mathbf{r}_{R,1}\}, \{\mathbf{r}_{R,2}\}, \cdots, \{\mathbf{r}_{R,\kappa}\}, \mathbf{S}_{\Theta^{(i)}}), \text{where } \Theta^{(i)} \in \mathsf{node}(t+1).$$

1.4   Related Works

Lattice-Based PAEKS. Boneh et al. constructed the concept of PEKS in 2004 [1]. Zhang et al. argued that its security model for keyword privacy is not complete and then defined a new security model [34]. However, the basic PEKS primitive cannot resist the IKGA since an inside adversary may deduce the keyword from a specific trapdoor. Huang et al. formalized a PAEKS protocol to solve this problem by combining keyword authentication with PEKS [5]. Nevertheless, Liu et al. and Cheng et al. introduced lattice-based PAEKS primitive to achieve quantum resistance [12,35]. Many researchers utilized the PAEKS scheme to preserve privacy for the Internet of Things [9,36,37].

Forward Security. Forward security (FS) in the public-key cryptosystem was initialized by [16]. Zeng et al. introduced the FS notation into the PEKS scheme for cloud computing [38]. Zhang et al. formalized the first lattice-based FS-PEKS primitive [19]. After that, Yang et al. extended the FS-PEKS and constructed a lattice-based FS identity-based encryption with PEKS, namely, FS-IBEKS [39]. Recently, Jiang et al. presented a forward secure public-key authenticated encryption with conjunctive keyword search [20], but without considering the quantum attacks.

1.5   Outline

The rest of this paper is structured as follows. Section 2 covers the preliminary knowledge. In Sect. 3, we present the syntax of forward-secure PAEKS primitive and its security models. The generic construction will be elaborated in Sect. 4, while the security analysis will be specified in Sect. 5. In Sect. 6, we give the lattice-based instantiation. The parameters setting with correctness and theoretical comparison are illustrated in Sects. 7 and 8, respectively. Section 9 shows two applications of FS-PAEKS. Finally, we conclude this paper in Sect. 10.

2 Preliminaries

2.1 Public-Key Encryption with Keyword Search Scheme

Public-key encryption with keyword search (abbr. PEKS) was initially proposed by Boneh et al. [1]. A standard PEKS scheme consists of four algorithms:

- $(\mathsf{pk}_{\mathsf{PEKS}}, \mathsf{sk}_{\mathsf{PEKS}}) \leftarrow \mathsf{KeyGen}(\lambda)$: Given a security parameter λ, this probabilistic-polynomial time (PPT) algorithm outputs $\mathsf{pk}_{\mathsf{PEKS}}$ and $\mathsf{sk}_{\mathsf{PEKS}}$ as a public key and secret key, respectively.
- $\mathsf{ct}_{\mathsf{PEKS},kw} \leftarrow \mathsf{PEKS}(\mathsf{pk}_{\mathsf{PEKS}}, kw)$: After inputting a public key $\mathsf{pk}_{\mathsf{PEKS}}$ and a keyword kw, this PPT algorithm will output a ciphertext $\mathsf{ct}_{\mathsf{PEKS},kw}$.
- $\mathbf{Trap}_{\mathsf{PEKS},kw'} \leftarrow \mathsf{Trapdoor}(\mathsf{sk}_{\mathsf{PEKS}}, kw')$: Given a secret key $\mathsf{sk}_{\mathsf{PEKS}}$ and a keyword kw', this PPT algorithm outputs a trapdoor $\mathbf{Trap}_{\mathsf{PEKS},kw'}$.
- (1 or 0) $\leftarrow \mathsf{Test}(\mathsf{ct}_{\mathsf{PEKS},kw}, \mathbf{Trap}_{\mathsf{PEKS},kw'})$: After input a ciphertext $\mathsf{ct}_{\mathsf{PEKS},kw}$ and a trapdoor $\mathbf{Trap}_{\mathsf{PEKS},kw'}$, this deterministic algorithm outputs 1 if $kw = kw'$; Otherwise, it outputs 0.

Security Models. A secure PEKS scheme must satisfy the following properties:

(1) Correctness: Given a security parameter λ, any valid public-secret key pairs $(\mathsf{pk}_{\mathsf{PEKS}}, \mathsf{sk}_{\mathsf{PEKS}})$, any keywords kw, kw', any ciphertexts generated by $\mathsf{PEKS}(\mathsf{pk}_{\mathsf{PEKS}}, kw)$, and any trapdoors generated by $\mathsf{Trapdoor}(\mathsf{sk}_{\mathsf{PEKS}}, kw')$, the PEKS scheme is correct if it satisfies:

If $kw = kw'$, $\Pr[\mathsf{Test}(\mathsf{ct}, \mathbf{Trap}) = 1] \approx 1$; and if $kw \neq kw'$, $\Pr[\mathsf{Test}(\mathsf{ct}, \mathbf{Trap}) = 0] \approx 1$.

(2) Ciphertext Indistinguiability: If it does not exist an adversary $\mathcal{A}$ can obtain any keyword information of the challenge ciphertext $\mathsf{ct}_{\mathsf{PEKS},kw}$, this PEKS scheme has ciphertext indistinguishability against chosen keyword attacks (IND-CKA).

2.2 Labelled Public-Key Encryption Scheme

Labelled public-key encryption (abbr. Labelled PKE) is one of the variants of public-key encryption [40]. We employ the Labelled PKE scheme for our construction and refer to it as PKE for brevity. A standard PKE scheme consists of three algorithms:

- $(\mathsf{pk}_{\mathsf{PKE}}, \mathsf{sk}_{\mathsf{PKE}}) \leftarrow \mathsf{KeyExt}(\lambda)$: Given a security parameter λ, this PPT algorithm outputs $\mathsf{pk}_{\mathsf{PKE}}$ and $\mathsf{sk}_{\mathsf{PKE}}$ as the public key and secret key for encryption and decryption, respectively.

- $\mathsf{ct}_{\mathsf{PKE}} \leftarrow \mathsf{Encrypt}(\mathsf{pk}_{\mathsf{PKE}}, \mathsf{label}, \mathsf{pt}_{\mathsf{PKE}}, \rho)$: Given a public key $\mathsf{pk}_{\mathsf{PKE}}$, a label label, a plaintext $\mathsf{pt}_{\mathsf{PKE}}$, and a randomness ρ, this PPT algorithm outputs the ciphertext $\mathsf{ct}_{\mathsf{PKE}}$.
- $(\mathsf{pt}_{\mathsf{PKE}} \text{ or } \perp) \leftarrow \mathsf{Decrypt}(\mathsf{sk}_{\mathsf{PKE}}, \mathsf{label}, \mathsf{ct}_{\mathsf{PKE}})$: Given a secret key $\mathsf{sk}_{\mathsf{PKE}}$, a label label, a ciphertext $\mathsf{ct}_{\mathsf{PKE}}$ and a randomness ρ, this deterministic algorithm outputs the plaintext ($\mathsf{pt}_{\mathsf{PKE}}$ or $\perp$).

Security Models. A secure PKE scheme must satisfy the following security properties:

(1) Correctness: Given a security parameter λ, a public key and secret key generated by $(\mathsf{pk}_{\mathsf{PKE}}, \mathsf{sk}_{\mathsf{PKE}}) \leftarrow \mathsf{KeyExt}(\lambda)$, a label label, a randomness ρ, a ciphertext generated by $\mathsf{ct}_{\mathsf{PKE}} \leftarrow \mathsf{Encrypt}(\mathsf{pk}_{\mathsf{PKE}}, \mathsf{label}, \mathsf{pt}_{\mathsf{PKE}}, \rho)$, the PKE scheme is correct if $\Pr[\mathsf{Decrypt}(\mathsf{sk}_{\mathsf{PKE}}, \mathsf{label}, \mathsf{ct}_{\mathsf{PKE}}) = \mathsf{pt}_{\mathsf{PKE}}] \approx 1$.
(2) IND-CPA/IND-CCA security: A secure PKE protocol satisfies the indistinguishability against chosen-plaintext attacks (IND-CPA) if it does not exist an adversary $\mathcal{A}$ can obtain any information of a challenge plaintext $\mathsf{pt}_{\mathsf{PKE}}$. In addition, it realizes indistinguishability against chosen-ciphertext attacks (IND-CCA) if $\mathcal{A}$ is permitted to access the decryption query for any ciphertext $\mathsf{ct}_{\mathsf{PKE}}$ excepting for querying the challenge ciphertext.

2.3 Basic Knowledge of Lattice and Trapdoors

Definition 1 (Lattice). *[41] Suppose that $\mathbf{b_1}, \mathbf{b_2}, \cdots, \mathbf{b_n} \in \mathbb{R}^m$ are n linearly independent vectors. The m-dimensional lattice Λ is generated by a set of linear combinations, denoted as $\Lambda = \Lambda(\mathbf{B}) = \{x_1 \cdot \mathbf{b_1} + x_2 \cdot \mathbf{b_2} + \cdots + x_n \cdot \mathbf{b_n} | x_i \in \mathbb{Z}\}$, where $\mathbf{B} = \{\mathbf{b_1}, \mathbf{b_2}, \cdots, \mathbf{b_n}\} \in \mathbb{R}^{m \times n}$ is the basis of Λ.*

Definition 2 (q-ary Lattices). *[42] Given $n, m, q \in \mathbb{Z}$, and $\mathbf{A} \in \mathbb{Z}_q^{n \times m}$, we define the following q-ary Lattices and a coset: $\Lambda_q(\mathbf{A}) := \{\mathbf{e} \in \mathbb{Z}^m | \exists \mathbf{s} \in \mathbb{Z}_q^n, \mathbf{A}^\top \mathbf{s} = \mathbf{e} \bmod q\}$, $\Lambda_q^\perp(\mathbf{A}) := \{\mathbf{e} \in \mathbb{Z}^m | \mathbf{A}\mathbf{e} = 0 \bmod q\}$, and $\Lambda_q(\mathbf{A^u}) := \{\mathbf{e} \in \mathbb{Z}^m | \mathbf{A}\mathbf{e} = \mathbf{u} \bmod q\}$.*

Definition 3 (Gaussian Distribution). *Given one positive parameter $\sigma \in \mathbb{R}^+$, one center $\mathbf{c} \in \mathbb{Z}^m$ and any $\mathbf{x} \in \mathbb{Z}^m$, we define $\mathcal{D}_{\sigma,\mathbf{c}} = \frac{\rho_{\sigma,\mathbf{c}(\mathbf{x})}}{\rho_{\sigma,\mathbf{c}(\Lambda)}}$ for $\forall \mathbf{x} \in \Lambda$ as the Discrete Gaussian Distribution over Λ with a center $\mathbf{c}$, where $\rho_{\sigma,\mathbf{c}(\mathbf{x})} = \exp(-\pi \frac{\|\mathbf{x}-\mathbf{c}\|^2}{\sigma^2})$ and $\rho_{\sigma,\mathbf{c}(\Lambda)} = \Sigma_{\mathbf{x} \in \Lambda} \rho_{\sigma,\mathbf{c}(\mathbf{x})}$. Specially, we say $\mathcal{D}_{\sigma,0}$ abbreviated as $\mathcal{D}_\sigma$ when $\mathbf{c} = 0$.*

Definition 4. *[43] We define Ψ_α as the probability distribution over $\mathbb{Z}_q$ for the random variable $\lfloor qx \rceil$ by selecting $x \in \mathbb{R}$ from the normal distribution with mean 0 and the standard deviation $\frac{\alpha}{\sqrt{2\pi}}$.*

Lemma 1 (TrapGen(n, m, q)). *[44] Taking $n, m, q \in \mathbb{Z}$ as input, this PPT algorithm returns $\mathbf{A} \in \mathbb{Z}_q^{n \times m}$ and $\mathbf{T_A} \in \mathbb{Z}_q^{m \times m}$, where $\mathbf{T_A}$ is a basis of $\Lambda_q^\perp(\mathbf{A})$ s.t. $\{\mathbf{A} : (\mathbf{A}, \mathbf{T_A}) \leftarrow \mathrm{TrapGen}(n, m, q)\}$ is statistically close to $\{\mathbf{A} : \mathbf{A} \xleftarrow{\$} \mathbb{Z}_q^{n \times m}\}$. In this way, we say $\mathbf{T_A}$ is a trapdoor of $\mathbf{A}$.*

Lemma 2 (SamplePre($\mathbf{A}, \mathbf{T_A}, \mathbf{u}, \sigma$)). *[45] Given a matrix $\mathbf{A} \in \mathbb{Z}_q^{n \times m}$ and its trapdoor $\mathbf{T_A} \in \mathbb{Z}_q^{m \times m}$, a vector $\mathbf{u} \in \mathbb{Z}_q^n$, and the parameter $\sigma \leq \|\tilde{\mathbf{T}}_\mathbf{A}\| \cdot \omega(\sqrt{\log(m)})$, where $m \geq 2n\lceil \log q \rceil$, this PPT algorithm publishes a sample $\mathbf{e} \in \mathbb{Z}_q^m$ statistically distributed in $\mathcal{D}_{\Lambda_q^\mathbf{u}(\mathbf{A}), \sigma}$ s.t. $\mathbf{Ae} = \mathbf{u} \mod q$.*

Lemma 3 (NewBasisDel($\mathbf{A}, \mathbf{R}, \mathbf{T_A}, \sigma$)). *[43] Taking a parameter $\sigma \in \mathbb{R}$, a matrix $\mathbf{A} \in \mathbb{Z}_q^{n \times m}$, a $\mathbb{Z}_q$-invertible matrix $\mathbf{R}$ sampled from the distribution $\mathcal{D}_{m \times m}$, and trapdoor $\mathbf{T_A}$ as input, this PPT algorithm will output a short lattice basis $\mathbf{T_B}$ of $\Lambda_q^\perp(\mathbf{B})$, where $\mathbf{B} = \mathbf{AR}^{-1}$.*

Lemma 4 (SampleLeft($\mathbf{A}, \mathbf{M}, \mathbf{T_A}, \mathbf{u}, \sigma$)). *[46] After input a matrix $\mathbf{A} \in \mathbb{Z}_q^{n \times m}$ and its corresponding trapdoor $\mathbf{T_A} \in \mathbb{Z}_q^{m \times m}$, a matrix $\mathbf{M} \in \mathbb{Z}_q^{n \times m_1}$, a vector $\mathbf{u} \in \mathbb{Z}_q^n$, and a parameter $\sigma \leq \|\tilde{\mathbf{T}}_\mathbf{A}\| \cdot \omega(\sqrt{\log(m + m_1)})$, this PPT algorithm will output a sample $t \in \mathbb{Z}^{m + m_1}$ from the distribution statistically close to $\mathcal{D}_{\Lambda_q^\mathbf{u}([\mathbf{A}|\mathbf{M}]), \sigma}$ s.t. $[\mathbf{A}|\mathbf{M}] \cdot t = \mathbf{u} \mod q$.*

Lemma 5 (ExtBasis($\mathbf{A}'', \mathbf{S}$)). *[25] For an input matrix $\mathbf{A} \in \mathbb{Z}_q^{n \times m}$, a basis $\mathbf{S} \in \mathbb{Z}_q^{m \times m}$ of $\Lambda^\perp(\mathbf{A})$, and a matrix $\mathbf{A}' \in \mathbb{Z}_q^{n \times m'}$, this deterministic algorithm outputs a basis $\mathbf{S}''$ of $\Lambda^\perp(\mathbf{A}'') \subseteq \mathbb{Z}_q^{m \times m''}$ s.t. $\|\tilde{\mathbf{S}}\| = \|\tilde{\mathbf{S}}''\|$, and $\mathbf{A}'' = \mathbf{A}\|\mathbf{A}'$, $m'' = m + m'$.*

3   Syntax and Security Models of FS-PAEKS

This sector presents syntax and security models of FS-PAEKS. Our scheme prohibits the use of a token to search for ciphertexts generated after the time period in which the token was generated.

3.1   Syntax of FS-PAEKS Scheme

We formalize the syntax of FS-PAEKS primitive (including seven algorithms), $\Pi = (\mathsf{Setup}, \mathsf{KeyGen}_S, \mathsf{KeyGen}_R, \mathsf{KeyUpdate}, \mathsf{FS\text{-}PAEKS}, \mathsf{Trapdoor}, \mathsf{Test})$.

- $\mathsf{pp} \leftarrow \mathsf{Setup}(\lambda, \mathsf{d})$: Given a security parameter λ and a depth d, this algorithm returns a public parameter pp.
- $(\mathsf{pk}_S, \mathsf{sk}_S) \leftarrow \mathsf{KeyGen}_S(\mathsf{pp})$: Given a public parameter pp, this algorithm publishes a public-secret key pair for a sender $(\mathsf{pk}_S, \mathsf{sk}_S)$.
- $(\mathsf{pk}_R, \mathsf{sk}_R) \leftarrow \mathsf{KeyGen}_R(pp)$: Given a public parameter pp, this algorithm outputs a public-secret key pair for a receiver $(\mathsf{pk}_R, \mathsf{sk}_R)$.
- $\mathsf{sk}_R(t + 1) \leftarrow \mathsf{KeyUpdate}(\mathsf{pp}, \mathsf{pk}_R, \mathsf{sk}_R, t, \mathsf{d})$: Given a public parameter pp, a public key of a receiver pk_R, a secret key of a sender $\mathsf{sk}_R(t)$ at time period t, and the depth of binary tree d as input, this algorithm outputs a new secret key of the sender $\mathsf{sk}_R(t + 1)$ at time period $t + 1$. Moreover, the former secret key of the receiver $\mathsf{sk}_R(t)$ has been deleted.

- ct ← FS-PAEKS(pp, pk_S, sk_S, pk_R, kw, t, d): Given a public parameter pp, a public key pk_S and a secret key sk_S of a sender, a public key pk_R, any keyword kw at time period t, and the depth of binary tree d, this algorithm returns a ciphertext ct of kw with time t as output.
- **Trap** ← Trapdoor(pp, pk_S, pk_R, $sk_R(t)$, kw'): Given a public parameter pp, a public key of a sender pk_S, a public key and a secret key of a receiver sk_R with time t, and a keyword kw', this algorithm outputs a trapdoor **Trap** of kw'.
- (1 or 0) ← Test(pp, ct, **Trap**): Given a public parameter pp, a ciphertext ct and a trapdoor **Trap**, this algorithm returns 1 if the ct and **Trap** is related to a same keyword, that is, $kw = kw'$ holds; Otherwise, it returns 0.

3.2 Security Models

The security criteria are that any probabilistic polynomial-time (PPT) adversary cannot obtain any keyword information from the ciphertext [1] and any (inside) PPT attacker cannot acquire any keyword information from the trapdoor [4,47]. We define ciphertext indistinguishability (CI) of forward-secure PAEKS under indistinguishability against chosen keywords attack (IND-CKA), the trapdoor privacy of forward-secure PAEKS under indistinguishability against inside keyword guessing attack (IND-IKGA), and the multi-ciphertext indistinguishability (MCI) of forward-secure PAEKS under indistinguishability against chosen multi-keywords attack (IND-Multi-CKA).

IND-CKA Game of Forward-Secure PAEKS

- **Setup**: After input a security parameter λ, the challenger C calls the Setup algorithm to obtain the public parameter pp. After that, C processes the KeyGen$_S$ and KeyGen$_R$ algorithms to compute the sender's and receiver's public-secret key pair (pk_S, sk_S) and (pk_R, sk_R). Ultimately, C sends pp, pk_S and pk_R to the adversary $\mathcal{A}$ and keeps the initial secret key sk_R secret.
- **Query 1**: In this query, $\mathcal{A}$ is permitted to adaptively access three oracles in polynomial times.
  - **KeyUpdate Oracle** $\mathcal{O}_{KU}$: If the time period $t < T - 1$, C will update the time period from t to $t+1$. If the time period $t = T-1$, which means the current period is the last period, C will return an empty string sk_T.
  - **Ciphertext Oracle** $\mathcal{O}_C$: $\mathcal{A}$ requires that the time period t is larger than the target time period t^* selected by an adversary. Given any keyword kw, C calls FS-PAEKS(pp, pk_S, sk_S, pk_R, kw, t, d) algorithm to obtain the ciphertext ct at time period t and returns it to $\mathcal{A}$.
  - **Trapdoor Oracle** $\mathcal{O}_T$: $\mathcal{A}$ requires that the time period t is larger than the target time period t^*. Given any keyword kw, C calls the Trapdoor(pp, pk_S, pk_R, $sk_R(t)$, kw') algorithm to obtain the trapdoor **Trap** in time period t and transmits it to $\mathcal{A}$. When $\mathcal{A}$ accesses $\mathcal{O}_{KU}$, $\mathcal{A}$ is forbidden to issue $\mathcal{O}_T$ for the past time periods.

- **Challenge**: In time period t^*, which has not been queried the $\mathcal{O}_T$, $\mathcal{A}$ selects two challenge keywords kw_0^* and kw_1^* and sends them to $\mathcal{C}$. This phase restricts that $\mathcal{A}$ never accesses the three oracles $(\mathcal{O}_{KU}, \mathcal{O}_C$ and $\mathcal{O}_T)$ for the challenge keywords kw_0^* and kw_1^*. After that, $\mathcal{C}$ selects a bit $b \in \{0,1\}$ at random and calls FS-PAEKS$(\mathsf{pp}, \mathsf{pk}_S, \mathsf{sk}_S, \mathsf{pk}_R, kw_b^*, t^*, \mathsf{d})$ algorithm to calculate the challenge ciphertext ct*. Finally, $\mathcal{C}$ sends ct* to $\mathcal{A}$.
- **Query 2**: $\mathcal{A}$ has the ability to continue those queries as similar as **Query 1** with a limitation that $\mathcal{A}$ is not allowed to query the challenge keywords (kw_0^*, kw_1^*).
- **Guess**: After finished the above phases, $\mathcal{A}$ will output a guess bit $b' \in \{0,1\}$. Therefore, we say that $\mathcal{A}$ wins the game if and only if $b = b'$.

We hereby define the advantage of $\mathcal{A}$ wins the above game as $Adv_{\mathcal{A}}^{IND\text{-}CKA}(\lambda) := |\Pr[b = b'] - \frac{1}{2}|$.

Definition 5 (IND-CKA secure of FS-PAEKS). *We say that an FS-PAEKS scheme satisfies forward-secure ciphertext indistinguishability (CI) under IND-CKA, if for any PPT adversary $\mathcal{A}$, the advantage $Adv_{\mathcal{A}}^{IND\text{-}CKA}(\lambda)$ is negligible.*

IND-IKGA Game of Forward Secure PAEKS

- **Setup**: This process is the same as the **IND-CKA Game**.
- **Query 1**: In this query, $\mathcal{A}$ is permitted to adaptively access three oracles $(\mathcal{O}_{KU}, \mathcal{O}_C$ and $\mathcal{O}_T$, are same as the **IND-CKA Game**) in some polynomial times.
- **Challenge**: In time period t^*, which has not been queried the $\mathcal{O}_T$, $\mathcal{A}$ selects two challenge keywords kw_0^* and kw_1^* and transmits them to $\mathcal{C}$. This phase restricts that $\mathcal{A}$ never accesses the three oracles $(\mathcal{O}_{KU}, \mathcal{O}_C$ and $\mathcal{O}_T)$ for the challenge keywords kw_0^* and kw_1^*. After that, $\mathcal{C}$ selects a bit $b \in \{0,1\}$ at random and calls Trapdoor$(\mathsf{pp}, \mathsf{pk}_S, \mathsf{pk}_R, \mathsf{sk}_R(t'), kw_b')$ algorithm to calculate the challenge trapdoor **Trap***. Finally, $\mathcal{C}$ sends **Trap*** to $\mathcal{A}$.
- **Query 2**: $\mathcal{A}$ has the ability to continue those queries as similar as **Query 1** with the limitation that $\mathcal{A}$ is not allowed to query the challenge keywords (kw_0^*, kw_1^*).
- **Guess**: After finished the above phases, $\mathcal{A}$ publishes a guess bit $b' \in \{0,1\}$. Thus, we say that $\mathcal{A}$ wins the game if and only if $b = b'$.

We define the advantage of $\mathcal{A}$ wins the above game as $Adv_{\mathcal{A}}^{IND-IKGA}(\lambda) := |\Pr[b = b'] - \frac{1}{2}|$.

Definition 6 (IND-IKGA secure of FS-PAEKS). *We say that an FS-PAEKS scheme satisfies forward-secure trapdoor privacy (TP) under IND-IKGA, if for any PPT adversary $\mathcal{A}$, the advantage $Adv_{\mathcal{A}}^{IND-IKGA}(\lambda)$ is negligible.*

IND-Multi-CKA Game of Forward Secure PAEKS

- **Setup**: This process is the same as the **IND-CKA Game**.
- **Query 1**: In this query, $\mathcal{A}$ is permitted to adaptively access three oracles ($\mathcal{O}_{KU}, \mathcal{O}_C$ and $\mathcal{O}_T$, same as the **IND-CKA Game**) in some polynomial times.
- **Challenge**: Given two tuples of challenge keywords $(kw_{0,1}^*, \cdots, kw_{0,n}^*)$, $\mathcal{C}$ firstly selects a tuple $(kw_{0,i}^*, kw_{1,i}^*)$ for some i s.t. $kw_{0,i}^* \neq kw_{1,i}^*$. After that, $\mathcal{C}$ selects a bit $b \in \{0,1\}$ randomly and calls FS-PAEKS($pp, pk_S, sk_S, pk_R, kw_b^*, t^*, d$) algorithm to calculate the challenge ciphertext ct^*. Moreover, $\mathcal{C}$ selects $n-1$ ciphertexts from the output space of FS-PAEKS algorithm, namely as, $(ct_1, ct_2, \cdots, ct_{i-1}, ct_{i+1}, ct_{i+2}, \cdots, ct_n)$.
- **Query 2**: $\mathcal{A}$ can continue the queries as in the **Query 1** with the restriction that $\mathcal{A}$ is not allowed to query the challenge keywords $kw_{i,j}^*$, where $i \in \{0,1\}$ and $j \in \{1, 2, \cdots, n\}$.
- **Guess**: After finished the above phases, $\mathcal{A}$ outputs a guess bit $b' \in \{0,1\}$ and $\mathcal{C}$ uses it as its output. We say that $\mathcal{A}$ wins the game if and only if $b = b'$.

Definition 7 (IND-Multi-CKA secure of FS-PAEKS). *We say that an FS-PAEKS scheme satisfies forward-secure multi-ciphertext under IND-Multi-CKA, if it satisfies CI under IND-CKA and it is a probabilistic algorithm.*

4 Our Proposed Construction

In this part, we illustrate the first generic construction of post-quantum FS-PAEKS based on the prototype of PEKS primitive, labelled PKE scheme, SPHF protocol, and binary tree architecture. Specifically, we define $\mathcal{KS}_{PEKS}$ as the keyword space and a standard PEKS scheme includes four algorithms (PEKS.KeyGen, PEKS.PEKS, PEKS.Trapdoor, PEKS.Test). Moreover, we define $\mathcal{PKS}_{PKE}$ and $\mathcal{PS}_{PKE}$ as the public key and plaintext space, respectively. Finally, we utilize a binary tree structure and the smallest minimal cover set to realize a secret key update for a receiver and we also employ ExtBasis algorithm to fulfill one-way secret key evolution.

A labelled PKE scheme consists of three algorithms (PKE.KeyGen, PKE.Encrypt, PKE.Decrypt). A SPHF protocol incorporates four algorithms (SPHF.KeyGen$_{Hash}$, SPHF.KeyGen$_{ProjHash}$, SPHF.Hash, SPHF.ProjHash). We first define the language of ciphertext as $(Para_l, Trap_l) = (pk_{PKE}, sk_{PKE})$, where $pk_{PKE} \in \mathcal{PKS}_{PKE}$, $\tilde{\mathcal{L}} := \{(label, ct_{PKE}, m_{PKE}) | \exists \rho, ct_{PKE} \leftarrow \text{Encrypt}(pk_{PKE}, label, m_{PKE}, \rho)\}$, and $\mathcal{L} := \{(label, ct_{PKE}, m_{PKE}) | \text{Decrypt}(sk_{PKE}, label, ct_{PKE}) = m_{PKE}\}$. Besides, we also define the witness relation $\tilde{\mathcal{K}}((label, ct_{PKE}, m_{PKE}), \rho) = 1$ if and only if we have $ct_{PKE} \leftarrow \text{Encrypt}(pk_{PKE}, label, m_{PKE}, \rho)\}$.

- Setup(λ, d): Given a security parameter λ and a depth d, this algorithm processes:
  - Calculates $(\mathbf{pk}_{PKE}, \mathbf{sk}_{PKE}) \leftarrow \text{PKE.KeyExt}(\lambda)$.
  - Selects a plaintext $m_{PKE} \xleftarrow{\$} \mathcal{PKS}_{PKE}$ and a label label $\xleftarrow{\$} \{0,1\}^*$ randomly.

- Selects two hash functions:

$$H_1 : \mathcal{PKS}_{\mathsf{PKE}} \times \mathcal{PS}_{\mathsf{PKE}} \times \{0,1\}^* \to \mathcal{PKS}_{\mathsf{PKE}}; \quad H_2 : \mathcal{KS}_{\mathsf{PEKS}} \times \{0,1\}^* \to \mathcal{KS}_{\mathsf{PEKS}}.$$

- Selects 2d matrices from $\mathbb{Z}_q^{n \times m}$ as Matrices.
- Outputs $\mathsf{pp} := (\lambda, \mathsf{mpk}, \mathsf{pk}_{\mathsf{PKE}}, \mathsf{m}_{\mathsf{PKE}}, \mathsf{label}, H_1, H_2, \mathsf{Matrices})$ as a public parameter.

- $\mathsf{KeyGen}_S(\mathsf{pp})$: Given a public parameter pp, this algorithm processes these operations:
  - Calculates $\mathbf{h}_S \leftarrow \mathsf{SPHF.KeyGen}_{\mathsf{Hash}}(\mathsf{mpk})$ and $\mathbf{p}_S \leftarrow \mathsf{SPHF.KeyGen}_{\mathsf{Proj}}(\mathbf{h}_S, \mathsf{mpk})$.
  - Calculates $\mathsf{ct}_{\mathsf{PKE},S} \leftarrow \mathsf{PKE.Encrypt}(\mathsf{mpk}, \mathsf{label}, \mathsf{m}_{\mathsf{PKE}}, \rho_S)$, where ρ_S is a randomly selected witness s.t. $\tilde{\mathcal{K}}((\mathsf{label}, \mathsf{ct}_{\mathsf{PKE},S}, \mathsf{m}_{\mathsf{PKE}}), \rho_S) = 1$.
  - Outputs $\mathsf{pk}_S := (\mathbf{p}_S, \mathsf{ct}_{\mathsf{PKE},S})$ and $\mathsf{sk}_S := (\mathbf{h}_S, \rho_S)$ as the public key and secret key of a sender, respectively.

- $\mathsf{KeyGen}_R(\mathsf{pp})$: Given a public parameter pp, this algorithm processes the following operations:
  - Calculates $\mathbf{h}_R \leftarrow \mathsf{SPHF.KeyGen}_{\mathsf{Hash}}(\mathsf{mpk})$ and $\mathbf{p}_R \leftarrow \mathsf{SPHF.KeyGen}_{\mathsf{Proj}}(\mathbf{h}_R, \mathsf{mpk})$.
  - Calculates $\mathsf{ct}_{\mathsf{PKE},R} \leftarrow \mathsf{PKE.Encrypt}(\mathsf{mpk}, \mathsf{label}, \mathsf{m}_{\mathsf{PKE}}, \rho_R)$, where ρ_R is a randomly selected witness s.t. $\tilde{\mathcal{K}}((\mathsf{label}, \mathsf{ct}_{\mathsf{PKE},R}, \mathsf{m}_{\mathsf{PKE}}), \rho_R) = 1$.
  - Calculates $(\mathsf{pk}_{\mathsf{PEKS}}, \mathsf{sk}_{\mathsf{PEKS}}) \leftarrow \mathsf{PEKS.KeyGen}(\lambda)$.
  - Outputs $\mathsf{pk}_R := (\mathbf{p}_R, \mathsf{ct}_{\mathsf{PKE},R}, \mathsf{pk}_{\mathsf{PEKS}})$ and $\mathsf{sk}_R := (\mathbf{h}_R, \rho_R, \mathsf{sk}_{\mathsf{PEKS}})$ as the public key and secret key of the receiver, respectively.

- $\mathsf{KeyUpdate}(\mathsf{pp}, \mathsf{pk}_R, \mathsf{sk}_R, t, \mathsf{d})$: Given a public parameter pp, a public key pk_R and a secret key sk_R of the initial receiver, a time period t, and a depth d, this algorithm processes as below:
  - Defines $F_{\Theta^{(i)}}$ as the corresponding matrix of $\Theta^{(i)}$.
  - For any $j < i$ where $j, i \in [1, d]$, calculates $\mathbf{S}_{\Theta^{(i)}} \leftarrow \mathsf{ExtBasis}(F_{\Theta^{(i)}}, \mathbf{S}_{\Theta^{(j)}})$, where $\mathbf{S}_{\Theta^{(j)}}$ is the trapdoor on time period j.
  - Defines $\mathsf{sk}_R(t) := (\mathsf{sk}_R, \mathbf{S}_{\Theta^{(i)}})$, where $\Theta^{(i)} \in \mathsf{node}(t)$.
  - Defines and outputs $\mathsf{sk}_R(t+1) := (\mathsf{sk}_R, \mathbf{S}_{\Theta^{(i)}})$, where $\Theta^{(i)} \in \mathsf{node}(t+1)$.

- $\mathsf{FS\text{-}PAEKS}(\mathsf{pp}, \mathsf{pk}_S, \mathsf{sk}_S, \mathsf{pk}_R, kw, t, \mathsf{d})$: Given a public parameter pp, a public key pk_S and a secret key sk_S of a sender, a public key pk_R of a receiver, a keyword $kw \in \mathcal{KS}_{\mathsf{FS\text{-}PAEKS}}$ the time period t, and the depth d, this algorithm processes the following operations:
  - Calculates $\mathsf{Hash}_S \leftarrow \mathsf{SPHF.Hash}(\mathbf{h}_S, \mathsf{mpk}, (\mathsf{ct}_{\mathsf{PKE},R}, \mathsf{m}_{\mathsf{PKE}}))$.
  - Calculates $\mathsf{ProjHash}_S \leftarrow \mathsf{SPHF.ProjHash}(\mathbf{p}_R, \mathsf{mpk}, (\mathsf{ct}_{\mathsf{PKE},S}, \mathsf{m}_{\mathsf{PKE}}), \rho_S)$.
  - Calculates $kw_S \leftarrow H_2(kw, \mathsf{Hash}_S \oplus \mathsf{ProjHash}_S)$
  - Calculates and outputs $\mathsf{ct} \leftarrow \mathsf{PEKS.PEKS}(\mathsf{pk}_{\mathsf{PEKS}}, kw_S)$.

- $\mathsf{Trapdoor}(\mathsf{pp}, \mathsf{pk}_S, \mathsf{pk}_R, \mathsf{sk}_R(t), kw')$: Given a public parameter pp, a public key pk_S of a sender, a public key pk_R and a secret key $\mathsf{sk}_R(t)$ of a receiver, a keyword $kw' \in \mathcal{KS}_{\mathsf{FS\text{-}PAEKS}}$, this algorithm processes the following operations:
  - Calculates $\mathsf{Hash}_R \leftarrow \mathsf{SPHF.Hash}(\mathbf{h}_R, \mathsf{mpk}, (\mathsf{ct}_{\mathsf{PKE},S}, \mathsf{m}_{\mathsf{PKE}}))$.
  - Calculates $\mathsf{ProjHash}_R \leftarrow \mathsf{SPHF.ProjHash}(\mathbf{p}_R, \mathsf{mpk}, (\mathsf{ct}_{\mathsf{PKE},R}, \mathsf{m}_{\mathsf{PKE}}), \rho_R)$.
  - Calculates $kw'_R \leftarrow H_2(kw', \mathsf{Hash}_R \oplus \mathsf{ProjHash}_R)$.

- Calculates $\mathbf{Trap_1} \leftarrow$ PEKS.Trapdoor($\mathsf{sk_{PEKS}}, kw'_R$), $\mathbf{Trap_2} \leftarrow$ SamplePre $(\mathbf{S}_{\Theta^{(t)}}, H_3(kw'), \sigma_3)$.
- Defines and outputs $\mathbf{Trap} := (\mathbf{Trap_1}, \mathbf{Trap_2})$.
- Test(pp, ct, **Trap**): Given a public parameter pp, a ciphertext ct, and a trapdoor **Trap**, this algorithm outputs PEKS.Test(ct, **Trap**).

5 Security Analysis

This section illustrates that the proposed FS-PAEKS construction satisfies CI under IND-CKA, TP under IND-IKGA, and MCI under IND-Multi-CKA. We specify the proofs of two theorems and give the analysis of a corollary.

Theorem 1. *The proposed* FS-PAEKS *scheme satisfies* CI *under* IND-CKA *if the* SPHF *protocol satisfies pseudo-randomness and the hash function* H_2 *is a random oracle.*

Proof. We finished the security analysis through four games as below.

Game 0: We simulate a real security game for the adversary $\mathcal{A}$ and define $Adv_{\mathcal{A}}^{\text{Game 0}}(\lambda) := \epsilon$. $\mathcal{A}$ has the ability to perform three oracle queries and the challenger $\mathcal{C}$ will reply to the following responses after receiving some keyword kw from $\mathcal{A}$.

- $\mathcal{O}_{\mathcal{KU}}$: If the time period $t < T - 1$, $\mathcal{C}$ updates $\mathsf{sk}_R(t + 1) \leftarrow$ KeyUpdate(pp, $\mathsf{pk}_R, \mathsf{sk}_R, t, \mathsf{d}$) and returns $\mathsf{sk}_R(t + 1)$ to $\mathcal{A}$. If the time period $t = T - 1$, $\mathcal{C}$ returns an empty string sk_T to $\mathcal{A}$.
- $\mathcal{O}_{\mathcal{C}}$: Given a keyword kw, $\mathcal{C}$ calculates ct $\leftarrow$ FS-PAEKS(pp, $\mathsf{pk}_S, \mathsf{sk}_S, \mathsf{pk}_R, kw, t, \mathsf{d}$) and returns ct to $\mathcal{A}$.
- $\mathcal{O}_{\mathcal{T}}$: Given a keyword kw, $\mathcal{C}$ calculates **Trap** $\leftarrow$ Trapdoor(pp, $\mathsf{pk}_S, \mathsf{pk}_R$, $\mathsf{sk}_R(t), kw'$) and returns **Trap** to $\mathcal{A}$.

Game 1: This game is identical to **Game 0**, except changing the calculation method of ct* in the **Challenge** query. To be more specific, $\mathcal{C}$ selects $\mathsf{Hash}_S \xleftarrow{\$} \mathcal{OS}_{\mathsf{Hash}_S}$ randomly ($\mathcal{OS}_{\mathsf{Hash}_S}$ is the output space of Hash_S) instead of calculating $\mathsf{Hash}_S \leftarrow$ SPHF.Hash($\mathsf{h}_S, \mathsf{mpk}, (\mathsf{ct_{PKE,R}}, \mathsf{m_{PKE}})$). For the view of $\mathcal{A}$, **Game 1** and **Game 0** are statistically indistinguishable due to the fact that the output of Hash_S satisfies pseudo-randomness. Hence, we acquire: $|Adv_{\mathcal{A}}^{\text{Game 1}}(\lambda) - Adv_{\mathcal{A}}^{\text{Game 0}}(\lambda)| \le \mathsf{negl}(\lambda)$.

Game 2: This game is identical to **Game 1**, except changing one more time of the calculation method for ct* in the **Challenge** query. In detail, $\mathcal{A}$ sends kw_0^* and kw_1^* to $\mathcal{C}$, $\mathcal{C}$ then selects a bit $b \in \{0, 1\}$ randomly and samples $kw_S \xleftarrow{\$} \mathcal{KS}_{\mathsf{PEKS}}$ randomly ($\mathcal{KS}_{\mathsf{PEKS}}$ is the keyword space of PEKS($\mathsf{pk_{PEKS}}, kw$) algorithm), instead of calculating $kw_S \leftarrow H_2(kw_b, \mathsf{Hash}_S \oplus \mathsf{ProjHash}_S)$. In this way, the output of $H_2(kw_b, \mathsf{Hash}_S \oplus \mathsf{ProjHash}_S)$ is random since Hash_S is randomly selected and H_2 is also a random oracle. Accordingly, in $\mathcal{A}$'s view,

$\widehat{\textbf{Game 2}}$ and $\widehat{\textbf{Game 1}}$ are statistically indistinguishable. Thus, we can say: $|Adv_{\mathcal{A}}^{\widehat{\text{Game}}\ 2}(\lambda) - Adv_{\mathcal{A}}^{\widehat{\text{Game}}\ 1}(\lambda)| \leq \textbf{negl}(\lambda)$.

$\widehat{\textbf{Game 3}}$: Till now, the keyword is generated by $kw_S \xleftarrow{\$} \mathcal{KS}_{\textsf{PEKS}}$ at random, the challenge ciphertext $\textsf{ct}^* = \textsf{ct}_{\textsf{PEKS},kw}$ is obtained from $\textsf{PEKS.PEKS}(\textsf{pk}_{\textsf{PEKS}}, kw_S)$ and $kw_S \xleftarrow{\$} \mathcal{KS}_{\textsf{PEKS}}$. Therefore, $\textsf{ct}^*$ does not divulge any information regarding to the challenge keywords (kw_0^*, kw_1^*). As for $\mathcal{A}$, the only way to acquire the keyword is by guessing absolutely. Consequently, we obtain: $|Adv_{\mathcal{A}}^{\widehat{\text{Game}}\ 3}(\lambda)| = 0$.

Theorem 2. *The proposed* FS-PAEKS *scheme satisfies* TP *under* IND-IKGA *if the* SPHF *protocol satisfies pseudo-randomness and the hash function H_2 is a random oracle.*

Proof. We finished the security analysis through four games as below.

$\widehat{\textbf{Game 0}}$: We simulate a real security game for the adversary $\mathcal{A}$ and define $Adv_{\mathcal{A}}^{\widehat{\text{Game}}\ 0}(\lambda) := \epsilon$. $\mathcal{A}$ has the ability to perform three oracle queries and the challenger $\mathcal{C}$ will reply to the responses (same as the proof of the former theorem) after receiving some keyword kw from $\mathcal{A}$.

$\widehat{\textbf{Game 1}}$: This game is identical to $\widehat{\textbf{Game 0}}$, except changing the calculation method of $\textbf{Trap}^*$ in the $\textbf{Challenge}$ query. To be more specific, $\mathcal{C}$ selects $\textsf{Hash}_R \xleftarrow{\$} \mathcal{OS}_{\textsf{Hash}_R}$ randomly ($\mathcal{OS}_{\textsf{Hash}_R}$ is the output space of $\textsf{Hash}_R$) instead of calculating $\textsf{Hash}_R \leftarrow \textsf{SPHF.Hash}(\textsf{h}_R, \textsf{mpk}, (\textsf{ct}_{\textsf{PKE},S}, \textsf{m}_{\textsf{PKE}}))$. For $\mathcal{A}$, $\widehat{\textbf{Game 1}}$ and $\widehat{\textbf{Game 0}}$ are statistically indistinguishable due to the fact that the output of $\textsf{Hash}_R$ satisfies pseudo-randomness. Hence, we acquire: $|Adv_{\mathcal{A}}^{\widehat{\text{Game}}\ 1}(\lambda) - Adv_{\mathcal{A}}^{\widehat{\text{Game}}\ 0}(\lambda)| \leq \textbf{negl}(\lambda)$.

$\widehat{\textbf{Game 2}}$: This game is identical to $\widehat{\textbf{Game 1}}$, except changing one more time of the calculation method for $\textbf{Trap}^*$ in the $\textbf{Challenge}$ query. In detail, $\mathcal{A}$ sends kw_0^* and kw_1^* to $\mathcal{C}$, $\mathcal{C}$ then selects a bit $b \in \{0, 1\}$ and samples $kw_R' \xleftarrow{\$} \mathcal{KS}_{\textsf{PEKS}}$ randomly, instead of calculating $kw_R' \leftarrow H_2(kw_b', \textsf{Hash}_R \oplus \textsf{ProjHash}_R)$. In this way, the output of $H_2(kw_b', \textsf{Hash}_R \oplus \textsf{ProjHash}_R)$ is random since $\textsf{Hash}_R$ is randomly selected and H_2 is a random oracle. Accordingly, in $\mathcal{A}$'s view, $\widehat{\textbf{Game 2}}$ and $\widehat{\textbf{Game 1}}$ are statistically indistinguishable. Thus, we can say: $|Adv_{\mathcal{A}}^{\widehat{\text{Game}}\ 2}(\lambda) - Adv_{\mathcal{A}}^{\widehat{\text{Game}}\ 1}(\lambda)| \leq \textbf{negl}(\lambda)$.

$\widehat{\textbf{Game 3}}$: Till now, the keyword is generated by $kw_R' \xleftarrow{\$} \mathcal{KS}_{\textsf{PEKS}}$ at random, the challenge trapdoor $\textbf{Trap}^* = (\textbf{Trap}_1^*, \textbf{Trap}_2^*)$ is generated from $\textsf{Trapdoor}(\textsf{pp}, \textsf{pk}_S, \textsf{pk}_R, \textsf{sk}_R(t), kw')$. Therefore, $\textbf{Trap}^*$ does not divulge any information regarding to the challenge keywords (kw_0^*, kw_1^*). As for $\mathcal{A}$, the only way to acquire the keyword is by guessing absolutely. Consequently, we obtain: $|Adv_{\mathcal{A}}^{\widehat{\text{Game}}\ 3}(\lambda)| = 0$.

Corollary 1. *The proposed* FS-PAEKS *scheme satisfies* MCI *under* IND-Multi-CKA *if it satisfies* CI *under* IND-CKA *and the* PEKS.PEKS *algorithm in our* FS-PAEKS *algorithm is probabilistic.*

Analysis. Our FS-PAEKS algorithm involves PEKS.PEKS algorithm. To the best of our knowledge, the existing PEKS.PEKS algorithm satisfies probabilistic [1,24]. Thus, our FS-PAEKS scheme is also probabilistic. In addition, we have proved that our scheme satisfies CI under IND-CKA. Consequently, the proposed FS-PAEKS scheme satisfies MCI under IND-Multi-CKA.

6 Lattice-Based Instantiation of FS-PAEKS

In this section, we construct the first post-quantum PAEKS with forward security instantiation based on the lattice hardness, namely FS-PAEKS, including seven algorithms.

- Setup(λ, d): Given a security parameter λ, the depth d of a binary tree, system parameters $q, n, m, \sigma_1, \sigma_2, \alpha, \sigma_3, T$, where q is a prime, σ_1, σ_2 and σ_3 are preimage sample parameters, α is a gaussian distribution parameter and $T = 2^d$ is the total number of time periods, this algorithm executes the following operations.

  - Calls $\kappa, \rho, \ell \leftarrow \mathsf{poly}(n)$ and selects $\mathbf{m} = m_1 m_2 \cdots m_\kappa \xleftarrow{\$} \{0,1\}^\kappa$ randomly.
  - Selects matrices $A_1^{(0)}, A_1^{(1)}, A_2^{(0)}, A_2^{(1)}, \cdots, A_d^{(0)}, A_d^{(1)} \in \mathbb{Z}_q^{n \times m}$.
  - Calls $\mathsf{TrapGen}(n, m, q)$ algorithm to generate a matrix $\mathbf{A_0}$ and the basis $\mathbf{T_{A_0}}$ of $\Lambda^\perp(\mathbf{A_0})$.
  - Sets $\mathbf{A_0}$ as a public key of PKE and $\mathbf{T_{A_0}}$ as a secret key of PKE.
  - Selects an element $u \xleftarrow{\$} \mathcal{U}$ randomly as the label of PKE.
  - Selects three Hash functions

  $$H_1 : \mathbb{Z}^{n \times m} \times \{0,1\}^\kappa \times \mathcal{U} \to \mathbb{Z}_q^{n \times m}; H_2 : \{1,-1\}^\ell \times \{0,1\}^\kappa \to \{1,-1\}^\ell; H_3 : \{1,-1\}^\ell \to \mathbb{Z}_q^n.$$

  - Selects an Injective function $H_4 : \mathcal{R} \to \mathbb{Z}_q^{n \times n}$.
  - Calculates the master public key of PKE: $\mathbf{A} \leftarrow H_1(\mathbf{T_{A_0}}, \mathbf{m}, u) \in \mathbb{Z}_q^{n \times m}$.
  - Ultimately, this algorithm returns a public parameter as $pp := (\lambda, q, n, m, \sigma_1, \sigma_2, \sigma_3, \kappa, \rho, \ell, \mathbf{T_{A_0}}, A_1^{(0)}, A_1^{(1)}, A_2^{(0)}, A_2^{(1)}, \cdots, A_d^{(0)}, A_d^{(1)}, \mathbf{A}, \mathbf{m}, u, H_1, H_2, H_3, H_4)$.

- KeyGen$_S(pp)$: Taking a public parameter pp as input, this algorithm will execute the following steps to generate the public key and secret key of the sender.

  - Sets gadget matrix $\mathbf{G} := \mathbf{I}_n \otimes \mathbf{g}^\top$, $\mathbf{g}^\top = [1, 2, \cdots, 2^k], k = \lceil \log q \rceil - 1$.
  - Defines and calculates $\mathbf{A}_{\mathsf{label}} = \mathbf{A} + \begin{bmatrix} 0 \\ \mathbf{G} H_4(u) \end{bmatrix} = \mathbf{A} + \begin{bmatrix} 0 \\ (\mathbf{I}_n \otimes \mathbf{g}^\top) H_4(u) \end{bmatrix}$.
  - Selects a matrix $\mathbf{h}_S \xleftarrow{\$} D_{\mathbb{Z},s}^m$ at random, and calculates the matrix $\mathbf{p}_S = \mathbf{A}_{\mathsf{label}} \cdot \mathbf{h}_S \in \mathbb{Z}_q^n$.
  - For $i = 1, 2, \cdots, \kappa$, selects vectors $\mathbf{s}_i \xleftarrow{\$} \mathbb{Z}_q$ and vectors $\mathbf{e}_{S,i} \xleftarrow{\$} D_{\mathbb{Z},t}^m$ randomly s.t. $\|\mathbf{e}_{S,i}\| \leq 2t\sqrt{m}$ and then calculates $\mathbf{c}_{S,i} = \mathbf{A}_{\mathsf{label}}^\top \cdot \mathbf{s}_i + \mathbf{e}_{S,i} + m_i[0, 0, \cdots, 0, \lceil \frac{q}{2} \rceil]^\top \bmod q$.

- Outputs $pk_S := (\mathbf{p}_S, \{\mathbf{c}_{S,1}\}, \{\mathbf{c}_{S,2}\}, \cdots, \{\mathbf{c}_{S,\kappa}\})$ and $sk_S :=$ $(\mathbf{h}_S, \{\mathbf{s}_1\}, \{\mathbf{s}_2\}, \cdots, \{\mathbf{s}_\kappa\})$ as a public key and a secret key of a sender, respectively.

- KeyGen$_R(pp)$: Taking a public parameter pp as input, it executes the following steps to compute the initial public key and initial secret key for a receiver.
  - Calls TrapGen(n, m, q) algorithm to generate a matrix $\mathbf{M}_R$ and the basis $\mathbf{S}_R$ of $\Lambda^\perp(\mathbf{M}_R)$.
  - For $i = 1, 2, \cdots, \ell$, selects matrices $\mathbf{M}_{R,i} \xleftarrow{\$} \mathbb{Z}_q^{n\times m}$ randomly.
  - Selects a matrix $\mathbf{C}_R \xleftarrow{\$} \mathbb{Z}_q^{n\times m}$ and a vector $\mathbf{r}_R \xleftarrow{\$} \mathbb{Z}_q^n$ at random.
  - Sets gadget matrix $\mathbf{G} := \mathbf{I}_n \otimes \mathbf{g}^\top$, $\mathbf{g}^\top = [1, 2, \cdots, 2^k]$, $k = \lceil \log q \rceil - 1$.
  - Defines and calculates $\mathbf{A}_{\mathsf{label}} = \mathbf{A} + \begin{bmatrix} 0 \\ \mathbf{G}H_4(u) \end{bmatrix} = \mathbf{A} + \begin{bmatrix} 0 \\ (\mathbf{I}_n \otimes \mathbf{g}^\top)H_4(u) \end{bmatrix}$.
  - Selects a matrix $\mathbf{h}_R \xleftarrow{\$} D_{\mathbb{Z},s}^m$ at random, and calculates the matrix $\mathbf{p}_R = \mathbf{A}_{\mathsf{label}} \cdot \mathbf{h}_R \in \mathbb{Z}_q^n$.
  - For $i = 1, 2, \cdots, \kappa$, selects vectors $\mathbf{r}_i \xleftarrow{\$} \mathbb{Z}_q$ and vectors $\mathbf{e}_{R,i} \xleftarrow{\$} D_{\mathbb{Z},t}^m$ randomly s.t. $\|\mathbf{e}_{R,i}\| \le 2t\sqrt{m}$ and then calculates $\mathbf{c}_{R,i} = \mathbf{A}_{\mathsf{label}}^\top \cdot \mathbf{r}_i + \mathbf{e}_{R,i} + m_i[0, 0, \cdots, 0, \lceil \frac{q}{2} \rceil]^\top \bmod q$.
  - Outputs $pk_R := (\mathbf{p}_R, \{\mathbf{c}_{R,1}\}, \{\mathbf{c}_{R,2}\}, \cdots, \{\mathbf{c}_{R,\kappa}\}, \mathbf{M}_R, \mathbf{M}_{R,1}, \mathbf{M}_{R,2}, \cdots, \mathbf{M}_{R,\ell}, \mathbf{C}_R, \mathbf{r}_R)$ and $sk_R := (\mathbf{h}_R, \{\mathbf{r}_1\}, \{\mathbf{r}_2\}, \cdots, \{\mathbf{r}_\kappa\})$ as the initial (root node) public key and secret key of the receiver, respectively.

- KeyUpdate(pp, pk_R, sk_R, t, d): Given a public parameter pp, time t, initial public key pk_R, and initial secret key sk_R, this algorithm processes the following steps.
  - Defines $t := (t_1 t_2 \cdots t_i)$, where t means the binary representation of time and $i \in [1, d]$, $t_i \in \{0, 1\}$, d is the depth of the binary tree.
  - Defines $\Theta^{(i)} := (\theta_1, \theta_2, \cdots, \theta_i) \in \mathsf{node}(t)$, where $i \in [1, d], \theta_i \in \{0, 1\}$ as the path from the root to the current node.
  - Defines $F_{\Theta^{(i)}} := [\mathbf{M}_R \| A_1^{(\theta_1)} \| A_2^{(\theta_2)} \| \cdots \| A_i^{(\theta_i)}]$ as the corresponding matrix of $\Theta^{(i)}$. For example, $F_{0100} = [\mathbf{M}_R \| A_1^0 \| A_2^1 \| A_3^0 \| A_4^0]$, $F_{101} = [\mathbf{M}_R \| A_1^1 \| A_2^0 \| A_3^1]$.
  - For any $j < i$, where $j, i \in [1, d]$, given the trapdoor $\mathbf{S}_{\Theta^{(j)}}$ on time j, calls ExtBasis$(F_{\Theta^{(i)}}, \mathbf{S}_{\Theta^{(j)}})$ to generate $\mathbf{S}_{\Theta^{(i)}}$, where $\Theta^{(i)} := (\theta_1, \theta_2, \cdots, \theta_j, \theta_{j+1}, \cdots, \theta_i)$. Thus, the updated trapdoor can be calculated by its any ancestor's trapdoor.
  - Define $sk_R(t) := (\mathbf{h}_R, \{\mathbf{r}_{R,1}\}, \{\mathbf{r}_{R,2}\}, \cdots, \{\mathbf{r}_{R,\kappa}\}, \mathbf{S}_{\Theta^{(i)}})$, where $\Theta^{(i)} \in \mathsf{node}(t)$ as the receiver's secret key on time t. Each node has the corresponding secret key in a binary tree.
  - Receiver updates $sk_R(t)$ to $sk_R(t+1)$ through calculating $sk_R(t+1) := (\mathbf{h}_R, \{\mathbf{r}_{R,1}\}, \{\mathbf{r}_{R,2}\}, \cdots, \{\mathbf{r}_{R,\kappa}\}, \mathbf{S}_{\Theta^{(i)}})$, where $\Theta^{(i)} \in \mathsf{node}(t+1)$. We show an example here, supposing that receiver updates $sk_R(1010)$ to $sk_R(1011)$. Given $sk_R(1010) = (\mathbf{h}_R, \{\mathbf{r}_{R,1}\}, \{\mathbf{r}_{R,2}\}, \cdots, \{\mathbf{r}_{R,\kappa}\}, \mathbf{S}_{101}, \mathbf{S}_{11})$, the updated secret key is $sk_R(1011) = (\mathbf{h}_R, \{\mathbf{r}_{R,1}\}, \{\mathbf{r}_{R,2}\}, \cdots, \{\mathbf{r}_{R,\kappa}\}, \mathbf{S}_{1011}, \mathbf{S}_{11})$.

- FS-PAEKS($pp, pk_S, sk_S, pk_R, kw, t, d$): Given a public parameter pp, the sender's public key and secret key pk_S, sk_S, the receiver's public key pk_R, a keyword $kw \in \{1, -1\}^\ell$, the time period t, and the depth of the binary tree d, this algorithm executes the following procedures.
  - For $i = 1, 2, \cdots, \kappa$, calculates

$$h_{S,i} \leftarrow \lfloor \frac{2(\mathbf{c}_{R,i}^\top \cdot \mathbf{h}_S(\bmod q))}{q} \rceil, p_{S,i} \leftarrow \lfloor \frac{2(\mathbf{s}_i^\top \cdot \mathbf{p}_R(\bmod q))}{q} \rceil.$$

  - Defines $y_{S,i} = h_{S,i} \cdot p_{S,i}$, and $\mathbf{y}_S = y_{S,1} y_{S,2} \cdots y_{S,\kappa} \in \{0, 1\}^\kappa$.
  - Defines and calculates $\mathbf{dk}_S = dk_{S,1} dk_{S,2} \cdots dk_{S,\ell} \leftarrow H_2(kw, \mathbf{y}_S) \in \{1, -1\}^\ell$.
  - Defines and calculates $\mathbf{M}_{dk} = \mathbf{C}_R + \sum_{i=1}^\ell dk_{S,i} \mathbf{M}_{R,i}$.
  - Calculates $\mathbf{F}_{dk} = [\mathbf{M}_R \| \mathbf{M}_{dk}] = [\mathbf{M}_R \| \mathbf{C}_R + \sum_{i=1}^\ell dk_{S,i} \mathbf{M}_{R,i}]$.
  - Defines $\mathbf{F}_t := [\mathbf{M}_R \| A_1^{t_1} \| A_2^{t_2} \| \cdots \| A_d^{t_d}]$.
  - For $j = 1, 2, \cdots, \rho$, processes the following operations as below:
    * Selects $b_j \xleftarrow{\$} \{0, 1\}$ and $\mathbf{s}_j \xleftarrow{\$} \mathbb{Z}_q^n$ randomly;
    * For $i = 1, 2, \cdots, \ell$, selects $\mathbf{R}_{i_j} \xleftarrow{\$} \{1, -1\}^{\frac{(d+3)m}{2} \times \frac{(d+3)m}{2}}$;
    * Defines and calculates $\bar{\mathbf{R}}_j = \sum_{i=1}^\ell dk_{S,i} \mathbf{R}_{i_j} \in \{-\ell, -\ell + 1, \cdots, \ell\}^{\frac{(d+3)m}{2} \times \frac{(d+3)m}{2}}$;
    * Selects $x_j \leftarrow \Psi_\alpha \in \mathbb{Z}_q$ and $\mathbf{y}_j \leftarrow \Psi_\alpha^{\frac{(d+3)m}{2}} \in \mathbb{Z}_q^{\frac{(d+3)m}{2}}$ as noise vectors;
    * Calculates $\mathbf{z}_j \leftarrow \bar{\mathbf{R}}_j^\top \mathbf{y}_j \in \mathbb{Z}_q^{\frac{(d+3)m}{2}}$, and $c_{0_j} = (\mathbf{r}_R^\top + H_3(kw)^\top)\mathbf{s}_j + x_j + b_j \lfloor \frac{q}{2} \rfloor \in \mathbb{Z}_q$.
    * Calculates $\mathbf{c_1}_j = (\mathbf{F}_{dk} \| \mathbf{F}_t)^\top \mathbf{s}_j + \begin{bmatrix} \mathbf{y}_j \\ \mathbf{z}_j \end{bmatrix} \in \mathbb{Z}_q^{(d+3)m}$.
  - Outputs a forward-secure searchable ciphertext $ct := (\{c_{0_j}, \mathbf{c_1}_j, b_j\}_{j=1}^\rho)$.
- Trapdoor($pp, pk_S, pk_R, sk_R(t), kw'$): After input a public parameter pp, the public key of the sender pk_S, the public key of the receiver pk_R, the secret key of the receiver $sk_R(t)$ with time t and a keyword $kw' \in \{1, -1\}^\ell$, this algorithm will process the following steps.
  - For $i = 1, 2, \cdots, \kappa$, calculates

$$h_{R,i} \leftarrow \lfloor \frac{2(\mathbf{c}_{S,i}^\top \cdot \mathbf{h}_R(\bmod q))}{q} \rceil, p_{R,i} \leftarrow \lfloor \frac{2(\mathbf{s}_{R,i}^\top \cdot \mathbf{p}_S(\bmod q))}{q} \rceil.$$

  - Defines $y_{R,i} = h_{R,i} \cdot p_{R,i}$, and $\mathbf{y}_R = y_{R,1} y_{R,2} \cdots y_{R,\kappa} \in \{0, 1\}^\kappa$.
  - Defines and calculates $\mathbf{dk}_R = dk_{R,1} dk_{R,2} \cdots dk_{R,\ell} \leftarrow H_2(kw', \mathbf{y}_R)$.
  - Defines and calculates $\mathbf{M}_{dk} = \mathbf{C}_R + \sum_{i=1}^\ell dk_{R,i} \mathbf{M}_{R,i}$.
  - Invokes SampleLeft($\mathbf{M}_R, \mathbf{M}_{dk}, \mathbf{S}_R, \mathbf{r}_R, \sigma_2$) algorithm to generate $\mathbf{Trap_1} \in \mathbb{Z}_q^{2m}$.
  - If $sk_R(t)$ includes the basis $\mathbf{S}_{\Theta(t)}$, this algorithm will continue the remainder procedures;
    If $sk_R(t)$ does not include the basis $\mathbf{S}_{\Theta(t)}$, this algorithm will call ExtBasis($F_{\Theta(t)}, \mathbf{S}_{\Theta(i)}$) to generate it and then continue the remainder procedures.

- Invokes $\mathsf{SamplePre}(\mathbf{S}_{\Theta^{(t)}}, H_3(kw'), \sigma_3)$ algorithm to generate $\mathbf{Trap_2} \in \mathbb{Z}_q^{(d+1)m}$.
- Outputs $\mathbf{Trap} := (\mathbf{Trap_1}, \mathbf{Trap_2})$.

- $\mathsf{Test}(pp, \mathsf{ct}, \mathbf{Trap})$:
  - For $j = 1, 2, \cdots, \rho$, calculates $v_j = c_{0_j} - \begin{pmatrix} \mathbf{Trap_1} \\ \mathbf{Trap_2} \end{pmatrix}^\top \mathbf{c}_{1_j}$.
  - Checks whether it satisfies $\lfloor v_j - \lfloor \frac{q}{2} \rfloor \rfloor$: If it holds, sets $v_j = 1$; Otherwise, sets $v_j = 0$.
  - This algorithm outputs 1 if and only if for $\forall j = 1, 2, \cdots, \rho$, it satisfies $v_j = b_j$, which implies the $\mathsf{Test}(pp, \mathsf{ct}, \mathbf{Trap})$ algorithm succeeds; Otherwise, it outputs 0, which implies the $\mathsf{Test}(pp, \mathsf{ct}, \mathbf{Trap})$ algorithm fails.

7 Parameters and Correctness

7.1 Parameters Setting

1. $m \geq 6n \log q$ to make $\mathsf{TrapGen}(n, m, q)$ algorithm process properly.
2. $s \geq \eta_\epsilon(\Lambda^\perp(\mathbf{A}_{\mathsf{label}}))$ for some $\epsilon = \mathsf{negl}(n)$ and $t = \sigma_1 \sqrt{m} \cdot (\sqrt{\log n})$ to make $\mathsf{KeyGen}_S(pp)$ and $\mathsf{KeyGen}_R(pp)$ run properly.
3. $\sigma_1 = 2\sqrt{n}$ and $q > \frac{2\sqrt{n}}{\alpha}$ to make the lattice reduction algorithm is correct.
4. $\sigma_2 > \ell \cdot m \cdot \omega(\sqrt{\log n})$ to let $\mathsf{SampleLeft}(\mathbf{A}, \mathbf{M}, \mathbf{T_A}, \mathbf{u}, \sigma)$ algorithm execute properly.
5. $m \geq 2n\lceil \log q \rceil$, $\sigma_3 \geq \| \tilde{\mathbf{B}} \| \cdot \omega(\sqrt{\log n})$ to let $\mathsf{SamplePre}(\mathbf{A}, \mathbf{T_A}, \mathbf{u}, \sigma)$ algorithm operate properly.
6. $\frac{(d+3)m}{2}$ is an integer to make $\mathsf{FS\text{-}PAEKS}(pp, pk_S, sk_S, pk_R, kw, t, d)$ algorithm work properly.
7. $q > \sigma_1 m^{\frac{3}{2}} \omega(\sqrt{\log n})$ to make first error term is bounded legitimately and $\mathbf{y}_S = \mathbf{y}_R$.
8. $\alpha < [\sigma_2 \ell m \omega(\sqrt{\log n})]^{-1}$, $q = \Omega(\sigma_2 m^{\frac{3}{2}})$ to make second error term is bounded legitimately.

7.2 Correctness

Theorem 3. *We initially consider the condition mentioned by Lemma 6.1 in reference [48] and $\epsilon = \mathsf{negl}(n)$ is negligible. That is, if the keywords hold $kw = kw'$ and the first error term $(\mathbf{r}_{R,i}^\top \cdot \mathbf{h}_{S,i}$ and $\mathbf{e}_{S,i}^\top \cdot \mathbf{h}_{R,i})$ is less than $\frac{\epsilon \cdot q}{8}$ with overwhelming probability, then we obtain the equality $\mathbf{dk}_S = \mathbf{dk}_R$.*

Proof. For $i = 1, 2, \cdots, \kappa$, calculates:

$$h_{S,i} = \lfloor \frac{2(\mathbf{r}_i^\top \cdot \mathbf{A}_{\mathsf{label}}) \cdot \mathbf{h}_S (\bmod q)}{q} + \underbrace{\frac{2\mathbf{r}_{R,i}^\top \cdot \mathbf{h}_S (\bmod q)}{q}}_{\text{first error term}} \rceil = \lfloor \frac{2((\mathbf{r}_i^\top \cdot \mathbf{A}_{\mathsf{label}}) \cdot \mathbf{h}_S (\bmod q))}{q} \rceil = p_{R,i};$$

$$h_{R,i} = \lfloor \frac{2(\mathbf{s}_i^\top \cdot \mathbf{A}_{\mathsf{label}}) \cdot \mathbf{h}_R (\bmod q)}{q} + \underbrace{\frac{2\mathbf{r}_{S,i}^\top \cdot \mathbf{h}_R (\bmod q)}{q}}_{\text{first error term}} \rceil = \lfloor \frac{2((\mathbf{r}_i^\top \cdot \mathbf{A}_{\mathsf{label}}) \cdot \mathbf{h}_R (\bmod q))}{q} \rceil = p_{S,i}.$$

For $i = 1, 2, \cdots, \kappa$, we have the following equalities: $y_{S,i} = h_{S,i} \cdot p_{S,i} = p_{R,i} \cdot p_{S,i} = p_{S,i} \cdot p_{R,i} = h_{R,i} \cdot p_{R,i} = y_{R,i}$. Therefore, we can say that $\mathbf{y}_S = \mathbf{y}_R$. In addition, because of $kw = kw'$, we obtain that $\mathbf{dk}_S = H_2(kw, \mathbf{y}_S) = H_2(kw', \mathbf{y}_S) = H_2(kw', \mathbf{y}_R) = \mathbf{dk}_R$.

Theorem 4. *If the* second error term $(x_j - \begin{pmatrix} \mathbf{Trap_1} \\ \mathbf{Trap_2} \end{pmatrix}^{\top} \begin{bmatrix} \mathbf{y}_j \\ \mathbf{z}_j \end{bmatrix})$ *has been bounded by* $((q \cdot \sigma_2 \cdot \ell \cdot m \cdot \alpha \cdot \omega(\sqrt{\log m}) + \mathcal{O}(\ell \sigma_2 m^{\frac{3}{2}})) \leq \frac{q}{5})$, *then the* Test$(pp, \mathsf{ct}, \mathbf{Trap})$ *algorithm outputs* 1, *and* b_j *is correct.*

Proof.

$$
v_j = c_{0_j} - \begin{pmatrix} \mathbf{Trap_1} \\ \mathbf{Trap_2} \end{pmatrix}^{\top} \mathbf{c}_{1_j} = (\mathbf{r}_R^{\top} + H_3(kw)^{\top})\mathbf{s}_j + x_j + b_j \lfloor \frac{q}{2} \rfloor - \begin{pmatrix} \mathbf{Trap_1} \\ \mathbf{Trap_2} \end{pmatrix}^{\top} \mathbf{c}_{1_j}
$$

$$
= \mathbf{r}_R^{\top}\mathbf{s}_j + x_j + b_j \lfloor \frac{q}{2} \rfloor + H_3(kw)^{\top}\mathbf{s}_j - \begin{pmatrix} \mathbf{Trap_1} \\ \mathbf{Trap_2} \end{pmatrix}^{\top} [(\mathbf{F}_{dk} \parallel \mathbf{F}_t)^{\top}\mathbf{s}_j + \begin{bmatrix} \mathbf{y}_j \\ \mathbf{z}_j \end{bmatrix}]
$$

$$
= \mathbf{r}_R^{\top}\mathbf{s}_j + x_j + b_j \lfloor \frac{q}{2} \rfloor + H_3(kw)^{\top}\mathbf{s}_j - (\mathbf{Trap_1}\mathbf{F}_{dk} + \mathbf{Trap_2}\mathbf{F}_t)\mathbf{s}_j - \begin{pmatrix} \mathbf{Trap_1} \\ \mathbf{Trap_2} \end{pmatrix}^{\top} \begin{bmatrix} \mathbf{y}_j \\ \mathbf{z}_j \end{bmatrix}
$$

$$
= b_j \lfloor \frac{q}{2} \rfloor + \underbrace{x_j - \begin{pmatrix} \mathbf{Trap_1} \\ \mathbf{Trap_2} \end{pmatrix}^{\top} \begin{bmatrix} \mathbf{y}_j \\ \mathbf{z}_j \end{bmatrix}}_{\text{second error term}}
$$

Therefore, as mentioned in Lemma 22 of reference [46], for $j = 1, 2, \cdots, \rho$, if the given keywords are absolutely identical, we can conclude that $v_j = b_j$.

8 Theoretical Comparison

We cryptanalyze and compare eight PEKS and PAEKS schemes with regards to six security properties in Table 1. Then, we compare the computational complexity and communication overhead with several post-quantum PEKS and PAEKS primitives in Tables 2 and 3.

Table 1. Security properties comparison with other existing PEKS and PAEKS schemes

Schemes	FS	CI	MCI	TP	PQ	WTA
Boneh et al. [1]	×	✓	✓	×	×	✓
Huang et al. [5]	×	×	×	×	×	✓
Behnia et al. [24]	×	✓	✓	×	✓	✓
Zhang et al. [49]	×	✓	✓	×	✓	×
Zhang et al. [19]	✓	✓	✓	×	✓	✓
Liu et al. [12]	×	✓	✓	✓	✓	✓
Emura [50]	×	✓	✓	✓	✓	✓
Cheng et al. [35]	×	✓	✓	✓	✓	✓
Our scheme	✓	✓	✓	✓	✓	✓

Notes. **PQ:** Post-quantum. **WTA:** Without trusted authority.

As for Table 2, the abbreviations are multiplication (T_{Mul}), hash function (T_{HF}), SampleLeft (T_{SL}), SamplePre (T_{SP}), and BasisDel (T_{BD}) algorithms. With regard to Table 3, we analyze the communication overhead in terms of ciphertext size and trapdoor size. d is the depth of a binary tree, ℓ is the length of a keyword kw, ρ, κ are related to the security parameter.

9   Potential Applications of FS-PAEKS

(1) **Combining with Electronic Medical Records (EMRs).** Numerous scholars have utilized PEKS primitive for doctors (data receiver) to search EMRs and protect the privacy of patients (data sender) [20,51,52]. However, a malicious attacker may recover the keyword kw from the previous search trapdoor **Trap** through keyword guessing attacks. Besides, if secret keys have been compromised, sensitive medical data may be disclosed. Compared with the existing schemes, our FS-PAEKS protocol completely avoids those problems and provides better security.

(2) **Combining with Industrial Internet of Things (IIoTs).** The PAKES protocol has been employed to safeguard the privacy of IIoTs while simultaneously achieving CI and TP security [37]. However, they failed to account for the potential risks of quantum computing attacks and the likelihood of secret key leakage during communication. Our FS-PAEKS primitive offers enhanced security features such as quantum resistance and elimination of secret key leakage. Besides, we realize MCI security, which addressed a previously unresolved issue of their work.

Table 2. Computational complexity comparison

Schemes	Ciphertext Generation	Trapdoor Generation	Test Generation
Behnia et al. [24]	$\rho(m^2 + 2nm + n + \ell + 1)T_{Mul}$	$\ell T_{Mul} + T_{SL}$	$2\rho m T_{Mul}$
Zhang et al. [19]	$T_{HF} + (\rho n + nm^2 + \rho)T_{Mul} + T_{SP}$	$T_{HF} + nm^2 T Mul$ $+T_{BD} + T_{SP}$	$T_{HF} + (\ell m + nm)T_M$
Liu et al. [12]	$T_{HF} + (\kappa(m + n + 1)$ $+\rho(m^2 + 2nm + n + \ell + 1))T_{Mul}$	$T_{HF} + (\kappa(m + n + 1)$ $+\ell)T_{Mul} + T_{SL}$	$2\rho m T_M$
Our scheme	$(\rho + 1)T_{HF} + (\kappa(m + n + 1)$ $+\rho(\frac{(d+3)^2 m^2}{4} + (d+3)nm$ $+2n + \ell + 1))T_{Mul}$	$2T_{HF} + (\kappa(m + n + 1)$ $+\ell)T_{Mul} + T_{SL} + T_{SP}$	$(d + 3)\rho m T_M$

Table 3. Communication overhead comparison

Schemes	Ciphertext Size	Trapdoor Size
Behnia et al. [24]	$\kappa(|q| + 2m|q| + 1)$	$2m|q|$
Zhang et al. [19]	$(\ell + m\ell + m)|q|$	$m|q|$
Liu et al. [12]	$\rho(|q| + 2m|q| + 1)$	$2m|q|$
Our scheme	$\rho(|q| + (d + 3)m|q| + 1)$	$(d + 3)m|q|$

10   Conclusion

In this paper, we generalize the first post-quantum public-key authenticated searchable encryption with forward security primitive, namely FS-PAEKS. The proposed scheme addresses the challenge of secret key exposure while enjoying quantum-safe security without trusted authorities. Technically speaking, we introduce the binary tree structure, the minimal cover set, and ExtBasis and SamplePre algorithms to achieve the post-quantum one-way secret key evolution. Moreover, we analyze it satisfies IND-CKA, IND-IKGA, and IND-Multi-CKA in a quantum setting. Besides, we also elaborate on the theoretical comparisons. Ultimately, we show two applications for FS-PAEKS to illustrate its feasibility. We hereby address an open problem of how to construct a post-quantum FS-PAEKS scheme without random oracle models.

Acknowledgements. Xue Chen interned as a Summer Research Assistant at HKU. This work is partially supported by HKU-SCF FinTech Academy, Shenzhen-Hong Kong-Macao Science and Technology Plan Project (Category C Project: SGDX20210823103537030), and Theme-based Research Scheme of RGC, Hong Kong (T35-710/20-R).

References

1. Boneh, D., Di Crescenzo, G., Ostrovsky, R., Persiano, G.: Public key encryption with keyword search. In: Cachin, C., Camenisch, J.L. (eds.) EUROCRYPT 2004. LNCS, vol. 3027, pp. 506–522. Springer, Heidelberg (2004). https://doi.org/10.1007/978-3-540-24676-3_30

2. Gang, X., et al.: A searchable encryption scheme based on lattice for log systems in blockchain. Comput. Mater. Continua **72**(3), 5429–5441 (2022)

3. Gang, X., et al.: PPSEB: a postquantum public-key searchable encryption scheme on blockchain for e-healthcare scenarios. Secur. Commun. Netw. **2022**, 13 (2022)

4. Byun, J.W., Rhee, H.S., Park, H.-A., Lee, D.H.: Off-line keyword guessing attacks on recent keyword search schemes over encrypted data. In: Jonker, W., Petković, M. (eds.) SDM 2006. LNCS, vol. 4165, pp. 75–83. Springer, Heidelberg (2006). https://doi.org/10.1007/11844662_6

5. Huang, Q., Li, H.: An efficient public-key searchable encryption scheme secure against inside keyword guessing attacks. Inf. Sci. **403**, 1–14 (2017)

6. Baodong Qin, Yu., Chen, Q.H., Liu, X., Zheng, D.: Public-key authenticated encryption with keyword search revisited: security model and constructions. Inf. Sci. **516**, 515–528 (2020)

7. Noroozi, M., Eslami, Z.: Public key authenticated encryption with keyword search: revisited. IET Inf. Secur. **13**(4), 336–342 (2019)

8. Qin, B., Cui, H., Zheng, X., Zheng, D.: Improved security model for public-key authenticated encryption with keyword search. In: Huang, Q., Yu, Yu. (eds.) ProvSec 2021. LNCS, vol. 13059, pp. 19–38. Springer, Cham (2021). https://doi.org/10.1007/978-3-030-90402-9_2

9. Yang, L., Li, J.: Lightweight public key authenticated encryption with keyword search against adaptively-chosen-targets adversaries for mobile devices. IEEE Trans. Mob. Comput. **21**(12), 4397–4409 (2021)

10. Pan, X., Li, F.: Public-key authenticated encryption with keyword search achieving both multi-ciphertext and multi-trapdoor indistinguishability. J. Syst. Architect. **115**, 102075 (2021)

11. Huang, Q., Huang, P., Li, H., Huang, J., Lin, H.: A more efficient public-key authenticated encryption scheme with keyword search. J. Syst. Architect. **137**, 102839 (2023)

12. Liu, Z.-Y., Tseng, Y.-F., Tso, R., Mambo, M., Chen, Y.-C.: Public-key authenticated encryption with keyword search: cryptanalysis, enhanced security, and quantum-resistant instantiation. In: Proceedings of the 2022 ACM on Asia Conference on Computer and Communications Security, pp. 423–436 (2022)

13. Bellare, M., Miner, S.K.: A forward-secure digital signature scheme. In: Wiener, M. (ed.) CRYPTO 1999. LNCS, vol. 1666, pp. 431–448. Springer, Heidelberg (1999). https://doi.org/10.1007/3-540-48405-1_28

14. Cao, Y., Shiyuan, X., Chen, X., He, Y., Jiang, S.: A forward-secure and efficient authentication protocol through lattice-based group signature in vanets scenarios. Comput. Netw. **214**, 109149 (2022)

15. Chen, X., Xu, S., He, Y., Cui, Y., He, J., Gao, S.: LFS-AS: lightweight forward secure aggregate signature for e-health scenarios. In: ICC 2022-IEEE International Conference on Communications, pp. 1239–1244. IEEE (2022)

16. Canetti, R., Halevi, S., Katz, J.: A forward-secure public-key encryption scheme. J. Cryptol. **20**, 265–294 (2007)

17. Chen, X., Shiyuan, X., Cao, Y., He, Y., Xiao, K.: AQRS: anti-quantum ring signature scheme for secure epidemic control with blockchain. Comput. Netw. **224**, 109595 (2023)

18. Xu, S., Chen, X., Kong, W., Cao, Y., He, Y., Xiao, K.: An efficient blockchain-based privacy-preserving authentication scheme in VANET. In: 2023 IEEE 97th Vehicular Technology Conference (VTC2023-Spring), pp. 1–6. IEEE (2023)

19. Zhang, X., Chunxiang, X., Wang, H., Zhang, Y., Wang, S.: FS-PEKS: lattice-based forward secure public-key encryption with keyword search for cloud-assisted industrial Internet of Things. IEEE Trans. Dependable Secure Comput. **18**(3), 1019–1032 (2021)

20. Zhe, J., Kai, Z., Liangliang, W., Jianting, N.: Forward secure public-key authenticated encryption with conjunctive keyword search. Comput. J. **66**, 2265–2278 (2022)

21. Shor, P.W.: Polynomial-time algorithms for prime factorization and discrete logarithms on a quantum computer. SIAM Rev. **41**(2), 303–332 (1999)

22. Shor, P.W.: Algorithms for quantum computation: discrete logarithms and factoring. In: Proceedings 35th Annual Symposium on Foundations of Computer Science, pp. 124–134. IEEE (1994)

23. Liu, Z.-Y., Tseng, Y.-F., Tso, R., Mambo, M., Chen, Y.-C.: Public-key authenticated encryption with keyword search: a generic construction and its quantum-resistant instantiation. Comput. J. **65**(10), 2828–2844 (2022)

24. Behnia, R., Ozmen, M.O., Yavuz, A.A.: Lattice-based public key searchable encryption from experimental perspectives. IEEE Trans. Depend. Secure Comput. **17**(6), 1269–1282 (2020)

25. Cash, D., Hofheinz, D., Kiltz, E., Peikert, C.: Bonsai trees, or how to delegate a lattice basis. J. Cryptol. **25**, 601–639 (2012)

26. Cramer, R., Shoup, V.: Universal hash proofs and a paradigm for adaptive chosen ciphertext secure public-key encryption. In: Knudsen, L.R. (ed.) EUROCRYPT 2002. LNCS, vol. 2332, pp. 45–64. Springer, Heidelberg (2002). https://doi.org/10.1007/3-540-46035-7_4

27. Katz, J., Vaikuntanathan, V.: Smooth projective hashing and password-based authenticated key exchange from lattices. In: Matsui, M. (ed.) ASIACRYPT 2009. LNCS, vol. 5912, pp. 636–652. Springer, Heidelberg (2009). https://doi.org/10.1007/978-3-642-10366-7_37

28. Canetti, R., Dachman-Soled, D., Vaikuntanathan, V., Wee, H.: Efficient password authenticated key exchange via oblivious transfer. In: Fischlin, M., Buchmann, J., Manulis, M. (eds.) PKC 2012. LNCS, vol. 7293, pp. 449–466. Springer, Heidelberg (2012). https://doi.org/10.1007/978-3-642-30057-8_27

29. Abdalla, M., Benhamouda, F., MacKenzie, P.: Security of the j-pake password-authenticated key exchange protocol. In: 2015 IEEE Symposium on Security and Privacy, pp. 571–587. IEEE (2015)

30. Jarecki, S., Krawczyk, H., Xu, J.: OPAQUE: an asymmetric PAKE protocol secure against pre-computation attacks. In: Nielsen, J.B., Rijmen, V. (eds.) EURO-CRYPT 2018. LNCS, vol. 10822, pp. 456–486. Springer, Cham (2018). https://doi.org/10.1007/978-3-319-78372-7_15

31. Erwig, A., Hesse, J., Orlt, M., Riahi, S.: Fuzzy asymmetric password-authenticated key exchange. In: Moriai, S., Wang, H. (eds.) ASIACRYPT 2020. LNCS, vol. 12492, pp. 761–784. Springer, Cham (2020). https://doi.org/10.1007/978-3-030-64834-3_26

32. Abdalla, M., Eisenhofer, T., Kiltz, E., Kunzweiler, S., Riepel, D.: Password-authenticated key exchange from group actions. In: Dodis, Y., Shrimpton, T. (eds.) Advances in Cryptology-CRYPTO 2022: 42nd Annual International Cryptology Conference, CRYPTO 2022, Santa Barbara, CA, USA, 15–18 August 2022, Proceedings, Part II, pp. 699–728. Springer, Cham (2022). https://doi.org/10.1007/978-3-031-15979-4_24

33. Katz, J., Vaikuntanathan, V.: Round-optimal password-based authenticated key exchange. J. Cryptol. **26**, 714–743 (2013)

34. Zhang, R., Imai, H.: Generic combination of public key encryption with keyword search and public key encryption. In: Bao, F., Ling, S., Okamoto, T., Wang, H., Xing, C. (eds.) CANS 2007. LNCS, vol. 4856, pp. 159–174. Springer, Heidelberg (2007). https://doi.org/10.1007/978-3-540-76969-9_11

35. Cheng, L., Meng, F.: Public key authenticated encryption with keyword search from LWE. In: Atluri, V., Di Pietro, R., Jensen, C.D., Meng, W. (eds.) Computer Security – ESORICS 2022. ESORICS 2022. Lecture Notes in Computer Science, vol. 13554, pp. 303–324. Springer, 2022. https://doi.org/10.1007/978-3-031-17140-6_15

36. Yao, L., et al.: Scalable CCA-secure public-key authenticated encryption with key-word search from ideal lattices in cloud computing. Inf. Sci. **624**, 777–795 (2023)

37. Pu, L., Lin, C., Chen, B., He, D.: User-friendly public-key authenticated encryption with keyword search for industrial internet of things. IEEE Internet of Things J. **10**, 13544–13555 (2023)

38. Zeng, M., Qian, H., Chen, J., Zhang, K.: Forward secure public key encryption with keyword search for outsourced cloud storage. IEEE Trans. Cloud Comput. **10**(1), 426–438 (2019)

39. Yang, X., Chen, X., Huang, J., Li, H., Huang, Q.: FS-IBEKS: forward secure identity-based encryption with keyword search from lattice. Comput. Stand. Inter-faces **86**, 103732 (2023)

40. Abdalla, M., Benhamouda, F., Pointcheval, D.: Public-key encryption indistin-guishable under plaintext-checkable attacks. IET Inf. Secur. **10**(6), 288–303 (2016)

41. Ajtai, M.: Generating hard instances of lattice problems. In: Proceedings of the Twenty-Eighth Annual ACM Symposium on Theory of Computing, pp. 99–108 (1996)
42. Peikert, C.: An efficient and parallel gaussian sampler for lattices. In: Rabin, T. (ed.) CRYPTO 2010. LNCS, vol. 6223, pp. 80–97. Springer, Heidelberg (2010). https://doi.org/10.1007/978-3-642-14623-7_5
43. Agrawal, S., Boneh, D., Boyen, X.: Lattice basis delegation in fixed dimension and shorter-ciphertext hierarchical IBE. In: Rabin, T. (ed.) CRYPTO 2010. LNCS, vol. 6223, pp. 98–115. Springer, Heidelberg (2010). https://doi.org/10.1007/978-3-642-14623-7_6
44. Micciancio, D., Peikert, C.: Trapdoors for lattices: simpler, tighter, faster, smaller. In: Pointcheval, D., Johansson, T. (eds.) EUROCRYPT 2012. LNCS, vol. 7237, pp. 700–718. Springer, Heidelberg (2012). https://doi.org/10.1007/978-3-642-29011-4_41
45. Gentry, C., Peikert, C., Vaikuntanathan, V.: Trapdoors for hard lattices and new cryptographic constructions. In: Proceedings of the Fortieth Annual ACM Symposium on Theory of Computing, pp. 197–206 (2008)
46. Agrawal, S., Boneh, D., Boyen, X.: Efficient lattice (H)IBE in the standard model. In: Gilbert, H. (ed.) EUROCRYPT 2010. LNCS, vol. 6110, pp. 553–572. Springer, Heidelberg (2010). https://doi.org/10.1007/978-3-642-13190-5_28
47. Rhee, H.S., Park, J.H., Susilo, W., Lee, D.H.: Trapdoor security in a searchable public-key encryption scheme with a designated tester. J. Syst. Software **83**(5), 763–771 (2010)
48. Li, Z., Wang, D.: Achieving one-round password-based authenticated key exchange over lattices. IEEE Trans. Serv. Comput. **15**(1), 308–321 (2019)
49. Zhang, X., Tang, Y., Wang, H., Chunxiang, X., Miao, Y., Cheng, H.: Lattice-based proxy-oriented identity-based encryption with keyword search for cloud storage. Inf. Sci. **494**, 193–207 (2019)
50. Emura, K.: Generic construction of public-key authenticated encryption with keyword search revisited: stronger security and efficient construction. In: Proceedings of the 9th ACM on ASIA Public-Key Cryptography Workshop, pp. 39–49 (2022)
51. Xu, G., et al.: AAQ-PEKS: an attribute-based anti-quantum public-key encryption scheme with keyword search for e-healthcare scenarios. Cryptology ePrint Archive (2023)
52. Li, H., Huang, Q., Huang, J., Susilo, W.: Public-key authenticated encryption with keyword search supporting constant trapdoor generation and fast search. IEEE Trans. Inf. Forensics Secur. **18**, 396–410 (2022)

Public Key Authenticated Encryption with Keyword Search Improved: Strong Security Model and Multi-keyword Construction

Guiquan Yang[1], Sha Ma[1(✉)], Hongbo Li[1], Husheng Yang[1], and Qiong Huang[1,2]

[1] College of Mathematics and Informatics, South China Agricultural University,
Guangzhou 510642, China
martin_deng@163.com, {hongbo,qhuang}@scau.edu.cn
[2] Guangzhou Key Lab of Intelligent Agriculture, Guangzhou 510642, China

Abstract. To efficiently and securely search encrypted files in cloud storage, Boneh et al. proposed the notion of Public Key Encryption with Keyword Search(PEKS) in 2004. However, original PEKS is susceptible to internal keyword guessing attacks(KGA) launched by server due to the limited keyword space. To resist this attack, Huang and Li introduced the notion of Public Key Authenticated Encryption with Keyword Search (PAEKS), which effectively resists KGA from server by additional authentication between the sender and receiver before encryption. Since both the sender and receiver can generate a common authentication key, a curious sender can use the authentication key to launch KGA, resulting in easily guessing keyword from a given trapdoor. To address this issue, we propose an improved security model for PAEKS that captures both offline KGA and online KGA launched by the curious sender. Then, we present a concrete Stronger Security Public Key Authenticated Encryption with Multi-keyword Search (S-PAEMKS) scheme, which not only supports multi-keyword search but also successfully counters KGA from curious senders. Finally, the experimental results show that our scheme achieves remarkable efficiency in the encryption phase and comparable efficiency in the trapdoor and testing phases.

Keywords: Searchable encryption · Keyword guessing attack · Multi-keyword search · Public key authenticated encryption

1 Introduction

As cloud computing technology progresses swiftly, a substantial volume of data is being stored in the cloud. The powerful computing capabilities and sufficient storage spaces of the cloud environment provide great convenience for various industries today. Nevertheless, in real-world scenarios, cloud storage service providers cannot be entirely trusted and may engage in the unauthorized sale of data or be susceptible to hacker attacks. Therefore, the pursuit of efficient file searching in the cloud while preserving data privacy remains an interesting topic.

© The Author(s), under exclusive license to Springer Nature Singapore Pte Ltd. 2024
C. Ge and M. Yung (Eds.): Inscrypt 2023, LNCS 14526, pp. 299–319, 2024.
https://doi.org/10.1007/978-981-97-0942-7_15

To address the challenge of efficiently searching encrypted files, Boneh et al. [2] introduced the notion of public key encryption with keyword search (PEKS), which seamlessly combines keyword search functionality with public key encryption. In the PEKS framework, a receiver can generate a trapdoor with a keyword and let the cloud server to test whether there are ciphertexts matching with the trapdoor. However, the limited keyword space of real-world applications makes it possible for adversaries to guess the keywords contained in a document namely keyword guessing attack (KGA) [4,31]. In detail, the adversary exhaustively tries every possible keyword to generate the ciphertext and tests it with the provided trapdoor. The adversary can deduce which keyword is encapsulated in the trapdoor based on the test results. As a result, the original PEKS framework inevitably faces the challenge of KGA from both external and internal adversaries.

In 2017, Huang and Li introduced the notion of Public Key Authenticated Encryption with Keyword Search (PAEKS) to successfully defend against KGA from both external and internal adversaries. Unlike original PEKS schemes, the PAEKS scheme includes authentication between the sender and receiver by utilizing an authenticating key derived from one party's secret key and the other party's public key. This effectively addresses the issue of KGA launched by a third party without the authenticating key. Subsequently, PAEKS has garnered significant attention from researchers, leading to the development of numerous variants under Public Key Infrastructure (PKI) framework [5,9,11,12,18,23,24,26,27,30], Identity Based Encryption (IBE) framework [13,17], and Certificateless Encryption (CLE) framework [8,16,19,21,29]. However, all security models in existing PAEKS schemes only focus on resisting external and internal adversaries without the authentication key. If a curious sender with the authentication key utilizes it to launch KGA, the trapdoor privacy of existing PAEKS schemes could be compromised. Assume Alice acts as the curious sender with a public/secret key pair $(pk_A = g^x, sk_A = x)$, and Bob acts as the receiver with a public/secret key pair $(pk_B = g^y, sk_B = y)$. Alice can monitor the trapdoors sent by the Bob to the server through public channel. We further illustrate how curious senders can launch three types of attacks as follows.

Attack I: Offline KGA of Curious Senders. In the existing PAEKS framework, a curious sender can deduce which keyword is hidden in the monitored trapdoor by offline KGA. Let's take Huang and Li's work [10] as an example to illustrate this attack:

- **Step1**: To retrieve files containing the keyword w from cloud storage, Bob uses w to generate the trapdoor T_w with pk_A and sk_B, and sends the trapdoor to the server by the public channel.
- **Step2**: Upon intercepting the trapdoor T_w from the public channel, Alice tries each possible keyword w' using pk_B and sk_A to generate the ciphertext C'_w and tests it with the intercepted trapdoor T_w. If C'_w matches T_w, Alice can infer that $w' = w$.

Attack II: Online KGA of Curious Senders. Assuming the curious sender's testing capability is restricted, it can deduce which keyword is hidden in the monitored trapdoor by utilizing the server's testing capability, namely online KGA. Let's take Li et al.'s work [13] scheme as an example to illustrate this attack:

- **Step1**: After intercepting the trapdoor T_w generated by Bob in the public channel, Alice uses sk_A and pk_B to encrypt possible keywords, generating a large number of ciphertexts $C_w = (C_{w,1} \ldots C_{w,i})$.
- **Step2**: Due to the limited testing capability, Alice seeks assistance only from the server. Thus, Alice uploads the encrypted file $C_f = (C_{f,1} \ldots C_{f,i})$ appended with $C_w = (C_{w,1} \ldots C_{w,i})$ to the server. Additionally, Alice continues to upload the intercepted trapdoor T_w to utilize the server's capability to match T_w with $C_{w,i}$.
- **Step3**: Based on the testing result from the server, Alice can deduce which keyword is hidden in the T_w. If the result contains $C_{f,i}\|C_{w,i}$, Alice can conclude that $w = w_i$.

Attack III: Leakage of Receiver's Secret Key. The curious sender can compute a part of knowledge about the secret key from the trapdoor by utilizing the authentication key. Assuming Alice's public/secret key pair as $(pk_A : \{g^{x_1}, g^{x_2}\}, sk_A : \{x_1, x_2\})$ and Bob's public/secret key pair as $(pk_B : \{g^{y_1}, g^{y_2}\}, sk_B : \{y_1, y_2\})$, let's take Lu et al.'s work [18] as an example to illustrate this attack:

- **Step1**: Alice intercepts the trapdoor $T_w = f_2(w, \lambda_1, \lambda_2)y_1$ generated by Bob in the public channel, where $\lambda_1 = f_1(g^{x_1}, g^{y_1}, g^{x_1 y_1})$, $\lambda_2 = f_1(g^{x_2}, g^{y_2}, g^{x_2 y_2})$.
- **Step2**: Alice tries possible keyword with sk_A and pk_B to compute $\phi = f_2(w', \lambda_1, \lambda_2)$. If $g^{T_w/\phi} = g^{y_1}$, Alice can not only determine that $w = w'$, but also compute y_1 by computing T_w/ϕ'.

All existing PAEKS schemes entirely trust the sender, without considering any guessing behavior towards the trapdoors generated by the receiver. However, in real-world scenarios, the sender may be interested in the trapdoors. If the curious sender utilizes the authenticated key to launch KGA on the trapdoors, the trapdoor privacy of all existing schemes cannot be guaranteed. This motivates us to address the issue of KGA launched by the curious sender.

1.1 Our Contributions

The contributions of our Stronger Security Public Key Authenticated Encryption with Multi-keyword Search (S-PAEMKS) scheme are summarized as follows:

1. Due to the inherent authenticated key in PAEKS construction, a curious sender can utilize this property to launch KGA on trapdoors successfully. The previous PAEKS schemes are shown to be ineffective in countering KGA launched by such an adversary.

2. To prevent KGA launched by curious senders, we present an improved security model for PAEKS that can capture both online and offline KGA from curious senders.

3. We propose a concrete S-PAEMKS scheme that not only supports multi-keyword search but also effectively counters KGA launched by curious senders. Furthermore, we prove its security under the improved security model based Computational Diffie Hellman (CDH) assumption in random oracle model.

4. The experimental results demonstrate that our scheme exhibits exceptional efficiency in the encryption phase and maintains a comparable efficiency in the trapdoor and testing phases.

1.2 Related Work

KGA Issue in PEKS. In 2004, Boneh et al. [2] proposed the first public-key searchable encryption with keyword search (PEKS) scheme. However, due to the limited space of keywords in real-world applications, Byun et al. [4] found an attack approach against PEKS schemes called offline KGA. Baek et al. [1] proposed a secure-channel-free PEKS scheme denoted by dPEKS, where only the designated tester is authorized to perform the testing algorithm, but it still cannot resist external offline KGA. To counter the external offline KGA, [28] improved the security model for dPEKS and provided schemes with indistinguishable trapdoors. However, Shao et al. [28] demonstrated that internal adversaries, such as a semi-honest server, can still launch offline KGA by using its secret key under both the PEKS and dPEKS frameworks. In addition, Yau et al. [31] described another possible attack called online KGA, where an external adversary can guess the keyword by monitoring the test results from the server. This attack can be applied to almost all existing PEKS or dPEKS schemes.

PAEKS and Its Variants. To solve the KGA issue posed by external and internal adversaries, Huang and Li [10] introduced the notion of public-key authenticated encryption with keyword search (PAEKS) under public key infrastructure (PKI) framework. Noroozi et al. [23] pointed out that [10] cannot withstand KGA in multi-user settings and proposed a modified scheme. Qin et al. [26] introduced two new security definitions namely multi-ciphertext indistinguishability(MCI) and multi-trapdoor privacy(MTP) for PAEKS and presented a concrete scheme that achieves MCI, but falls short of achieving MTP. Following Qin et al. [26], Pan and Li [24] proposed another PAEKS scheme that claims to achieve both MCI and MTP. However, it was subsequently pointed by Chen et al. [6] that this scheme can not achieve MCI and MTP. Chen et al. [5] introduced a PAEKS scheme that relies on dual servers, eliminating the need for costly bilinear pairing. Lu et al. [18] proposed a no-pairing PAEKS scheme based on a single server. More recently, Huang et al. [9] introduced inverted index technology into PAEKS to improve retrieval speed. Li et al. [12] proposed a PAEKS scheme with constant trapdoors, supporting fast search and further enhancing efficiency in the searching phase. In Identity-based Encryption (IBE) framework, Li et al. [13] and liu et al. [17] proposed identity-based public-key authenticated encryption with keyword search(IBAEKS) schemes, which can resolve the complex problem of public key certification management in PKI. However, the key escrow problem naturally exists in IBE construction. In Certificateless Encryption (CLE) framework, He et al. [8] proposed a certificateless public-key authenticated encryption with keyword search (CLPAEKS) scheme to address both the issues of key escrow and certificate management. In addition, many schemes [19,21,29] have been developed based on CLPEAKS.

Multi-keyword Search in PEKS. Park et al. [25] proposed public-key encryption with multi-keyword search (PEMKS), which extends the PEKS scheme from single keyword search to multi-keyword search. Jiang et al. [11] incorporated forward security technology [32] and multi-keyword search technology into PAEKS and proposed a forward secure public-key authenticated encryption with multi-keyword search (FS-PAEMKS) scheme. Both [11,25] require an index of keyword positions for searching. Zhang et al. [33] proposed a PEMKS scheme that eliminates the need for a keyword position index. However, Yang et al. [30] pointed out that [33] cannot resist selective keyword and chosen keyword attacks. They subsequently proposed a PAEMKS scheme that achieves both MCI and MTP security. Additionally, other PEMKS or variant schemes have been presented [7,14,22].

1.3   Paper Organization

In the next section, we provide the preliminaries and the assumptions. In Sect. 3, we present the definition of our S-PAEMKS scheme and its security models. In Sect. 4, we provide a detailed explanation of our S-PAEMKS scheme. In Sect. 5, the security proof is demonstrated. In Sect. 6, we compared our scheme with related work and present experimental results. In the last section, we draw conclusions for our scheme.

2   Preliminaries

2.1   Bilinear Pairing

Let $\mathbb{PG} = (\mathbb{G}_1, \mathbb{G}_T, g, p, \hat{e})$ be a symmetric-pairing group. $\mathbb{G}_1$ and $\mathbb{G}_T$ are cyclic groups of prime order p. For all $g, h \in \mathbb{G}_1$ and $a, b \in Z_p^*$, $\hat{e} : \mathbb{G}_1 \times \mathbb{G}_1 \to \mathbb{G}_T$ is a map satisfying the following three properties ?.

1) Bilinear: $\hat{e}(g^a, h^b) = \hat{e}(g, h)^{ab}$.
2) Non-degenerate: $\hat{e}(g, h) \neq 1_{\mathbb{G}_T}$, where $1_{\mathbb{G}_T}$ is the identity of $\mathbb{G}_T$.
3) Computable: There is an efficient algorithm to compute $\hat{e}(g, h)$.

2.2 0/1-Encoding

Lin et al. [15] proposed 0/1-encoding methods to address Millionaires' Problem (MP), effectively transforming integer comparison into an intersection set operation. Let $a = a_n a_{n-1} \ldots a_1 \in \{0,1\}^n$ be a n-bit binary string. Then, the 0/1-encoding approach proceeds as follow:

$$S_a^0 = \{a_n a_{n-1} \ldots a_{i+1} 1 | a_i = 0, 1 \le i \le n\},$$
$$S_a^1 = \{a_n a_{n-1} \ldots a_i | a_i = 1, 1 \le i \le n\}.$$

To compare the values of two integers x and y, we first encode x using the 0-encoding algorithm to obtain S_x^0, and encode y using the 1-encoding algorithm to obtain S_y^1. If the intersection of S_x^0 and S_y^1 is not empty, we conclude that $x < y$. Otherwise, we conclude that $x \ge y$. Formally, it is denoted as $S_x^0 \cap S_y^1 = \varnothing \Leftrightarrow x < y$.

For example, let $x = 5 = (0101)_2$ and $y = 10 = (1010)_2$ be two 4-bit strings. We encode x with 0-encoding and y with 1-encoding. This yields $S_x^0 = \{011, 1\}$ and $S_y^1 = \{101, 1\}$. Since $S_x^0 \cap S_y^1 \ne \varnothing$, we conclude that $x < y$.

2.3 CDH Assumption [3]

For any PPT adversary, given (g, g^a, g^b), where $a, b \in Z_p^*, g \in \mathbb{G}_1$, it is hard to compute the value g^{ab}. This can be formally described as follows:

$$|\Pr[\mathcal{A}(g, g^x, g^y) = g^{xy}]| \le negl(1^\lambda),$$

where $negl(\cdot)$ is a negligible function.

3   System Model and Definitions

3.1   System Model

As shown in Fig. 1, the system model comprises three entities: the data sender, the data receiver, and the designated server tester. The data sender extracts keywords from files and generates ciphertexts for files and keywords, uploading them to the cloud. When the data receiver wants to search for files on the cloud server, it generates trapdoors using keywords and uploads them to the cloud. After accepting the trapdoors, the designated server tester matches them with ciphertexts to search for the corresponding files and sends the search results back to the receiver.

3.2   Definitions

Our Strong Security Public Key Authenticated Encryption with Multi-keyword Search(S-PAEMKS) scheme consists of the following (probabilistic) polynomial-time algorithms.

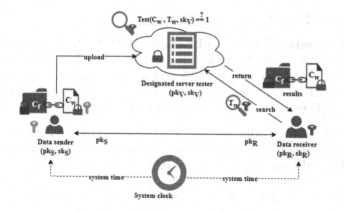

Fig. 1. Our S-PAEMKS model

- **Setup(1^λ)**: This algorithm is executed by the server. It takes the security parameter λ as input, and outputs global system parameter gp.
- **UserKeyGen(gp)**: This algorithm is executed by the user(sender/receiver). It takes the global parameter gp as input, and outputs the user's public/secret key pair (pk_U, sk_U).
- **ServerKeyGen (gp)**: This algorithm is executed by the server. It takes the global parameter gp as input, and outputs the public/secret key pair (pk_V, sk_V) of the server.
- **Enc (gp, W, sk_S, pk_R, t)**: This algorithm is executed by the sender. It takes the global parameter gp, a keywords set W, the receiver's public key pk_R, the sender's secret key sk_S, and the system time t as inputs, and outputs a ciphertext CT.
- **TrapGen ($gp, Q, sk_R, pk_S, pk_V, t'$)**: This algorithm is executed by the receiver. It takes the global parameter gp, a keywords set Q, the sender's public key pk_S, the receiver's secret key sk_R, and the system time t' as inputs, and outputs a trapdoor TD.
- **Test (gp, TD, CT, sk_V)**: This algorithm is executed by the server. It takes the global parameter gp, a trapdoor TD, a ciphertext CT, and the server's secret key sk_V as inputs. It outputs 1 if $Q \subseteq W$ and TD is generated after CT, where Q and W are the keywords sets hidden in TD and CT, respectively. Otherwise, it outputs 0.

Correctness. Using the above notions, if $Q \subseteq W$ and $t < t'$, then $\Pr[\text{Test}(gp, TD, CT, sk_V) = 1] = 1$; otherwise, $\Pr[\text{Test}(gp, TD, CT, sk_V) = 0] = 1 - negl(\lambda)$, where $negl(\cdot)$ is a negligible function.

3.3   Security Model

Game I: Ciphertext Indistinguishability (CI). Ciphertext indistinguishability simulates the behavior of a semi-trusted server, denoted as $\mathcal{A}_1$, in distinguishing which of the two keywords sets a given ciphertext corresponds to, assuming that $\mathcal{A}_1$ has no knowledge of the secret keys of the sender and receiver. This game is designed for $\mathcal{A}_1$ and the challenger $\mathcal{C}$ as follows:

- **Setup:** Given a security parameter λ, compute the global parameter gp using the $Setup(1^\lambda)$ algorithm. Then, compute the public/secret key pairs (pk_S, sk_S) and (pk_R, sk_R) for the sender and receiver, respectively, using the $UserKeyGen(gp)$ algorithm. Compute the public/secret key pair (pk_V, sk_V) for the server using the $ServerKeyGen(gp)$ algorithm. Finally, $\mathcal{C}$ provides $(gp, pk_S, pk_R, pk_V, sk_V)$ to $\mathcal{A}_1$.
- **Phase1:** $\mathcal{A}_1$ can adaptively issue the following queries.
  Ciphertext Oracle $\mathcal{O}_C$: Given a keywords set W and system time t submitted by $\mathcal{A}_1$, $\mathcal{C}$ computes the ciphertext $CT \leftarrow Enc(gp, W, sk_S, pk_R, t)$ and outputs CT.
  Trapdoor Oracle $\mathcal{O}_T$: Given a keywords set Q and system time t' submitted by $\mathcal{A}_1$, $\mathcal{C}$ computes the trapdoor $TD \leftarrow TrapGen(gp, Q, sk_R, pk_S, pk_V, t')$ and outputs TD.
- **Challenge:** $\mathcal{A}_1$ submits two keywords sets W_0^*, W_1^*, and the system time t^* to $\mathcal{C}$, with the requirements that $\mathcal{A}_1$ has not queried W_0^* or W_1^* with any time t in $\mathcal{O}_C$, and has not queried any subset of W_0^* or W_1^* with a time t' in $\mathcal{O}_T$, where $t' > t^*$. Then $\mathcal{C}$ randomly selects a bit $b \in \{0, 1\}$, generates challenge ciphertext $CT^* \leftarrow Enc(gp, W_b^*, sk_S, pk_R, t^*)$, and outputs CT^* to $\mathcal{A}_1$.
- **Phase2:** $\mathcal{A}_1$ can query oracles $\mathcal{O}_C$ and $\mathcal{O}_T$, with the same restrictions as in the challenge phase.
- **Guess:** Finally, $\mathcal{A}_1$ outputs its guess $b' \in \{0, 1\}$, and wins the game if and only if $b = b'$. The advantage that $\mathcal{A}_1$ wins the game I is defined as:

$$Adv_{\mathcal{A}_1}^{SPAEMKS\text{-}CI}(1^\lambda) = |\Pr[b' = b] - \frac{1}{2}|.$$

Definition 1 (CI-Security). For any PPT adversary $\mathcal{A}_1$ in the security parameter λ, our scheme achieves CI-security if the advantage $Adv_{\mathcal{A}_1}^{PAEMKS\text{-}CI}(1^\lambda)$ is negligible.

Game II: Trapdoor Indistinguishability (TI). Trapdoor indistinguishability simulates the semi-trusted server, denoted as $\mathcal{A}_2$, in distinguishing which of the two keywords sets a given trapdoor corresponds to, assuming that $\mathcal{A}_2$ has no knowledge of the sender and receiver's secret keys. This game is designed for $\mathcal{A}_2$ and the challenger $\mathcal{C}$ as follows:

- **Setup:** Given a security parameter λ, compute the global parameter gp using the $Setup(1^\lambda)$ algorithm. Then, compute the public/secret key pairs (pk_S, sk_S) and (pk_R, sk_R) for the sender and receiver, respectively, using the

$UserKeyGen(gp)$ algorithm. Compute the public/secret key pair (pk_V, sk_V) for the server using the $ServerKeyGen(gp)$ algorithm. Finally, $\mathcal{C}$ provides $(gp, pk_S, pk_R, pk_V, sk_V)$ to $\mathcal{A}_2$.

- **Phase1:** $\mathcal{A}_2$ can adaptively issue the following queries.
  Ciphertext Oracle $\mathcal{O}_{\mathcal{C}}$: Same as Game I.
  Trapdoor Oracle $\mathcal{O}_{\mathcal{T}}$: Same as Game I.
- **Challenge:** $\mathcal{A}_2$ submits two keywords sets Q_0^*, Q_1^*, and the system time t^* to $\mathcal{C}$, with the requirements that $\mathcal{A}_2$ has not queried Q_0^* or Q_1^* with any time t' in $\mathcal{O}_{\mathcal{T}}$, and has not queried W that contain Q_0^* or Q_1^* with a time t in $\mathcal{O}_{\mathcal{C}}$, where $t < t^*$. Then $\mathcal{C}$ randomly selects a bit $b \in \{0,1\}$, generates challenge trapdoor $TD^* \leftarrow TrapGen(gp, Q_b^*, sk_R, pk_S, pk_V, t^*)$, and outputs TD^* to $\mathcal{A}_2$.
- **Phase2:** $\mathcal{A}_2$ can query oracles $\mathcal{O}_{\mathcal{C}}$ and $\mathcal{O}_{\mathcal{T}}$, with the same restrictions as in the challenge phase.
- **Guess:** Finally, $\mathcal{A}_2$ outputs its guess $b' \in \{0,1\}$, and wins the game if and only if $b = b'$. The advantage of $\mathcal{A}_2$ wins the game II is defined as:

$$Adv_{\mathcal{A}_2}^{SPAEMKS\text{-}TI}(1^\lambda) = |\Pr[b' = b] - \frac{1}{2}|.$$

Definition 2 (TI-Security). For any PPT adversary $\mathcal{A}_2$ in the security parameter λ, our scheme achieves TI-security if the advantage $Adv_{\mathcal{A}_2}^{SPAEMKS\text{-}TI}(1^\lambda)$ is negligible.

Game III: Designated Testability (DT). Designated testability simulates the curious sender, denoted as $\mathcal{A}_3$, in distinguishing which of the two keywords sets a given trapdoor corresponds to, assuming that $\mathcal{A}_3$ has no knowledge of server's secret key. This game is designed for $\mathcal{A}_3$ and the challenger $\mathcal{C}$ as follows:

- **Setup:** Given a security parameter λ, compute the global parameter gp using the $Setup(1^\lambda)$ algorithm. Then, compute the public/secret key pairs (pk_S, sk_S) and (pk_R, sk_R) for the sender and receiver, respectively, using the $UserKeyGen(gp)$ algorithm. Compute the public/secret key pair (pk_V, sk_V) for the server using the $ServerKeyGen(gp)$ algorithm. Finally, $\mathcal{C}$ provides $(gp, pk_S, pk_R, pk_V, sk_S)$ to $\mathcal{A}_3$.
- **Phase1:** $\mathcal{A}_3$ can adaptively issue the following queries.
  Ciphertext Oracle $\mathcal{O}_{\mathcal{C}}$: Same as Game I.
  Trapdoor Oracle $\mathcal{O}_{\mathcal{T}}$: Same as Game I.
- **Challenge:** $\mathcal{A}_3$ submits two keywords sets Q_0^*, Q_1^*, and the system time t^* to $\mathcal{C}$, with the requirements that $\mathcal{A}_3$ has not queried Q_0^* or Q_1^* with any time t' in $\mathcal{O}_{\mathcal{T}}$. Then $\mathcal{C}$ randomly selects a bit $b \in \{0,1\}$, generates challenge trapdoor $TD^* \leftarrow TrapGen(gp, Q_b^*, sk_R, pk_S, pk_V, t^*)$, and outputs TD^* to $\mathcal{A}_3$.
- **Phase2:** $\mathcal{A}_3$ can query oracles $\mathcal{O}_{\mathcal{C}}$ and $\mathcal{O}_{\mathcal{T}}$, with the same restrictions as in the challenge phase.
- **Guess:** Finally, $\mathcal{A}_3$ outputs its guess $b' \in \{0,1\}$, and wins the game if and only if $b = b'$. The advantage of $\mathcal{A}_3$ wins the game III is defined as:

$$Adv_{\mathcal{A}_3}^{SPAEMKS\text{-}DT}(1^\lambda) = |\Pr[b' = b] - \frac{1}{2}|.$$

Remark. In contrast to Game I and Game II, there are no restrictions on querying the two challenge keywords sets in $\mathcal{O}_C$. This means that $\mathcal{A}_3$ can obtain the ciphertexts corresponding to the challenge keywords sets by the $\mathcal{O}_C$.

Definition 3 (DT-security). For any PPT adversary $\mathcal{A}_3$ in the security parameter λ, our scheme achieves DT-security if the advantage $Adv_{\mathcal{A}_3}^{SPAEMKS\text{-}DT}(1^\lambda)$ is negligible.

4 The Proposed S-PAEMKS Scheme

4.1 The Concrete Construction

- **Setup** (1^λ): Given a security parameter λ, the algorithm randomly chooses two multiplicative cyclic groups $\mathbb{G}_1$ and $\mathbb{G}_T$ with the same order p, satisfying the bilinear map $\hat{e} : \mathbb{G}_1 \times \mathbb{G}_1 \to \mathbb{G}_T$. The algorithm randomly selects a generator g for $\mathbb{G}_1$ and generates three hash functions $H_1 : \{0,1\}^* \to Z_p^*$, $H_2 : \{0,1\}^* \to \mathbb{G}_1$, and $H_3 : \mathbb{G}_1 \to Z_p^*$. Then, it sets l_1 to indicate the search mode. In this context, $l_1 = 1$ represents the single keyword search mode, while $l_1 > 1$ represents the multi-keyword search mode. Finally, return global parameters $gp = (\mathbb{G}_1, \mathbb{G}_T, \hat{e}, g, p, H_1, H_2, H_3, l_1)$.

- **UserKeyGen**(gp): Given gp, it generates (pk_U, sk_U) as a public/secret key pair of user. Here, it randomly selects $\alpha_1, \alpha_2 \leftarrow Z_p^*$ and returns $(pk_S = g^{\alpha_1}, sk_S = \alpha_1)$ and $(pk_R = g^{\alpha_2}, sk_R = \alpha_2)$ as the public/secret key pairs for the receiver and sender, respectively.

- **ServerKeyGen**(gp): Given gp, it randomly selects $v \leftarrow Z_p^*$ and returns $(pk_V = g^v, sk_V = v)$ as the public/secret key pair for the server.

- **Enc**(gp, W, sk_S, pk_R, t): Given gp, $W = (w_1 \ldots w_{l_1})$, sk_S, pk_R and t, it randomly selects $r_1, r_2 \leftarrow Z_p^*$ and computes as follows:
  a) Encode the system time t to a set $T_t^0 = (t_1 \ldots t_i)$ by the *0-Encoding* algorithm. For $i \in [1, |T_t^0|]$, compute $CT_{t_i} = H_2(t_i)^{r_1}$.
  b) For $i \in [1, l_1]$, compute $h_i = H_1(w_i, pk_R^{sk_S})$. Then, use $h_1 \ldots h_{l_1}$, r_1, and r_2 to build a $l_1 + 1$ degree polynomial $f(x)$, and extract $\vec{a} = (a_0 \ldots a_{l_1+1})$ as follows:

$$f(x) = (x - r_2) \prod_{i=1}^{l_1} (x - h_i) + r_1 = a_{l_1+1}x^{l_1+1} + \cdots + a_0 x^0.$$

  Remark. If the size of W is less than l_1, random values $r_j \leftarrow Z_p^*$ are selected to pad the polynomial.
  Finally, output the ciphertext $CT = (\{CT_t\}, \vec{a}, t)$.

- **TrapGen**$(gp, Q, sk_R, pk_S, pk_V, t')$: Given gp, $Q = (w_1' \ldots w_{l_2}')$, sk_R, pk_S, pk_V, and t', it randomly selects $s_0 \ldots s_{l_1+1}, \beta \leftarrow Z_p^*$, and computes as follows:
  a) Encode the system time t' to a set $T_{t'}^1 = (t_1' \ldots t_i')$ by the *1-Encoding* algorithm. For $i \in [1, |T_{t'}^1|]$, compute $TD_{t_i} = H_2(t_i')^{1/\beta}$.
  b) For $i \in [0, l_1 + 1]$, $j \in [1, l_2]$, compute $h_j = H_1(w_j', pk_S^{sk_R})$, and use these h_j to compute $x_i = \sum_{j=1}^{l_2} h_j^i$.

c) For $i \in [0, l_1 + 1]$, compute $TD_{1,i} = g^{s_i}$ and $TD_{2,i} = g^{\beta x_i H_3(pk_V^{s_i})}$. Finally, output the trapdoor $TD = (\{TD_t\}, \{TD_1\}, \{TD_2\}, l_2, t')$.

- **Test**(gp, TD, CT, sk_V): Parse the ciphertext CT as $(\{CT_t\}, \vec{a}, t)$ and the trapdoor TD as $(\{TD_t\}, \{TD_1\}, \{TD_2\}, l_2, t')$. It uses the server's secret key sk_V to perform the matching as follows:

  a) If $t < t'$, it must exist the elements $TD_{t_j} = H_2(t'_j)^{1/\beta}$ and $CT_{t_j} = H_2(t_i)^{r_1}$, where $H_2(t_i) = H_2(t'_j)$. Otherwise, it returns 0.

  b) For $i \in [0, l_1 + 1]$, compute $g^{\beta x_i} = TD_{2,i}^{1/H_3(TD_{1,i}^{sk_V})}$.

  c) For $i \in [0, l_1 + 1]$, compute $g^{\beta r_1 l_2} = \prod_{i=0}^{l_1+1} g^{\beta x_i a_i}$.

  d) If $\hat{e}(g^{l_2}, CT_{t_i}) = \hat{e}(g^{\beta r_1 l_2}, TD_{t_j})$, it can deduce that $Q \subseteq W$, where Q and W are the sets of keywords hidden in TD and CT, respectively. In this case, the algorithm returns 1; otherwise, it returns 0.

4.2 Correctness

Parsing CT as $(\{CT_t\}, \vec{a}, t)$ and TD as $(\{TD_t\}, \{TD_1\}, \{TD_2\}, l_2, t')$, the correctness of the scheme is demonstrated as follows:

a) For $i \in [0, l_1 + 1]$, $g^{\beta x_i} = TD_{2,i}^{1/H_3(TD_{1,i}^{sk_V})} = g^{\beta x_i H_3(pk_V^{s_i})/H_3(TD_{1,i}^{sk_V})}$.

b) For $i \in [0, l_1 + 1]$, if $Q \subseteq W$, $g^{\beta r_1 l_2} = \prod_{i=0}^{l_1+1} g^{\beta x_i a_i}$ shows such as:

$$\sum_{i=0}^{l_1+1} x_i a_i = \sum_{j=1}^{l_2} (a_0 h_j^0 + a_1 h_j^1 + \cdots + a_{l_1+1} h_j^{l_1+1}) = r_1 l_2,$$

so it have the equation $\prod_{i=0}^{l_1+1} g^{\beta x_i a_i} = g^{\beta \sum_{i=0}^{l_1+1} x_i a_i} = g^{\beta r_1 l_2}$; otherwise, it is unable to obtain $g^{\beta r_1 l_2}$ and cannot proceed correctly to the next step.

c) If $t < t'$, there must exist the elements $TD_{t_j} = H_2(t'_j)^{1/\beta}$ and $CT_{t_i} = H_2(t_i)^{r_1}$, where $H_2(t_i) = H_2(t'_j)$. In this case, it can obtain $\hat{e}(g^{l_2}, CT_{t_i}) = \hat{e}(g^{\beta r_1 l_2}, TD_{t_j})$ such as:

$$\hat{e}(g^{l_2}, H_2(t_i)^{r_1}) = \hat{e}(g^{\beta r_1 l_2}, H_2(t'_j)^{1/\beta}).$$

Otherwise, if there is no equation $H_2(t_i) = H_2(t'_j)$, it cannot obtain $\hat{e}(g^{l_2}, CT_{t_i}) = \hat{e}(g^{\beta r_1 l_2}, TD_{t_j})$, and returns 0.

Therefore, our S-PAEMKS scheme is correct.

5 Security Proof

Theorem 1. *The proposed S-PAEMKS scheme satisfies ciphertext indistinguishability if CDH assumption holds.*

Remark. Due to the similarity in the security models of S-PAEMKS and [11, 25], if *Theorem 1* is proven to be valid, it can also be shown that the scheme satisfies forward security.

Proof. Under the CI security model, there is an algorithm $\mathcal{B}$ that solves the CDH problem based on the following game played with a PPT adversary denoted as $\mathcal{A}_1$. Given a problem instance $(g, g^{\alpha_1}, g^{\alpha_2}) \in \mathbb{G}_1$, $\mathcal{B}$ performs the following works by controlling the random oracle and running $\mathcal{A}_1$ as a subroutine.

- **Setup:** Let $gp = \{\mathbb{G}_1, \mathbb{G}_T, \hat{e}, g, p, H_2, H_3, l_1\}$ be the global parameter and H be a random oracle. $\mathcal{B}$ sets $pk_S = g^{\alpha_1}$, $pk_R = g^{\alpha_2}$, $sk_V = v$, and $pk_V = g^v$, and send $(gp, pk_S, pk_R, sk_V, pk_V)$ to $\mathcal{A}_1$.
- **Phase1:** $\mathcal{A}_1$ can query the following oracles polynomially many times.
  Hash Oracle $\mathcal{O}_{\mathcal{H}}$: Inputting K_i and w_i, $\mathcal{B}$ performs the following steps:
  a) If $\hat{e}(g^{\alpha_1}, g^{\alpha_2}) = \hat{e}(g, K_i)$, $\mathcal{B}$ gets the answer of the problem instance $(K_i, g^{\alpha_1}, g^{\alpha_2})$ and quits.
  b) If the tuple $\langle K_i, w_i, h_i \rangle$ is already in L_H, $\mathcal{B}$ simply returns $h_i = H(K_i, w_i)$. Otherwise, $\mathcal{B}$ randomly selects $\phi_i \leftarrow Z_p^*$ and sets $h_i = \phi_i$.
  Finally, $\mathcal{B}$ adds the tuple $\langle K_i, w_i, \phi_i \rangle$ to L_H and outputs h_i.
  Ciphertext Oracle $\mathcal{O}_C$: Inputting $K = (K_1 \ldots K_{l_1})$, $W = (w_1 \ldots w_{l_1})$, and t, the algorithm randomly selects $r_1, r_2 \leftarrow Z_p^*$ and performs the following steps:
  a) Encode t to $T_t^0 = (t_1 \ldots t_i)$ by the *0-Encoding* algorithm, and compute $CT_{t_i} = H_2(t_i)^{r_1}$, where $i \in [1, |T_t^0|]$.
  b) For $i \in [1, l_1]$, query (K_i, w_i) in $\mathcal{O}_{\mathcal{H}}$ to obtain h_i.
  c) Use these $r_1, r_2, h_1 \ldots h_{l_1}$ values to build a $l_1 + 1$ degree polynomial $f(x) = (x - r_2) \prod_{i=1}^{l_1}(x - h_i) + r_1$, and extract $\vec{a} = (a_0 \ldots a_{l_1+1})$.
  Finally, return the ciphertext $CT = (\{CT_t\}, \vec{a}, t)$ to $\mathcal{A}_1$.
  Trapdoor Oracle $\mathcal{O}_T$: Inputting $K = (K_1 \ldots K_{l_2})$, $Q = (w_1 \ldots w_{l_2})$, and t', the algorithm randomly selects $\beta, s_0 \ldots s_{l_1+1} \leftarrow Z_p^*$ and performs the following steps:
  a) Encode t' to $T_{t'}^1 = (t'_1 \ldots t'_i)$ by the *1-Encoding* algorithm, and compute $TD_{t_i} = H_2(t'_i)^{1/\beta}$, where $i \in [1, |T_{t'}^1|]$.
  b) For $j \in [1, l_2]$, query (K_j, w_j) in $\mathcal{O}_{\mathcal{H}}$ to obtain h_j.
  c) For $i \in [0, l_1 + 1]$, $j \in [1, l_2]$, compute $x_i = \sum_{j=1}^{l_2} h_j^i$, $TD_{1,i} = g^{s_i}$, and $TD_{2,i} = g^{\beta x_i H_1(pk_V^{s_i})}$.
  Finally, return the trapdoor $TD = (\{TD_t\}, \{TD_1\}, \{TD_2\}, l_2, t')$ to $\mathcal{A}_1$.
- **Challenge:** $\mathcal{A}_1$ submits $W_0^* = (w_{0,1}^* \ldots w_{0,l_1}^*)$, $W_1^* = (w_{1,1}^* \ldots w_{1,l_1}^*)$, and t^* to $\mathcal{B}$, with the requirement that $\mathcal{A}_1$ has not queried W_0^* or W_1^* with any t in $\mathcal{O}_C$, and has not queried any subset of W_0^* or W_1^* with t' in $\mathcal{O}_T$, where $t' > t^*$. Then $\mathcal{B}$ randomly selects a bit $b \in \{0, 1\}$ and $r_1^*, r_2^* \leftarrow Z_p^*$, and performs the following steps:
  a) Encode t^* to $T_{t^*}^0 = (t_1^* \ldots t_i^*)$ by the *0-Encoding* algorithm, and compute $CT_{t_i}^* = H_2(t_i^*)^{r_1}$, where $i \in [1, |T_{t^*}^0|]$.
  b) For $i \in [1, l_1]$, query $(*, w_{b,i}^*)$ in $\mathcal{O}_{\mathcal{H}}$ to obtain h_i^*.
  c) Use these $r_1^*, r_2^*, h_1^* \ldots h_{l_1}^*$ values to build a $l_1 + 1$ degree polynomial $f(x) = (x - r_2^*) \prod_{i=1}^{l_1}(x - h_i^*) + r_1^*$, and extract $\vec{a}^* = (a_0^* \ldots a_{l_1+1}^*)$.

Finally, return the ciphertext $CT^* = (\{CT_t^*\}, \vec{a}^*, t^*)$ to $\mathcal{A}_1$.

- **Phase2:** $\mathcal{A}_1$ can continue to query $\mathcal{O}_C$ and $\mathcal{O}_T$ with the same limitation as in challenge phase.
- **Guess:** $\mathcal{A}_1$ outputs a guess b'.

Advantage of Breaking the Challenge Ciphertext. We denote by $\mathbf{E}_1$ the event that $\mathcal{A}_1$ has queried $(g^{\alpha_1 \alpha_2}, w_{b,i}^*)$ in $\mathcal{O}_{\mathcal{H}}$. In case $\mathbf{E}_1$ happens, the algorithm $\mathcal{B}$ aborts the game and solves the CDH problem with full advantage based on $\mathcal{A}_1$'s input. In other case, if the query $(g^{\alpha_1 \alpha_2}, w_{b,i}^*)$ is not made, $H_1(g^{\alpha_1 \alpha_2}, w_{b,i}^*)$ is random. $\mathcal{A}_1$ has no advantage in breaking the challenge ciphertext. Hence, the probability of $\mathcal{A}_1$ to win this game is:

$$
\begin{aligned}
| \Pr[\mathcal{A}_1^{\mathrm{win}}]| &= | \Pr[\mathcal{A}_1^{\mathrm{win}} \wedge \overline{\mathbf{E}_1}] + \Pr[\mathcal{A}_1^{\mathrm{win}} \wedge \mathbf{E}_1]| \\
&= | \Pr[\mathcal{A}_1^{\mathrm{win}} \mid \overline{\mathbf{E}_1}] \cdot \Pr[\overline{\mathbf{E}_1}] + \Pr[\mathcal{A}_1^{\mathrm{win}} \mid \mathbf{E}_1] \cdot \Pr[\mathbf{E}_1]| \\
&= \frac{1}{2} \cdot (1 - ne.g.l(1^\lambda)) + \Pr[\mathcal{A}_1^{\mathrm{win}} \mid \mathbf{E}_1] \cdot negl(1^\lambda) \\
&\le \frac{1}{2} + ne.g.l(1^\lambda).
\end{aligned}
$$

Theorem 2. *The proposed S-PAEMKS scheme satisfies trapdoor indistinguishability if CDH assumption holds.*

The proof of Theorem 2 is similar to that of Theorem 1, which is omitted here.

Theorem 3. *The proposed S-PAEMKS scheme satisfies designated testability if CDH assumption holds.*

Proof. Under the DT security model, there is an algorithm $\mathcal{B}$ that solves the CDH problem based on the following game played with a PPT adversary denoted as $\mathcal{A}_3$. Set $gp = (\mathbb{G}_1, \mathbb{G}_T, \hat{e}, g, p, H_1, H_2, l_1)$ be the global parameter and H be a random oracle. Given a problem instance $(g, g^v, g^{s_0^*} \dots g^{s_{l_1+1}^*}) \in \mathbb{G}_1$, $\mathcal{B}$ performs the following works by controlling the random oracle and running $\mathcal{A}_3$ as a subroutine.

- **Setup:** $\mathcal{B}$ sets $pk_S = g^{\alpha_1}$, $sk_S = \alpha_1$, $pk_R = g^{\alpha_2}$, and $pk_V = g^v$, and sends $(gp, pk_S, sk_S, pk_R, pk_V)$ to $\mathcal{A}_3$.
- **Phase1:** $\mathcal{A}_3$ can query the following oracles polynomially many times.
  Hash Oracle $\mathcal{O}_{\mathcal{H}}$: Inputting g^{s_i} and K_i, $\mathcal{B}$ performs the following steps:
  a) If $\hat{e}(pk_V, g^{s_i}) = \hat{e}(g^v, K_i)$, $\mathcal{B}$ gets an answer to the CDH problem instance as $K_i = g^{s_i v}$ and quits.
  b) If the tuple $\langle g^{s_i}, K_i, \phi_i \rangle$ is already in L_H, $\mathcal{B}$ simply responds with ϕ_i. Otherwise, $\mathcal{B}$ randomly selects $\phi_i \leftarrow Z_p^*$, and sets $H(K_i) = \phi_i$.
  Finally, $\mathcal{B}$ adds the tuple $\langle g^{s_i}, K_i, \phi_i \rangle$ to L_H and outputs ϕ_i.
  Ciphertext Oracle $\mathcal{O}_C$: Inputting t and $W = (w_1 \dots w_{l_1})$, the algorithm randomly selects $r_1, r_2 \leftarrow Z_p^*$ and performs the following steps:
  a) Encode t to $T_t^0 = (t_1 \dots t_i)$ by the *0-Encoding* algorithm, and compute $CT_{t_i} = H_2(t_i)^{r_1}$, where $i \in [1, |T_t^0|]$.

b) For $i \in [1, l_1]$, compute $h_i = H_1(w_i, g^{\alpha_1 \alpha_2})$.

c) Use these $r_1, r_2, h_1 \ldots h_{l_1}$ values to build a $l_1 + 1$ degree polynomial $f(x)$ $= (x - r_2) \prod_{i=1}^{l_1} (x - h_i) + r_1$, and extract $\vec{a} = (a_0 \ldots a_{l_1+1})$.

Finally, return the ciphertext $CT = (\{CT_t\}, \vec{a}, t)$ to $\mathcal{A}_3$.

Trapdoor Oracle $\mathcal{O}_T$: Inputting $K = (K_0 \ldots K_{l_1+1})$, $Q = (w_1 \ldots w_{l_2})$, and t', the algorithm randomly selects $\beta, s_0 \ldots s_{l_1+1} \leftarrow Z_p^*$ and performs the following steps:

a) Encode t' to $T_{t'}^1 = (t_1' \ldots t_i')$ by the *1-Encoding* algorithm, and compute $TD_{t_i} = H_2(t_i')^{1/\beta}$, where $i \in [1, |T_{t'}^1|]$.

b) For $i \in [0, l_1 + 1], j \in [1, l_2]$, compute $h_j = H_1(w_j, g^{\alpha_1 \alpha_2})$ and $x_i = \sum_{j=1}^{l_2} h_j^i$.

c) For $i \in [0, l_1 + 1]$, compute $TD_{1,i} = g^{s_i}$, query (g^{s_i}, K_i) in $\mathcal{O}_{\mathcal{H}}$ to obtain ϕ_i, and then compute $TD_{2,i} = g^{\beta x_i \phi_i}$.

Finally, return the trapdoor $TD = (\{TD_t\}, \{TD_1\}, \{TD_2\}, l_2, t')$ to $\mathcal{A}_3$.

- **Challenge:** $\mathcal{A}_3$ submits two keyword sets $Q_0^* = (w_{0,1}^* \ldots w_{0,l_2}^*)$, $Q_1^* = (w_{1,1}^* \ldots w_{1,l_2}^*)$ and t^* to $\mathcal{B}$, with the requirement that $\mathcal{A}_3$ has not queried Q_0^* or Q_1^* with any t' in $\mathcal{O}_T$. Then $\mathcal{B}$ randomly selects a bit $b \in \{0, 1\}$ and $\beta \leftarrow Z_p^*$, and computes as follows:

  a) Encode t^* to $T_{t^*}^1 = (t_1^* \ldots t_i^*)$ by the *1-Encoding* algorithm, and compute $TD_{t_i} = H_2(t_i^*)^{1/\beta}$, where $i \in [1, |T_{t^*}^0|]$.

  b) For $i \in [0, l_1 + 1]$, $j \in [1, l_2]$, compute $h_j^* = H_1(w_{b,j}^*, g^{\alpha_1 \alpha_2})$, and use these h_j^* to compute $x_i^* = \sum_{j=1}^{l_2} h_j^{*i}$.

  c) For $i \in [0, l_1 + 1]$, set $TD_{1,i}^* = g^{s_i^*}$, query $(g^{s_i^*}, *)$ in $\mathcal{O}_{\mathcal{H}}$ to obtain ϕ_i^*, and compute $TD_{2,i}^* = g^{\beta x_i^* \phi_i^*}$.

  Finally, return the trapdoor $TD^* = (\{TD_t^*\}, \{TD_1^*\}, \{TD_2^*\}, l_2, t^*)$ to $\mathcal{A}_3$.

- **Phase2:** $\mathcal{A}_3$ can continue to query $\mathcal{O}_C$ and $\mathcal{O}_T$ with the same limitation as in challenge phase.

- **Guess:** $\mathcal{A}_3$ outputs a guess b'.

Advantage of Breaking the Challenge Trapdoor. We denote by $\mathbf{E_3}$ the event that $\mathcal{A}_3$ has queried $(g^{s_i^*}, g^{s_i^* v})$ in $\mathcal{O}_{\mathcal{H}}$. In case $\mathbf{E_3}$ happens, the algorithm $\mathcal{B}$ aborts the game and solves the CDH problem with full advantage based on $\mathcal{A}_3$'s input. In other case, if the query $(g^{s_i^*}, g^{s_i^* v})$ is not made, $H_3(g^{s_i^* v})$ is random. $\mathcal{A}_3$ has no advantage in breaking the challenge trapdoor. Hence, the probability of $\mathcal{A}_3$ to win this game is $|\Pr[\mathcal{A}_3^{win}]| \leq \frac{1}{2} + negl(1^\lambda)$.

6   Experiments and Comparison

Table 1 compares the features of our S-PAEMKS scheme with those of related schemes, including Park-PEMKS [25], HL-PAEKS [10], Jiang-PAEMKS [11], Yang-PAEMKS [30], Lu-PAEKS [18], Li-Fast-PAEKS [12], MA-CLPAEMKS [22], He-CLPAEKS [8], Qin-PAEKS [26], and Li-DIBAEKS [13]. The comparison shows that our scheme has better properties than related work. In particular, our scheme has exceptional advantages in security, as it effectively counters KGA launched by curious senders and achieves forward security.

Table 1. Comparisons of features

Schemes	DT	MK	FS	KGA-I	KGA-S
Park-PEMKS [25]	×	√	×	×	×
HL-PAEKS [10]	×	×	×	√	×
Jiang-PAEMKS [11]	×	√	√	√	×
Li-DIBAEKS [13]	√	×	×	√	×
Yang-PAEMKS [30]	√	√	×	√	×
Lu-PAEKS [18]	√	×	×	√	×
Qin-PAEKS [26]	×	×	×	√	×
Li-Fast-PAEKS [12]	×	×	×	√	×
He-CLPAEKS [8]	×	×	×	√	×
MA-CLPAEMKS [22]	×	√	×	√	×
Ours PAEKS	√	√	√	√	√

* DT: Designated tester. MK: Multi-keyword. FS: Forward security. KGA-I: Resist keyword guessing attack from internal adversary. KGA-S: Resist keyword guessing attack from curious senders.

6.1 Efficiency Analysis

Considering that our scheme shares several similar features with some schemes, we make a comparison with these schemes [10,11,13,18,25,30] in term of computational and storage cost. Table 2 offers the computational and storage cost for theoretical evaluation, while Table 3 displays the time cost of basic operations and the storage cost of data types. As our scheme incorporates time into the ciphertext and trapdoor, we configure the system clock to span the range of $[1, 2^{12}]$ (approximately 10 years), providing sufficient coverage. Assume that t_0 and t_1 are 6, the half of length of system time, where t_0 and t_1 represent the size of T using the *0-Encoding* algorithm and the *1-Encoding* algorithm, respectively. Additionally, let n and m be 10, representing the number of keywords in a ciphertext and a trapdoor, respectively. Our focus is on evaluating the efficiency of the **Enc**, **TrapGen**, and **Test** algorithms, and comparing the computational and storage cost of our scheme with related schemes as follows.

Comparison of Computation Cost. Our **Enc** algorithm consumes a theoretical time of $(n + t_0)h + (t_0 + 1)e_1$, which is calculated as $16h + 6e_1$ based on the aforementioned instantiations, when n and m are 10, and t_0 and t_1 are 6. When comparing the cost of our scheme with [10,11,13,18,25,30], which are calculated as $10h + 30e_1$, $26h + 29e_1$, $10h + 30e_1 + 20p$, $40h + 50e_1$, $10h + 12e_1 + 10p$, and $10h + 15e_1$ respectively, our scheme exhibits similarities with [30] and incurs lower costs than the others. This comparison leads us to a preliminary conclusion that our **Enc** algorithm demonstrates high efficiency.

In terms of **Test** algorithms, our scheme consumes a theoretical time of $(n+2)h+(2n+4)e_1+2p$ calculated as $12h+24e_1+2p$. When compared to other multi-keyword search schemes, both [11,25], as well as our scheme, require a constant number of symmetric bilinear pairing operations, each of which costs 10 ms. In contrast, [30] requires $m+3$ asymmetric bilinear pairing operations, with each operation costing 20 ms, as shown in Table 3. Consequently, [30] achieves MCI and MTP at the expense of sacrificing search efficiency. When compared with [11,25], which are calculated as e_1+p and $6e_1+p$ respectively, our scheme incurs higher costs because [11,25] require an index containing the position of each keyword. However, this approach can be limiting when it comes to keywords of the same type. For instance, if "Dog" and "Cat" are keywords of the same type and have the same position indexes, it is necessary to perform two searches to find files that contain both of these keywords simultaneously. In contrast, our scheme overcomes this limitation. In summary, our scheme achieves multi-keyword search without relying on an additional index of keyword positions, unlike [11,25], and without significant efficiency sacrifices compared to [30].

Table 2. Comparisons of computation cost and communication cost.

Schemes	Computation cost			Communication cost	
	Enc	TrapGen	Test	Ciphertext	Trapdoor
[25] [a]	$np+nh+(n+2)e_1$	$mh+e_1$	e_1+p	$2|G_1|+n|G_T|$	$|G_1|+|Z_p|$
[10] [a]	$n\cdot(3e_1+h)$	$m\cdot(e_1+h+p)$	$m\cdot(2p)$	$n\cdot(2|G_1|)$	$m\cdot|G_T|$
[11] [a]	$(2n+t_0+1)h+$ $(4+2n+t_0)e_1$	$t_1h+(4+2m)e$	$(t_0+1)e_1+3p$	$(t_0+n+1)|G_1|$	$3|G_1|+$ $t_0(|S|+|Z_p|)$
[13] [a]	$n\cdot(2h+3e_1+2p)$	$m\cdot(2e_1+2h+p)$	$m\cdot(2e_1+2p)$	$n\cdot(2|G_1|+|G_T|)$	$m\cdot2|G_1|$
[30] [b]	$nh+(n+5)e_1$	$mh+(n+5)e_2$	$2e_2+(n+3)p$	$(n+3)|G_1|$	$(n+4)|G_2|$
[18] [a]	$n\cdot(4h+5e_1)$	$m\cdot(3h+2e_1)$	$m\cdot(2e_1+h)$	$n\cdot(|G_1|+|Z_p|)$	$m\cdot|Z_p|$
Ours [a]	$(n+t_0)h+$ $(t_0+1)e_1$	$(t_1+n+m+2)h$ $+(t_1+3n+6))e_1$	$(n+2)h+$ $(2n+4)e_1+2p$	$t_0|G_1|+$ $(n+2)|Z_p|$	$(t_1+2n+4)|G_1|$

* a: Symmetric bilinear pairing. b: Asymmetric bilinear pairing.
h: A hash operation. t_0: The size of T_t^0 by 0-encoding. t_1: The size of T_t^1 by 1-encoding. n: The number of keywords in a file. m: The number of search keywords.

Table 3. The time cost of basic operations and the storage cost of basic data types.

Symmetric bilinear pairing					Asymmetric bilinear pairing						
Time cost(ms)		Storage cost(bit)			Time cost(ms)			Storage cost(bit)			
e_1	p	Z_p	G_1	G_T	e_1	e_2	p	Z_p	G_1	G_2	G_T
2.8	10	160	1024	1024	1.5	8	20	160	960	960	960

* Symmetric bilinear pairing: $G_1 \times G_1 \to G_T$. Asymmetric bilinear pairing: $G_1 \times G_2 \to G_T$.
e_1: A modal exponential operation of G_1. e_2: A modal exponential operation of G_2. p: A bilinear pair operation.

In terms of the **TrapGen** algorithms, our scheme consumes a theoretical time complexity of $(t_1 + n + m + 2)h + (t_1 + 3n + 7)e_1$ calculated as $28h + 42e_1$. When compared to [10,13], which are calculated as $10e_1 + 10h + 10p$ and $20e_1 + 20h + 10p$ respectively, our scheme has a lower cost thanks to the absence of symmetric bilinear pairing operations. When compared to recently works [11,30] calculated as $6h + 24e_1$ and $10h + 15e_2$, respectively, our scheme incurs a higher cost of more than 50% and 25%. In summary, compared to recent similar schemes, our **TrapGen** maintains a comparable efficiency while achieving stronger trapdoor privacy.

Comparison of Communication Cost. The ciphertext and trapdoor of our scheme consume a theoretical storage of $t_0|\mathbb{G}_1| + (n+2)|Z_p|$ and $(t_1 + 2n + 4)|\mathbb{G}_1|$ respectively. As shown in Fig. 2(b), we can conclude that our ciphertext has the shortest length, while our trapdoor has the longest length. Therefore, our scheme exhibits comparable storage and communication costs to other schemes.

6.2   Experimental Performance

Our scheme is implemented using the Multi-precision Integer and Rational Arithmetic C/C++ Library (MIRACL). The experimental setup consists of a host machine equipped with a 6-Core AMD Ryzen 53600 CPU, 8 GB DDR4 RAM, running on the Windows 10 operating system. The security parameter is set to a length of 80.

Based on the assumptions made in the previous section, we set the values of n and m to 10, and the system time t to a length of 12. We perform the **Enc**, **TrapGen**, and **Test** algorithms 100 times to simulate a cloud storage and search environment. In Fig. 2(a), the experimental results demonstrate that our **Enc** algorithm exhibits higher efficiency compared to [10,11,13,18,25], and is similar to [30]. Our **TrapGen** algorithm demonstrates similar performance to [11,18,30], and surpasses [10,13]. In the **Test** algorithm, our efficiency significantly outperforms compared with [10,13,30], and is inferior to [11,18,25]. Consequently, our experimental results support the analysis presented in the theoretical analysis section, affirming that our scheme exhibits remarkable efficiency in the encryption phase, while its efficiency in the trapdoor and testing phases is comparable with other schemes.

To provide a more intuitive exhibition of the impact of the number of keywords, we set the X-axis label to the number of keywords. In Fig. 3(a), our **Enc** algorithm demonstrates a minimal slope, in contrast to [10,11,13,20,25], which display a linear progression as the number of keywords increases. In Fig. 3(b),(c), the efficiency of our **TrapGen** and **Test** algorithms is at a moderate level. There is a decreasing trend in the slope of our scheme as the number of keywords increases. Based on theoretical analysis and experimental results, our scheme performs well in executing multi-keyword search.

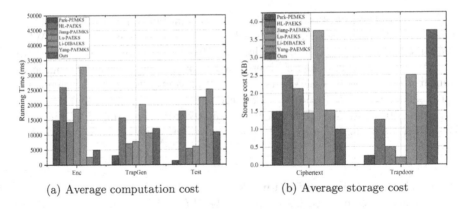

(a) Average computation cost   (b) Average storage cost

Fig. 2. Cost of Computation and Communication

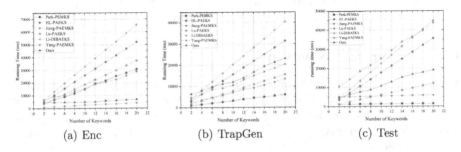

(a) Enc   (b) TrapGen   (c) Test

Fig. 3. The Impact of Keywords Number on Running Time

7   Conclusion and Future Works

In this paper, we addressed the issue of keyword guessing attack (KGA) launched by curious senders in previous PAEKS schemes and improved the previous security model of PAEKS to capture KGA from curious senders. We proposed a concrete Stronger Security Public Key Authenticated Encryption with Multi-keyword Search (S-PAEMKS) scheme that supports multi-keyword search without relying on an additional index of keyword positions and counters KGA from curious senders. The comparison demonstrated that our scheme achieves excellent performance, particularly in terms of security. The experimental results confirm its high efficiency in the encryption phase. Our trapdoor phase and test phase sacrificed a certain degree of efficiency to achieve more strong security in trapdoor privacy. As part of our future work, we aim to further enhance the security of our scheme by achieving multi-ciphertext indistinguishability (MCI) and multi-trapdoor privacy (MTP).

Acknowledgement. This work is supported in part by the National Natural Science Foundation of China under Grant 61872409, Grant 61872152 and Grant 62272174, in part by Guangdong Basic and Applied Basic Research Foundation under Grant 2020A1515010751, in part by the Guangdong Major Project of Basic and Applied Basic Research under Grant 2019B030302008, and in part by the Science and Technology Program of Guangzhou under Grant 201902010081.

References

1. Baek, J., Safavi-Naini, R., Susilo, W.: Public key encryption with keyword search revisited. In: Gervasi, O., Murgante, B., Laganà, A., Taniar, D., Mun, Y., Gavrilova, M.L. (eds.) ICCSA 2008. LNCS, vol. 5072, pp. 1249–1259. Springer, Heidelberg (2008). https://doi.org/10.1007/978-3-540-69839-5_96
2. Boneh, D., Di Crescenzo, G., Ostrovsky, R., Persiano, G.: Public key encryption with keyword search. In: Cachin, C., Camenisch, J.L. (eds.) EUROCRYPT 2004. LNCS, vol. 3027, pp. 506–522. Springer, Heidelberg (2004). https://doi.org/10.1007/978-3-540-24676-3_30
3. Boyen, X.: The uber-assumption family. In: Galbraith, S.D., Paterson, K.G. (eds.) Pairing 2008. LNCS, vol. 5209, pp. 39–56. Springer, Heidelberg (2008). https://doi.org/10.1007/978-3-540-85538-5_3
4. Byun, J.W., Rhee, H.S., Park, H.-A., Lee, D.H.: Off-line keyword guessing attacks on recent keyword search schemes over encrypted data. In: Jonker, W., Petković, M. (eds.) SDM 2006. LNCS, vol. 4165, pp. 75–83. Springer, Heidelberg (2006). https://doi.org/10.1007/11844662_6
5. Chen, B., Wu, L., Zeadally, S., He, D.: Dual-server public-key authenticated encryption with keyword search. IEEE Trans. Cloud Comput. **10**(1), 322–333 (2019)
6. Cheng, L., Meng, F.: Security analysis of pan et al.'s public-key authenticated encryption with keyword search achieving both multi-ciphertext and multi-trapdoor indistinguishability. J. Syst. Architect. **119**, 102248 (2021)
7. Guan, Z., et al.: Cross-lingual multi-keyword rank search with semantic extension over encrypted data. Inf. Sci. **514**, 523–540 (2020)
8. He, D., Ma, M., Zeadally, S., Kumar, N., Liang, K.: Certificateless public key authenticated encryption with keyword search for industrial internet of things. IEEE Trans. Industr. Inf. **14**(8), 3618–3627 (2017)
9. Huang, Q., Huang, P., Li, H., Huang, J., Lin, H.: A more efficient public-key authenticated encryption scheme with keyword search. J. Syst. Architect. **137**, 102839 (2023)
10. Huang, Q., Li, H.: An efficient public-key searchable encryption scheme secure against inside keyword guessing attacks. Inf. Sci. **403**, 1–14 (2017)
11. Jiang, Z., Zhang, K., Wang, L., Ning, J.: Forward secure public-key authenticated encryption with conjunctive keyword search. Comput. J. **66**, 2265–2278 (2022)
12. Li, H., Huang, Q., Huang, J., Susilo, W.: Public-key authenticated encryption with keyword search supporting constant trapdoor generation and fast search. IEEE Trans. Inf. Forensics Secur. **18**, 396–410 (2022)
13. Li, H., Huang, Q., Shen, J., Yang, G., Susilo, W.: Designated-server identity-based authenticated encryption with keyword search for encrypted emails. Inf. Sci. **481**, 330–343 (2019)

14. Li, H., Huang, Q., Susilo, W.: A secure cloud data sharing protocol for enterprise supporting hierarchical keyword search. IEEE Trans. Dependable Secure Comput. **19**(3), 1532–1543 (2020)

15. Lin, H.-Y., Tzeng, W.-G.: An efficient solution to the millionaires' problem based on homomorphic encryption. In: Ioannidis, J., Keromytis, A., Yung, M. (eds.) ACNS 2005. LNCS, vol. 3531, pp. 456–466. Springer, Heidelberg (2005). https://doi.org/10.1007/11496137_31

16. Liu, X., Li, H., Yang, G., Susilo, W., Tonien, J., Huang, Q.: Towards enhanced security for certificateless public-key authenticated encryption with keyword search. In: Steinfeld, R., Yuen, T.H. (eds.) ProvSec 2019. LNCS, vol. 11821, pp. 113–129. Springer, Cham (2019). https://doi.org/10.1007/978-3-030-31919-9_7

17. Liu, Z.Y., Tseng, Y.F., Tso, R., Chen, Y.C., Mambo, M.: Identity-certifying authority-aided identity-based searchable encryption framework in cloud systems. IEEE Syst. J. **16**(3), 4629–4640 (2021)

18. Lu, Y., Li, J.: Lightweight public key authenticated encryption with keyword search against adaptively-chosen-targets adversaries for mobile devices. IEEE Trans. Mob. Comput. **21**(12), 4397–4409 (2021)

19. Lu, Y., Li, J., Wang, F.: Pairing-free certificate-based searchable encryption supporting privacy-preserving keyword search function for IIoTs. IEEE Trans. Industr. Inf. **17**(4), 2696–2706 (2020)

20. Lu, Y., Wang, G., Li, J., Shen, J.: Efficient designated server identity-based encryption with conjunctive keyword search. Ann. Telecommun. **72**, 359–370 (2017)

21. Ma, M., He, D., Khan, M.K., Chen, J.: Certificateless searchable public key encryption scheme for mobile healthcare system. Comput. Electr. Eng. **65**, 413–424 (2018)

22. Ma, Y., Kazemian, H.: Public key authenticated encryption with multiple keywords search using Mamdani system. Evol. Syst. **12**(3), 687–699 (2021)

23. Noroozi, M., Eslami, Z.: Public key authenticated encryption with keyword search: revisited. IET Inf. Secur. **13**(4), 336–342 (2019)

24. Pan, X., Li, F.: Public-key authenticated encryption with keyword search achieving both multi-ciphertext and multi-trapdoor indistinguishability. J. Syst. Architect. **115**, 102075 (2021)

25. Park, D.J., Kim, K., Lee, P.J.: Public key encryption with conjunctive field keyword search. In: Lim, C.H., Yung, M. (eds.) WISA 2004. LNCS, vol. 3325, pp. 73–86. Springer, Heidelberg (2005). https://doi.org/10.1007/978-3-540-31815-6_7

26. Qin, B., Chen, Y., Huang, Q., Liu, X., Zheng, D.: Public-key authenticated encryption with keyword search revisited: security model and constructions. Inf. Sci. **516**, 515–528 (2020)

27. Qin, B., Cui, H., Zheng, X., Zheng, D.: Improved security model for public-key authenticated encryption with keyword search. In: Huang, Q., Yu, Yu. (eds.) ProvSec 2021. LNCS, vol. 13059, pp. 19–38. Springer, Cham (2021). https://doi.org/10.1007/978-3-030-90402-9_2

28. Shao, Z.Y., Yang, B.: On security against the server in designated tester public key encryption with keyword search. Inf. Process. Lett. **115**(12), 957–961 (2015)

29. Shiraly, D., Pakniat, N., Noroozi, M., Eslami, Z.: Pairing-free certificateless authenticated encryption with keyword search. J. Syst. Architect. **124**, 102390 (2022)

30. Yang, P., Li, H., Huang, J., Zhang, H., Au, M.H.A., Huang, Q.: Secure channel free public key authenticated encryption with multi-keyword search on healthcare systems. Futur. Gener. Comput. Syst. **145**, 511–520 (2023)

31. Yau, W.C., Phan, R.C.W., Heng, S.H., Goi, B.M.: Keyword guessing attacks on secure searchable public key encryption schemes with a designated tester. Int. J. Comput. Math. **90**(12), 2581–2587 (2013)

32. Zeng, M., Qian, H., Chen, J., Zhang, K.: Forward secure public key encryption with keyword search for outsourced cloud storage. IEEE Trans. Cloud Comput. **10**(1), 426–438 (2019)
33. Zhang, Y., Wang, Y., Li, Y.: Searchable public key encryption supporting semantic multi-keywords search. IEEE Access **7**, 122078–122090 (2019)

Identity-Based Proxy Re-encryption Based on SM9

Hang Liu[ID], Yang Ming[(✉)][ID], Chenhao Wang[ID], and Yi Zhao[ID]

School of Information Engineering, Chang'an University,
Xi'an 710064, Shaanxi, China
yangming@chd.edu.cn

Abstract. Proxy re-encryption, as a cryptographic primitive, allows an untrusted proxy to transform a ciphertext encrypted with the data owner's public key to a ciphertext encrypted with the authorized user's public key, without any knowledge of the underlying plaintext, which achieves the sharing of ciphertext data. As an identity-based cryptosystem, SM9 has been adopted as a Chinese national standard and an ISO/IEC international standard. However, the SM9 encryption algorithm can only achieve the function of data encryption without considering the ciphertext transformation. In this paper, based on SM9, we first propose an identity-based proxy re-encryption scheme (termed IBPRE-I). IBPRE-I has the same user secret key as SM9, so it can be effectively integrated with SM9-based systems. Security proof indicates that IBPRE-I achieves the ciphertext indistinguishability against selective identity and chosen plaintext attack, and the secret key leakage resistance against collusion attack in the random oracle model. Then, by extending the IBPRE-I scheme, we present our second scheme IBPRE-II to achieve the security under chosen ciphertext attack. Finally, the performance is evaluated and the results show that the proposed schemes are practical.

Keywords: Proxy re-encryption · identity-based cryptography · SM9 · CPA secure · CCA secure

1 Introduction

With the rapid development of cloud computing technology, cloud storage has become an essential part of modern network architecture, which provides users with convenient data storage and data sharing services [8,24]. However, untrusted cloud servers may leak the data without the permission of the user. The most effective approach to solve this problem is to encrypt the data before uploading it to the cloud servers [25]. Thus, only authorized users can decrypt the ciphertext.

In traditional public key cryptography (PKC), a certificate authority is responsible for issuing the certificate, which binds the user's identity and public

© The Author(s), under exclusive license to Springer Nature Singapore Pte Ltd. 2024
C. Ge and M. Yung (Eds.): Inscrypt 2023, LNCS 14526, pp. 320–339, 2024.
https://doi.org/10.1007/978-981-97-0942-7_16

key to ensure the validity of the public key. However, it consumes heavy storage costs and suffers from complex certificate management problems. To solve this issue, Shamir [29] presented identity-based cryptography (IBC) by utilizing the user's identity (or email address) as the public key, in which a private key generator is introduced to generate the private key for the user. Subsequently, based on bilinear pairing, Boneh et al. [4] proposed the first provably secure and practical identity-based encryption (IBE) scheme. In 2016, the State Password Administration of China officially released the SM9 algorithms [14], which consist of the digital signature algorithm, key exchange protocol, key encapsulation mechanism, and identity-based encryption algorithm. At present, SM9 has officially become the Chinese national and ISO/IEC international standards.

Although IBE is able to protect the privacy of data, how to share encrypted data with others has become a new challenge. To mitigate this issue, Blaze et al. proposed the concept of proxy re-encryption (PRE) [2] to achieve ciphertext transformation securely. Specifically, the data owner generates a re-encryption key when it intends to share the ciphertext with some authorized users. This key can be used by an untrusted proxy to transform the ciphertext under the data owner's public key to the ciphertext under the authorized user's public key. Furthermore, the transformation process doesn't leak any information about the plaintext. In order to address the certificate management problem in the traditional PKC-based PRE scheme, Green et al. [15] introduced the notion of identity-based proxy re-encryption (IBPRE) and proposed two concrete constructions. Although many IBPRE schemes [11,13,16,17,22,23,26,31–35] have been put forward, there is no IBPRE scheme based on SM9. Therefore, it is urgent to design an IBPRE scheme compatible with the SM9 algorithm.

Our Contributions. First, the identity-based proxy re-encryption scheme (IBPRE-I) based on SM9 is proposed based on the characteristics and the user secret key form of the SM9 encryption algorithm. Second, in the random oracle, IBPRE-I is proven to be secure against chosen plaintext attack and collusion attack under the GDDHE and q-SDH assumptions, respectively. Third, based on the IBPRE-I, we present a novel scheme IBPRE-II to withstand chosen ciphertext attack. Finally, the theoretical analysis and simulation results show the feasibility of the proposed schemes.

The rest of this paper is organized as follows. We review the related work in Sect. 2. Section 3 gives some preliminaries. Section 4 describes the construction and security proof of IBPRE-I in detail, respectively. We present the CCA-secure scheme IBPRE-II in Sect. 5. Section 6 evaluates the performance of our schemes. Finally, we conclude this paper in Sect. 7.

2   Related Work

Since Blaze et al. [2] introduced the notion of PRE in 1998, PRE has been widely investigated and applied. In the scheme [2], PRE can be classified into two categories, i.e. bidirectional and unidirectional. In a bidirectional PRE scheme, the re-encryption key allows for the transformation of ciphertext from the data owner to the authorized user and vice versa. Furthermore, based on the number of re-encryption operations that could be performed, PRE schemes also can be divided into single-hop and multi-hop [6]. The former statement indicates that re-encrypted ciphertext cannot be re-encrypted again, whereas the latter statement implies that re-encrypted ciphertext is capable of undergoing multiple rounds of re-encryption. In consideration of practicality and security, the research emphasis was on unidirectional and single-hop PRE schemes [10,12,30]. However, these schemes are built on the traditional PKC, thus suffering from the certificate management problem and consuming heavy storage costs.

To address the above problems, Green *et al.* [15] put forward the identity-based PRE (IBPRE) following the idea of IBC and constructed two concrete IBPRE schemes. One is secure against chosen plaintext attack (CPA) and the other is secure against chosen ciphertext attack (CCA). However, they are vulnerable to collusion attack, that is, the untrusted proxy and authorized user can collaborate to compute the secret key of the data owner. Later on, collusion resistant IBPRE schemes were proposed in [26,33]. Subsequently, IBPRE was extensively studied to provide different properties and functionality, including fine-grained transformation [23,31], revocation of ciphertexts and keys [13,22], one-to-many transformation [11,32,34], data deduplication [17], verifiability of re-encryption [16], resistance to backdoor attack [35], etc.

Since SM9 became the Chinese national and ISO/IEC international standards, it has been investigated extensively by scholars. Cheng *et al.* [9] formally proved the security of the SM9 algorithm. Lai *et al.* [21] optimized the SM9 key encapsulation algorithm and proved the security under weaker assumptions. By introducing a trusted third party that can quickly revoke and update user access rights, Qin *et al.* [27] proposed the mediated IBE. To achieve multi-user data sharing, Lai *et al.* [18,19] proposed the identity-based broadcast encryption schemes based on SM9. Re *et al.* [28] presented the traceable and accountable access control protocol. Incorporating the SM9 signature and encryption algorithms, Lai *et al.* [20] constructed the identity-based signcryption scheme.

3 Preliminaries

3.1 Bilinear Pairing

Let $e : \mathbb{G}_1 \times \mathbb{G}_2 \rightarrow \mathbb{G}_T$ be a bilinear pairing, where $\mathbb{G}_1$, $\mathbb{G}_2$ and $\mathbb{G}_T$ are three cyclic groups with the same prime order N, It has the following properties.

- Bilinearity: For any $P \in \mathbb{G}_1$, $Q \in \mathbb{G}_2$ and $\alpha, \beta \in \mathbb{Z}_N^*$, there is $e(\alpha P, \beta Q) = e(P, Q)^{\alpha\beta}$.
- Non-degeneracy: For any generator $P \in \mathbb{G}_1$ and $Q \in \mathbb{G}_2$, $e(P, Q)$ is a generator of $\mathbb{G}_T$.
- Computability: For any $P \in \mathbb{G}_1$ and $Q \in \mathbb{G}_2$, there is an efficient algorithm to compute $e(P, Q)$.

For the bilinear pairing e, if $\mathbb{G}_1 = \mathbb{G}_2$, e is a symmetric bilinear pairing (Type I), otherwise an asymmetric bilinear pairing (Type II and III). In Type II bilinear pairing, there exists a valid and publicly computable isomorphic $\psi : \mathbb{G}_2 \to \mathbb{G}_1$, satisfying $\psi(Q) = P$, where P and Q are the generator of $\mathbb{G}_1$ and $\mathbb{G}_2$, respectively. SM9 is based on Type II bilinear pairing.

3.2 Definition of Identity-Based Proxy Re-Encryption

The IBPRE scheme consists of the following algorithms.

Setup(λ). On inputting the security parameter λ, this algorithm outputs the master public key mpk and the master secret key msk.

Extract(msk, id). On inputting the master secret key msk and the identity id, this algorithm outputs the secret key of identity id.

Encrypt(id_i, m). On inputting the identity id_i and the message m, this algorithm outputs the first level ciphertext C_i.

Re-KeyGen(sk_{id_i}, id_j). On inputting the secret key sk_{id_i} and the identity id_j, this algorithm outputs the re-encryption key $rk_{i \to j}$.

Re-Encrypt($C_i, rk_{i \to j}$). On inputting the first level ciphertext C_i and the re-encryption key $rk_{i \to j}$, this algorithm outputs the second level ciphertext $\widetilde{C}_j$ or the symbol $\perp$.

Decrypt$_1$(C_i, sk_{id_i}). On inputting the first level ciphertext C_i and the secret key sk_{id_i}, this algorithm outputs the message m' or the symbol $\perp$.

Decrypt$_2$($\widetilde{C}_j, sk_{id_j}$). On inputting the second level ciphertext $\widetilde{C}_j$ and the secret key sk_{id_j}, this algorithm outputs the message m' or the symbol $\perp$.

3.3 Security Model of IBPRE

For the security of IBPRE, the interactive games between a challenger $\mathcal{C}$ and an adversary $\mathcal{A}$ are defined to capture the first level ciphertext indistinguishability against selective identity and chosen plaintext attack (IND-sID-CPA-1), the second ciphertext indistinguishability against selective identity and chosen plaintext attack (IND-sID-CPA-2), the first level ciphertext indistinguishability against selective identity and chosen ciphertext attack (IND-sID-CCA-1), the second ciphertext indistinguishability against selective identity and chosen ciphertext attack (IND-sID-CCA-2), and the secret key leakage resistance against collusion attack (SKLR-CA).

Game IND-sID-CPA-1. This game is interactive between $\mathcal{C}$ and $\mathcal{A}$.

Initialization. $\mathcal{A}$ outputs the challenge identity id^*.

Setup. $\mathcal{C}$ generates the master public key mpk and the master secret key msk. Finally, $\mathcal{C}$ returns mpk to $\mathcal{A}$.

Phase 1. $\mathcal{A}$ can make a polynomial bounded number of queries adaptively.

- Hash queries: Given an hash query, $\mathcal{C}$ returns a random value.
- Secret key extract queries: Given a secret key extract query on $id_i \neq id^*$, $\mathcal{C}$ returns the secret key sk_{id_i}.

– Re-encryption key extract queries: Given a re-encryption key extract query on $\{id_i, id_j\}$ satisfying $id_i \neq id^*$, $\mathcal{C}$ returns the re-encryption key $rk_{i \rightarrow j}$.

Challenge. $\mathcal{A}$ submits two messages $\{m_0, m_1\}$ to $\mathcal{C}$ as its challenge. $\mathcal{C}$ randomly selects $b \in \{0,1\}^*$, computes the challenge first level ciphertext C_b^* and returns to $\mathcal{A}$.

Phase 2. $\mathcal{A}$ can continue to make queries as in Phase 1.

Guess. Finally, $\mathcal{A}$ outputs its guess $b' \in \{0,1\}$. If $b' = b$, $\mathcal{A}$ wins.

The advantage of $\mathcal{A}$ in game IND-sID-CPA-1 is defined as

$$\mathrm{Adv}_{\mathcal{A}}^{\mathrm{IND\text{-}sID\text{-}CPA\text{-}1}} = |\Pr[b' = b] - 1/2|.$$

Game IND-sID-CPA-2. This game is the same as the game IND-sID-CPA-1, except that $\mathcal{C}$ returns the challenge second level ciphertext $\widetilde{C}_b^*$ to $\mathcal{A}$ in **Challenge.**

The advantage of $\mathcal{A}$ in the game IND-sID-CPA-2 is defined as

$$\mathrm{Adv}_{\mathcal{A}}^{\mathrm{IND\text{-}sID\text{-}CPA\text{-}2}} = |\Pr[b' = b] - 1/2|.$$

Definition 1. *If $Adv_{\mathcal{A}}^{IND\text{-}sID\text{-}CPA\text{-}1}$ and $Adv_{\mathcal{A}}^{IND\text{-}sID\text{-}CPA\text{-}2}$ are negligible for any PPT adversary $\mathcal{A}$, the IBPRE scheme is IND-sID-CPA secure.*

Game IND-sID-CCA-1. This game is interactive between $\mathcal{C}$ and $\mathcal{A}$.

Initialization. Same as in Game IND-sID-CPA-1.

Setup. Same as in Game IND-sID-CPA-1.

Phase 1. $\mathcal{A}$ can make a polynomial bounded number of queries adaptively.

– Hash queries: Same as in Game IND-sID-CPA-1.
– Secret key extract queries: Same as in Game IND-sID-CPA-1.
– Re-encryption key extract queries: Same as in Game IND-sID-CPA-1.
– Re-encrypt queries: Given a re-encrypt query on $\{C_i, id_i, id_j\}$ satisfying $id_i \neq id^*$, $\mathcal{C}$ returns the second level ciphertext $\widetilde{C}_j$.
– Decrypt$_1$ queries: Given a decrypt$_1$ query on $\{C_i, id_i\}$ satisfying $id_i \neq id^*$, $\mathcal{C}$ returns the decryption result m' or $\bot$.
– Decrypt$_2$ queries: Given a decrypt$_2$ query on $\{\widetilde{C}_j, id_j\}$ satisfying $id_j \neq id^*$, $\mathcal{C}$ returns the decryption result m' or $\bot$.

Challenge. $\mathcal{A}$ submits two messages $\{m_0, m_1\}$ to $\mathcal{C}$ as its challenge. $\mathcal{C}$ randomly selects $b \in \{0,1\}^*$, computes the challenge first level ciphertext C_b^* and returns to $\mathcal{A}$.

Phase 2. Same as in Game IND-sID-CPA-1.

Guess. Same as in Game IND-sID-CPA-1.

The advantage of $\mathcal{A}$ in game IND-sID-CCA-1 is defined as

$$\mathrm{Adv}_{\mathcal{A}}^{\mathrm{IND\text{-}sID\text{-}CCA\text{-}1}} = |\Pr[b' = b] - 1/2|.$$

Game IND-sID-CCA-2. This game is the same as the game IND-sID-CCA-1, except that $\mathcal{C}$ returns the challenge second level ciphertext $\widetilde{C}_b^*$ to $\mathcal{A}$ in **Challenge.**

The advantage of $\mathcal{A}$ in game IND-sID-CCA-2 is defined as

$$\mathrm{Adv}_{\mathcal{A}}^{\mathrm{IND\text{-}sID\text{-}CCA\text{-}2}} = |\Pr[b' = b] - 1/2|.$$

Definition 2. *If $Adv_{\mathcal{A}}^{IND\text{-}sID\text{-}CCA\text{-}1}$ and $Adv_{\mathcal{A}}^{IND\text{-}sID\text{-}CCA\text{-}2}$ are negligible for any PPT adversary $\mathcal{A}$, the IBPRE scheme is IND-sID-CCA secure.*

Game SKLR-CA. This game is interactive between $\mathcal{C}$ and $\mathcal{A}$.
Initialization. Same as in Game IND-sID-CPA-1.
Setup. Same as in Game IND-sID-CPA-1.
Phase 1. $\mathcal{A}$ can make a polynomial bounded number of queries adaptively.

- Hash queries: Same as in Game IND-sID-CPA-1.
- Secret key extract queries: Same as in Game IND-sID-CPA-1.
- Re-encryption key extract queries: Given a re-encryption key extract query on $\{id_i, id_j\}$, $\mathcal{C}$ returns the secret key $rk_{i \to j}$.

Output. $\mathcal{A}$ outputs the secret key sk' of id^*. If $sk' = sk_{id^*}$, $\mathcal{A}$ wins.
The advantage of $\mathcal{A}$ in game SKLR-CA is defined as

$$\mathrm{Adv}_{\mathcal{A}}^{\mathrm{SKLR\text{-}CA}} = |\Pr[sk' = sk_{id^*}]|.$$

Definition 3. *If $Adv_{\mathcal{A}}^{SKLR\text{-}CA}$ is negligible for any PPT adversary $\mathcal{A}$, the IBPRE scheme is SKLR-CA secure.*

3.4 Security Assumptions

The security assumptions are given as follows.

(f, h)-general Diffie-Hellman exponent (GDDHE) problem [18]: For unknown $\theta, k \in \mathbb{Z}_N^*$, given the elements $\{P_0, \theta P_0, \theta^2 P_0, \cdots, \theta^{2n} P_0, kf(\theta)P_0 \in \mathbb{G}_1, Q_0, \theta Q_0, \theta^2 Q_0, \cdots, \theta^{t-1} Q_0, \theta^2 h(\theta) Q_0, k\theta^2 h(\theta) Q_0 \in \mathbb{G}_2, Z \in \mathbb{G}_T\}$, the (f, h)-GDDHE problem is to determine whether $Z = e(P_0, Q_0)^{k\theta h(\theta)}$.

(f, h)-GDDHE assumption [18]: It is difficult for the PPT algorithm to solve the (f, h)-GDDHE problem with non-negligible advantage.

q-strong Diffie-Hellman (q-SDH) problem [3]: For unknown $\theta \in \mathbb{Z}_N^*$, given the elements $\{P_0 \in \mathbb{G}_1, Q_0, \theta Q_0, \theta^2 Q_0, \cdots, \theta^q Q_0 \in \mathbb{G}_2\}$, the q-SDH problem is to find the pair $(k, \frac{1}{k+\theta} P_0)$ where $k \in \mathbb{Z}_N^*$.

q-SDH assumption [3]: It is difficult for the PPT algorithm to solve the q-SDH problem with non-negligible advantage.

3.5 SM9 Identity-Based Encryption

The SM9 identity-based encryption (SM9-IBE) [14] is defined as follows.
Setup. Given the security parameter λ, select a bilinear pairing $e : \mathbb{G}_1 \times \mathbb{G}_2 \to \mathbb{G}_T$, where the generator of $\mathbb{G}_1$ and $\mathbb{G}_2$ be P and Q, respectively. Randomly select $s \in \mathbb{Z}_N^*$, and compute $P_{pub} = s \cdot P$, $g = e(P_{pub}, Q)$. The secure hash function $H_1 : \{0,1\}^* \to \mathbb{Z}_N^*$ and key derivation function $KDF : \{0,1\}^* \to \{0,1\}^{klen}$ are

selected. Furthermore, choose a secret key function identifier hid and a secure message authentication code MAC. Finally, the master public key is $mpk = \{\mathbb{G}_1, \mathbb{G}_2, \mathbb{G}_T, e, N, P, Q, P_{pub}, g, H_1, KDF, hid, MAC\}$ and the master secret key is $msk = \{s\}$.

Extract. Given the master secret key msk and the identity id, compute $sk_{id} = \frac{s}{s+H_1(id||hid,N)} \cdot Q$ as the secret key of identity id.

Encrypt. Given the identity id and the message m, select a random number $\alpha \in \mathbb{Z}_N^*$ and compute $u = g^\alpha, c_0 = \alpha \cdot (P_{pub} + H_1(id_i||hid, N) \cdot P), K = KDF(c_0||u||id, klen) = K_1||K_2, c_1 = m \oplus K_1, c_2 = MAC(K_2, c_1)$. Return the ciphertext $C = \{c_0, c_1, c_2\}$.

Decrypt. Given the ciphertext C and the secret key sk_{id}, compute $u' = e(c_0, sk_{id})$, $K' = KDF(c_0||u'||id, klen) = K_1'||K_2'$, $m' = c_1 \oplus K_1'$, $c_2' = MAC(K_2', c_1)$. If $c_2' = c_2$, return the message m' and $\bot$ otherwise.

In the random oracle, SM9-IBE has been proved secure against chosen ciphertext attack under Gap-τ-BCAA1 assumption [9].

4   Chosen Plaintext Secure IBPRE

In this section, based on SM9, the construction and security proof of IBPRE-I is provided. Constructing an IBPRE directly from the CCA-secured SM9-IBE is difficult, so we take a slight detour. Specifically, we first discard the part of SM9-IBE that achieves ciphertext validity checking (only CPA security is considered), and then realize the ciphertext transformation function for it. In Sect. 5, we will consider how to convert CPA-secure IBPRE-I to CCA-secure IBPRE-II.

4.1   Construction of IBPRE-I

The details of IBPRE-I are as follows.

Setup. Given the security parameter λ, select a bilinear pairing $e : \mathbb{G}_1 \times \mathbb{G}_2 \to \mathbb{G}_T$, where the generator of $\mathbb{G}_1$ and $\mathbb{G}_2$ are P and Q, respectively. Randomly select $s \in \mathbb{Z}_N^*$, $Q' \in \mathbb{G}_2$ and compute $P_{pub} = s \cdot P$, $g = e(P_{pub}, Q)$. Two independent secure hash functions $H_1 : \{0,1\}^* \to \mathbb{Z}_N^*$ and $H_2 : \mathbb{G}_T \to \mathbb{Z}_N^*$ are selected. Furthermore, choose a secret key function identifier hid. Finally, the master public key is $mpk = \{\mathbb{G}_1, \mathbb{G}_2, \mathbb{G}_T, e, N, P, Q', P_{pub}, g, H_1, H_2, hid\}$ and the master secret key is $msk = \{s, Q\}$.

Extract. Given the master secret key msk and the identity id, compute $sk_{id} = \frac{s}{s+H_1(id||hid,N)} \cdot Q$ as the secret key of identity id.

Encrypt. Given the identity id_i and the message m, select a random number $\alpha \in \mathbb{Z}_N^*$ and compute $c_{i,0} = m \cdot g^\alpha$, $c_{i,1} = \alpha \cdot (P_{pub} + H_1(id_i||hid, N) \cdot P)$, $c_{i,2} = \alpha \cdot Q'$. Return the first level ciphertext $C_i = \{c_{i,0}, c_{i,1}, c_{i,2}\}$.

Re-KeyGen. Given the secret key sk_{id_i} and the identity id_j, randomly pick $\beta, \gamma \in \mathbb{Z}_N^*$, and compute $k_{id_j} = H_2(g^\gamma)$, $rk_0 = \gamma \cdot (P_{pub} + H_1(id_j||hid, N) \cdot P)$, $rk_1 = \beta \cdot (P_{pub} + H_1(id_i||hid, N) \cdot P)$, $rk_2 = sk_{id_i} + \beta \cdot k_{id_j} \cdot Q'$. Return the re-encryption key $rk_{i \to j} = \{rk_0, rk_1, rk_2\}$.

Re-Encrypt. Given the first level ciphertext C_i and the re-encryption key $rk_{i \to j}$, compute $\tilde{c}_{j,0} = c_{i,0} \cdot e(c_{i,1}^{-1}, rk_2) = m \cdot e(\alpha \cdot (P_{pub} + H_1(id_i \| hid, N) \cdot P), \beta \cdot k_{id_j} \cdot Q')^{-1}$, $\tilde{c}_{j,1} = e(rk_1, c_{i,2}) = e(\beta \cdot (P_{pub} + H_1(id_i \| hid, N) \cdot P), \alpha \cdot Q')$, $\tilde{c}_{j,2} = rk_0 = \gamma \cdot (P_{pub} + H_1(id_j \| hid, N) \cdot P)$. Return the second level ciphertext $\tilde{C}_j = \{\tilde{c}_{j,0}, \tilde{c}_{j,1}, \tilde{c}_{j,2}\}$.

Decrypt₁. Given the first level ciphertext C_i and the secret key sk_{id_i}, compute $m' = c_{i,0} \cdot e(c_{i,1}^{-1}, sk_{id_i})$. Return the message m'.

Decrypt₂. Given the second level ciphertext $\tilde{C}_j$ and the secret key sk_{id_j}, compute $k'_{id_j} = H_2(e(\tilde{c}_{j,2}, sk_{id_j}))$, $m' = \tilde{c}_{j,0} \cdot \tilde{c}_{j,1}^{k'_{id_j}}$. Return the message m'.

4.2 Security Proof of IBPRE-I

Next, we formally prove the IND-sID-CPA security and SKLR-CA security for IBPRE-I. For the sake of descriptive convenience, we utilize $H_1(id)$ to substitute for $H_1(id \| hid, N)$ in the subsequent proofs.

Theorem 1. *The proposed IBPRE-I scheme is IND-sID-CPA-1 secure in the random oracle if the (f, h)-GDDHE assumption holds.*

Proof. Suppose the PPT adversary $\mathcal{A}$ is able to break the IND-sID-CPA-1 security of IBPRE-I with non-negligible advantage ϵ, then an algorithm $\mathcal{B}$ can be constructed to solve the (f, h)-GDDHE problem with non-negligible advantage $\epsilon' = \epsilon$. Assume the t is the total number of H_1 and secret key extract queries. Given the (f, h)-GDDHE instance $\{P_0, \theta P_0, \theta^2 P_0, \cdots, \theta^{2n} P_0, kf(\theta)P_0, \theta Q_0, \theta^2 Q_0, \cdots, \theta^t Q_0, \theta^2 h(\theta)Q_0, k\theta^2 h(\theta)Q_0, Z\}$, the target of $\mathcal{B}$ is to determine whether $Z = e(P_0, Q_0)^{k\theta h(\theta)}$.

Define the following notations.

$h(x) = \prod_{i=1}^{t}(x + \lambda_i)$, $f(x) = \prod_{i=t+1}^{t+n}(x + \lambda_i)$, where $\lambda_1, \cdots, \lambda_{t+n} \in \mathbb{Z}_N^*$.

$f_i(x) = \frac{f(x)}{x + \lambda_i}$ for $i \in [t+1, t+n]$, which is a ploynomial of degree $n - 1$.

$h_i(x) = \frac{h(x)}{x + \lambda_i}$ for $i \in [1, t]$, which is a ploynomial of degree $t - 1$.

Initialization. $\mathcal{A}$ outputs the challenge identity id^*.

Setup. $\mathcal{B}$ implicitly sets $s = \theta$, $Q = h(\theta)Q_0$, computes $P = \prod_{i=t+2}^{t+n}(\theta + \lambda_i)P_0$, $P_{pub} = \theta \prod_{i=t+2}^{t+n}(\theta + \lambda_i)P_0$, $g = e(P_0, Q_0)^{\theta h(\theta) \prod_{i=t+2}^{t+n}(\theta + \lambda_i)}$, and $Q' = a\theta^2 h(\theta)Q_0$, where a is a random number in $\mathbb{Z}_N^*$. Finally, $\mathcal{B}$ returns $mpk = \{\mathbb{G}_1, \mathbb{G}_2, \mathbb{G}_T, e, N, P, Q', P_{pub}, g\}$ to $\mathcal{A}$.

Phase 1. $\mathcal{A}$ can make the following queries adaptively.

- H_1 queries: $\mathcal{B}$ maintains the initially empty list L_1 which consists of tuples (id_i, λ_i). When $\mathcal{A}$ submits a H_1 query on id_i, $\mathcal{B}$ returns λ_i to $\mathcal{A}$ if (id_i, λ_i) is in L_1. Otherwise, $\mathcal{B}$ performs as follows.
  - If $id_i = id^*$, $\mathcal{B}$ sets $H_1(id_i) = \lambda_{t+1}$, inserts (id_i, λ_{t+1}) to L_1, and returns λ_{t+1} to $\mathcal{A}$.
  - If $id_i \neq id^*$, $\mathcal{B}$ sets $H_1(id_i) = \lambda_i$, inserts (id_i, λ_i) to L_1, and returns λ_i to $\mathcal{A}$.

- H_2 queries: $\mathcal{B}$ maintains the initially empty list L_2 which consists of tuples (σ_i, H_i). When $\mathcal{A}$ submits a H_2 query on σ_i, $\mathcal{B}$ returns H_i to $\mathcal{A}$ if (σ_i, H_i) is in L_1. Otherwise, $\mathcal{B}$ randomly selects $H_i \in \mathbb{Z}_N^*$, inserts (σ_i, H_i) to L_2, and returns H_i to $\mathcal{A}$.
- Secret key extract queries: $\mathcal{B}$ maintains the initially empty list L_{sk} which consists of tuples (id_i, sk_{id_i}). When $\mathcal{A}$ submits a secret key extract query on any $id_i \neq id^*$, $\mathcal{B}$ returns sk_{id_i} to $\mathcal{A}$ if (id_i, sk_{id_i}) is in L_{sk}. Otherwise, $\mathcal{B}$ computes $sk_{id_i} = \theta h_i(\theta) Q_0$, inserts (id_i, sk_{id_i}) to L_{sk}, and returns sk_{id_i} to $\mathcal{A}$.
- Re-encryption key extract queries: When $\mathcal{A}$ submits a re-encryption key extract query on $\{id_i, id_j\}$ satisfying $id_i \neq id^*$, $\mathcal{B}$ checks whether (id_i, sk_{id_i}) is in L_{sk}. If not, it queries the secret key extract query on id_i. Then, $\mathcal{B}$ randomly selects $\beta, \gamma \in \mathbb{Z}_N^*$, computes $k_{id_j} = H_2(g^\gamma)$, $rk_0 = \gamma(P_{pub} + H_1(id_j) \cdot P)$, $rk_1 = \beta(P_{pub} + H_1(id_i) \cdot P)$, $rk_2 = sk_{id_i} + \beta \cdot k_{id_j} \cdot Q'$. Then, $\mathcal{B}$ returns $rk_{i \to j} = \{rk_0, rk_1, rk_2\}$ to $\mathcal{A}$.

Challenge. $\mathcal{A}$ submits two messages $\{m_0, m_1\}$ to $\mathcal{B}$ as its challenge. $\mathcal{B}$ randomly selects $b \in \{0,1\}^*$, computes $T = Z^{\prod_{i=t+2}^{t+n} \lambda_i} \cdot e(\frac{1}{\theta}(\prod_{i=t+2}^{t+n}(\theta + \lambda_i) - \prod_{i=t+2}^{t+n} \lambda_i)P_0, k\theta^2 h(\theta)Q_0)$, $c_0^* = m_b \cdot T$, $c_1^* = kf(\theta)P_0$, $c_2^* = a \cdot k\theta^2 h(\theta)Q_0$. Then, $\mathcal{B}$ returns $C^* = \{c_0^*, c_1^*, c_2^*\}$ to $\mathcal{A}$.

Phase 2. $\mathcal{A}$ can continue to make queries as in Phase 1.

Guess. Finally, $\mathcal{A}$ outputs its guess $b' \in \{0,1\}$. If $b' = b$, $\mathcal{B}$ outputs 1 as the solution to the instance of (f, h)-GDDHE problem. Otherwise, $\mathcal{B}$ outputs 0.

If $Z = e(P_0, Q_0)^{k\theta h(\theta)}$, we have

$$T = e(P_0, Q_0)^{k\theta h(\theta) \prod_{i=t+2}^{t+n} \lambda_i} \cdot e(\frac{1}{\theta}(\prod_{i=t+2}^{t+n}(\theta + \lambda_i) - \prod_{i=t+2}^{t+n} \lambda_i)P_0, k\theta^2 h(\theta)Q_0)$$

$$= e(P_0, Q_0)^{k\theta h(\theta) \prod_{i=t+2}^{t+n} \lambda_i} \cdot e(P_0, Q_0)^{k\theta h(\theta) \prod_{i=t+2}^{t+n}(\theta + \lambda_i) - \prod_{i=t+2}^{t+n} \lambda_i}$$

$$= e(P_0, Q_0)^{k\theta h(\theta) \prod_{i=t+2}^{t+n}(\theta + \lambda_i)} = g^k,$$

$$c_0^* = m_b \cdot g^k,$$

$$c_1^* = k \prod_{i=t+1}^{t+n}(\theta + \lambda_i)P_0 = k(\theta + \lambda_{t+1}) \prod_{i=t+2}^{t+n}(\theta + \lambda_i)P_0 = k \cdot P_{pub} + kH_1(id^*) \cdot P,$$

$$c_2^* = k \cdot a\theta^2 h(\theta)Q_0 = k \cdot Q'.$$

Thus, C^* is a valid ciphertext, then $\Pr[b' = b] = \epsilon + \frac{1}{2}$.

If $Z \neq e(P_0, Q_0)^{k\theta h(\theta)}$, C^* is the encryption of a random message because Z is a random element of $\mathbb{G}_T$, then $\Pr[b' = b] = \frac{1}{2}$.

Therefore, the advantage of $\mathcal{B}$ in solving (f, h)-GDDHE problem is $\epsilon' = |\Pr[b' = b|Z = e(P_0, Q_0)^{k\theta h(\theta)}] - \Pr[b' = b|Z \neq e(P_0, Q_0)^{k\theta h(\theta)}]| = |\epsilon + \frac{1}{2} - \frac{1}{2}| = \epsilon.$ ∎

Theorem 2. *The proposed IBPRE-I is IND-sID-CPA-2 secure in the random oracle if the (f, h)-GDDHE assumption holds.*

Proof. The proof is the same as the proof in Theorem 1, except that **Challenge** phase.

Challenge. $\mathcal{A}$ submits two messages $\{m_0, m_1\}$ to $\mathcal{B}$ as its challenge. $\mathcal{B}$ randomly selects $b \in \{0,1\}^*$, $\alpha^* \beta^* \in \mathbb{Z}_N^*$, $(id_i, sk_{id_i}) \in L_{sk}$, computes $T = Z^{\prod_{i=t+2}^{t+n} \lambda_i} \cdot e(\frac{1}{\theta}(\prod_{i=t+2}^{t+n}(\theta + \lambda_i) - \prod_{i=t+2}^{t+n} \lambda_i)P_0, k\theta^2 h(\theta)Q_0)$, $\tilde{c}_0^* = m_b \cdot e(\alpha^* \cdot (P_{pub} + H_1(id_i) \cdot P), \beta^* \cdot H_2(T) \cdot Q')$, $\tilde{c}_1^* = e(\alpha^* \cdot (P_{pub} + H_1(id_i) \cdot P), \beta^* \cdot Q')$, $\tilde{c}_2^* = kf(\theta)P_0$. Then, $\mathcal{B}$ returns $\tilde{C}_b^* = \{\tilde{c}_0^*, \tilde{c}_1^*, \tilde{c}_2^*\}$ to $\mathcal{A}$.

Similar to the analysis of Theorem 1, the advantage of $\mathcal{B}$ in solving (f,h)-GDDHE problem is $\epsilon' = \epsilon$. ∎

Theorem 3. *The proposed IBPRE-I is SKLR-CA secure in the random oracle if the q-SDH assumption holds.*

Proof. Suppose the PPT adversary $\mathcal{A}$ is able to break the SKLR-CA security of IBPRE-I with non-negligible advantage ϵ, then an algorithm $\mathcal{B}$ can be constructed to solve the q-SDH problem with non-negligible advantage $\epsilon' = \epsilon$. Assume the q is the total number of H_1 and secret key extract queries. Given the q-SDH instance $\{P_0, Q_0, \theta Q_0, \theta^2 Q_0, \cdots, \theta^q Q_0\}$, the target of $\mathcal{B}$ is find the pair $(k, \frac{1}{k+\theta}P_0)$ where $k \in \mathbb{Z}_N^*$.

Define the following notations.

$f(x) = \prod_{i=1, i \neq i^*}^{q}(x + \lambda_i)$, where $i^* \in [1, q], \lambda_1, \cdots, \lambda_q \in \mathbb{Z}_N^*$.

$f_i(x) = \frac{f(x)}{x + \lambda_i}$ for $i \in [1, q]$ and $i \neq i^*$, which is a ploynomial of degree $q - 2$.

Initialization. Same as in Theorem 1.

Setup. $\mathcal{B}$ implicitly sets $s = \theta$, computes $Q = f(\theta)Q_0$, $P = \psi(Q)$, $P_{pub} = \psi(\theta f(\theta)Q_0) = \theta P$, $g = e(P_{pub}, Q)$, and $Q' = Q_0$. Finally, $\mathcal{B}$ returns $mpk = \{\mathbb{G}_1, \mathbb{G}_2, \mathbb{G}_T, e, N, P, Q', P_{pub}, g\}$ to $\mathcal{A}$.

Phase 1. $\mathcal{A}$ can make the following queries adaptively.

- H_1 queries: $\mathcal{B}$ maintains the initially empty list L_1 which consists of tuples (id_i, λ_i). When $\mathcal{A}$ submits a H_1 query on id_i, $\mathcal{B}$ returns λ_i to $\mathcal{A}$ if (id_i, λ_i) is in L_1. Otherwise, $\mathcal{B}$ performs as follows.
  - If $id_i = id^*$, $\mathcal{B}$ sets $H_1(id_i) = \lambda_{i^*}$, inserts (id_i, λ_{i^*}) to L_1, and returns λ_{i^*} to $\mathcal{A}$.
  - If $id_i \neq id^*$, $\mathcal{B}$ sets $H_1(id_i) = \lambda_i$, inserts (id_i, λ_i) to L_1, and returns λ_i to $\mathcal{A}$.
- H_2 queries: Same as in Theorem 1.
- Secret key extract queries: $\mathcal{B}$ maintains the initially empty list L_{sk} which consists of tuples (id_i, sk_{id_i}). When $\mathcal{A}$ submits a secret key extract query on any $id_i \neq id^*$, $\mathcal{B}$ returns sk_{id_i} to $\mathcal{A}$ if (id_i, sk_{id_i}) is in L_{sk}. Otherwise, $\mathcal{B}$ computes $sk_{id_i} = Q - H_1(id_i)f_i(\theta)Q_0$, inserts (id_i, sk_{id_i}) to L_{sk}, and returns sk_{id_i} to $\mathcal{A}$.
- Re-encryption key extract queries: When $\mathcal{A}$ submits a re-encryption key extract query on $\{id_i, id_j\}$, $\mathcal{B}$ checks whether (id_i, sk_{id_i}) is in L_{sk}. If not, it queries the secret key extract query on id_i. Then, $\mathcal{B}$ performs as follows.
  - If $id_i \neq id^*$, $\mathcal{B}$ randomly selects $\beta, \gamma \in \mathbb{Z}_N^*$, computes $k_{id_j} = H_2(g^\gamma)$, $rk_0 = \gamma(P_{pub} + H_1(id_j) \cdot P)$, $rk_1 = \beta(P_{pub} + H_1(id_i) \cdot P)$, $rk_2 = sk_{id_i} + \beta \cdot k_{id_j} \cdot Q'$. Then, $\mathcal{B}$ returns $rk_{i \to j} = \{rk_0, rk_1, rk_2\}$ to $\mathcal{A}$.

- If $id_i = id^*$, $\mathcal{B}$ randomly selects $\beta', \gamma \in \mathbb{Z}_N^*$, computes $k_{id_j} = H_2(g^\gamma)$, $rk_0 = \gamma(P_{pub} + H_1(id_j) \cdot P)$, $rk_1 = \frac{1}{k_{id_j}}(\beta' \cdot (P_{pub} + H_1(id_i) \cdot P) - \theta f(\theta)P)$, $rk_2 = \beta' \cdot Q'$. Then, $\mathcal{B}$ returns $rk_{i \to j} = \{rk_0, rk_1, rk_2\}$ to $\mathcal{A}$.

Note that when $id_i = id^*$, we define the random number $\beta = \frac{1}{k_{id_j}}(\beta' - \frac{\theta f(\theta)}{\theta + \lambda_{i^*}})$, therefore

$$\beta \cdot (P_{pub} + H_1(id_i) \cdot P) = \frac{1}{k_{id_j}}(\beta' - \frac{\theta f(\theta)}{\theta + \lambda_{i^*}}) \cdot (P_{pub} + H_1(id_i) \cdot P)$$

$$= \frac{1}{k_{id_j}}(\beta' \cdot (P_{pub} + H_1(id_i) \cdot P) - \theta f(\theta)P) = rk_1,$$

$$sk_{id_i} + \beta \cdot k_{id_j} \cdot Q' = \frac{\theta f(\theta)}{\theta + \lambda_{i^*}} Q_0 + \frac{1}{k_{id_j}}(\beta' - \frac{\theta f(\theta)}{\theta + \lambda_{i^*}}) \cdot k_{id_j} \cdot Q'$$

$$= \beta' \cdot Q' = rk_2.$$

Thus, $rk_{i \to j}$ is a valid re-encryption key.

Output. $\mathcal{A}$ outputs the secret key sk' of id^*, satisfying $e(P_{pub} + \lambda_{i^*} \cdot P, sk') = g$. By using long division technology, the polynomial $F(x) = xf(x)$ can be defined as $F(x) = (x + \lambda_{i^*}) \cdot h(x) + \upsilon$, where $h(x) = \sum_{i=1}^{q-1} h_i x^i$, $h_1, \cdots, h_{q-1}, \upsilon \in \mathbb{Z}_N^*$. Thus, $\mathcal{B}$ outputs $(\lambda_{i^*}, T = \frac{1}{\upsilon}\psi(sk' - h(\theta) \cdot Q_0))$ as the solution to the instance of q-SDH problem.

Due to $sk' = \frac{\theta f(\theta)}{\theta + \lambda_{i^*}} Q_0$, thus $T = \frac{1}{\upsilon}\psi(sk' - h(\theta) \cdot Q_0) = \frac{1}{\upsilon}\psi(\frac{\theta f(\theta)}{\theta + \lambda_{i^*}} \cdot Q_0 - h(\theta) \cdot Q_0) = \frac{1}{\upsilon} \cdot (\frac{F(\theta)}{\theta + \lambda_{i^*}} - h(\theta)) \cdot P_0 = \frac{1}{\theta + \lambda_{i^*}} P_0$.

Accordingly, the advantage of $\mathcal{B}$ in solving q-SDH problem is $\epsilon' = \epsilon$.   ■

5   Chosen Ciphertext Secure IBPRE

As the above analysis, the proposed IBPRE-I scheme can only wistand the chosen plaintext attack and collusion attack. Although it is practical enough, how to resist the stronger chosen ciphertext attack is also important. CHK transform [7] is an effective technique which could transform a CPA-secure IBE scheme into a CCA-secure IBE scheme via computing a publicly-verifiable signature to achieve the ciphertext validity check. In this section, we extend the IBPRE-I scheme to present the CCA-secure IBPRE-II by CHK transform and BLS short signature [5].

5.1   Construction of IBPRE-II

The detail construction of IBPRE-II is given as follows.

Setup. Given the security parameter λ, select a bilinear pairing $e : \mathbb{G}_1 \times \mathbb{G}_2 \to \mathbb{G}_T$, where the generator of $\mathbb{G}_1$ and $\mathbb{G}_2$ are P and Q, respectively. Randomly select $s \in \mathbb{Z}_N^*$, $Q' \in \mathbb{G}_2$ and compute $P_{pub} = s \cdot P$, $g = e(P_{pub}, Q)$. Five independent secure hash functions $H_1 : \{0,1\}^* \to \mathbb{Z}_N^*$, $H_2 : \{0,1\}^* \to \mathbb{Z}_N^*$,

$H_3 : \mathbb{G}_T \to \{0,1\}^l$, $H_4 : \{0,1\}^* \to \mathbb{G}_1$, and $H_5 : \mathbb{G}_T \to \mathbb{Z}_N^*$ are selected. Furthermore, choose a secret key function identifier hid. Finally, the master public key is $mpk = \{\mathbb{G}_1, \mathbb{G}_2, \mathbb{G}_T, e, N, P, Q', P_{pub}, g, H_1, H_2, H_3, H_4, H_5, hid\}$ and the master secret key is $msk = \{s, Q\}$.

Extract. Given the master secret key msk and the identity id, compute $sk_{id} = \frac{s}{s + H_1(id||hid, N)} \cdot Q$ as the secret key of identity id.

Encrypt. Given the identity id_i and the message m, select a random element $\sigma \in \mathbb{G}_T$ and compute $\alpha = H_2(m, \sigma)$, $c_{i,0} = m \oplus H_3(\sigma)$, $c_{i,1} = \alpha \cdot (P_{pub} + H_1(id_i||hid, N) \cdot P)$, $c_{i,2} = \sigma \cdot g^\alpha$, $c_{i,3} = \alpha \cdot Q'$, $c_{i,4} = \alpha \cdot H_4(c_{i,0}, c_{i,1}, c_{i,2}, c_{i,3})$. Return the first level ciphertext $C_i = \{c_{i,0}, c_{i,1}, c_{i,2}, c_{i,3}, c_{i,4}\}$.

Re-KeyGen. Given the secret key sk_{id_i} and the identity id_j, randomly pick $\beta, \gamma \in \mathbb{Z}_N^*$ and compute $k_{id_j} = H_5(g^\gamma)$, $rk_0 = \gamma \cdot (P_{pub} + H_1(id_j||hid, N) \cdot P)$, $rk_1 = \beta \cdot (P_{pub} + H_1(id_i||hid, N) \cdot P)$, $rk_2 = sk_{id_i} + \beta \cdot k_{id_j} \cdot Q'$. Return the re-encryption key $rk_{i \to j} = \{rk_0, rk_1, rk_2\}$.

Re-Encrypt. Given the first level ciphertext C_i and the re-encryption key $rk_{i \to j}$, verify whether the following equation holds

$$e(H_4(c_{i,0}, c_{i,1}, c_{i,2}, c_{i,3}), c_{i,3}) = e(c_{i,4}, Q'). \tag{1}$$

If it holds, compute $\widetilde{c}_{j,0} = c_{i,0} = m \oplus H_3(\sigma)$, $\widetilde{c}_{j,1} = c_{i,2} \cdot e(c_{i,1}^{-1}, rk_2) = \sigma \cdot e(\alpha \cdot (P_{pub} + H_1(id_i||hid, N) \cdot P), \beta \cdot k_{id_j} \cdot Q')^{-1}$, $\widetilde{c}_{j,2} = c_{i,3} = \alpha \cdot Q'$, $\widetilde{c}_{j,3} = rk_0 = \gamma \cdot (P_{pub} + H_1(id_j||hid, N) \cdot P)$, $\widetilde{c}_{j,4} = rk_1 = \beta \cdot (P_{pub} + H_1(id_i||hid, N) \cdot P)$. Return the second level ciphertext $\widetilde{C}_j = \{\widetilde{c}_{j,0}, \widetilde{c}_{j,1}, \widetilde{c}_{j,2}, \widetilde{c}_{j,3}, \widetilde{c}_{j,4}\}$.

Decrypt$_1$. Given the first level ciphertext C_i and the secret key sk_{id_i}, check whether the Eq. 1 holds. If it doesn't hold, return $\perp$. Otherwise, compute $\sigma' = c_{i,2} \cdot e(c_{i,1}^{-1}, sk_{id_i})$, $m' = c_{i,0} \oplus H_3(\sigma')$, $\alpha' = H_2(m', \sigma')$. If $c_{i,3} = \alpha' \cdot Q'$, return m' and $\perp$ otherwise.

Decrypt$_2$. Given the second level ciphertext $\widetilde{C}_j$ and the secret key sk_{id_j}, compute $k'_{id_j} = H_2(e(\widetilde{c}_{j,3}, sk_{id_j}))$, $\sigma' = \widetilde{c}_{j,1} \cdot e(\widetilde{c}_{j,4}^{k'_{id_j}}, \widetilde{c}_{j,2})$, $m' = \widetilde{c}_{j,0} \oplus H_3(\sigma')$, $\alpha' = H_2(m', \sigma')$. If $\widetilde{c}_{j,2} = \alpha' \cdot Q'$, return m' and $\perp$ otherwise.

5.2 Security Proof of IBPRE-II

Theorem 4. *The proposed IBPRE-II is IND-sID-CCA-1 secure in the random oracle if the (f, h)-GDDHE assumption holds.*

Proof. Suppose the PPT adversary $\mathcal{A}$ is able to break the IND-sID-CCA-1 security of IBPRE-II with non-negligible advantage ϵ, then an algorithm $\mathcal{B}$ can be constructed to solve the (f, h)-GDDHE problem with non-negligible advantage $\epsilon' = \epsilon$. Assume the t is the total number of H_1 and secret key extract queries. Given the (f, h)-GDDHE instance $\{P_0, \theta P_0, \theta^2 P_0, \cdots, \theta^{2n} P_0, kf(\theta)P_0, \theta Q_0, \theta^2 Q_0, \cdots, \theta^t Q_0, \theta^2 h(\theta)Q_0, k\theta^2 h(\theta)Q_0, Z\}$, the target of $\mathcal{B}$ is to determine whether $Z = e(P_0, Q_0)^{k\theta h(\theta)}$.

Define the following notations.

$h(x) = \prod_{i=1}^{t}(x + \lambda_i)$, $f(x) = \prod_{i=t+1}^{t+n}(x + \lambda_i)$, where $\lambda_1, \cdots, \lambda_{t+n} \in \mathbb{Z}_N^*$.

$f_i(x) = \frac{f(x)}{x+\lambda_i}$ for $i \in [t + 1, t + n]$, which is a ploynomial of degree $n - 1$.

$h_i(x) = \frac{h(x)}{x+\lambda_i}$ for $i \in [1, t]$, which is a ploynomial of degree $t - 1$.

Initialization. $\mathcal{A}$ outputs the challenge identity id^*.

Setup. $\mathcal{B}$ implicitly sets $s = \theta$, $Q = h(\theta)Q_0$, computes $P = \prod_{i=t+2}^{t+n}(\theta+\lambda_i)P_0$, $P_{pub} = \theta \prod_{i=t+2}^{t+n}(\theta+\lambda_i)P_0$, $g = e(P_0, Q_0)^{\theta h(\theta) \prod_{i=t+2}^{t+n}(\theta+\lambda_i)}$, and $Q' = a\theta^2 h(\theta)Q_0$, where a is a random number in $\mathbb{Z}_N^*$. Finally, $\mathcal{B}$ returns $mpk = \{\mathbb{G}_1, \mathbb{G}_2, \mathbb{G}_T, e, N, P, Q', P_{pub}, g\}$ to $\mathcal{A}$.

Phase 1. $\mathcal{A}$ can make the following queries adaptively.

- H_1 queries: $\mathcal{B}$ maintains the initially empty list L_1 which consists of tuples (id_i, λ_i). When $\mathcal{A}$ submits a H_1 query on id_i, $\mathcal{B}$ returns λ_i to $\mathcal{A}$ if (id_i, λ_i) is in L_1. Otherwise, $\mathcal{B}$ performs as follows.
  - If $id_i = id^*$, $\mathcal{B}$ sets $H_1(id_i) = \lambda_{t+1}$, inserts (id_i, λ_{t+1}) to L_1, and returns λ_{t+1} to $\mathcal{A}$.
  - If $id_i \neq id^*$, $\mathcal{B}$ sets $H_1(id_i) = \lambda_i$, inserts (id_i, λ_i) to L_1, and returns λ_i to $\mathcal{A}$.
- H_2 queries: $\mathcal{B}$ maintains the initially empty list L_2 which consists of tuples (m_i, σ_i, τ_i). When $\mathcal{A}$ submits a H_2 query on (m_i, σ_i), $\mathcal{B}$ returns τ_i to $\mathcal{A}$ if (m_i, σ_i, τ_i) is in L_2. Otherwise, $\mathcal{B}$ randomly selects $\tau_i \in \mathbb{Z}_N^*$, inserts (m_i, σ_i, τ_i) to L_2, and returns τ_i to $\mathcal{A}$.
- H_3 queries: $\mathcal{B}$ maintains the initially empty list L_3 which consists of tuples (σ_i, ς_i). When $\mathcal{A}$ submits a H_3 query on σ_i, $\mathcal{B}$ returns H_i to $\mathcal{A}$ if (σ_i, ς_i) is in L_3. Otherwise, $\mathcal{B}$ randomly selects $\varsigma_i \in \{0, 1\}^l$, inserts (σ_i, ς_i) to L_3, and returns ς_i to $\mathcal{A}$.
- H_4 queries: $\mathcal{B}$ maintains the initially empty list L_4 which consists of tuples $(c_{i,0}, c_{i,1}, c_{i,2}, c_{i,3}, \Phi_i, \phi_i)$. When $\mathcal{A}$ submits a H_4 query on $(c_{i,0}, c_{i,1}, c_{i,2}, c_{i,3})$, $\mathcal{B}$ returns Φ_i to $\mathcal{A}$ if $(c_{i,0}, c_{i,1}, c_{i,2}, c_{i,3}, \Phi_i, \phi_i)$ is in L_4. Otherwise, $\mathcal{B}$ randomly selects $\phi_i \in \mathbb{Z}_N^*$, computes $\Phi_i = \phi_i \cdot f(\theta)P_0$, inserts $(c_{i,0}, c_{i,1}, c_{i,2}, c_{i,3}, \Phi_i, \phi_i)$ to L_4, and returns Φ_i to $\mathcal{A}$.
- H_5 queries: $\mathcal{B}$ maintains the initially empty list L_4 which consists of tuples (Ψ_i, ζ_i). When $\mathcal{A}$ submits a H_5 query on Ψ_i, $\mathcal{B}$ returns ζ_i to $\mathcal{A}$ if (Ψ_i, ζ_i) is in L_5. Otherwise, $\mathcal{B}$ randomly selects $\zeta_i \in \mathbb{Z}_N^*$, inserts (Ψ_i, ζ_i) to L_5, and returns ζ_i to $\mathcal{A}$.
- Secret key extract queries: $\mathcal{B}$ maintains the initially empty list L_{sk} which consists of tuples (id_i, sk_{id_i}). When $\mathcal{A}$ submits a secret key extract query on any $id_i \neq id^*$, $\mathcal{B}$ returns sk_{id_i} to $\mathcal{A}$ if (id_i, sk_{id_i}) is in L_{sk}. Otherwise, $\mathcal{B}$ computes $sk_{id_i} = \theta h_i(\theta)Q_0$, inserts (id_i, sk_{id_i}) to L_{sk}, and returns sk_{id_i} to $\mathcal{A}$.
- Re-encryption key extract queries: When $\mathcal{A}$ submits a re-encryption key extract query on $\{id_i, id_j\}$ satisfying $id_i \neq id^*$, $\mathcal{B}$ checks whether (id_i, sk_{id_i}) is in L_{sk}. If not, it queries the secret key extract query on id_i. Then, $\mathcal{B}$ randomly selects $\beta, \gamma \in \mathbb{Z}_N^*$, computes $k_{id_j} = H_5(g^\gamma)$, $rk_0 = \gamma \cdot (P_{pub} + H_1(id_j) \cdot P)$, $rk_1 = \beta \cdot (P_{pub} + H_1(id_i) \cdot P)$, $rk_2 = sk_{id_i} + \beta \cdot k_{id_j} \cdot Q'$. Then, $\mathcal{B}$ returns $rk_{i \to j} = \{rk_0, rk_1, rk_2\}$ to $\mathcal{A}$.
- Re-encrypt queries: When $\mathcal{A}$ submits a re-encrypt query on $\{C_i, id_i, id_j\}$ satisfying $id_i \neq id^*$, $\mathcal{B}$ checks whether (id_i, sk_{id_i}) is in L_{sk}. If not, it queries the

secret key extract query on id_i. Then, $\mathcal{B}$ parses C_i as $\{c_{i,0}, c_{i,1}, c_{i,2}, c_{i,3}, c_{i,4}\}$ and checks whether $e(H_4(c_{i,0}, c_{i,1}, c_{i,2}, c_{i,3}), c_{i,3}) = e(c_{i,4}, Q')$ holds. If it doesn't hold, $\mathcal{B}$ returns $\perp$. Otherwise, $\mathcal{B}$ queries the re-encryption key extract query on $\{id_i, id_j\}$ to obtain $rk_{i \to j}$, computes $\widetilde{c}_{j,0} = c_{i,0}$, $\widetilde{c}_{j,1} = c_{i,2} \cdot e(c_{i,1}, rk_2)^{-1}$, $\widetilde{c}_{j,2} = c_{i,3}$, $\widetilde{c}_{j,3} = rk_0$, $\widetilde{c}_{j,4} = rk_1$. Then, $\mathcal{B}$ returns $\widetilde{C}_j = \{\widetilde{c}_{j,0}, \widetilde{c}_{j,1}, \widetilde{c}_{j,2}, \widetilde{c}_{j,3}, \widetilde{c}_{j,4}\}$ to $\mathcal{A}$.

- Decrypt$_1$ queries: When $\mathcal{A}$ submits a decrypt$_1$ query on $\{C_i, id_i\}$ satisfying $id_i \neq id^*$, $\mathcal{B}$ checks whether (id_i, sk_{id_i}) is in L_{sk}. If not, it queries the secret key extract query on id_i. Then, $\mathcal{B}$ parses C_i as $\{c_{i,0}, c_{i,1}, c_{i,2}, c_{i,3}, c_{i,4}\}$ and checks whether $e(H_4(c_{i,0}, c_{i,1}, c_{i,2}, c_{i,3}), c_{i,3}) = e(c_{i,4}, Q')$ holds. If it doesn't hold, $\mathcal{B}$ returns $\perp$. Otherwise, $\mathcal{B}$ computes $\sigma_i' = c_{i,2} \cdot e(c_{i,1}, sk_{id_i})^{-1}$, $m_i' = c_{i,0} \oplus H_3(\sigma_i')$, $\alpha_i' = H_2(m_i', \sigma_i')$. If $c_{i,3} = \alpha_i' \cdot Q'$, $\mathcal{B}$ returns m_i' to $\mathcal{A}$ and $\perp$ otherwise.

- Decrypt$_2$ queries: When $\mathcal{A}$ submits a decrypt$_2$ query on $\{\widetilde{C}_j, id_j\}$ satisfying $id_j \neq id^*$, $\mathcal{B}$ checks whether (id_j, sk_{id_j}) is in L_{sk}. If not, it queries the secret key extract query on id_j. Then, $\mathcal{B}$ parses $\widetilde{C}_j$ as $\{\widetilde{c}_{j,0}, \widetilde{c}_{j,1}, \widetilde{c}_{j,2}, \widetilde{c}_{j,3}, \widetilde{c}_{j,4}\}$ and checks whether $e(H_4(c_{i,0}, c_{i,1}, c_{i,2}, c_{i,3}), c_{i,3}) = e(c_{i,4}, Q')$ holds. If it doesn't hold, $\mathcal{B}$ returns $\perp$. Otherwise, $\mathcal{B}$ computes $k_{id_j}' = H_2(e(\widetilde{c}_{j,3}, sk_{id_j}))$, $\sigma_j' = \widetilde{c}_{j,1} \cdot e(\widetilde{c}_{j,4}, \widetilde{c}_{j,2})^{k_{id_j}'}$, $m_j' = \widetilde{c}_{j,0} \oplus H_3(\sigma_j')$, $\alpha_j' = H_2(m_j', \sigma_j')$. If $\widetilde{c}_{j,2} = \alpha_j' \cdot Q'$, $\mathcal{B}$ returns m_j' to $\mathcal{A}$ and $\perp$ otherwise.

Challenge. $\mathcal{A}$ submits two messages $\{m_0, m_1\}$ to $\mathcal{B}$ as its challenge. $\mathcal{B}$ randomly selects $b \in \{0,1\}^*$, $\phi^* \in \mathbb{Z}_N^*$, $\sigma^* \in \mathbb{G}_T$, computes $T = Z^{\prod_{i=t+2}^{t+n} \lambda_i} \cdot e(\frac{1}{\theta}(\prod_{i=t+2}^{t+n}(\theta + \lambda_i) - \prod_{i=t+2}^{t+n} \lambda_i) P_0, k\theta^2 h(\theta) Q_0)$, $c_0^* = m_b \oplus H_3(\sigma^*)$, $c_1^* = kf(\theta)P_0$, $c_2^* = \sigma^* \cdot T$, $c_3^* = a \cdot k\theta^2 h(\theta) Q_0$, $c_4^* = \phi^* \cdot kf(\theta)P_0$. Then, $\mathcal{B}$ inserts $(c_0^*, c_1^*, c_2^*, c_3^*, \phi^* \cdot f(\theta)P_0, \phi^*)$ to L_4 and returns $C_b^* = \{c_0^*, c_1^*, c_2^*, c_3^*, c_4^*\}$ to $\mathcal{A}$.

Phase 2. $\mathcal{A}$ can continue to make queries as in Phase 1.

Guess. Finally, $\mathcal{A}$ outputs its guess $b' \in \{0,1\}$. If $b' = b$, $\mathcal{B}$ outputs 1 as the solution to the instance of (f, h)-GDDHE problem. Otherwise, $\mathcal{B}$ outputs 0. If $Z = e(P_0, Q_0)^{k\theta h(\theta)}$, we have

$$T = e(P_0, Q_0)^{k\theta h(\theta) \prod_{i=t+2}^{t+n} \lambda_i} \cdot e(\frac{1}{\theta}(\prod_{i=t+2}^{t+n}(\theta + \lambda_i) - \prod_{i=t+2}^{t+n} \lambda_i) P_0, k\theta^2 h(\theta) Q_0)$$

$$= e(P_0, Q_0)^{k\theta h(\theta) \prod_{i=t+2}^{t+n} \lambda_i} \cdot e(P_0, Q_0)^{k\theta h(\theta) \prod_{i=t+2}^{t+n}(\theta + \lambda_i) - \prod_{i=t+2}^{t+n} \lambda_i}$$

$$= e(P_0, Q_0)^{k\theta h(\theta) \prod_{i=t+2}^{t+n}(\theta + \lambda_i)} = g^k,$$

$$c_0^* = m_b \oplus H_3(\sigma^*),$$

$$c_1^* = k \prod_{i=t+1}^{t+n}(\theta + \lambda_i) P_0 = k(\theta + \lambda_{t+1}) \prod_{i=t+2}^{t+n}(\theta + \lambda_i) P_0 = kP_{pub} + kH_1(id^*)P,$$

$$c_2^* = \sigma^* \cdot g^k,$$

$$c_3^* = k \cdot a\theta^2 h(\theta) Q_0 = kQ',$$

$$c_4^* = k \cdot \phi^* f(\theta) P_0 = kH_4(c_0^*, c_1^*, c_2^*, c_3^*).$$

Thus, C_b^* is a valid ciphertext, then $\Pr[b' = b] = \epsilon + \frac{1}{2}$.

If $Z \neq e(P_0, Q_0)^{k\theta h(\theta)}$, C_b^* is the encryption of a random message because Z is a random element of $\mathbb{G}_T$, then $\Pr[b' = b] = \frac{1}{2}$.

Therefore, the advantage of $\mathcal{B}$ in solving (f, h)-GDDHE problem is $\epsilon' = |\Pr[b' = b | Z = e(P_0, Q_0)^{k\theta h(\theta)}] - \Pr[b' = b | Z \neq e(P_0, Q_0)^{k\theta h(\theta)}]| = |\epsilon + \frac{1}{2} - \frac{1}{2}| = \epsilon$. ∎

Theorem 5. *The proposed IBPRE-II is IND-sID-CCA-2 secure in the random oracle if the (f, h)-GDDHE assumption holds.*

Proof. The proof is the same as the proof in Theorem 4, except that **Challenge** phase.

Challenge. $\mathcal{A}$ submits two messages $\{m_0, m_1\}$ to $\mathcal{B}$ as its challenge. $\mathcal{B}$ randomly selects $b \in \{0,1\}^*$, $\alpha^* \beta^* \in \mathbb{Z}_N^*$, $\sigma^* \in \mathbb{G}_T$, $(id_i, sk_{id_i}) \in L_{sk}$, computes $T = Z^{\prod_{i=t+2}^{t+n} \lambda_i} \cdot e(\frac{1}{\theta}(\prod_{i=t+2}^{t+n}(\theta + \lambda_i) - \prod_{i=t+2}^{t+n} \lambda_i)P_0, k\theta^2 h(\theta)Q_0)$, $\tilde{c}_0^* = m_b \oplus H_3(\sigma^*)$, $\tilde{c}_1^* = \sigma^* \cdot e(\alpha^* \cdot (P_{pub} + H_1(id_i) \cdot P), \beta^* \cdot H_2(T) \cdot Q')$, $\tilde{c}_2^* = a \cdot k\theta^2 h(\theta)Q_0$, $\tilde{c}_3^* = kf(\theta)P_0$, $\tilde{c}_4^* = \beta^* \cdot (P_{pub} + H_1(id_i) \cdot P)$. Then, $\mathcal{B}$ returns $\tilde{C}_b^* = \{\tilde{c}_0^*, \tilde{c}_1^*, \tilde{c}_2^*, \tilde{c}_3^*, \tilde{c}_4^*\}$ to $\mathcal{A}$.

Similar to the analysis of Theorem 4, the advantage of $\mathcal{B}$ in solving (f, h)-GDDHE problem is $\epsilon' = \epsilon$. ∎

Theorem 6. *The proposed IBPRE-II is SKLR-CA secure in the random oracle if the q-SDH assumption holds.*

Proof. The proof is the same as the proof in Theorem 3. ∎

6 Performance Evaluation

6.1 Theoretical Analysis

The performance of our schemes and the related schemes [13,15,26,33] is evaluated from a theoretical perspective, where our schemes are based on asymmetric bilinear pairing $e : \mathbb{G}_1 \times \mathbb{G}_2 \to \mathbb{G}_T$, and the schemes [13,15,26,33] utilize symmetric bilinear pairing $\bar{e} : \mathbb{G} \times \mathbb{G} \to \overline{\mathbb{G}}_T$.

Table 1. Computational cost and security comparison of IBPRE schemes

Schemes	[15]	[33]	[13]	IBPRE-I
Encrypt	$p + sm + e + H$	$p + 3sm + e + H$	$3sm + e$	$2sm_1 + sm_2 + e_1$
Re-KeyGen	$p + 2sm + e + 2H$	$3sm + 2H$	$p + 6sm + e + H$	$4sm_1 + sm_2 + e_1$
Re-Encrypt	p	$4p$	$2p + e$	$2p_1 + e_1$
Decrypt$_1$	p	$2p$	$p + e$	$p_1 + e_1$
Decrypt$_2$	$2p + H$	$2p$	$3p + 3sm + 2e$	$p_1 + e_1$
Security	CPA	CPA,CA	CPA,CA	CPA,CA
Schemes	[15]	[33]	[26]	IBPRE-II
Encrypt	$p + 3sm + 2H$	$p + 4sm + e + 2H$	$p + 4sm + H$	$3sm_1 + sm_2 + e_1 + H_1$
Re-KeyGen	$p + 2H$	$3sm + 2H$	$p + 5sm + H$	$4sm_1 + sm_2 + e_1$
Re-Encrypt	$4p + 2sm + H$	$6p + H$	$3p + H$	$3p_1 + sm_1 + H_1$
Decrypt$_1$	$2p + 4sm + H$	$4p + sm + H$	$5p + sm + H$	$3p_1 + sm_1 + sm_2 + H_1$
Decrypt$_2$	$2p + sm + 2H$	$2p + sm$	$2p + sm + e$	$2p_1 + sm_1 + sm_2$
Security	CCA	CCA,CA	CCA,CA	CCA,CA

Table 1 gives the computational cost and security comparison result, in which p_1, sm_1, sm_2, e_1, H_1, p, sm, e, H, CPA, CA, and CCA denote the time of asymmetric bilinear pairing, scale multiplication in $\mathbb{G}_1$, scale multiplication in $\mathbb{G}_2$, modular exponentiation in $\mathbb{G}_T$, map-to-point hash in $\mathbb{G}_1$, symmetric bilinear pairing, scale multiplication in $\mathbb{G}$, modular exponentiation in $\overline{\mathbb{G}}_T$, map-to-point hash in $\mathbb{G}$, security against chosen plaintext attack, security against collusion attack, and security against chosen ciphertext attack, respectively. As shown in Table 1, our schemes avoid the time-consuming pairing operation in algorithms Encrypt and Re-KeyGen, so as to achieve a lower computational cost. The computational cost of algorithms Decrypt$_2$ in IBPRE-I is more superior to the schemes [13,15,33]. IBPRE-II and the scheme [26] utilize the fewer bilinear pairing operation to execute the algorithm Re-Encrypt. Also, it is worth noting that IBPRE-II has a higher efficiency than the schemes [26,33] in decrypting first level ciphertext.

Let l be the length of message in CCA-secure schemes, $|\mathbb{G}_1|$, $|\mathbb{G}_2|$, $|\mathbb{G}_T|$, $|\mathbb{G}|$, and $|\overline{\mathbb{G}}_T|$ be the element length of in $\mathbb{G}_1$, $\mathbb{G}_2$, $\mathbb{G}_T$, $\mathbb{G}$, and $\overline{\mathbb{G}}_T$, respectively. The communication overhead comparison result is shown in Table 2. It can be observed that IBPRE-I has less communication overhead of re-encryption key and second level ciphertext in comparison with the scheme [13]. At the same time, IBPRE-II is comparable in communication overhead to the schemes [15,26,33].

Table 2. Communication overhead comparison of IBPRE schemes

Schemes	First level ciphertext	Re-encryption key	Second level ciphertext
[15]	$|\mathbb{G}| + |\overline{\mathbb{G}}_T|$	$2|\mathbb{G}| + |\overline{\mathbb{G}}_T|$	$2|\mathbb{G}| + 2|\overline{\mathbb{G}}_T|$
[33]	$3|\mathbb{G}| + |\overline{\mathbb{G}}_T|$	$2|\mathbb{G}|$	$2|\mathbb{G}| + |\overline{\mathbb{G}}_T|$
[13]	$2|\mathbb{G}| + |\overline{\mathbb{G}}_T|$	$5|\mathbb{G}| + |\overline{\mathbb{G}}_T|$	$4|\mathbb{G}| + 2|\overline{\mathbb{G}}_T|$
IBPRE-I	$|\mathbb{G}_1| + |\mathbb{G}_2| + |\mathbb{G}_T|$	$2|\mathbb{G}_1| + |\mathbb{G}_2|$	$|\mathbb{G}_1| + 2|\mathbb{G}_T|$
[15]	$l + 2|\mathbb{G}| + |\overline{\mathbb{G}}_T|$	$l + |\mathbb{G}|$	$2l + |\mathbb{G}| + |\overline{\mathbb{G}}_T|$
[33]	$l + 4|\mathbb{G}| + |\overline{\mathbb{G}}_T|$	$2|\mathbb{G}|$	$l + 2|\mathbb{G}| + |\overline{\mathbb{G}}_T|$
[26]	$l + 3|\mathbb{G}| + |\overline{\mathbb{G}}_T|$	$3|\mathbb{G}|$	$l + 3|\mathbb{G}| + |\overline{\mathbb{G}}_T|$
IBPRE-II	$l + 2|\mathbb{G}_1| + |\mathbb{G}_2| + |\mathbb{G}_T|$	$2|\mathbb{G}_1| + |\mathbb{G}_2|$	$l + 2|\mathbb{G}_1| + |\mathbb{G}_2| + |\mathbb{G}_T|$

6.2 Experimental Tests

In this section, we simulate the proposed schemes and the related schemes [13, 15,26,33] on a Linux virtual machine, where the RAM is 4 GB, and the CPU is Intel(R) Core(TM) i5-10400. We utilize the Python programming language and Charm crypto library [1] to implement the schemes.

Under 128 bits security level, BN256 curve $E(F_q) : y^2 = x^3 + 5$ is utilized in asymmetric bilinear pairing-based schemes (e.g., IBPRE-I and IBPRE-II), and Type-A curve $E(F_{\overline{q}}) : y^2 = x^3 + x$ is selected in symmetric bilinear pairing-based schemes [13,15,26,33], where l, $|\mathbb{G}_1|$, $|\mathbb{G}_2|$, $|\mathbb{G}_T|$, $|\mathbb{G}|$, and $|\overline{\mathbb{G}}_T|$ are 1024, 512,

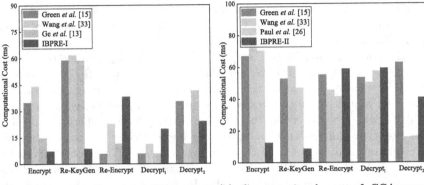

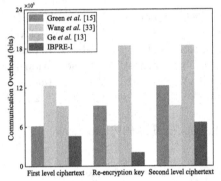

(a) Computational cost of CPA-secure schemes.

(b) Computational cost of CCA-secure schemes.

(c) Communication overhead of CPA-secure schemes.

(d) Communication overhead of CCA-secure schemes.

Fig. 1. Practical performance analysis of IBPRE schemes

1024, 3072, 3072 and 3072 bits, respectively. Figure 1 depicts the experimental result with respect to computational cost and communication overhead.

As shown in Figs. 1(a) and 1(b), the computational costs of algorithms Encrypt and Re-KeyGen in IBPRE-I and IB-PRE-II are much lower than that of the schemes [13,15,33] and the schemes [15,26,33], respectively. This is owing to the fact that the time-consuming pairing and map-to-point hash operations are avoided in our schemes. Moreover, the computational costs of algorithms Re-KeyGen, $Decrypt_1$, and $Decrypt_1$ are comparable to the schemes [13,15,33] and the schemes [15,26,33], respectively. Specifically, IBPRE-I cost 7.2533, 8.7107, 38.0451, 19.7624, and 23.9430 ms in algorithms Encrypt, Re-KeyGen, Re-Encrypt, $Decrypt_1$ and $Decrypt_2$, respectively, while IBPRE-II requires 12.3706, 8.6692, 58.9234, 59.3467, and 40.7583 ms. Therefore, the proposed schemes are feasible in practical scenarios from the perspective of computational cost.

It can be observed that our schemes are superior to the schemes [13,15,26,33] with regard to communication overhead, as illustrated in Figs. 1(c) and 1(d). It is mainly explained by the fact that the proposed schemes are constructed based on SM9 and utilize asymmetric bilinear pairing with shorter element lengths. In detail, the lengths of first level ciphertext, re-encryption key, and second level ciphertext are 4608, 2048, and 6656 bits in IBPRE-I, and 6144, 2048, and 6144 bits in IBPRE-II, respectively. This significantly reduces the communication overhead and storage costs in real-world applications.

7   Conclusion and Future Work

In this paper, we proposed two identity-based proxy re-encryption schemes based on SM9. In the proposed schemes, the user secret key form is the same as in SM9, thus making them easy to integrate with SM9. The formal security proof demonstrated that the first scheme can resist chosen plaintext and collusion attacks, while the second scheme withstands chosen ciphertext and collusion attacks. The theoretical analysis and experimental tests simultaneously shown that the proposed schemes are practical in terms of computational cost and communication overhead.

It is worth noting that the proposed schemes only achieve the basic ciphertext transformation functionality and the security against chosen plaintext, chosen ciphertext, and collusion attacks. Therefore, how to apply them to real-world scenarios where more functionality, e.g., one-to-many transformation, revocation, and fine-grained transformation, is desired is our future work.

Acknowledgement. This work is supported by the National Natural Science Foundation of China under Grant 62072054, the Key Research and Development Program of Shaanxi Province under Grants 2022GY-032 and 2024GX-YBXM-078, the Xi'an Science and Technology Planning Program under Grant 23ZDCYJSGG0009-2022, and the Fundamental Research Funds for the Central Universities, CHD, under Grant 300102242201.

References

1. Akinyele, J.A., et al.: Charm: a framework for rapidly prototyping cryptosystems. J. Cryptogr. Eng. **3**, 111–128 (2013). https://doi.org/10.1007/s13389-013-0057-3
2. Blaze, M., Bleumer, G., Strauss, M.: Divertible protocols and atomic proxy cryptography. In: Nyberg, K. (ed.) EUROCRYPT 1998. LNCS, vol. 1403, pp. 127–144. Springer, Heidelberg (1998). https://doi.org/10.1007/BFb0054122
3. Boneh, D., Boyen, X.: Short signatures without random oracles. In: Cachin, C., Camenisch, J.L. (eds.) EUROCRYPT 2004. LNCS, vol. 3027, pp. 56–73. Springer, Heidelberg (2004). https://doi.org/10.1007/978-3-540-24676-3_4
4. Boneh, D., Franklin, M.: Identity-based encryption from the Weil pairing. In: Kilian, J. (ed.) CRYPTO 2001. LNCS, vol. 2139, pp. 213–229. Springer, Heidelberg (2001). https://doi.org/10.1007/3-540-44647-8_13
5. Boneh, D., Lynn, B., Shacham, H.: Short signatures from the Weil pairing. In: Boyd, C. (ed.) ASIACRYPT 2001. LNCS, vol. 2248, pp. 514–532. Springer, Heidelberg (2001). https://doi.org/10.1007/3-540-45682-1_30

6. Canetti, R., Hohenberger, S.: Chosen-ciphertext secure proxy re-encryption. In: CCS 2007, pp. 185–194. ACM, New York (2007). https://doi.org/10.1145/1315245. 1315269

7. Canetti, R., Halevi, S., Katz, J.: Chosen-ciphertext security from identity-based encryption. In: Cachin, C., Camenisch, J.L. (eds.) EUROCRYPT 2004. LNCS, vol. 3027, pp. 207–222. Springer, Heidelberg (2004). https://doi.org/10.1007/978-3-540-24676-3_13

8. Cao, N., Wang. C., Li. M.: Privacy-preserving multi-keyword ranked search over encrypted cloud data. IEEE Trans. Parallel Distrib. Syst. **25**(1), 222–233 (2013). https://doi.org/10.1109/TPDS.2013.45

9. Cheng, Z.: Security analysis of SM9 key agreement and encryption. In: Guo, F., Huang, X., Yung, M. (eds.) Inscrypt 2018. LNCS, vol. 11449, pp. 3–25. Springer, Cham (2019). https://doi.org/10.1007/978-3-030-14234-6_1

10. Chow, S.S.M., Weng, J., Yang, Y., Deng, R.H.: Efficient unidirectional proxy re-encryption. In: Bernstein, D.J., Lange, T. (eds.) AFRICACRYPT 2010. LNCS, vol. 6055, pp. 316–332. Springer, Heidelberg (2010). https://doi.org/10.1007/978-3-642-12678-9_19

11. Deng, H., et al.: Identity-based encryption transformation for flexible sharing of encrypted data in public cloud. IEEE Trans. Inf. Forensics Secur. **15**, 3168–3180 (2020). https://doi.org/10.1109/TIFS.2020.2985532

12. Deng, R.H., Weng, J., Liu, S., Chen, K.: Chosen-Ciphertext secure proxy re-encryption without pairings. In: Franklin, M.K., Hui, L.C.K., Wong, D.S. (eds.) CANS 2008. LNCS, vol. 5339, pp. 1–17. Springer, Heidelberg (2008). https://doi.org/10.1007/978-3-540-89641-8_1

13. Ge, C., Liu, Z., Xia, J., Fang, L.: Revocable identity-based broadcast proxy re-encryption for data sharing in clouds. IEEE Trans. Dependable Secure Comput. **18**(3), 1214–1226 (2021). https://doi.org/10.1109/TDSC.2019.2899300

14. GM/T0044-2016: Identity-based cryptographic algorithm SM9. (2016)

15. Green, M., Ateniese, G.: Identity-based proxy re-encryption. In: Katz, J., Yung, M. (eds.) ACNS 2007. LNCS, vol. 4521, pp. 288–306. Springer, Heidelberg (2007). https://doi.org/10.1007/978-3-540-72738-5_19

16. Jiang, L., Alazab, M., Qin, Z.: Secure task distribution with verifiable re-encryption in mobile crowdsensing assisted emergency IoT system. IEEE Internet Things J. (2023). https://doi.org/10.1109/JIOT.2023.3272070

17. Kan, G., Jin, C., Zhu, H., Xu, Y., Liu, N.: An identity-based proxy re-encryption for data deduplication in cloud. J. Syst. Archit. **121**, 102332 (2021). https://doi.org/10.1016/j.sysarc.2021.102332

18. Lai, J., Huang, X., He, D.: An efficient identity-based broadcast encryption scheme based on SM9 (in Chinese). Chin. J. Comput. **44**(5), 897–907 (2021). https://doi.org/10.11897/SP.J.1016.2021.00897

19. Lai, J., Huang, X., He, D., Ning, J.: CCA secure broadcast encryption based on SM9 (in Chinese). J. Soft. **34**(7), 3354–3364 (2023). https://doi.org/10.13328/j.cnki.jos.006531

20. Lai, J., Huang, X., He, D., Wu, W.: An efficient identity-based signcryption scheme based on SM9 (in Chinese). J. Cryptol. Res. **8**(2), 314–329 (2021). https://doi.org/10.13868/j.cnki.jcr.000440

21. Lai, J., Huang, X., He, D., Wu, W.: Security analysis of SM9 digital signature and key encapsulation (in Chinese). Sci. China Inf. Sci. **51**(11), 1900–1913 (2021). https://doi.org/10.1360/SSI-2021-0049

22. Liang, K., Liu, J.K., Wong, D.S., Susilo, W.: An efficient cloud-based revocable identity-based proxy re-encryption scheme for public clouds data sharing. In: Kutyłowski, M., Vaidya, J. (eds.) ESORICS 2014. LNCS, vol. 8712, pp. 257–272. Springer, Cham (2014). https://doi.org/10.1007/978-3-319-11203-9_15

23. Liang, K., Liu, Z., Tan, X., Wong, D.S., Tang, C.: A CCA-secure identity-based conditional proxy re-encryption without random oracles. In: Kwon, T., Lee, M.-K., Kwon, D. (eds.) ICISC 2012. LNCS, vol. 7839, pp. 231–246. Springer, Heidelberg (2013). https://doi.org/10.1007/978-3-642-37682-5_17

24. Ming, Y., Zhang, W., Liu, H., Wang, C.: Certificateless public auditing scheme with sensitive information hiding for data sharing in cloud storage. J. Syst. Archit. **143**, 102965 (2023). https://doi.org/10.1016/j.sysarc.2023.102965

25. Ming, Y., et al.: Blockchain-enabled efficient dynamic cross-domain deduplication in edge computing. IEEE Internet Things J. **9**(17), 15639–15656 (2022). https://doi.org/10.1109/JIOT.2022.3150042

26. Paul, A., Srinivasavaradhan, V., Sharmila Deva Selvi, S., Pandu Rangan, C.: A CCA-secure collusion-resistant identity-based proxy re-encryption scheme. In: Baek, J., Susilo, W., Kim, J. (eds.) ProvSec 2018. LNCS, vol. 11192, pp. 111–128. Springer, Cham (2018). https://doi.org/10.1007/978-3-030-01446-9_7

27. Qin, B., Zhang, B., Bai, X.: Mediated SM9 identity-based encryption algorithm (in Chinese). Chin. J. Comput. **45**(2), 412–426 (2022). https://doi.org/10.11897/SP.J.1016.2022.00412

28. Ren, K., Jiang, P., Gai, K., Zhu, L., Huang, J.: SM9-based traceable and accountable access control for secure multi-user cloud storage. In: IEEE International Conference on Smart Cloud, pp. 13–18. IEEE (2021). https://doi.org/10.1109/SmartCloud52277.2021.00010

29. Shamir, A.: Identity-based cryptosystems and signature schemes. In: Blakley, G.R., Chaum, D. (eds.) CRYPTO 1984. LNCS, vol. 196, pp. 47–53. Springer, Heidelberg (1985). https://doi.org/10.1007/3-540-39568-7_5

30. Shao, J., Cao, Z.: CCA-secure proxy re-encryption without pairings. In: Jarecki, S., Tsudik, G. (eds.) PKC 2009. LNCS, vol. 5443, pp. 357–376. Springer, Heidelberg (2009). https://doi.org/10.1007/978-3-642-00468-1_20

31. Shao, J., Wei, G., Ling, Y., Xie, M.: Identity-based conditional proxy re-encryption. In: IEEE ICC 2011, pp. 1–5 (2011). https://doi.org/10.1109/icc.2011.5962419

32. Sun, J., Xu, G., Zhang, T., Cheng, X., Han, X., Tang, M.: Secure data sharing with flexible cross-domain authorization in autonomous vehicle systems. IEEE Trans. Intell. Transp. Syst. **24**(7), 7527–7540 (2023). https://doi.org/10.1109/TITS.2022.3157309

33. Wang, L., Wang, L., Mambo, M., Okamoto, E.: New identity-based proxy re-encryption schemes to prevent collusion attacks. In: Joye, M., Miyaji, A., Otsuka, A. (eds.) Pairing 2010. LNCS, vol. 6487, pp. 327–346. Springer, Heidelberg (2010). https://doi.org/10.1007/978-3-642-17455-1_21

34. Xu, P., Jiao, T., Wu, Q., Wang, W., Jin, H.: Conditional identity-based broadcast proxy re-encryption and its application to cloud email. IEEE Trans. Comput. **65**(1), 66–79 (2016). https://doi.org/10.1109/TC.2015.2417544

35. Zhou, Y., Zhao, L., Jin, Y., Li, F.: Backdoor-resistant identity-based proxy re-encryption for cloud-assisted wireless body area networks. Inf. Sci. **604**, 80–96 (2022). https://doi.org/10.1016/j.ins.2022.05.007

Security and Privacy

SecCDS: Secure Crowdsensing Data Sharing Scheme Supporting Aggregate Query

Yuxi Li[1(✉)], Fucai Zhou[2], Zifeng Xu[3], and Dong Ji[4]

[1] School of Computer Science and Engineering, Northeastern University,
Shenyang 110819, China
eliyuxi@gmail.com
[2] Software College, Northeastern University, Shenyang 110819, China
[3] School of Cybergram, Hainan University, Haikou 570228, China
[4] National Frontiers Science Center for Industrial Intelligence and Systems
Optimization, Northeastern University, Shenyang 110819, China

Abstract. This paper presents SecCDS, a secure crowdsensing data
sharing scheme that supports aggregate queries ensuring location privacy and hiding query patterns. In crowdsensing environment, how to
balance the trade-off of the sensor data applicability and the leakage
abuse of participants' location is a critical issue needed to pay attention. Aim at this and to cater to the demands of real-world crowdsensing
workloads, we deployed a 2-server collaboration architecture in SecCDS,
which protects participants' location and query privacy against arbitrary
misbehavior by one of the servers. SecCDS incorporates a recently developed cryptographic tool–*function secret sharing* to allow a participant to
secret-share real-time location in an obfuscated structure, without compromising the effectiveness of aggregate queries. The theoretical analysis
demonstrates that SecCDS achieves correctness while satisfying adaptive $\mathcal{L}$-semantic security. The experimental evaluation with two servers
demonstrates that SecCDS could conduct highly parallelizable aggregate
queries which is efficient for diverse crowdsensing applications.

Keywords: Crowdsensing · Location Privacy · Secure Sharing ·
Aggregate Queries · Semantic Security

1 Introduction

The proliferation of sensor-rich mobile devices has played a crucial role in driving
technological advancements across various fields within the crowdsensing environment. The amalgamation of observations with temporal and spatial information in crowdsensed data has resulted in a continuous augmentation of the
crowd-sensed database managed by the crowdsensing service provider. The esca-
lating demand for crowdsensing applications has consequently led to a substantial growth in the querying of mobile crowdsensed data. This trend has fostered

C. Ge and M. Yung (Eds.): Inscrypt 2023, LNCS 14526, pp. 343–359, 2024.
https://doi.org/10.1007/978-981-97-0942-7_17

the rapid emergence and widespread popularity of crowdsensing [1,2]. Notably, Fig. 1 illustrates a crowdsensed data query framework, wherein a server assumes the role of the crowdsensing service provider, overseeing the management of the crowdsensing database. Additionally, a querier, whether an individual or an organization, possesses the capability to solicit aggregate results pertaining to location-based sensory data, which is continually updated by multiple participants. This ability to access and analyze crowdsensed data enhances various processes such as forecasting, decision-making, and resource allocation.

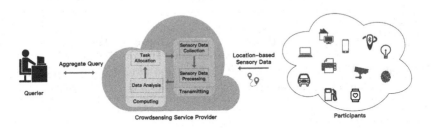

Fig. 1. Crowdsensed Data Query Framework

The advancement of crowdsensed data querying has brought about a noteworthy trade-off between privacy protection and usability. The rapid proliferation of devices and the activities of cybercriminals have led to privacy violations, while corporations engage in invasive behavioral advertising. Technological safeguards have faced difficulties in keeping pace with the ever-expanding scope and volume of crowdsensed data collected from end-users, as well as the development of privacy-enhancing crowdsensed data analytics tools necessary for processing and leveraging such data. Consequently, these advancements have introduced substantial new challenges, including:

(1) In the majority of mobile crowdsensing systems, location information is considered the most critical data. Participants continuously contribute their location and sensory data to the system, which poses potential risks of privacy breaches. To address these concerns, privacy-enhancing technologies have been developed within crowdsensing systems to empower participants with control over the collection, sharing, and utilization of their location data.

Wang et al. [3] explored location privacy by employing k-anonymity to mitigate the risk of disclosing location information. They aimed to ensure that individuals' locations cannot be easily distinguished from a group of at least $k-1$ other participants. Sucasas et al. [4] proposed a novel pseudonym-based signature scheme that enabled unlinkable-yet-accountable pseudonymity. This scheme facilitated anonymous authentication in crowdsensing systems, ensuring participants' identities remain protected. Niu et al. [5] introduced a real-time crowdsensing data collection mechanism that achieved w-event ϵ-differential privacy for participants. Their approach aimed to provide location privacy with lower complexity. However, it should be noted that the obfuscation of information in their method may potentially compromise the accuracy and integrity of the data. Yang et al. [6] leveraged differential privacy techniques to obfuscate location information while minimizing the loss in data quality. However, their approach overlooked the potential leakage of query patterns that could result from the sensory data itself, which may still pose privacy risks.

(2) Besides privacy preserving requirement, the sharing of location data with untrusted parties must be conducted securely and under controlled conditions. Queriers often aim to protect their query patterns during query execution while obtaining statistically meaningful location-based crowdsensing results. However, it is crucial to recognize that the obfuscation of locations, driven by privacy concerns, can impact the accuracy of aggregate query results. As a result, there is a critical need for secure query mechanisms that can effectively safeguard query patterns.

Gao et al. [7] and Arivarasi et al. [8] have both explored the use of end-to-end encryption as a means to protect users' location privacy against local eavesdroppers. Their approaches focus on ensuring that location information remains confidential throughout the data transmission process. Zhang et al. [9] have leveraged searchable encryption techniques to preserve location privacy. They proposed a novel spatial task matching framework in crowdsensing, which not only protects location privacy but also enables the accomplishment of geometric range queries.

These studies highlight the importance of incorporating secure mechanisms to safeguard query patterns and preserve location privacy in privacy-preserving crowdsensing environments. However, deploying these techniques in practice within MCS contexts remains challenging, and their feasibility is yet to be definitively determined.

1.1 Contributions

In this paper, we propose SecCDS, a secure crowdsensing data sharing scheme that supports aggregate queries. It protects participants' location and query privacy in semi-honest model.

To satisfy real-world scenario, we build a 2-server collaboration architecture for SecCDS. Inspired by the construction of a new cryptographic tool—function secret sharing for distributed point function, we give core protocols of SecCDS which requires no public-key cryptography (except for secure channels), nor general-purpose multiparty computation. SecCDS allows participants to secret-share their real-time locations in an obfuscated structure to the server-side, querier can request for aggregate result such as sum, count, variance est. while preventing query pattern leakage.

SecCDS achieves correctness and adaptive $\mathcal{L}$-semantic security in semi-honest model. The experimental evaluation demonstrates that SecCDS could conduct highly parallelizable aggregate queries which is efficient for diverse crowdsensing applications.

2   Preliminaries

Function Secret Sharing. Our solution is built on the concept of function secret sharing (FSS) [10]. FSS allows a dealer to divide a secret value into 2 shares, one for each of 2 parties, such that none of the parties can individually gain any insight into the secret value, yet both 2 shares contain enough information to reconstruct it. More pricisely, FSS allows for the splitting of a function $g : \{0,1\}^n \rightarrow \mathcal{G}$ from a function class $\mathcal{F}$ into two succinct function shares g_1, g_2. These shares are succinctly described by keys g_0, g_1 respectively. Each key g_b conceals the function f, and for every $x \in 0,1^n$, we have $\mathcal{F}(x) = g_0(x) + g_1(x)$.

Geohash. Geohash [12] is a geocoding system that provides a convenient way to encode a location's latitude and longitude into an alphanumeric string. The length of the geohash determines the precision of the encoding. It employs a hierarchical spatial data structure, dividing geographical areas into grid-like buckets. One notable feature of geohash is its ability to achieve arbitrary precision. By gradually removing characters from the end of the geohash, its length can be reduced while sacrificing precision. The spatial proximity between two locations can be inferred by comparing the common prefix of their geohashes - the longer the shared prefix, the closer the locations are [13].

3   The Model of SecCDS

3.1   Architecture

As illustrated in Fig. 2, SecCDS consists several entities: a set of *participants* $\mathcal{P}_1, \ldots, \mathcal{P}_U$, *querier* $\mathcal{Q}$, two servers $\mathcal{S}_0, \mathcal{S}_1$.

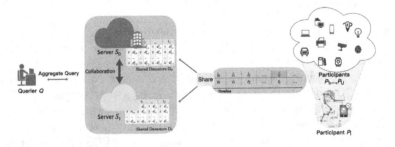

Fig. 2. Architechture

- **Participants:** Participants, denoted as $\mathcal{P}_1, \ldots, \mathcal{P}_U$, represent a collection of distributed entities in the system. These entities have limited computational capabilities and storage capacity. Each participant, $\mathcal{P}_i$, continuously gathers sensory data related to a specific target area, alongside the corresponding timestamps. The acquired data is then divided into shares and uploaded to servers for subsequent processing and analysis. This division into shares allows for efficient distribution and utilization of resources while maintaining the privacy and security of the data.

- **Querier:** Querier $\mathcal{Q}$ has the capability to make aggregate queries about a particular location and timestamp from the database, to obtain targeted insights and analysis based on the collected data.
- **Server $\mathcal{S}_0$:** $\mathcal{S}_0$, assumes the role of the primary coordinating entity within the system. It oversees and governs the overall operation of the crowdsensing service, supervises the data collection process from the participating entities, and facilitates the dissemination of aggregated data to the edge servers.
- **Server $\mathcal{S}_1$:** $\mathcal{S}_1$, function as a collaborated server for the crowdsensing database. Their primary mandate involves hosting and maintaining distinct subsets of the data gathered by the participants. In addition, these servers possess the requisite capability to perform aggregate queries on behalf of queriers, effectively retrieving and processing pertinent information from the crowdsensing database.

We assume that the two servers are semi-honest and do not engage in collusion. This precautionary measure prevents any server from acquiring knowledge about both the participants' location information and the query patterns.

3.2 Syntax

SecCDS is a triple of algorithms/protocols (Init, Share, Query). The formal description of SecCDS's syntax is as follows:

- Init(1^λ) $\rightarrow$ (D_0, D_1): On input the security parameter λ, the server $\mathcal{S}_0$ and $\mathcal{S}_1$ initializes D_0 and D_1 to empty;
- Share($\mathcal{P}_i : l_i^j, t^j ; \mathcal{S}_b : D_b$) $\rightarrow$ ($\perp ; D_b'$): a participant $\mathcal{P}_i$ executes with $\mathcal{S}_0$ and $\mathcal{S}_1$ to upload his real-time location. $\mathcal{P}_i$ inputs his the location l_i and timestamp t_i, $\mathcal{S}_0$ inputs D_0, and $\mathcal{S}_1$ inputs D_1, the output of $\mathcal{S}_0$ is the updated D_0', the output of $\mathcal{S}_1$ is the updated D_1'.
- Query($\mathcal{Q} : t_q, l_q ; \mathcal{S}_0 : D_0 ; \mathcal{S}_1 : D_1$) $\rightarrow$ ($R; \perp; \perp$): a querier $\mathcal{Q}$ executes with $\mathcal{S}_0$ on input t_q and l_q, $\mathcal{S}_0$ interacts with $\mathcal{S}_1$ to query D_0 and D_1. The final output for the querier $\mathcal{Q}$ is the result R.

3.3 Security Model

SecCDS addresses the following security requirements:

- **Correctness**: Correctness implies that, given any logical query request, Query protocol will always output the correct aggregate result for the given query token.
- **Location Privacy**: participants' location and its metadata remain confidential and inaccessible to servers and unauthorized parties, including the query phase.

- **Query Privacy**: Servers cannot learning the exact query pattern associated with the query request(which item match a given query), this feature helps maintain the anonymity of matched participants and their trajectories.

We formalize the security requirements in the following definitions.

Definition 1 (Correctness). *For all* 1^λ, *all* (D_0, D_1) *generated by* $Init(1^\lambda)$, *all sequences of Share and Query protocols, for all* $l_i^j \in \mathcal{L}$ *and* $t^j \in \mathcal{T}$, $Query(\mathcal{Q} : t_q, l_q; \mathcal{S}_0 : D_0; \mathcal{S}_1 : D_1)$ *will always output result* R *that:* R *is the summation of* $d_i \in D$ *where* $l_i = l_q$ *and* $t_i = t_q$, *which satisfies the true the traffic flow result, representing the number of matched participants who is in location* l_q *at time* t_q. *That is:*

$$Pr[Query(t_q, l_q, D) \to R = \Sigma v_i : l_i = l_q \wedge t_i = t_q] = 1.$$

Suppose $\mathcal{A}$ is an adversary with pseudo-random polynomial time (PPT) computation ability, who is given the security parameter k. We introduce the formulation of two distinct probabilistic experiments: $Real(1^\lambda)$ and $Ideal(1^\lambda)$ [16]. $Real(1^\lambda)$ represents the execution of the core protocol in SecCDS in a real-world scenario, $Ideal(1^\lambda)$ simulates an ideal-world execution, wherein the parties interact with a trusted functionality $\mathcal{F}_{SecCDS}$. $\mathcal{F}_{SecCDS}$ is parameterized with the leakage profile $\mathcal{L} = (\mathcal{L}_1, \mathcal{L}_2)$ and interacts with a client $\mathcal{C}$ and the simulator Sim, where $\mathcal{L}_1(D, (share, l, t))$ and $\mathcal{L}_2(D, (query, l, t))$.

Definition 2 (Adaptive $\mathcal{L}$-Semantic Secure). *SecCDS is adaptive $\mathcal{L}$-semantic secure, if, for all polynomial time $\mathcal{A}$, there exists polynomial time simulator Sim such that the following two distribution ensembles are computationally indistinguishable:* $Output_{\mathcal{A}}^{Real(1^\lambda)} \approx Output^{Ideal(1^\lambda)}$.

4   The Construction of SecCDS

Inspired by the FSS construction on distributed point functions (DPF) [10], we design the core protocols of SecCDS to allow participants to partition location data into two additive shares in an obfuscated structure. The shares stores in two server's databases separately while reveal no information about the participant's actual location. Employing this approach, SecCDS enables query functionality while protect the participants' location and concealing the underlying query pattern. By evaluating both shares on the query location value, the original location's evaluation can be reconstructed if time and location both match. The content of the raw data is customized based on the supported queries, with the default query configuration of SecCDS supporting operations such as sum, count, mean, and variance.

4.1   Initialization

Let λ denotes security parameter. Let $\mathcal{F} : \{0,1\}^\lambda \to \{0,1\}^{2(\lambda+1)}$ be a pseudorandom generator [11], and $H_{\mathcal{G}} : \{0,1\}^n * \{0,1\}^n \to \{0,1\}^l$ be the geohash encoding algorithm to translate two n-bit strings into a l-bit value [19]. The two servers $\mathcal{S}_0$ and $\mathcal{S}_1$ initialize key-value crowdsensing databases D_0 and D_1 initialized to be empty, as the distributed crowdsensing datastore. In D_0 and D_1, each key represents the timestamp, and the values are the shares participants' locations of different timestamps.

4.2 Share

Participant $\mathcal{P}_i$ extracts his real-time GPS coordinates (x, y) from his device continuously, which includes the longitude $x \in \{0, 1\}^i$, latitude $y \in \{0, 1\}^j$. $\mathcal{P}_i$ encodes (x, y) by the geohash encoding function $H_{\mathcal{G}}(x, y)$ into a l-bit location value $l_i^j \in \{0, 1\}^l$ at timestamp t_j. Let $l_i^j = r_1, ..., r_l$ be the bit decomposition of l_i^j.

As illustrated in Fig. 3, $\mathcal{P}_i$ generates a pair of location shares (α_0^i, α_1^i) to hide his location l_i^j from the server-layer. Each share α_b^i includes a random PRG seed s_b and l shared keys $\{k(1), ..., k(l)\}$, which defines a GGM-style binary tree with 2^l leaves. Each node in a tree will be labeled by a bit t and a λ-bit seed s, where the label of each node is fully determined by the label of its parent. These shares (α_0^i, α_1^i) are such that 1 is the only value present at the l_i^j-th position, while all other positions are set to 0.

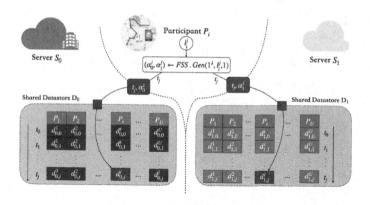

Fig. 3. Share Phase Illustration

$\mathcal{P}_i$ sampled random $s_0^{(0)} \leftarrow \{0, 1\}^\lambda$ and $s_1^{(0)} \leftarrow \{0, 1\}^\lambda$, let $t_0^{(0)} = 0$ and $t_1^{(0)} = 1$. To generated the shared trees, the two labels of a node should be divided into a mod-2 additive secret sharing of its label, suppose that the labels of the i-th node n_i on the evaluation path are $[s]^{(i)}, [t]^{(i)}$, consisting of shares $[s]^{(i)} = (s_0^{(i)}, s_1^{(i)})$, $[t]^{(i)} = (t_0^{(i)}, t_1^{(i)})$. For $i = 1$ to l, $\mathcal{P}_i$ computes $s_b^{L,(i)} \| t_b^{L,(i)} \| s_b^{R,(i)} \| t_b^{R,(i)} \leftarrow \mathcal{F}(s_b^{(i-1)})$. The construction ensures that the "sum" $t_0^{(i)} \oplus t_1^{(i)}$ over all nodes leading to an input r_i that is exactly equal to 1. To compute the labels of the $(i+1)$-th node, the servers start by locally computing

$\mathcal{F}([s]^{(i)}) = [s^{L,(i)}, t^{L,(i)}, s^{R,(i)}, t^{R,(i)}]$. The labels of the left child are $s^{L,(i)}, t^{L,(i)}$ and the labels of the right child are $s^{R,(i)}, t^{R,(i)}$.

S_0 and S_1 should share the same seed for all nodes except for the node along the path to leaf l_i^j. To do so, $\lambda + 2$ bits correction keys $k(i)$ for each level i are included: $s_k^{(i)} \leftarrow s_0^{L,(i)} \oplus s_1^{L,(i)}$ and two bits $(t_k^{L,(i)}, t_k^{R,(i)})$. The participant only needs to consider the case that the node is on the path to l_i^j where $t = 1$, in which case the calculation will be applied. At level i, if $r_i = 1$, $s_k^{(i)} \leftarrow s_0^{L,(i-1)} \oplus s_1^{L,(i-1)}$, $t_k^{L,(i)} \leftarrow t_0^{L,(i-1)} \oplus t_1^{L,(i-1)} \oplus 1$, $t_k^{R,(i)} \leftarrow t_0^{R,(i-1)} \oplus t_1^{R,(i-1)}$, then $s_b^{(i)} \leftarrow s_b^{R,(i-1)} \oplus t_b^{(i-1)} * s_k$ and $t_b^{(i)} \leftarrow t_b^{R,(i-1)} \oplus t_b^{(i-1)} * t_k^{R,(i-1)}$. If $r_i = 0$, $s_k^{(i)} \leftarrow s_0^{R,(i-1)} \oplus s_1^{R,(i-1)}$, $t_k^{L,(i)} \leftarrow t_0^{L,(i-1)} \oplus t_1^{L,(i-1)}$, $t_k^{R,(i)} \leftarrow t_0^{R,(i-1)} \oplus t_1^{R,(i-1)} \oplus 1$, then $s_b^{(i)} \leftarrow s_b^{L,(i-1)} \oplus t_b^{(i-1)} * s_k$ and $t_b^{(i)} \leftarrow t_b^{L,(i-1)} \oplus t_b^{(i-1)} * t_k^{L,(i-1)}$.

Therefore, the l correction values $k(i)$ are computed from the root labels by applying the above iterative computation along the path to l_i^j, and are included in both keys (α_0^i, α_1^i). That is, α_b^i as $s_b^{(0)} || k(1) || ... || k(l)$. $\mathcal{P}_i$ sends the share α_b to $\mathcal{S}_b$. $\mathcal{S}_b$ appends $D_b[t_j][l_i]' \leftarrow D_b[t_i][l_i] \cup \alpha_b^i$. The Share protocol is shown in Algorithm 1.

Algorithm 1. Share$(\mathcal{P}_i : l_i^j, t^j; \mathcal{S}_b : D_b) \rightarrow (\bot; D_b')$

Require: $\mathcal{P}_i : l_i^j, t^j; \mathcal{S}_b : D_b$
Ensure: $\bot; D_0'; D_1'$
1: $\mathcal{P}_i$ parses l_i^j as $r_1, ..., r_l$
2: $\mathcal{P}_i$ samples random $s_0^{(0)} \leftarrow \{0,1\}^\lambda$ and $s_1^{(0)} \leftarrow \{0,1\}^\lambda$
3: Let $t_0^{(0)} = 0$ and $t_1^{(0)} = 1$
4: **for** $i = 1$ to l, $\mathcal{P}_i$ does
5:     $s_b^{L,(i)} || t_b^{L,(i)} || s_b^{R,(i)} || t_b^{R,(i)} \leftarrow \mathcal{F}(s_b^{(i-1)})$
6:     **if** $r_i = 0$ **then**
7:         $s_k^{(i)} \leftarrow s_0^{R,(i-1)} \oplus s_1^{R,(i-1)}$
8:         $t_k^{L,(i)} \leftarrow t_0^{L,(i-1)} \oplus t_1^{L,(i-1)}$
9:         $t_k^{R,(i)} \leftarrow t_0^{R,(i-1)} \oplus t_1^{R,(i-1)} \oplus 1$
10:        $k(i) \leftarrow s_k^i || t_k^{L,i} || t_k^{R,i}$
11:        $s_b^{(i)} \leftarrow s_b^{L,(i-1)} \oplus t_b^{(i-1)} * s_k^{(i)}$
12:        $t_b^{(i)} \leftarrow t_b^{L,(i-1)} \oplus t_b^{(i-1)} * t_k^{L,(i-1)}$.
13:    **else**
14:        $s_k^{(i)} \leftarrow s_0^{L,(i-1)} \oplus s_1^{L,(i-1)}$
15:        $t_k^{L,(i)} \leftarrow t_0^{L,(i-1)} \oplus t_1^{L,(i-1)} \oplus 1$
16:        $t_k^{R,(i)} \leftarrow t_0^{R,(i-1)} \oplus t_1^{R,(i-1)}$
17:        $k(i) \leftarrow s_k^i || t_k^{L,i} || t_k^{R,i}$
18:        $s_b^{(i)} \leftarrow s_b^{R,(i-1)} \oplus t_b^{(i-1)} * s_k^{(i)}$
19:        $t_b^{(i)} \leftarrow t_b^{R,(i-1)} \oplus t_b^{(i-1)} * t_k^{R,(i-1)}$
20: **end for**
21: Let $\alpha_b^i \leftarrow s_b^{(0)} || k(1) || ... || k(l)$
22: $\mathcal{P}_i$ sends α_b^i to $\mathcal{S}_b$
23: $\mathcal{S}_b$ appends $D_b[t_j][l_i]' \leftarrow D_b[t_i][l_i] \cup \alpha_b^i$

4.3 Query

To query the aggregate result (such as the traffic flow in a specific time and location) in the crowdsensing databases, a querier $\mathcal{Q}$ constructs a query token $\tau = (l_q, t_q)$ which consists of timestamp $t_q \in \{0,1\}^n$ and location $l_q \in \{0,1\}^l$, then transmits them to the two servers $\mathcal{S}_b$, as illustrated in Fig. 4, $\mathcal{S}_b$ sets $R_b \leftarrow \perp$, extracts all the shares corresponding to the query timestamp t_q in D_b, denoted as $\{d_b^1, \ldots, d_b^U\} \leftarrow D_b[t_q]$, then evaluated each share d_b^i with the query location l_q.

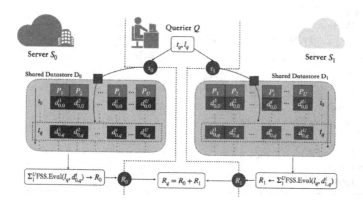

Fig. 4. Query Phase Illustration

More precisely, the query process involves comparing l_q to a private value d_b^i in D_b, and it goes as follows: For each $d_b^i \in D_b[t_q]$, $\mathcal{S}_b$ parses d_b^i as $s_b^{(0)} || k(1) || \ldots || k(l)$, sets $t_b^{(0)} = 0$. For $j = 1$ to l, $\mathcal{S}_b$ parses $k(j) = s_k^{(j)} || t_k^{L,(j)} || t_k^{R,(j)}$, computes $\tau_b^{(j)} \leftarrow \mathcal{F}(s_b^{(j-1)}) \oplus (t_b^{(j-1)} * [s_k^{(j)} || t_k^{L,(j)} || s_k^{(j)} || t_k^{R,(j)}])$, and gets parse $\tau_b^{(j)} = s_b^{L,(j)} || t_b^{L,(j)} || s_b^{R,(j)} || t_b^{R,(j)} \in \{0,1\}^{2\lambda+2}$. If $r_j = 0$ then $s_b^{(j)} \leftarrow s_b^{L,(j)}, t_b^{(j)} \leftarrow t_b^{L,(j)}$; if $r_j = 1$, then $s_b^{(j)} \leftarrow s_b^{R,(j)}, t_b^{(j)} \leftarrow t_b^{R,(j)}$. At the end of the computation, each server outputs t_b. By evaluation of all value in $D_b[t_q]$, both servers compute $R_b = \Sigma_1^U t_b^j$ and send R_b to $\mathcal{Q}$.

Upon receiving the results R_b from $\mathcal{S}_b$, the querier $\mathcal{Q}$ employs modular addition to aggregate the share results R_0 and R_1 into a unified final result denoted as $R \leftarrow R_0 + R_1$. When the servers' outputs are summed, the query resulting value is the aggregate sum result, representing the number of matched participants who is in location l_q at time t_q. The Query protocol is shown in Algorithm 2.

Aggregate Query Beyond Summation. SecCDS supports various aggregate query types in addition to summation queries:

Algorithm 2. Query($\mathcal{Q} : t_q, l_q; \mathcal{S}_0 : \mathsf{D}_0; \mathcal{S}_1 : \mathsf{D}^1) \to (R; \bot; \bot)$

Require: $\mathcal{Q} : t_q, l_q; \mathcal{S}_0 : \mathsf{D}_0; \mathcal{S}_1 : \mathsf{D}_0$
Ensure: $R; \bot; \bot$

1: $\mathcal{Q}$ generates $\tau \leftarrow (l_q, t_q)$
2: $\mathcal{Q}$ sends τ to $\mathcal{S}_b$
3: $\mathcal{S}_b$ sets $R_b \leftarrow \bot$
4: $\mathcal{S}_b$ retrieves $\{d_b^1, \ldots, d_b^U\} \leftarrow \mathsf{D}_b[t_q]$
5: For $1 \leq i \leq |U|$, $\mathcal{S}_b$ does
6:     Parse $d_b^i = s_b^{(0)} || k(1) || \ldots || k(l)$
7:     Let $t_b^{(0)} = 0$
8:     For $j = 1$ to l
9:         Parse $k(j) = s_k^{(j)} || t_k^{L,(j)} || t_k^{R,(j)}$
10:         $\tau_b^{(j)} \leftarrow \mathcal{F}(s_b^{(j-1)}) \oplus (t_b^{(j-1)} * [s_k^{(j)} || t_k^{L,(j)} || s_k^{(j)} || t_k^{R,(j)}])$
11:         Parse $\tau_b^{(j)} = s_b^{L,(j)} || t_b^{L,(j)} || s_b^{R,(j)} || t_b^{R,(j)} \in \{0,1\}^{2\lambda+2}$
12:         If $r_j = 0$ then $s_b^{(j)} \leftarrow s_b^{L,(j)}, t_b^{(j)} \leftarrow t_b^{L,(j)}$
13:         Else $s_b^{(j)} \leftarrow s_b^{R,(j)}, t_b^{(j)} \leftarrow t_b^{R,(j)}$
14:     End for
15:     $\mathcal{S}_b$ computes $R_b \leftarrow R_b \cup t_b^{(l)}$
16: end for
17: $\mathcal{S}_b$ sends R_b to $\mathcal{Q}$
18: $\mathcal{Q}$ sets $R \leftarrow \bot$
19: $\mathcal{Q}$ computes $R \leftarrow R_0 + R_1$

- **Average Query:** To query the average value of sensor data matching a given location l_q and t_q, each participant $\mathcal{P}_i$ is instructed to generate $(\beta_i^0, \beta_i^1) \leftarrow$ Share(l_i, v_i) and include them in the sensor record. Servers $\mathcal{S}_0$ and $\mathcal{S}_1$ are instructed to output the following: $\mathcal{S}_0$ and $\mathcal{S}_1$ evaluate $\{n_1^0, \ldots, n_U^0\} \leftarrow$ Query($l_q, \Sigma_i^U \alpha_i^0$) and $\{n_1^1, \ldots, n_U^1\} \leftarrow$ Query($l_q, \Sigma_i^U \alpha_i^1$), with $N = \Sigma_i^U (n_i^0 + n_i^1)$ representing the number of matched participants. $\mathcal{S}_0$ and $\mathcal{S}_1$ evaluate $\{R_1^0, \ldots, R_U^0\} \leftarrow$ Query($l_q, \Sigma_i^U \beta_i^0$) and $\{R_1^1, \ldots, R_U^1\} \leftarrow$ Query($l_q, \Sigma_i^U \beta_i^1$), with $R = \Sigma_i^U (R_i^0 + R_i^1)$ denoting the summation of the matched records. By dividing the summation result R by the number of matched participants N, $\mathcal{S}_0$ can obtain the mean value, i.e., $M = R/N$.

- **Variance Query:** To query the variance of sensor values within a location l_q and t_q, each participant $\mathcal{P}_i$ is instructed to generate $(\gamma_i^0, \gamma_i^1) \leftarrow$ Share(l_i, v_i^2) and also include them in the sensor record. The variances of the location-matched data stream values can be computed as follows: $\mathcal{S}_0$ and $\mathcal{S}_1$ evaluate $\{R_1^0, \ldots, R_U^0\} \leftarrow$ Query($l_q, \Sigma_i^U \beta_i^0$) and $\{R_1^1, \ldots, R_U^1\} \leftarrow$ Query($l_q, \Sigma_i^U \beta_i^1$), with $R = \Sigma_i^U (R_i^0 + R_i^1)$ denoting the summation of the matched records. $\mathcal{S}_0$ and $\mathcal{S}_1$ evaluate $\{V_1^0, \ldots, V_U^0\} \leftarrow \Sigma_i^U$ Query($l_q, \Sigma_i^U \gamma_i^0$) and $\{V_1^1, \ldots, V_U^1\} \leftarrow$ Query($l_q, \Sigma_i^U \gamma_i^1$), with $V = \Sigma_i^U (V_i^0 + V_i^1)$ denoting the summation of the matched records' squares. The variance Var can be obtained by calculating $Var = R^2 - V$.

5   Theoretical Analysis

5.1   Correctness

Theorem 1. *If the construction of pseudo-random generator [11] is correct, and the adversary is passive and follows the protocol, then the SecCDS construction satisfies correctness, which is defined in Definition 1.*

Proof Sketch: First of all, by conducting Share protocol, $\mathcal{P}_i$ generates and sends the location shares (α_0^i, α_1^i) corresponding to (l_i, t_j). Each α_b^i consists of $(s_b^{(0)}, k(1), ..., k(l))$, each $k(i)$ consists $s_k^{(i)}$ and two bits $(t_k^{L,(i)}, t_k^{R,(i)})$. It defines a GGM-style binary tree with 2^l leaves by chosen the keys as following way: the two seeds s_0 and s_1 on the first node off the path are identical, and the sum of $t_0 \oplus t_1$ along the whole path to n_i is exactly 1 if the departure is the path to l_i, i.e. $l_q = l_i$, and is 0 if the departure is not the path to l_i. Therefore, these shares (α_0^i, α_1^i) are such that 1 is the only value present at the l_i^j-th position, while all other positions are set to 0.

For each level i, $\mathcal{P}_i$ uses PRG $\mathcal{F}$ to compute $\mathcal{F}(s_b^{(i)}) = [s_b^{L,(i)}, t_b^{L,(i)}, s_b^{R,(i)}, t_b^{R,(i)}]$.

- If $(s_0^{L,(i)}, t_0^{L,(i)}) = (s_1^{L,(i)}, t_1^{L,(i)})$ and $(s_0^{R,(i)}, t_0^{R,(i)}) = (s_1^{R,(i)}, t_1^{R,(0)})$: sets $(s_0^{(i)}, t_i, k(i))$ arbitrarily, and then sets $s_1^{(i)} = s_0^{(i)}$ and $t_1^{(i)} = t_0^{(i)}$. A straightforward calculation confirms that the resulting construction satisfies the correctness.

- If $(s_0^{L,(0)}, t_0^{L,(0)}) \neq (s_1^{L,(0)}, t_1^{L,(0)})$ or $(s_0^{R,(0)}, t_0^{R,(0)}) \neq (s_1^{R,(0)}, t_1^{R,(0)})$: chooses $s_1^{(}i), s_0^{(}i)$, and t_0 arbitrarily, set $k(i)$ as $k(i) \leftarrow s_k^i \| t_k^{L,i} \| t_k^{R,i}$ or $k(i) \leftarrow s_k^i \| t_k^{L,i} \| t_k^{R,i}$. The calculation confirms that in both cases the resulting construction satisfies the correctness. In this calculation, we will consider the case of $(s_0^{L,(0)}, t_0^{L,(0)}) \neq (s_1^{L,(0)}, t_1^{L,(0)})$ or $(s_0^{R,(0)}, t_0^{R,(0)}) = (s_1^{R,(0)}, t_1^{R,(0)})$. The calculations for the other case is completely symmetric. The correction key $k(i)$ is conditionally applied to both child seeds of a node. This modifies the child seeds such that afterward, the two children of each node along the path to leaf l_i, for which S_0 and S_1's seeds differ, one is "deactivated" (i.e. S_0 and S_1's seeds at that position are made identical), and the other is not.

This correction is performed in such a way that neither server can determine which branch has been deactivated.

If the query token is (l_q, t_q), server $\mathcal{S}_b$ evaluates all the shares at t_q for location l_q. $\mathcal{S}_b$ evaluates d_b^j on the query l_q, which requires traversing the tree generated by each share d_b^i from the root to the leaf representing l_q by calculating the labels of all nodes on the path to l_q, and summing up the label of the leaf t_b. Each server $\mathcal{S}_b$ starts from the root, at each level i goes down one node in the tree and generate $(i+1)$-th labels depending on the bit l_q^i using a common correction key $k(i)$. Consequently, the construction ensures that the "sum" $t_0 \oplus t_1$ over all nodes leading to an input l_i that is exactly equal to $f_{l_i,1}(l_q)$, therefore R should equal the summation of the matched participants whose locations evaluate to l_i.

Hence, by performing this operation, the desired equivalence to the original function is preserved. If SecCDS returns R as the query result, it implies that it yields the correct summation where $l_i = l_q$ and $t_i = t_q$.

5.2   Security

Theorem 2. *If the construction of pseudo-random generator [11] is semantic secure, and the two servers S_I and S_∞ are semi-honest, then SecCDS satisfies adaptive $\mathcal{L}$-semantic secure, which is defined in Definition 2.*

Proof Sketch: Consider the simulator Sim that simulates $\mathcal{A}$ in the Ideal(1^λ) environment while receiving the leakage from the ideal functionality $\mathcal{F}_{\text{SecCDS}}$. We now aim to demonstrate that the simulated view of $\mathcal{A}$ in Ideal(1^λ) is computationally indistinguishable from the adversary's view in Real(1^λ).

To show $\mathcal{L}$-semantic secure we reduce the security to that of the output of Share being indistinguishable from the output of a truly random function. This will be done via a sequence of steps, where in each step we replace another correction key $k(i)$ within the share from being honestly generated to being random. The high-level security will go as follows:

- Each share begins with a random seed s_b^0 that is completely unknown to the other server. For $i = 1$ to l, the parties apply G to their seed $s_b^{(i-1)}$ to generate $s_b^{L,(i)} || t_b^{L,(i)} || s_b^{R,(i)} || t_b^{R,(i)} \leftarrow \mathcal{F}(s_b^{(i-1)})$. This process will always be performed on a seed which appears completely random; because of this, the security of the PRG $\mathcal{F}$ guarantees that the resulting values appear similarly random. The correction key $k(i)$ will adapt the randomness of $t_b^{L,(i)}$ and $t_b^{R,(i)}$, and the seed corresponding to the path to l: i.e. $s_b^{L,(i)}$ if $l_i = 1$. The remaining other seed still appears random.
- Given the query location l_q and two related items d_0 and d_1 in the two datastores, any seed s_b is computationally indistinguishable from a random string, which guarantees that for any correctly constructed (d_0, d_1) for location string l, Query(d_0, l_q) + Query$(d_1, l_q) = \beta$ only if $l_q = l$, and the output is zero otherwise. Even if an attacker compromises one of the two servers, they gain no knowledge about the secret index α or the location l embedded in the share.

Therefore, for all polynomial time $\mathcal{A}$, there exists PPT simulator Sim such that Real(1^λ) is computationally indistinguishable from Ideal(1^λ).

We can demonstrate that the proposed scheme satisfies adaptive $\mathcal{L}$-semantic secure in the random oracle model, which is defined in Definition 2.[1]

5.3   Complexity

Computation Complexity. The basic functions in SecCDS are the length-doubling PRG operations $\mathcal{F}$ expanding $s \in \{0,1\}^\lambda$ to $2\lambda + 2$ bits, which can be

---

[1] Interested readers can read the security proof in Boyle et al.'s manuscript [10].

implemented by AES in counter mode, i.e. $\mathcal{F}(s) = \text{AES}_{s||0}(0)||\text{AES}_{s||0}(1)$. Share requires two AES operations per PRG expansion since it uses the whole expanded string, but Query requires only one AES operation per PRG invocation since the evaluation uses either the left or the right half of the expanded string, depending on the next bit of l_q. Therefore, for each Share phase for n-bit sensory value, the computation complexity for a participant is $O(n)$, which is roughly $4n$ AES calls.

Storage Complexity. The storage complexity for servers is $O(\lambda n)$, which is related to the length of roughly λn bits for both data shares sent to servers. The computation and communication cost of Query between servers is roughly $O(|U|*n)$, which contains n AES calls multiply the number of participants, where both can be implemented using fixed-key AES.

Communication Complexity. The participant to server communication consists of a single share $O(l)$. The querier to server communication consists of a query token $O(1)$. The server to server communication requires the elements of partial query result proportional to the number of participants that a single timestamp, which is $O(|U|)$.

5.4   Comparision

Table 1 provides a comparison of SecCDS with related works [3, 6, 9, 14, 15] which are privacy-preserving solutions for the crowdsensing environment. Notably, [3, 6] utilize k-anonymity and differential privacy techniques to protect location privacy but suffer from decreased Query accuracy due to location obfuscation, while only [6] and SecCDS consider the privacy of both location and sensory data content. Overall, based on the comparison in Table 1, SecCDS surpasses the other works in terms of its overall performance and features, which maintains the performance and functionality requirements of large-scale data systems.

Table 1. Comparison

	[3]	[9]	[6]	[14]	[15]	SecCDS
Privacy Techniques	k-anonymous	SSE	DP	BlockChain	ORAM	PRG
Update Cost	low	high	high	–	high	high
Query Cost	low	high	mediem	high	high	mediem
Query Expression	low	low	midiem	low	low	high
Location Privacy	●	●	●	●	●	●
Sensory Data Privacy	●	○	○	○	●	●
Query Pattern Preserving	○	○	○	○	●	●
Trusted Server	●	○	○	○	●	○
Load Balancing	–	–	–	○	●	–

SSE: Symmetric Searchable Encryption; DP: Differential Privacy; ORAM: Oblivious RAM; PRG: Pseudo-Random Generation.

6   Experimental Evaluation

The implementation of SecCDS is carried out in C++ programming language, consisting of approximately 3,000 lines of code. To ensure robust security, a 256-bit security parameter is used. The PRG component employs AES in counter mode [17], taking advantage of AES-NI-enabled CPUs for efficient PRG evaluations. Geohash encoding in SecCDS is implemented using an existing geohash encoding algorithm sourced from a static library [19]. To evaluate the performance and effectiveness of SecCDS, simulations are conducted using real-world datasets, specifically the Gowalla check-in dataset [18]. Users and their check-in spots represent participants and sensing locations, respectively. Each experiment is run multiple times (between 10 to 100 times), and the average results are reported to provide a comprehensive analysis of SecCDS's performance.

Client Performance. Our client(participants and queriers) experiments run on computers in Linux Ubuntu 18.04.2 64-Bit version with Intel Core i7-2600 quad-core processors (3.4 GHz) and 8 GB of memory. In Share protocol, a client sends two location shares to the servers, which have size linear in the length of the location strings. During the experiments, the client's running time to generate a pair of location shares remains constant at 18.75 ms. It should be noted that this timing is observed for practical geohash values represented by l in the domain $\{0, 1\}^{80}$.

These results indicate the efficiency of the Share protocol in generating location shares within a practical time frame, even for geohash values commonly encountered in real-world scenarios (Table 2).

Table 2. Evaluation of Client Performance

Location Domain	$\{0,1\}^{16}$	$\{0,1\}^{25}$	$\{0,1\}^{48}$	$\{0,1\}^{80}$
Computation Cost(ms)	11.24	13.32	16.82	18.75
Communication Cost(kb)	2.80	3.93	5.86	11.45

Servers Performance. We used two AWS c5.xlarge instances in the Asia Pacific region. In the evaluation of server performance, the storage inflation was assessed by varying the number of location shares in the range of 200 to 1000, assuming geohash values in the domain $\{0, 1\}^{80}$. The results are presented in Fig. 5, indicating the storage cost at the server end. It can be seen that the server's storage cost increased almost linearly with the increase in the number of shares, which is inflated with the plain solution.

To measure the running time of the Query protocol, we initiated the process after the server received the query token from the clients. Figure 6 compares the execution times of Query in different aggregate query type. It is observed

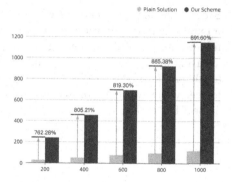

Fig. 5. Server's storage cost by varying the number of location shares

that as the number of records grows, the gain in running time becomes moderately decreased. Moreover, the summation query runs faster by between 40% to 50% than the other two query types, but overall the running times are all within acceptable limits, which demonstrate the SecCDS's ability to handle different query requests, thus support its practicality and suitability for real-world scenarios.

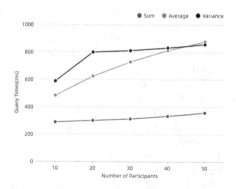

Fig. 6. Query times by varying aggregate query types

7 Conclusions

In this paper, we propose SecCDS, a secure crowdsensing data sharing scheme that supports aggregate queries. We build a collaboration architecture for Sec-CDS with two servers to act as the service provider. SecCDS protects participants' location and query privacy against arbitrary misbehavior by one of the servers. SecCDS allows a participant to secret-share the real time locations in a obfuscated binary tree-style structure without compromising the effectiveness of aggregate queries. SecCDS achieves correctness while satisfying adaptive $\mathcal{L}$-semantic security. The experimental evaluation with two servers demonstrates that SecCDS could conduct highly parallelizable aggregate queries which is efficient for diverse crowdsensing applications. A limitation of SecCDS is that the computation cost for participants to generate location shares is slight expensive for resource limited device, which we have drawn attention and conduct efficiency improvement for SecCDS without compromise of location privacy in the future work.

References

1. Liu, Y., Kong, L., Chen, G.: Data-oriented mobile crowdsensing: a comprehensive survey. IEEE Commun. Surv. Tutor. **21**(3), 2849–2885 (2019a)
2. [Kucuk, K., Bayilmis, C., Sonmez, A.F., Kacar, S.: Crowd sensing aware disaster framework design with IoT technologies. J. Ambient Intell. Humaniz. Comput. **11**, 1709–1725 (2020)
3. Wang, X., Liu, Z., Tian, X., Gan, X., Guan, Y., Wang, X.: Incentivizing crowdsensing with location-privacy preserving. IEEE Trans. Wireless Commun. **16**(10), 6940–6952 (2017)
4. Sucasas, V., Mantas, G., Bastos, J., et al.: A signature scheme with unlinkable-yet-accountable pseudonymity for privacy-preserving crowdsensing[J]. IEEE Trans. Mob. Comput. **19**(4), 752–768 (2019)
5. Niu, X., Huang, H., Li, Y.: A real-time data collection mechanism with trajectory privacy in mobile crowdsensing. IEEE Commun. Lett. **24**(10), 2114–2118 (2020)
6. Yang, Q., Chen, Y., Guizani, M., Lee, G.M.: Spatiotemporal location differential privacy for sparse mobile crowdsensing. In: Proceedings of the International Wireless Communications and Mobile Computing, Harbin City, China (2021)
7. Gao, J., Fu, S., Luo, Y., et al.: Location privacy-preserving truth discovery in mobile crowd sensing. In: 2020 29th International Conference on Computer Communications and Networks (ICCCN), pp. 1–9. IEEE (2020)
8. Arivarasi, A., Ramesh, P.: An improved source location privacy protection using adaptive trust sector-based authentication with honey encryption algorithm in WSN. J. Ambient Intell. Humanized Comput. 1–13 (2021). https://doi.org/10.1007/s12652-021-03021-2
9. Zhang, C., Zhu, L., Xu, C., et al.: Location privacy-preserving task recommendation with geometric range query in mobile crowdsensing. IEEE Trans. Mob. Comput. **21**(12), 4410–4425 (2021)
10. Boyle, E., Gilboa, N., Ishai, Y.: Function secret sharing: improvements and extensions. Cryptology ePrint Archive (2018)
11. Goldreich, O., Goldwasser, S., Micali, S.: How to construct random functions. J. ACM (JACM) **33**(4), 792–807 (1986)
12. Geohash. https://en.wikipedia.org/wiki/Geohash
13. Moussalli, R., Srivatsa, M., Asaad, S.: Fast and flexible conversion of geohash codes to and from latitude/longitude coordinates. In: 2015 IEEE 23rd Annual International Symposium on Field-Programmable Custom Computing Machines, IEEE (2015)
14. Zou, S., Xi, J., Xu, G., Zhang, M., Lu, Y.: CrowdHB: a decentralized location privacy-preserving crowdsensing system based on a hybrid blockchain network. IEEE Internet Things J. **9**(16), 14803–14817 (2021)

15. Reichert, L., Brack, S., Scheuermann, B.: Privacy-preserving contact tracing of COVID-19 patients. Cryptology ePrint Archive (2020)
16. Ran, C.: Universally composable security: a new paradigm for cryptographic protocols. In: Proceedings 42nd IEEE Symposium on Foundations of Computer Science, pp. 136–145. IEEE (2001)
17. The OpenSSL Project. OpenSSL: The Open Source Toolkit for SSL/TLS. (2015). http://www.openssl.org/. Accessed May 2023
18. Gowalla (2021). https://snap.stanford.edu/data/loc-gowalla.html. Accessed 13 Mar 2023
19. libgeohash. https://github.com/simplegeo/libgeohash

An Improved Method for Evaluating Secret Variables and Its Application to WAGE

Weizhe Wang, Haoyang Wang, and Deng Tang[✉]

Shanghai Jiao Tong University, Shanghai 200240, China
{SJTUwwz,haoyang.wang}@sjtu.edu.cn, dtang@foxmail.com

Abstract. The cube attack is a powerful cryptanalysis technique against symmetric ciphers, especially stream ciphers. The adversary aims to recover secret key bits by solving equations that involve the key. To simplify the equations, a set of plaintexts called a cube is summed up together. Traditional cube attacks use only linear or quadratic superpolies, and the size of cube is limited to an experimental range, typically around 40. However, cube attack based on division property, proposed by Todo et al. at CRYPTO 2017, overcomes these limitations and enables theoretical cube attacks on many lightweight stream ciphers. For a given cube I, they evaluate the set J of secret key bits involved in the superpoly and require $2^{|I|+|J|}$ encryptions to recover the superpoly. However, the secret variables evaluation method proposed by Todo et al. sometimes becomes unresponsive and fails to solve within a reasonable time. In this paper, we propose an improvement to Todo's method by breaking down difficult-to-solve problems into several smaller sub-problems. Our method retains the efficiency of Todo's method while effectively avoiding unresponsive situations. We apply our method to the WAGE cipher, an NLFSR-based authenticated encryption algorithm and one of the second round candidates in the NIST LWC competition. Specifically, we successfully mount cube attacks on 29-round WAGE, as well as on 24-round WAGE with a sponge constraint. To the best of our knowledge, this is the first cube attack against the WAGE cipher, which provides a more accurate characterization of the WAGE's resistance against algebraic attacks.

Keywords: Cube attack · Division property · WAGE · MILP

1 Introduction

The cube attack, proposed by Dinur and Shamir [6], is an algebraic attack technique against stream ciphers. Its main idea is to obtain simple equations about the key by summing a set of plaintexts, called a cube C_I, and then solve these equations to retrieve partial key information. Cube attacks consist of two phases: the offline phase involves constructing proper cubes and recovering their corresponding superpolies, while the online phase involves encrypting $2^{|I|}$ plaintexts

C. Ge and M. Yung (Eds.): Inscrypt 2023, LNCS 14526, pp. 360–378, 2024.
https://doi.org/10.1007/978-981-97-0942-7_18

under the real key and summing up them to obtain values of the superpolies. Afterward, the equations are solved, and a brute-force search attack is performed on the remaining key. It is vital to construct cubes in cube attacks. In traditional cube attacks, superpolies are often required to be linear or quadratic. Both properties can only be probabilistically determined through practical tests. This limits the size of cube to about 40.

Division property is an accurate characterization for the sum property of certain set, which was proposed by Todo [23]. In [24], Todo et al. combined cube attacks with division property. The link between division trail and the algebraic normal form (ANF) of superpoly was established. For a given cube I, they proposed an algorithm to evaluate the set J of secret variables involved in superpoly. A cube attack is available when the restriction $|I| + |J| < n$ is met, where n is the length of key. The combination of cube attacks and division property eliminates the size limitation of the cube and leads to theoretical cube attacks. The capability and applicability of cube attacks were greatly enhanced. Subsequently, more and more improved techniques have been proposed, such as flag technique [26], three-subset division property without unknown set [10], monomial prediction technique [12]. These developments have significantly improved the effectiveness and scope of cube attacks and have made it an important tool for attacking stream ciphers. In current research, cube attacks based on division property have primarily targeted simple stream ciphers such as Trivium [4] and Grain-128a [2]. To trace the propagation of division property effectively, original cryptoanalytic problems are often transformed into mixed-integer linear programming (MILP) problems and solved using optimizers. Some research [5,13,20] has also been conducted on other ciphers with intricate components. However, as the components of targeted cipher become complex, the model to be solved also becomes more complex. Thus, how to handle complex models becomes a crucial aspect in the research of cube attacks based on division property.

Authenticated Encryption with Associated Data (AEAD) is a type of encryption that provides both confidentiality and authenticity of data. It is commonly used to transmit confidential messages over insecure channels. In 2018, the National Institute of Standards and Technology (NIST) called for algorithms to be considered for lightweight cryptographic standards with AEAD and optional hashing functionalities. The aim of the competition was to identify and standardize lightweight cryptographic algorithms suitable for use in constrained environments, such as Internet of Things devices. A total of 57 candidates were submitted to NIST, and after selection, 32 submissions were chosen as Round 2 candidates. WAGE [3], submitted by AlTawy et al., was one of the 32 candidates. The WAGE permutation is used in the unified sponge-duplex mode to achieve the authenticated encryption functionality that provides 128-bit security with at most 2^{64} bits of allowed data per key. In [3], the designers analyzed the diffusion, algebraic, differential, and linear properties of the WAGE permutation and provided a clear security claim against differential and linear attacks. However, the description of WAGE's resistance to algebraic attacks is relatively subjective and lacks specific experiments to support it. In [7], Fei et al. applied

Correlation Power Analysis (CPA) technique to WAGE and recovered the key up to 12 out of 111 rounds.

In this paper, we conduct a detailed study of the secret variables evluation method, and explore the security level of WAGE against cube attacks. Compared to Trivium and Grain-128a, WAGE has a more complex feedback function and a larger state, making its corresponding MILP model more complex and challenging to solve. Applying Todo's method [24] directly to certain rounds of WAGE can result in unresponsiveness, which impedes the process of cube attacks. Thus, we propose an improved method to address this issue and successfully construct some useful cubes, as shown in Table 4. Our implementation is available in the following Github repository: https://github.com/SJTUwwz/WAGE_cube_attack.git. In particular, our contributions can be summarized in the following two aspects:

1. We improve the secret variables evaluation method proposed by Todo et al. [24]. In our improved method, we use a limit for solving time to judge whether the MILP problem is difficult to solve or not. If the time of solving process exceeds the limit, we break down the MILP problem into several sub-problems explicitly. This improvement effectively avoids the issue of unresponsiveness, which can enable higher round attacks.
2. Cube attacks are mounted on 29-round WAGE, as well as on 24-round WAGE with a sponge constraint with time complexity 2^{124}. This is the first cube attack on the initialization phase of WAGE and it provides a clear evaluation of the security level of WAGE by cube attacks.

The remainder of this paper is origanized as follows. In Sect. 2, we provide a review of the concept of cube attacks, division property, and fully linear integer inequality characterizations. We then introduce Todo's secret variables evaluation method in Sect. 3.1 and propose our improved method in Sect. 3.2. Section 4.1 offers a brief description of WAGE. In Sect. 4.2, we present a detailed description of cube attacks on the initialization phase of WAGE. Finally, Sect. 5 concludes the paper.

2 Preliminaries

In this paper, we will use the following notations. Let $\mathbb{F}_2$ be the field with two elements $\{0, 1\}$ and $\mathbb{F}_2^n$ be the vector space of n-tuple over $\mathbb{F}_2$. We use bold italic letters to represent bit vectors, $\mathbf{0}$ and $\mathbf{1}$ represent bit vectors with all coordinates being 0 and 1, respectively. We denote $\boldsymbol{u} = (u_0, u_1, \ldots, u_{n-1}) \in \mathbb{F}_2^n$ an n-bit vector over $\mathbb{F}_2$. The Hamming weight of $\boldsymbol{u}$ is defined as $wt(\boldsymbol{u}) = \#\{0 \leq i \leq n-1 : u_i \neq 0\} = \sum_{i=0}^{n-1} u_i$. We use $\oplus$ (resp. $\bigoplus$) to denote the addition (resp. multiple sums) in $\mathbb{F}_2$ or $\mathbb{F}_2^n$. Moreover, $\boldsymbol{u} \succeq \boldsymbol{v}$ represents $u_i \geq v_i$ for all $i \in \{0, 1, \ldots, n-1\}$. Let $f : \mathbb{F}_2^n \to \mathbb{F}_2$ be a Boolean function in $\mathbb{F}_2[x_0, x_1, \ldots, x_{n-1}]/(x_0^2 - x_0, x_1^2 - x_1, \ldots, x_{n-1}^2 - x_{n-1})$ whose algebraic normal form (ANF) is

$$f(\boldsymbol{x}) = f(x_0, x_1, \ldots, x_{n-1}) = \bigoplus_{\boldsymbol{u} \in \mathbb{F}_2^n} a_{\boldsymbol{u}} \boldsymbol{x}^{\boldsymbol{u}},$$

where $a_u \in \mathbb{F}_2$ and $\boldsymbol{x}^u = \pi_u(\boldsymbol{x}) = \prod_{i=0}^{n-1} x_i^{u_i}$ is called a monomial.

2.1 Cube Attack

The cube attack [6] was first introduced by Dinur and Shamir at EUROCRYPT 2009, which is the extension of the higher-order differential cryptanalysis [15] and integral cryptanalysis [14]. Let $\boldsymbol{x} = (x_0, x_1, \ldots, x_{n-1})$ and $\boldsymbol{v} = (v_0, v_1, \ldots, v_{m-1})$ be n secret variables and m public variables, respectively. Then we can represent the symmetric-key cryptosystem as $f(\boldsymbol{x}, \boldsymbol{v})$, where f is a function from $\mathbb{F}_2^{n+m}$ to $\mathbb{F}_2$, $\boldsymbol{x}$ is the secret variable (key), $\boldsymbol{v}$ is the public variable (initialization vector (IV) or nonce). The main idea of cube attacks is to simplify the polynomial $f(\boldsymbol{x}, \boldsymbol{v})$ by computing its higher order differential on public variables $\boldsymbol{v}$. Let $I = \{v_{i_1}, v_{i_2}, \ldots, v_{i_d}\}$ be a subset of public variables. Then function f can be rewritten as

$$f(\boldsymbol{x}, \boldsymbol{v}) = t_I \cdot p_I(\boldsymbol{x}, \boldsymbol{v}) \oplus q_I(\boldsymbol{x}, \boldsymbol{v}),$$

where $t_I = \prod_{v \in I} v$. As noted in [6], after the summation of the 2^d values of f by assigning all the possible values to d variables in I, the value of p_I is computed, that is

$$\bigoplus_{(v_{i_1}, v_{i_2}, \ldots, v_{i_d}) \in C_I} f(\boldsymbol{x}, \boldsymbol{v}) = p_I(\boldsymbol{x}, \boldsymbol{v}).$$

The public variables in I are called cube variables and the remaining public variables are called non-cube variables. The set C_I that contains all 2^d assignments of cube variables is called a cube. The dimension of C_I is d and all the non-cube variables are set to constants, usually all zeros. The simplified polynomial p_I is called the superpoly of C_I in f. In the absence of ambiguity, we would call p_I the superpoly of I in f for convenience.

The cube attack consists of the offline phase and the online phase. In the offline phase, attackers need to find cubes whose superpoly is useful. Useful superpolies can be used to directly recover partial information of key or help to filter out wrong keys. In the online phase, attackers would query the encryption oracle to get the cube summation under the real key for each cube obtained in the offline phase. By solving the equations of superpolies, we can recover some key bits. Finally, a brute-force attack would be applied to recover the whole key.

2.2 Division Property

Division property was first proposed in [23]. Then, the conventional bit-based division property and the bit-based division property using three subsets were introduced in [25]. Three-subset division property without unknown subset was introduced in [10]. In this paper, we will focus on the conventional bit-based division property. The definition of the conventional bit-based division property is as follows.

Definition 1 (Bit-Based Division Property). *Let $\mathbb{X}$ be a multiset whose elements take a value of $\mathbb{F}_2^n$, and $\mathbb{K}$ be a set whose elements take an n-dimensional* *bit vector. When the multiset* $\mathbb{X}$ *has the division property* $\mathcal{D}_{\mathbb{K}}^{1^n}$, *it fulfils the following conditions:*

$$\bigoplus_{x \in \mathbb{X}} \pi_u(x) = \begin{cases} unknown, & \text{if there are } k \in \mathbb{K} \text{ s.t. } u \succeq k, \\ 0, & \text{otherwise.} \end{cases}$$

Assume that $\mathbb{X}$ is the input set with the division property $\mathcal{D}_{\mathbb{K}_0}^{1^n}$. Let $\mathbb{Y}$ be the output set obtained by encrypting r rounds on $\mathbb{X}$. It is difficult to evaluate the division property of $\mathbb{Y}$, denoted by $\mathcal{D}_{\mathbb{K}_r}^{1^n}$, directly. In [25,28], the propagation rules of division property on basic operations were given. Based on those rules, $\mathcal{D}_{\mathbb{K}_0}^{1^n}$ can be computed by iteratively evaluating the propagation on round function. The concept of division trail was first introduced in [28], which facilitates the application of the MILP method to the division property and is defined as follows.

Definition 2 (Division Trail). *Consider the propagation of the division property* $\{k\} = \mathbb{K}_0 \to \mathbb{K}_1 \to \mathbb{K}_2 \to \cdots \to \mathbb{K}_r$. *For any vector* k_i^* *in* $\mathbb{K}_i$ $(i \geq 1)$, *there must exist an vector* k_{i-1}^* *in* $\mathbb{K}_{i-1}$ *such that* k_{i-1}^* *can propagate to* k_i^* *by division property propagation rules. Furthermore, for* $(k_0, k_1, \ldots, k_r) \in \mathbb{K}_0 \times \mathbb{K}_1 \times \cdots \times \mathbb{K}_r$, *if* k_{i-1} *can propagate to* k_i *for all* $i \in \{1, 2, \ldots, r\}$, *we call* $(k_0, k_1, \ldots, k_r)$ *an r-round division trail.*

In [28], the authors described the propagation rules for AND, COPY, and XOR using MILP models. For detailed information, please refer to [28].

In [24], the authors applied the division property to cube attacks. Instead of finding zero-sum integral distinguishers, they used the division property to analyze the ANF coefficients of a Boolean function f. The relation between division property and ANF coefficient is given in the following lemma and proposition.

Lemma 1. *Let* $f(x)$ *be a boolean function from* $\mathbb{F}_2^n$ *to* $\mathbb{F}_2$ *and* $a_u^f \in \mathbb{F}_2(u \in \mathbb{F}_2^n)$ *be the ANF coefficients. Let* k *be an n-dimensional bit vector. Then, assuming there is no division trail such that* $k \xrightarrow{f} 1$, a_u^f *is always 0 for* $u \succeq k$.

Proposition 1. *Let* $f(x, v)$ *be a boolean function from* $\mathbb{F}_2^{n+m}$ *to* $\mathbb{F}_2$, *where* x *and* v *denote the secret and public variables, respectively. For a set of indices* $I = \{i_1, i_2, \ldots, i_{|I|}\} \subset \{1, 2, \ldots, m\}$, *let* C_I *be a set of* $2^{|I|}$ *values where the variables in* $\{v_{i_1}, v_{i_2}, \ldots, v_{i_{|I|}}\}$ *are taking all possible combinations of values. Let* k_I *be an m-dimensional bit vector such that* $v^{k_I} = t_I = v_{i_1} v_{i_2} \cdots v_{i_{|I|}}$, *i.e.* $k_i = 1$ *if* $i \in I$ *and* $k_i = 0$ *otherwise. Assuming there is no division trail such that* $(e_j, k_I) \xrightarrow{f} 1$, x_j *is not involved in the superpoly of the cube* C_I.

Based on Lemma 1 and Proposition 1, attackers can find all related secret variables J in the superpoly $p_I(x, v)$. Then, the superpoly could be recovered with time complexity $2^{|I|+|J|}$. Degree estimation and term enumeration techniques were introduced in [26]. With these thechniques, the time complexity of recovering the superpoly can be reduced to $2^{|I|} \times \binom{|J|}{\leq d}$, where d is the upper bound of the degree of the superpoly.

2.3 Full Linear Integer Inequality Characterization

To apply MILP to cryptanalytic problems, attackers need to describe the fundamental components of ciphers using linear inequalities. This leads to the concept of full linear integer inequality characterization.

Definition 3 (FLIIC [8]). *Let $S \subset \mathbb{Z}_2^n$ and L be a set of linear integer inequalities:*

$$\begin{cases} a_{0,0}x_0 + a_{0,1}x_1 + \cdots + a_{0,n-1}x_{n-1} + b_0 \geq 0 \\ a_{1,0}x_0 + a_{1,1}x_1 + \cdots + a_{1,n-1}x_{n-1} + b_1 \geq 0 \\ \quad\quad\quad\quad \vdots \\ a_{m-1,0}x_0 + a_{m-1,1}x_1 + \cdots + a_{m-1,n-1}x_{n-1} + b_{m-1} \geq 0 \end{cases},$$

where $a_{i,j}$ and b_i are integers for $0 \leq i \leq m-1$, $0 \leq j \leq n-1$. L is called a full linear integer inequality characterization (FLIIC, in short) of S if the solution set of L on $\mathbb{Z}_2^n$ is S exactly. We also say L fully characterizes S, and m is called the cardinality of L, denoted by $|L|$.

The FLIIC of a complex component like the S-box can be obtained by directly combining basic operations. However, this method would result in a large number of inequalities and variables, making the model inefficient to solve. A better approach is to construct the FLIIC directly based on the given set S. The entire problem can be solved in two steps. The first step involves generating a sufficient number of high-quality inequalities. Then, in the second step, redundancies are removed and a minimal number of inequalities are selected.

In the first step, inequalities can be constructed using the H-representation method proposed in [21], the logical condition method described in [1], or the SuperBall method introduced in [16]. In the second step, we encounter a Set Covering Problem (SCP). In existing research, SCP is typically solved using either a greedy algorithm or MILP techniques [19]. In [8], the authors established a complete theoretical system to solve the problem of fully characterizing a given set with the minimal number of inequalities. They provided an algorithm of enumerating all plain closures for a given S-box, which supports point sets with high dimension up to 18 and is the fastest at present.

3 Evaluating Secret Variables in Superpoly

The critical step in cube attacks is constructing useful cubes during the offline phase. Our objective is to construct cubes that satisfy the condition $|I|+|J| < n$. In this section, we begin by presenting the secret variables evaluation method based on division property, which was initially proposed in [24]. Subsequently, we introduce *our improved secret variables evaluation method* and provide a detailed explanation of why it is an improvement over Todo's method.

3.1 Previous Secret Variables Evaluation Method

Based on the insights provided by Lemma 1 and Proposition 1, Todo et al. [24] introduced a framework that enables the evaluation of secret variables associated with the superpoly of a given cube. Algorithm 1 is the concrete algorithm supported by MILP.

Algorithm 1. Evaluate secret variables based on division property

---
1: **procedure** DPEVAL(MILP model M, cube indices I)
2:    Let x be n MILP variables of M corresponding to secret variables.
3:    Let v be m MILP variables of M corresponding to public variables.
4:    $M.con \leftarrow v_i = 1$ for all $i \in I$
5:    $M.con \leftarrow v_i = 0$ for all $i \in (\{0, 1, \ldots, m - 1\} - I)$
6:    $M.con \leftarrow \sum_{i=0}^{n-1} x_i = 1$
7:    $J = \emptyset$
8:    solve MILP model M
9:    **while** M is solved **do**
10:       pick index $j \in \{0, \ldots, n - 1\}$ s.t. $x_j = 1$
11:       $J = J \cup \{j\}$
12:       $M.con \leftarrow x_j = 0$
13:       solve MILP model M
14:    **end while**
15:    **return** J
16: **end procedure**

The input model M is the MILP model of target cipher by the context of division property and the cube is represented as a set I. In line 4–6, the input division property is contrained to the form (e_j, k_I). Line 7–14 is the core idea of Algorithm 1. When model M is feasible, a satisfying division trail (e_j, k_I) can be found, which means that x_j is involved in the superpoly. Then, the index j is added to the set J, and a new constraint is included to exclude this specific point. The process is repeated until the model becomes infeasible. Finally, the set J containing the indices of the secret variables involved in the superpoly is obtained.

3.2 An Improved Secret Variables Evaluation Method

In addition to Todo's method, it is evident that a more intuitive approach exists. This alternative method is to verify (e_j, k_I) input division property for all $0 \leq j \leq m - 1$ individually. The details of this intuitive method are presented in Algorithm 2.

When comparing Algorithm 1 and Algorithm 2, it is expected that Algorithm 1 will outperform Algorithm 2, since the former's iteration count is $|J| \leq n$ while the latter's iteration count is n. However, there is another important factor to consider. That is, the MILP problems that need to be solved during the iteration

---

Algorithm 2. Evaluate each secret variables individually

1: **procedure** INDEVAL(MILP model M, cube indices I)
2:     Let $\boldsymbol{x}$ be n MILP variables of M corresponding to secret variables.
3:     Let $\boldsymbol{v}$ be m MILP variables of M corresponding to public variables.
4:     $M.con \leftarrow v_i = 1$ for all $i \in I$
5:     $M.con \leftarrow v_i = 0$ for all $i \in (\{0, 1, \ldots, m - 1\} - I)$
6:     $M.con \leftarrow \sum_{i=0}^{n-1} x_i = 1$
7:     $J = \emptyset$
8:     **for** j from 0 to $n - 1$ **do**
9:         $M.con \leftarrow x_j = 1$
10:        solve MILP model M
11:        **if** M is solved **then**
12:            $J = J \cup \{j\}$
13:        **end if**
14:        $M.con \rightarrow x_j = 1$ ▷ "$\rightarrow$" means removing constraint.
15:    **end for**
16:    **return** J
17: **end procedure**

---

process are not the same. More precisely, the constraints on input secret variables differ between the two methods. Specially, in the i-th iteration, Todo's method has constraints

$$\sum_{j=0}^{n-1} x_j = 1 \text{ and } x_j = 0, \forall j \in J,$$

while the intuitive method has constraints

$$x_i = 1 \text{ and } x_j = 0, \forall j \neq i, j \in \{0, 1, \ldots, n\}.$$

It is clear that the latter's constraints are stronger. This difference will also have an impact on the efficiency of algorithms. In order to compare the efficiency of the two methods, we conducted a series of experiments. The results indicated that in marjority of cases, Todo's method required less time than the intuitive method. Nevertheless, in certain situations, Todo's method was unable to produce results within a reasonable timeframe. Upon further investigation, we discovered that such issue was due to the difficulty in optimizing the MILP model after eliminating all feasible solutions. Moreover, this problem did not arise when using intuitive method. By combining the strengths of Todo's method and intuitive method, we have developed an improved secret variables evaluation method, which not only maintains the high efficiency, but also avoids the issue of unresponsiveness. Algorithm 3 gives the details of our new method.

Compared to Todo's method, our improved method makes use of the *TimeLimit* parameter of Gurobi solver. Lines 2–15 correspond to the first part of procedure. In this part, Todo's method is applied directly. If the solver has not stopped when time is up, the model-solving process is forcibly terminated. Then, the unsolved set $\bar{J}$ will be solved by intuitive method one by one. This

---

Algorithm 3. An improved secret variables evaluation method

1: **procedure** NEWEVAL(MILP model M, cube indices I, limit of time t)
2:     Let $\boldsymbol{x}$ be n MILP variables of M corresponding to secret variables.
3:     Let $\boldsymbol{v}$ be m MILP variables of M corresponding to public variables.
4:     $M.TimeLimit \leftarrow t$
5:     $M.con \leftarrow v_i = 1$ for all $i \in I$
6:     $M.con \leftarrow v_i = 0$ for all $i \in (\{0, 1, \ldots, m-1\} - I)$
7:     $M.con \leftarrow \sum_{i=0}^{n-1} x_i = 1$
8:     $J = \emptyset$
9:     solve MILP model M
10:     **while** M is solved **do**
11:         pick index $j \in \{0, \ldots, n-1\}$ s.t. $x_j = 1$
12:         $J = J \cup \{j\}$
13:         $M.con \leftarrow x_j = 0$
14:         solve MILP model M
15:     **end while**
16:     **if** M is not solved within t **then**   ▷ The MILP model is difficult to solve.
17:         $\bar{J} = \{0, 1, \ldots, n-1\} - J$
18:         **for all** $j \in \bar{J}$ **do**
19:             $M.con \leftarrow x_j = 1$
20:             solve MILP model M
21:             **if** M is solved **then**
22:                 $J = J \cup \{j\}$
23:             **end if**
24:             $M.con \rightarrow x_j = 1$
25:         **end for**
26:     **end if**
27:     **return** J
28: **end procedure**

---

is the second part of procedure, corresponding to lines 16–26. Since the MILP model in the intuitive method is simpler, it is hopeful that the problem can be solved within a reasonable time. Actually, we manually divide the original complex MILP model into several simpler MILP models and solve them individually in the second part of the process. A similar idea was used to recover superpoly in [11].

If the MILP model M in the first part can be solved within the time limit, the second part of Algorithm 3 will not be activated. This ensures that our method maintains high efficiency, similar to Todo's method in most cases. In situations where Todo's method does not perform well, our method will continue to work with simpler MILP models. In summary, our new method represents a significant improvement over Todo's method.

4 Experiment and Result

We apply our new method to the lightweight authenticated cipher WAGE [3]. In this section, we will first provide a concise description of WAGE. Subsequently, we will present the details of our experiments and the corresponding results.

4.1 Description of WAGE

The authenticated cipher WAGE-$\mathcal{AE}$-128 is built upon the WAGE permutation, which is specifically designed to be lightweight and hardware-friendly. The WAGE permutation operates on a state size of 259 bits over the finite field $\mathbb{F}_{2^7}$. The design of the WAGE function adopts the structure of the (nonlinear) initialization phase of the WG stream cipher family [18]. The designer of WAGE claims that the permutation achieves full bit diffusion in 28 rounds. Due to the complex nonlinear feedback function, the algebraic degree in WAGE grow rapidly. As a result, WAGE exhibits robust resistance against algebraic attacks, such as integral and cube attacks.

The WAGE Permutation. The core components of the WAGE permutation include two different S-boxes (WGP and SB) defined over $\mathbb{F}_{2^7}$, a nonlinear feedback, five word-wise XORs, and a pair of 7-bit round constants (rc_1^i, rc_0^i). Figure 1 presents a high-level overview of the round function of the WAGE permutation. The state consists of 37 7-bit words and is denoted by $S^i = (S_{36}^i, \ldots, S_0^i)$ at the beginning of i-th round. The round function takes as inputs the current state S^i and the round constant tuple (rc_1^i, rc_0^i), and updates the state in a Galois NLFSR fashion with the following three steps:

1. Computing linear feedback. The feedback computation is given by

$$fb = S_{31}^i \oplus S_{30}^i \oplus S_{26}^i \oplus S_{24}^i \oplus S_{19}^i \oplus S_{13}^i \oplus S_{12}^i \oplus S_8^i \oplus S_6^i \oplus (\omega \otimes S_0^i).$$

where the representation of $\omega \otimes x$ is given by

$$\omega \otimes (x_0, x_1, x_2, x_3, x_4, x_5, x_6) \rightarrow (x_6, x_0 \oplus x_6, x_1 \oplus x_6, x_2 \oplus x_6, x_3, x_4, x_5).$$

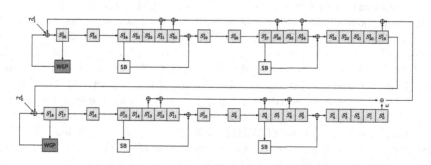

Fig. 1. A block diagram of the WAGE's round function

2. Updating intermediate words and adding round constants.

$$S_5^i \leftarrow S_5^i \oplus SB(S_8^i), S_{11}^i \leftarrow S_{11}^i \oplus SB(S_{15}^i), S_{19}^i \leftarrow S_{19}^i \oplus WGP(S_{18}^i) \oplus rc_0^i$$

$$S_{24}^i \leftarrow S_{24}^i \oplus SB(S_{27}^i), S_{30}^i \leftarrow S_{30}^i \oplus SB(S_{34}^i), \boldsymbol{fb} \leftarrow \boldsymbol{fb} \oplus WGP(S_{36}^i) \oplus rc_1^i.$$

3. Shifting the register contents and update the last word.

$$S_j^{i+1} \leftarrow S_{j+1}^i, j \in 0, 1, \ldots, 35,$$

$$S_{36}^{i+1} \leftarrow \boldsymbol{fb}.$$

The WGP S-box is a unique Welch-Gong permutation that achieves low differential uniformity and high nonlinearity [9,17]. The SB S-box is constructed iteratively using nonlinear transformations and bit permutations. The maximum algebraic degree of both S-boxes is 6. The hexadecimal representations of the WGP and SB S-boxes are provided in Table 1 and Table 2, respectively, in a row-major order. Round constants are generated by an LFSR of length 7 with feedback polynomial $x^7 + x + 1$. The WAGE permutation contains 111 rounds in total.

Table 1. WGP's hexadecimal representation

00	12	0a	4b	66	0c	48	73	79	3e	61	51	01	15	17	0e
7e	33	68	36	42	35	37	5e	53	4c	3f	54	58	6e	56	2a
1d	25	6d	65	5b	71	2f	20	06	18	29	3a	0d	7a	6c	1b
19	43	70	41	49	22	77	60	4f	45	55	02	63	47	75	2d
40	46	7d	5c	7c	59	26	0b	09	03	57	5d	27	78	30	2e
44	52	3b	08	67	2c	5	6b	2b	1a	21	38	07	0f	4a	11
50	6a	28	31	10	4d	5f	72	39	16	5a	13	04	3c	34	1f
76	1e	14	23	1c	32	4e	7b	24	74	7f	3d	69	64	62	6f

The Authenticated Cipher WAGE-$\mathcal{AE}$-128. WAGE operates in the unified sponge duplex mode to provide authenticated encryption with associated data functionality. The authenticated cipher WAGE-$\mathcal{AE}$-128 supports key, nonce, and tag sizes of 128 bits, and processes 64 bits per call of the WAGE permutation. The 259-bit internal state is represented as a string $(\boldsymbol{X}, \boldsymbol{Y})$, where $\boldsymbol{X}$ and $\boldsymbol{Y}$ denote the 64-bit rate and 195-bit capacity part of the state, respectively. Specifically, the rate part contains 9 words, $S_{8,9,15,16,18,27,28,34,35}$, and the first bit of word S_{36}. With a sponge constraint, we can only get the value of the rate part.

During the initialization of WAGE-$\mathcal{AE}$-128, the state is first loaded with a 128-bit nonce $\boldsymbol{N} = (n_0, \ldots, n_{127})$ and a 128-bit key $\boldsymbol{K} = (k_0, \ldots, k_{127})$. The key $\boldsymbol{K}$ is then divided into two key blocks, $\boldsymbol{K}_0 = k_0, \ldots, k_{63}$ and $\boldsymbol{K}_1 = k_{64}, \ldots, k_{127}$.

Table 2. SB's hexadecimal representation

2e	1c	6d	2b	35	07	7f	3b	28	08	0b	5f	31	11	1b	4d
6e	54	0d	09	1f	45	75	53	6a	5d	61	00	04	78	06	1e
37	6f	2f	49	64	34	7d	19	39	33	43	57	60	62	13	05
77	47	4f	4b	1d	2d	24	48	74	58	25	5e	5a	76	41	42
27	3e	6c	01	2c	3c	4e	1a	21	2a	0a	55	3a	38	18	7e
0c	63	67	56	50	7c	32	7a	68	02	6b	17	7b	59	71	0f
30	10	22	3d	40	69	52	14	36	44	46	03	16	65	66	72
12	0e	29	4a	4c	70	15	26	79	51	23	3f	73	5b	20	5c

The two key blocks are then absorbed into the state with the WAGE permutation applied each time. The steps of initialization are described as follows:

$$(X, Y) \leftarrow WAGE(load(N, K))$$
$$(X, Y) \leftarrow WAGE(X \oplus K_i, Y), i = 0, 1,$$

The *load* function is explicitly given in Table 3. In Table 3, we denote $k_i, k_{i+1}, \ldots, k_{i+t}$ as k_{i-i+t}. In this paper, we will focus on the attack of the WAGE permutation and the initialization phase of WAGE-$\mathcal{AE}$-128. Consequently, we will not provide a detailed decription of other aspects of WAGE-$\mathcal{AE}$-128. Readers who are interested can refer to [3] for more information.

Table 3. The $load(N, K)$ procedure of WAGE-$\mathcal{AE}$-128.

S_0	S_1	S_2	S_3	S_4	S_5	S_6	S_7
k_{0-6}	k_{14-20}	k_{28-34}	k_{42-48}	k_{56-62}	k_{71-77}	k_{85-91}	k_{99-105}

S_8	S_9	S_{10}	S_{11}	S_{12}	S_{13}	S_{14}	S_{15}
$k_{113-119}$	n_{7-13}	n_{21-27}	n_{35-41}	n_{49-55}	n_{64-70}	n_{78-84}	n_{92-98}

S_{16}	S_{17}	S_{18}		S_{19}	S_{20}
$n_{120-126}$	$n_{106-112}$	$k_{63}, k_{127}, n_{63}, n_{127}, 0, 0, 0$		k_{7-13}	k_{21-27}

S_{21}	S_{22}	S_{23}	S_{24}	S_{25}	S_{26}	S_{27}	S_{28}
k_{35-41}	k_{49-55}	k_{64-70}	k_{78-84}	k_{92-98}	$k_{106-112}$	$k_{120-126}$	n_{0-6}

S_{29}	S_{30}	S_{31}	S_{32}	S_{33}	S_{34}	S_{35}	S_{36}
n_{14-20}	n_{28-34}	n_{42-48}	n_{56-62}	n_{71-77}	n_{85-91}	n_{99-105}	$n_{113-119}$

4.2 Cube Attacks on WAGE Using MILP

As previously mentioned, the cube attack consists of offline phase and online phase. The most challenging part of the attack lies in constructing useful cubes.

A cube C_I is deemed *"useful"* when it statisfies the condition $|I| + |J| < n$, where $|I|$ is the dimension of cube, $|J|$ is the number of secret variables involved in its superpoly and n is the length of key. Once a useful cube is obtained, it can be leveraged to construct an effective cube attack. In this section, we will introduce how to construct a theoretical cube attack on WAGE based on our new method. All our experiments were completed on a PC (Intel Core i5-10400 CPU with 6 cores, 16 GB memory, Windows 11). The source code of this work can be found in https://github.com/SJTUwwz/WAGE_cube_attack.git.

Constructing MILP Model. The first step of our attck is to construct MILP model simulating the propagation of division property. Generally, we will construct the MILP model round by round. The round function of WAGE consists of shift, XOR, ω, addition of round constants and S-box operations. The propagation on the first three operations can be fully characterized by two basic rules: COPY and XOR [28]. The corresponding constraint of ω operataion is shown in Algorithm 4. Furthermore, the addition of round constants would not affect the division property. Therefore, our focus is to find the FLIICs of nonlinear components, WGP and SB, to construct the characterization of the entire round function.

Algorithm 4. MILP model for the ω operation in WAGE

1: **procedure** ω(MILP model M, input variables $\boldsymbol{x}$, output variables $\boldsymbol{y}$)
2:     $M.var \leftarrow a_1, a_2, a_3, a_4$ as binary.
3:     $M.con \leftarrow a_1 + a_2 + a_3 + a_4 = x_6$
4:     $M.con \leftarrow y_0 = a_0$
5:     **for** $i \in \{4, 5, 6\}$ **do**
6:         $M.con \leftarrow y_i = x_{i-1}$
7:     **end for**
8:     **for** $i \in \{1, 2, 3\}$ **do**
9:         $M.con \leftarrow y_i = x_{i-1} + a_i$
10:     **end for**
11: **end procedure**

Firstly, we calculate the ANFs of WGP and SB using the Möbius transform. With the Algorithm 2 in [28], we can obtain the division trails of WGP and SB, which we denote as S_{WGP} and S_{SB}, respectively. Subsequently, we use SageMath [22] to generate the H-representations and candidate inequalities of S_{WGP} and S_{SB}. During this process, we obtain $3,204$ candidate inequalities for S_{WGP} and $400,781$ for S_{SB}. Given the size of the SCP problem, we employ different techniques to compute the minimal FLIIC of each set. Specifically, we compute the minimal FLIIC of S_{WGP} with MILP techniques and find a FLIIC with 14 inequalities. For S_{SB}, we use a greedy algorithm and obtain a FLIIC with 46 inequalities. Based on the existing conditions, we can begin building the overall model of WAGE. For ease of description, we will use the notation $OP(inputvariable, outputvariable)$ to represent the specific constraints that need to be added for a given operation. The details of the process are shown in Algorithm 5.

In Algorithm 5, $A - H, Z_1, Z_2$ are temporary 7-bit variables. Lines 4–35 corresponds to the propagation of division trail through round function. The lines 5–15, 16–33, and 34 correspond to the three steps of the round function: linear feedback calculation, intermediate state update, and byte shifting, respectively. Upon this model, we can incorporate additional input constraints and objective functions to enable functionality such as algebraic degree estimation and secret variables evaluation.

Constructing Useful Cubes and Key Recovery. In cube attacks, it is important to construct useful cubes with simple superpoly. Usually, superpoly with lower algebraic degrees tends to be simpler and more likely to satisfy $|I| + |J| < n$. A heuristic algorithm of constructing cube with linear super-poly was proposed in [30]. Moreover, they extended a small cube by adding "steep variable" and "gentle variable" properly. However, directly applying their method on WAGE is not practical due to the length of nonce. To address this challenge, we propose the idea of "steep word variable". The definition is given as follow.

Definition 4 (Steep Word Variable). *Let $I = \{v_{i_1}, v_{i_2}, \ldots, v_{i_l}\}$ be a set containing $l \times w$ cube variables, where w is the length of word. Then, a word $t \in B$ is called a steep word variable of I if*

$$ds(I \cup \{t\}) = \min\{ds(I \cup \{v\})|v \in B\},$$

where $B = \{v_0, v_1, \ldots, v_{m-1}\}\backslash I$ and $ds(I)$ is the degree of the superpoly of I.

We opt for the word-based version of "steep variable" for several reasons. Firstly, the nonce length of the WAGE is 128 bits, which leads to an unmanageably large search space if we include bit-by-bit. Secondly, the WAGE itself is word-based and searching at the word level is already sufficiently precise. Finally, from an analysis of division property, when the input division property of an S-box is **1**, its output division property will also be **1**, which facilitates a longer division trails.

In this paper, we would use the degree evaluation method based on division property to determine the steep word variable. Based on the MILP model constructed by Algorithm 5, we present Algorithm 6 to estimate the algebraic degree of superpoly on WAGE.

During the process of constructing cubes, we employ an algorithm similar to depth-first search. Specifically, in each iteration, we add the steep word variable to the cube. This process is similar to the first stage of the Algorithm 3 in [30]. This method will help us find the "path" of fastest algebraic degree descent. Unlike the approach in [30], we start from empty set directly. Table 3 indicates that the nonce words are S_{9-17} and S_{28-36}, from which we can select cube variables only. Since WAGE adopts an NLFSR based design, the word at position

---

Algorithm 5. MILP model for the R round WAGE permutation

1: **procedure** $WAGEModel$(The number of round R, the index of target bit $tindex$)
2:     Prepare empty MILP model M
3:     $M.var \leftarrow S^0 = (S_0^0, \ldots, S_{258}^0)$ as binary $\triangleright S^0 = (S_0^0, \ldots, S_{36}^0)$
4:     **for** $r = 0$ to $R - 1$ **do**
5:         $M.var \leftarrow A = (a_0, \ldots, a_6)$ as binary
6:         $M.con \leftarrow \omega(S_0^0, A)$
7:         $XorExpr = [A]$
8:         **for** $i \in \{6, 8, 12, 13, 19, 24, 26, 30, 31\}$ **do**
9:             $M.var \leftarrow B = (b_0, \ldots, b_6), C = (c_0, \ldots, c_6)$ as binary
10:             $M.con \leftarrow COPY(S_i^r, (B, C))$
11:             $S_i^r = B$
12:             $XorExpr.append(C)$
13:         **end for**
14:         $M.var \leftarrow fb = (fb_0, \ldots, fb_6)$ as binary
15:         $M.con \leftarrow XOR(XorExpr, fb)$
16:         **for** $(i_1, i_2) \in \{(5, 8), (11, 15), (24, 27), (30, 34)\}$ **do**
17:             $M.var \leftarrow D = (d_0, \ldots, d_6), E = (e_0, \ldots, e_6)$ as binary
18:             $M.con \leftarrow COPY(S_{i_2}^r, (E, F))$
19:             $S_{i_2}^r = E$
20:             $M.var \leftarrow G = (g_0, \ldots, g_6), H = (h_0, \ldots, h_6)$
21:             $M.con \leftarrow SB(S_{i_1}^r, G)$
22:             $M.con \leftarrow XOR((G, F), H)$
23:             $S_{i_1}^r = H$
24:         **end for**
25:         **for** $(Z_1, Z_2) \in \{(S_{18}^r, S_{19}^r), (fb, S_{36}^r)\}$ **do**
26:             $M.var \leftarrow D = (d_0, \ldots, d_6), E = (e_0, \ldots, e_6)$ as binary
27:             $M.con \leftarrow COPY(Z_2, (E, F))$
28:             $Z_2 = E$
29:             $M.var \leftarrow G = (g_0, \ldots, g_6), H = (h_0, \ldots, h_6)$
30:             $M.con \leftarrow WGP(Z_1, G)$
31:             $M.con \leftarrow XOR((G, F), H)$
32:             $Z_1 = H$
33:         **end for**
34:         $S^{r+1} = (S_1^r, S_2^r, \ldots, S_{36}^r, fb)$
35:     **end for**
36:     **for** i from 0 to 258 **do**
37:         **if** $i \neq tindex$ **then**
38:             $M.con \leftarrow S_i^R = 0$
39:         **else**
40:             $M.con \leftarrow S_i^R = 1$
41:         **end if**
42:     **end for**
43: **end procedure**

Algorithm 6. MILP model for the R round WAGE permutation

1: **procedure** $WAGEDeg$(cube indices I, The number of round R, the index of target bit $tindex$)
2:　　$M \leftarrow WAGEModel(R, tindex)$
3:　　$K \leftarrow \{0, 1, \ldots, 62\} \cup \{126, 127\} \cup \{133, 134, \ldots, 195\}$
4:　　$N \leftarrow \{63, 64, \ldots, 125\} \cup \{128, 129\} \cup \{196, 197, \ldots, 258\}$
5:　　$M.con \leftarrow S_i^0 = 1$ for all $i \in I$
6:　　$M.con \leftarrow S_i^0 = 0$ for all $i \in N - I$
7:　　**for** $i \in \{130, 131, 132\}$ **do**
8:　　　　$M.con \leftarrow S_i^0 = 0$
9:　　**end for**
10:　　Set the objective function $M.obj \leftarrow \max \sum_{i \in K} S_i^0$
11:　　Solve MILP model M
12:　　**return** The solution of M
13: **end procedure**

---

0 is mixed at a slower rate slower than others. With a sponge constraint, we can only get the value of $S_{8,9,15,16,18,27,28,34,35}$, and the first bit of word S_{36}. With division property, we successfully demonstrate that WAGE achieves full bit diffusion in 28 rounds. Besides, we also demonstrate that S_8 achieves full bit diffusion in 23 rounds. Therefore, when constructing cube, we focus output position on S_0 and S_8. By applying our method, we successfully construct some useful cubes at S_0 and S_8 in 29 rounds and 24 rounds, respectively. The details of cubes are shown in Table 4.

Table 4. Useful cubes constructed by our method

Position	Round	Cube variables	Index of involved key bit	Deg	$|J|$	$|I|+|J|$
S_0	29	S_{9-16}	7–13,21–27,35–41,49–	48	65	121
		$S_{9-15,17}$	55,63–70,			
S_8	24	S_{9-16}	78–84,92–98,106–			
		$S_{9-15,17}$	112,120–127			

To compared our method with Todo's method, we conducted the same experiments using Todo's method. We found that Todo's method resulted in unresponsiveness when the cube was $S_{9-15,17}$, the round number was 29 and the indices of target bit were 0 and 6. A similar situation occurred when the cube was S_{9-16} and the indices of target bit were 2 and 5. This phenomenon demonstrates the superiority of our method.

From Table 4, we know that each useful cube satisfies $|I| + |J| = 121 < 128$. Moreover, we can compute 7 superpolies simultaneously because their involved key bits are the same. Therefore, we can obtain 7 superpolies with $2^{|I|} \times 7 \times \binom{|J|}{\leq d} \approx 2^{123.81}$ requests. With the assumption in [24], it is hopeful that we can recover

7 bits secret information from 7 superpolies. Although there is evidence [27,29] suggesting that the assumptions would not hold true in certain cases, it is worth nothing that these cases often occur when the superpoly has low algebraic degree and relates to few secret variables. However, the superpoly we found has high algebraic degree and numerous related secret variables, making it highly unlikely to degenerate into a constant function. Besides, it would be easy to find a non-cube constant that makes the superpoly a balanced function. Hence, we can use these useful cubes to implement cube attacks on WAGE.

For the sake of time complexity, when conducting cube attacks on WAGE, we only need to use one cube from the Table 4. During the offline phase, 7 balanced superpolies are obtained through $2^{123.81}$ requests. In the online phase, we can recover 7 bits secret infromation based on the superpolies and then perform a exhaustive search on the remaining 121 bits key information. The time complexity is $2^{123.81} + 2^{121} \approx 2^{124}$. In summary, we have successfully mounted cube attacks on 29-round WAGE, as well as on 24-round WAGE with a sponge constraint.

5   Conclusion

In this paper, we proposed an improved method for evaluating secret variables in cube attacks. Our method's improvement lies in explicitly breaking down difficult-to-solve problems into sub-problems, which helps to avoid the issue of unresponsiveness to a certain extent. As an application, we used our improved method to attack WAGE and successfully mounted two cube attacks on 29-round WAGE and 24-round WAGE with a sponge constraint. Although this result does not violate WAGE's security claims, it provides a clear security level of WAGE against cube attacks. We also believe that our improved method will facilitate the implementation of cube attacks on other ciphers.

Acknowledgements. We are grateful to Xiutao Feng and Shengyuan Xu for their valuable suggestions on FLIIC. We also thank the anonymous reviewers for their helpful comments. The work of Deng Tang was supported in part by the National Key Research and Development Project 2020YFA0712300 and NSFC (No. 62272303).

References

1. Abdelkhalek, A., Sasaki, Y., Todo, Y., Tolba, M., Youssef, A.M.: MILP modeling for (large) s-boxes to optimize probability of differential characteristics. IACR Trans. Symmetric Cryptol. **2017**(4), 99–129 (2017). https://doi.org/10.13154/tosc.v2017.i4.99-129
2. Ågren, M., Hell, M., Johansson, T., Meier, W.: Grain-128a: a new version of grain-128 with optional authentication. Int. J. Wirel. Mob. Comput. **5**(1), 48–59 (2011). https://doi.org/10.1504/IJWMC.2011.044106

3. AlTawy, R., Gong, G., Mandal, K., Rohit, R.: WAGE: an authenticated encryption with a twist. IACR Trans. Symmetric Cryptol. **2020**(S1), 132–159 (2020). https://doi.org/10.13154/tosc.v2020.iS1.132-159

4. De Canniére, C., Preneel, B.: Trivium. In: Robshaw, M., Billet, O. (eds.) New Stream Cipher Designs. LNCS, vol. 4986, pp. 244–266. Springer, Heidelberg (2008). https://doi.org/10.1007/978-3-540-68351-3_18

5. Derbez, P., Fouque, P.: Increasing precision of division property. IACR Trans. Symmetric Cryptol. **2020**(4), 173–194 (2020). https://doi.org/10.46586/tosc.v2020.i4.173-194

6. Dinur, I., Shamir, A.: Cube attacks on tweakable black box polynomials. In: Joux, A. (ed.) EUROCRYPT 2009. LNCS, vol. 5479, pp. 278–299. Springer, Heidelberg (2009). https://doi.org/10.1007/978-3-642-01001-9_16

7. Fei, Y., et al.: Correlation power analysis and higher-order masking implementation of WAGE. In: Dunkelman, O., Jacobson, Jr., M.J., O'Flynn, C. (eds.) SAC 2020. LNCS, vol. 12804, pp. 593–614. Springer, Cham (2021). https://doi.org/10.1007/978-3-030-81652-0_23

8. Feng, X., Tian, Y., Wang, Y., Xu, S., Zhang, A.: Full linear integer inequality characterization of set over $\mathbb{Z}_2^n$. CSTR:32003.36.ChinaXiv. 202210.00055.V2 (2023). http://www.chinaxiv.org/abs/202210.00055

9. Gong, G., Youssef, A.M.: Cryptographic properties of the welch-gong transformation sequence generators. IEEE Trans. Inf. Theory **48**(11), 2837–2846 (2002). https://doi.org/10.1109/TIT.2002.804043

10. Hao, Y., Leander, G., Meier, W., Todo, Y., Wang, Q.: Modeling for three-subset division property without unknown subset. In: Canteaut, A., Ishai, Y. (eds.) EUROCRYPT 2020. LNCS, vol. 12105, pp. 466–495. Springer, Cham (2020). https://doi.org/10.1007/978-3-030-45721-1_17

11. Hu, K., Sun, S., Todo, Y., Wang, M., Wang, Q.: Massive superpoly recovery with nested monomial predictions. In: Tibouchi, M., Wang, H. (eds.) ASIACRYPT 2021. LNCS, vol. 13090, pp. 392–421. Springer, Cham (2021). https://doi.org/10.1007/978-3-030-92062-3_14

12. Hu, K., Sun, S., Wang, M., Wang, Q.: An algebraic formulation of the division property: revisiting degree evaluations, cube attacks, and key-independent sums. In: Moriai, S., Wang, H. (eds.) ASIACRYPT 2020. LNCS, vol. 12491, pp. 446–476. Springer, Cham (2020). https://doi.org/10.1007/978-3-030-64837-4_15

13. Hu, K., Wang, Q., Wang, M.: Finding bit-based division property for ciphers with complex linear layers. IACR Trans. Symmetric Cryptol. **2020**(1), 396–424 (2020). https://doi.org/10.13154/tosc.v2020.i1.396-424

14. Knudsen, L., Wagner, D.: Integral cryptanalysis. In: Daemen, J., Rijmen, V. (eds.) FSE 2002. LNCS, vol. 2365, pp. 112–127. Springer, Heidelberg (2002). https://doi.org/10.1007/3-540-45661-9_9

15. Lai, X.: Higher order derivatives and differential cryptanalysis. In: Communications and Cryptography: Two Sides of One Tapestry, pp. 227–233 (1994)

16. Li, T., Sun, Y.: Superball: a new approach for MILP modelings of boolean functions. IACR Trans. Symmetric Cryptol. **2022**(3), 341–367 (2022). https://doi.org/10.46586/tosc.v2022.i3.341-367

17. Mandal, K., Gong, G., Fan, X., Aagaard, M.D.: Optimal parameters for the WG stream cipher family. Cryptogr. Commun. **6**(2), 117–135 (2014). https://doi.org/10.1007/s12095-013-0091-0

18. Nawaz, Y., Gong, G.: WG: a family of stream ciphers with designed randomness properties. Inf. Sci. **178**(7), 1903–1916 (2008). https://doi.org/10.1016/j.ins.2007.12.002

378   W. Wang et al.

19. Sasaki, Yu., Todo, Y.: New impossible differential search tool from design and cryptanalysis aspects. In: Coron, J.-S., Nielsen, J.B. (eds.) EUROCRYPT 2017. LNCS, vol. 10212, pp. 185–215. Springer, Cham (2017). https://doi.org/10.1007/978-3-319-56617-7_7

20. Sun, L., Wang, W., Wang, M.: Automatic search of bit-based division property for arx ciphers and word-based division property. In: Takagi, T., Peyrin, T. (eds.) ASIACRYPT 2017. LNCS, vol. 10624, pp. 128–157. Springer, Cham (2017). https://doi.org/10.1007/978-3-319-70694-8_5

21. Sun, S., Hu, L., Wang, P., Qiao, K., Ma, X., Song, L.: Automatic security evaluation and (Related-key) differential characteristic search: application to SIMON, PRESENT, LBlock, DES(L) and other bit-oriented block ciphers. In: Sarkar, P., Iwata, T. (eds.) ASIACRYPT 2014. LNCS, vol. 8873, pp. 158–178. Springer, Heidelberg (2014). https://doi.org/10.1007/978-3-662-45611-8_9

22. The Sage Developers: SageMath, the Sage Mathematics Software System (Version 9.1) (2020). https://www.sagemath.org

23. Todo, Y.: Structural evaluation by generalized integral property. In: Oswald, E., Fischlin, M. (eds.) EUROCRYPT 2015. LNCS, vol. 9056, pp. 287–314. Springer, Heidelberg (2015). https://doi.org/10.1007/978-3-662-46800-5_12

24. Todo, Y., Isobe, T., Hao, Y., Meier, W.: Cube attacks on non-blackbox polynomials based on division property. In: Katz, J., Shacham, H. (eds.) CRYPTO 2017. LNCS, vol. 10403, pp. 250–279. Springer, Cham (2017). https://doi.org/10.1007/978-3-319-63697-9_9

25. Todo, Y., Morii, M.: Bit-based division property and application to SIMON family. In: Peyrin, T. (ed.) FSE 2016. LNCS, vol. 9783, pp. 357–377. Springer, Heidelberg (2016). https://doi.org/10.1007/978-3-662-52993-5_18

26. Wang, Q., Hao, Y., Todo, Y., Li, C., Isobe, T., Meier, W.: Improved division property based cube attacks exploiting algebraic properties of superpoly. In: Shacham, H., Boldyreva, A. (eds.) CRYPTO 2018. LNCS, vol. 10991, pp. 275–305. Springer, Cham (2018). https://doi.org/10.1007/978-3-319-96884-1_10

27. Wang, S., Hu, B., Guan, J., Zhang, K., Shi, T.: MILP-aided method of searching division property using three subsets and applications. In: Galbraith, S.D., Moriai, S. (eds.) ASIACRYPT 2019. LNCS, vol. 11923, pp. 398–427. Springer, Cham (2019). https://doi.org/10.1007/978-3-030-34618-8_14

28. Xiang, Z., Zhang, W., Bao, Z., Lin, D.: Applying MILP method to searching integral distinguishers based on division property for 6 lightweight block ciphers. In: Cheon, J.H., Takagi, T. (eds.) ASIACRYPT 2016. LNCS, vol. 10031, pp. 648–678. Springer, Heidelberg (2016). https://doi.org/10.1007/978-3-662-53887-6_24

29. Ye, C., Tian, T.: Revisit division property based cube attacks: key-recovery or distinguishing attacks? IACR Trans. Symmetric Cryptol. 2019(3), 81–102 (2019). https://doi.org/10.13154/tosc.v2019.i3.81-102

30. Ye, C.-D., Tian, T.: A practical key-recovery attack on 805-round trivium. In: Tibouchi, M., Wang, H. (eds.) ASIACRYPT 2021. LNCS, vol. 13090, pp. 187–213. Springer, Cham (2021). https://doi.org/10.1007/978-3-030-92062-3_7

Exploring Emotion Trends in Product Reviews: A Multi-modal Analysis with Malicious Comment Filtering and User Privacy Protection

Biyun Chen[1,2] , Lin Jiang[1] , Xin Pan[3], Guoquan Zhou[1], Aihua Sun[1], and Dafang Li[4(✉)]

[1] Yancheng Teachers University, Yancheng 224002, China
`chenby@yctu.edu.cn`
[2] Nanjing University of Posts and Telecommunications, Nanjing 210023, China
[3] Aviation University Air Force, Changchun 130022, China
[4] Nanjing University of Finance and Economics, Nanjing 210023, China
`df.li@nufe.edu.cn`

Abstract. In this paper, we introduce an innovative approach that combines multi-modal sentiment analysis with mechanisms for safeguarding user information security. Our objective is to effectively combat harmful comments and precisely forecast trends in product sentiment. Initially, we detect and secure sensitive user information by implementing regular expressions to ensure user confidentiality and security. First, we apply statistical analysis and K-means++ algorithms to screen users who post malicious reviews. Next, we develop a novel multi-modal sentiment analysis and prediction model that incorporates the pre-trained BERT model and Swin Transformer model for feature extraction from comment text and image data. Furthermore, the expressive capability of image features is enhanced with the aid of the SENet model. We input the image features, improved by the SENet model, as well as the text features, extracted by the BERT model, into the Transformer model for fusion, and the classification probability is determined using the SoftMax function. We employ the Prophet method to combine sentiment indicators and time series features, which allows us to predict the upcoming sentiment trends of product reviews. The algorithm is implemented in the evaluation of the Amazon book review datasets and is compared to other algorithms such as Bert, yielding an accuracy of 94.15%. This study is of significant value for enabling real-time monitoring of product sentiment trends, filtering malicious reviews, and enhancing both product management and user experience.

Keywords: Multi-modal Sentiment Analysis · Time Series Forecasting · Malicious Criticism Classification · Data Privacy and Security

1 Introduction

Sentiment analysis provides insight into users' preferences and emotional attitudes towards items or content. Predicting customer sentiment trends based on sentiment analysis is important for corporations to provide valuable information for consumer insights,

C. Ge and M. Yung (Eds.): Inscrypt 2023, LNCS 14526, pp. 379–396, 2024.
https://doi.org/10.1007/978-981-97-0942-7_19

market feedback, brand management and opinion management. The rise of social media has generated a rise in multi-modal comments, such as images, text, audio and more. This shift towards multi-modal sentiment analysis of a single modality data has been observed [1, 2]. By taking a holistic view of the data from different modalities, it becomes possible to achieve a more detailed and accurate understanding of the user's sentiment and attitude towards the product. Recent research has concentrated on the combination of image and text, given that review data commonly exists in both formats.

Textual sentiment analysis involves analyzing and processing written content to determine the emotional information or sentiment contained within it. This is an essential application within the field of Natural Language Processing, as it enables the interpretation and comprehension of affective tendencies and emotional states in written texts. The primary methods employed are the Lexicon-based approach [3], the machine learning based approach [4], and a hybrid approach that combines the two [5]. Lexicon-based approaches are split into dictionary-based [6–11] and corpus-based methods [12–14]. While the Lexicon-based model has advantages in simplicity and efficiency, it does have limitations in dealing with complex sentiment, context, and lexical deletions. These limitations often require the use of other methods, such as machine learning, to improve processing. Machine learning methods are widely employed in text sentiment analysis, particularly to model complex sentiment. Nonetheless, they usually necessitate substantial quantities of training data and feature engineering and exhibit comparatively weak model interpretability.

Image visual sentiment analysis involves examining the composition of an image with the objective of identifying and interpreting the emotional state conveyed by its contents. Rule-based and machine learning-based methods are two categories of techniques used in this process. A Transformer model proposed by Bengio's team has revolutionized the field, leveraging an attention mechanism to boost deep learning models' training speed. As a result, this approach is now widely adopted in various fields [15]. As Swin Transformer and Bert are deep learning frameworks based on Transformer, it is only necessary to extract the embedded features of images and texts and input them into the Transformer to achieve satisfactory results for sentiment analysis. A deep bidirectional representation model is pre-trained in an unsupervised manner by codecs using unlabeled features, and ultimately, the user's sentiment index is obtained through supervised fine-tuning.

Currently, multi-modal sentiment trend prediction based on multi-modal sentiment faces some challenges, such as the difficulty of correlation analysis between different modal data and a large number of malicious false comments that lead to a decrease in the credibility of the model, etc. At the same time, we should be aware that we must ensure that we comply with relevant privacy legislation when collecting, storing and processing data. For personally identifiable information, additional privacy measures are required.

And the contributions of this paper are as follows:

(1) We have established a security mechanism for user information that preserves the use of regular expressions to detect and protect user information such as phone numbers, addresses, e-mail and IP addresses.

(2) We selected key statistical features of time difference as well as ratings based on users' reading cycles and book preferences, and used cluster analysis to filter malicious user reviews;

(3) We propose a novel multi-modal sentiment analysis prediction. By combining the BERT model and the Swin Transformer model with feature enhancement and fusion using the SENet model, the intrinsic relationship between text and images is captured more accurately, thus improving the performance and accuracy of the sentiment analysis task;

(4) Incorporate time series to predict existing consumer sentiment, analyze future consumer sentiment trends, and support sentiment-driven product optimization and marketing strategy development.

The rest of the paper is organized as follows. First, we will discuss current work in sentiment analysis in Sect. 2, followed by presenting the details of our multi-modal sentiment analysis model in Sect. 3. The experimental setting and evaluation metrics will be presented in Sect. 4, Sect. 5 analyzes and discusses the experimental results, while the conclusions and future work will be presented in Sect. 6.

2 Related Work

2.1 Image Visual Sentiment Analysis

The earliest model proposal for image sentiment analysis was a rule-based approach. Chen et al. [16] utilized object-based conceptual and semantic knowledge to develop a classifier for analyzing sentiments in images. They found connections between objects and their characteristics by extracting adjective-noun pairs (ANPs) from image labels. Yuan et al. [17] proposed the "Sentribute" framework, which provides more explanatory results. Borth et al. [18] developed "Senti-Bank" [19] based on web mining and psychological theories, etc. Rule-based approaches usually rely on a priori knowledge and manually-defined rules, which may not be able to accurately deal with complex sentiment expressions. Machine learning-based methods, on the other hand, utilize a large amount of well-labeled image data for training and construct classifiers or deep neural network models to learn the association between images and emotions [20–22]. In recent years, with the rapid development of deep learning, deep neural network-based methods have made many breakthroughs in visual emotion analysis. These methods can learn higher-level abstract features from raw image data and obtain better emotion classification performance through structures such as convolutional neural networks (CNN) or recurrent neural networks (RNN). For instance, PCNN's end-to-end approach for visual sentiment analysis using fine-tuned convolutional neural networks on Tumblr and Twitter image datasets was introduced by You et al. [23], while Campos et al. [24] suggested utilizing Café Net CNN architecture to extract valuable features for recognizing visual sentiment in Twitter image datasets from social media platforms. In this paper, Swin Transformer based on sliding window mechanism is used for image processing.

2.2 Text Sentiment Analysis

Pang et al. [25] were the pioneers in proposing research on sentiment classification approach using machine learning based approach, they used Naïve Bayes, support vector machines and maximum entropy classifier on IMDB movie review datasets and verified its accuracy. Considering the respective limitations of machine learning and Lexicon-Based Approach, the Lexicon-Based Approach proposed by Poria et al. [26] has been enhanced by integrating machine learning techniques, demonstrating its superior performance deep learning is at the forefront of ongoing research and development Deep learning techniques can achieve more advanced and abstract semantic representations by performing various semantic operations at multiple levels. And incorporate feature extraction into the process of creating the model to decrease the lack of thoroughness and repetition of manually created features [27]. However, deep learning methods require huge datasets and rely on contextual relationships, and pre-trained language representation models such as Bert can integrate left and right contextual information for deep bi-directional linguistic representations to mine the deep features of text reviews [28]. The book review datasets in this paper's experiments has a large sample size and is feature rich, so further fine-tuning based on the pre-trained BERT network on the categorization task is used to extract features to improve the accuracy of sentiment analysis.

2.3   Multi-modal Sentiment Fusion Analysis

The effective utilization of sentiment information in multi-modal user reviews from social media has become a prominent research subject, given the diverse forms of reviews available. This research aims to enhance the accuracy and comprehensiveness of evaluating and recommending commodities. Considering different modalities, multi-modal sentiment fusion can be categorized into: image-text union [29], text-audio [30], video-audio union, and text-image-audio tri-modal union [31, 32]. Morency et al. [31] proposed a sentiment analysis architecture that utilizes video, audio, and text features from the Spanish YouTube datasets. The architecture comprises three modalities. It achieved an accuracy rate of 55.3%. Wollmer et al. [30] designed a multi-modal sentiment analysis framework based on text and audio features and used SVM and Bi-LSTM classifiers to analyze the sentiment of a movie review video datasets with 73.2% accuracy. Poria et al. [33] proposed a deep CNN-based multi-kernel learning method for multi-modal sentiment analysis with 88.6% accuracy. You et al. [29] proposed a method based on sentence parsing and attentional mechanisms for sentiment classification of textual and visual information. They achieved 90.2% accuracy on Getty, Twitter, and VSO-VT datasets. Pereira et al. [32] proposed a method that fuses audio, text, and visual cues for multi-modal sentiment analysis with 84% accuracy. Majumder et al. [34] used a hierarchical fusion feature fusion strategy to design a multi-modal sentiment classification method with 80% accuracy. They conducted experiments on IEMOCAP and CMU-MOSI datasets. Huang et al. [35] developed a framework for multi-modal sentiment analysis of image-text data, which achieved 86.9% accuracy on datasets extracted from Getty Images, Twitter and Flickr. Huddar et al. [36] proposed an attention-based multi-modal context fusion strategy to extract contextual information from IEMOCAP and CMU-MOSI datasets. The research in this paper is based on bimodal fusion of image and text.

3 Algorithm Design

The basic idea of the algorithm in this paper is as follows (Fig. 1):

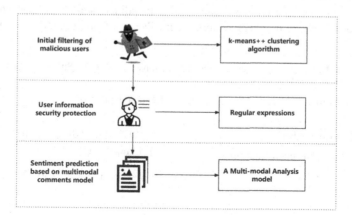

Fig. 1. General framework of the algorithm

First, the selection of key statistical features including time difference and ratings based on users' reading cycle and book preferences is combined with the support vector machine method to filter out malicious user reviews. Second, sensitive user information is protected using the regularization expression. Finally, a multi-modal review prediction model relying on sentiment analysis is established to analyze the future emotional trend of the products.

3.1 Initial Filtering of Malicious Users

To screen for malicious user reviews, we analyzed the review samples in detail and selected five key features for extraction: mean and standard deviation of time difference, mean and standard deviation of rating, and verification of purchase status. The selection of these five features is based on typical characterization of malicious user reviews and research experience. The time difference and rating reflect the reviewer's behavioral pattern and evaluation attitude, while the verified purchase status provides information about the reviewer's authentication. In order to facilitate the modeling, the data features are analyzed to see whether the distribution of features is uniform or not, if not, Box-Cox transform is used with the following Eq. (1).

$$y(\lambda) = \begin{cases} \frac{y^{\lambda}-1}{\lambda}, & \text{if } \lambda \neq 0 \\ log(y), & \text{if } \lambda = 0 \end{cases} \tag{1}$$

where y is the normalized input feature matrix. λ It is our features that determine the form of the transformation. At that time $\lambda = 0$, the logarithmic transformation is used; when $\lambda \neq 0$, power transformation is used. The processed data is easy to model and then the review samples are classified into different clusters using the k-means++ clustering algorithm.

3.2 User Information Security Protection

The use of regular expressions can be effective in detecting and protecting user information and ensuring user privacy and security. Regular expressions are powerful text matching and processing tools that can be used to validate and extract data in specific formats, such as phone numbers, addresses, emails, and IP addresses (Table 1).

Table 1. Examples of Regularized Expressions for Common Phone Numbers

Regular expressions for common phone number formats	Regular expression
for the US phone number	^(\ +?1)?(\([-)\.]?\d{3}\)?[-\.)]?){2}\d{4}$
Chinese mainland the phone number	^(1[3–9]\d{9})$
landline phone number	^0\d{2,3}-\d{7,8}(-\d{1,6})?$

3.3 Sentiment Prediction Based on Multi-modal Comments Model

The framework of the multi-modal sentiment analysis prediction algorithm is shown in Fig. 2. Firstly, sentiment classification is conducted on the text data employing Text-Blob to create novel features, with BERT employed to extract the embedded feature matrix for combination classification. Then, the uploaded image data uses Swin Transformer to extract the embedded feature matrix. The Transformer processes both the embedded feature matrices of the text and image data for sentiment analysis, producing sentiment indicators. The sentiment indicators are subsequently subjected to time clustering, and sentiment prediction is carried out.

Multi-modal Emotion Feature Extraction

Firstly, text sentiment feature extraction is carried out, in this paper, Text Blob is used for initial annotation, and lexicality, negation, degree adverbs, punctuation and sentiment symbols are considered comprehensively in calculating the sentiment value. In each text message, the 'sentiment' attribute returns a named tuple in the form of "Sentiment (polarity, subjectivity)". After labeling, this paper adopts Word Piece algorithm in Bert for word vector encoding training, and finally extracts the deep features of text emotion. Then image emotion feature extraction, first of all need to extract the features in multiple images, this paper uses Swin Transformer model is used to process the image input, so as to extract the high dimensional features in the image.

Multi-modal Feature Fusion

For text input, we obtained the text embedding of the BERT model and used it as input for subsequent processing. For image input, after processing by Swin Transformer model, we obtain the visual embedding. In order to further improve the expression of image features, this paper introduces the SENet model to provide richer information for the subsequent feature fusion process. Next, we pass the visual embeddings enhanced by

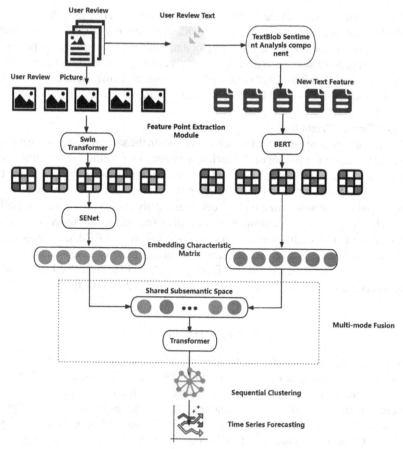

Fig. 2. Framework of the multi-modal sentiment analysis prediction algorithm

the SENet model and the text embeddings extracted by the BERT model to the Concat-DenseSE block to achieve feature fusion. The Concat-DenseSE block first splices the two embeddings in terms of feature dimensions, and then performs dimensionality transformations and dimensionality reduction through the linear layer to obtain the fused feature representation. Then, the fused feature representation is again augmented by the SENet model to further enhance the feature representation. Finally, the Transformer model is used for feature training and learning classification. By combining the BERT model and the Swin Transformer model and utilizing the SENet model for feature enhancement and fusion, we are able to more accurately capture the intrinsic relationship between text and images, thus improving the performance and accuracy of the sentiment analysis task.

Time Series Clustering

In this paper, K-Shape algorithm is used for time series clustering analysis. By applying the K-Shape algorithm for time series clustering analysis, time series with similar sentiment change trends can be grouped into the same cluster. This helps to identify underlying patterns in the review data and provides a deeper understanding of sentiment change patterns. By analyzing the clustering of data within the same day, it is possible to obtain comprehensive sentiment data for the day's comment collection. Such an analysis can provide insights into the overall sentiment trends and characteristics of the day's review content, helping to provide a deeper understanding of the day's review collection.

Affective Timing Prediction

In the case where a large number of reviews exist within the same day, and there may still be discontinuities in the timing of the review data after integrating the data through K-Shape clustering analysis, we use the additional Prophet framework to forecast the time series data. Prophet is a process of forecasting time series data based on an additional model of nonlinear trends with annual, weekly, and daily seasonality as well as holiday effects. The design and implementation of Prophet focuses on circumventing several drawbacks present in traditional time series models such as ARIMA, such as insufficient handling of anomalous data, difficulty in modeling trends and seasonal variations, etc. Prophet is the time-series additive model, which can be given by Eq. 2, and the Prophet algorithm is the one that is fitted to cumulatively obtain the time-series forecast values.

$$y(t) = g(t) + s(t) + h(t) + \varepsilon(t) \tag{2}$$

In this model, $g(t)$ represents the trend of the time series in terms of non-periodicity; whereas $s(t)$ represents the cyclical or seasonal term, which is usually used in cycles measured in weeks or years; and $h(t)$ represents the holiday term, which denotes the impact of potential, non-fixed-period holidays on the predicted values; $\varepsilon(t)$ i.e., the error term or known as the residual term, which represents the fluctuations not predicted by the model. $\varepsilon(t)$ Obeying the Gaussian distribution, in this paper $g(t)$ employs a segmented linear function to predict the general trend of future sentiment.

4   Experimental Environment and the Evaluation Index

4.1   Test Environment

The hardware and software platform are a PC using Inter Core I7-9803.33 GHz, with a GPU using GTX 3090 and 32G memory. The experimental conditions are listed The experimental conditions are listed in Table 2.

4.2   Evaluation Indicators

This study selected traditional evaluation indexes: precision, recall rate, accuracy, and scoring. The model's judgment result is indicated by P(Positive) and N(Negative), while the correctness of the judgment result is indicated by T(True) and F(False). The symbols

Table 2. Experimental hardware and software environment

Heading level	Name	Edition
hardware environment	CPU	Intel i7-980 $\times$ 3.33
	GPUs	GTX 3090
	Internal storage	32G
	operating system	Windows 10
software environment	Machine learning framework	Tslearn, Sklearn
	Deep learning framework	Torch
	Data processing library	Numpy 1.20.1/Pandas 1.2.4
	Program editor	Python 3.8

P and N represent the outcomes of the model's judgment, while T and F indicate the accuracy of those judgments. The outcome of the calculation is provided below.

$$
\begin{aligned}
Precision &= \frac{TP}{TP + FP} \\
Recall &= \frac{TP}{TP + FN} \\
F1 &= \frac{2\,Precision * Recall}{Precision + Recall} \\
Accuracy &= \frac{TP + TN}{TP + TN + FP + FN}
\end{aligned}
\tag{3}
$$

where TP is the number of samples correctly classified as positive, FP is the number of samples incorrectly assigned as active, and FN is the number of samples that originally belonged to the negative category but were assigned to another category. FP is the number of samples incorrectly assigned as active, and FN is the number of samples that originally belonged to the negative category but were assigned to another category.

$$
\begin{aligned}
MSE &= \frac{1}{n} \sum_{i=1}^{n} (\hat{y}_i - y_i)^2 \\
MAE &= \frac{1}{n} \sum_{i=1}^{n} |\hat{y}_i - y_i|
\end{aligned}
\tag{4}
$$

To further describe the accuracy of the model, we selected the mean squared error (MSE) and mean absolute error (MAE). For MSE and MAE, when the predicted value is exactly consistent with the real value, it is equal to 0, which is the perfect model. The larger the error, the greater the value. Where is the predicted value of the sample and is the true value of the i-th sample.

5   Experimental Results and Analysis

5.1   Datasets

As the classic Amazon Review Datasets of the recommendation system, this datasets records users' comments on products on the Amazon website. The datasets are divided into sub-datasets of Books, Electronics, Movies and TV, CDs and Vinyl. These sub-datasets contain two types of information: commodity information and user-score record information.

The data used in this paper are books data, from which it contains 40 thousand images and 27 million reviews data. All scoring information covers the period from 1990 to 2018. The Table 3 lists the relevant properties of the datasets. The Amazon Datasets labels is shown in Table 3.

Table 3. The Amazon datasets labels

Label	Tag instructions
Overall	Comment on the star
Verified	Whether to pass the verification
Vote	Comments support quantity
Style	Book style
Review Time	Date of comment
Reviewer ID	The only comment on ID
Asin	Product unique model ID
Reviewer Name	Comment on the name
Image	Comment on the picture URL address
Summary	Long review summary
Review Text	Long comments
Unix Review Time	Comment on the timestamp

5.2   User Information Security Protection

Weed out data containing sensitive user information, such as user phone number, IP, email, etc. by regular expressions. For example, matching common phone number format: $^\d\{3\}-\d\{3\}-\d\{4\}$. Since the comment text data on raw features consists of a thousand to thousands of words, the data features are relatively redundant, and the computational complexity can be reduced by using their mapping on low-dimensional summary data for initial classification.

5.3 Malicious User Comment Filtering

First, based on the previous analysis, five key features were selected: the mean and standard deviation of the time difference, the mean and standard deviation of the ratings, and the validation of the purchase status. The findings from the histogram analysis are presented in Fig. 3(left), illustrating a non-uniform allocation of the chosen characteristics.

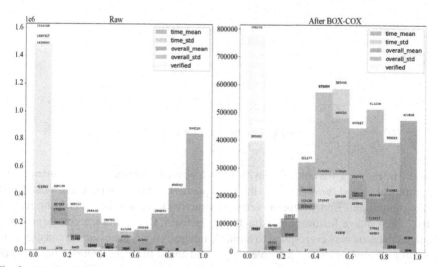

Fig. 3. Distribution of key features of malicious user comments (left: original distribution; right: distribution after BOX-COX processing)

The result of the transformation is shown in Fig. 3(right), which converts the features to a near normal distribution. This makes normally distributed data more suitable for statistical analysis and modeling. Next, we use k-means++ clustering algorithm to classify the review samples into different clusters and the results are shown in Fig. 4.

From the Fig. 4 we can clearly see that malicious users are screened out, indicating that our method is highly accurate and reliable in identifying malicious user comments. According to the clustering results we randomly selected a malicious false user David and extracted his comment data, and found that his comments are highly appreciated and highly recommended, with obvious false components, in comparison with a non-malicious false comment user carol, we found that his comments are more pertinent and credible. In summary, our study successfully screens and filters malicious user reviews through feature extraction, data transformation and clustering analysis, and provides strong support for e-commerce platforms to improve user experience and product quality.

5.4 Multi-modal Sentiment Analysis Prediction

Next, we perform Multi-modal sentiment analysis prediction, firstly, extracts the text sentiment features, constructs a new feature T using Text Blob, and normalizes the new

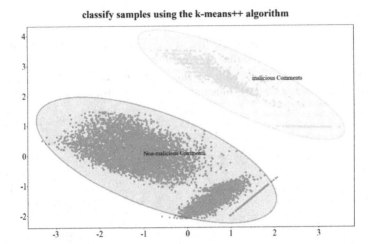

Fig. 4. Results of cluster analysis

feature. The range of T is controlled within [0,1], when T is closer to 0, the more negative the sentiment is, and the closer to 1, the more positive the sentiment is. Then the T text matrix is input into Bert within the feature extraction to obtain the Embedding feature matrix. Then image features are extracted using Swin Transformer, a comment in the comment datasets may correspond to multiple images, so it is necessary to construct the Embedding feature matrix of multiple images and adjust the weight ratio of the features between the image modality and the text modality, so that the data features are aligned. Finally, the obtained Embedding feature matrices of text and images are input into the Transformer for Encoder and Decoder, and the final emotion scores e-score are output through SoftMax, where e-score is between [0,1], the closer to 0, the more negative, the closer to 1, the more positive.

Experiment 1: Selection of Time Series Forecasting Algorithms
We select the number "B017WJ5PR4" for trial, we can get the emotion score time series of the book from 1998 to 2018, as shown in Fig. 5.

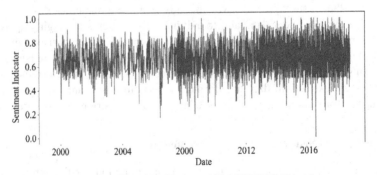

Fig. 5. Emotional distribution of "B017WJ5PR4" books

In order to better make time series prediction, we used different algorithms of Prophet, ARIMA, SARIMA and LSTM for modeling analysis, and conducted the results are shown in Table 4 below.

Table 4. Comparison of prediction accuracy of four algorithms

Algorithm	MAE	MSE
Prophet	0.093854	0.013827
ARIMA	0.107660	0.018912
SARIMA	0.105364	0.016604
LSTM	0.104919	0.019959

From Table 4, we found that Prophet has the highest prediction accuracy, and the accuracy of both MAE and MSE is optimal, So Prophet is chosen as our temporal prediction model.

Experiment 2: Comparison of User Sentiment Trends Toward Different Books
Next, we used the Prophet algorithm to predict and analyze two different books: "B017WJ5PR4" and "1508582211", and obtained the emotional data and emotional trends of the two books in the next year.

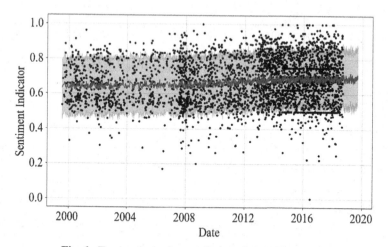

Fig. 6. Temporal emotion prediction of "B017WJ5PR4"

From Fig. 6 and 7, analyzing the emotional data and emotional trends in the coming year, it is not difficult to see that the buying sentiment of the book category "B017WJ5PR4" is increasing, further reflecting that the book is more and more popular with the public.

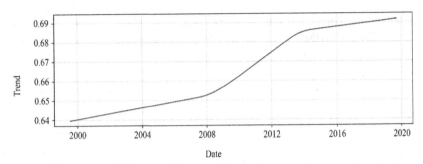

Fig. 7. Emotional trends for "B017WJ5PR4"

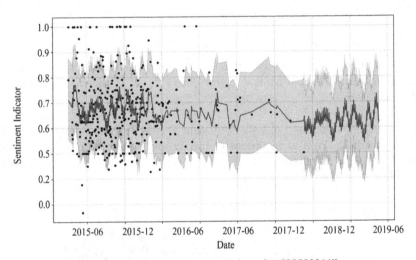

Fig. 8. Temporal emotion prediction of "1508582211"

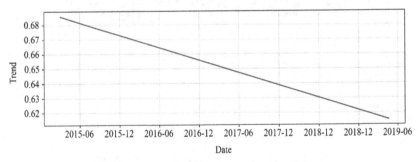

Fig. 9. Emotional trends for "1508582211"

At the same time, the combined forecast of "1508582211" books, as shown in Fig. 8, is predicted that the purchasing mood is gradually decreasing analyzing the trend, as shown in Fig. 9, it is found that the mood of buyers shows a downward trend, indicating that the book may not be liked by the public, and the store needs to change its sales strategy.

Ablation Test

The accuracy of multi-modal sentiment analysis is as high as 94.15%. To ensure the effectiveness of the multi-modal sentiment analysis, this study performed an ablation test. The test results are listed in Table 5 below.

Table 5. Comparison of different algorithms

Algorithm	Precision	Accuracy	Recall	F1
Multi-modal	0.9420	0.9415	0.9405	0.9407
Fast-Text	0.6054	0.6070	0.5973	0.5687
Bert	0.2600	0.5099	0.5100	0.3416
ConvNeXt	0.5492	0.9460	0.5217	0.5349
RestNet50	0.6154	0.9282	0.5957	0.5937

The experiments show that using the Fast-Text algorithm, the accuracy are only 60.7%, while using the Bert deep learning sentiment classification method, the precision and accuracy are 26% and 50.99% respectively. This paper then moves on to separate recognition of image data using the ConvNeXt algorithm with a precision of only 54.92% and an accuracy of 94.6%. Although the recognition is not precise enough due to more features, it still has a reduced accuracy. When ResNet50 is used for image recognition, the precision and accuracy are 61.54% and 92.82% respectively, which is a slight improvement over the ConvNeXt results, but still not comparable to the multi-modal fusion technique.

The ablation test showed that multi-modal fusion technology is more accurate in the emotion recognition of comments, ensuring the accuracy of the later prediction model.

6 Conclusion

In this study, we propose an approach that fuses multi-modal sentiment analysis with user information security protection mechanisms, focusing on effectively fending off malicious comments and accurately predicting product sentiment trends. Through experimental validation, we draw the following conclusions. Regular expressions can effectively detect and protect user information, such as phone numbers, addresses, emails, and IP addresses, thus ensuring user privacy and security. Statistical analysis and K-means++ algorithms can initially filter users who post malicious reviews and improve the credibility of reviews. The multi-modal sentiment analysis and prediction model we constructed successfully combines the pre-trained BERT model, Swin Transformer model, and SENet model to effectively extract and enhance the features of comment text and image data. After feature fusion and feature enhancement, our model achieves

94.15% accuracy on the Amazon book review datasets. Combining sentiment indicators and time series features, the Prophet method can effectively predict the future sentiment trends of product reviews, providing an important reference for real-time monitoring of product sentiment and user experience.

In summary, the method proposed in this study has significant value in real-time monitoring of product sentiment trends, filtering malicious comments, improving product management and user experience, and providing a useful reference for further improving product sentiment analysis and user information security protection. However, there are still some challenges to overcome, such as handling large-scale data and considering more text and image features. Because review data now presents multipolarity, and video information such as audio and voice also exist in the icons of textual information expression, the algorithm can be improved in future by using visual modal recognition models, speech modal recognition, etc. to achieve more mode fusion and further extract emotional features, so as to make the model results closer to reality, more accurate and robust.

Acknowledgments. The authors want to thank editors and unknown reviewers for providing useful suggestions. The authors also thank the Government of China to provide the required financial resources to complete the proposed project.

Funding. This research was funded by the National Natural Science Foundation of China (Grant No. 11901509), the Natural Science Foundation of the Jiangsu Higher Education Institutions of China (Grant No. 21KJB510009), National Nature Sciences Foundation of China with (Grant No. 42250410321) and the Natural Science Foundation of the Jiangsu Higher Education Institutions of China (Grant No. 19KJB110023).

Data Availability Statement. The data that support the findings of this study are available from the first author upon reasonable request.

Conflicts of Interest. The authors declare no conflict of interest.

References

1. Ringki, D., Thoudam, D.S.: Multimodal sentiment analysis: a survey of methods, trends, and challenges. ACM Comput. Surv. **55**(13s), 1–38 (2023). Article No.: 270
2. Srinivasan, K., Raman, K., Chen, J., Bendersky, M., Najork, M., Pang, L.: Wit: Wikipedia-based image text dataset for multi-modal multilingual machine learning. In: Proceedings of the 44th International ACM SIGIR Conference on Research and Development in Information Retrieval, pp. 2402–2406 (2021)
3. Meng, X., Wei, F., Liu, X., Zhou, M., Xu, G., Wang, H.: Cross-lingual mixture model for sentiment classification. In: Proceedings of the 50th Annual Meeting of the Association for Computational Linguistics, Volume 1: Long Papers, pp. 572–581 (2012)
4. Xu, R., Xu, J., Wang, X.: Instance level transfer learning for cross lingual opinion analysis. In: Proceedings of the 2nd Workshop on Computational Approaches to Subjectivity and Sentiment Analysis (WASSA 2011), pp. 182–188 (2011)
5. Appel, O., Chiclana, F., Carter, J., et al.: A hybrid approach to the sentiment analysis problem at the sentence level. Knowl.-Based Syst. **108**, 110–124 (2016)

6. Kim, S., Hovy, E.: Determining the sentiment of opinions. In: Proceedings of the 20th International Conference on Computational Linguistics, pp. 1367–1373 (2004)
7. Miller, G.A.: WordNet: a lexical database for English. Commun. ACM **38**(11), 39–41 (1995)
8. Mohammad, S., Dunne, C., Dorr, B.: Generating high-coverage semantic orientation lexicons from overtly marked words and a thesaurus. In: Proceedings of the 2009 Conference on Empirical Methods in Natural Language Processing, pp. 599–608 (2009)
9. Taboada, M., Brooke, J., Toiloski, M., Voll, K., Stede, M.: Lexicon-based methods for sentiment analysis. Comput. Linguist. **37**(2), 267–307 (2011)
10. Pandey, P., Govilkar, S.: A framework for sentiment analysis in Hindi using HSWN. Int. J. Comput. Appl. **119**(19) (2015)
11. Qiu, G., He, X., Zhang, F., Shi, Y., Bu, J., Chen, C.: DASA: dissatisfaction-oriented advertising based on sentiment. Expert Syst. Appl. **37**(9), 6182–6191 (2010)
12. Nasukawa, T., Yi, J.: Sentiment analysis: capturing favorability using natural language processing. In: Proceedings of the 2nd International Conference on Knowledge Capture, pp. 70–77 (2003)
13. Turney, P.: Thumbs up or thumbs down? Semantic orientation applied to unsupervised classification of reviews. In: Proceedings of the 40th Annual Meeting of the Association for Computational Linguistics, Philadelphia, Pennsylvania, USA, pp. 417–424. Association for Computational Linguistics (2002). https://doi.org/10.3115/1073083.1073153
14. Lu, Y., Kong, X., Quan, X., Liu, W., Xu, Y.: Exploring the sentiment strength of user reviews. In: Chen, L., Tang, C., Yang, J., Gao, Y. (eds.) WAIM 2010. LNCS, vol. 6184, pp. 471–482. Springer, Heidelberg (2010). https://doi.org/10.1007/978-3-642-14246-8_46
15. Dai, Z., Yang, Z., Yang, Y., et al.: Attentive Language Models beyond a Fixed-Length Context. arXiv preprint arXiv:1901.02860 (2019). https://doi.org/10.48550/arXiv.1901.02860
16. Chen, T., Yu, F.X., Chen, J., Cui, Y., Chen, Y.Y., Chang, S.F.: Object-based visual sentiment concept analysis and application. In: Proceedings of the 22nd ACM International Conference on Multimedia (MM 2014), pp. 367–376 (2014). Association for Computing Machinery, New York (2014). https://doi.org/10.1145/2647868.2654935
17. Yuan, J., McDonough, S., You, Q., Luo, J.: Sentribute: image sentiment analysis from a mid-level perspective. In: Proceedings of the Second International Workshop on Issues of Sentiment Discovery and Opinion Mining, pp. 1–8 (2013)
18. Borth, D., Ji, R., Chen, T., Breuel, T., Chang, S.F.: Large-scale visual sentiment ontology and detectors using adjective noun pairs. In: Proceedings of the 21st ACM International Conference on Multimedia, pp. 223–232 (2013)
19. Borth, D., Chen, T., Ji, R., Chang, S.F.: Sentibank: large-scale ontology and classifiers for detecting sentiment and emotions in visual content. In: Proceedings of the 21st ACM International Conference on Multimedia, pp. 459–460 (2013)
20. Barbosa, L., Feng, J.: Robust sentiment detection on twitter from biased and noisy data. In: Coling 2010: Poster Volume, pp. 36–44 (2010)
21. Davidiv, D., Tsur, O., Rappoport, A.: Enhanced sentiment learning using twitter hashtags and smileys. In: Coling 2010: Poster Volume, pp. 23–27 (2010)
22. Go, A., Bhayani, R., Huang, L.: Twitter Sentiment Classification using Distant Supervision (2009)
23. You, Q., Luo, J., Jin, H., Yang, J.: Robust image sentiment analysis using progressively trained and domain transferred deep networks. In: Twenty-Ninth AAAI Conference on Artificial Intelligence (2015)
24. Campos, V., Jou, B., Giro-i Nieto, X.: From pixels to sentiment: fine-tuning CNNs for visual sentiment prediction. Image Vis. Comput. **65**, 15–22 (2017)

25. Pang, B., Lee, L., Vaithyanathan, S.: Thumbs up?: sentiment classification using machine learning techniques. In: Proceedings of the ACL-02 Conference on Empirical Methods in Natural Language Processing, vol. 10, pp. 79–86. Association for Computational Linguistics (2002)
26. Poria, S., Cambria, E., Winterstein, G., Huang, G.-B.: Sentic patterns: dependency-based rules for concept-level sentiment analysis. Knowl.-Based Syst. **69**, 45–63 (2014)
27. Bayer, M., Kaufhold, M.A., Reuter, C.: A survey on data augmentation for text classification. ACM Comput. Surv. **55**(7), 1–39 (2022)
28. Tenney, I., Das, D., Pavlick, E.: BERT rediscovers the classical NLP pipeline. arXiv preprint arXiv:1905.05950 (2019)
29. You, Q., Cao, L., Jin, H., Luo, J.: Robust visual-textual sentiment analysis: when attention meets tree-structured recursive neural networks. In: Proceedings of the 24th ACM International Conference on Multimedia, pp. 1008–1017 (2016)
30. Wöllmer, M., et al.: YouTube movie reviews. Sentiment analysis in an audio-visual context. IEEE Intell. Syst. **28**(3), 46–53 (2013)
31. Morency, L.-P., Mihalcea, R., Doshi, P.: Towards multimodal sentiment analysis: harvesting opinions from the web. In: Proceedings of the 13th International Conference on Multimodal Interfaces, pp. 169–176 (2011)
32. Pereira, M.H.R., Pádua, F.L.C., Pereira, A.C.M., Benevenuto, F., Dalip, D.H.: Fusing audio, textual, and visual features for sentiment analysis of news videos. In: Tenth International AAAI Conference on Web and Social Media (2016)
33. Poria, S., Cambria, E., Gelbukh, A.: Deep convolutional neural network textual features and multiple kernel learning for utterance-level multimodal sentiment analysis. In: Proceedings of the 2015 Conference on Empirical Methods in Natural Language Processing, pp. 2539–2544 (2015)
34. Majumder, N., Hazarika, D., Gelbukh, A., Cambria, E., Poria, S.: Multimodal sentiment analysis using hierarchical fusion with context modeling. Knowl.-Based Syst. **161**, 124–133 (2018)
35. Huang, F., Zhang, X., Zhao, Z., Xu, J., Li, Z.: Image-text sentiment analysis via deep multimodal attentive fusion. Knowl.-Based Syst. **167**, 26–37 (2019)
36. Huddar, M.G., Sannakki, S.S., Rajpurohit, V.S.: Attention-based multimodal contextual fusion for sentiment and emotion classification using bidirectional LSTM. Multimedia Tools Appl. **80**(9), 13059–13076 (2021)

XPORAM: A Practical Multi-client ORAM Against Malicious Adversaries

Biao Gao[1,2] , Shijie Jia[1,2(✉)], Jiankuo Dong[3], and Peixin Ren[1,2]

[1] State Key Laboratory of Information Security, Institute of Information
Engineering, Chinese Academy of Sciences, Beijing, China
{gaobiao,jiashijie,renpeixin}@iie.ac.cn

[2] School of Cyber Security, University of Chinese Academy of Sciences, Beijing,
China

[3] School of Computer Science, Nanjing University of Posts and Telecommunications,
Nanjing, China

Abstract. Oblivious RAM (ORAM) was proposed to solve the problem of memory disclosure, preventing the system from reverse engineering attacks. Naturally, researchers apply ORAM into the out-sourced storage scenarios widely to protect the users' access patterns, including the sequence, the time, the correlation of the accesses, etc., which might compromise the users' private information and be utilized by malicious adversaries to launch attacks. ORAM typically protect user information by transforming a single access to the target item into a sequence accesses to multiple items, periodically reshuffling the accessed data. However, these extra operations bring about extra storage, computation and communication cost. Especially when applied to the multi-client scenarios, the overhead will be usually multiplied considering both the security and the performance. Current multi-client ORAM schemes suffer from the large overhead because of complicated architecture or cryptographic primitive, such as fully-homomorphic encryption, private information retrieval. This paper presents XPORAM, an efficient Oblivious RAM scheme appropriate for practical multi-client scenarios against malicious adversaries. Using the architecture of the non-colluding model, our scheme constructs multi-party secure communication while achieving obliviousness. Our security analysis guarantees the secure deployment of XPORAM and our experimental results demonstrate the $O(1)$ communication overhead and $O(\log N)$ computation overhead without requiring any trustworthy proxy.

Keywords: Oblivious RAM · Multi-Client ORAM · Privacy Security · Access Pattern

1 Introduction

Encryption algorithms ensure the confidentiality and integrity of the outsourced data, thus constituting the basic ingredients of secure storage systems. Unfortunately, encryption-only storage systems are definitely insufficient to provide

© The Author(s), under exclusive license to Springer Nature Singapore Pte Ltd. 2024
C. Ge and M. Yung (Eds.): Inscrypt 2023, LNCS 14526, pp. 397–417, 2024.
https://doi.org/10.1007/978-981-97-0942-7_20

comprehensive data protection, as the disclosure of data access pattern also significantly compromises the data security in oblivious data structure [28,38], oblivious storage [29], oblivious file system [1,11,40], secure multi-party computation [37,42], secure processor design [19,22,39], etc. According to the statistical analysis approach, the adversary can infer a lot of sensitive information through the data access pattern. For instance, Islam et al. [16] observed the data access to a publicly available remote encrypted database [17] and finally identified approximately 80% of the sensitive keyword search queries by analyzing the correlations of access behaviors.

To protect access pattern protection, Goldreich et al. firstly proposed the concept of Oblivious Random Access Machine (ORAM) [12] and proposed two classical prototypes: square-root ORAM and hierarchical ORAM [13]. Based on the seminal work of classical ORAMs, Shi et al. [30] designed tree-based ORAM, which constitutes the fundamental component of most subsequent ORAMs, e.g., Path ORAM [31] significantly simplified and reduced the overhead of Tree ORAM. Currently, ORAM has become a systematic cryptographic primitive for access pattern protection.

On an untrusted database, the physical accesses to data are publicly available information. The primary purpose of ORAM is to prevent adversaries (or privileged auditors) from acquiring sensitive information regarding the *logical* access, while still allowing adversaries to observe the *physical* access behaviors. This is achieved primarily by incorporating a substantial amount of dummy data blocks and introducing additional memory accesses. For more than three decades, researchers strive to conceal the client's access pattern by applying various techniques, such as reshuffle [10,13,30,31,35,42], eviction [21,31,37], secret sharing scheme [5,14], private information retrieval [6,24,25], homomorphic encryption [2,9]. However, existing ORAMs naturally suffer from a high overhead because of these massive dummy operations of complicated obfuscation to hide *logical* access to data blocks.

Consequently, one line of ORAM researches is designing delicate ORAMs and conducting theoretical analyses of their overhead, e.g., Larsen et al. [18] in CRYPTO '18 and Asharov et al. [3] in J.ACM'23 proved that the $\Omega(\log N)$ overhead in memory accesses is theoretically indispensable for any online ORAM to ensure computational security, where N is the number of data blocks. Another line involves adapting and employing ORAM in various scenarios while concurrently reducing costs. Moreover, traditional single-client-single-server model is unable to effectively cope with the increasing demands for collaboration caused by the rising computing requirements, data volume, and the number of devices involved. This inadequacy can significantly amplify the overall cost of ORAM implementation when scaling traditional schemes up to multi-server or multi-client models. Despite numerous ORAMs have been proposed and implemented in the literature, there are still some deficiencies in feasibility when deploying ORAMs in specific real-world scenarios.

Firstly, although numerous works [7,14,15,21,32–34,36,41] focused on multi-server cases, researchers primarily leveraged powerful servers only as building modules to handle the large computation and storage overhead. However, these server-centric schemes are insufficient to address the emerging challenges that arise when multiple clients involved. Common collaborative databases such as OneDrive and Dropbox allow multiple clients to access to and collaborate on the same database, but not all involved parties (including the server) are trustworthy. Any user's committed data will face the potential risk at being observed by other malicious users who access to the same database. Furthermore, the mutual communication channels among the clients and server introduce additional risk, such as potential man-in-the-middle attack, which could lead to the disclosure of access behaviors. Therefore, it is crucial to develop a system that prevents the disclosure of access pattern in multi-client scenarios through any means.

Table 1. Comparison metrics for related multi-client ORAMs and our design in different criteria. The "Comm.", "Comp." and "TTP." respectively denote the communication complexity, the computation complexity and whether there is a requirement for a trusted third-party proxy. N is the number of blocks, B is the block size (in terms of # bits)

Work	Cache	Reshuffling	Comm.	S.Comp	C.Comp	TTP.
TaoStore [29]	$\omega(\log N)$	–	$O(\log N)$	$O(\log N)$	$O(1)$	required
Tianji [5]	$O(\log N)$	–	$O(B + \log N)$	$O(B \cdot \log N)$	$O(B + \log N)$	required
PIRMC [24]	$O(\sqrt{N})$	–	$O(\sqrt{N})$	$O(N)$	$O(\sqrt{N})$	–
Blass [4]	$O(\sqrt{N})$	$O(N \log^2 N)$	$O(\log N)$	$O(N \log^2 N)$	$O(\log N)$	–
XPORAM (Our design)	$O(1)$	–	$O(1)$	$O(\log N)$	$O(\log N)$	–

Secondly, despite the typically inferior performance of the client compared to the server, the potential benefits of multiple clients remain largely untapped. The limited number of existing multi-client ORAMs [4,5,24,29] have only achieved a weak balance among the overhead, the data security and the practical application. On the one hand, certain multi-client schemes [5,29] have demonstrated good performance but heavily rely on a trusted third-party proxy (TTP) to ensure security and minimize storage and computation costs. For example, Cheng et al. [5] recently designed Shamir-based ORAM called "*Tianji*" to support asynchronous multi-client scenarios. Their scheme effectively manages an amortized overhead of $O(\log N)$ but relies on a TTP to enhance the security against malicious adversaries. It is noted that the presence of a trusted third proxy is a stringent requirement in real-world settings, which introduces extra overhead and poses challenges towards its secure fulfillment. On the other hand, while some other schemes [4,24] do not demand a TTP, they entail larger overall costs. For instance, Maffei et al. [24] formalized the notion of maliciously secure multi-client ORAM and proposed an ORAM based on Private Information Retrieval (PIR), which further enhances the access control mechanism. However, with no trusted proxy, this solution only achieved large overhead of $O(\sqrt{N})$. Therefore, it still remains an open question whether there is a multi-client ORAM construction that can defend against malicious adversaries while achieving $O(1)$ or $O(poly \log N)$ overhead of storage, communication and computation without any requirement of extra trusted third proxy.

Aiming to solve the above problems, we propose XPORAM, an efficient and practical multi-client ORAM against malicious adversaries without requirement of third trust-party proxy. We conclude the key insights of XPORAM as follows: 1) Leverage the obliviousness of the non-colluding parties in multi-client scenario to ensure the security and eliminate the requirement of TTP; 2) Leverage XOR technique and design message structures to reduce the communication overhead; 3) Leverage a greedy approach to reduce the computation overhead. More specifically, our XPORAM focuses on the multi-client ORAM system and if the participants in the system are collusive, multi-client-single-server model will degrade into the single-client-single-server one that has been studied in many previous traditional works. A client in system can delegate data transmission to other clients that do not collude with the server, which help eliminate the requirement of a TTP. Besides, when requesting blocks from the server, we utilize the XOR technique of Burst ORAM [8] to emerge the response messages into only one block, which helps hide the sensitive information about the real *logic* access and reduce the communication overhead. Subsequently, when uploading blocks back to the server, we are inspired by Path ORAM [31] and make the server determinate the location of writing back in a greedy method. With the help of obliviousness of non-colluding parties, we can eliminate time-consuming operations (e.g., shuffling that are deemed important in other ORAMs) to reduce the computation overhead. The corresponding analysis of security and experiments of XPORAM will be discussed in Sect. 5 and 6.2, showing that XPORAM outperforms the state-of-the-art multi-client ORAM both in theory and in practice. We draw a systematic and intuitive overhead comparison of the most representative related multi-client ORAMs with our design (cf. Table 1). Here, we will not distinguish whether the storage overhead stems from the server or clients because simply shifting the storage burden from clients to the server has little influence on the entire performance and currently the storage capability of clients has been improved significantly. In summary, the major contributions of this paper are as follows:

- We propose XPORAM, a practical multi-client ORAM, which protects access pattern against malicious adversaries from the server and multiple clients.
- We utilize the knowledge on the obliviousness of non-colluding parties to eliminate the demand for TTP. Leveraging the XOR technique and greedy approach, we achieve $O(1)$ communication overhead and $O(\log N)$ computation overhead.
- We provide a rigorous security analysis of XPORAM and the detailed experimental results demonstrate the significant performance improvement of XPORAM, which is consistent with the theoretical analysis.

2   Background

In this section, we give a brief but important background knowledge which we leverage to construct our **XPORAM**. On the one hand, we utilize the XOR technique, which is firstly proposed by Dautrich et al. [8], to reduce the communication cost significantly. On the other hand, we employ the insight of the greedy algorithm inspired by Path ORAM [31] to eliminate a part of server computation overhead while still guaranteeing the security under the scenario of non-colluding parties.

2.1   XOR Technique

The XOR technique [8] merges multiple blocks into a single block with XOR operation. Among these blocks, only one block corresponds to the ciphertext of the target block that the client intends to access while the remaining blocks serve as dummy blocks (referred to as dummy data hereafter without further distinction). The dummy blocks are generated by symmetrically encrypting "000...000" with various unique random initial vectors on the client side locally. All the blocks can be recovered by the local client through computation. Upon retrieval of the requests from the client, the server returns only a single block of data to the client. Subsequently, the client calculates the corresponding dummy blocks according to the locally stored random values separately, and successively performs XOR operation with the returned block to obtain the ciphertext of the target data. Also using the random value corresponding to the target block, the client can decrypt the result to obtain the plaintext.

2.2   Path ORAM

The Path ORAM [31] is based on the Tree ORAM [30], where each block is assigned to a randomly selected leaf node. This construction simplifies the overall tree-based framework and affords researchers greater flexibility to optimize the structure and the performance of ORAM. When the client intends to access the target block B from the server, Path ORAM retrieves all the blocks along the entire path where B resides. This operation reads and stores $O(\log N)$ blocks, including the target block B, in the cache. Regardless of whether the access is for reading or writing purposes, the client re-encrypts all these $O(\log N)$ blocks and updates them into another randomly selected path. Conventionally, these blocks are written back to the root node, and as the procedure performs, they are evicted into the buckets along the paths towards their respective leaf nodes. Specifically, Path ORAM follows a greedy strategy with the server writing the updated block as close to the leaf as possible. Moreover, the selected path originates from the common ancestor of the block's original leaf node and newly selected leaf node. This greedy algorithm saves the overhead significantly from evicting blocks along the path.

3   System Model

In this section, we will provide a clear description of assumptions in our system model to facilitate the better construction of XPORAM in the following section.

Firstly, we assume the advantage to be negligible to compromise the confidentiality of encryption algorithms and communication channels. Because our XPORAM targets at protecting the access pattern from disclosure, we ignore the possibility of other kinds of information leakage in this work. In other words, the adversaries are computationally bounded and all the encrypted data are indistinguishable. Moreover, the messages that flow through the channels are delivered successfully to corresponding receivers.

Secondly, our XPORAM targets at defending against malicious adversary. Typically, adversaries in the semi-honest model are characterized as "curious but honest", meaning they execute each step of the ORAM scheme correctly while also being curious to uncover sensitive information about the transmitted data. In our XPORAM, we allow the adversary to be more "dangerous" (*malicious model*), i.e., the adversary may refuse to perform the system operations correctly and desires to infer the sensitive information about data through all the information acquired in the protocol.

Thirdly, all the parties in the protocol do not trust each other. The client that initiates the requests may face the potential adversaries from other clients and the untrusted server. We, however, assume that these untrusted parties are *non-colluding* server and clients, i.e., even though all these parties probably desire to compromise the protocol, they share no acquired or inferred information except those publicly exposed ones. We consider this assumption to be reasonable. Otherwise, the untrustworthy clients and server can be regarded as single party, and such a scenario will result in the model being degenerated to a single server-client scenario, which has been studied in many seminal works [8,26,27,30,31,34].

4   The **XPORAM** protocol

The insight behind the design of XPORAM arises from the observation that, regardless of the presence of untrustworthy clients, leveraging multi-client obliviousness towards the server can effectively reduce the overall cost of the ORAM and help eliminate the requirement of TTP. Furthermore, this obliviousness property also serves as the important guarantee for the security of our design, which will be illustrated in Sect. 5.

4.1   Overview

In the existing systems of multi-party ORAM, a server's ability in multi-client scenarios is usually limited, even if the system multiplies the number of servers. Besides, most existing multi-client schemes either suffer from high overheads or rely on a stringent requirement of TTP to make schemes secure and practical. Our work focuses on the multi-client scenario against malicious adversaries and achieve practical performance in the meanwhile. The obliviousness of non-colluding parties enables our XPORAM to eliminate the need for a TTP. By employing the XOR technique and a greedy write-back approach design, XPORAM can significantly reduce the communication and computation overheads to $O(1)$ and $O(\log N)$ respectively. We assume that there is a group of M clients whose data is stored on a remote server (denoted as S). A requester is a client who initiates accesses to the server while assistors are helpers picked at random among the remaining clients by the requester. In this group, when a client initiates an access request to the server, it assumes the role of requester while the remaining clients are potential assistors. The requester C_1 requests S for a target block and re-encrypts the returned block locally. Subsequently, the requester and assistors will jointly upload distinct data in accordance with our XPORAM protocol, wherein all information is linked to the reconstructed block while the assistors' data is exclusively generated by the requester. It is noteworthy that throughout the entire process, neither the server S nor the assistors $(C_2, C_3, \cdots)$ knows any knowledge regarding which block the requester accesses and whether the access is *read* or *write*. On the one hand, although the requested blocks are all located in the same path as the target block, the server receives indistinguishable messages including the re-encrypted data blocks from the requester and assistors, which prevents the server from inferring the association between the requested blocks and the updated ones. On the other hand, the location of the updated blocks will be determined by the server and carry no sensitive information about the data that the requester accesses.

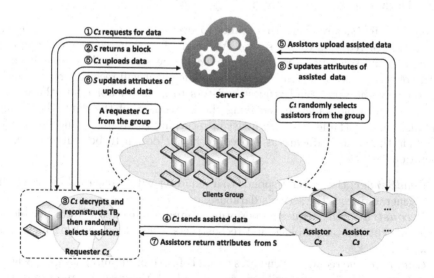

Fig. 1. The structure of XPORAM.

4.2   Storage Structures

Server Storage. The data storage mechanism in XPORAM resembles those of traditional tree-based ORAM schemes [30,31]. The user has the flexibility to determine the number of tree branches, and we choose binary tree for simplicity. Let N be the total number of distinct data blocks, thus the binary tree is organized at a height of $H = \lfloor \log_2 N \rfloor$, where the Level 0 (namely top level) means the root node while the Level $H = L - 1$ (namely bottom level) denotes the level of leaf nodes. Every node in the tree is considered as a bucket consisting of a fixed number of blocks. Specially, each leaf node has only one specific path from the root node to this leaf node and the path can be regarded as public information for each data block. In other word, the assigned path for each block serves as a public attribute that can be shared among all parties involved in the ORAM protocol.

Client Storage. Each client in the working group needs a position map to locate its data on the server, including the corresponding leaf nodes (i.e., paths) and offsets. Besides, the random initialization vectors (*IVs*) chosen to encrypt data are also stored in each client. The requester takes corresponding *IVs* into the decryption algorithm after downloading the actually requested encrypted data blocks.

4.3   Data Access

In our XPORAM, any client that wants to *access* a target block, will initiate a sequence of requests to the server. Although the other requested blocks are located in the same path as the target block, the server will be actually not aware of which one is the real target block. The client will receive a result block returned by the server and request assistors to assist in uploading the newly generated data blocks. After verifying the correctness of the data, the server will also request the assistors to assist in returning the response messages. We conclude the entire data *access* procedure in our design to be four main data operations as below:

- *ReadServer*: the server responds to a requester with a returned block which is generated from the server's database.
- *Reconstruct*: the requester performs computation on the returned block to decrypt the target block and reconstructs a new block waiting for being written back.
- *Generate*: the requester generates a serial of (real or dummy) datasets, where the dummy datasets are utilized to confuse both the assistors and the server about the information of the real updated block. The requester separately sends different generated datasets to other randomly selected assistors no matter whether the data is real or dummy.
- *WriteBack*: all the generated data sets will be uploaded to the server by the requester and the assistors. The server performs computation on the uploaded

data to verify the correctness and obtain the uploaded blocks to be written back. After writing these blocks into the database in a greedy manner, the server will send the corresponding offsets to the requester and the assistors, all of which will be obtained by the requester finally.

Table 2. Notations of the XPORAM.

N	The number of total blocks in the remote server
m	The number of clients involved in a single access in all M clients
$H = \lfloor \log_2 N \rfloor$	Height of the tree
$L = H + 1$	The number of total levels of the tree
PM	The position map stored in the client
P_i (or $\mathcal{P}(j)$)	The path where block B_i (or block j) is located
LN_i	The leaf node of the path P_i
R_i	The random number assigned to block B_i
$\textit{offs}_j$	The offset of block j
$GA(B_i)$	The algorithm to store B_i greedily

We provide a general structure of XPORAM in Fig. 1 and give detailed description of these four operations in the following. The corresponding notations are shown in Table 2.

ReadServer. The "Read" operation (see Step ① and Step ② Fig. 1) constitutes the first step of accessing to the server. When a client C_1 wants to access a target block TB, C_1 looks up the position map (PM) to obtain both the corresponding leaf node (i.e., its specific path l) and offset of TB. Then C_1 randomly select another $L - 1 = \lfloor \log_2 N \rfloor$ blocks in the same path l and obtain their offsets. Regardless of whether these $L - 1$ blocks store valid data, requester C_1 treats them as dummy blocks. All these L offsets together with the id of path (l) consist of a data stream that will be sent to S. The server correspondingly reads these blocks from path l according to the offsets and merges them into only one result block using XOR, with which the server S responds to C_1.

Reconstruct. The "Reconstructing blocks" operation (consisting of Step ③ in Fig. 1) constitutes the second step of an *access*. The random initialization vectors (IVs) of requested blocks are all locally stored in client C_1, with which C_1 reconstructs all the dummy blocks by using the same symmetric encryption algorithm (e.g., AES-128). Specifically, dummy block reconstruction can be performed in parallel with the "ReadServer" operation to reduce the time cost. In the same way as server S, the requester C_1 XORs these reconstructed blocks together with the returned block from S in sequence to retrieve the interested block. C_1 finally decrypts such a block to obtain the real value of target block.

Generate. The "Generating uploaded data" operation (consisting of Step ③ in Fig. 1) constitutes the third step of an *access*. The requester C_1 re-encrypts TB with a new random IV_1 to get a ciphertext TB_1 (also B_1 for the sake of presentation). In the meanwhile, C_1 randomly chooses $m-1$ clients from the client group as assistors, to which $m-1$ newly generated dummy blocks $B_2, \cdots, B_m$ are separately assigned. Then C_1 randomly chooses m new paths $P_1, P_2, \cdots, P_m$ and corresponding m random values $R_1, R_2, \cdots, R_m$ for blocks $B_1, B_2, \cdots, B_m$ respectively, i.e., $\forall i \in \{1, \cdots, m\}$, the block B_i is located in the path P_i, with R_i as a specific mark, from the root node to the leaf node LN_i.

WriteBack. The "Writing back blocks" operation (consisting of Step ④ to Step ⑦ in Fig. 1) constitutes the fourth part of an *access*. From the m clients (C_1 included) in "Generate", the requester C_1 choose a random client (denoted as C_R) to upload real data B_1, and the rest assist in uploading dummy blocks. Subsequently, XPORAM performs the protocol from Step ④ to Step ⑦) according to the determination of m and C_R. We present a detailed intuitive description of XPORAM in Fig. 2, taking $m=2$ as an example for simplicity.

Requester C_1	Server S	Assistor C_2

INPUT: target block TB, $m=2$
$(\mathcal{P}(TB), \mathit{offs}_{TB}) \leftarrow PM$
$(\mathit{offs}_{k_1}, \cdots, \mathit{offs}_{k_{L-1}}) \sim PM$,
where $\forall j \in \{1, \cdots, L-1\}, \mathcal{P}(k_j) = \mathcal{P}(TB)$

$Q := (\mathcal{P}(TB), \mathit{offs}_{TB}, \mathit{offs}_{k_1}, \cdots, \mathit{offs}_{k_{L-1}})$ $\xrightarrow{Q}$ $(TB, B_{k_1}, \cdots, B_{k_{L-1}}) \leftarrow Database$

$B_{k_j} = Enc(\{0\}^{length}, IV_{k_j})$ $\xleftarrow{Res_{req}}$ $Res_{req} := TB \oplus \sum_{j=1}^{L-1} B_{k_j}$
$TB = Dec(Res \oplus \sum_{j=1}^{L-1} B_{k_j}, IV_{k_{TB}})$
$B_1 := TB_1 = Enc(TB, IV_1)$
$B_2 = Enc(\{0,1\}^{length}, IV_2)$
$(P_1, P_2) \sim \{\mathcal{P}(LN_0), \cdots, \mathcal{P}(LN_{2^H-1})\}$
$(R_1, R_2) \sim \{0,1\}^{256}$
$Hash(P_1 || B_1) = SHA\text{-}256(P_1 || B_1)$
$Hash(P_2 || B_2) = SHA\text{-}256(P_2 || B_2)$

CASE 1: $C_R = C_1$

$\xrightarrow{\qquad B_2, R_1, R_2, Hash(P_2||B_2) \qquad}$

$\xrightarrow{B_1, P_1 \oplus R_1, P_2 \oplus R_2, Hash(P_1||B_1)}$ $P_1' = (P_1 \oplus R_1) \oplus R_1$ $\xleftarrow{B_2, R_1, R_2, Hash(P_2||B_2)}$
$P_2' = (P_2 \oplus R_2) \oplus R_2$
verify $Hash(P_1||B_1) == Hash(P_1'||B_1)$
verify $Hash(P_2||B_2) == Hash(P_2'||B_2)$

Store $\mathit{offs}_{B_1}, \mathit{offs}_{B_2}$ in PM $\xleftarrow{\mathit{offs}_{B_1}}$ $\mathit{offs}_{B_1} = GA(B_1), \mathit{offs}_{B_2} = GA(B_2)$ $\xrightarrow{\mathit{offs}_{B_2}}$
$\xleftarrow{\qquad\qquad\qquad\qquad}$ $\xrightarrow{\qquad \mathit{offset}_{B_2} \qquad}$

CASE 2: $C_R = C_2$
C_1 exchanges the messages, which are sent to C_2 and S in **CASE 1**. Then the offs_{B_1} and offs_{B_2} will be also exchanged correspondingly. However, it should be noted that the server still cannot differentiate between the messages received from C_1 and C_2, and therefore, it cannot distinguish the relationship between their corresponding offsets and the original requested blocks.

Fig. 2. The XPORAM protocol for $m=2$.

5   Security Analysis

As indicated in [16,29], repeated accesses to the same block can threaten the access pattern privacy since the adversary tries to infer the correlations between this block and others through these accesses, which will be utilized to compromise the security. However, in our XPORAM, for each access to a block, there will be at least one dummy block written back to the server. Moreover, the requester and the assistors will re-encrypt the blocks, making it impossible for a computationally-bounded adversary to determine whether a real data block is uploaded or which block, if any, corresponds to the originally accessed real data.

The standard definition of ORAM security [34] is expressed as: for any two sequences of request for the target blocks, their access patterns are computationally indistinguishable. In other words, the security of a reliable ORAM scheme depends on whether adversary can distinguish the access pattern from the client's access sequences. We give a detailed analysis on the access behaviors of the client, based on which we illustrate the security of our XPORAM from the perspectives of each phase of "Access" in turn. For the sake of presentation, we also take $m = 2$ as an example because the number of m has no influence on the prove the security of our XPORAM.

5.1   Semi-honest Model

We first consider the case of the semi-honest model, i.e., the parties (including the server and all clients) in the protocol are all legitimate participants who will not deviate from the predetermined protocol but will attempt to infer all possible information from legitimately received messages, e.g., one of which keeps a record of all its intermediate computations and tries to decrypt the ciphertexts.

ReadServer operation reveals no extra information that can be inferred from the legitimate messages. When the requester C_1 wants to access the server, the path and the offsets of the requested blocks are all obtained from C_1's local storage. All these blocks have the same path and conform to a random distribution due to the random choices of dummy blocks. Although the target block is specific, it is hidden in the dummy blocks and one block will not influence the randomness of these L blocks in a round of access. Notably, all these chosen blocks were previously written to database in a public greedy algorithm, as a result, the offsets of these blocks leak no private information about themselves. Then the returned block, calculated by XORing these blocks and TB, has no private information. Therefore, the **ReadServer** operation leaks no extra private information.

Reconstruct operation reveals no extra information that can be inferred from the legitimate messages. It is obvious that this phase is all completed locally. Therefore, our focus lies solely on the intermediate data. C_1 utilizes random vector to re-encrypt TB and we can consider TB_1 and TB indistinguishable based on the assumption of computationally bounded adversary. Therefore, the **Reconstruct** operation leaks no extra private information.

Generate operation reveals no extra information that can be inferred from the legitimate messages. The new dummy blocks to be assigned to assistors are generated by encrypting "000 ⋯ 000" with new random vectors, rendering them independent of the real block. In the meanwhile, the assistors are also randomly selected, which cannot be predicted in advance. Therefore, the **Generate** operation leaks no extra private information.

WriteBack operation reveals no extra information that can be inferred from the legitimate messages. Since the choice of C_R only influence which client will upload the real block, we still take the example of $C_R = C_1$ in the following detailed illustrations.

- Firstly, we consider C_2, to which the data set sent by C_1 consists of four items in total: an encrypted block B_2, B_2's corresponding random value R_2, another random value R_1 and a hash value $Hash(P_2||B_2)$. On the one hand, we can consider the encrypted block as indecipherable based to the system model. Moreover, since the remaining three items are perceived as random values from C_2's perspective, it is impossible for C_2 to deduce any additional private information from the messages of these four items collectively. On the other hand, we recall that P_1 (or P_2) is obtained by XORing $P_1 \oplus R_1$ (or $P_2 \oplus R_2$) with R_1 (or R_2) by the server S. Therefore, C_2 is not aware of the path of B_1 (or B_2) due to the fact that C_2 and S are non-colluding parties, i.e., C_2 cannot infer more extra private information from the behaviors of transmitting these four items.
- Secondly, we consider S, whose datasets come from C_1 and C_2. As described in the analysis of **Reconstruct**, S cannot distinguish the new block B_1 from the original block TB, and the remaining items sent by C_1 to S are random values in the view of S, i.e., S cannot recognize whether the data sent by C_1 is real or dummy data. In addition, the behaviors of C_1 and C_2 are both the same in the view of S. As a result, S has no more information both from the perspectives of messages and behaviors.
- Finally, in the Step 6 to Step 7, the returned offsets come from a public greedy algorithm, which is used to write blocks to the database, i.e., although C_2 knows the returned offset of B_2, C_2 still has no way of knowing specific location of B_2 since C_2 cannot calculate the path P_2.

Therefore, the **WriteBack** operation leaks no extra private information. In conclusion, our XPORAM is secure under the semi-honest model.

5.2 Malicious Model

Besides the semi-honest model, we then consider the case of the malicious model, i.e., the clients (except requester C_1) and the server S are potential malicious adversaries, which can deviate from our XPORAM, e.g., changing the messages transmitted, directly aborting our protocol, etc.

Firstly, we consider the case of a malicious server, i.e., S dose not exactly follow the protocol in the Step 2 and Step 6. If S does not perform rightly in Step

2, then C_1 will discover the malicious behavior of S because C_1 cannot decrypt ciphertexts rightly. And for the same reason, if S does not perform rightly in Step 6, S will be exposed when C_1 requests for such a block which were written wrongly by S in Step 6. Therefore, our XPORAM can discover the malicious behavior of the server S.

Secondly, we consider the case of a malicious assistor, i.e., C_2 does not exactly follow the protocol in Step 5 and Step 7. If Step 7 is executed incorrectly by C_2, then the offset of B_2 is aborted or a wrong offset of B_2 is sent to C_1. It is obvious that C_1 will find out the malicious behavior of C_2 immediately in the former situation or when C_1 requests such a B_2 with a wrong offset in a next round (i.e., cannot decrypt rightly) in the latter situation. However, if C_2 does not exactly perform the Step 5, we divide the messages in Step 5 into two parts: the "$B_2, R_2, Hash(P_2||B_2)$" and "R_1":

- $B_2, R_2, Hash(P_2||B_2)$: S needs $P_2 \oplus R_2$ and R_2 to get P_2. Because of the system model that C_2 and S are non-colluding parties, C_2 cannot calculate P_2 without $P_2 \oplus R_2$. Furthermore, due to the assumption that C_2 does not have unbounded computation power, C_2 cannot forge new $B_2', R_2', Hash(P_2'||B_2')$ so that $(P_2 \oplus R_2) \oplus R_2' = P_2$, $Hash(P_2'||B_2') = Hash(P_2||B_2')$, which means that C_2's malicious behavior involved with B_2, R_2, $Hash(P_2||B_2)$ will be found out.
- R_1: C_2 cannot obtain correct P_1 calculated by S for the same reason, and as a result, C_2 cannot forge R_1' to obtain a P_1' so that $Hash(P_1'||B_1)$ equals $Hash(P_1||B_1)$ in the server, which means that C_2's malicious behavior involved with R_1 will be found out.

Therefore, XPORAM can discover the malicious behavior of the assistor C_2. In conclusion, our XPORAM is still secure against the malicious model.

6 Implementation and Evaluation

We implemented the prototype of our XPORAM in C++ on Windows 10. In this section, we first describe the details of our experimental setup and illustrate the evaluation metrics and methodology, followed by the multi-dimensional comparison between our XPORAM and S^3ORAM^+, which is the state-of-the-art multi-user ORAM constructing *Tianji* [5]. In tandem with figures, we will furnish a more precise and elaborate interpretation of the experimental results.

6.1 Experimental Setup

Software Setting. XPORAM works with three external libraries on Windows: 1) OpenSSL library v3.0.5 for pseudo-random number generation and AES-128-CBC encryption because of its optimized computation; 2) Mongocxx library v3.6.7 as an engine for database access like [15,20]; 3) Boost library v1.80.0 for handling the data types beyond those in the standard C/C++ libraries.

Hardware Setting. We deployed our clients on two types of devices: 1) 4*Intel CPUs i7-6700, 24 GB RAM, and 2TB HDD (also the same as our server); 2) 6*Intel CPUs i7-8750H, 16 GB RAM, and 500 GB SSD. All the server and clients are connected to the Ethernet with 34.66 Mbps download, 9.62 Mbps upload throughput and 8.34 ms round-trip latency.

Database. Using Mongocxx driver, we generated random binary data as the databases with size ranging from 1 GB to 64 GB, where each block size ranges from 4 KB to 256 KB.

6.2 Evaluation Metrics and Methodology

Similar to the technique in [32] and [33], we warmed up our XPORAM with N blocks stored in the full-binary-tree databases. We conducted our experiments to assess the impact of different database and block sizes on the end-to-end delay, which directly reflects the performance of an ORAM. The delay mainly depends on the overhead of four modules: 1) client-server communication; 2) server computation; 3) client computation; 4) disk I/O. We also measured the concrete time of these four metrics respectively to give an intuitive view of their influence.

6.3 Experimental Results and Evaluation

In this subsection, we will analyze the experimental results horizontally and vertically to determine the causes and optimization directions. Many existing papers focus on the response time, number of operations, etc., where the former varies from system to system and from device to device, while the latter generally depends only on the design performance of the solution itself and does not vary by experimental configuration.

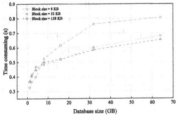
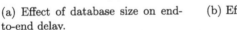
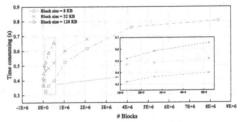

(a) Effect of database size on end-to-end delay.

(b) Effect of block size on end-to-end delay.

Fig. 3. End-to-end delay for varying database sizes and block sizes.

End-to-End Delay. We provide the end-to-end delay under three different block size settings in Fig. 3 and the results are consistent with our theoretical overhead analysis. We scale up the size of our ORAM by increasing the height of the fundamental tree and the logarithmic curve trend illustrates that the cost of end-to-end delay is $O(\log N)$. For instance, XPORAM took around 0.324 s to access a 1 GB database and the delay increased logarithmically to 0.805 s when accessing a 64 GB database. Such growth mainly stems from the logarithmic computation overhead on the server side. In contrast, the computation time on client side is nearly negligible (see Sect. 6.3). Considering that larger block sizes will result in fewer data blocks within a given database size, we take the database size and the number of blocks respectively as horizontal axes of the two subfigures to eliminate the potential misleading of different block sizes' impact for the same database size on the delay. The partial zoom in Fig. 3b depicts an intuitive vertical comparison of the effect of various block sizes on the delay.

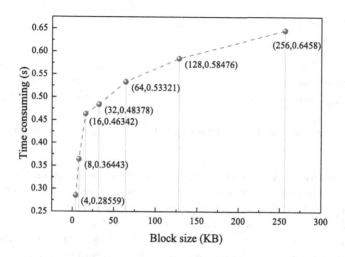

Fig. 4. The effect of block size on the end-to-end delay with $N = 262144$.

Although the block size should have no influence on the delay in our XPORAM design, the Fig. 4 still shows that, for the same number of blocks (taking $N = 262144$ as an example), the average delay exhibits a logarithmic-like growth as the block size increases. This is because we store all the data in binary format in MongoDB and the block size will be directly involved in nearly all the calculation of the data when accessing to the MongoDB, which increases the time of operations. Besides, the larger the block size is, the easier it is to perform the system operations on data blocks. Therefore, the curve shows a logarithmic-like growth rather than a linear growth. The optimizations of our implementation will be one of our future work. Nonetheless, we note that the design of S^3ORAM+ in *Tianji* leads to a linear growth of the end-to-end delay (cf. Fig. 4 in [5]) as the block size increase and has significantly larger overhead than our XPORAM.

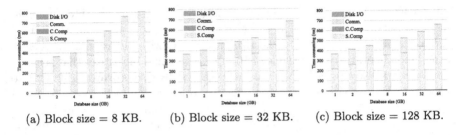

(a) Block size = 8 KB.   (b) Block size = 32 KB.   (c) Block size = 128 KB.

Fig. 5. The cost breakdown of XPORAM for three different block sizes.

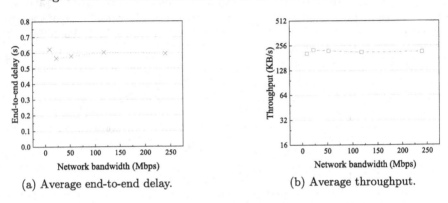

(a) Average end-to-end delay.   (b) Average throughput.

Fig. 6. End-to-end delay and throughput for varying network bandwidth.

Cost Breakdown. As described in Sect. 6.2, the overhead of end-to-end delay mainly comes from four modules and Fig. 5 shows the cost breakdown of the delay for three kinds of block size. Although the client-side computational complexity is $O(\log N)$, the time spent on both client computation and disk I/O accounts for a negligible portion of the overall end-to-end delay, with the former representing approximately 0.7% and the latter 0.4% on average. In comparison, the computation time of the server consumes the largest portion and grows up logarithmically as the database size increases. The Mongocxx driver is responsible for performing disk I/O operations to read from and write to the database. The client computation mainly consists of requester's looking up the local position map, reconstructing the blocks, constructing write-back messages along with calculating the hash values. The server computation overhead is mainly from XORing the fetched blocks from the database, calculating the paths of uploaded data, verifying the write-back messages and determining their offsets.

Additionally, the client-server communication time ranks second in terms of its proportion to the overall delay (also see Fig. 5). We can further observe from Fig. 6 that the communication overhead remains stable and it has little influence on the end-to-end delay nor the system throughput. The design of lowering communication costs boosts the scalability of our XPORAM. Even our typical home network bandwidth is never a bottleneck of performance when we raise the database size and block size.

7 Related Work

Traditional Single-client-Single-server ORAM. The first ORAM could be traced back to the research on mitigating the reverse engineering attacks on local memory data by obfuscating access patterns. Goldreich et al. [13] pioneered the ORAM researches, aiming to conceal access pattern information pertaining to specific blocks. Both of their proposed classical ORAMs, namely square-root ORAM and hierarchical ORAM, consumed large overheads (amortized $O(\sqrt{N})$ and $O(\log^3(N)$, respectively). This was primarily due to the intricate operations involved in shuffling, eviction, and storage mechanisms, etc. Based on the hierarchical ORAM, Shi et al. designed Tree ORAM [30], which is further significantly simplified by Path ORAM [31] to achieve a polylogarithmic-level overhead. However, preliminary ORAMs were primarily tailored for clients with limited storage capacities and treated the server as a mere storage module, consuming high communication and storage costs. As the increase of the involved devices and the need for collaborative scenarios, the entire overhead will be further amplified, posing more challenges for ORAMs.

Multi-client ORAM without TTP. Some researchers (e.g., [4,5,10,23,24, 29]) enabled the server involved in computation, trying to reduce the overall cost of multi-client scenario. The [24] formalized the notion of maliciously secure multi-client ORAM and proposed a PIR-based multi-client ORAM, which further combined the public-key cryptography and zero-knowledge proofs for access control. However, all the techniques of [24] were time-consuming (e.g., the communication cost is amortized $O(\sqrt{N})$) and therefore impractical. Similar to [24], Blass et al. [4] also designed a multi-client ORAM. They separated client accesses into two parts which can be checked more carefully to reveal the malicious behaviors. Besides, they employed the classical ORAM as a building block to store the Path ORAM's meta data to achieve a multi-client secure version of *read* protocol. However, [4] still suffered from large cost of $O(N \log^2 N)$ computation overhead caused by the complicated shuffling.

Multi-client ORAM with TTP. TaoStore [29] achieved a tree-based asynchronous oblivious store for multi-client scenario with a trusted proxy mediating client-cloud communication. They leveraged the request map to keep track of all concurrent requests for the same block so that they could manage the asynchronous requests. Besides, they designed a *fresh-subtree* to keep the data in stash always up-to-date. Although TaoStore achieved $O(\log N)$ computation and communication costs, it only considered the semi-honest adversary and still demand for a TTP. Recently in TDSC'23, Cheng et al. proposed the state-of-the-art maliciously secure multi-client ORAM, namely *Tianji* [5], which extended the Shamir-based S^3ORAM and incorporated the new extension, namely S^3ORAM$^+$, into their storage system. They eliminated the cost of eviction and reached the computation overhead of $O(\log N)$. However, *Tianji* was built on a trusted proxy server, which is a stringent requirement in real-world scenarios and will introduce additional overhead towards its secure fulfillment.

8   Conclusion

We propose a practical secure multi-client ORAM scheme, XPORAM, which achieves $O(1)$ communication overhead and amortized $O(\log N)$ computation overhead. XPORAM works under the non-colluding-parties situation, which helps eliminate the stringent requirement of any TTP. We utilize the XOR technique to compress the transmitted data, extremely reducing the communication cost. We provide the adequate and rigorous analysis of security and correctness to illustrate that, the large overhead caused by cumbersome operations like complicated cryptographic primitives is unnecessary in XPORAM. We eliminate these operations and smartly design message structures to achieve great computation performance. We implement the prototype of XPORAM and carry out extensive experiments to demonstrate the progressive performance and advantages of XPORAM.

Acknowledgments. This work was supported by National Key Research and Development Program of China (No.2021YFB3101100) and National Natural Science Foundation of China (No.62272457, No.62302238).

References

1. Ahmad, A., Kim, K., Sarfaraz, M.I., Lee, B.: OBLIVIATE: a data oblivious filesystem for intel SGX. In: NDSS (2018)
2. Apon, D., Katz, J., Shi, E., Thiruvengadam, A.: Verifiable oblivious storage. In: Krawczyk, H. (ed.) PKC 2014. LNCS, vol. 8383, pp. 131–148. Springer, Heidelberg (2014). https://doi.org/10.1007/978-3-642-54631-0_8
3. Asharov, G., Komargodski, I., Lin, W.K., Nayak, K., Peserico, E., Shi, E.: Optorama: optimal oblivious ram. J. ACM **70**(1), 1–70 (2022)
4. Blass, E.-O., Mayberry, T., Noubir, G.: Multi-client oblivious RAM secure against malicious servers. In: Gollmann, D., Miyaji, A., Kikuchi, H. (eds.) ACNS 2017. LNCS, vol. 10355, pp. 686–707. Springer, Cham (2017). https://doi.org/10.1007/978-3-319-61204-1_34
5. Cheng, W., Sang, D., Zeng, L., Wang, Y., Brinkmann, A.: TIANJI: securing a practical asynchronous multi-user ORAM. IEEE Trans. Depend. Secure Comput. **20**, 5143–5155 (2023)
6. Chor, B., Goldreich, O., Kushilevitz, E., Sudan, M.: Private information retrieval. In: Proceedings of IEEE 36th Annual Foundations of Computer Science, Wisconsin, USA, pp. 41–50. IEEE (1995). https://doi.org/10.1109/SFCS.1995.492461
7. Dauterman, E., Feng, E., Luo, E., Popa, R.A., Stoica, I.: {DORY}: An encrypted search system with distributed trust. In: 14th USENIX Symposium on Operating Systems Design and Implementation (OSDI 20), pp. 1101–1119 (2020)
8. Dautrich, J., Stefanov, E., Shi, E.: Burst ORAM: minimizing ORAM response times for bursty access patterns. In: 23rd USENIX Security Symposium (USENIX Security 14), Berkley, CA, pp. 749–764. USENIX Association (2014)

9. Devadas, S., van Dijk, M., Fletcher, C.W., Ren, L., Shi, E., Wichs, D.: Onion ORAM: a constant bandwidth blowup oblivious RAM. In: Kushilevitz, E., Malkin, T. (eds.) TCC 2016. LNCS, vol. 9563, pp. 145–174. Springer, Heidelberg (2016). https://doi.org/10.1007/978-3-662-49099-0_6
10. Franz, M., et al.: Oblivious outsourced storage with delegation. In: Danezis, G. (ed.) FC 2011. LNCS, vol. 7035, pp. 127–140. Springer, Heidelberg (2012). https://doi.org/10.1007/978-3-642-27576-0_11
11. Gao, B., Chen, B., Jia, S., Xia, L.: EHIFS: an efficient history independent file system. In: Proceedings of the 2019 ACM Asia Conference on Computer and Communications Security, pp. 573–585 (2019)
12. Goldreich, O.: Towards a theory of software protection and simulation by oblivious rams. In: Proceedings of the Nineteenth Annual ACM Symposium on Theory of Computing, New York, NY, USA, pp. 182–194. STOC '87, Association for Computing Machinery (1987)
13. Goldreich, O., Ostrovsky, R.: Software protection and simulation on oblivious rams. J. ACM (JACM) 43(3), 431–473 (1996)
14. Hoang, T., Guajardo, J., Yavuz, A.A.: MACAO: a maliciously-secure and client-efficient active ORAM framework. In: 27th Annual Network and Distributed System Security Symposium, NDSS 2020, San Diego, California, USA, February 23–26 (2020)
15. Huang, Y., et al.: ThinORAM: towards practical oblivious data access in fog computing environment. IEEE Trans. Serv. Comput. 13(4), 602–612 (2020)
16. Islam, M.S., Kuzu, M., Kantarcioglu, M.: Access pattern disclosure on searchable encryption: ramification, attack and mitigation. In: NDSS, vol. 20, p. 12 (2012)
17. Klimt, B., Yang, Y.: The Enron corpus: a new dataset for email classification research. In: Boulicaut, J.-F., Esposito, F., Giannotti, F., Pedreschi, D. (eds.) ECML 2004. LNCS (LNAI), vol. 3201, pp. 217–226. Springer, Heidelberg (2004). https://doi.org/10.1007/978-3-540-30115-8_22
18. Larsen, K.G., Nielsen, J.B.: Yes, there is an oblivious RAM lower bound! In: Shacham, H., Boldyreva, A. (eds.) CRYPTO 2018. LNCS, vol. 10992, pp. 523–542. Springer, Cham (2018). https://doi.org/10.1007/978-3-319-96881-0_18
19. Liu, C., Wang, X.S., Nayak, K., Huang, Y., Shi, E.: OBLIVM: a programming framework for secure computation. In: 2015 IEEE Symposium on Security and Privacy, pp. 359–376. IEEE (2015)
20. Liu, Z., Huang, Y., Li, J., Cheng, X., Shen, C.: DivORAM: towards a practical oblivious ram with variable block size. Inf. Sci. 447, 1–11 (2018)
21. Liu, Z., Li, B., Huang, Y., Li, J., Xiang, Y., Pedrycz, W.: NewMCOS: towards a practical multi-cloud oblivious storage scheme. IEEE Trans. Knowl. Data Eng. 32(4), 714–727 (2019)
22. Maas, M., et al.: Phantom: practical oblivious computation in a secure processor. In: Proceedings of the 2013 ACM SIGSAC Conference on Computer & Communications Security, pp. 311–324 (2013)
23. Maffei, M., Malavolta, G., Reinert, M., Schröder, D.: Privacy and access control for outsourced personal records. In: 2015 IEEE Symposium on Security and Privacy, pp. 341–358. IEEE (2015)
24. Maffei, M., Malavolta, G., Reinert, M., Schröder, D.: Maliciously secure multi-client ORAM. In: Gollmann, D., Miyaji, A., Kikuchi, H. (eds.) ACNS 2017. LNCS, vol. 10355, pp. 645–664. Springer, Cham (2017). https://doi.org/10.1007/978-3-319-61204-1_32

25. Mayberry, T., Blass, E., Chan, A.H.: Efficient private file retrieval by combining ORAM and PIR. In: 21st Annual Network and Distributed System Security Symposium, NDSS. The Internet Society (2014)

26. Pinkas, B., Reinman, T.: Oblivious RAM revisited. In: Rabin, T. (ed.) CRYPTO 2010. LNCS, vol. 6223, pp. 502–519. Springer, Heidelberg (2010). https://doi.org/10.1007/978-3-642-14623-7_27

27. Ren, L., et al.: Constants count: Practical improvements to oblivious RAM. In: 24th USENIX Security Symposium (USENIX Security 15), Washington, D.C., pp. 415–430. USENIX Association (2015)

28. Roche, D.S., Aviv, A., Choi, S.G.: A practical oblivious map data structure with secure deletion and history independence. In: 2016 IEEE Symposium on Security and Privacy (SP), pp. 178–197. IEEE (2016)

29. Sahin, C., Zakhary, V., El Abbadi, A., Lin, H., Tessaro, S.: Taostore: overcoming asynchronicity in oblivious data storage. In: 2016 IEEE Symposium on Security and Privacy (SP), pp. 198–217. IEEE (2016)

30. Shi, E., Chan, T.-H.H., Stefanov, E., Li, M.: Oblivious RAM with $O((\log N)^3)$ worst-case cost. In: Lee, D.H., Wang, X. (eds.) ASIACRYPT 2011. LNCS, vol. 7073, pp. 197–214. Springer, Heidelberg (2011). https://doi.org/10.1007/978-3-642-25385-0_11

31. Stefanov, E., et al.: Path ORAM: an extremely simple oblivious ram protocol. In: Proceedings of the 2013 ACM SIGSAC Conference on Computer & Communications Security. CCS 2013, New York, NY, USA, pp. 299–310. Association for Computing Machinery (2013)

32. Stefanov, E., Shi, E.: Multi-cloud oblivious storage. In: Proceedings of the 2013 ACM SIGSAC Conference on Computer & Communications Security. CCS 2013, New York, NY, USA, pp. 247–258. Association for Computing Machinery (2013)

33. Stefanov, E., Shi, E.: ObliviStore: high performance oblivious cloud storage. In: 2013 IEEE Symposium on Security and Privacy, pp. 253–267. IEEE (2013)

34. Stefanov, E., Shi, E., Song, D.X.: Towards practical oblivious RAM. In: 19th Annual Network and Distributed System Security Symposium, NDSS 2012, San Diego, California, USA,, Reston, VA, USA 5–8 February, pp. 1–40. The Internet Society (2012)

35. Tople, S., Jia, Y., Saxena, P.: Pro-ORAM: practical read-only oblivious ram. In: RAID, pp. 197–211 (2019)

36. Vadapalli, A., Henry, R., Goldberg, I.: DuORAM: a bandwidth-efficient distributed ORAM for 2-and 3-party computation. In: 32nd USENIX Security Symposium (2023)

37. Wang, X.S., Huang, Y., Chan, T.H., Shelat, A., Shi, E.: ScORAM: oblivious ram for secure computation. In: Proceedings of the 2014 ACM SIGSAC Conference on Computer and Communications Security. CCS 2014, pp. 191–202 (2014)

38. Wang, X.S., et al.: Oblivious data structures. In: Proceedings of the 2014 ACM SIGSAC Conference on Computer and Communications Security, pp. 215–226 (2014)

39. Wang, Y., Malluhi, Q.M.: Privacy preserving computation in cloud using reusable garbled oblivious rams. In: Susilo, W., Chen, X., Guo, F., Zhang, Y., Intan, R. (eds.) ISC 2022. LNCS, vol. 13640, pp. 3–19. Springer, Cham (2022). https://doi.org/10.1007/978-3-031-22390-7_1

40. Williams, P., Sion, R., Tomescu, A.: PrivateFS: a parallel oblivious file system. In: Proceedings of the 2012 ACM Conference on Computer and Communications Security, pp. 977–988 (2012)

41. Xu, W., Zhang, J., Yuan, Y., Wang, X.: Symmetric searchable encryption with supporting search pattern and access pattern protection in multi-cloud. Concurr. Comput. Pract. Exp. **35**(9), e7651 (2023)
42. Zahur, S., et al.: Revisiting square-root ORAM: efficient random access in multi-party computation. In: 2016 IEEE Symposium on Security and Privacy (SP), pp. 218–234. IEEE (2016)

A Multi-scene Webpage Fingerprinting Method Based on Multi-head Attention and Data Enhancement

Lixia Xie[1], Yange Li[1], Hongyu Yang[1,2(✉)], Peng Wang[1], Ze Hu[2(✉)],
Xiang Cheng[3,4(✉)], and Liang Zhang[5]

[1] School of Computer Science and Technology, Civil Aviation University of China,
Tianjin 300300, China
yhyxlx@hotmail.com
[2] School of Safety Science and Engineering, Civil Aviation University of China,
Tianjin 300300, China
zhu@cauc.edu.cn
[3] School of Information Engineering, Yangzhou University, Yangzhou 225127, China
huozhai9527@126.com
[4] Information Security Evaluation Center of Civil Aviation, Civil Aviation University of China,
Tianjin 300300, China
[5] School of Information, University of Arizona, Tucson, AZ 85721, USA

Abstract. Aiming the problems of the high segmentation error of multi-tab webpage traffic and unreasonable use of mixed regions in the current Tor webpage fingerprinting methods and the poor recognition effect of webpage fingerprinting caused by lack of information on incomplete webpage traffic, a multi-scene webpage fingerprinting method based on multi-head attention and data enhancement was proposed. In the multi-tab webpage browsing scenario, sequence embedding and block division were used to transfer the original multi-tab webpage traffic sequence into a block matrix that preserves the original access order. Then, the global features of different mixed types of webpages were extracted from the block matrix based on multi-head attention for webpage recognition. In incomplete webpage browsing scenario, the original incomplete webpage traffic sequence was preprocessed to generate sequence samples. Then, incomplete sequences were interpolated through generative adversarial imputation nets to achieve data enhancement. The interpolated complete sequence was used for webpage recognition. The experiment results demonstrate that the proposed method has good performance in both webpage browsing scenarios.

Keywords: Webpage Fingerprinting · Multi-tab Webpage · Multi-head Attention · Incomplete Webpage · Data Enhancement

1 Introduction

Webpage fingerprinting [1] (WF) identifies Tor webpages [2, 3] by extracting fingerprint information from monitoring traffic for webpage matching, to achieve deanonymization of communication targets. It provides technical support for regulatory governance for

C. Ge and M. Yung (Eds.): Inscrypt 2023, LNCS 14526, pp. 418–432, 2024.
https://doi.org/10.1007/978-981-97-0942-7_21

network regulatory law enforcement agencies and has become a research hotspot in Tor anonymous communication systems. Initially, research on WF primarily focused on single-tab webpage browsing scenarios, assuming users accessed one webpage at a time, and the recognizer could collect the complete traffic accessing that webpage [4–7]. However, the ideal assumption of traditional single-tab WF methods makes them unable to adapt to complex user behavior and often fails in real-world scenarios [8].

In this paper, we focus on two webpage browsing scenarios: multi-tab webpage browsing and incomplete webpage browsing. In the multi-tab webpage browsing scenario, users open multiple tabs to access multiple webpages concurrently, and there is an apart, continuous, or overlapping relationship between the traffic of multiple webpages. In incomplete webpage browsing scenario, users close a webpage midway through its access, resulting in a missing head or tail of webpage traffic. The current multi-tab WF methods often transform the multi-tab recognition problem into the single-tab recognition problem through traffic segmentation. However, the mixing of multiple webpage traffic, the error of split point recognition, and the error of traffic splitting algorithm bring interference to webpage recognition. In addition, most studies only focus on overlapping multi-tab webpage traffic and do not make reasonable use of mixed regions. They simply discard the mixed regions or treat them equally with other regions, resulting in information loss or confusion. The current incomplete WF methods lack mining and supplementation of fingerprint information. The lack of information on incomplete webpage traffic affects the access patterns of the same webpage and the differences between different webpage traffic, leading to a serious decrease in webpage recognition accuracy.

To address the above problems, we propose a multi-scene WF method, and conducted research on WF in two Tor webpage browsing scenarios. In the multi-tab webpage browsing scenario, a multi-head attention-based multi-tab webpage fingerprinting (MAMWF) is proposed. In the incomplete webpage browsing scenario, a data enhancement-based webpage fingerprinting (DEWF) is proposed.

In summary, the main contributions of this paper are as follows:

- In multi-tab WF, sequence embedding and block division are proposed. Sequence embedding automatically captures relevant features from the directional sequence of the original multi-tab webpage traffic. Block division then partitions the resulting embedding vector into distinct blocks. To differentiate sequences belonging to different webpages, positional encoding is incorporated. They effectively mitigate interference from sequence splitting errors during webpage recognition.
- In multi-tab WF, a multi-head attention-based global feature extraction method is proposed. Three encoders are designed to handle three specific types of mixed webpage separately. Each encoder captures the correlation between blocks and assigns varying degrees of attention to them. This approach ensures the effective utilization of mixed regions and significantly improves the accuracy of webpage recognition.
- In incomplete WF, data enhancement-based webpage fingerprinting is proposed. An incomplete webpage traffic sequence data enhancement model based on generative adversarial imputation nets (GAIN) [9] is designed to impute missing elements in incomplete webpage sequences. The complete webpage sequence after imputation is more in line with the data distribution of real webpage sequences. The fingerprint

information in it is used for webpage recognition and can effectively improve the accuracy of webpage recognition.

2 Related Work

In the absence of defense, the accuracy and recall of Deep Fingerprinting (DF) [10] were better than the previous deep learning method. In lightweight defense scenarios [11, 12], it also achieved a good recognition result. However, the assumption that users can only browse on one tab and webpage traffic can be fully captured is not always tenable. Zou et al. [3] highlighted the significance of mitigating the user behavior hypothesis in real-world WF scenarios. They emphasized that it is necessary to study more complex user action settings.

Xu et al. [13] introduced a multi-tab WF approach that leverages split point recognition as a central element of their method. To tackle the problem of data imbalance, they employed the BalanceCascade [14] undersampling method and constructed an XGBoost [15] classifier to identify split points between two overlapping webpages. However, this method does not consider webpage classification after the first segmentation points, and errors in the segmentation process can negatively impact the overall classification performance. Cui et al. [16] proposed a splitting algorithm for identifying multi-tab and incomplete webpages. They segmented a webpage traffic sequence and conducted webpage recognition on each segment. To determine the final category of the webpage, a majority vote was employed. However, it treats these mixed regions equally with other regions and fails to consider the relevance and importance of the mixed regions in determining the webpage category. Mixed regions containing information from multiple webpages can interfere with the recognition results. Moreover, segments from incomplete webpage sequences result in more limited information, leading to poor recognition results. Guan et al. [17] proposed a block attention profiling model (BAPM), which focuses on overlapping webpage traffic. Firstly, they generated tab-aware representations from directional sequences and performed block division. Then, blocks belonging to the same webpage were grouped based on attention. Finally, multiple webpages were recognized simultaneously in the global view. But as the number of webpages increases, BAPM faces the challenge of dynamically adapting the number of attention heads, which introduces instability to the network structure and leads to more parameters. In addition, BAPM only considers a single scenario of overlapping visits and cannot adapt to more complex browsing scenarios.

3 Proposed Methodology

Guan et al. [17] categorized multi-tab webpage traffic sequences into the following three types: The first is apart traffic sequences. The user first opens the first webpage, waits for the page to be fully loaded, then briefly browses it, and then opens the second webpage. The second is a continuous traffic sequence. The user first opens the first webpage, waits for the webpage to load completely, and then immediately clicks the second webpage. The third is the overlapping traffic sequence. The user first opens the first webpage, and clicks the second webpage when the first webpage is not fully loaded.

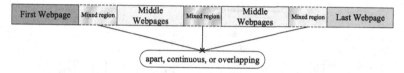

Fig. 1. The classification of webpages in multi-tab webpage traffic sequences.

As shown in Fig. 1, to use a unified method to handle the three types of multi-tab webpage traffic sequences mentioned above, we divide the webpages in the multi-tab webpage traffic sequence into three categories based on the different mixing modes of the webpage sequences. The first webpage, its tail mixed with other webpages, and its category are recorded as $webpage_{first}$. The middle webpages, their head and tail mixed with other webpages, and their category are recorded as $webpage_{middle}$. The last webpage, its head mixed with other webpages, and its category is recorded as $webpage_{last}$. The mixed relationships between various webpage traffic sequences include apart, continuous, and overlapping. When the recognizer can only listen to a portion of webpage traffic, the head or tail of the webpage traffic sequence is missing, and its category is recorded as $webpage_{inco}$.

The overall framework of the multi-scene webpage fingerprinting method based on multi-head attention and data enhancement proposed in this paper is shown in Fig. 2. MAMWF is composed of three parts: sequence embedding, block division, and multi-tab WF. DEWF is composed of three parts: sequence preprocessing, data enhancement, and incomplete WF.

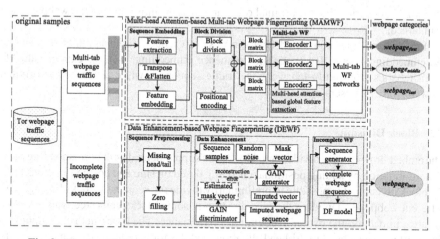

Fig. 2. The overall framework of the multi-scene webpage fingerprinting method.

4 Multi-head Attention-Based Multi-Tab WF

4.1 Sequence Embedding

The process of sequence embedding is shown in Fig. 3, and its process is as follows:

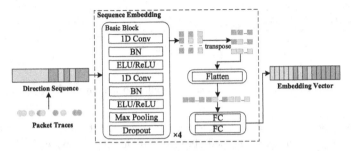

Fig. 3. The process of sequence embedding.

Firstly, the convolutional neural network is used to extract features from the original direction sequence. In this part of the network, the convolution basic block consists of two one-dimensional convolution layers. Following each one-dimensional convolution layer, there are batch normalization and activation operations incorporated. These operations play a crucial role in accelerating the training process of the deep network effectively. The utilization of max pooling layers and dropout operations can effectively aggregate sequence characteristics and prevent overfitting. Specifically, the first basic block employs the ELU activation function [18]. This choice is particularly beneficial for handling negative values present in the original sequence.

Secondly, to maintain the correspondence between each row in the two-dimensional feature representation and the features obtained through channel-wise convolution of the original sequence, we transpose the two-dimensional feature representation before flattening it, ensuring that the original order and relationships between the webpages are maintained.

Finally, two fully connected layers are used to reduce dimensionality to generate the embedding vector. By leveraging sequence embedding, we can extract valuable characteristics from multi-tab webpage traffic sequences while retaining the original browsing order of users.

4.2 Block Division

The embedding vector is divided into blocks and supplemented with corresponding position information by adding positional encoding based on sine and cosine functions [19]. By block division, it is possible to preliminarily divide the sequence blocks belonging to different webpages. Dividing the mixed region in some blocks can effectively avoid its negative impact on the overall recognition performance. The block matrix is input into three different groups of multi-head attention modules for parallel processing to identify all webpages in the multi-tab webpage traffic sequence.

4.3 Multi-tab WF

Based on the classification of webpages in multi-tab webpage traffic sequences, three encoders based on multi-head attention mechanism are constructed to extract global features for three types of webpages, each containing 8 attention heads. The three encoders

(Encoder1, Encoder2, and Encoder3) extract global features from the first webpage with a mixed tail, middle webpages with mixed headers and tails, and the last webpage with a mixed head, respectively. The encoders recognize and utilize the correlation between blocks related to classification tasks by automatically learning and adjusting parameters. Following iterative model training, Encoder1 focuses more on the blocks at the head of the block matrix that has a strong correlation with its classification targets, allocates less attention to the mixed blocks situated within the middle of the block matrix, and assigns the least attention to blocks that contain unrelated sequences of webpages, ensuring a reasonable utilization of information from each block.

A multi-tab WF network is used to classify all webpages in the multi-tab webpage traffic sequence. The multi-tab WF network constructs multiple fully connected layers, categorizing the webpages based on their global characteristics, and employs diverse activation functions to generate the probability of classification. The classification methods for various webpages are:

$$webpage_{first} = \text{softmax}\left(\text{FC}\left(feature_{first}\right)\right) \tag{1}$$

$$webpage_{middle} = \text{sigmoid}(\text{FC}(feature_{middle})) \tag{2}$$

$$webpage_{last} = \text{softmax}(\text{FC}(feature_{last})) \tag{3}$$

where FC (.) is the fully connected operation in the multi-tab WF network. $Feature_{first}$, $feature_{middle}$, and $feature_{last}$ are global features extracted by Encoder1, Encoder2, and Encoder3, respectively.

The global features extracted by Encoder1 and Encoder3 are input into the softmax function to classify the first and last webpage, respectively. The global features extracted by Encoder2 are passed through a sigmoid function to perform multi-classification of the middle webpages. For instance, in the scenario where there are two middle webpages, we determine the classification results by selecting the two webpage categories with the highest probabilities of classification.

5   Data Enhancement-Based WF

5.1   Sequence Preprocessing

The publicly available single-tab dataset is used as a pretraining sample for the GAIN model, and some elements in the original sample are randomly masked using mask vectors. In WF, due to the midway shutdown behavior of users during webpage access or the monitoring restrictions of the listener, the head or tail of the monitored webpage traffic sequence is missing. Assuming the missing proportion (the proportion of missing partial sequences to the total sequence length) is a known condition, incomplete webpage sequences with missing heads or tails are used as test samples. In the process of generating the original sequence samples, 0 is filled at the missing position of the sequence based on the missing proportion first. Then, for the sequences that do not meet the original sample dimension, 0 is intercepted or filled at the tail until they meet the sequence sample dimension.

5.2 Data Enhancement

GAIN is built based on the standard Generative adversarial network [20] architecture, which can be changed according to specific problems. To ensure that the results of the adversarial process meet expectations, GAIN uses "hint" mechanism to provide additional information to the discriminator. The architecture of the incomplete webpage traffic sequence data enhancement model is shown in Fig. 4.

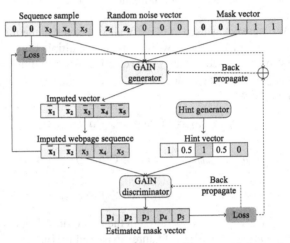

Fig. 4. The architecture of the incomplete webpage traffic sequence data enhancement model.

Assuming that the preprocessed sequence sample is a d-dimensional vector $X = (x_1, ..., x_d)$, the mask vector $M = (m_1, ..., m_d)$ is used to reflect the missing status of each element in the sequence sample X. The value of each element in M is 0 or 1, where 1 indicates that the element is not missing, and 0 indicates that the element is missing. The interpolation values are generated using a random noise vector $Z = (z_1, ..., z_d)$, whose elements are randomly sampled from a uniform distribution of [0,1).

Firstly, the positions of the corresponding missing elements in Z are masked by M, and then X, Z, and M are input into the GAIN generator. The GAIN generator generates an interpolation value for each element in X, resulting in the imputed vector $\overline{X}$. The missing elements in X are replaced with the interpolation values in $\overline{X}$ to obtain the imputed webpage sequence $\hat{X}$. Its calculation method is:

$$\hat{X} = M \odot X + (1 - M) \odot \overline{X} \tag{4}$$

where $\odot$ represents multiplication by elements.

Then, $\hat{X}$ and the hint vector are input into the GAIN discriminator to predict the probability of each element not missing in the imputed webpage sequence and obtain the estimated mask vector.

The GAIN generator and discriminator are both constructed using fully connected neural networks. The generator performs backpropagation to minimize the loss of real elements in sequence samples and imputed webpage sequences, as well as the negative loss between mask vectors and estimated mask vectors. The discriminator performs backpropagation to minimize the error between the mask vectors and the estimated mask vectors. After several iterations, the imputed webpage sequence is generated that is more in line with the distribution of real webpage sequence data.

5.3 Incomplete WF

The specific identification process of incomplete webpage traffic sequences is as follows:

Firstly, the sequence sample is generated by filling 0 to the positions of the missing elements in the incomplete sequence based on the missing proportion, and the imputed webpage sequence is obtained using the trained GAIN generator.

Secondly, the imputed webpage sequence is input into the sequence generator. Since the Tor webpage direction sequence only contains ± 1, the imputed elements in the imputed webpage sequence are transformed into:

$$w_i = \begin{cases} 1, & \bar{x}_i \geq 0.5 \\ -1, & \bar{x}_i < 0.5 \end{cases} \tag{5}$$

Finally, the complete webpage sequence is input into the DF model, and the relatively complete fingerprint information is used for webpage recognition to obtain incomplete webpage classification results.

6 Experiments and Results

6.1 Experimental Setup

Dataset. The research of WF typically explores two well-acknowledged experimental scenarios [21]: Closed-World (CW) and Open-World (OW). In the experiment, a single-tab webpage dataset [12] was utilized to manually construct a multi-tab webpage dataset and an incomplete webpage dataset. The single-tab webpage dataset was collected in 2016 using Tor 0.2.8.1 on Tor Browser 6.0, using the homepage of Alex's top 108 websites as monitored webpages and 10291 other webpages as unmonitored webpages.

Performance Metrics. In the experiment, accuracy, macro average precision (macro_P), and macro average recall (macro_R) are employed as performance metrics to evaluate the proposed method. Macro average precision and macro average recall represent the arithmetic mean of precision and recall for all webpage categories, respectively.

6.2 Experimental Results and Analysis of Multi-tab WF

Performance Evaluation Experiments. To verify the recognition performance of the proposed method MAMWF, it was compared with BAPM [17], Cui-Sectioning [16], Xu-Splitting [13], and Multi-DF for overlapping two-tab WF in CW. Where Multi-DF is the deformation of the classic single-tab WF model DF [10] to adapt to the multi-tab

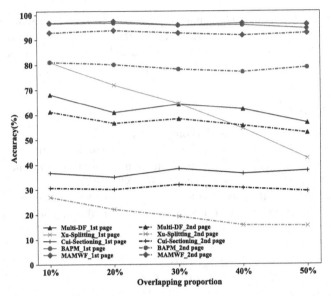

Fig. 5. Results of two-tab WF with different overlapping proportions in CW.

scenario. The results of two-tab WF with different overlapping proportions in CW are shown in Fig. 5.

By analyzing the experimental results presented in Fig. 5, several conclusions can be drawn:

1. The recognition accuracy of the second webpage is lower than that of the first webpage. Since users are required to establish a connection with the server when initiating access to a webpage, the substantial amount of information transmitted during this period plays a significant role in distinguishing different webpages. The head of the second webpage mixes with another webpage, resulting in poor recognition accuracy of the second webpage.

2. The performance of Multi-DF in terms of recognition is unsatisfactory, suggesting that the single-tab WF approach cannot be directly extended to multi-tab scenario. Xu-Splitting had the worst recognition performance on the last webpage, and as the overlapping proportion increased, the recognition accuracy on the first webpage significantly decreased. BAPM has a high recognition accuracy on the first webpage. However, when recognizing webpages with high overlapping proportions and the second webpage with a mixed head, its accuracy is low.

3. In various types of webpage recognition, MAMWF is superior to the comparison method, and as the overlapping proportion increases, the recognition effect remains basically stable. MAMWF can allocate more attention to the regions that are specifically associated with its classification goals, and integrate the correlation features between mixed regions and other regions in multiple subspaces to improve recognition performance.

To verify the recognition performance of MAMWF in simulated real environments, the two-tab WF experiments with different open-world scales were conducted in OW. The experimental results are shown in Table 1.

Table 1. Results of two-tab WF with different open-world scales in OW.

Metrics	$webpage_{first}$			$webpage_{last}$		
	4000	6000	8000	4000	6000	8000
Accuracy	93.0%	91.8%	90.9%	88.8%	90.9%	86.4%
macro_P	94.6%	92.1%	81.7%	80.6%	91.7%	76.5%
macro_R	84.6%	82.0%	80.1%	80.1%	80.1%	75.1%

The experimental results demonstrate that MAMWF exhibits good webpage when it comes to identifying webpages under different open-world scales. However, as the size of the open world scale increases, i.e. the number of unmonitored webpage categories increases, various indicators gradually decrease. The reason is that a larger collection of unmonitored webpages has a more similar data distribution pattern to monitored webpages, making webpage recognition more difficult.

To assess the generalization ability of MAMWF, a series of four-tab WF experiments were conducted on different types of multi-tab webpage sequences (including apart, continuous, overlapping, and complex types). The experimental results are presented in Fig. 6.

The experimental results in Fig. 6 demonstrate that MAMWF exhibits excellent recognition performance across diverse types of multi-tab webpage traffic, thereby substantiating its robustness and ability to identify all types of multi-tab webpage traffic. The design of the MAMWF network structure is based on the classification of webpages in multi-tab webpage traffic sequences, and each webpage is mixed with the other two webpages at most. When the number of webpages increases, no new mixing situation occurs. Therefore, without changing the model structure, MAMWF still achieves good recognition results in four-tab WF.

Ablation Experiments. Table 2 displays the results of two ablation experiments that were conducted to evaluate the significance of each component in MAMWF. In Table 2, MAMWF\E&D is a comparison method that removes sequence embedding and block division based on MAMWF, and MAMWF\A is a comparison method that removes multi-head attention-based global feature extraction based on MAMWF.

Compared to MAMWF, the recognition accuracy of MAMWF\E&D notably declined for the last webpage. It suggests that the sequence embedding and block division components in MAMWF play an important role in capturing and utilizing the relevant information related to the final webpage in multi-tab browsing sessions. Because they can extract the inherent characteristics of mixed regions and isolate them from other regions to maximize the utilization of mixed regions. MAMWF\A is equivalent to a simple multi-tab classifier, so the recognition accuracy of it is lower than that of MAMWF.

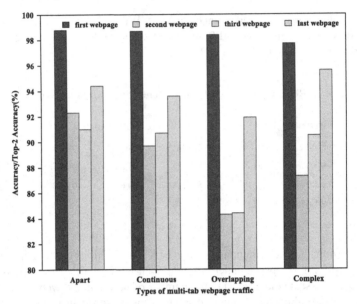

Fig. 6. Results of four-tab WF.

Table 2. Results of ablation experiments for multi-tab WF.

Methods	$webpage_{first}$			$webpage_{last}$		
	Accuracy	macro_P	macro_R	Accuracy	macro_P	macro_R
MAMWF	97.0%	97.0%	96.9%	96.2%	96.6%	96.3%
MAMWF\E&D	87.1%	86.0%	86.7%	24.2%	25.6%	24.0%
MAMWF\A	60.1%	61.0%	60.1%	53.7%	54.2%	53.7%

6.3 Experimental Results and Analysis of Incomplete WF

Performance Evaluation Experiments. To verify the recognition performance of the proposed method DEWF, a comparative experiment was conducted on incomplete WF between DEWF and Cui-Sectioning [16]. The results of incomplete WF with different missing proportions in CW are shown in Fig. 7. We can observe the following results from the experimental results in Fig. 7:

1. As the missing proportion increases, the recognition accuracy of head-missing webpages decreases by 20.7%, and the recognition accuracy of tail-missing webpages decreases by 6.2%. The experimental results indicate that the head of a webpage sequence is more important than the tail in WF. Because users need to send many HTTP requests at the beginning of establishing a connection with the server, the patterns and differences among them can help distinguish different webpages.
2. The recognition effect of Cui-Sectioning is poor, and with the increase of the missing proportion, the accuracy marked decline. Sequence splitting in Cui-Sectioning makes

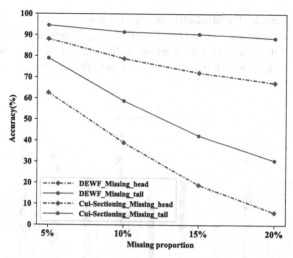

Fig. 7. Results of incomplete WF with different missing proportions in CW.

the information contained in each segment more limited, resulting in poor recognition performance.

3. The recognition accuracy of DEWF is better than that of the comparison method. The experimental results indicate that DEWF can make the generated imputed webpage sequence more consistent with the data distribution of real webpage sequences, achieving effective recognition of incomplete webpage sequences.

Table 3 shows the results of incomplete WF experiments with different open-world scales conducted in OW to verify the recognition performance of DEWF in simulated real environments.

Table 3. Results of incomplete WF with different open-world scales in OW.

Metrics	Missing_head			Missing_tail		
	4000	6000	8000	4000	6000	8000
Accuracy	89.6%	90.1%	91.0%	95.1%	95.9%	93.1%
macro_P	86.3%	83.0%	84.3%	93.7%	93.9%	93.6%
macro_R	85.3%	84.5%	84.2%	93.1%	93.6%	93.4%

The experimental results show that under different open-world scales, the recognition performance of DEWF for incomplete webpages remains basically stable. In an open-world scale with 8000 unmonitored webpage categories, the head-missing webpage sequence can still achieve a macro average precision rate and macro average recall rate of over 80%, indicating that DEWF has good recognition performance in simulated real environments.

Ablation Experiments. The ablation experiment is designed to verify the effectiveness of the data enhancement section in DEWF, and the experimental results are shown in Fig. 8. In Fig. 8, DEWF\DE is a comparison method that removes data enhancement based on DEWF, which means it directly identifies partially missing incomplete webpage sequences.

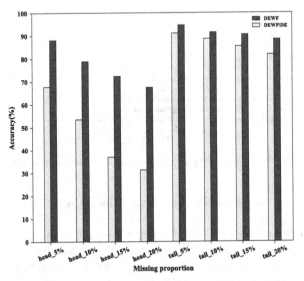

Fig. 8. Results of ablation experiments for incomplete WF.

The experimental results show that the recognition accuracy of the webpage traffic sequence with missing heads has been improved by 20.4% −36.1% and the recognition accuracy of webpage traffic sequences with missing tails is improved by 2.8% −6.6% after data enhancement. This indicates that data enhancement can effectively improve the recognition accuracy of incomplete webpage sequences.

7 Conclusion

To address the problems of high segmentation errors and unreasonable use of mixed regions in multi-tab webpage traffic, and incomplete webpage traffic resulting in poor WF performance, this paper proposes a multi-scene webpage finger-printing method on Tor.

In a multi-tab browsing scenario, MAMWF uses sequence embedding to mine the potential features of the original direction sequence and generates the embedding vectors through block division. Based on multi-head attention, MAMWF extracts corresponding global features of different mixed types of webpages for WF. The experimental results show that MAMWF has outstanding performance in multi-tab WF.

In incomplete webpage browsing scenario, DEWF utilizes the incomplete webpage traffic sequence data enhancement model based on GAIN to enhance the preprocessed incomplete sequence data and recognizes the imputed webpage sequence through the DF model. Experiments showed that DEWF can effectively improve the recognition rate of incomplete webpages.

In future research, we will attempt to break the constraints of existing experimental scenarios and conduct experiments using more diverse datasets to verify the effectiveness of Tor WF methods more accurately.

Acknowledgments. This work was supported by the National Natural Science Foundation of China (No. 62201576, No. U1833107), the Fundamental Research Funds for the Central Universities (No. 3122022050), the Open Fund of the Information Security Evaluation Center of Civil Aviation University of China (ISECCA-202202), and the Discipline Development Funds of Civil Aviation University of China.

References

1. Sun, X.F., Huang, A.S., Luo, X.T., et al.: Webpage fingerprinting identification on tor: a survey. J. Comput. Res. Dev. **58**(8), 1773–1788 (2021)
2. Zhao, N.F., Su, J.S., Zhao, B.T., et al.: A survey on hidden service location technologies in anonymous communication system. Chin. J. Comput. **45**(2), 393–411 (2022)
3. Zou, H.F., Su, J.S., Wei, Z.T., et al.: A review of the research of website fingerprinting identification and defense. Chin. J. Comput. **45**(10), 2243–2278 (2022)
4. Wang, T.F., Cai, X.S., Nithyanand, R.T., et al.: Effective attacks and provable defenses for website fingerprinting. In: 23rd USENIX Security Symposium (USENIX Security 14), pp. 143–157. USENIX Association, San Diego (2014)
5. Hayes, J.F., Danezis, G.S.: k-fingerprinting: a robust scalable website fingerprinting technique. In: USENIX Security Symposium, pp. 1187–1203. USENIX Association, Austin (2016)
6. Panchenko, A.F., Lanze, F.S., Pennekamp, J.T., et al.: Website fingerprinting at internet scale. In: 23rd Network and Distributed System Security Symposium (NDSS), pp. 1–15. ISOC, California (2016)
7. Rimmer, V.F., Preuveneers, D.S., Juarez, M.T., et al.: Automated website fingerprinting through deep learning. arXiv preprint arXiv:1708.06376 (2017)
8. Juarez, M.F., Afroz, S.S., Acar, G.T., et al.: A critical evaluation of website fingerprinting attacks. In: Proceedings of the 2014 ACM SIGSAC Conference on Computer and Communications Security, pp. 263–274. ACM, AZ, USA (2014)
9. Yoon J.F., Jordon J.S., Schaar M.T.: Gain: missing data imputation using generative adversarial nets. In: International Conference on Machine Learning, pp. 5689–5698. ACM, Stockholm (2018)
10. Sirinam, P.F., Imani, M.S., Juarez, M.T., et al.: Deep fingerprinting: undermining website fingerprinting defenses with deep learning. In: Proceedings of the 2018 ACM SIGSAC Conference on Computer and Communications Security, pp. 1928–1943. ACM, Toronto (2018)
11. Juarez, M., Imani, M., Perry, M., Diaz, C., Wright, M.: Toward an efficient website fingerprinting defense. In: Askoxylakis, I., Ioannidis, S., Katsikas, S., Meadows, C. (eds.) ESORICS 2016. LNCS, vol. 9878, pp. 27–46. Springer, Cham (2016). https://doi.org/10.1007/978-3-319-45744-4_2
12. Wang, T.F., Goldberg, I.S.: Walkie-Talkie: an efficient defense against passive website fingerprinting attacks. In: USENIX Security Symposium, pp. 1375–1390. USENIX Association, Vancouver, BC, Canada (2017)

13. Xu, Y.F., Wang, T.S., Li, Q.T., et al.: A multi-tab website fingerprinting attack. In: Proceedings of the 34th Annual Computer Security Applications Conference, pp. 327–341. IEEE, San Juan (2018)

14. Liu, X.F., Wu, J.S., Zhou, Z.T.: Exploratory undersampling for class-imbalance learning. IEEE Trans. Syst. Man Cybern. **39**(2), 539–550 (2008)

15. Chen T.F., Guestrin C.S.: XGBoost: a scalable tree boosting system. In: Proceedings of the 22nd ACM SIGKDD International Conference on Knowledge Discovery and Data Mining, pp. 785–794. ACM, San Francisco (2016)

16. Cui, W.F., Chen, T.S., Fields, C.T., et al.: Revisiting assumptions for website fingerprinting attacks. In: Proceedings of the 2019 ACM Asia Conference on Computer and Communications Security, pp. 328–339. ACM, London (2019)

17. Guan, Z.F., Xiong, G.S., Gou, G.T., et al.: BAPM: block attention profiling model for multi-tab website fingerprinting attacks on tor. In: Annual Computer Security Applications Conference, pp. 248–259. IEEE, USA (2021)

18. Clevert, D.A.F., Unterthiner, T.S., Hochreiter, S.T.: Fast and accurate deep network learning by exponential linear units (elus). arXiv preprint arXiv:1511.07289 (2015)

19. Vaswani, A.F., Shazeer, N.S., Parmar, N.T., et al.: Attention is all you need. In: Advances in Neural Information Processing Systems, vol. 30, pp. 5998–6008 (2017)

20. Creswell, A., White, T., Dumoulin, V., Arulkumaran, K., Sengupta, B., Bharath, A.A.: Generative adversarial networks: an overview. IEEE Signal Process. Mag. **35**(1), 53–65 (2018). https://doi.org/10.1109/MSP.2017.2765202

21. Wang, Y., Haitao, X., Guo, Z., Qin, Z., Ren, K.: SnWF: website fingerprinting attack by ensembling the snapshot of deep learning. IEEE Trans. Inf. Forensics Secur. **17**, 1214–1226 (2022). https://doi.org/10.1109/TIFS.2022.3158086

A Lightweight Access Control Scheme Supporting Policy Hidden Based on Path Bloom Filter

Chao Luo[1], Jiaoli Shi[1,2,3]([✉]), Minchen Xie[1], Chao Hu[1,2,3], Lihua Wang[1], Zhuolin Mei[1,2,3], Shimao Yao[1], and Hui Li[4]

[1] School of Computer and Big Data Science, Jiujiang University, Jiujiang 332005, Jiangxi, China
shijiaoli@whu.edu.cn
[2] Jiujiang Key Laboratory of Network and Information Security, Jiujiang 332005, Jiangxi, China
[3] Institute of Information Security, Jiujiang University, Jiujiang 332005, Jiangxi, China
[4] Shenzhen Graduate School Peking University, Shenzhen, China

Abstract. Traditional CP-ABE (Ciphertext-Policy Attribute-Based Encryption) schemes require the access policy to be uploaded to the cloud along with the ciphertext, but access policies often also involve some private information, which can lead to privacy leakage. Moreover, the decryption cost of the traditional CP-ABE scheme is too high, which is not suitable for source-limited end devices, such as medical monitoring terminals. To achieve *policy hiding*, *decryption lightening*, and *high expressiveness of access policy* all at the same time, we present a new CP-ABE scheme, in which a PBF (Path Bloom Filter) is designed based on ROBDD (Reduced Ordered Binary Decision Diagram). The ROBDD, as the access structure, can provide more vital and more flexible expressiveness. Then the PBF can hide the access policy, reduce the decryption cost, and accelerate the decryption speed. Analysis and simulation study show that our proposed scheme is secure under Decisional q-BDHE assumption and superior to previous schemes concerning computational cost.

Keywords: Ciphertext-Policy Attribute-Based Encryption · Policy Hiding · Reduced Ordered Bifurcated Decision Diagrams · Path Bloom Filter

1 Introduction

CP-ABE (Ciphertext-Policy Attribute-Based Encryption) binds the access policy to the data and the user's private key can be decrypted if it matches with the access policy, and can be used to realize fine-grained access control. However, CP-ABE is not suitable to be used in various scenarios in practice where terminal resources are limited because CP-ABE spends too high decryption cost on users. Therefore, there are several methods to reduce the decryption cost at the terminal, such as: 1) Decryption process is divided into two parts: offline and online, such as [1]. The preparation work is completed offline first, and users only need to complete the online part when they go online. This method

C. Ge and M. Yung (Eds.): Inscrypt 2023, LNCS 14526, pp. 433–451, 2024.
https://doi.org/10.1007/978-981-97-0942-7_22

can reduce the user latency. 2) The part of decryption computation is transferred to a third party to reduce the decryption cost on users, such as [2]. 3) More flexible access structures, such as ROBDD (Reduced Ordered Binary Decision Diagrams), can also mitigate decryption costs, such as [3].

The ROBDD has high expressiveness. However, doing policy hiding on ROBDD is computationally expensive. Unlike access structures such as with or gates, access trees and access matrices, ROBDD is a recursive algorithm that must verify that a node attribute is secretly owned before it can go to the next node attribute for verification. The previous three can be computationally verified directly. This means that if the access policy is hidden, then it is necessary to try to decrypt all possible results in the ROBDD access structure.

Access policy in CP-ABE discloses sensitive ciphertext information. In an attribute-based access control scheme, the end user first defines access policies for the data and encrypts the data according to these access policies. Only users whose attributes satisfy the access policy are eligible to decrypt the data. They all suffer from one problem: access policies can compromise privacy. This is because the access policy is associated with encrypted data in plaintext form, and after encryption is complete, the policy is uploaded to the cloud along with the ciphertext. From the plaintext of the access policy, the attacker can obtain some private information about the end user. For example, to open a locked box and access its contents, we can see the lock on the box whether we can open it or not, and even if we cannot open the box, we can still derive relevant information by looking at the lock.

Currently, there are several approaches to policy privacy protection for CP-ABE: 1) Migrate the access policy verification process and outsource it to the cloud, but in this approach, the cloud server is not fully trusted and there is still a risk of privacy leakage. 2) Migrate the access policy authentication part to other difficult problems, this approach increases the decryption cost to the end user. 3) Hide the attribute values of the access policy, but when decrypting, the user still needs to resort to the access policy. So, after hiding the attribute values in the access policy, decryption will be very difficult for the user.

In summary, although there have been studies on lightweight access control, policy hiding, and ROBDD, no scheme comprehensively considers these three aspects. This paper perfectly integrates lightweight, privacy protection, and rich expression by designing PBF and combining ROBDD.

1.1 Our Contributions

Our contributions can be summarized as follows.

1) A Lightweight Access Control Scheme Supporting Policy Hidden based on ROBDD and Path Bloom Filter, called LACS-PRP, is proposed, which not only achieves full expression of the access policy, but also takes into account the hiding of the access policy, with rich expression capability.

2) The Path Bloom filter (PBF) is constructed to help a user match his attribute set quickly with an access policy when decrypting. The PBF is adopted to achieve the hiding of the access policy to protect the user's privacy while saving the user's decryption time.

1.2 Related Work

In 1984, Shamir [4] proposed the IBE (Identity-Based Encryption), and the first IBE scheme was implemented in 2001 by Dan Boneh et al. [5] using bilinear mappings on elliptic curves. Then Sihai et al. [6] proposed ABE on the basis of IBE. In ABE, the encryptor constructs the access structure and binds it with his data. The decryptor can decrypt if his own attribute set matches the access structure bound with a data.

In order to represent access control policies more flexibly, CP-ABE(Ciphertext-Policy ABE) [7] and KP-ABE(Key-Policy ABE) [8] have subsequently emerged. In 2014, Zhang et al. [9] proposed a CP-ABE scheme with constant computational cost and constant ciphertext length. In CP-ABE solutions, a quality access structure can often make a huge difference to the efficiency of the system. Waters et al. [10] proposed several CP-ABE schemes on the basis of LSSS access structures, which by construction can basically satisfy arbitrary Boolean operations, but still lack flexibility as their properties can only appear once in the access matrix.

The emergence of OBDD (Ordered Binary Decision Diagrams) [11] solves these problems perfectly, with the ability to perfectly express arbitrary forms of Boolean expressions without the need to integrate other access structures. Li et al. [12] proposed a CP-ABE scheme based on OBDD in 2017, supporting with or without gates, thresholds and positive and negative values, and based on prime order bilinear multiplicative cyclic groups, with complexity assumptions based on DBDH assumptions and security based on CPA. In 2021, Wang et al. [13] proposed a scheme based on the OBDD access structure, supporting the expression of arbitrary Boolean expressions and positive and negative values of attributes, based on the DBDH assumption, supporting the selection of plaintext attacks on CSPs under the standard model, and also supporting white-box traceability for prime order bilinear cyclic groups.

Subsequently, in order to be able to simplify the OBDD, the ROBDD (Reduced Ordered Bifurcation Decision Diagram was proposed to solve the problem of the OBDD being too cumbersome. Affum et al. [14] supported efficient attribute expressions by constructing ROBDD schemes. Li et al. [3] proposed a CP-ABE scheme based on ROBDD, which achieves fast decryption and a fixed length of private key.

However, none of the above solutions prevent policy leakage, and the same protection is needed as there is a possibility of confidentiality in the access policy. There are multiple security options for policy hiding, with the ability to set up trusted third-party servers and migrate and outsource the access policy validation process to the cloud to make access policies invisible to users.

K. Edemacu et al. [15] proposed a secure scheme by outsourcing the encryption and decryption and adding virtual attributes, which supports selective security. The access policy may or may not be encrypted, converting the adversary's access policy authentication component to some other form and migrating it to other difficult problems. Affum et al. [14] implemented a secure scheme for CP-ABE in conjunction with the R-LWE problem in the Content-Centric Networking / Named Data Networking (CCN/NDN) scenario. To prevent privacy leakage in access policies, a simple way is to hide the attributes in the access policy. Li et al. [16] achieved attribute value hiding by replacing attribute values with hash values.

But when attributes are hidden, neither unauthorized nor authorized users have any way of knowing which attributes are involved in the access policy, which makes decryption a challenging problem. As for lightening of access control, Lai et al. [17] proposed a fully secure ciphertext policy attribute-based encryption (CP-ABE) scheme with a partially hidden access policy. However, the scheme is limited to specific access policies. In 2016, Yang et al. [18] proposed an efficient fine-grained big data access control scheme with privacy-preserving policies and a new Attribute Bloom Filter (ABF). In 2018, Chen et al. [19] proposed a hidden policy attribute base encryption based on a bilinear group of meromorphic order and proved its security under selective plaintext attacks using a dual system encryption mechanism. In 2018, Han et al. [20] achieved efficient and robust attribute-based encryption and support access policies hidden in the IoT by using Oblivious Transfer and building ABF. In 2020, Li et al. [21] proposed a traceable ciphertext policy hiding ABE scheme based on prime order group construction. In 2021, Zhang et al. [22] designed a online decryption test algorithm and a testing key for user to make the decryption cost on users comparable to traditional CP-ABE. However, their scheme reveals the attribute name and the access matrix. In 2023, Wang et al. [23] established a blockchain platform for healthcare centers to share their EHR. The decryption cost on users just needs 2 pairing operation, 1 multiplication operation and 1 division operation. However, they do not say how the access structure is delivered to the user.

However, most of the above schemes are based on LSSS (Linear Secret Sharing Scheme), which lacks certain flexibility. Based on the above schemes, we propose a policy hidden attribute-based encryption scheme based on ROBDD structure.

2   Background and Assumptions

2.1   Reduced Ordered Binary Decision Diagram

The BDD(Binary Decision Diagram) was proposed by Akers [24]. And Bryant [11] attached variable order and simplification constraints to BDD, making them become a canonical type of Boolean expression formulation, called OBDD (Ordered Binary Decision Diagram). And subsequent introduction of some simplification rules to form a ROBDD (Reduced Ordered Binary Decision Diagram).

(1) BDD (Binary Decision Diagram)

BDD is a rooted directed acyclic graph. It includes a root node, internal nodes, and terminal nodes. Usually, a node nd is used to denote the non-terminal node. And all non-terminal nodes have 4 sets of attributes (f_{nd}, var,low,$high$), the f_{nd} denotes the Boolean function of nd, $f_{nd} \in (x_1, x_2, x_3..., x_n)$; var denotes the marker variable for nd; low denotes the 0-branch sub-node of the node nd when $nd.var = 0$, called a 0-edge, and is represented by a dashed line in the decision diagram; $high$ denotes the 1-branch sub-node of node nd when $nd.var = 1$, called a 1-edge, and is represented by a solid line in the decision diagram. A terminal node is denoted by v and is also called a leaf node. Its Boolean constant can be expressed as $v.value \in \{0, 1\}$. Each variable appears at most once on any directed path in the decision diagram.

(2) OBDD (Ordered Binary Decision Diagram)

The difference between OBDD and BDD is that the order of occurrence of each variable remains the same on any of its paths from the root node to the terminal node.

(3) ROBDD (Reduced Ordered Binary Decision Diagram)

Generated on the basis of the OBDD, two simplified rules are introduced: **Consolidation rule** (Fig. 1): If two nodes are terminal nodes and have the same label, or are internal nodes and have the same child nodes, they are merged. **S-deletion rule** (Fig. 2): For the node nd, if $nd.low = nd.high$, the node is removed from the graph and its parent node is redirected to a child node.

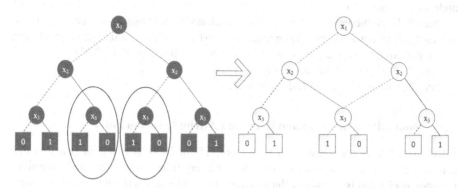

Fig. 1. Consolidation rule

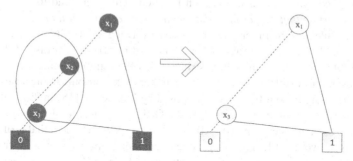

Fig. 2. S-deletion rule

2.2 Construction of ROBDD

Step 1: Present the access structure: $ROBDD = \left\{ Node_{id_i}^{attr_i} \middle| attr_i \in U, id_i \in ID \right\}$, id_i represents the node number in the ROBDD, $attr_i$ represents the attribute in ROBDD, U represents the set of contained attributes, ID represents the set of non-terminal node numbers.

Step 2: Obtain the relevant data and requirements for the corresponding access policy. For example, the attribute $attr_i$ required in the access policy, the number of attributes required x, and the policy to be satisfied between attributes.

Step 3: Construct a full binary tree of depth x based on the number of attribute secrets x.

Step 4: Traversal nodes from the root node to the terminal node. Each node at each level is assigned the corresponding attribute $attr_i$ in turn, the root node is assigned attribute $attr_1$, the two nodes at the second level are assigned attribute $attr_2$, the four nodes at the third level are assigned attribute $attr_3$, ..., and each leaf node is assigned attribute $attr_i$.

Step 5: Construct a full binary tree of depth 2 for each leaf node, with each leaf node as the root. The left branch is a dashed line, called a 0-output arc, pointing to a node with a value of 0; The right branch is a solid line, called a 1-output arc and points to a node with a value of 1.

Step 6: Mark 0-edges and 1-edges under each node according to the access policy to be satisfied between attributes. Then indicate them by dashed and solid lines respectively.

Step 7: Simplify the access structure according to the rules of ROBDD.

Step 8: Assign the node number to each node.

Step 9: Complete the ROBDD construction.

2.3 Bloom Filter, Garble Bloom Filter and Attribute Bloom Filter

BF (Bloom Filter) was introduced by Bloom [25] in 1970. It is a data structure that can save storage space and reduce insertion or query time, and can be used to retrieve whether an element is in a set. If the location of an element x is 0 after h hash functions have been mapped, then the element does not exist, and if it is 1, it may exist. This is because hash collisions occur in the hash function, which can lead to *false positives*. That is, *it is certain that it does not exist, but it is not certain that it does.*

GBF (Garble Bloom Filter) was proposed by Dong et al. [26] in 2013. GBF is a variation of BF that uses arrays of arrays instead of arrays of arrays, reducing the number of *false positives* by matching strings rather than simply seeing if the value is 0 or 1. However, it is unable to locate the row number of the attribute in the access matrix.

ABF (Attribute Bloom Filter) was proposed by Yang et al. [18] in 2016. It is based on the GBF, with certain improvements to the GBF, and is able to pinpoint the position of the attributes in the access matrix. ABF proposes a special element that is of length λ, and consists of two fixed-length strings, one string representing a line number of length L_{row} and the other string representing an attribute of length L_{att} and $L_{row} + L_{att} = \lambda$. This ABF not only determines whether an attribute is in a set, but also the row number of the attribute in the access matrix by L_{row}.

2.4 Decisional q-BDHE Assumption

Theorem 1 (Decisional q-BDHE Assumption): Choose the group G of prime order p according to the safety parameter λ. Set $a, s \in Z_p^*$ to be arbitrarily chosen and g to be the generating element of G. Set g_i to denote g^{a^i}. When given $\vec{y} = (g, g_1, \cdots, g_q, g_{q+2}, \cdots, g_{2q}, g^s)$ one must distinguish $\hat{e}(g, g)^{a^{q+1}s} \in G_T$ from a random element g in G_T. Algorithm has an advantage in solving the decisional q-BDHE assumption in G if the following conditions are satisfied:

$$| \Pr[B(\overrightarrow{y}, T = \hat{e}(g, g)^{a^{q+1}s}) = 0] - \Pr[B(\overrightarrow{y}, T = R) = 0]| \geq \varepsilon$$

If no polynomial-time algorithm has a non-negligible advantage in solving the q-BDHE problem, then we say that the q-BDHE assumption is judged to hold.

3 Definitions of Our LACS-PRP

3.1 Definition of System Model

This scheme will create a system for access policy hiding through PBF. The system consists of four entities: AA (Attribute Authorities), CSP (Cloud Service Provider), DO (Data Owner), and DU (Data User), shown as Fig. 3.

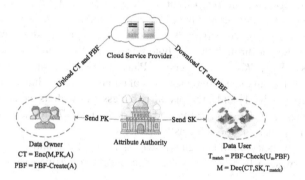

Fig. 3. System model

AA is an attribute authorization, responsible for managing all attributes in the system, assigning attributes to users, and also working as a key generation centre, generating public params as well as public keys, and issuing private keys to users according to their different attributes in the system, acting as a fully trusted authority in this system.

CSP is a cloud service provider that provides users with efficient computing power, as well as data storage, data sharing, data backup and other functions. In this system, it is responsible for storing ciphertext, plaintext, access policies, etc. The cloud server is not fully trusted and exists as a semi-trusted organization.

DO is a data owner. The Data Owner is the producer or owner of the data and is responsible for uploading the data to the cloud server and encrypting the uploaded data as well as defining the access structure and implementing access control over the data. It is also responsible for enforcing the hiding of access policies in this system and is a fully trusted entity.

DU is a data user that downloads the data it needs from the cloud server and can only decrypt the encrypted data with its own private key if it meets a threshold of a set of attributes in the access policy.

3.2 Security Requirements

Access Policy Hidden. The user cannot get more information from the access policy when decrypting it.

Collusion Resistance. Two legitimate users cannot modify permissions that they do not have individually by combining their private keys.

Data Confidentiality. The data submitted by the Data Owner is stored encrypted on the server side. And the contents of the data are not accessible to the CSP or the unauthorized users.

3.3 Security Model

The proposed scheme is secure if the maximum advantage of an adversary wining the following security game is negligible in polynomial time.

Setup: Challenger runs the *Setup* algorithm to generate the *MPK* and the *MSK*, where the *MSK* is kept by Challenger and the *MPK* is provided to Adversary.

Phase 1: In this phase, Adversary continuously sends private key queries related to attributes to Challenger through the attribute sets $S_1, S_2, S_3...$, and Challenger C sends private keys $SK_1, SK_2, SK_3...$ to Adversary. Phase 1 can be repeated several times.

Challenge: Adversary sends two messages of equal length to Challenger. Challenger randomly selects $\eta \in \{0, 1\}$ and encrypts the two messages with its own access structure to generate ciphertext CT_η, and finally sends the ciphertext CT_η to Adversary.

Phase 2: The process is the same as for phase 1.

Guess: An adversary outputs a guess $\eta'(\eta' \in \{0, 1\})$ for η and the adversary wins if $\eta' = \eta$, otherwise Adversary loses. The success rate of Adversary in the game is: $Adv(A) = \left| \Pr[\eta' = \eta] - 1/2 \right|$.

4 Construction of Our LACS-PRP

4.1 Main Idea

Path Bloom Filter (PBF) is first proposed by us based on ABF, it is used for the first time with ROBDD (Reduced Ordered Binary Decision Diagram) to put the paths in its access policy into PBF, which can achieve fast matching. The PBF consists of two parts. Both of which are fixed length strings. The former indicates the node number using a length $L_{nodenum}$ bit string, and the latter indicates the attribute secret with a length L_{att} bit string. The designed structure can determine quickly whether an attribute is in the ROBDD access policy and its node number is in the access structure. This design can help to achieve policy hiding and determine quickly whether an attribute meets the decryption requirements.

Table 1. Notations

Symbols	Description
MPK, MSK	the master public/private key
U, U_u, U_c	the system attribute set, the attribute set of the user u, the attribute set bound on a ciphertext
n, n_u, n_c	$|U|, |U_u|, |U_c|$
SK_u	the private key of the user u
M, A	the plaintext and the access policy
T_{match}	a matched path
$Attr_i, id_i$	the attribute and its sequence number
$n_{path}, n_{path,attr}$	number of paths, the number of attributes in a path
$\{H_j\}_{j\in[1,h]}$	hash functions for generate the position in BPF

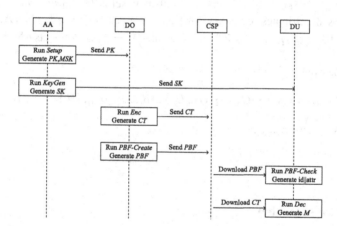

Fig. 4. Framework of LACS-PRP

4.2 Definition of Our LACS-PRP

The main notations are listed in Table 1.

Our scheme consists of 6 algorithms (*Setup, KeyGen, PBF-Create, Enc, PBF-Check* and *Dec*) shown as Fig. 4.

Setup$(1^s) \rightarrow (MPK, MSK)$: The *Setup* algorithm takes the security parameter as input and outputs the master public key MPK as well as the master private key MSK. MPK is the default input for each algorithm.

KeyGen$(U_u, MSK) \rightarrow (SK_u)$: The AA runs the *KeyGen* algorithm to generate user private keys for individual users. With the inputs of U_u (the attribute set of the user u) and the MSK, AA outputs the user's private key SK_u.

Enc$(M, A) \rightarrow (CT)$: In this phase it is responsible for encrypting the plaintext. Input the plaintext M and the access policy A and output the encrypted ciphertext CT.

PBF-Create(A) → (PBF): *PBF-Create* algorithm takes as input the access policy A and outputs the *PBF*.

PBF-Check(U_u, PBF) → (T_{match}): Taking a user's attributes set U_u and *PBF* as input, this algorithm outputs a matched path $T_{match} = \{nodenum_i \| Attr_i\}_{i \in [1, n_{path}]}$.

Dec(CT, SK_u, T_{match}) → (M): The *Dec* algorithm takes the ciphertext CT and the user's private key SK_u as input and outputs the plaintext M.

4.3 Detail Design of our LACS-PRP

4.3.1 *Setup* Algorithm

The algorithm runs on AA. The algorithm takes the security parameter ς as input and outputs a master public key *MPK* and a master private key *MSK*. Firstly, G_1, G_2 and G_T are three p-order cyclic groups (p is a large prime number) and $e : G_1 \times G_2 \to G_T$, g_1 and g_2 are generating elements of G_1 and G_2 respectively. $e(g_1, g_2) = e(g_2, g_1) = 1$, $e(g_1, g_1) \neq 1$, $e(g_2, g_2) \neq 1$. Secondly, AA selects random numbers: $\alpha, \beta \in Z_p^*$, and calculates $Y = e(g_1^\alpha, g_1^\beta)$. The system attribute set is $U = \{attr_1, attr_2, ..., attr_n\}$. AA generates all attributes secret keys $\{a_i\}_{i \in [1, n]} \in Z_q^*$, and $B_i = g_1^{a_i}$. Then AA chooses random numbers $\{x_i, r_i\}_{i \in [1, n]} \in Z_p^*$, and calculates $X_i = g_2^{x_i}$. AA selects h hash functions $\{H_j\}_{j \in [1, h]}$.

The master public key is:

$$MPK = (g_1, g_2, G_1, G_2, G_T, U, e, \{B_i, X_i\}_{i \in [1, n]}, \{H_j\}_{j \in [1, h]}, Y)$$

The master private key is:

$$MSK = (\{a_i, x_i, r_i\}_{i \in [1, n]}, \alpha, \beta)$$

4.3.2 *KeyGen* Algorithm

KeyGen algorithm runs on AA. Assuming that the user has n_u attributes, and $n_u \leq n$, the set of attributes for that user is $U_u = \{s_1, s_2, \cdots, s_{n_u}\}$. The user sends the information related to the attributes they have to the AA, which selects $r_u \in Z_p^*$ for different users, and issues the user's private key as follows.

$$sk_0 = g_1^{\alpha\beta} \cdot g_2^{r_u \sum_{i \in [1, n_u]} x_i - r_i}, \quad sk_{1,i} = g_1^{a_i r_u} \cdot g_2^{-r_i},$$

$$sk_{2,i} = \begin{cases} B_i^{r_u} \cdot g_2^{-r_u}, & s_i \in U_u \\ B_i^{r_u} \cdot g_2^{-r_i}, & s_i \notin U_u \end{cases}$$

$$SK_u = (sk_0, \{sk_{1,i}, sk_{2,i}\}_{i \in [1, n_u]})$$

4.3.3 *Enc* Algorithm

DO input plaintext M and access structure A. The access structure ROBDD is constructed as $ROBDD = \left\{ Node_{id_i}^{attr_i} \middle| attr_i \in U_c, id_i \in ID \right\}$, wherein id_i represents the node numbers in the ROBDD, $attr_i$ represent the attributes in the ROBDD, U_c represent the set of contained attributes, and ID represent the set of non-terminal node numbers. Then DO chooses random numbers $s, \{v_i\}_{i \in [1, n_c]} \in Z_p^*$.

$$C_0 = g_1 \cdot g_2^s, \quad C' = M \cdot Y,$$

$$C_{k,i,1} = \begin{cases} B_i^{-v_i s} \cdot X_i^s, & t_{k,i} \in U_c \\ B_i^{-v_i} \cdot X_i^s, & t_{k,i} \notin U_c \end{cases}, \quad C_{k,i,2} = g_1^{v_i s} \cdot g_2^{x_i s}$$

$$CT = \left(C_0, C', \{ C_{k,i,1}, C_{k,i,2} \}_{i \in [1, n_{path,attr}], k \in [1, n_{path}]} \right)$$

4.3.4 *PBFCreat* Algorithm

We construct a new type of Bloom filter (BF), called the Path Bloom Filter (PBF). Its structure is shown in the Fig. 5. The reasons for this construction are stated as follows. GBF (Garbled Bloom Filter) has been constructed based on the secret sharing method. In contrast to the traditional Bloom Filter, the GBF is constructed which uses a λ-*bit* string instead of a *1-bit*. This reduces the number of false positives that occur when determining whether an element belongs to a subset. The low false alarm rate allows the Garble Bloom Filter to be used in the age of big data.

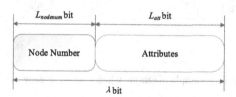

Fig. 5. Structure of an element in *PBF*

In this phase, the data owner will calculate the corresponding access policy $T_k = \{attr_{k,1}, attr_{k,2}, \cdots, attr_{k,j} \cdots, , attr_{k,n_{k,attr}}\}_{k \in [1, n_{path}]}$ through the ROBDD access structure based on the type of data required by the user, wherein T_k denotes the k available path which are from the root node to the final decision node with a value of 1, $attr_{k,j}$ denotes the node j that is passed through included in the T_k. n_{path} denotes the number of available paths in the access structure. $n_{k,attr}$ denotes the number of attributes included in T_k.

The main processes are as follows.

Step 1: Bind the attributes and node numbers in the generated path Tk to generate: $e_i = \{Nodenum_i \| attr_i\}$.

Step 2: Generate randomly $h-1$ strings $\{r_{1,e}, r_{2,e} \ldots r_{h-1,e}\}$, all of which have length of λ bit, and calculate: $r_{h,e} = r_{1,e} \oplus r_{2,e} \oplus \cdots \oplus r_{h-1,e} \oplus e_i$.

Step 3: The current attribute is then hashed with the h hash functions $\{H_1(*), H_2(*), \cdots, H_h(*)\}$ and the result is the position in the array called as PBF. The position means the subscript, which guides where random numbers are stored in the array.

$$r_{1,e} \rightarrow PBF[H_1(e_i)]$$
$$r_{2,e} \rightarrow PBF[H_2(e_i)]$$
$$\vdots$$
$$r_{h,e} \rightarrow PBF[H_h(e_i)]$$

Step 4: If there is only one attribute on the path, h' perturbed elements are incorporated into the array.

Step 5: If a string already exists at some array position, the existing string is used as the new randomly generated string, which is shown in Fig. 6. When the new $r'_{1,e}$ is inserted, $r_{2,e}$ is already stored in the array element. The $r'_{1,e}$ will be set as $r_{2,e}$, and $r'_{h,e}$ will be recalculated as $r'_{h,e} = r_{2,e} \oplus r'_{2,e} \oplus \cdots \oplus r'_{h-1,e} \oplus e'_i$.

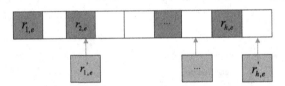

Fig. 6. Example diagrams when a string already exists

Step 6: Repeat the above steps for each path, then generate an array of n_{path}.

Algorithm *PBF-Create*

Input: $\{T_k = \{attr_{k,1}, attr_{k,2}, attr_{k,3}, \cdots, attr_{k,n_{path,attr}}\}\}_{k \in [1, n_{path}]}$

Output: $\{PBF_k\}_{k \in [1, n_{path}]}$

For all $\{T_k\}_{k \in [1, n_{path}]}$ **do**

For $i = 1$ **to** $n_{k,attr}$ **do**

    $e_i = Nodenum_i \parallel attr_i$

    Select $h-1$ random strings: $r_{k,1}, r_{k,2}, \cdots, r_{k,h-1}$

    Compute: $r_{k,h} = r_{k,1} \oplus r_{k,2} \oplus \cdots \oplus r_{k,h-1} \oplus e_i$

    For $j = 1$ **to** h **do**

        Compute: $H_j(e_i)$ is the location of $r_{k,j}$ in the *PBF*

        If $PBF_k[H_j(e_i)] == NULL$

            $PBF_k[H_j(e_i)] = r_{k,j}$

        Else

            $r_{k,j} = PBF_k[H_j(e_i)]$

            $r_{k,h} = r_{k,1} \oplus r_{k,2} \oplus \cdots \oplus PBF[H_j(e_i)] \oplus r_{k,h-1} \oplus e_i$

            $PBF_k[H_h(e_i)] = r_{k,h}$

        EndIf

    EndFor

EndFor

EndFor

4.3.5 *PBFCheck* Algorithm

The user does h hash functions $\{H_1(*), H_2(*), \cdots, H_h(*)\}$ on his own attributes and its *nodenum* in ROBDD to obtains the specific j locations in the *PBF*. Then the user gets h values $\{r_{1,e}, r_{2,e}, \cdots, r_{h-1,e}, r_{h,e}\}$ stored in these locations.

$$r_{1,e} \leftarrow PBF[H_1(nodenum_i \parallel attr_i)]$$
$$r_{2,e} \leftarrow PBF[H_2(nodenum_i \parallel attr_i)]$$
$$\vdots$$
$$r_{h,e} \leftarrow PBF[H_h(nodenum_i \parallel attr_i)]$$

After obtaining all these h values, the user performs the calculation as below:

$$nodenum_i \parallel attr_i = r_{1,e} \oplus r_{2,e} \oplus \cdots \oplus r_{h-1,e} \oplus r_{h,e}$$

The user compares the result of the calculation with the $L_{att} - bit$ string in the first path in the *PBF*. If both are the same, the user continues comparing subsequent other attributes in order. If all the $L_{att} - bit$ strings in that path are matched, this access policy is matched successfully, and the ciphertext can be decrypted.

Algorithm *PBF-Check*

Input: $\{attr_{u,i}\}_{i\in[1,n_u]}$

Output: *Nodenum*

For $\{attr_{u,i}\}_{i\in[1,n_u]}$ **do**

    For $l=1$ to h **do**

        $r_1 \leftarrow H_1(Nodenum_i \parallel attr_{u,i})$,

        $r_2 \leftarrow H_2(Nodenum_i \parallel attr_{u,i})$,

        $\cdots$

        $r_h \leftarrow H_h(Nodenum_i \parallel attr_{u,i})\}$

        $e^* = r_1 \oplus r_2 \oplus \cdots \oplus r_{h-1} \oplus r_h$

        Compare e^* with the e: $Nodenum_i \parallel attr_i$ in ROBDD in CT

        If $e^* = e$

            pass the node check

        EndIf

    EndFor

EndFor

Dec algorithm: If the user is able to pass all nodes in a feasible path, the ciphertext is decrypted according to the access policy obtained.

$$M = \frac{C'}{e(C_0, sk_0) \cdot \Pi_{i=1}^n e(C_{k,i,1}, sk_{1,i}) \cdot e(C_{k,i,2}, sk_{2,i})}$$

5 Analysis of Our LACS-PRP

5.1 Correctness Analysis

$$M = \frac{C'}{e(C_0, sk_0) \cdot \Pi_{i=1}^n e(C_{k,i,1}, sk_{1,i}) \cdot e(C_{k,i,2}, sk_{2,i})}$$

$$= \frac{M \cdot Y}{e(g_1 \cdot g_2^s, g_1^{\alpha\beta} \cdot g_2^{r_u \sum_{i\in[1,n_u]} x_i - r_i}) \cdot \Pi_{i=1}^n e(B_i^{-v_i s} \cdot X_i^s, g_1^{a_i r_u} \cdot g_2^{-r_i}) \cdot e(g_1^{v_i s} \cdot g_2^{x_i s}, B_i^{r_u} \cdot g_2^{-r_u})}$$

$$= \frac{M \cdot e(g_1, g_1)^{\alpha\beta}}{e(g_1, g_1)^{\alpha\beta} \cdot e(g_2^s, g_2^{r_u \sum_{i\in[1,n_u]} x_i - r_i}) \cdot \Pi_{i=1}^n e(g_1^{-a_i v_i s} \cdot g_2^{x_i s}, g_1^{r_u} \cdot g_2^{r_u}) \cdot e(g_1^{v_i s} \cdot g_2^{r_i s}, g_1^{a_i r_u} \cdot g_2^{-r_u})}$$

$$= \frac{M}{e(g_2, g_2)^{r_u s \sum_{i\in[1,n_u]} x_i - r_i} \cdot \Pi_{i=1}^n e(g_1, g_1)^{-a_i v_i r_u s} e(g_2, g_2)^{r_u x_i s} \cdot e(g_1, g_1)^{a_i v_i r_u s} e(g_2, g_2)^{-r_u r_i s}}$$

$$= M$$

5.2 Security Analysis

5.2.1 Security Analysis of Policy Hiding

In this section, we demonstrate the security of our scheme for policy hiding. Recall that we combine the ROBDD and ABE scheme with our proposed PBF to design the secure policy hiding method. To formally analyze the private-preserving policy guarantee, we define the setup leakage L^{PBF} as $L^{PBF} = (k, |PBF_k|, n^*_{path,attr})$, where k denotes the number of feasible paths. $|PBF_k|$ denotes the length of the array PBF_k. $n^*_{path,attr}$ is the number of non-zero array elements in $PBF_k[]$. The $n^*_{path,attr}$ is less than $n_{path,attr}$ which is the number attributes in a feasible path.

Apart from the above leakage, we also define the leakage using repeated queries $L^{repeat} = (M_{q\times q}, R_q)$, where $M_{q\times q}$ denotes the symmetric bit matrix that records repeated q queries and R_q denotes the result set.

Give the security model defined in Sect. 3.3, we provide the formal security proof.

Definition 1. The proposed scheme is a secure scheme with (L^{PBF}, L^{repeat}) leakages under the random-oracle model if $\{H_j\}_{j\in[1,h]}$ are secure.

Proof. We first define random oracles $\{F_{H_j}\}_{j\in[1,h]}$. From leakage L^{PBF}, the simulator ς simulates one of arrays $\{\overline{PBF}_k\}_{k\in[1,n_{path}]}$, which have the same size as the real one. The arrays contain a dictionary with n entries and a set with x elements. Each entry contains $n_{path,attr}$ random strings.

When the first query sample $(\overline{r}_{k,1}, \overline{r}_{k,2}, \cdots, \overline{r}_{k,h-1})$ is sent, ς generates simulated $\overline{r}_{k,h}$. After that, the random oracle $\{F_{H_j}\}$ are operated in the $\{\overline{PBF}_k[F_{H_j}(\overline{r}_{k,j})] \leftarrow \overline{r}_{k,j}\}$ to fill the elements of the array $\overline{PBF}_k$.

We consider the most dangerous scenarios that there is just one attribute in a feasible path. That is to say, the adversary knows $h + h' - 1$ random strings to try to calculate the h element. From L^{repeat}, ς updates $M_{1\times 1} = 1$ and adds $(\overline{r}_{k,1}, \overline{r}_{k,2}, \cdots, \overline{r}_{k,h-1})$ into R_q.

For the subsequent queries, if L^{repeat} indicates the query repeat, ς will select the same h element to return. Meanwhile, it will update $M_{q\times q}$. Due to the pseudo-randomness of Hash function, an adversary cannot distinguish the calculated result and a random string.

5.2.2 Discussion on Policy Hiding

Based on the analysis of GBF in Dong et al. [18], false positives for PBF are of negligible probability. Specifically, a false positive occurs only when the attribute $attr$ is not in the set S, but the output of the PBF is equal to y. In our scheme, only data consumers who have attributes can obtain attribute strings from the attribute space U. An attacker who does not know the attribute string cannot launch a brute force attack in polynomial time to guess the attribute string. Therefore, they cannot obtain private information from the access policy consisting of the PBF. Data users are only allowed to check that the attributes they own are in the access policy. Data consumers cannot check all attributes from the attribute space in the system unless they have all the attributes of the attribute space. Since the PBF is constructed with a GBF in which the λ-bit string is embedded in the BF, the probability of a false positive for the PBF can be reduced to $(1/2^\lambda)$.

5.2.3 Discussion on Collusion Resistance

Legitimate users cannot decrypt the ciphertext by colluding with each other and using a combined private key. When generating a user's private key, a scrambling factor is added to make the private key different from one user to another, so that even if the private keys are combined, no more privileges can be obtained.

5.2.4 Discussion on Data Confidentiality

The plaintext is encrypted into a *CT* stored in the server by a symmetric encryption algorithm and the *PBF* is also encrypted in the server by a specific algorithm. Only the user whose key carries a set of attributes matching the *PBF* can decrypt the *CT*. Unauthorized users will not be able to recover plaintext *M* even if they obtain *CT* and *PBF*.

6 Performance Analysis

Table 2 compares the calculation cost of each algorithm between existing schemes (Zhang's [9], Han's [20]) and our proposed LACS-PRP scheme. Wherein, *Ee* denotes the computation of an exponential operation on a group, *Ep* denotes the computation of a pairing operation on a group, E_H denotes the computation of a hash operation, n_u denotes the number of attributes carried by the user attribute private key, *l* denotes the number of attributes managed by AA, the authorization authority associated with the ciphertext, *n* denotes the number of attributes in the system; and *t* denotes the number of hash values in the *PBF*. The comparison in Table 1 ignores the computational cost of multiplication and division.

Table 2. Comparison of Calculation Cost

	Zhang's [9]	Han's [20]	Our LACS-PRP
Setup	$Ep + Ee$	$Ep + Ee$	$Ep + (2n + 2)Ee$
KeyGen	$(4n_u + 3)Ee$	$((3k + 1)n_u + 3)Ee$	$(2n_u + 2n + 3)Ep$
Encrypt	$(5n + 2)Ee$	$(5n + 2)Ee + ltE_H$	$(2n + 6)Ee + ltE_H$
Decrypt	$(2n_u + 1)Ee+$ $(3n_u + 1)Ep$	$(2n_u + 1)Ee+$ $(3n_u + 1)Ep + n_utE_H$	$(1 + 2n_u)Ep + n_utE_H$

According to the analysis on Table 1, our proposed scheme has a smaller computational cost in encryption and decryption when compared with Zhang's [9] and Han's [20]. Our scheme uses fewer operations to run the *Decrypt* algorithm on the user side, which is more in line with the general trend towards lightweight terminals. It can also be seen that the amount of computing used by the data owner to run the *Encrypt* algorithm has a significant advantage over other solutions, which is ideal for end nodes with weak computing power, in line with the current environment where a large number of low computing power network nodes are deployed for the rapid development of the IoT in the 5G era. Our scheme uses a larger amount of computing in the *KeyGen* algorithm phase of the authorization server, and the user's waiting time after requesting a key is theoretically longer than in other schemes, but in a network with more stable data interactions, this difference may be smaller or negligible for an authorization server with strong computing power in the network environment. To keep concise, Table 2 has not shown the computational time for the *PBFCreate* and *PBFCheck* algorithms. The computation required for both algorithms is hE_H. As for the communication cost, both algorithms require $k * n_{path,attr}|e_i|$, where $|e_i|$ represents the size of $Nodenum_i$ plus the size of $attr_i$.

7 Simulation

The Ubuntu operating system is used as the platform for the simulation experiments. PBC (Pairing Based Cryptography Library [27]) is used for the arithmetic library and GMP (The GNU MP Bignum Library [28]) is used for the large integer database. The simulation of the computational cost on the user side of the encryption and decryption process is shown in Fig. 7, where the elliptic curve is chosen α, the order of the group is all 160 bits, and the size of the domain is 512 bits. The number of attributes in the access policy and the number of attributes contained in the user attribute private key are set to 200 by default. In order to make the experimental results stable, the running times are averaged over 100 runs.

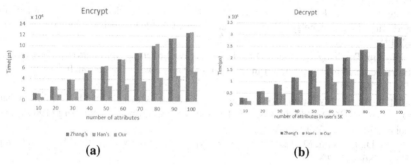

Fig. 7. a Encryption time and number of attributes in the system. b Decryption time and number of attributes in user private key.

Figure 7a shows the simulation results of the encryption process at the Data Owner's end. It can be seen that the encryption time of all three schemes is linearly related to the number of attributes in the system. At the same time, the encryption cost of this scheme is much smaller than that of the comparison scheme. The reason why Han's [20] scheme is slightly more costly than Zhang's [9] is that the Attribute Bloom Filter (ABF) needs to be constructed during the encryption process, which requires multiple hash function operations.

Figure 7b shows the simulation results of the decryption process on the Data User side. As can be seen, our scheme is still far less expensive to decrypt than the comparison scheme. The decryption cost of Han's [20] is still slightly higher than that of Zhang's [9], again because the former needs to verify the user attributes before decrypting them and determine whether they are in the ABF.

8 Conclusion

We achieve *policy hiding, decryption high efficiency* and *high expressiveness of access policy* all at the same time. After analyses of the current CP-ABE access structures and policy hiding schemes, we propose an access policy hiding scheme based on the ROBDD access structure and PBF. The access structure has high expressiveness, and its privacy is protected using PBF, which is first proposed. These two methods are adopted smartly to match a user's attribute set quickly with an access policy to save the user decryption time while hiding the policy.

Acknowledgment. This work was supported by the National Science Foundation of China [No. 62062045, No. 61962029], the Jiangxi Provincial Natural Science Foundation of China (No. 20202BAB212006).

References

1. Liu, Z., Jiang, Z.L., Wang, X., Xinyi Huang, S.M., Yiu, K.S.: Offline/online attribute-based encryption with verifiable outsourced decryption. Concurrency Comput. Pract. Exp. **29**(7), e3915 (2017). https://doi.org/10.1002/cpe.3915
2. Yang, K., Jia, X., Ren, K., Zhang, B.: DAC-MACS: effective data access control for multi-authority cloud storage systems. In: Proceedings of the 2013 IEEE INFOCOM, Turin, Italy (2013)
3. Li, L., Gu, T., Chang, L., Xu, Z., Qian, J.: Expressive ciphertext-policy attribute-based encryption scheme with fast decryption and constant-size secret keys. J. Electron. Inf. Technol. **40**(7), 1661–1668 (2018)
4. Shamir, A.: Identity-based cryptosystems and signature schemes. In: Blakley, G.R., Chaum, D. (eds.) CRYPTO 1984. LNCS, vol. 196, pp. 47–53. Springer, Heidelberg (1985). https://doi.org/10.1007/3-540-39568-7_5
5. Boneh, D., Franklin, M.: Identity-based encryption from the Weil pairing. SIAM J. Comput. **32**(3), 586–615 (2003)
6. Sahai, A., Waters, B.: Fuzzy identity-based encryption. In: Cramer, R. (ed.) Advances in Cryptology – EUROCRYPT 2005, pp. 457–473. Springer Berlin Heidelberg, Berlin, Heidelberg (2005). https://doi.org/10.1007/11426639_27
7. Bethencourt, J., Sahai, A., Waters, B.: Ciphertext-policy attribute-based encryption. In: 2007 IEEE Symposium on Security and Privacy (SP 2007), pp. 321–334. IEEE (2007)
8. Goyal, V., Pandey, O., Sahai, A., Waters, B.: Attribute-based encryption for fine-grained access control of encrypted data. In: Proceedings of the 13th ACM Conference on Computer and Communications Security, pp. 89–98 (2006)
9. Zhang, Y., Zheng, D., Chen, X., Li, J., Li, H.: Computationally efficient ciphertext-policy attribute-based encryption with constant-size ciphertexts. In: Chow, S.S.M., Liu, J.K., Hui, L.C.K., Yiu, S.M. (eds.) Provable Security, pp. 259–273. Springer International Publishing, Cham (2014). https://doi.org/10.1007/978-3-319-12475-9_18
10. Waters, B.: Ciphertext-policy attribute-based encryption: An expressive, efficient, and provably secure realization. In: Catalano, D., Fazio, N., Gennaro, R., Nicolosi, A. (eds.) Public Key Cryptography – PKC 2011, pp. 53–70. Springer Berlin Heidelberg, Berlin, Heidelberg (2011). https://doi.org/10.1007/978-3-642-19379-8_4
11. Bryant, R.E.: Graph-based algorithms for boolean function manipulation. Computers, IEEE Transactions on **100**(8), 677–691 (1986)
12. Li, L., Gu, T., Chang, L., Xu, Z., Liu, Y., Qian, J.: A ciphertext-policy attribute-based encryption based on an ordered binary decision diagram. IEEE Access **5**, 1137–1145 (2017)
13. Wang, Q., Ou, Y.: Traceable and revocable CP-ABE scheme OBDD-based access structure. Appl. Res. Comput. **38**(4), 1185–1189 (2021)

14. Affum, E., Zhang, X., Wang, X., Ansuura, J.B.: Efficient lattice CP-ABE AC scheme supporting reduced-OBDD structure for CCN/NDN. Symmetry 12(1), 166 (2020)

15. Edemacu, K., Jang, B., Kim, J.W.: CESCR: CP-ABE for efficient and secure sharing of data in collaborative ehealth with revocation and no dummy attribute. PLoS ONE 16(5), e0250992 (2021)

16. Li, J., Ren, K., Zhu, B., Wan, Z.: Privacy-aware attribute-based encryption with user account-ability. In: Samarati, P., Yung, M., Martinelli, F., Ardagna, C.A. (eds.) Information Security, pp. 347–362. Springer Berlin Heidelberg, Berlin, Heidelberg (2009). https://doi.org/10.1007/978-3-642-04474-8_28

17. Lai, J., Deng, R.H., Li, Y.: Fully secure cipertext-policy hiding CP-ABE. In: Bao, F., Weng, J. (eds.) Information Security Practice and Experience, pp. 24–39. Springer Berlin Heidelberg, Berlin, Heidelberg (2011). https://doi.org/10.1007/978-3-642-21031-0_3

18. Yang, K., Han, Q., Li, H., Zheng, K., Su, Z., Shen, X.: An efficient and fine-grained big data access control scheme with privacy-preserving policy. IEEE Internet Things J. 4(2), 563–571 (2016)

19. Chen, D., Tang, B.: An attribute-based encryption scheme with hidden policy based on LSSS. Comput. Technol. Dev. 28(2), 119–124 (2018)

20. Han, Q., Zhang, Y., Li, H.: Efficient and robust attribute-based encryption supporting access policy hiding in internet of things. Futur. Gener. Comput. Syst. 83, 269–277 (2018)

21. Li, J., Zhang, Y., Ning, J., Huang, X., Poh, G.S., Wang, D.: Attribute based encryption with privacy protection and accountability for CloudIoT. IEEE Trans. Cloud Comput. 10(2), 762–773 (2020)

22. Zhang, Z., Zhang, W., Qin, Z.: A partially hidden policy CP-ABE scheme against attribute values guessing attacks with online privacy-protective decryption testing in IoT assisted cloud computing. Futur. Gener. Comput. Syst. 123, 181–195 (2021)

23. Wang, M., Guo, Y., Zhang, C., Wang, C., Huang, H., Jia, X.: MedShare: a privacy-preserving medical data sharing system by using blockchain. IEEE Trans. Serv. Comput. 16(1), 438–453 (2023)

24. Akers: Binary decision diagrams. IEEE Trans. Comput. C–27(6), 509–516 (1978). https://doi.org/10.1109/TC.1978.1675141

25. Bloom, B.H.: Space/time trade-offs in hash coding with allowable errors. Commun. ACM 13(7), 422–426 (1970)

26. Dong, C., Chen, L., Wen, Z.: When private set intersection meets big data: an efficient and scalable protocol. In: Proceedings of the 2013 ACM SIGSAC Conference on Computer & Communications Security, pp. 789–800 (2013)

27. Lynn, B.: PBC Library Manual 0.5.14 (2022). https://crypto.stanford.edu/pbc/

28. Granlund, T., Team, T.G.D.: The GNU Multiple Precision Arithmetic Library (2023). https://gmplib.org/

MFL-RAT: Multi-class Few-Shot Learning Method for Encrypted RAT Traffic Detection

Yijing Zhang[1,2], Jianhuan Zhuo[1,2], Jianjun Lin[1,2], Xiaoyu Liu[1,2],
Weilin Gai[3,4,6], Xiaodu Yang[1,2], Yinliang Yue[5(✉)], and Bo Sun[6(✉)]

[1] Institute of Information Engineering, Chinese Academy of Sciences, Beijing, China
[2] School of Cyber Security, University of Chinese Academy of Sciences, Beijing, China
{zhangyijing,zhuojianhuan,linjianjun,liuxiaoyu,yangxiaodu}@iie.ac.cn
[3] Institute of Software, Chinese Academy of Sciences, Beijing, China
[4] School of Computer Science and Technology, University of Chinese Academy of Sciences, Beijing, China
[5] Zhongguancun Laboratory Beijing, Beijing, People's Republic of China
yueyl@zgclab.edu.cn
[6] National Computer Network Emergency Response Technical Team/Coordination Center of China, Beijing, China
{gwl,sunbo}@cert.org.cn

Abstract. Remote Access Trojan (RAT) poses a significant risk in today's network environment. These malware are commonly employed by hacking groups to monitor victims' activities and illicitly obtain sensitive personal information from targeted computers. With the rapid upgrade of RAT, obtaining sufficient network traffic samples of newly emerging RATs is difficult in a short period. Unfortunately, the existing malicious traffic detection methods typically rely on a large volume of traffic samples for effective learning, resulting in a limited ability to recognize newly emerging RATs effectively. Thus, we propose a novel multiclass encrypted RAT traffic detection method called "MFL-RAT" based on the meta-learning model Model-Agnostic Meta-Learning (MAML). In addition to distinguishing RAT traffic from benign traffic as before, our approach further considers classifying traffic from different new RAT classes, which is more practical in real-world scenarios. MFL-RAT leverages prior knowledge, generalizing from original RATs with sufficient network traffic samples, and develops a robust generalization model. It then quickly fine-tunes the model through a handful of new RAT traffic samples, and the fine-tuned model enjoys a high detection accuracy for new RATs. MFL-RAT employs a multimodal feature extraction network that generates flow sequence and packet payload embeddings. By combining these embeddings through feature fusion, MFL-RAT maximizes the utilization of information from limited resources. MFL-RAT performs better than existing works with at least a precision of 96.8% and a recall rate of 96.1% when dealing with different new RATs.

C. Ge and M. Yung (Eds.): Inscrypt 2023, LNCS 14526, pp. 452–471, 2024.
https://doi.org/10.1007/978-981-97-0942-7_23

Keywords: Network malicious traffic detection · RAT · Few-shot learning · Meta-learning · Feature fusion

1   Introduction

In recent years, the rapid development of the Internet has brought significant challenges to network security. Trojans are one of the primary malicious attacks in online activities. Remote Access Trojan (RAT) is a kind of trojan that can steal confidential data and execute malicious commands under the control of hackers. With more and more TLS-encrypted traffic on the Internet, an increasing number of RATs are using TLS to hide their tracks. Deep packet inspection (DPI)-based methods [1] is a popular method to detect malicious traffic using predefined patterns as signatures. However, it is very likely to fail due to the encryption technique since extracting effective signatures from encrypted payload content is difficult. Recently, researchers have tended to use traditional machine learning (TML)-based methods to tackle the identification problem of malicious encrypted traffic [2–5]. However, TML-based methods need to be designed upon a careful-designed feature set. Thus, TML-based methods rely sincerely on expert experience. To reduce the model's dependence on feature engineering, several deep learning (DL)-based methods have emerged to realize end-to-end learning by extracting features from network traffic automatically [6–9].

Nowadays, the network environment is constantly changing, and the upgrade of RATs is rapid. It is difficult for security agencies to obtain sufficient network traffic samples of newly emerging RATs in a short period. Moreover, generating a reliable dataset takes a long time in data gathering and labeling. The corresponding RAT may become obsolete even after experts have prepared a sufficient and well-labeled dataset. Thus, developing models that can be trained on limited network traffic samples is essential to identify new types of RATs. Unfortunately, traditional methods for detecting malicious traffic, especially those based on deep learning (DL), require a large number of samples to train the model. Without sufficient RAT traffic samples in the training dataset, these approaches suffer from severe overfitting, and their effectiveness declines significantly. Furthermore, the challenge becomes more complicated when trying to distinguish between multiple types of new RATs with only a small number of traffic samples for each type. It is difficult for models to be trained on such limited samples and successfully differentiate between different variants of new RATs.

In this work, we aim to address the challenge of developing a model that can be trained on limited malicious traffic samples for encrypted RAT traffic detection. To tackle this issue, we propose a novel multi-class few-shot learning method called MFL-RAT, based on Model-Agnostic Meta-Learning (MAML) [10]. MAML is a classical and widely used meta-learning approach that enables rapid generalization to new tasks with limited training samples by leveraging prior knowledge. The motivation for using meta-learning in this context comes from the human learning process. Cybersecurity experts are often able to identify new types of network traffic with only a limited number or even a single sample, thanks to their extensive domain knowledge. Similarly, while obtaining sufficient traffic samples of new RATs is challenging, there are usually large numbers of original RATs traffic samples available from which we can learn prior domain knowledge. Previous few-shot learning methods for malicious traffic detection have mainly focused on data augmentation-based [11,12] and metric-learning-based [13,14] approaches. The data augmentation-based methods use Generative Adversarial Networks (GAN) to generate new traffic data to complement the training dataset. The metric-learning-based methods adopt different sampling strategies to balance the number of benign and malicious traffic samples. However, these methods do not fully exploit the valuable information in the traffic samples from original RATs. In contrast, MFL-RAT integrates the concept of meta-learning to leverage prior knowledge from original RATs traffic samples and quickly generalize to new RATs with limited samples. The proposed MFL-RAT method builds on the foundation of MAML, which is relatively new to malicious traffic detection. The only existing work that utilizes MAML is FCAD [15], which focuses on identifying unseen anomaly traffic from benign traffic. Unlike FCAD, MFL-RAT extends the application of MAML to the multi-class classification field, allowing it to distinguish traffic from different RATs. This extension makes MFL-RAT more practical and useful in real-world scenarios, as it provides the ability to identify and categorize different types of attacks.

MAML is a model-independent few-shot learning scheme; thus, we design our encrypted RAT traffic detection model based on a multimodal feature extraction network. The model extract features from flow sequences and packet payload bytes for capturing comprehensive information about network behaviors, which is particularly useful when dealing with limited resources in few-shot scenarios. Unlike our model, FCAD extracts feature embedding only from the flow sequence and ignores packet payload-based features, which are also helpful information for RAT traffic detection. Additionally, we employ a feature fusion method to extract inter-modularity information for discrimination. MFL-RAT consists of meta-training and meta-testing phases, similar to the basic MAML algorithm. The meta-training process is conducted on several M-way K-shot classification tasks to obtain prior knowledge generalizing from original RATs. However, different from the basic MAML algorithm, in the meta-testing phase, we generate multiple tasks to handle the possible imbalance in the sample size of different new RAT classes. It allows the model to adapt and fine-tune its knowledge to these new classes, enabling effective few-shot learning.

In summary, the main contributions of this paper are as follows:

- We propose a novel multi-class few-shot learning method (MFL-RAT) for encrypted RAT traffic detection with MAML. Our proposed detection model is pre-trained during the meta-learning phase on multi-class classification tasks generated from original RAT traffic. The detection model is then fine-tuned with new RAT samples during the meta-testing phase. We also generate multiple tasks in meta-testing to handle the imbalance in new RAT class samples.

- A multimodal feature extraction network generates embeddings from flow sequences and packet payloads bytes simultaneously. We use feature fusion to combine generated embeddings to utilize as much information as possible from limited resources to detect new RATs.
- We implement the MFL-RAT framework and conduct extensive experiments to evaluate its performance. The results reveal that it can achieve superior multi-class RAT traffic detection compared with baseline methods. At the same time, our model achieves over 99% precision rate and 98% recall rate in detecting malicious RAT traffic, outperforming the baseline methods in the binary classification of RAT and benign traffic.

The paper is organized as follows: Section 2 provides a comprehensive explanation of our method, outlining the steps and procedures followed in our study. Section 3 focuses on the experimental setup we used to test our method and analyze the experimental results we obtained. Section 4 reviews the related work, and finally, Sect. 5 draws conclusions based on our findings.

2 Architecture of MFL-RAT

In this section, we describe our proposed framework MFL-RAT. The framework utilizes two datasets that we can obtain: The large meta-training dataset D^{train}, which contains M classes of original RATs with sufficient traffic samples, and the meta-testing dataset D^{test}, which contains N classes of new RATs with insufficient traffic samples. MFL-RAT aims to learn a general multi-class RAT traffic detection model from D^{train} by training the model on D^{train}. The general RAT detection model is not specific to identifying a particular RAT class. Instead, it can be generalized to detect the traffic of any new RAT class. To address the new RAT traffic detection problem, we fine-tune the general detection model on the meta-testing dataset D^{test}.

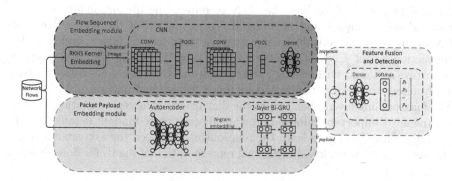

Fig. 1. The architecture of multi-class RAT traffic detection model.

2.1   Multi-class RAT Traffic Detection Model

The detail of the multi-class encrypted RAT traffic detection model is presented in Fig. 1. It contains two feature extraction modules: (1) the Flow Sequence Embedding module and (2) the Packet Payload Embedding module. The Flow Sequence Embedding module focuses on the characteristics of the flow sequence, which vary between RAT and benign traffic flow. It extracts a feature vector, $v_{sequence}$, that captures these discriminative characteristics. The Packet Payload Embedding module, on the other hand, captures the characteristics of packet payload bytes and the interrelationships between them. These characteristics also contribute to the identification of RAT traffic. The Packet Payload Embedding module generates a feature vector representing these characteristics, denoted as $v_{payload}$. The model then fuses the two feature vectors and classifies the encrypted traffic.

Flow Sequence Embedding Module. The Flow Sequence Embedding module employs the feature extraction method used by the module TEM in our previous work ER-ERT [16]. It aims to extract features from the flow sequence in network traffic to model the specific network behavior characteristics. The flow sequence consists of three types of data: packet inter-arrival time sequence $\Delta t_1, \Delta t_2, ..., \Delta t_n$, packet length sequence $s_1, s_2, ..., s_n$, and packet direction sequence $d_1, d_2, ..., d_n$. N represents the packet number in the flow. These sequences capture important characteristics of the network traffic. The Reproducing Kernel Hilbert Space (RKHS) embedding method [17] is used to realize a transformation from the three input sequences to a 3-channel image. We choose to use the RKHS embedding method instead of a Long Short-Term Memory (LSTM) to process the sequential data because the RKHS embedding method can capture the information of the marginal distribution of a specific flow attribute. The marginal distribution provides an accurate and compact representation of the characteristics of a flow sequence.

The 3-channel image converted by the RKHS embedding method is highly dimensional, so it is fed into the CNN to reduce the dimensionality and generate a more compact and meaningful representation of the traffic flow. The CNN comprises two convolutional layers, two max-pooling layers, and three full connection layers. CNN is suitable for dealing with data in the form of multiple arrays and data with strong local correlations [18]. The convolutional layers apply filters to the input image, detecting various local patterns and features. The max-pooling layers then reduce the dimension of the representation, capturing the most important information while discarding redundant details. Finally, the fully connected layers learn the relationships between the extracted features and generate a hidden low-dimensional representation of the traffic flow, denoted as $v_{sequence}$.

Packet Payload Embedding Module. The Packet Payload Embedding module employs the feature extraction method used by the module SPA in our previous work ER-ERT [16]. It aims to extract features from the packet payload bytes in the network flow. It discovers the impact of packet interrelationships on identifying malicious RAT traffic. The overall procedure of the Packet Payload Embedding module is depicted in Fig. 2.

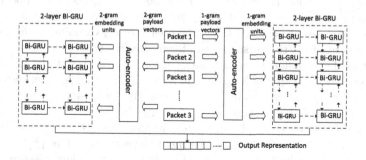

Fig. 2. The feature extraction procedure of packet payload.

The packet sequence of a flow f, denoted by $f = (p_1, p_2, ..., p_l)$, is treated as the input to the Packet Payload Embedding module. We first use a sliding window of length n to form n-gram payload vectors ($n \in \{1, 2\}$). Autoencoders are then used to compress the n-gram payload vectors while preserving the essential information in the packet payload. The compression reduces the complexity of the data and allows for more efficient subsequent processing. The outputs of the autoencoders are 1-gram and 2-gram embedding units.

We utilize two separate Bi-GRUs to deal with the 1-gram and 2-gram embeddings units. The 1-gram and 2-gram embeddings model the local dependencies between adjacent packets while Bi-GRUs capture long-term dependencies of the packet payload. The Bi-GRU is adopted to incorporate contextual information of the embedding unit sequence by summarizing sequential information from both directions. To form the final representation of the whole flow $v_{payload}$, the outputs of the two Bi-GRUs with the input 1-gram embedding unit sequence and 2-gram embedding unit sequence are concentrated. A more detailed description of the feature extraction method for packet payload is in [16].

Feature Fusion and Detection. Through intramodal learning, the Flow Sequence Embedding module and the Packet Payload Embedding module output the feature vectors $v_{sequence}$ and $v_{payload}$, respectively. The multi-class encrypted RAT traffic detection model performs feature fusion to combine these feature vectors. Shared presentation layers called FusionNet learn the relationships between the modalities and classify the traffic as either belonging to a benign application or different types of RATs. A softmax layer is added to generate a vector representing the probability of the traffic category, from which the predicted label can be obtained.

2.2   Training Process of Detection Model with MAML

We train our multi-class RAT traffic detection model based on the MAML algorithm. The training process is depicted in Fig. 3. We generate the meta-training task set $\{T_i\}_{i=1}^{H}$ from dataset D^{train}. Each task T_i consists of a support set S_i and a query set Q_i. The support set S_i contains traffic from N classes of original RATs and samples of benign traffic. The query set Q_i contains traffic from the same N classes of RATs and samples of benign traffic. $\theta_{initial}$ denotes the initial parameters of the model. The temporary parameter θ_{temp} is obtained by training the model on S_i through gradient descent for each task T_i. Then meta-loss across tasks is calculated based on all the query sets. By optimizing the meta-loss, we obtain the model with parameter θ_{meta}, which is the output of the meta-training phase. In the meta-testing phase, traffic samples from D^{test} are used to train the model with parameter θ_{meta}. The meta-testing task set is $\{S_i^{new}\}_{i=1}^{d}$. We fine-tune the model by training it on $\{S_i^{new}\}_{i=1}^{d}$ using gradient descent, resulting in the model parameter $\theta_{fine-tuned}$. We will describe our training process from task generation, meta-training, and meta-testing phases.

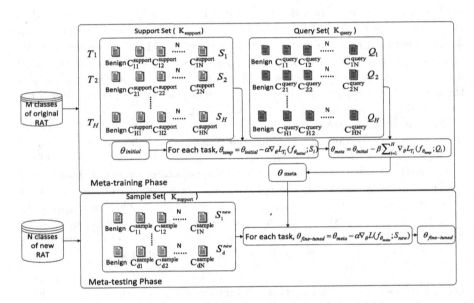

Fig. 3. The training process of the detection model.

Task Generation. In the meta-training phase, to meet the goal of detecting and classifying the RATs, we generate multiple multi-class classification tasks by randomly sampling N classes of original RATs from dataset D^{train}. We define the task $T_i = \{S_i, Q_i\}$, in which S_i and Q_i are the support and query sets, respectively. The support set $S_i = \{C_{i1}^{support}, C_{i2}^{support}, ..., C_{iN}^{support}, C_{benign}^{support}\}$, in which $C_{in}^{support}$ indicates $K_{support}$ samples randomly selected from RAT class n and $C_{in}^{support} = \{(x_1, y_1), (x_2, y_2), ..., (x_{K_{support}}, y_{K_{support}})\}$. $C_{benign}^{support}$ indicates $K_{support}$ samples randomly selected from benign traffic. The query set $Q_i = \{C_{i1}^{query}, C_{i2}^{query}, ..., C_{iN}^{query}, C_{benign}^{query}\}$, in which C_{in}^{query} indicates K_{query} samples randomly selected from RAT class n and $C_{in}^{query} = \{(x_1, y_1), (x_2, y_2), ..., (x_{K_{query}}, y_{K_{query}})\}$. C_{benign}^{query} indicates K_{query} samples randomly selected from benign traffic. In the meta-testing phase, we aim to adapt our model to distinguish new RATs traffic from benign traffic. Thus, we construct the task S_i^{new} in the meta-testing phase by selecting $K_{support}$ traffic samples from each new RAT class and $K_{support}$ benign traffic. These meta-testing tasks are used to fine-tune the model to generate the final training result.

Meta-training Phase. The meta-training phase aims to train a model that can quickly adapt to new tasks using only a few training samples and iterations. To accomplish the goal, we train our initial model with parameter $\theta_{initial}$ on the meta-training tasks and generate the model with parameter θ_{meta}. The parameter $\theta_{initial}$ is randomly initialized. We use the support sets in the tasks to compute the first-order gradient and the query sets in the tasks to compute the second-order gradient to update the parameters in the model. The meta-training algorithm is depicted in Algorithm 1.

Algorithm 1: Meta-training for few-shot multi-class RAT traffic detection

---

Input: Hyper-parameters α, β
1 Randomly initialize parameter $\theta_{initial}$ of the meta-model $f_{\theta_{initial}}$;
2 **while** *not done* **do**
3   Sample batch of tasks $\{T_i\}_{i=1}^{H}$. T_i contains N classes of RAT traffic $\{C_{ij}\}_{j=1}^{N}$ and benign traffic;
4   **foreach** T_i **do**
5   Construct the support set S_i by sampling $K_{support}$ labeled flows from each RAT class in $\{C_{ij}\}_{j=1}^{N}$ and $K_{support}$ benign flows;
6   Construct the query set Q_i by sampling K_{query} labeled flows from each RAT class in $\{C_{ij}\}_{j=1}^{N}$ and K_{query} benign flows;
7   **end**
8   **foreach** T_i **do**
9   Compute the loss function $\mathcal{L}_{T_i}(f_{\theta_{initial}}; S_i)$;
10   Generate the temporary parameter $\theta_{temp} = \theta_{initial} - \alpha \nabla_{\theta} \mathcal{L}_{T_i}(f_{\theta_{initial}}; S_i)$;
11   **end**
12   Update the meta parameter $\theta_{meta} = \theta_{initial} - \beta \sum_{i=1}^{H} \nabla_{\theta} \mathcal{L}_{T_i}(f_{\theta_{temp}}; Q_i)$;
13 **end**

We represent our model as f, which maps observations of network traffic flows to predicted class labels. By computing the first-order gradient, we can generate the model's temporal parameter θ_{temp}. Following the MAML algorithm, we define the loss function on the support set S_i in task T_i:

$$\mathcal{L}_{T_i}(f_{\theta_{initial}}; S_i) = \sum_{(x_i, y_i) \in S_i} L(f_{\theta_{initial}}(x_i), y_i) \tag{1}$$

where L is the cross entropy error function that measures the difference between the prediction class $f_{\theta_{initial}}(x_i)$ and the actual class label y_i. We then figure out the parameter θ_{temp} from $\theta_{initial}$:

$$\theta_{temp} = \theta_{initial} - \alpha \nabla_\theta \mathcal{L}_{T_i}(f_{\theta_{initial}}; S_i) \tag{2}$$

where α is the learning rate and $\nabla_\theta \mathcal{L}_{T_i}(f_{\theta_{initial}}; S_i)$ indicates the first-order gradient for each task.

To get the output model parameter θ_{meta} of the meta-training phase, we need to calculate the second-order gradient by taking into account of all the sampled tasks. We define the loss function on the query set Q_i in task T_i:

$$\mathcal{L}_{T_i}(f_{\theta_{temp}}; Q_i) = \sum_{(x_i, y_i) \in Q_i} L(f_{\theta_{temp}}(x_i), y_i) \tag{3}$$

Then we update the initial parameter $\theta_{initial}$ rather than the temporal parameter θ_{temp}:

$$\theta_{meta} = \theta_{initial} - \beta \sum_{i=1}^{H} \nabla_\theta \mathcal{L}_{T_i}(f_{\theta_{temp}}; Q_i) \tag{4}$$

where β is the learning rate and $\nabla_\theta \mathcal{L}_{T_i}(f_{\theta_{temp}}; Q_i)$ indicates the second-order gradient for each task.

Meta-testing Phase. After the meta-training process, we get the pre-trained model with parameter θ_{meta}. During the meta-testing phase, we fine-tune the pre-trained model on each task from the meta-testing task set $\{S_i^{new}\}_{i=1}^d$. S_i^{new} contains $K_{support}$ samples for each new RAT class and benign traffic. We figure out the parameter $\theta_{fine-tuned}$ by updating the model through gradient descent of each meta-testing task:

$$\theta_{fine-tuned} = \theta_{meta} - \alpha \nabla_\theta \mathcal{L}_{S_i^{new}}(f_{\theta_{meta}}; S_i^{new}) \tag{5}$$

The model with parameter $\theta_{fine-tuned}$ is the final model training result.

3   Performance Evaluation

In this section, we describe experimental details and provide the experimental results and analysis. We design a series of experiments to verify MFL-RAT from multiple perspectives based on the following questions:

Q1: How does MFL-RAT perform in few-shot RAT traffic detection compared to the state-of-the-art TML-based and DL-based methods?

Q2: How does MFL-RAT perform in original RAT traffic detection compared to the state-of-the-art TML-based and DL-based methods? We adopt the original RAT traffic in the D^{train} dataset to test the model (i.e., the training and testing set contain the same original RAT classes and have large samples).

Q3: Does MFL-RAT perform better than other few-shot malicious traffic detection methods?

Q4: How is MFL-RAT's performance affected by the selection of K value, with the K-shot meta-learning procedure applied in our model training (K represents $K_{support}$ in our framework)?

Q5: How much do MFL-RAT's different embedding modules contribute to performance? Does the multimodal feature extraction and feature fusion mechanism improve the model's performance in few-shot scenarios?

3.1 Experimental Setup

Dataset. The RAT traffic dataset used for meta-training called R_1, consists of traffic from 10 different RATs. The details of R_1 are provided in Table 1. The traffic of trojan TrickBot, Emotet, Dridex, Trickster, and Upatre is selected from the Stratosphere project [19], collected between 2015 and 2018. We remove the traffic flow that is too short or incomplete (usually less than ten packets) to eliminate noise interference. To enrich the variety and quantity of the RAT traffic dataset, we also collect traffic from trojans Pupy, Recoms, Gh0st, DarkCome, and NanoCore, which are open-source RATs commonly used in recent attacks. The collection is done by using a client with Windows 10 operating system as the victim and a RAT server with Ubuntu 16.04 operating system. The traffic between the server and the client is recorded. The RAT traffic dataset used for meta-testing, called R_2, consists of trojan traffic from CTU-13 [20]. CTU-13 contains traffic from 7 different types of trojans. We only select the Command and Control(C&C) traffic according to the dataset description. Thus, 5 trojans are chosen for meta-testing because they have C&C traffic available. More details of R_2 can be found in Table 1. The traffic dataset of each RAT in R_2 is divided into a 0.2:0.8 ratio for model training and testing (e.g., 8 out of 40 traffic flows of Sogou and 554 out of 2771 traffic flows of Neris are used for model training).

Table 1. An Overview of R_1 and R_2 dataset.

R_1				R_2	
Public		Self-collected			
Trojan	Session Num	Trojan	Session Num	Trojan	Session Num
TrickBot	78980	Pupy	4680	Neris	2771
Emotet	95643	Recoms	5899	Murio	1070
Dridex	53309	Gh0st	2810	Menti	198
Trickster	8764	DarkCome	6634	Virut	58
Upatre	65550	NanoCore	7689	Sogou	40

The benign section of our dataset is from the open dataset USTC-TFC2016 [21]. It contains 3.71 GB of traffic generated by 10 normal applications, including BitTorrent, Facetime, FTP, Gmail, MySQL, Outlook, Skype, SMB, Weibo, and WorldOfWarcraft. It is organized into 14 PCAP files and consists of 345,470 sessions.

Baseline Method. We select several state-of-the-art TML-based and DL-based approaches for comparison. The first baseline method proposed by Stergiopoulos et al. [5]. utilizes the CART algorithm to classify encrypted traffic. It uses five side-channel features extracted from the traffic to make predictions. The second baseline method, BGRUA, was proposed by Liu et al. [6] and employs a Bi-GRU and attention mechanism to capture both forward and backward dependencies in the byte sequences of a session. It aims to classify HTTPS traffic. The third baseline method, FS-Net, proposed by Liu et al. [9], adopts a multi-layer encoder-decoder structure to generate embeddings from packet length sequences. This method focuses on capturing the temporal dependencies in the traffic flow and has shown promising results in traffic classification.

We also make comparisons with multiple detection methods adapting to the few-shot condition. For multi-class RAT traffic detection, baseline method TA-GAN [12] is chosen for comparison. TA-GAN is an end-to-end framework that integrates the generation of the minority traffic samples with the training of the target classifier. It generates traffic samples of multiple classes by GAN. For binary-class RAT traffic detection, three baselines, KitNET [22], RENOIR [14], and FCAD [15], are chosen for comparison. KitNET uses an ensemble of autoencoders to differentiate between normal and abnormal traffic patterns collectively. RENOIR employs the Triplet network, a classic metric learning approach, for intrusion detection. It processes the flow-based characteristics of the network traffic data to detect signs of malicious activities. FCAD applies MAML-based few-shot anomaly detection like our method MFL-RAT, but it can only identify unseen anomaly traffic from benign traffic.

Evaluation Metrics. The evaluation metrics are precision rate (PR), recall rate (RC), and F1 score, which are the most widely used metrics to quantify the performance of a model. The PR is calculated as the ratio of correct predictions over the total number of predictions, which measures the model's ability to classify correctly. The RC is calculated as the ratio of the number of true positives over the total number of positives, which measures the model's ability to identify the actual labels of samples. The F1 score considers the PR and the RC simultaneously to form a compositive metric of the designed model.

Implementation Details. The experimental hardware platform is a computer equipped with a CPU of ADM RYZEN 5800H × 3.2 GHz and 16 GB of memory. The GPU accelerator is NVIDIA GeForce GTX 1660. The framework runs on Python 3.7, and the deep learning platform is Tensorflow 2.5.

There are several hyperparameters in the meta-learning process in our framework. We fix the number of iterations in the meta-training phase at 100 and the size of the task set at 1000 for each iteration. We equate $K_{support}$ and K_{query} in our meta-training process. The learning rates α and β are set to 0.001. In the meta-testing phase, we fix the size of the task set at 50.

In the meta-learning process, we use N-way classification tasks to train the model for multi-class classification of RATs traffic. If the model is trained for distinguishing new RAT traffic from benign traffic, i.e., binary classification, we set the value of N to be 1. It means that for each meta-training or meta-testing task, only one class of RAT is randomly sampled from D^{train} or D^{test}. However, if the model is trained to identify traffic from different new RAT classes, we set N as the number of new RAT classes in D^{test}. In the meta-training phase, we randomly sample the same number of original RAT classes from the D^{train} as the number of new RAT classes in D^{test}. In the meta-testing phase, $K_{support}$ traffic flows are sampled for each new RAT class.

3.2   Experimental Results

To answer Q1, we evaluate the overall effectiveness of MFL-RAT by comparing its performance with the TML- and DL-based baseline methods. The comparison results are depicted in Table 2 and Table 3. As shown in Table 2, our model outperforms other models in detecting various types of new RAT traffic, as evidenced by the PR and RC scores. The performance of CART, FS-Net, and BGRUA decline sharply from trojan Neris to Sogou due to the decrease in the number of samples for each trojan. It indicates that the performance of TML- and DL-based methods heavily depends on the distribution of the dataset used for training. These methods require a large number of multi-class malicious traffic samples to achieve good detection results. In contrast, our model maintains high PR and RC among different new RAT classes, even with varying training sample sizes. It is because we pre-train our model on a collection of K-way-M-shot classification tasks generated from the original RATs with sufficient traffic training samples. The pre-training allows our model to learn a general multi-class RAT traffic detection model. The general RAT detection model can be generalized into detecting the traffic of any new RAT class by fine-tuning it with only a few new RAT traffic samples. In addition, we generate multiple tasks in the meta-testing phase to balance the sample size of new RAT classes. As a result, the performance of MFL-RAT is not restricted by the distribution of the training dataset. It can achieve excellent detection results for RATs even with very limited training samples, such as Sogou and Virut.

Table 3 shows that MFL-RAT is far superior to the TML-and DL-based approaches in distinguishing both new and original RAT traffic from benign traffic. Unlike Table 2, which shows the models' performance in multi-class classification, Table 3 depicts the models' performance in binary classification. In new RAT traffic detection, the baseline methods CART, FS-Net, and BGRUA show a higher PR and RC on benign traffic than on RAT traffic. It is because there are sufficient benign training samples for the model to be trained on, making it easier for the TML- and DL-based models to learn the features of benign traffic than new RAT traffic. New RAT classes lack training samples, making it more challenging for these models to detect new RAT traffic accurately. On the other hand, our model maintains high PR and RC for both benign traffic detection and RAT traffic detection, proving that the size of the training dataset does not limit the effectiveness of MFL-RAT.

464   Y. Zhang et al.

Table 2. Comparison of MFL-RAT with state-of-the-art TML-based and DL-based methods for multi-class new RAT traffic detection. The highlight value is the **overall best method**.

Metrics	Methods	RATs					
		Neris	Murli	Menti	Virut	Sogou	Benign
PR	CART	0.724	0.754	0.543	0.556	0.512	0.823
	FS-Net	0.815	0.820	0.690	0.648	0.650	0.905
	BGRUA	0.834	0.809	0.694	0.612	0.654	0.934
	MFL-RAT (before fine-tuning)	0.978	0.964	0.967	0.969	0.959	0.981
	MFL-RAT (after fine-tuning)	**0.983**	**0.986**	**0.973**	**0.980**	**0.968**	**0.986**
RC	CART	0.669	0.684	0.590	0.495	0.417	0.796
	FS-Net	0.796	0.761	0.709	0.580	0.563	0.879
	BGRUA	0.780	0.796	0.743	0.612	0.578	0.926
	MFL-RAT (before fine-tuning)	0.972	0.963	0.965	0.949	0.950	0.986
	MFL-RAT (after fine-tuning)	**0.981**	**0.974**	**0.967**	**0.961**	**0.976**	**0.989**

Table 3. Comparison of MFL-RAT with state-of-the-art TML-based and DL-based methods for new and original RAT traffic detection.

Methods	New RAT detection						Original RAT detection					
	Benign			RAT			Benign			RAT		
	PR	RC	F1	PR	RC	F1	PR	RC	F1	PR	RC	F1
CART	0.897	0.765	0.826	0.713	0.697	0.705	0.905	0.893	0.899	0.823	0.801	0.812
FS-Net	0.912	0.932	0.922	0.794	0.708	0.749	0.938	0.932	0.935	0.917	0.946	0.931
BGRUA	0.933	0.955	0.944	0.756	0.738	0.747	0.952	0.949	0.950	0.944	0.963	0.953
MFL-RAT	**0.992**	**0.989**	**0.990**	**0.990**	**0.983**	**0.986**	**0.981**	**0.991**	**0.986**	**0.987**	**0.984**	**0.985**

To verify the adaptability of our model in processing the original RAT traffic classes(Q2), we use dataset R_1 as both the meta-training dataset and the testing set through standard training/testing set division. The results are shown in Table 3. It can be observed that our method MFL-RAT performs better than the state-of-the-art baseline methods in detecting original RAT traffic. It is worth noting that the DL-based methods FS-Net and BGRUA achieve relatively satisfactory results in detecting the original RAT traffic since the training and testing datasets share the same data distribution and RAT classes. However, our model performs better in detection since it leverages the heterogeneity of the network flow by simultaneously learning embeddings from flow sequences and packet payload bytes. On the other hand, FS-Net and BGRUA utilize a single-modularity representation learning approach, which is less effective in this task.

In addition to comparing our model with TML- and DL-based methods, we also evaluate its performance against some few-shot malicious traffic detection methods to address Q3. The comparison results are depicted in Table 4 and 5. Table 4 presents the comparison results with the baseline method TA-GAN. Since TA-GAN is a multi-class few-shot classification method, we train our model as a multi-class new RAT traffic detection model for comparison. Table 5 shows the comparison results with the baseline methods KitNET, RENOIR, and FCAD. Since KitNET, RENOIR, and FCAD can only detect anomaly traffic from benign

Table 4. Comparison of MFL-RAT with TA-GAN.

Classes	PR		RC	
	TA-GAN	MFL-RAT	TA-GAN	MFL-RAT
Neris	0.905	**0.983**	0.919	**0.981**
Murli	0.912	**0.986**	0.929	**0.974**
Menti	0.864	**0.973**	0.891	**0.967**
Virut	0.808	**0.980**	0.778	**0.961**
Sogou	0.769	**0.968**	0.706	**0.976**
Benign	0.952	**0.986**	0.938	**0.989**

traffic, we train our model for binary classification of RAT and benign traffic. It can be seen in the tables that our model outperforms these few-shot malicious traffic detection methods. The performance of TA-GAN, which employs GAN for traffic sample generation to augment the dataset, is limited by the sample size of the RAT class. For RAT classes with tiny sample sizes, such as Virut and Sogou, the generation of samples using GAN does not yield satisfactory results, resulting in poor detection performance.

Table 5. Comparison of MFL-RAT with KitNET, RENOIR and FCAD.

Methods	Benign			RAT		
	PR	RC	F1	PR	RC	F1
KitNET	0.972	0.967	0.969	0.854	0.892	0.873
RENOIR	0.925	0.937	0.931	0.955	0.909	0.931
FCAD	0.959	0.969	0.964	0.962	0.954	0.958
MFL-RAT	**0.992**	**0.989**	**0.990**	**0.990**	**0.983**	**0.986**

The results in Table 5 demonstrate that our model performs better than KitNET, RENOIR, and FCAD. Our model achieves a PR of 99.0% and an RC of 98.3% on malicious RAT traffic and a PR of 99.2% and an RC of 98.9% on benign traffic. KitNET, an unsupervised machine-learning-based method, only uses benign traffic for training. As a result, it exhibits poorer performance compared to our supervised machine-learning-based method. RENOIR is a metric-based intrusion detection model that relies on sampling from benign and RATs traffic to compute distances. However, due to the tiny sample size available for some new RAT classes (e.g., Sogou and Virut), RENOIR has difficulties sampling from these classes, which ultimately affects its overall performance. In contrast to our detection model, FCAD only utilizes the feature embedding generated from the flow sequence. Our model, on the other hand, generates embeddings from both the flow sequence and packet payloads. The multimodal feature extraction and feature fusion enable the model to capture more hidden information from network traffic by considering intra-modality and inter-modality dependencies. By leveraging limited resources to incorporate as much information as possible, we are able to enhance the accuracy of malicious RAT traffic detection.

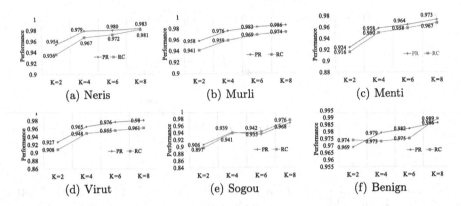

Fig. 4. The performance of MFL-RAT on classes (a) to (f) with respect to different K values.

In our experiment on the hyperparameters of MFL-RAT, we focused on the number of training samples (K) for each RAT class. We found that this parameter influences the performance of the model. Meanwhile, the value of K is limited by the new RAT class with the most miniature training sample set, which is Sogou in our dataset, containing only 8 flows for model training. Thus, K is assigned the values 2, 4, 6, and 8 for comparison (Q4). The results are shown in Fig. 4. With the increase of the K value, we observed an improvement in the model's ability to detect traffic of different RATs. Since more samples are involved in each training iteration, it is easier for our model to learn the discriminative features of each new RAT class. Therefore, the model obtains better multi-class classification results.

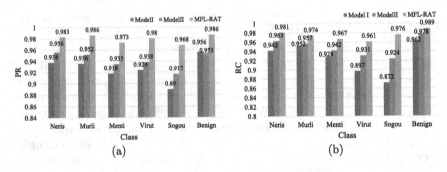

Fig. 5. (a) the PR and (b) the RC of Model I, Model II, and MFL-RAT on different RAT classes and benign traffic.

To evaluate the effectiveness of two feature extraction modules (Q5), we create two baseline models called Model I and Model II to assess the benefits of different modules. Model I eliminates the embeddings generated by the

Packet Payload Embedding module, while Model II eliminates the embeddings generated by the Flow Sequence Embedding module. Compared with the integrated MFL-RAT model, Model I and Model II are created by removing feature fusion and learning representation from a single modularity. All three models are trained and tested under the same circumstance, and the results are shown in Fig. 5. We can see that the removal of different components in Model I and Model II leads to varying degrees of decline in performance. Comparing MFL-RAT with Model I and Model II, it is clear that the introduction of representation learned from packet payload or flow sequence benefits the detection capacity. It also can be seen that the performance gaps brought by the two modules differ among different RAT classes, and these gaps increase when the training sample size of the RAT class decreases. For example, for Neris, the packet payload embedding improves the PR by 4.5%, and the flow sequence embedding improves it by 2.7%. While for Sogou, the packet payload embedding improves the PR by 7.8%, and the flow sequence embedding improves it by 5.1%. It suggests that the multimodal feature extraction and feature fusion mechanism performs better for new RAT classes with fewer training samples. The comparison between Model I and Model II reveals that the Packet Payload Embedding module outperforms the Flow Sequence Embedding module. Model II has an average PR and RC that are 1.5% and 2.3% higher than Model I, respectively.

4   Related Work

4.1   Malicious Traffic Detection

The existing methods of malicious traffic detection can be divided into three main categories: DPI-based, TML-based, and DL-based approaches. The DPI-based methods use predefined patterns like regular expressions as signatures to detect malicious traffic [1]. Since most malware, including RAT, encrypts their network flow like normal applications, the actual contents of IP packet payloads are invisible, and it is hard to extract effective signatures from encrypted payload content. The DPI-based detection methods are significantly challenged and usually lose functionality in detecting encrypted malicious traffic. TML-based methods are often used with a careful-designed feature set to deal with the problem of malicious traffic identification. These methods include Random Forest (RF) [2], Support Vector Machine (SVM) [3], XGBoost [4], Classification and Regression Tree (CART) [5], and so on. Feature engineering is essential to guarantee the performance of these TML-based methods. However, it is costly with the requirements of careful engineering and considerable domain expertise. DL-based methods can automatically generate feature representations from network traffic data. Thus, it realizes end-to-end learning without the need to design manual features. Some DL-based methods learn representations from packet payload bytes [6,7] while others generate embeddings from flow sequences [8,9]. Few DL-based methods extract features from flow sequence and packet payload bytes simultaneously.

4.2   Few-Shot Learning

FSL methods can be categorized into data augmentation-based, metric-learning-based, and meta-learning-based approaches. The data augmentation-based methods use prior knowledge to augment the training dataset by increasing the number of training samples [23]. Metric-learning-based methods focus on learning feature embeddings or distance measurements of dataset samples. They classify an unseen sample based on its distance to labeled samples [24]. Meta-learning-based methods address the data problem by leveraging prior learning experiences from multiple learning episodes. They extract meta-knowledge from these episodes, which often cover the distribution of related tasks, and use this knowledge to learn new tasks more quickly. The research in meta-learning can be categorized into metric-based, model-based, and optimization-based methods. In [25], metric-based meta-learning methods are introduced to acquire meta-knowledge in the form of a good feature space or distance metric that can be used for various new tasks. In [26], the model-based meta-learning methods are proposed to maintain an internal state of the model. The internal states, chosen dynamically according to different scenarios, can capture relevant task-specific information and are used to make predictions for new task inputs. In [27], optimization-based methods are used to model meta-learning as a two-level optimization problem, i.e., inner and outer levels. At the inner level, a base learner makes task-specific updates. While at the outer level, the performance across tasks is optimized. Optimization-based meta-learning is designed for fast adaption and performs better in generalizing to out-of-distribution tasks. The most frequently used optimization-based method is MAML [10].

4.3   Malicious Traffic Detection with Insufficient Labeled Samples

For malicious traffic detection, many researchers have noticed the lack of sufficient labeled samples due to the difficulties of collecting malicious traffic in cyberspace, especially for new attacks. Thus, some researchers have used data augmentation-based methods to address the training data insufficiency problem [11,12]. These methods use Generative Adversarial Networks (GAN) to generate new traffic data similar to the training dataset samples, which are treated as a complement to the training dataset. However, it is hard for GAN to generate discrete network traffic data since it suffers a performance degradation when facing discrete data like text. Except for data augmentation-based methods, some researchers have turned to unsupervised scenarios to deal with the data insufficiency problem. For example, Yisroel et al. [22] proposed Kitsune's core algorithm (KitNET), which used an ensemble of autoencoders to collectively differentiate between normal and abnormal traffic patterns. Zavrak et al. [28] adopted an intrusion detection system with variational autoencoders using flow features. These methods assume that most network traffic data in training datasets are benign and train the neural networks with only benign traffic flow data. Thus, the unsupervised models cannot identify the specific type of malicious traffic and tend to have lower precision than supervised models. The metric-based few-shot learning methods have also been used for malicious traffic detection [13,14]. These methods adopt different sampling strategies to balance the number of benign and malicious traffic samples. However, these methods are highly dependent on the sampling strategies. A simple sampling strategy could cause an under-fitting problem in the model, while a complex sampling strategy could lead to over-fitting and slow convergence.

Meta-learning is relatively new to malicious traffic detection, and the related researches are not perfect and need to be improved. Feng et al. [15] applied a MAML-based few-shot anomaly detection method FCAD to detect traffic from a before unseen anomaly class with only a few samples.

5 Conclusion

Most existing approaches proposed to address the problem of encrypted malicious traffic detection need a large number of labeled samples to train the models. Thus, they typically fail when facing new RAT classes with insufficient training samples. To address this limitation, we propose a novel method MFL-RAT based on MAML. MFL-RAT leverages the power of few-shot learning and meta-learning to develop a model for encrypted RAT traffic detection with limited training samples. By incorporating prior knowledge from original RATs traffic samples and enabling multi-class classification, MFL-RAT offers an effective and practical solution for detecting and categorizing different new types of RAT traffic in real-world scenarios. We also employ a multimodal embedding generation method and a feature fusion mechanism to combine these multimodal embeddings. This enables the model to generate a comprehensive and robust representation of network flow, which improves resource utilization efficiency.

References

1. Finsterbusch, M., Richter, C., Rocha, E., Muller, J.-A., Hanssgen, K.: A survey of payload-based traffic classification approaches. IEEE Commun. Surv. Tutorials **16**(2), 1135–1156 (2013)
2. Meghdouri, F., Vázquez, F.I., Zseby, T.: Cross-layer profiling of encrypted network data for anomaly detection. In: 2020 IEEE 7th International Conference on Data Science and Advanced Analytics (DSAA), pp. 469–478. IEEE (2020)
3. Han, W., Xue, J., Yan, H.: Detecting anomalous traffic in the controlled network based on cross entropy and support vector machine. IET Inf. Secur. **13**(2), 109–116 (2019)
4. Shekhawat, A.S., Di Troia, F., Stamp, M.: Feature analysis of encrypted malicious traffic. Exp. Syst. Appl. **125**, 130–141 (2019)
5. Stergiopoulos, G., Talavari, A., Bitsikas, E., Gritzalis, D.: Automatic detection of various malicious traffic using side channel features on TCP packets. In: Lopez, J., Zhou, J., Soriano, M. (eds.) ESORICS 2018. LNCS, vol. 11098, pp. 346–362. Springer, Cham (2018). https://doi.org/10.1007/978-3-319-99073-6_17
6. Liu, X., et al.: Attention-based bidirectional GRU networks for efficient https traffic classification. Inf. Sci. **541**, 297–315 (2020)

7. Lotfollahi, M., Siavoshani, M.J., Zade, R.S.H., Saberian, M.: Deep packet: a novel approach for encrypted traffic classification using deep learning. Soft Comput. **24**(3), 1999–2012 (2020)

8. Shapira, T., Shavitt, Y.: FlowPic: encrypted internet traffic classification is as easy as image recognition. In: IEEE INFOCOM 2019-IEEE Conference on Computer Communications Workshops (INFOCOM WKSHPS), pp. 680–687. IEEE (2019)

9. Liu, C., He, L., Xiong, G., Cao, Z., Li, Z.: FS-Net: a flow sequence network for encrypted traffic classification. In: IEEE INFOCOM 2019-IEEE Conference on Computer Communications, pp. 1171–1179. IEEE (2019)

10. Finn, C., Abbeel, P., Levine, S.: Model-agnostic meta-learning for fast adaptation of deep networks. In: International Conference on Machine Learning, pp. 1126–1135. PMLR (2017)

11. Ring, M., Schlör, D., Landes, D., Hotho, A.: Flow-based network traffic generation using generative adversarial networks. Comput. Secur. **82**, 156–172 (2019)

12. Guo, Y., Xiong, G., Li, Z., Shi, J., Cui, M., Gou, G.: TA-GAN: GAN based traffic augmentation for imbalanced network traffic classification. In: 2021 International Joint Conference on Neural Networks (IJCNN), pp. 1–8. IEEE (2021)

13. Cai, S., Han, D., Yin, X., Li, D., Chang, C.-C.: A hybrid parallel deep learning model for efficient intrusion detection based on metric learning. Connect. Sci. **34**(1), 551–577 (2022)

14. Andresini, G., Appice, A., Malerba, D.: Autoencoder-based deep metric learning for network intrusion detection. Inf. Sci. **569**, 706–727 (2021)

15. Feng, T., Qi, Q., Wang, J., Liao, J.: Few-shot class-adaptive anomaly detection with model-agnostic meta-learning. In: 2021 IFIP Networking Conference (IFIP Networking), pp. 1–9. IEEE (2021)

16. Zhang, Y.: ER-ERT: a method of ensemble representation learning of encrypted RAT traffic. In: 2023 IFIP Networking Conference (IFIP Networking), pp. 1–10 (2023)

17. Fukumizu, K., Song, L., Gretton, A.: Kernel Bayes' rule: Bayesian inference with positive definite kernels. J. Mach. Learn. Res. **14**(1), 3753–3783 (2013)

18. Wang, W., Zhu, M., Wang, J., Zeng, X., Yang, Z.: End-to-end encrypted traffic classification with one-dimensional convolution neural networks. In: 2017 IEEE International Conference on Intelligence and Security Informatics (ISI), pp. 43–48 (2017)

19. Stratosphere: Stratosphere laboratory datasets (2022). https://www.stratosphereips.org/datasets-overview. Accessed 14 Mar 2022

20. Garcia, S., Grill, M., Stiborek, J., Zunino, A.: An empirical comparison of botnet detection methods. Comput. Secur. **45**, 100–123 (2014)

21. Ring, M., Wunderlich, S., Scheuring, D., Landes, D., Hotho, A.: A survey of network-based intrusion detection data sets. Comput. Secur. **86**, 147–167 (2019)

22. Mirsky, Y., Doitshman, T., Elovici, Y., Shabtai, A.: Kitsune: an ensemble of autoencoders for online network intrusion detection. arXiv preprint arXiv:1802.09089 (2018)

23. Schwartz, E.: Delta-encoder: an effective sample synthesis method for few-shot object recognition. In: Advances in Neural Information Processing Systems, vol. 31 (2018)

24. Sung, F., Yang, Y., Zhang, L., Xiang, T., Torr, P.H.S., Hospedales, T.M.: Learning to compare: relation network for few-shot learning. In: Proceedings of the IEEE Conference on Computer Vision and Pattern Recognition, pp. 1199–1208 (2018)

25. Vinyals, O., Blundell, C., Lillicrap, T., Wierstra, D., et al.: Matching networks for one shot learning. In: Advances in Neural Information Processing Systems, vol. 29 (2016)
26. Gidaris, S., Komodakis, N.: Dynamic few-shot visual learning without forgetting. In: Proceedings of the IEEE Conference on Computer Vision and Pattern Recognition, pp. 4367–4375 (2018)
27. Li, Z., Zhou, F., Chen, F., Li, H.: Meta-SGD: learning to learn quickly for few-shot learning. arXiv preprint arXiv:1707.09835 (2017)
28. Zavrak, S., İskefiyeli, M.: Anomaly-based intrusion detection from network flow features using variational autoencoder. IEEE Access **8**, 108346–108358 (2020)

Author Index

Printed in the United States
by Baker & Taylor Publisher Services